Ohio State
University Press

February
1981

JOURNAL OF MONEY, CREDIT AND BANKING

US ISSN 0022-2879

JOURNAL OF MONEY, CREDIT AND BANKING

ISSN 0022-2879.

JOURNAL OF MONEY, CREDIT AND BANKING

VOLUME XIII NUMBER 1 FEBRUARY 1981

ARTICLES

Adjustment Lags Versus Information Lags: A Test of Alternative Explanations of the Phillips Curve Phenomenon — *Charles R. Nelson* 1

Theory and Implications of Currency Substitution — *Lance Girton and Don Roper* 12

The Federal Reserve System and Control of the Money Supply in the 1970s — *Robert L. Hetzel* 31

The Term Structure of Interest Rates in a Small Open Economy — *Michael Beenstock and J. Andrew Longbottom* 44

Measuring the Effect of Callability on Bond Yields — *Jess B. Yawitz and William J. Marshall* 60

The Leverage Structure of Interest Rates — *Enrique R. Arzac, Robert A. Schwartz, and David K. Whitcomb* 72

NOTES, COMMENTS, REPLIES

A Tribute to Clark Warburton, 1896-1979 — *A Note by Thomas F. Cargill* 89

Sluggish Price Adjustments and the Effectiveness of Monetary Policy Under Rational Expectations — *A Comment by Roman Frydman* 94

Sluggish Price Adjustments and the Effectiveness of Monetary Policy Under Rational Expectations — *A Reply by Bennett T. McCallum* 103

A Possible Error in the Expectations Theory — *A Comment by Frans J. Ballendux and Marius J. L. Jonkhart* 105

A Possible Error in the Expectations Theory — *A Rejoinder by Yakov Amihud* 107

The Bank Failures of 1930-31 — *A Comment by Robert F. Stauffer* 109

BOOK REVIEWS

Financing Black Economic Development, by Timothy Bates and William Bradford — *Reviewed by Harold Black* 114

The International Monetary Tangle: Myths and Realities, by Guillaume Guindey
Reviewed by Harlan M. Smith 115

Bankruptcy Risk in Financial Depository Intermediaries, by Michael F. Koehn
Reviewed by Karl H. Borch 117

An Unformalized Forecasting Model, by Aleksander Markowski
Reviewed by Gary Smith 118

Substitution Effects, Speculation and Exchange Rate Stability, by Patrick Minford
Reviewed by Robert J. Hodrick 121

On the Generality of Keynesian Economics, by Jukka Pekkarinen
Reviewed by J. A. Kregel 124

The U.S. Balance of Payments and the Sinking Dollar, by Wilson E. Schmidt
Reviewed by Hubertus Müller-Groeling 127

The Equity Funding Papers, by Lee J. Seidler, Frederick Andrews, and Marc J. Epstein
Reviewed by David L. Bickelhaupt 129

The Pay Board's Progress: Wage Controls in Phase II, by Arnold R. Weber and Daniel J. B. Mitchell
Reviewed by Charles C. Cox 132

JOURNAL OF MONEY, CREDIT, AND BANKING (ISSN 0022-2879). Published quarterly in February, May, August, and November by the Ohio State University Press, 2070 Neil Avenue, Columbus, Ohio 43210. Richard C. Rose, Managing Editor; Kummi Ranjit, Production Editor; Lisa Satterfield, Assistant Editor; Lois Fausnaugh, Subscriptions Manager; Jeanette White, Secretary to the Editor, Department of Economics, Ohio State University. Second-class postage paid at Columbus, Ohio, and at additional mailing offices.

SUBSCRIPTIONS. Individual: U.S.$20.00 per year; library: U.S.$25.00; student: U.S.$16.00; additional subscriptions to the same address: U.S.$16.00 per subscription. Postage outside the United States: add $2.00 per year. Sustaining Subscriptions: U.S.$500 per year. Supporting Subscriptions: U.S.$100 per year. Claims for missing issues must be made within four months of the date of publication. Allow six weeks for address change. Checks should be made payable to the Ohio State University Press, 2070 Neil Avenue, Columbus, Ohio 43210.

BACK ISSUES, REPRINTS, AND MICROFILM. Back issues in print are listed in the May and November issues and may be obtained from the Ohio State University Press. Microfilms of back volumes and reprints of articles and out-of-print issues may be obtained from University Microfilms International, 300 North Zeeb Road, Ann Arbor, Michigan 48106.

MANUSCRIPTS. Manuscripts are to be submitted in triplicate to the Editor, *Journal of Money, Credit, and Banking,* Department of Economics, Ohio State University, 1775 College Road, Columbus, Ohio 43210. Submission fee: individual subscribers U.S.$15; nonsubscribers U.S.$25. Checks are to be made payable to the Journal of Money, Credit, and Banking and enclosed with submitted manuscripts. Complete instructions for preparing text and illustrations may be obtained from the editor.

CHARLES R. NELSON*

Adjustment Lags Versus Information Lags

A Test of Alternative Explanations of the Phillips Curve Phenomenon

IT IS PERHAPS A TRUISM that without lags either in the adjustment of prices and wages or in the transmission of information about prices and wages there would be no business "cycle," but rather employment and output would follow presumably smooth paths determined by demographic factors, capital accumulation, and other long-run processes.

The observation that movements in wages and prices are correlated with output and employment, and the hypothesis that this phenomenon may be accounted for by adjustment lags in prices and wages are not new and certainly predate both the Phillips [25] paper in 1958 and the Keynesian revolution in macroeconomics. For example, Irving Fisher [5, 6] presented both empirical and theoretical analyses along these lines more than a decade before publication of Keynes' *General Theory* [15] in 1936. Milton Friedman's [8] analysis of the Phillips curve phenomenon parallels Fisher's thinking quite closely, both emphasizing an hypothesized lag in factor prices behind final product prices attributed at least partially to the existence

*I am indebted to Paul Evans, Milton Friedman, Clive Granger, William Haraf, Levis Kochin, John Makin, and referees of this journal for helpful and insightful comments, but responsibility for errors remains entirely my own. This research has been supported by a grant from the National Science Foundation.

CHARLES R. NELSON *is professor and chairman, Department of Economics, University of Washington.*

0022-2879/81/0281-0001$00.50/0
JOURNAL OF MONEY, CREDIT, AND BANKING, vol. 13, no. 1 (February 1981)

of long-term contracts. Hume [14] anticipated the essential idea of lagged adjustment and its connection with fluctuations in real activity when he wrote in 1752 "that though the high price of commodities be a necessary consequence of the encrease of gold and silver, yet it follows not immediately upon that encrease. It is easy to trace the money in its progress through the whole commonwealth; where we shall find that it must first quicken the diligence of every individual, before it encrease the price of labour." Interestingly, Hume was clearly of the opinion that the *level* of activity would be raised *permanently* by a steady increase in the quantity of money, prices, and wages. Hume was therefore a believer in stable, long-run Phillips curves and perhaps the only serious economist to have so committed himself in print! If adjustment lags are finite there need be no long-run trade-off between inflation and output, but the potential for counter cyclical monetary policy may still remain, as Fisher [7] and Phelps and Taylor [24] have demonstrated.

The information lag hypothesis put forward by Lucas [17, 18] postulates, on the other hand, flexible wages and prices but assumes that economic agents must assess the relative prices of their outputs without knowledge of the current aggregate price level. Lucas shows that if the information available to each agent is limited each period to the current price of his own output and *past* aggregate data and if expectations are rational, then aggregate supply of output will respond only to the discrepancy between the actual current aggregate price level and its expected value. While both adjustment and information lags are capable of generating business cycles (or more correctly, pseudo-cycles), the information lag hypothesis implies that there is *no* constructive role for monetary policy, rather an active monetary policy can only increase the variance of output. Consequently, two questions of considerable practical as well as scientific interest are (1) whether the observable implications of the information lag hypothesis differ from those of the adjustment lag hypothesis, and if so (2) which hypothesis is favored by the data?

1. GRANGER-CAUSALITY RELATIONSHIPS IN THE INFORMATION LAG MODEL

The aggregate supply function derived by Lucas from the information lag hypothesis takes the special form

$$\tilde{q}_t = \gamma[p_t - E_{t-1}p_t] + \sum_{i=1}^{\infty} \lambda_i \tilde{q}_{t-i} + \epsilon_t, \tag{1}$$

where $\tilde{q}_t$ is the deviation of the log of output or employment from its natural rate, p_t is the log of the aggregate price level, $E_{t-1}p_t$ is the expectation of p_t given all available information in the prior period, and ϵ_t is a random disturbance. The testability of the information lag hypothesis depends crucially on the fact that while past levels of output appear in this supply function, past price "surprises" $[p_t - E_{t-1}p_t]$ do not. The absence of past price surprises in the supply function along with the hypothesis that expectations incorporate all relevant information imply, as

Sargent [27] has noted, that exogenous or policy variables cannot "cause" $\tilde{q}$ in the purely predictive sense defined by Granger [11].[1] Since $E_{t-1}p_t$ incorporates all relevant information about p_t, it must be that past values of those variables cannot be useful in predicting the surprise $[p_t - E_{t-1}p_t]$ and therefore cannot be useful in predicting $\tilde{q}_t$ once past values of $\tilde{q}$ have been taken into account. Using the unemployment rate as a measure of $\tilde{q}$ and the narrowly defined money supply and various government fiscal measures as exogenous variables, Sargent found some evidence of unemployment being Granger-caused, although the results were mixed. It is readily apparent that the Lucas model also implies that $\tilde{q}$ cannot be Granger-caused by other endogenous variables in the system since that information is also incorporated in $E_{t-1}p_t$. Thus, finding that the past rates of change in prices or nominal spending (GNP, say) helped to predict the unemployment rate would be inconsistent with the information lag hypothesis, though in general unemployment rates will Granger-cause both prices and nominal spending in a system in which the current price level and the current unemployment rate are simultaneously determined as in Sargent's "Prototype Model" [27, p. 209].

The presence of lagged values of $\tilde{q}$ in (1) is implied by the well-documented serial correlation present in measures of output and employment. These lagged values might be attributed to accelerated effects from capital accumulation [19], inventory dynamics [12], or costs of adjusting output rates toward desired levels. For example, if desired output were linear in perceived relative price and costs were quadratic in the change in output and the difference between actual and desired output, then the Lucas supply function would take the form of the standard partial adjustment model with one lagged value of $\tilde{q}$. Regardless of the explanation for persistence in output, it is clearly implicit in [1] that current output decisions depend on the state of the system at the beginning of the period and current perceived relative price and not on past perceived relative prices per se. But as McCallum [20] has written "it is hard to imagine ways in which past expectational errors could have direct effects on current behavior—bygones are, after all, bygones."

2. GRANGER-CAUSALITY RELATIONSHIPS IN A PRICE ADJUSTMENT LAG MODEL

An alternative class of models with very different Granger-causal implications are the lagged price adjustment "monetarist" models in the tradition of Friedman [9] and Andersen and Carlson [1]. In these models the level of nominal spending is shifted by exogenous shocks, primarily resulting from money supply movements. The division of a change in nominal spending between changes in prices and output depends on the "inertia" in prices and on the discrepancy between actual output and the "natural" or "full-employment" level of output. The relative importance of

[1]The use of the word "cause" in this context refers only to the predictive definition given by Granger [11]. Ths issue of causation in the sense employed by philosophers of science is not a relevant one here. Exogenous variables, or at least their unexpected parts, do presumably cause movement in real variables in the latter sense.

inertia versus demand pressure determines the degree of price flexibility in these models and indicates in an important sense how "Keynesian" the model is. By that measure, the "St. Louis" model of Andersen and Carlson is very Keynesian indeed since the price level adjusts very slowly to shifts in aggregate spending (see Beveridge [3] and Nelson [22]). These models do in general imply a role for stabilization policies, but do not necessarily imply long run tradeoffs between inflation and output as long as the sources of lagged adjustment (such as contracts) are recognized to be a product of the ambient monetary environment. The price level adjustment equation in these models can be expressed as

$$p_t = f_p(p_{t-1}, \ldots; y_t, y_{t-1}, \ldots; \bar{q}_t, \bar{q}_{t-1}, \ldots) + \eta_t, \tag{2}$$

where y is the log of nominal spending, $\bar{q}$ is the log of the natural rate of output or employment, and η is a disturbance term. It is clear from the presence of lagged spending in the price equation that the price level will in general be Granger-caused by nominal spending, although spending will not be caused by prices if variation in spending is due to exogenous monetary factors. Since the price adjustment equation along with a given level of nominal spending completely determine output and employment, it is clear that adjustment lag models also imply that both output and employment (or unemployment) are Granger-caused by nominal spending, but not vice versa.

3. EMPIRICAL TESTS AND DISCUSSION

Drawing on the implications of the preceding section, we can discriminate between the information lag and adjustment lag hypotheses on the basis of observed Granger-causal relations. Following Sargent [27] and Barro [2], we take the unemployment rate (hereafter "UR") as the relevant measure of $\tilde{q}$. Nominal spending is measured by GNP and the price level by the deflator for GNP, both seasonally adjusted and in first differences of natural logs. The data is quarterly for the U.S., 1954-1970. As Sargent [27] noted, it is clear from Granger's definition that if a time series X does not cause another time series Y in the Granger sense, then lagged values of X added to an autoregression in Y should not result in a statistically significant improvement in fit. On the other hand, a significant improvement in fit would imply causation in the Granger sense from X to Y. A recent Monte Carlo study [23] shows that then direct tests compare favorably relative to other proposed tests in terms of power against a plausible range of causal structures. To carry out these direct tests a set of regressions were run in which four lags of the dependent variable and successively zero, one, and four lags of another were included. Four lags of the dependent variable allow for seasonal as well as nonseasonal autocorrelation, recognizing that seasonal adjustment often fails to remove all seasonality. The results are summarized in Table 1.

Contrary to the information lag hypothesis, GNP is strongly significant in predicting the UR both in one lag and four lag tests. There is also some evidence of the price deflator predicting the UR from the four lag test. These relationships are both consistent with the price adjustment lag hypothesis. Also consistent with the price adjustment lag hypothesis is the lack of evidence of Granger causation running from

TABLE 1
DIRECT TESTS FOR GRANGER CAUSALITY 1954–1970: TEST STATISTICS FOLLOWED BY SIGNIFICANCE LEVELS

Unemployment Rate on:	*GNP*	Price Deflator
One Lag: *t*	−4.04	−0.64
	0.0002	0.52
Four Lags: *F*	4.17	1.953
	0.005	0.11
Price Deflator on:	***GNP***	**Unemployment Rate**
One Lag: *t*	2.39	−1.17
	0.02	0.24
Four Lags: *F*	1.66	2.42
	0.17	0.06
***GNP* on:**	**Price Deflator**	**Unemployment Rate**
One Lag: *t*	−0.14	0.28
	0.89	0.78
Four Lags: *F*	0.96	0.29
	0.44	0.88

NOTE: t with 57 *d.f.*, F with 4 and 54 *d.f.*

either prices or the UR to GNP and the positive evidence of Granger causation running from GNP to the price deflator in the one lag test. Granger causation from the UR to prices is indicated by the four lag test and is consistent with either hypothesis.

The empirical results strongly suggest, therefore, that lags in the transmission of price information cannot account for the lead-lag relations we observe in the movement of spending, employment, and prices. A number of caveats, however, are in order. Equations (1) and (2) each represent strong and simplified versions of the underlying theories and incorporate therefore a number of maintained hypotheses that if untrue could lead to rejection of the primary hypothesis. For example, the information lag hypothesis as stated assumes that individual supply functions aggregate into a macro supply function of the same form. Similarly, some monetarists would not be distressed by departure from the recursivity assumption of the St. Louis model that makes nominal spending exogenous to prices and output. Also implicit in the tests are the assumptions that the standard operational variables used are faithful to the concepts of the theory (which cannot be strictly true), and that quarterly intervals and seasonal adjustment procedures are appropriate. The popularity of the unemployment rate as a measure of deviations from a natural rate of output [2, 27] is perhaps due to the vagaries of extracting the "full employment" level or "natural rate" from series such as industrial production, real GNP, or total employment.

While correspondence with descriptive reality is not an adequate test of a theory,

I find the plausibility of the information lag hypothesis strained by the fact that a great deal of price information is available to firms, workers, and consumers on a virtual real-time basis. A typical firm is constantly in the market for inputs and outputs, receiving bids and offers on a daily or even hourly basis. Prices of many basic raw materials are available daily in the financial press and virtually instantaneously through the electronic communication systems that link geographically separated markets. A firm unable to distinguish the real and inflation components of a particular change in demand can consult the stock exchange for an "efficient" estimate of the firm's current value. The consumer is aware not only of current wage levels but is exposed daily to a wide range of spot prices that must proxy very well for much of the variation in the overall cost of living. Of course, the official consumer price index is produced with a lag of roughly a month, but less comprehensive indexes are available weekly; for example, the BLS spot price indexes published in *Business Week;* and even daily, for example, the Dow Jones Commodity Index published in *The Wall Street Journal*. What one does observe directly, of course, are numerous contracting arrangements by which nominal or sometimes real wages and prices are fixed for substantial periods of time. The concern here is not with the reasons for the existence of such arrangements but rather with such rigidities as a competing explanation for aggregate fluctuations.

4. A DYNAMIC PHILLIPS CURVE

If movements in aggregate spending do have predictable effects on real activity as the results of section 3 suggest, it would be useful to have a description of the dynamics of that relationship. In particular, the length of the lags involved as well as the long-run slope are of special interest. For this purpose I have constructed a rational distributed lag or transfer function model with the change in the unemployment rate (ΔUR) as the dependent variable and the change in the log of nominal spending (ΔGNP) as the independent variable. The cross-correlations between the residuals in this relationship and *future* prewhitened values of *GNP* provide the basis for an additional test to detect Granger causation from the *UR* to *GNP*, following the procedure suggested by Pierce and Haugh [26]. Previous univariate analysis of the *UR* series [21] has indicated that mean-reversion in the series is not strong; hence, I have dealt with the first differences in the *UR* to assure stationarity.

The transfer function model relating ΔUR to ΔGNP is of the form

$$\Delta UR = \frac{\lambda(L)}{\delta(L)} \Delta GNP + \text{const.} + e, \tag{3}$$

where $\lambda(L)$ and $\delta(L)$ are polynomials of finite degree in the lag operator L and e is a stochastic error possibly autocorrelated with an ARMA representation. The effect of a ΔGNP at time t on the ΔUR at time $(t + k)$ is given by the kth coefficient in the expansion of $[\lambda(L)/\delta(L)]$ as a polynomial in L. These coefficients are called lag weights or impulse response weights and their sum is the long run slope or steady state gain of the model. The steady state gain can be interpreted as the long-run effect of a ΔGNP at one point in time on the *level* of the unemployment rate since it sums up all subsequent ΔURs traceable to that change in spending.

Preliminary estimates of the lag weights were computed from cross-correlations between ΔUR and ΔGNP after both were transformed by the univariate (prewhitening) model for ΔGNP described in [22], following a general procedure described by Box and Jenkins [4].[2] The resulting preliminary estimates were

Lag	0	1	2	3	4	5	6	7	8
Weight	−0.22	−0.15	−0.04	0.01	0.03	0.05	0.03	0.01	0.02

with *UR* expressed in fractional form to be comparable to ΔGNP. These weights continue to be small but predominantly positive at longer lags. This slow decay suggests the presence in $\delta(L)$ of a root close to unity, since $\delta(L) = 0$ is the difference equation that generates the lag weights given initial conditions determined by $\lambda(L)$. The sum of lag weights, or gain, is $[\lambda(1)/\delta(1)]$ which will be zero if the long-run effect on *UR* of a change in *GNP* is zero. This suggests that $\lambda(L)$ will also have a root close or equal to unity. The initial conditions reflected in the negative weights at lags 0 through 2 suggest that $\lambda(L)$ will be at least of order 2. Estimating by nonlinear least squares, satisfactory results in terms of the diagnostics for residual autocorrelation and crosscorrelation were obtained with both polynomials being of second degree and no ARMA structure on the error term. The model estimated under the constraint that the gain be zero is

$$\Delta UR = \frac{(-0.23 + 0.14L + 0.09L^2)}{1 - 1.30L + 0.34L^2} \Delta GNP + 0.0009 + e, \tag{4}$$

where

$$\begin{aligned}
\text{Std. error} &= 0.19 \times 10^{-2};\ R^2 = 0.79;\ \bar{R}^2 = 0.78 \\
F(4,60) &= 57.75;\ p \text{ value} = 7 \times 10^{-20} \\
Q(12) &= 15.7,\ p \text{ value} = 0.21;\ S(0,12) = 8.9, \\
&\ p \text{ value} = 0.45 \\
S(-1,-12) &= 9.6,\ p \text{ value} = 0.65 \\
F - \text{stat. on gain constraint} &= 2.40;\ p \text{ value} = 0.13.
\end{aligned}$$

The lag weights implied by the fitted model are displayed in Table 2 and closely resemble the preliminary estimates given above. The pattern is one of large negative initial effects followed after four quarters by small but highly persistent positive effects. The degree of persistence reflects the fact that the roots of (1-1.3L +

[2]Calculations reported in this section were performed by programs CROSSCORR and TRANSEST.

$0.34L^2) = 0$ are real, numerically 2.78 and 1.07, and that one of them is close to unity. When the constraint that the gain or long-run effect of ΔGNP on ΔUR be zero is relaxed there is little apparent effect on the parameter estimates or on the implied lag weights except that they are even more persistently positive. The estimated gain is +0.55 which would imply that the long-run effect of a given spending increase at one point in time is to *raise* the level of the unemployment rate. The F-statistic on the constraint, as reported above under equation (4), is significant only at the 0.13 level. Hence, evidence against a zero long-run trade-off is not strong, but what evidence there is points in the direction of an unfavorable trade-off. This is consistent with evidence I have presented elsewhere [22] on the long-run dynamics of spending and inflation. Friedman [10] has suggested some plausible explanations for a positively sloped long-run Phillips curve that have received empirical support in a recent paper by Levi and Makin [16].

TABLE 2

Distributed Lag Weights on Nominal Spending Implied by the Dynamic Model

Lag in Quarters	Weight
0	−0.232
1	−0.159
2	−0.037
3	0.005
4	0.019
5	0.023
6	0.024
7	0.023
8	0.021
>8	$\beta_k \simeq 0.935\, \beta_{k-1}$

As a check for serial correlation in the residuals I have used the Box-Pierce Q statistic which for the twelve lags reported will be chi-square with twelve degrees of freedom under the null hypothesis of no autocorrelation. It is 15.7 in this case with a p value (significance level) of 0.21 and thus is satisfactory. The $S(0,12)$ statistic is constructed from cross-correlations between model residuals and the current and past twelve lags of prewhitened *GNP*. It is designed to check for misspecification of the transfer function [4] and will be chi-square under the null hypothesis of correct specification. In this case the value is 8.9 with nine degrees of freedom, implying a p value of only 0.45. Finally, the $S(-1,-12)$ statistic uses cross-correlations in the forward direction to try to detect Granger causal feedback from the *UR* to *GNP* and will be chi-square with twelve degrees of freedom if no feedback is present [13]. The statistic is 9.6 with a p value of 0.65 and therefore provides no evidence of feedback. To cover the possibility that evidence of feedback is present but only at very short lags, we note that the individual cross-correlation at lag (−1) quarter (forward one quarter) was only −0.001 with a standard error of 0.12.

Since both the numerator and denominator polynomials of the fitted transfer function contain roots not far from unity (or exactly unity for the numerator when the gain is constrained to be zero), it is reasonable to question whether those polynomials contain redundant factors that can be canceled out with little sacrifice in fit. To check this out I have estimated a transfer function with one less term in each polynomial. Starting values for the iterations were obtained by dividing the numerator and denominator of (4) by $(1-L)$ which has a root exactly equal to unity. The result was a fall in R^2 from 0.79 to 0.005. The $S(0,12)$ statistic was 60.9 with a p-value below the tabulation capability of the program indicating severe misspecification. Similarly indicative of specification error is the $Q(1,12)$ statistic of 39.3 which reflects strong autocorrelation in residuals. Interestingly, there is still no evidence of feedback from *UR* to *GNP* since the $S(-1,-12)$ statistic is only 3.5 which would have a p-value of 0.99 in a well-specified model. What the data seem to be telling us is that a gain close to zero, which corresponds to a root close to unity in the numerator, and slow decay in the effect of a spending shock on the *UR*, which corresponds to a root close to unity in the denominator, are essential attributes of the relationship. This would seem to be strong affirmation of two predictions of the adjustment lag hypothesis.

To interpret the dynamic Phillips curve appropriately it is important to keep in mind the monetary environment of the 1954–1960 period. Log changes in nominal spending as measured by *GNP* were strongly mean-reverting. While they did display some autocorrelation on a quarterly basis, it is weak; 0.36 at one-quarter lag and 0.05 at two quarters. If the dynamic regression represented by (4) held under any circumstances, it would be possible in principle to engineer a permanent decrease in unemployment by generating an appropriately chosen rate of change in spending. For example, since the partial sum of the lag weights is negative at any finite lag, it is easy to see that a policy raising the rate of growth of spending to a permanently higher level would result in a sequence of ever smaller decreases in the *UR* and hence a lower level of the *UR* in the long run. It is important to realize, however, that the environment in which this relation held was not characterized by long-run changes in the growth of spending but rather by a sequence of essentially transitory changes. It is hard to believe that contracting practices and like sources of adjustment lags would not adapt to change in the monetary environment in such a way as to eliminate any positive long-run trade-off.

5. SUMMARY AND CONCLUSIONS

The objective of the paper has been to test the theory developed by Lucas that states that macroeconomic fluctuations are due to lags in information about the aggregate price level against the hypothesis that these fluctuations are due to lags in the adjustment of wages and prices. The latter hypothesis has deep roots in the classical tradition, though in extreme form has become identified as the sine qua non of the Keynesian position. The tests used in this paper are based on the differing implications of information lags as opposed to adjustment lags in regard to Granger-causal relationships among measures of employment, the aggregate price level, and nominal spending. The evidence presented here is consistent with the adjustment lag hypothesis but not with the information lag hypothesis. The dynamic Phillips curve implied by a transfer function analysis of unemployment and nominal spending indicates that the initial negative impact of a spending increase on unemployment will be followed after a few quarters by small but highly persistent *positive* changes in unemployment. The total long-run impact is estimated to be positive though not significantly so.

LITERATURE CITED

1. Andersen, Leonall C., and Keith M. Carlson. "A Monetarist Model for Economic Stabilization." *Review of the Federal Reserve Bank of St. Louis,* 52 (April 1970), 7-25.
2. Barro, Robert J. "Unanticipated Money Growth and Unemployment in the United States." *American Economic Review,* 67 (March 1977), 101-15.
3. Beveridge, Stephen. "An Evaluation of the St. Louis Model." Ph.D. dissertation, University of Chicago, 1975.
4. Box, George E. P., and Gwilym M. Jenkins. *Time Series Analysis: Forecasting and Control.* San Francisco: Holden-Day, 1970.
5. Fisher, Irving. "Our Unstable Dollar and the So-called Business Cycle." *Journal of the American Statistical Association,* 20 (June 1925), 179-202.
6. ———. "A Statistical Relation Between Unemployment and Price Changes." *International Labour Review,* 13 (June 1926), 785-92.
7. Fischer, Stanley. "Long Term Contracts, Rational Expectations, and the Optimal Money Supply Rate." *Journal of Political Economy,* 85 (February 1977), 191-205.
8. Friedman, Milton. "The Role of Monetary Policy." *American Economic Review,* 58 (March 1968), 1-17.
9. ———. "A Theoretical Framework for Monetary Analysis." *Journal of Political Economy,* 78 (March/April 1970), 193-238.
10. ———. "Nobel Lecture; Inflation and Unemployment." *Journal of Political Economy,* 85 (Junc 1977), 451-72.
11. Granger, Clive W. J. "Investigating Causal Relations by Econometric Models and Cross-Spectral Methods." *Econometrica,* 37 (July 1969), 424-38.
12. Haraf, William S. "Inventories, Orders, and the Persistent Effects of Monetary Shocks." *Proceedings of the 1978 West Coast Academic/Federal Reserve Economic Research Seminar.* San Francisco: San Francisco Federal Reserve Bank, 1979.
13. Haugh, Larry D. "The Identification of Time Series Interrelationships with Special Reference to Dynamic Regression." Ph.D. dissertation, University of Wisconsin, 1972.
14. Hume, David. "Of Money." In *Political Discourses.* Edinburgh, 1752.
15. Keynes, John M. *The General Theory of Employment, Interest, and Money.* New York: Harcourt, Brace, and Company, 1936.
16. Levi, Maurice D., and John H. Makin. "Inflation Uncertainty and the Phillips Curve: Some Empirical Evidence." *American Economic Review,* 68 (December 1978), 801-12.
17. Lucas, Robert E., Jr. "Expectations and the Neutrality of Money." *Journal of Economic Theory,* 4 (April 1972), 103-24.
18. ———. "Some International Evidence on Output-Inflation Trade-offs." *American Economic Review,* 63 (June 1973), 326-34.
19. ———. "An Equilibrium Model of the Business Cycle." *Journal of Political Economy,* 83 (December 1975), 1113-44.

20. McCallum, Bennett T. "On the Observational Inequivalence of Classical and Keynesian Models." *Journal of Political Economy,* 87 (April 1979), 395–402.

21. Nelson, Charles R. "The Prediction Performance of the FRB-MIT-PENN Model of the U.S. Economy." *American Economic Review,* 62 (December 1972), 902–17.

22. ______. "Recursive Structure in U.S. Income, Prices, and Output." *Journal of Political Economy,* 87 (December 1979), 1307–27.

23. Nelson, Charles R., and G. William Schwert. "Tests for Granger/Wiener Causality: A Monte Carlo Investigation." University of Washington discussion Paper No. 79-15, September 1979.

24. Phelps, Edmund S., and John B. Taylor. "Stabilizing Powers of Monetary Policy Under Rational Expectations." *Journal of Political Economy,* 85 (February 1977), 163–90.

25. Phillips, Alban W. "The Relation Between Unemployment and the Rate of Change of Money Wage Rates in the U.K., 1861–1957." *Economica* (November 1958), 283–99.

26. Pierce, David A., and Larry D. Haugh. "Causality in Temporal Systems: Characterizations and a Survey." *Journal of Econometrics,* 5 (May 1977), 265–94.

27. Sargent, Thomas J. "A Classical Macroeconometric Model for the United States." *Journal of Political Economy,* 84 (April 1976), 207–37.

28. Sims, Christopher A. "Money, Income, and Causality." *American Economic Review,* 62 (September 1972), 540–52.

LANCE GIRTON
DON ROPER*

Theory and Implications of Currency Substitution

> Thus if currency notes were to be deprived of their liquidity-premium by the stamping system, a long series of substitutes would step into their shoes—bank-money, debts at call, foreign money, jewelery and the precious metals generally, and so forth. (John M. Keynes [18, p. 358])

MONETARY THEORY HAS TRADITIONALLY ASSUMED that one currency circulates in each country. The relaxation of the one-currency-per-country assumption allows currency questions to be separated from questions dealing primarily with international and interregional trade. Just as the pure theory of international trade abstracts from monetary phenomena, the pure theory of multiple currencies can be investigated independently of the number of countries or regions.

The theory of substitutable monies developed here is applicable to several monies circulating in one country and to several monies circulating internationally. Consideration of issues involving CS (currency substitution) cuts across the usual distinction (based on political or governmental jurisdictions) between "domestic" and "international" monetary economics. Consequently, the literature on substitutable

*This paper has benefited from helpful suggestions from Dale Henderson, Tom Grennes, George Moore (for material in Appendix B), Stephen Turnovsky, and two anonymous referees. The authors appreciate the comments and support from members of the IIES (Institute for International Economic Studies) at the University of Stockholm, where the first draft of the paper was completed in 1974. Helpful discussions over subsequent drafts followed seminars at ANU, Chase Manhattan Bank, University of North Carolina, Monash University, Princeton University, and UCLA. Our work was stimulated by conversations with Russell Boyer at the Federal Reserve Board in the summers of 1972 and 1973. An earlier version of the paper was circulated under the same title in 1976.

LANCE GIRTON AND DON ROPER *are professors of economics, University of Utah.*

0022-2879/81/0281-0012$00.50/0
JOURNAL OF MONEY, CREDIT, AND BANKING, vol. 13, no. 1 (February 1981)

monies comes from domestic monetary economics [e.g., 2, 4, 20, 25, 32] and international monetary economics [e.g., 3, 5, 15, 16, 19, 21, 22, 23, 24, 28, 33]. A brief survey is given in [6].

The paper is organized as follows: In section 1 a two-currency model of the exchange rate is developed under the assumption that (the paths of) the quantities of monies are exogenous. The exchange rate between monies is shown to be "unstable" in the sense that movements in the exchange rate necessary to maintain monetary equilibrium become larger without limit as CS increases. In addition, the exchange rate is indeterminate with perfect CS. In contrast with CS, an increase in substitution between bonds does not produce an "unstable" bond-exchange rate and perfect bond substitution does not produce indeterminacy. CS is different from substitution between other financial assets because the yield on money is independent of the value of money. This independence is, as argued in section 2, due to the choice of units in which financial contracts are specified. The fact that the interest payment on money is denominated in terms of itself (money) and that the interest payment on bonds is not denominated in terms of bonds provides a distinction between money and bonds which, we argue, is more fundamental than the usual view of the money-bond distinction. In section 3 the behavior of money issuers in response to CS is characterized as the choice between fixing exchange rates or competing in the production of monies. It is shown that there is no externality in the production of money such that the usual implication of competition, allocative efficiency, is as applicable to money as to other commodities. When the behavior of money issuers is endogenized, the presence of CS is found to eliminate rather than cause exchange rate instability. In the summary it is concluded that the usual fixed-money-growth rule will lead to an inferior, depreciating money if the public is offered competitively produced substitutes.

1. AN ASSET DEMAND MODEL OF CURRENCY SUBSTITUTION

The model of CS developed here contains two money-demand functions which, together with exogenous money supplies, are used to analyze the money exchange rate. A third nonmonetary asset is implicit in the model, but the balance sheet constraint makes the market equilibrium condition for this asset redundant.

CS can be modeled by the inclusion of real returns on both monies in both money-demand functions. Defining r_1 and r_2 as the anticipated real returns on monies one and two, the demands for real balances can be expressed as

$$M_k/P_k = L_k(r_1, r_2, r, w), \qquad (k = 1,2) \tag{1}$$

where M_k is the nominal quantity of currency k, P_k is the price of goods in terms of currency k, r is the anticipated real return on the nonmonetary asset, and w is a scale variable such as real wealth. w and r are taken as exogenous. Money holders are assumed to hold both monies so the same scale variable, w, is used in both L_1 and L_2.[1]

In keeping with standard specifications, money-demands are assumed to depend on differential returns:

$$L_1(r_1-r,\ r_1-r_2,\ w) \quad \text{and} \quad L_2(r_2-r,\ r_2-r_1,\ w). \tag{2}$$

To simplify the argument, the demand functions are assumed to have exponential specifications. The equilibrium condition for currency one is,[2]

$$M_1/P_1 = \theta_1(w)\exp[\alpha_1(r_1-r) + \sigma_1(r_1-r_2)], \qquad (\alpha_1,\ \sigma_1 > 0) \tag{3}$$

where σ_1 is a coefficient of substitution between monies one and two and α_1 is a coefficient of substitution between money one and the nonmonetary asset.

The monetary equilibrium conditions in logarithmic form are

$$\ln M_1 - \ln P_1 = \ln\theta_1 + \alpha_1(r_1-r) + \sigma_1(r_1-r_2) \tag{4a}$$

$$\ln M_2 - \ln P_2 = \ln\theta_2 + \alpha_2(r_2-r) + \sigma_2(r_2-r_1). \tag{4b}$$

Implications of CS can be obtained by focusing on the relative values of the two monies. To find the expression determining the relative value of the monies, subtract (4b) from (4a) and rearrange terms to obtain

$$\ln(P_1/P_2) = \ln[(M_1/\theta_1)/(M_2/\theta_2)] - \alpha(r_1 - r_2) - 2\sigma(r_1 - r_2), \tag{5}$$

where the following symmetry conditions have been imposed: $\alpha_1 = \alpha_2 = \alpha$ and $\sigma_1 = \sigma_2 = \sigma$. The assumption $\sigma_1 = \sigma_2$ identifies CS with the single parameter, σ, and the condition $\alpha_1 = \alpha_2$ makes the relative value of monies invariant to changes in r, the yield on the nonmonetary asset.

Equation (5) can be used to determine the exchange rate between the two monies if some relation between P_1/P_2 and E (the exchange market price of money two in

[1]The money-demand functions L_1 and L_2 are defined by currency, not by country. Most BOP (balance of payments) models are based on the assumption of one currency-per-country and therefore do not distinguish between money demand defined by country of residence and money demand defined by currency. When defined by country, money-demand functions are appropriate for explaining the multiregional or interregional BOP. When defined by currency, they are appropriate for explaining the multicurrency concept of exchange market pressure, defined as that combination of reserve and exchange rate changes that is independent of central bank intervention. A measure of EMP with equal weights is given in [11].

Standard BOP accounting does not distinguish between these two concepts of the BOP. Data is collected for above-the-line-entries on the basis of country residency. The official settlements definition of the BOP, a measure (when the exchange rate is fixed) of exchange market pressure, is entered below the line.

[2]$\alpha_1(r_1-r)$ is the usual interest rate term found in money-demand functions. This becomes clear if r_1 is expressed as the difference between the market or nominal interest rate on money one, i_1, and the anticipated rate of inflation in terms of money one, π_1. Substituting $i_1-\pi_1$ for r_1 converts $\alpha_1(r_1-r)$ to $-\alpha_1(r+\pi_1) + \alpha_1 i_1$, where $\alpha_1 i_1$ is usually assumed constant and therefore suppressed. Equation (3), therefore, is a typical *LM* equation with the addition of the substitution effect between the two monies.

terms of money one) is imposed. The obvious condition to use is that $E = P_1/P_2$. This looks like and might well be regarded as purchasing power parity, but it is not based on the usual arbitrage assumption associated with PPP. Rather than the usual condition that arbitrage takes place across space or between regions, the multicurrency version of PPP requires that arbitrage take place between currencies. This condition means that neither money is discriminated against, or discounted relative to the other, when used as a medium of exchange. When two prices are quoted for the same good, the ratio of the prices must equal the rate at which the currencies are traded in the exchange market.

Defining $e = \ln E$ and imposing the condition that $e = \ln(P_1/P_2)$, equation (5) can be expressed as

$$e = \tilde{e} - \eta\,\delta, \tag{6}$$

where $\tilde{e} = \ln[(M_1/\theta_1)/(M_2/\theta_2)]$, $\eta = \alpha + 2\sigma$, and $\delta = r_1 - r_2$. Exogenous money supplies and demand factors are contained in the term $\tilde{e}$.[3] CS is reflected in the σ-parameter such that η will vary from α to infinity as CS ranges from zero to infinity.

The differential anticipated real return on monies is equal to the differential nominal return minus the differential anticipated rate of inflation:

$$\begin{aligned}\delta &= r_1 - r_2 = (i_1 - \pi_1) - (i_2 - \pi_2)\\ &= (i_1 - i_2) - (\pi_1 - \pi_2).\end{aligned} \tag{7}$$

Assuming anticipations are formed in a manner consistent with (the multicurrency version of) PPP, the anticipated rate of change in the exchange rate, x, will equal the difference between the anticipated inflation rates such that equation (7) can be expressed as

$$\delta = i_1 - i_2 - x. \tag{7$'$}$$

Substituting this expression for δ into the exchange rate equation (6) produces

$$e = \tilde{e} - \eta(i_1 - i_2 - x). \tag{8}$$

Since equation (8) will be used to derive implications of CS, it is worth summarizing the assumptions used in the derivation of this relationship. First, the nominal interest rates on monies, i_1 and i_2, are assumed fixed. This assumption will be discussed in section 2. Second, the money supplies are taken as exogenous and are contained in $\tilde{e}$. The assumption of exogenous money supplies will be relaxed in

[3]We are assuming that $\tilde{e}$ is independent of e. A sufficient condition to assure this independence is that any exchange-rate induced wealth effects have proportional impacts on θ_1 and θ_2.

In contrast to an arbitrage version of PPP, we could have assumed the neutrality version of PPP, viz., the real exchange rate is independent of nominal variables. This would complicate the definition of $\tilde{e}$ but leave the conclusions unaffected.

section 3. Third, the anticipated rate of change of the exchange rate x is taken as exogenous. When x is endogenized using rational expectations in Appendix A or using adaptive expectations in [10], the results are consistent with the conclusions of this section.

There are two basic implications of CS, given the assumptions of this section. One implication relates directly to a policy issue and the other concerns the foundations of monetary theory. First, CS will cause exchange rate "instability" in the sense that shifts in the anticipated rate of change of the exchange rate lead to larger exchange rate movements with greater degrees of CS. Second, perfect CS implies that the exchange rate is indeterminate.

Consider first the impact of a shift in the anticipated rate of change of the exchange rate x. Taking the derivative of expression (8),

$$\partial e/\partial x = \eta = \alpha + 2\sigma. \tag{8'}$$

The greater the degree of CS (i.e., the larger the value of σ), the larger the change in e needed to satisfy monetary equilibrium for a given shift in x. The movement in the exchange rate needed to satisfy the monetary equilibrium conditions approaches infinity as substitution becomes perfect (i.e., as η approaches infinity).

From equation (8), the impact of $\tilde{e}$ on e, given by $\partial e/\partial \tilde{e} = 1$, holds for all finite value of CS. Since money supplies are included in $\tilde{e}$, changes in the supplies or composition of monies have a proportional impact on the exchange rate for all finite degrees of CS. CS increases the impact of x (or δ) on e but leaves the impact of money supplies on e unaffected, so exchange market intervention becomes a relatively less effective instrument for offsetting shifts in x. The fact that e is more sensitive to i_1 and i_2 as CS increases motivates the assumption in section 3 that, when money issuers compete for larger market shares, they do so by offering more attractive rates on their liabilities.

The second implication concerns the theoretical question of exchange rate determination under perfect CS.[4] In order for both monies to circulate, their values (in terms of goods) must be finite. This means the exchange rate must be nonzero and finite. In order for the exchange rate to be finite and greater than zero, the rate of return δ must be zero. But equal real returns do not impose any condition on the exchange rate because δ is independent of P_1 and P_2 and, therefore, of the exchange rate. The remaining condition to which one might appeal is $e = \tilde{e}$. But with perfect CS, the individual money-demands in $\tilde{e}$ are no longer defined. Consequently, any exchange rate is an equilibrium rate when CS is perfect.[5]

[4]The implications of perfect CS for exchange rate determination are also found in [2, 3, 10, 15, 16]. We assume that monies (like other financial assets) are distinguished by issuer, and counterfeiting is effectively prohibited. (See [20, 33, 12].) Perfect substitution does not imply indistinguishability.

[5]It should be noted that there is no inconsistency in the proposition that, when CS is perfect, the exchange rate is both unstable and indeterminate. Instability does not presuppose determinacy as can be seen with the following argument: Suppose that two perfectly substitutable currencies have the same initial real yields and are exchangeable at some initial finite exchange rate, e^0. Now suppose that δ is changed from its initial zero value. This shock will cause e to go to plus or minus infinity (E will go to plus infinity or to zero). The infinite movement in e reflects instability under perfect CS. But e^0 was completely arbitrary. It is not necessary to determine the initial value of e to determine that the (limit of the) derivative $\partial e/\partial x$, is infinite.

To see that these implications of CS are peculiar to money, per se, we will contrast CS with bond substitution. With slight changes in the expression for δ, equation (8) can be used to examine substitution between two bonds, A and B. The only assumption that makes the preceding specification of δ unique to money is that the market yields i_1 and i_2 have been taken as exogenous. Rather than being fixed, bond market yields vary inversely with the values of the bonds. For convenience, the bonds are assumed to be perpetuities paying a constant and continuous stream of interest denoted as C_a and C_b. The market yields on the bonds are

$$i_a = C_a/Q_a \quad \text{and} \quad i_b = C_b/Q_b,$$

where Q_a and Q_b are the bond prices. Both bond prices and their stream of interest payments are measured in terms of a single background numeraire needing no further specification for our purposes.

Retaining the symbols η and x from the money-equation (8), the counterpart bond-equation is

$$R = \tilde{R} - \eta(C_a/Q_a - C_b/Q_b - x), \tag{8b}$$

where R is the (log of the) bond-exchange rate, $\ln(Q_b/Q_a)$, and x is the anticipated rate of change of R. Supply and demand factors are embedded in $\tilde{R}$ exactly as they were in $\tilde{e}$ such that $\tilde{R}$ is the value of R when the anticipated differential return is zero.

It is clear from the construction of the money-equation (8) and the bond-equation (8b) that the only difference between the determination of the money-exchange rate (e) and the bond-exchange rate (R) is that the values of bonds effect the differential bond yield whereas the values of monies do not influence the differential money yield.

Equation (8b) can be used to contrast the implications of CS with the implications of bond substitution. First, we found that the change in e necessary to accommodate a change in the anticipated rate of change of e, as given by $\partial e/\partial x$, approaches infinity as CS becomes perfect. In contrast, the change in R necessary to accommodate a change in the differential bond return is

$$\partial R/\partial x = \eta/(1+\eta i), \tag{9}$$

where the derivative has been simplified by evaluating it at the point where $C_a/Q_a = C_b/Q_b = i$. The derivative $\partial R/\partial x$ approaches $1/i$ as bond substitution becomes perfect. Thus, changes in x have a limited impact on the bond-exchange rate. If, for example, bond holders suddenly expect bond B to appreciate relative to bond A, their effort to sell A and purchase B increases the yield on A and decreases the yield on B until holders are satisfied with the existing quantities of bonds. This is not the case for two monies since values of monies have no influence on the market yields on monies.

Finally, consider the determination of the bond-exchange rate, R, when bonds A

and B are perfect substitutes. Just as individual money demands are no longer defined ($\tilde{e}$ is undefined) when CS is perfect, individual bond demands are no longer defined ($\tilde{R}$ is undefined) when bond substitution is perfect. But in the case of perfect bond substitution, R is determined by the requirement that the differential return is zero. Setting the parenthesis on the right-hand side of (8b) to zero constrains the bond-exchange rate since Q_a and Q_b are determinants of the differential yield. In contrast, P_1 and P_2 did not appear in the differential yield formula for monies. For perpetuity bonds with continuous interest payments, the bond-exchange rate equals the ratio of interest payments, that is, $Q_b/Q_a = C_b/C_a$.[6] Perfect bond substitution rigidly fixes the bond-exchange rate whereas perfect CS leaves the money-exchange rate indeterminate.

Although indeterminacy is a logical implication of a model that utilizes widely accepted money-demand functions, we regard it as a consequence of abstracting from transactions costs and not of immediate concern for policy. The macro model used in this section abstracts from the costs of posting multiple prices or converting prices stated in one money to another money. Examples of *perfect* substitution of which we are aware, for example, Federal Reserve notes of different districts, exhibit *unitary* exchange rates. This suggests that transactions costs at exchange rates other than unity (or perhaps multiples of ten) may be an important constraint on the rate of exchange between perfectly substitutable currencies.

2. THE DISTINCTION BETWEEN MONEY AND BONDS

In the preceding section the implications of CS were contrasted with the implications of bond substitution. It was emphasized that the peculiarity of the CS implications is due to the invariance of the market yields on monies with respect to their values. The economic rationale for this distinguishing characteristic of money will be examined in this section.

It will be sufficient to focus on only one bond and one money. The analysis is simplified with the assumption of perfect foresight. With this assumption, r_m and r_b are used to represent both the anticipated and actual real returns on the money and the bond, respectively. The procedure will be to examine the yield formulas for r_b and r_m to determine exactly why r_b depends on the value of the bond and why r_m does not depend on the value of money.

The formula for the instantaneous real return on a bond can be expressed as

$$r_b = C_b/Q_b + g, \tag{10}$$

[6]With perfect substitution between bonds A and B, their anticipated real yields will be equal, which implies that

$$C_a/Q_a + g_a = C_b/Q_b + g_b,$$

where g_a and g_b are the capital gains. If capital gains are equal, the equality of real yields immediately implies that the bond-exchange rate equals the ratio of the interest payments. This solution is also derived in Appendix B, where the capital gains are not assumed equal.

where g represents the capital gain against goods (which could be decomposed into the appreciation of the money price of the bond minus the rate of change of the money price of goods). Using π to represent the rate of inflation, the instantaneous real yield on money is

$$r_m = i_m - \pi. \tag{11}$$

To understand why i_m is "constant" requires explicit recognition of the difference between the interest *payment* and the interest *rate* on money.[7] By denoting the money value of the interest payment as C_m, formula (11) can be expressed as

$$r_m = C_m/1 - \pi, \tag{12}$$

where $-\pi$ is, like g in equation (10), the capital gain against goods. C_m is the (fraction of) units of money paid per time period per unit of money. The price of money that must be used to deflate C_m is, as the dimensions indicate, the price of money in terms of itself, viz., unity.

A comparison of the yield formulas (10) and (12) reemphasizes the earlier argument that the yield on a bond depends inversely on its value Q_b, whereas the yield on money does not depend on its value (whether measured in terms of goods P^{-1}, or in terms of bonds Q_b^{-1}). To explain the difference between money and bonds, we will briefly consider how the yield formulas would be written if the interest payments on both bonds and money were tied to the price level or indexed against inflation. Suppose that the interest payment on a bond were indexed against inflation such that the real interest payment were constant. Then the appropriate expression for the real bond return would be

$$r_b = c_b/q_b + g, \tag{10'}$$

where $c_b = C_b/P$, $q_b = Q_b/P$, and P is the money price of goods. If c_b is constant, then (10′) shows that r_b depends not on Q_b per se, but on q_b.

Similarly, if the coupon or interest payment on money were fixed in real terms, then the appropriate real return formula for money would be

$$r_m = c_m/P^{-1} - \pi, \tag{12'}$$

where c_m is the constant real interest payment. The denominator P^{-1} is the goods value of money. Equation (12′), in contrast to (12), shows that the yield on money *does* depend on the (goods) value of money when the interest payment is contracted

[7]In this section we assume that the interest *payment* on money is fixed and use the fixed interest payment to explain the fixed interest rate i_m. In a broader analysis in which other variables are endogenized, neither the interest rate nor the interest payment would need to be fixed. i_m could vary but, if the model were neutral (with respect to the level of nominal variables), then r_m and, therefore, i_m would be independent of P. The invariance of i_m with respect to P is consistent with the observable, positive relation between bank deposit rates (that are not subject to ceilings) and the *rate-of-change* of P.

in terms of goods. When contrasted with (10) and (12), equations (10′) and (12′) show that the yield on an asset depends inversely on the value of the asset measured in the units in which the interest payments are fixed.

One observes that most contractual obligations are specified in terms of the units in which the medium of exchange is measured. Escalated contracts and other forms of indexation are the exceptions, not the rule. Interest payments on money, when they are nonzero, are specified in terms of money units.[8] Interest payments on bonds are not specified in bond units. As Keynes pointed out, "it is the essence of debt [in contrast to what Keynes called "money proper"] to be enforceable in terms of something other than itself" [17, p. 6]. Conversely, it is the essence of money that its own return be contracted in the same units used to measure the asset itself. And this defining characteristic of money explains the differences in the implications generated by CS and those generated by bond substitution.

The distinction developed here between money and bonds contrasts sharply with the current view in the theoretical literature. A widely accepted statement of the money-bond distinction is given by Tobin [30, 31]. According to Tobin, the nominal interest rate on money is "exogenously fixed." But the only items fixed are the coupons or interest payments on both money and bonds. And the interest *rate* on money is "fixed" (i.e., invariant to the value of money), not because the interest payment is fixed, but because interest on money is specified in terms of itself. It is not the fixity of the interest payment but the units in which it is fixed that makes i_m invariant to the value of money. If the interest payment on money were fixed in terms of any other commodity or asset, then money, like other assets, would have a market yield dependent on its value and the implications of CS would be similar to the implications of substitution between other financial assets. Further research should provide more insight into why contracts are specified in units in which the medium of exchange is measured.[9] But it is unnecessary to accept the invariance of i_m as an institutional datum.

3. IMPLICATIONS OF CS FOR THE BEHAVIOR OF MONEY ISSUERS

In section 1 CS was associated with instability in the sense that, for a given shift in anticipated exchange rate movements, greater CS produced larger exchange rate

[8] We have thus far considered only the pecuniary yield on money. To determine the relation between the value of money and its *total* return, it is necessary to consider the nonpecuniary yield on money and payments in kind (e.g., bank services to large depositors). As long as real behavioral functions are homogeneous of degree zero in nominal variables, these considerations do not alter the invariance of money's return to the value of money.

[9] Opinions differ over priority of the unit-of-account and medium-of-exchange properties of money. We conjecture that the medium-of-exchange property is fundamental to the unit-of-account because creditors can be paid off in any exchange medium as long as the market value of the medium satisfies the contract. If this is true, then, contrary to prevailing opinion, the medium-of-exchange property *is* embedded in models of the financial sector through the standard assumption that i_m is fixed. If the medium-of-exchange property is fundamental, then it is both the source of indeterminacy (through its determination of the units in which interest-payment contracts are specified) and a source of resolution of the indeterminacy issue (through the transactions costs of using more than one exchange media without unitary exchange rates).

Other authors (e.g., Keynes [17]) have argued that the unit-of-account property is fundamental to the medium-of-exchange property. Resolution of this question is outside the scope of this paper.

fluctuations. One of the crucial assumptions underlying the model in section 1 was that money issuers were assumed to alter neither the nominal quantity of money, M, nor the nominal yield on money, i_m, in response to exchange rate fluctuations. By altering either the explicit interest paid on money or the quantity of money (and imposing a capital gain or loss on money holders), a money issuer could alter the real return (r_m) and induce the changes in currency demand necessary to eliminate or at least dampen fluctuations in the exchange rate. It is particularly appropriate for an issuer of substitutable money to use the real money yield as the monetary control variable because, as was shown in section 1, the impact of a change in r_m on the exchange rate becomes greater as CS increases. In this section, the behavior of money issuers is endogenized and their response to demand shifts is shown to eliminate the instability associated with CS in the model of section 1.

There are a multitude of objectives leading money issuers to respond to exchange market pressure. With an increase in CS, the role of profit or seigniorage considerations should become more important in the determination of monetary policy. Central banks with policies more expansionary than the average would find their monetary control seriously eroded if they acted as if their seigniorage position was unimportant when their liabilities are substitutes with other currencies. The model developed in this section will, consequently, assume profit-maximization.

With substitutable monies, market pressure will force individual money issuers to make their monies attractive relative to alternative monies available to money holders. But the implications of CS will depend on the market structure in which substitutable monies are issued. Of particular interest are a competitive market structure and a cartel market structure.[10]

Money issuers may cooperatively determine a joint monetary policy through a cartel agreement to retain market shares.[11] To reduce the incentive for money holders to shift between monies, a formal cartel would likely include a fixed exchange rate agreement to help ensure that cartel members property coordinate their policies. If, for example, one member bank attempted to pursue a less inflationary policy (and pay a higher real yield), the demand for its currency would increase. In order to keep its currency from appreciating against member currencies, the bank would have to reverse its tight policy and create money against the purchase of the weaker currencies. Similarly, commercial banks' traditional commitment to maintain a fixed exchange rate between their deposit liabilities and central bank money restrains competition between the central and commercial banks. A cartel would stabilize exchange rates without providing money holders lower inflation rates or higher real yields.

A primary purpose of this section is to develop the implications of competitively supplied money.[12] Authors such as Friedman [7] and Pesek and Saving [26] have

[10]Rather than compete or form a cartel, money issuers could be protected through the institution of currency controls. The absence of such controls was implicitly assumed in section 1 when (the multicurrency version of) purchasing-power-parity was introduced, and that assumption is continued here. If governments protect central banks' monopoly position by prohibiting the use of "foreign" monies, then the arbitrage condition underlying PPP will be violated.

[11]As we have argued in [13], the European Monetary Union is an example of monetary cooperation facilitated through the use of a fixed-exchange-rate regime.

[12]Monetary competition has been introduced in a general neoclassical framework by Thompson [29].

argued that competition in the production of money is not viable because the value of money will be driven to its marginal cost of physical production. If this occurred, a commodity money would be the result and the advantages of a fiduciary system would be lost.

Since the marginal cost of paper and ink or maintenance of accounting entries necessary to physically produce other debt instruments (e.g., bonds) is, like money, near zero, we should ask why a similar conclusion has not been deduced for the supply of other financial instruments. The primary cost of producing a bond is, obviously, the interest and principal obligation, not the trivial cost of paper and ink. But the contractual payments represent a cost to a bond issuer only because the coupons are fixed in terms of another asset, usually money. On the other hand, the physical cost of production appears as the only cost for a monopoly issuer of fiat money because money holders must accept interest payments determined by contracts expressed in units of the money issuers own liability, if interest is paid at all. The fact that contracts are traditionally specified in money units explains why it is frequently argued that competitively supplied money will be issued until it becomes worthless and why a similar argument is not (to our knowledge) generally made for competition in the supply of other debt instruments.

Money holders choose between monies on the basis of anticipated real rates of return and, consequently, banks compete through their offers of real returns. Since the real return on money is $r_m = i_m - \pi$, a bank can change its real return by altering either the nominal yield i_m or the capital gain or loss on money, π. The theoretical results of this section are independent of the particular way a money issuer chooses to offer a given real return. But the institutional arrangements for rate-of-return competition are interesting in their own right. A brief discussion of possible arrangements will motivate a key assumption in the model that follows.

Under existing institutional arrangements, the monetary liabilities of commercial banks are convertible into the liabilities of a national central bank. But if commercial banks were not required to link their deposits to central bank liabilities, they could make their deposits convertible into any assets or goods they might choose. A bank concerned with seigniorage would choose assets that would have the greatest appeal to money holders. Since money holders are presumed interested in real rather than nominal values, they would prefer convertibility into real assets or assets with stable purchasing power. If the bank were able to, in effect, hold a portfolio of real assets, then the convertibility of the bank's deposit liabilities into real assets would insure depositors against real capital loss.[13] In short, profit considerations would induce banks to offer monetary liabilities convertible into assets with stable real values. This would be a return to a real (but not necessarily gold) standard.

At the abstract level of the model developed here the assets available for the banks of issue to hold are limited to capital goods paying a real yield of r. The assumption that banks maintain convertibility of their deposit liabilities into bank-

[13]Banks would presumably hold correspondent balances at other banks and deposit withdrawals could take the form of checks on other banks rather than convertibility into the actual assets of the first bank. The convertibility arrangement would be like a modern open-ended mutual fund or money market fund.

held assets implies that the bank's monetary liabilities are fixed against (capital) goods. This implies that the value of bank liabilities are guaranteed against capital loss in terms of goods.[14]

To make our model compatible with previous work on the revenue from inflation, we assume the nominal interest payment on money is zero ($i_m = 0$) such that the entire real return r_m is paid through deflation. This is equivalent to the institutional arrangement described above (in which money issuers maintain convertibility of their liabilities into assets with stable real purchasing power) if the convertibility feature is modified. Rather than maintaining a fixed parity between its liabilities and its (real) assets, a bank maintains convertibility at a price changing at a constant rate, $r_m = -\pi$. The bank of issue stands ready to redeem its liabilities at a price-path whose slope is (minus) the real return that the bank offers on its monetary liabilities.[15]

A profit-maximizing model for the behavior of a single money issuer will be developed for all degrees of CS. We depart from earlier literature on the revenue from inflation by dividing the flow of earnings into two parts. The first is the flow of net real income from issuing new money. The gross flow is $\dot{M}/P$. Part of the new money issued is used to purchase and hold real assets to provide a redemption fund to back the liabilities being created. Thus, the flow of net real income is $\dot{M}/P - \dot{m} = \pi m$ where $\dot{m} = d(M/P)/dt$. The second part of the bank's earnings is the return on the redemption fund, rm. Total net real revenue at time t, measured as an instantaneous rate is, therefore,

$$\pi m + rm = im, \qquad (13)$$

where im is the area under the usual liquidity preference schedule. The area is a maximum (or minimum) where the elasticity of the demand for real balances with respect to the market rate on the alternative asset is (minus) unity.[16] The elasticity, $m'(i)[i/m]$, is unitary when

[14]According to Friedman [8], it is not feasible for monetary policy to stabilize a price index given the current state of economic knowledge; hence, a stable rate of monetary growth is preferable to an active policy to stabilize P. Friedman is implicitly assuming that money issuers hold nominal assets. As we argue in the text, a bank that is serious about controlling the real value of its monetary liabilities would hold real, not nominal, assets. Just as money issuers once maintained the gold value of their liabilities by holding gold assets, they can maintain the real value of their liabilities by holding real assets. This would allow for price stabilization at the present state of economic knowledge.

[15]The assumption that the bank of issue guarantees a price path is equivalent to Auernheimer's [1] concept of an "honest" bank.

The question of the honesty or deception of money issuers in a competitive market has been given detailed attention by Klein [20]. He treats money as a consumer durable and argues that a long-run profit maximizing bank will limit current deception and hold down the current inflation rate in order to not erode consumer confidence in its money. Banks will act to create (what Klein calls) "brand name capital." In Klein's model with costly information it will be profitable, even under conditions of perfect competition, to have nonzero deception. We differ from Klein in that we assume banks can costlessly write binding contracts if they so desire, these contracts can be costlessly enforced, and default can be insured against. Under these conditions only firms that offer a goods-back-guarantee (along a price path) will be able to attract money holders.

[16]The present value of a bank offering a return $r_m = -\pi$ and facing an initial money-demand, $m(i,w(0))$, is $\int im(i,w(\tau))\exp(-r\tau)d\tau$, where integration is from zero to T, w is real wealth growing at an exogenous rate γ, and r is assumed greater than γ to assure convergence. Auernheimer [1] has a

$$i = m/m'(i) \quad \text{or} \quad \pi = m/m' - r. \tag{14}$$

A maximum is assured (i.e., $\partial^2[im(i)]/\partial i^2 < 0$) when an exponential specification for the demand for money is used. Assuming market interest rates on other monies are unchanged, the exponential specification used in section 1 (equation (3)) implies the relation $m'(i) = -(\alpha + \sigma)m$. Substituting this relation into (14) yields

$$i = 1/(\alpha + \sigma) \quad \text{or} \quad \pi = 1/(\alpha+\sigma) - r. \tag{15}$$

Several implications of CS follow immediately from equation (15). Beginning from a position in which each bank has a complete monopoly ($\sigma = 0$), equation (15) implies $\pi = 1/\alpha - r$, a result which has been derived by Phelps [27] and Auernheimer [1].

With substitution between the liabilities of money issuers, their ability to maintain monopolies in segmented markets is undermined. As inspection of equation (15) shows, the profit-maximizing inflation rate falls with larger values of σ. The greater the degree of CS, the more easily a money issuer can capture a larger share of the market by offering a lower rate of inflation. As substitution between monies becomes perfect ($\sigma \rightarrow \infty$), a competitive money issuer engineers a deflation equal to the alternative real return, r. Another way to express the condition is that the alternative asset's nominal yield is zero, that is, $r + \pi = 0$. With perfect CS, therefore, the opportunity cost of holding money becomes equal to the (assumed) zero marginal cost of production. This condition was introduced by Friedman [9] for an optimal quantity of real money balances.[17] Resource allocation between money creation and other activities should be efficient when money issuers compete and their liabilities are perfect substitutes in demand.[18]

---

similar present value formula for the limiting case, $T \rightarrow \infty$. As long as $m(i,w)$ is "separable" in i and w as in equation (3) of section 1, then the maximization of the flow, $im(i,w(t))$, at every point in time will assure the maximization of its present value. The discussion in the text is based on this assumption.

The upper limit of integration, T, is the date at which the bank is assumed to retire all of its liabilities outstanding. The preceding present value expression equals

$$m(0) + \int(\dot{M}/P)\exp(-r\tau)d\tau - m(T)\exp(-rT),$$

where integration is from 0 to T, $m(T)$ is short hand for $m(i,w(T))$, and the last term is the present value of the cost of converting $M(T)$ into $m(T)$ goods at the price $P(T) = P(0)\exp(\pi T)$. When the partial derivative of the present value is taken with respect to π and set to zero, the result is equation (14), which is independent of the value of T.

The assumption of an explicit redemption fund is expositionally convenient but not logically necessary. Regardless of the resources a bank might or might not retain in order to be able to maintain convertibility along the announced price path, the discounted value of the monetary liability, $m(T)\exp(-rT)$, must be substracted out to correctly ascertain the firm's net worth.

[17]Literature on the optimum quantity of money is usually expressed in terms of *the* optimum quantity of money. But the marginal conditions for Pareto efficiency can hold for different levels of real balances if other variables, such as the distribution of wealth, are considered. Consequently, it is more accurate to refer to the marginal conditions for *an* optimum quantity of money. The marginal condition ($i = 0$) assures efficiency in the production of money if efficiency conditions are not violated elsewhere, and, in particular, if other sources of government revenue are nondistorting. These issues are dealt with in an optimal tax framework by Phelps [27].

[18]Competition does not produce efficiency if, as has been argued, there is an externality involved in the holding of money. The usual argument (e.g., Friedman [9]) is that an individual who increases his cash balances must forgo consumption. Given a fixed nominal quantity of money, others in the community are able to temporarily consume more than their income as the value of their real balances is increased. Thus,

The solution found for no CS or for a monopoly bank, viz., that $\pi = 1/\alpha - r$, is also applicable to a cartel of money issuers whose liabilities are linked with fixed rates. A cartel produces money with a low or negative real return and suboptimal real balances.

The results of this section can be cast in more general terms by relaxing the assumption that the bank pays no explicit interest on its liabilities. The market or nominal yield on the alternative nonmonetary asset can be represented by $i = r + \pi$. If no interest is paid on money, then i is equal to the differential real yield. In symbols,

$$r - r_m = (i - \pi) - (i_m - \pi) = i - i_m \tag{16}$$

is equal to i if i_m is zero. If the more general expression $r - r_m$ is substituted for i in the profit-maximizing condition (15), the result is

$$r_m = r - 1/(\alpha + \sigma). \tag{15'}$$

If the interest payment on money is not taken as exogenous, then i_m and π can take on an infinity of values without violating the competitive profit-maximizing condition (15′). (*cf.* also [20].) When there are no exogenous nominal rates, a homogeneous model such as ours determines the difference in nominal rates but not their absolute levels.[19]

If the nominal returns on monies are equal, whether at zero or otherwise, then the equality of real returns assures equal inflation rates and secularly stable exchange rates.[20] The regime of fixed rates imposed by a cartel bears only a superficial

---

the person who acquires more real balances confers an external benefit on others in the community for which he receives no compensation. This argument is based on the assumption of an exogenous money supply.

When money is endogenized with the assumption that the bank of issue accommodates any changes in real demand, it becomes clear that an externality is not inherent in the holding of money. The bank issues more fiduciary currency in return for the goods (or equities) that the first person sells to acquire more cash balances. The individual must consume less only if the bank is not competitive. If the bank is competitive, money holders receive the real rate of return, r, and the individual's consumption does not fall. In short, there is no externality involved in the holding of money. What has appeared as an externality is due to the fixed money supply assumption. (A similar point has been developed in [33].)

[19]The original revenue function (13) can be redeveloped under the assumption that i_m is nonzero. The gross revenue is $M/P - i_m m$ and the net flow of real revenue is $M/P - i_m m - \dot{m}$ which equals $-r_m m$. The stream of real returns from the redemption fund remains $r \cdot m$ such that the total net flow of real revenue is

$$-r_m m + rm = [r - r_m]\cdot m(r-r_m). \tag{13'}$$

Maximization of (13′) with respect to the differential real return yields (15′).

Our results are consistent with Hayek's [14] argument that competition in the provision of currencies (that he calls "concurrent currencies") will produce a stable price level if it is assumed that i_m is equal to r. If there is no explicit interest on money, then competition should produce deflation rather than stable prices.

[20]With only one real asset in our model, the banks offer the same real return on their monetary liabilities and hold only the single real asset. An extended model would allow for many goods and diversity of tastes among money holders. In the more complex model, banks might offer monies with different characteristics and hold different assets. With the possibility of banks holding different asset bundles and offering real returns measured against different bundles of goods, the exchange rate between monies would vary as the relative price indices of the different bundles of goods changed.

resemblance to the stable rates under competition. While the real returns on monies will be equal in either situation, the level of the returns will be very different.

4. SUMMARY

Two fundamental implications of CS were derived in section 1. CS was found to produce instability in the sense that shifts in the anticipated rate of exchange rate change produce larger movements in the exchange rate and these movements are unbounded as CS increases. The second implication was that, if two monies are perfect substitutes in demand, their rate of exchange is indeterminate.

The indeterminacy of the exchange rate between two perfectly substitutable monies is a logical consequence of an asset-demand model utilizing standard money-demand assumptions. But we suspect that the exchange rate would be determinate (probably at the value of unity) if transactions costs were developed more fully in aggregate money-demand functions. Further research appears necessary before policy prescriptions can be based on the finding of indeterminacy.

The instability found in section 1 was eliminated when the behavior of money issuers was endogenized in section 3. The original instability was implied by a model with exogenous nominal returns and exogenous nominal money supplies. When the response of money issuers to CS is incorporated in the analysis, the nominal returns and/or nominal supplies change in response to demand shifts. The pressures of CS induce coordination of monetary policies or rate-of-return competition. In either case, the exchange rate should be stable or follow a stable path. In the absence of CS, money issuers can engage in independent monetary policies resulting in fluctuating exchange rates. It is the absence of CS, not its presence, that allows for unstable exchange rates.

Boyer [3] and Kareken and Wallace [15] have argued, and some of the remarks by Mundell [23, 24] suggest, that the instability associated with CS should be countered with fixed exchange rates. But as was shown in section 3, fixing exchange rates is a method whereby money issuers agree to coordinate monetary policies to avoid market pressure and maintain market shares. The chief disadvantage of the cartel solution is that it allows money issuers, by collective action, to frustrate money holders' search for superior monies and is consistent with the high inflation rates experienced with the demise of the gold standard.

It is widely believed that one solution to the problem of inflation is to replace discretionary monetary policy with a rule for a fixed money growth rate. In the absence of CS, such a rule might eliminate exchange rate instability. But in the presence of CS, money-growth rate rules (in conjunction with fixed nominal yields on monies) would, as shown in section 1, cause exchange rate instability. Moreover, monies with fixed growth rates would be seen as inferior to competitively supplied currencies. Interestingly enough, these rules have come from economists (e.g., Milton Friedman and Henry Simons) who have been staunch advocates of the free market. The fear of eliminating government supported monopolies in the production of money stems from the view that competitively supplied money would be issued in such quantities that it would become valueless. But to attract ultimate wealth holders faced with a choice in monies, banks would have to issue monies convertible into real assets to assure money holders against capital loss. Rather than the competively supplied money becoming worthless, it would be convertible into real goods such that risk against capital loss would be minimal. A fixed money growth rule can be applied to a monopoly or a cartel. But a money supplied at a fixed rate of growth would be driven from circulation if the public is offered substitutable convertible currencies.

APPENDIX A

The Exchange Rate with Rational Expectations

In the text the expected rate of change in the exchange rate x is taken as exogenous. In this appendix the expected rate of change of the exchange rate is endogenized using the assumption of rational expectations, that is, the expected rate of change in the exchange rate is equal to the rate of change in the exchange rate determined in the model. It will be demonstrated that if dynamic stability is assumed, the rational expectations assumption is a special case of the model developed in the text.

The assumption of rational expectations can be imposed by substituting $\dot{e}$ for x in equation (8) of the text:

$$e(t) = \tilde{e}(t) - \eta(i_1 - i_2) + \eta\dot{e}(t), \tag{A1}$$

where e and $\tilde{e}$ are written as explicit functions of time. In order to solve the differential equation (A1) we need to specify how $\tilde{e}(t) = \ln[(M_1(t)/\theta_1(t))/(M_2(t)/\theta_2(t))]$ moves over time. We assume that $\tilde{e}(t)$ is a linear function of time,

$$\tilde{e}(t) = \tilde{e}(0) + kt. \tag{A2}$$

Substituting (A2) into (A1) we obtain

$$e(t) = \tilde{e}(0) + kt - \eta(i_1 - i_2) + \eta\dot{e}(t), \tag{A3}$$

which is a nonautonomous, linear differential equation with constant coefficients.

The general solution of (A3) is

$$e(t) = [\tilde{e}(0) - \eta(i_1 - i_2) + \eta k] + kt + C\exp(t/\eta), \tag{A4}$$

where

$$\dot{e}(t) = k + (C/\eta)\exp(t/\eta).$$

The characteristic root is positive, $1/\eta > 0$, so the autonomous part of the solution for $e(t)$ (A4) is unstable unless $C = 0$. The initial condition implies $C = e(0) - [\tilde{e}(0) - \eta(i_1 - i_2 - k)]$. Thus for the exchange rate to be on a nonexplosive time path $e(0) = \tilde{e}(0) - \eta(i_1 - i_2 - k)$. That is, stability requires that the level of the exchange rate jump instantaneously to its equilibrium value, $e(0)$, following any shock to the system. Dynamic stability implies the time path of e is given by

$$e(t) = [\tilde{e}(0) + kt] - \eta(i_1 - i_2 - k), \tag{A5}$$

where

$$\dot{e}(t) = k.$$

Equation (A5) produces the same implications as equations (8) in the text, with the proviso that x is equal to k, rather than being set arbitrarily, and where $\tilde{e}(t)$ is separated into the level of $\tilde{e}(t)$ at time zero, $\tilde{e}(0)$, and the growth of $\tilde{e}(t)$ after $t = 0$, $kt = (\tilde{e}(t) - \tilde{e}(0))$. Monetary changes are then separated into jumps in the levels of money supplies (and exogenous components of money demands), and changes in the rate of growth of $\tilde{e}(t)$:

$$de(t) = d\tilde{e}(t) - \eta d(i_1 - i_2) + \eta dk. \tag{A6}$$

As in the text, jumps in $\tilde{e}$ (exogenous changes in money supplies and demands) produce proportional changes in e independently of the degree of CS. Changes in the anticipated relative rate of return (changes in the is and in k) produce effects on e in proportion to the CS parameter η. In particular higher degrees of CS require larger jumps in e for given changes in the anticipated differential rate of return.

APPENDIX B

Determination of the Bond-Exchange Rate

The bond-exchange rate is the ratio Q_b/Q_a, where Q_a and Q_b are found as the capitalized values of the streams of future interest payments. Since the instantaneous bond yields may vary over time, a variable-yield capitalization formula must be used to determine Q_a and Q_b.

The instantaneous capital gain on bonds A and B will be denoted as $\hat{Q}_a$ and $\hat{Q}_b$, where $\hat{}$ indicates the percent change or instantaneous logarithmic time derivative. By definition, $x = (\hat{Q}_b - \hat{Q}_q)^*$ and we assume that the latter term is equal to $\hat{Q}_b^* - \hat{Q}_a^*$, where * represents an anticipated magnitude. The condition that $\delta = 0$ for all t therefore implies that $C_a/Q_a + \hat{Q}_a^* = C_b/Q_b + \hat{Q}_b^*$ for all t. The instantaneous yields are inclusive of capital gains and will be denoted as

$$\hat{\phi}_j(t) = d\ln\phi_j/dt = C_j/Q_j + \hat{Q}_j^*, \qquad (j = a,b),$$

where ϕ_j is the discount factor used in the capitalization formula, and

$$Q_j(t) = \int C_j \phi_j(\tau)\, d\tau \,/\, \phi_j(t), \qquad (j = a,b)$$

where integration is from t to infinity and the discount factor has the initial condition $\phi_j(0) = 1$. Perfect bond-substitution implies that $\phi_a(t) = \phi_b(t)$ holds for all t. Consequently, the ratio of $Q_b(t)$ to $Q_a(t)$, both found from the capitalization formula, equals C_b/C_a. Were the bonds not perpetuities, the bond-exchange rate would not generally equal the ratio of the interest payments, but it would nevertheless be fully determinate.

LITERATURE CITED

1. Auernheimer, Leonardo. "The Honest Government's Guide to the Revenue from the Creation of Money." *Journal of Political Economy,* 82 (May/June 1974), 598–606.

2. Boyer, Russell S. "Nickles and Dimes." Unpublished manuscript, Federal Reserve Board, 1972.

3. ______. "Currency Mobility and Balance of Payments Adjustment." In *The Monetary Approach to International Adjustment,* edited by Bluford H. Putnam and D. Sykes Wilford, pp. 184–98. New York: Praeger, 1978.

4. Bronfenbrenner, Martin. "The Currency-Choice Defense." *Challenge,* 22 (January/February 1980), 31–36.

5. Calvo, Guillermo A., and Carlos A. Rodriguez. "A Model of Exchange Rate Determination Under Currency Substitution and Rational Expectations." *Journal of Political Economy,* 85 (June 1977), 617–25.

6. Connolly, Michael. "The Monetary Approach to an Open Economy: The Fundamental Theory." In *The Monetary Approach to International Adjustment,* edited by Bluford H. Putnam and D. Sykes Wilford, pp. 6–18. New York: Praeger, 1978.

7. Friedman, Milton. *A Program for Monetary Stability.* New York: Fordham University Press, 1959.

8. ______. "The Role of Monetary Policy." *American Economic Review,* 58 (March 1968), 1–17.

9. ______. "The Optimum Quantity of Money." In *The Optimum Quantity of Money and Other Essays,* edited by Milton Friedman, pp. 1–50. Chicago: Aldine, 1969.

10. Girton, Lance, and Don Roper. "Theory and Implications of Currency Substitution." *International Financial Discussion Papers,* Federal Reserve Board, 1976.

11. ______. "A Monetary Model of Exchange Market Pressure Applied to the Post-War Canadian Experience." *American Economic Review,* 67 (September 1977), 537–48.

12. ______. "Substitutable Monies and the Monetary Standard." In *The Political Economy of Policy Making,* edited by Michael Dooley, Herbert Kaufman, and Raymond Lombra, pp. 233–46. Beverly Hills, Calif.: Sage, 1979.

13. ______. "A Theory of Currency Substitution and Monetary Unification." *Economie Appliquee,* 1980.

14. Hayek, Frederick A. *Denationalization of Money: An Analysis of the Theory and Practice of Concurrent Currencies.* London: Institute of Economic Affairs, 1976.

15. Kareken, John, and Neil Wallace. "Samuelson's Consumption-Loan Model with Country-Specific Fiat Monies." *Staff Report,* No. 24, Federal Reserve Bank of Minneapolis, July 1978.

16. ______. "International Monetary Reform: The Feasible Alternatives." *Quarterly Review,* Federal Reserve Bank of Minneapolis, Summer 1978.

17. Keynes, John Maynard. *A Treatise on Money: The Pure Theory of Money.* London: Macmillan, 1930.

18. ______. *The General Theory of Employment Interest and Money.* New York: Harcourt, Brace and Company, 1936.

19. King, David, Bluford H. Putnam, and D. Sykes Wilford. "A Currency Portfolio Approach to Exchange Rate Determination: Exchange Rate Stability and the Independence of Monetary Policy." In *The Monetary Approach to International Adjustment,* edited by Bluford H. Putnam and D. Sykes Wilford, pp. 119–214. New York: Praeger, 1978.

20. Klein, Benjamin. "The Competitive Supply of Money." *Journal of Money, Credit, and Banking,* 6 (November 1974), 423–53.

21. Miles, Marc A. "Currency Substitution, Flexible Exchange Rates, and Monetary Independence." *American Economic Review,* 68 (June 1978), 428–36.

22. ______. "Currency Substitution: Perspective, Implications, and Empirical Evidence." In *The Monetary Approach to International Adjustment,* edited by Bluford H. Putnam and D. Sykes Wilford, pp. 170–83. New York: Praeger, 1978.

23. Mundell, Robert A. *International Economics.* New York: Macmillan, 1968.

24. ______. *Monetary Theory; Inflation, Interest, and Growth in the World's Economy.* Pacific Palisades; Calif.: Goodyear, 1971.

25. Parkin, Michael. "Price and Output Determination in an Economy with Two Media of Exchange and a Separate Unit of Account." In *Recent Issues in Monetary Economics,* edited by Emil Claassen and Pascal Salin, pp. 74–98. Amsterdam: North-Holland, 1976.

26. Pesek, Boris P., and Thomas R. Saving. *Money, Wealth, and Economic Theory.* New York: Macmillan, 1967.

27. Phelps, Edmund S. "Inflation in the Theory of Public Finance." *Swedish Journal of Economics,* 75 (March 1973), 67–82.

28. Takayama, Akira, and Y. N. Shieh. "Flexible Exchange Rates Under Currency Substitution and Rational Expectations—Two Approaches to the Balance of Payments." Texas A&M University, manuscript, 1980.

29. Thompson, Earl. "The Theory of Money and Income Consistent with Orthodox Value Theory." In *Trade Stability and Macroeconomics,* edited by George Horwich and Paul A. Samuelson, pp. 427–51. New York: Academic Press, 1974.

30. Tobin, James. "Commercial Banks as Creators of Money." In *Banking and Monetary Studies,* edited by Deane Carson, pp. 408–19. Homewood, Ill.: Irwin, 1963.

31. ______. "A General Equilibrium Approach to Monetary Theory." *Journal of Money, Credit, and Banking,* 1 (February 1969), 15–29.

32. Tullock, Gordon. "Competing Monies." *Journal of Money, Credit, and Banking,* 7 (November 1975), 491–97.

33. Vaubel, Roland. "Free Currency Competition." *Weltwirtschaftliches Archiv,* 113 (October 1977), 435–59.

ROBERT L. HETZEL*

The Federal Reserve System and Control of the Money Supply in the 1970s

1. INTRODUCTION

THIS PAPER ADDRESSES THE QUESTION of whether the Federal Reserve System in the 1970s used the money supply as its predominant intermediate target of policy.[1] Did the Federal Reserve "control" the money supply in the 1970s, where "control" is defined as requiring that the behavior of the money supply accurately reflect the stance of monetary policy desired by the Federal Open Market Committee (FOMC) of the Federal Reserve System? The question just posed is approached through an examination of the system's operating procedures for implementing monetary policy in the 1970s. What intermediate target of policy was the FOMC trying to achieve, as inferred by its choice of operating procedures?[2]

*The author is indebted for critical comments to Neil Berkman, J. Alfred Broaddus, Raymond Lombra, Thomas Mayer, Paul Meek, Ann-Marie Meulendyke, Clark Warburton, Roy Webb, Robert Weintraub, and three anonymous referees. The views expressed in this paper are those of the author. They should not be attributed to the preceding individuals, to the Federal Reserve System, or the Federal Reserve Bank of Richmond.

[1]Feige and McGee [3] and Benjamin Friedman give an affirmative answer. Friedman wrote of the Federal Reserve's October 6, 1979, actions, "many observers of monetary policy believe that the new policy amounts to adopting a monetary growth target strategy for monetary policy where none existed before. Instead . . . the Federal Reserve has changed the method of using open market operations to implement the monetary growth target strategy that it has had throughout most of the past decade. The general policy of pursuing monetary growth targets remains" [4, p. 9]. DeRosa and Stern reach an ambiguous conclusion [2]. Poole gives a negative answer [8].

[2]Information about the operating procedures of the Federal Reserve can be derived from three sources. The first is the annual reviews of open market operations published in the *Review* of the Federal Reserve Bank of New York. The second is the *Record of Policy Actions of the FOMC* published in the *Federal Reserve Bulletin*. The *Record* contains the directive issued by the FOMC to the Desk and a summary of the discussion that produced the directive. The third is the document entitled *Monetary Aggregates and*

ROBERT L. HETZEL *is economist, Federal Reserve Bank of Richmond.*

0022-2879/81/0281-0031$00.50/0
JOURNAL OF MONEY, CREDIT, AND BANKING, vol. 13, no. 1 (February 1981)

If the FOMC had viewed the money supply as its primary intermediate target of policy, it would have put into place a set of operating procedures that would have ensured control of the money supply. Such a set of operating procedures must possess the following three characteristics. First, long-run money supply targets that are operationally significant must exist. Operationally significant money supply targets are defined to be targets that, once established, remain invariant with respect to the subsequent actual behavior of the money supply and thus can serve as a benchmark for assessing the actual behavior of the money supply. Second, short-run money supply targets that are derived from the long-run targets must exist. These targets provide for the System Open Market Account Manager (the Desk) a guide for week-to-week actions that will ensure that the long-run money supply targets are achieved. Third, the Desk must possess the ability to alter its operating variable sufficiently in order to eliminate deviations of actual values of the money supply from the targeted values.

2. LONG-RUN MONEY SUPPLY TARGETS

Did the Federal Reserve's money supply targets in the 1970s possess operational significance? Beginning in 1970, the FOMC specified targets for the rate of growth of the money supply over intervals of one quarter. At the first monthly meeting in a quarter, a target was set for the current quarter. At the second and third monthly meetings, a target was set for the current and for the succeeding quarter. Beginning in September 1972, the target for the money supply was specified as a rate of growth over an interval of two quarters. At the first and second monthly meetings in a quarter, a target was set for the current and succeeding quarter combined. At the third meeting, a target was set for the succeeding two quarters combined. (The M1 targets were not publicly announced until April 1975. The targets before this date are listed in an appendix to this paper available from the author.) A realized monthly value for the money supply was used as the base to which to apply the targeted rate of growth. This base was changed each quarter. Consequently, a deviation in the realized value of the money supply from its previously targeted value would be incorporated into the new base. (This characteristic came to be known as "base drift.") In the absence of offsetting changes in the targeted growth rate, base drift vitiates money supply targets of operational significance. Targets move in line with misses and thus cannot serve as a benchmark for assessing the actual behavior of the money supply. The question of whether the FOMC offset the phenomenon of base drift by changes in the targeted rates of growth of the money supply is examined initially for the period from the second quarter of 1970 to the first quarter of 1975.

Money Market Conditions (called the *Bluebook*) prepared by the staff of the Board of Governors and the Federal Reserve Bank of New York and circulated to members of the FOMC before each of their meetings. The first section of the *Bluebook* evaluates recent financial developments with reference to the predictions and targets for financial variables associated with the directive issued at the last meeting. The second section suggests alternative directives for the Desk for the coming period and details the implications of each for conditions in the money markets and the behavior of the monetary and credit aggregates. This document is available publicly (upon request) with a five-year lag. For an example of a careful examination of the manner in which the *Bluebook* was used by the FOMC, see [6].

A regression was run (eq. (1)), using quarterly observations, of changes in targeted rates of growth of the money supply ($TG_1 - TG_O$) on the difference, over the preceding period, between actual (AG_O) and targeted (TG_O) rates of growth of the money supply. If the FOMC's money supply targets were varied in order to endow them with operational significance, the coefficient on the right-hand side variable would be significantly negative. For example, errors incorporated into the base when the actual exceeded the targeted growth of M1 would be offset by decreases in the long-run targets. Future targets for M1, expressed in level form, would then not have been affected by the vagaries of quarterly misses in money supply targets. The regression (1) exhibits a positive rather than a negative coefficient on the right-hand side variable, indicating that before 1975 the FOMC's money supply targets could not be used as benchmarks against which to assess the realized behavior of the money supply.[3]

$$(TG_1 - TG_O) = \underset{(0.02)}{0.01} + \underset{(1.8)}{0.32}\,(AG_O - TG_O) + U \qquad (1)$$

observations = 19; RSQ = 0.16; SER = 1.9; D-W = 2.9 (t statistics in par entheses).

House Concurrent Resolution 133, passed by Congress March 24, 1975, expressed the will of Congress that the Federal Reserve System report to it the system's objectives for growth of the money supply over four-quarter periods. In response, the FOMC made three minor changes in its procedures for specifying targets for growth of the money supply. It began specifying targets as a range, rather than as a single value; it began specifying targets for one year, rather than for two-quarter intervals; and it began using a quarter, rather than a month, as the base value against which to apply its targets for growth rates. These changes did nothing, however, to ensure the FOMC's targets of operational significance. From April 1975 through October 1978, the FOMC, each quarter, set four-quarter targets for the rate of growth of M1. The realized four-quarter rate of growth of M1 fell short of the target range in the third quarter of 1976 and exceeded the target range from the third quarter of 1977 through the fourth quarter of 1978. In no case was the target range adjusted in order to compensate for base drift. In October 1978, Congress passed the Full Employment and Balanced Growth Act of 1978. Its implementation

[3]The left-hand side variable is first-differences of the targeted rate of growth of M1 chosen in the last monthly meeting of each quarter. From the second quarter of 1970 to the fourth quarter of 1972, M1 targets were set for one-quarter intervals. For this period, the right-hand side variable equals the actual rate of growth of M1 (projected to occur as of the last month of the quarter) over the interval from the last month of the preceding quarter to the last month of the current quarter minus the rate of growth of M1 targeted for this interval at the last monthly meeting of the preceding quarter. From the first quarter of 1973 to the first quarter of 1975, M1 targets were set for two-quarter intervals. For this period, the right-hand side variable equals the actual rate of growth of M1 (projected to occur as of the last month of the quarter) over the interval from the last month of the quarter two quarters ago to the last month of the current quarter minus the rate of growth of M1 targeted for this interval at the last monthly meeting two quarters ago. (The projected growth of M1 was obtained from the *Bluebook.*) Until the fourth quarter of 1972, TG_o is identical on both sides of (1), potentially biasing the multiplicative coefficient positively. If the Federal Reserve actually hit its money supply targets apart from random error, however, the right-hand side term ($AG_O - TG_O$) would be uncorrelated with TG_O on the left-hand side, and there would be no bias.

required that the base to which the targeted rate of growth of the money supply was applied be kept unchanged over the course of a year. This requirement went far toward eliminating the characteristic of base drift from money supply targets.

3. SHORT-RUN MONEY SUPPLY TARGETS

Did the FOMC furnish the Desk with short-run money supply targets, derived from the long-run targets, in order to guide the week-to-week actions of the Desk in a way that promoted hitting the long-run target? The FOMC did so before October 1972. In the 1970s, the targeted rate of growth of the money supply was accompanied by a tracking path consisting of monthly values of the money supply in level form. Until October 1972, the benchmark for M1 that guided the actions of the Desk between FOMC meetings was a weekly tracking path for M1 derived from the monthly tracking path. The Federal Reserve's operating procedures changed in 1972, however, as a result of an abortive attempt to control the money supply with the reserve aggregate, reserves available to support private deposits (RPDs). It is necessary to review this change in operating procedures before addressing the question just posed.

Beginning in February 1972, the FOMC, at its monthly meetings, selected the path for RPDs implied by its money supply target. In order to smooth the data on reserves that were to guide the actions of the Desk between FOMC meetings, the FOMC did not specify a weekly tracking path for RPDs. It specified instead a range of acceptable values of rates of growth over the two-month interval ending the month following the FOMC meeting. During the interval between FOMC meetings, if the projection of the two-month rate of growth of RPDs fell outside this range, the Desk was to vary the nonborrowed reserves of banks appropriately.

The FOMC constrained the extent to which the Desk could vary nonborrowed reserves in response to misses in RPD targets by specifying a range of permissible variation in the funds rate target. This range was not made public until the FOMC meetings beginning January 1974, but the *Record of Policy Actions* indicated its restrictiveness in 1972 by a statement, typically, indicating that the Desk had been instructed "to avoid a marked firming in money market conditions and unduly sharp increases in interest rates." It became apparent immediately that the magnitude of the change in the funds rate the FOMC was willing to permit was insufficient to allow actual RPD growth to be brought into line with targeted RPD growth. The tolerance ranges for two-month rates of growth of RPDs came to be viewed not as targets to be achieved, but rather as a device for indicating to the Desk when it should vary the funds rate target between FOMC meetings. They were, however, unsatisfactory even in this limited role. The relationship between RPD growth and growth in the money supply proved impossible to predict. Furthermore, because of lagged reserve accounting, RPD growth in the current statement week reflected deposit growth two weeks earlier, not current deposit growth.

In October 1972, in order to supplement the RPD tolerance range, the FOMC began specifying tolerance ranges for the rate of growth of M1 over the two-month interval ending the month following an FOMC meeting. The relationship of projections of two-month rates of growth of M1 to the specified tolerance range for growth of M1 then became the dominating determinant of when to change the funds rate target between FOMC meetings. Since 1970, the FOMC had issued two kinds of directives, which came to be distinguished as money-market and monetary-aggregates directives. The former called for a minor change in conditions in the money market if, over the interval between FOMC meetings, the money supply differed significantly from a benchmark value. The latter called for a larger change in conditions in the money market in response to smaller deviations of the money supply from the benchmark value. In early 1977, the informal difference between a monetary-aggregates and a money-market directive was quantified with respect to the use of the ranges of tolerance for two-month rates of growth of the money supply. With a monetary-aggregates directive, the Desk was to vary the funds rate target when the projected two-month growth rates for M1 and M2 exceeded the midpoints of their tolerance ranges by 1-¼ percentage points. With a money-market directive, the Desk was to vary the funds rate target when the projected two-month growth rates for M1 and M2 fell outside their tolerance ranges. Because the tolerance range was generally 4 percentage points wide, the funds rate was varied when the projection differed from the midpoint of the tolerance range by more than 2 percentage points.[4]

Changes in the federal funds rate target could then occur in two ways after 1972. First, the FOMC could explicitly change the target at an FOMC meeting or during a telephone conference between meetings. Second, the FOMC could effect changes as a consequence of instructions to the Desk to change the target contingent upon the behavior, over the interval between FOMC meetings, of projections of the two-month rate of growth of the money supply relative to the specified tolerance range for two-month rates of growth. Contingent changes in the funds rate were somewhat more important than explicit changes. For the period from November 1972 to February 1978, the standard deviation of explicit monthly changes was 0.29 and the standard deviation of contingent monthly changes was 0.35.[5]

Did the tolerance ranges for two-month rates of growth of M1 serve as short-run money supply targets? First, the FOMC stated that the M1 tolerance ranges, like the

[4]The authors noted in footnote 1 who argue that the Federal Reserve shifted to a monetary-aggregates strategy in the 1970s point to the positive statistical correlation between changes in the funds rate and growth of the money supply over short intervals of time that these operating procedures produced. This paper emphasizes that such a correlation does not imply control of the money supply in the absence of the three criteria listed in the second paragraph of the introduction.

[5]The series for each type of change in the funds rate target is derived by reading the *Record of Policy Actions*. The chairmanship of the FOMC changed in March 1978. After this time, all changes in the funds rate target were in fact explicit changes by the FOMC even though the tolerance ranges for M1 and M2 continued to be set. The Desk no longer altered the funds rate target when such an alteration was indicated by the projection for the two-month rate of growth of the money supply. A telephone conference of members of the FOMC was called instead, and the FOMC decided whether to alter the target. As indicated in the *Record of Policy Actions*, from March 1978 to September 1979, the operating procedures that triggered changes in the funds rate target during the interval between FOMC meetings in response to money supply projections called for a change in the target twelve times, but the change was overruled by the FOMC seven times.

RPD tolerance ranges they replaced, were not money supply targets, but rather were a device for indicating to the Desk when to alter the funds rate target between FOMC meetings. (The following excerpt is from the June 1978 *Record of Policy Actions*.) ''It was noted that, perhaps because of the manner in which the directive was worded, the 2-month ranges of tolerance for M1 and M2 were subject to misinterpretation as embodying the Committee's short-run targets for these aggregates, intended to be achieved by appropriate changes in the Federal funds rate. . . . The purpose of the 2-month ranges was to provide the manager with an indicator for determining when changes in the funds rate were appropriate.'' Second, no procedure was established for deriving the ranges of tolerance for M1 growth rates from the FOMC's target for the money supply.

How were the tolerance ranges for two-month rates of growth of M1 set? At its meetings, the FOMC had available an estimate, in the form of a range, of two-month rates of growth of M1 that were projected to be consistent with the prevailing funds rate. (This range is publicly available through 1975 and is listed, along with the M1 tolerance ranges actually adopted, in an appendix available from the author.) Examination of the data suggests that the FOMC set the actual M1 tolerance range slightly below this range when it considered the rate of growth of M1 to be too high and slightly above this range when it considered the rate of growth of M1 to be too high and slightly above this range when it considered the rate of growth of M1 to be too low.

From March 1973 through September 1979, out of seventy-seven FOMC meetings, the magnitude of the difference between the midpoint of the range of two-month rates of growth of M1 projected to be consistent with the prevailing funds rate and the midpoint of the adopted M1 tolerance range exceeded one percentage point only twelve meetings and exceeded 1.5 percentage points only four meetings. During the combined interval October 1972 to August 1974, April 1975 to October 1975, and February 1977 to September 1979, the difference between the midpoint of the range of two-month rates of growth of M1 projected to be consistent with the prevailing funds rate and the midpoint of the adopted M1 tolerance range was positive forty-four times and negative only four times (zero twelve times). As indicated by the behavior of the funds rate target set at each of the FOMC meetings, the FOMC considered the rate of growth of M1 to be too high in this combined interval.[6] Changes in the funds rate target set at these FOMC meetings were positive thirty-seven times and negative only seven times (zero fifteen times). During the combined interval September 1974 to March 1975 and November 1975 to January 1977, the difference between the midpoint of the range of two-month rates of growth of M1 projected to be consistent with the prevailing funds rate and the midpoint of the adopted M1 tolerance range was positive only three times and negative fourteen times (zero five times). In this combined interval, the FOMC considered the rate of growth of M1 to be too low as judged by the fact that changes

[6]The interval April 1975 to October 1975 contained the high rates of growth of M1 associated with the tax rebate. Although near the trough of the recession, the FOMC resisted these growth rates.

in the funds rate target set at FOMC meetings were positive only four times and negative thirteen times (zero five times). (The series on the funds rate target set at FOMC meetings is contained in an appendix to this paper available from the author.)

A set of regressions was run in order to determine whether the tolerance range for two-month rates of growth of M1 was derived in part from the long-run target for M1. The top, *TTR,* (bottom) of the adopted tolerance range for two-month rates of growth of M1 was regressed on (1) a constant; (2) the long-run target growth rate for M1, *T* (after 1975, the midpoint of the four-quarter target range); (3) the difference between the rate of growth of M1 over the six-month interval ending in the month of a particular FOMC meeting, as estimated at the time of the FOMC meeting, and the long-run target growth rate for M1, *D;* and (4) the top, *TTRFR,* (bottom) of the range of two-month rates of growth of M1 projected to be consistent with the prevailing funds rate. If the FOMC derived the tolerance range for two-month rates of growth of M1 from the long-run money supply target, the first three variables should enter the regression in a statistically significant fashion. For example, the top of the M1 tolerance range would be set equal to the long-run target for the rate of growth of M1 plus a positive constant. This value would then be adjusted in order to correct for recent deviations in the money supply from its targeted value. The regressions were run over the two periods given in the preceding paragraph as periods when the rate of growth of the money supply was considered to be "high" and "low." The following regression (2), using the upper bound of the M1 tolerance range, is for the "high" money growth period. The regression for the "low" money growth period using the upper M1 bound and the regressions for the "high" and "low" money growth periods using the lower M1 bound are similar to the regression shown. In no case does the long-run target for M1, T, enter with a statistically significant positive coefficient (in two cases the coefficients are statistically insignificant and negative).

$$\underset{}{TTR} = \underset{(3.9)}{1.8} + \underset{(0.4)}{0.03}\,T - \underset{(-2.8)}{0.10}\,D + \underset{(19.8)}{0.71}\,TTRFR \qquad (2)$$

observations = 60; RSQ = 0.88; SER = 0.55; D-W(2) = 1.7 (*t* statistics in parentheses).

The top of the range of two-month rates of growth of M1 projected to be consistent with the prevailing funds rate (*TTRFR*) does enter regression (2) with a statistically significant positive coefficient.[7,8] Discrepancies between actual and targeted

[7]There is considerable seasonal in the "seasonally adjusted" monthly figures for M1. The reason is that M1 is seasonally adjusted with constant historical seasonal adjustment factors, but the factors that put seasonality into the money supply, like tax rebates, vary from year to year. Movements in the range of two-month rates of growth of M1 projected to be consistent with the prevailing funds rate capture in part this residual seasonality. Adjusting the tolerance range for two-month rates of growth of M1 in light of this range could in principle have kept the system's operating procedures from imparting the seasonal in the money supply to the funds rate. As shown in [5], this effort was unsuccessful.

[8]The multiplicative coefficient on *TTRFR* exaggerates the extent to which the adopted tolerance range for M1 was adjusted downward in the "high" money growth periods relative to the range of two-month

rates of growth of the money supply D enter with a statistically significant negative coefficient. (These results continue to obtain when the regression is run with the bottom of the M1 tolerance range and for "low" money growth periods.) These results, in conjunction with the failure of the long-run targeted rate of growth of M1 to appear in a statistically significant manner, accord with the observation made above about how the FOMC set the M1 tolerance range.

The FOMC started with the range of two-month rates of growth of M1 projected to be consistent with the prevailing funds rate and then adjusted this range modestly downward if it felt that a sustained positive deviation in the rate of growth of M1 from its long-run targeted value had occurred or modestly upward if it felt that a negative deviation had occurred. Use of the estimated rate of growth of M1 over the three-month, rather than six-month, interval ending with the month of a particular FOMC meeting in calculating discrepancies between actual and targeted rates of growth of M1 causes the coefficient on such discrepancies in (2) to lose statistical significance. The t value on the coefficient of D becomes -0.6. It is concluded from this fact that the FOMC reacted to undesired increases in the rate of growth of the money supply only after it determined that such increases would not be self-correcting at the given funds rate target.[9]

The tolerance ranges for two-month rates of growth of M1 were not money supply targets. They were not specified with the intention that the Desk would vary the funds rate in order to cause the actual growth of the money supply to fall within their lower and upper bounds. They served the more limited role of indicating to the Desk when to change the funds rate target during the interval between FOMC meetings. They were a device for effecting changes in the funds rate target in the direction necessary in order to bring the actual rate of growth of the money supply into line with its targeted rate of growth. Although they served this role, they lacked the operational significance of money supply targets. Because the specification of the M1 tolerance ranges depended upon the range of M1 growth rates projected to be consistent with the prevailing funds rate, they were high when actual rates of growth of M1 were high and low when actual rates of growth of M1 were low. They did not yield a measure of the discrepancy between the actual value of the money supply and a value of the money supply consistent with the long-run targeted rate of growth of the money supply. (The subtle role played by the M1 tolerance ranges is elaborated on in section 5.)

---

rates of growth of M1 projected to be consistent with the prevailing funds rate. A more accurate measure comes from regressing *TTR* on *TTRFR* without the constant term.

$$TTR = \underset{(76.6)}{0.93}\ TTRFR \tag{3}$$

observations = 60; RSQ = 0.75; SER = 0.75; D-W(2) = 1.1 (t statistics in parentheses).

The only data used in regressions (2) and (3) that are not publicly available are the observations on *TTRFR* from 1976 through 1979.

[9]Over the "low" growth periods, this result was reversed. Discrepancies calculated using three-month, but not six-month, estimated rates of growth of M1 entered with a statistically significant negative coefficient. The total length of the "low" growth periods was twenty-two months. The "high" growth periods accounted for sixty months.

4. CHANGES IN THE FUNDS RATE TARGET

With respect to the third criterion given at the end of the introduction, was the Desk able to alter its operating target sufficiently in order to hit long-run money supply targets? The FOMC in the 1970s imposed constraints on the sign and magnitude of changes in the funds rate target. The first kind of constraint arose because the FOMC viewed the funds rate and the level of short-term interest rates as indicators of the stance of monetary policy, as illustrated by the following two quotations. "If the Federal Reserve tried to maintain a rigid monetary growth rate . . . interest rates could fluctuate widely, and to no good end. The costs of financial intermediation would be increased, and the course of monetary policy might be misinterpreted" [1, p. 557]. "Monetary policy also moved clearly in the direction of restraint during 1978. Interest rates for short-term market instruments rose about 3 to 4 percentage points. . . . These appreciable advances in market rates reflect a monetary policy that continues in its efforts to foster financial conditions consistent with a moderation in the pace of economic activity and a slowing of inflation" [7, p. 227]. Identification of changes in the funds rate with changes in the stance of monetary policy produced a strong desire on the part of the FOMC for changes in the funds rate to be unidirectional over extended periods of time. It was felt that changes in the funds rate that were reversed shortly after they were made would be construed by the public as evidence of erratic monetary policy.

First differences were taken of the series of the funds rate target set by the FOMC at each of its monthly meetings from October 1972 to September 1979. The differenced series changes sign only eight times in eighty-one meetings. No change in sign in the differenced series occurred from January 1977 to September 1979. (As a point of reference, the differenced series of monthly observations of the market rate of interest on three-month Treasury bills changes sign frequently as evidenced by the low first-order autocorrelation of this series, 0.15, calculated over the above interval.) If the funds rate had been viewed solely as an operating variable for controlling the money supply and if it had been set each month according to an unbiased estimate of what was required to keep the money supply on a chosen target path, changes in the funds rate target would have changed signs more frequently.

The FOMC also constrained the magnitude of changes in the funds rate target that could be effected by the Desk in the interval between FOMC meetings. In general, because the initial value of the funds rate target after an FOMC meeting was in the center of the range of permissible variation established by the FOMC, the Desk could vary the funds rate target during the interval between FOMC meetings by only half of this range. Dividing by half the funds rate range specified by the FOMC at its monthly meetings, including subsequent modifications in this range during telephone conferences, shows that the Desk had the freedom to vary the funds rate in one direction on average by fifty-eight basis points from October 1972 to December 1974, by forty-three basis points from January 1975 to February 1977, and by only twenty-eight basis points from March 1977 to September 1979.

Summarizing sections 2, 3, and 4, before 1979 the Federal Reserve System did not possess long-run targets for the money supply that could serve as a benchmark against which to assess the actual behavior of the money supply. After 1972, it did not possess short-run targets for the money supply to guide the actions of the Desk. Finally, it closely constrained the behavior of the funds rate for reasons unrelated to control of the money supply. The funds rate was modified when the actual rate of growth of the money supply was deviating in a persistent way from its targeted rate of growth. Given the above three characteristics of the system's operating procedures, however, this latter fact could only fortuitously produce control of the money supply. (Again, "control" as defined here requires that the behavior of the money supply represent accurately the stance of monetary policy desired by the FOMC.)

5. RATIONALIZING THE FOMC'S CHOICE OF OPERATING PROCEDURES

The FOMC's choice of operating procedures in the 1970s cannot be rationalized under the assumption that the FOMC viewed the money supply as its predominant intermediate target of policy.[10] The FOMC's choice of operating procedures can be rationalized under the assumption that the FOMC viewed both the rate of growth of the money supply and the level of short-term interest rates as important intermediate targets of policy in their own right. Policymaking in the 1970s centered around an ongoing process whereby each month desirable targets for the rate of growth of the money supply and for the level of short-term interest rates, when each of these two variables was considered in isolation, were compromised in order to arrive at mutually compatible targets. The federal funds rate was used both as an operating target and as an intermediate target. In its former role, it could be varied in order to determine the behavior of the money supply. In its latter role, it had an importance in itself as a determinant of the level of short-term interest rates and the spending decisions of the public. The system's operating procedures allowed the funds rate to be changed in order to affect the behavior of the money supply, but they also imparted an inertia to movements in the funds rate that allowed the funds rate to serve as an intermediate target of policy in its own right.[11]

Nothing in the FOMC's operating procedures defined what would constitute an overshoot or shortfall in the money supply when it was measured in level form. The spirit of achieving money supply targets was that when the actual differed from the desired rate of growth of the money supply, the funds rate would be gradually altered in order to bring the actual into line with the desired rate of growth. There was never any intention of correcting for overshoots or shortfalls in the money

[10]There is of course a diversity of opinion among members of the FOMC. The FOMC must, however, choose unique values for its operating target. In order to understand the particular choice of values that occurred in the 1970s, an effort was made to construct a point of view that could explain the collective actions of the members of the FOMC. Alternatively, one could view the FOMC as a heterogeneous group trying to arrive at a compromise value for its policy variable, the funds rate. The need to compromise could have imparted an inertia to movements in the funds rate. The inertia, in turn, could have accounted for the behavior of the money supply in the 1970s.

[11]It is an empirical question whether the operating procedures adopted in the 1970s improved "control" of the money supply, where control is assessed by reference to a reduction in the procyclical behavior of the money supply. A section deleted from the original paper because of considerations of length concluded that the money supply was not controlled more closely in the 1970s than in the 1960s.

supply that occurred in the process of aligning actual with desired rates of growth of the money supply. For example, from the time the FOMC began specifying tolerance ranges for the two-month rate of growth of M1 in October 1972 through September 1979, never did it set a range with a negative lower bound. This fact is evidence that the tolerance ranges were not manipulated in order to offset overshoots in M1. This approach toward targeting the money supply, and the operating procedures compatible with it, built an inertia into changes in the funds that can only be explained by a desire to maintain the level of short-term interest rates as an intermediate target of policy in its own right.

This approach toward targeting the money supply is illustrated by an example of how the tolerance ranges for two-month rates of growth of M1 were used in practice. Assume the FOMC felt, at some meeting in the 1970s, that the rate of growth of M1 had been undesirably high over the last couple months. Assume that the range of two-month rates of growth of M1 projected to be consistent with the prevailing funds rate was 2 to 6 percent, with a midpoint of 4 percent. (With no change in the funds rate, the two-month rate of growth of M1 ending the following month would be less than 4 percent with a 50 percent probability.) Typically in this situation, the FOMC would have left the funds rate unchanged, but would have set the midpoint of the tolerance range for two-month rates of growth of M1 1 percentage point below the midpoint of the above range, that is at 3 percent, and would have set a tolerance range of 1 to 5 percent. With a monetary-aggregates directive, a projection during the interval between meetings in excess of 4-¼ percent (the midpoint 3 percent plus 1-¼) would have triggered an increase in the funds rate, typically ⅛ to ¼ of a percentage point. A money-market directive would have required a projection in excess of 5 percent. (In either case, the probability of an increase in the funds rate target would have been less than 50 percent.)

It was in fact impossible to predict when a significant, persistent change in the magnitude of the rate of growth of the money supply would occur. In the situation just described, if a sustained increase in the rate of growth of the money supply had occurred, the money supply would in general have turned out to be higher than predicted. Over the course of the subsequent and ensuing intervals between FOMC meetings, the updating of projections of two-month rates of growth of the money supply in response to incoming data on the money supply would have triggered changes in the funds rate target. In practice, the procedure of specifying tolerance ranges for the rate of growth of the money supply gave the FOMC a means of effecting consecutive monthly changes in the funds rate that cumulated to a significant total change in response to a sustained change in the rate of growth of the money supply, but avoided significant changes in the funds rate in response to temporary changes in the rate of growth of the money supply.

6. SYSTEM ACTIONS OCTOBER 6, 1979

The Federal Reserve System formulated monetary policy in the first half of 1979 in an environment of anticipated recession. In this environment, the FOMC allowed the funds rate to rise by only one-half of a percentage point between February and July 1979, while M1 grew at an annualized rate of 9.7 percent over this interval. By September, M1 and M2 were at the top of the intrayearly ranges implied by their four-quarter target ranges. The anticipated recession, however, did not materialize. By September, inflation and the depreciation of the dollar emerged as the primary concern of monetary policy. In the changed environment, it became imperative that the FOMC hit its money supply targets. Accordingly, the FOMC became willing on October 6, 1979, to drop the level of short-term interest rates as an intermediate target of policy and to concentrate on the money supply. This change in intermediate targets of policy prompted the shift in operating procedures whereby nonborrowed reserves rather than the funds rate became the system's operating variable. The FOMC, however, continued to specify a range of permissible variation for the funds rate, in effect, preserving the option of returning the level of short-term interest rates to the status of an intermediate target of policy.

The post-October 1979 spirit within the Federal Reserve is that the four-quarter targets for growth of the monetary aggregates must be achieved. These targets, nevertheless, give the FOMC considerable latitude to try to influence the level of short-term interest rates. First, they need only be achieved over a four-quarter interval. Second, they are expressed as a range of from 2-½ to 3 percentage points. Third, there are targets for $M1 - A$, $M1 - B$, and M2.[12] During periods of reintermediation and disintermediation, the rates of growth of these three aggregates will diverge significantly, and the relationship among the rates of growth will be difficult to predict. At these times, it is likely that the target growth range for at least one of the monetary aggregates will be achieved, even if the FOMC is trying to influence the level of interest rates.

At the time of writing of this paper, the May 1980 FOMC meeting was the most recent meeting for which a *Record of Policy Actions* was available. The monetary aggregates had fallen below their intrayearly target paths. The majority of the FOMC expressed the concern that moving the aggregates back to path quickly was undesirable because the consequent decline in the funds rate would exacerbate inflationary expectations, exert a strong adverse effect on the foreign exchange value of the dollar, and possibly require a reversal of the decline that would lead to "significant increases in interest rates in a period of substantial weakness of the economy." At this time, it is too early to tell whether the money supply will become the predominant intermediate target of policy, or whether the money supply and the level of short-term interest rates will both continue as important targets of policy.

LITERATURE CITED

1. Burns, Arthur. "Statement" before the Committee on Banking and Currency, House of Representatives, July 30, 1974. In *Federal Reserve Bulletin,* 60 (August 1974), 554-60.

[12]Roughly, $M1-B$ is $M1-A$ plus NOW accounts, ATS, and credit union share drafts. M2 is $M1-B$ plus savings and small-denomination time deposits at all depository institutions, overnight repurchase agreements, and money market mutual funds.

2. DeRosa, Paul, and Gary Stern. ''Monetary Control and the Federal Funds Rate.'' *Journal of Monetary Economics,* 3 (April 1977), 217-30.

3. Feige, Edgar L., and Robert McGee. ''Has the Federal Reserve Shifted from a Policy of Interest Rate Targets to a Policy of Monetary Aggregate Targets?'' *Journal of Money, Credit, and Banking,* 11 (November 1979), 381-404.

4. Friedman, Benjamin M. ''A Policy for the 1980s.'' Testimony before the House Committee on Banking, Finance, and Urban Affairs, reprinted in *American Banker,* December 28, 1979, p. 4.

5. Lawler, Thomas A. ''Federal Reserve Policy Strategy and Interest Rate Seasonality.'' *Journal of Money, Credit, and Banking,* 11 (November 1979), 494-99.

6. Lombra, Raymond, and Michael Moran. ''Policy Advice and Policymaking at the Federal Reserve,'' *Journal of Monetary Economics Conference Series on Public Policy,* 13 (Autumn 1980), 9-68.

7. Miller, G. William. ''Statement'' before the Committee on the Budget, Senate, February 22, 1979. In *Federal Reserve Bulletin,* 65 (March 1979), 225-28.

8. Poole, William. ''Burnsian Monetary Policy: Eight Years of Progress?'' *The Journal of Finance,* 34 (May 1979), 473-84.

MICHAEL BEENSTOCK
J. ANDREW LONGBOTTOM*

The Term Structure of Interest Rates In a Small Open Economy

1. INTRODUCTION

PREVIOUS RESEARCH INTO THE TERM STRUCTURE of interest rates has largely focused upon two broad hypotheses, the neoclassical or expectations theory as suggested by Hicks [10], Lutz [12], and others, and the market segmentation or preferred habitat theory as suggested by Modigliani and Sutch [15]. Both of these principal theories and their derivatives are essentially concerned with the case of a closed economy where the term structure is treated as a domestic matter that is not directly related to financial considerations outside the country in question.

On the other hand, there is an extensive body of theory and evidence, for example, Hodjera [11] and Beenstock [2], which suggests that domestic capital markets are closely related to their external counterparts. If this is so, the domestic term structure of interest rates cannot be independent of the external or world term structure of interest rates. Indeed, as shall be argued in the next section, the interest parity hypothesis suggests that, in the case of a small open economy, the domestic term structure will be dominated by the world term structure. Under such circumstances the two principal hypotheses will not be applicable to the domestic term structure; instead, what might be called the "international theory" of the term structure would seem to be more appropriate. At the very least this theory presents an alternative to the traditional hypotheses.

*We should like to thank without implication Charles Goodhart for his comments on an earlier draft of this paper. The financial support of the Social Science Research Council is gratefully acknowledged.

MICHAEL BEENSTOCK *is senior research fellow, and* J. ANDREW LONGBOTTOM *is research officer, Centre for Economic Forecasting, London Graduate School of Business Studies.*

0022-2879/81/0281-0044$00.50/0
JOURNAL OF MONEY, CREDIT, AND BANKING, vol. 13, no. 1 (February 1981)

In section 2 the ''international theory'' is described and is juxtaposed with respect to the traditional approaches. In section 3 the ''international theory'' is tested using the U.K. as an example of a small open economy. It is shown that the world term structure has had an important bearing upon the U.K. term structure and it is suggested that the ''international theory'' may well be an important complement to existing theories of the term structure.

2. THE INTERNATIONAL THEORY

Asset Substitution

The starting point for much of the recent analysis of international capital movements has been the hypothesis that agents hold financial assets (and liabilities) of different currency denominations in their portfolios [4]. Thus the share of domestic financial assets (D) held in the portfolio depends on the difference between the rate of interest on domestic assets (R) and the rate of interest on assets abroad (R_w). In addition it will depend on the expected rate of appreciation of domestic currency. Thus

$$\frac{D}{W} = F\left(R - R_w + \frac{S^e - S}{S}\right), \qquad F' > 0 \tag{1}$$

where W is the size of the portfolio, S denotes the exchange rate, and S^e the expected exchange rate. Thus $(S^e - S)/S$ is the expected rate of appreciation of domestic currency vis-à-vis world currency. Equation (1) states that if the expected return on domestic assets rises, the share of domestic assets in portfolios will increase generating a capital inflow on the balance of payments. The value of F' will depend upon the elasticity of substitution between internationally traded financial assets; the greater the substitutability the greater will be F'. If assets are perfect substitutes the expected return on domestic assets, allowing for expected exchange rate movements, must be equal in equilibrium to the return on overseas assets, or

$$R + \frac{S^e - S}{S} = R_w . \tag{2}$$

Equation (2) will be recognized as the interest parity condition derived, for example, by Frankel [8] who has also shown that it commands widespread empirical support in the context of international financial markets.

If the domestic financial system is ''small'' relative to the world financial system, R_w may be regarded as exogenous in which case according to equation (3) the domestic rate of interest is wholly influenced by the world rate of interest for a given expected rate of exchange rate appreciation. When assets are perfect substitutes, domestic considerations such as the quantity of money or bonds cannot directly influence the domestic rate of interest independently of their possible effects on expected exchange rate movements. The expected rate of exchange rate appreciation will be equal to the differential between the expected rates of domestic and world inflation since the exchange rate will tend to move to equate purchasing power parity.

Term Structure Analysis·

While equation (2) applies to the level of the domestic rate of interest it is readily applicable to the determination of the domestic term structure. We may write separate equilibrium conditions for shorts and longs as

$$RS + \gamma_1 \left(\frac{S_s^e - S}{S} \right) = RS_w \tag{3}$$

$$RL + \gamma_2 \left(\frac{S_L^e - S}{S} \right) = RL_w , \tag{4}$$

where *RS* and *RL* are short- and long-term interest rates, respectively, while S_s^e represents the exchange rate expected to prevail when shorts mature and S_L^e is its counterpart when longs mature. γ_1 and γ_2 are normalizing coefficients since all interest rates are expressed as annual rates. Equations (3) and (4) imply that the domestic term structure as measured by the difference between long- and short-rates is equal to the world term structure adjusted for the term structure of exchange rate expectations:

$$RL - RS = RL_w - RS_w + \frac{\gamma_1 S_s^e - \gamma_2 S_L^e}{S} + \gamma_2 - \gamma_1 . \tag{5}$$

If the term structure of exchange rate expectations is flat the analysis implies that the domestic term structure will be the same as the world term structure. If instead the expected rate of depreciation is greater in the longer term, the domestic term structure will be steeper than the world term structure since longs will have to command a premium over shorts to the international investor. It therefore follows that in the case of the small open economy the term structure is determined by international considerations, and equation (5) may be regarded as an alternative hypothesis to the neoclassical and market segmentation hypotheses.

Juxtaposing the "International Theory"

We begin by juxtaposing the "international theory" with its neoclassical precursor. It turns out that if the world term structure is determined along neoclassical lines, equation (5) implies that the domestic term structure will also reflect neoclassical considerations. This may be seen using a simple two-period example. According to the neoclassical analysis, the world long rate will be an average of the current short term rate and the short rate expected to prevail in the second period, or

$$RL_w = \frac{RS_{w1} + RS_{w2}}{2} . \tag{6}$$

Equation (4) may be rewritten as

$$RL + \frac{\dot{S}_1 + \dot{S}_2}{2} = RL_w , \tag{4'}$$

where $\dot{S}_1$ and $\dot{S}_2$ are the expected rate of exchange rate appreciation in the first and second periods, respectively. But equation (3) implies that

$$RS_i + \dot{S}_i = RS_{wi}, \qquad i = 1,2 \tag{3'}$$

from which we can deduce that

$$RL = \frac{RS_1 + RS_2}{2} , \tag{7}$$

or, the domestic long rate is an average of the domestic short rates. Thus the international efficient markets condition implies that the domestic term structure will have neoclassical properties provided that the world term structure has these properties.

This does not of course imply that the international and neoclassical theories are equivalent. First of all, as we shall discuss, the world term structure may not be determined along neoclassical lines. Under such circumstances equation (7) would not be valid although equation (5) might still be applicable. Second, equation (7) does not stand on its own two feet since the flow of causality emanates from external considerations. Instead, it is simply a consequence of the international arbitrage model.

If the world term structure reflects market segmentation considerations, the international theory suggests that these factors will be communicated to the domestic term structure as may be inferred directly from equation (5). However, it could be argued that if the neoclassical restrictions do not apply to the world term structure it would be unreasonable to expect the international efficient markets conditions to apply. If, for example, international investors have preferred habitats with respect to different maturities in the world term structure, it might also be the case that they have preferred habitats with respect to assets of different currency denominations. If so, these assets will no longer be perfect substitutes and equations (3) and (4) will no longer apply. Nevertheless, even under such an argument the domestic term structure would still reflect the world term structure to some degree but domestic considerations would also be influential. On the other hand, it could be argued that internationally traded assets are perfect substitutes at given maturities despite the fact that investors are not indifferent to equal yielding assets of different maturities.

These considerations suggest that the "international theory" provides an independent medium for the analysis of the term structure of interest rates in open economies.

3. U.K. EVIDENCE

Exchange Rate Expectations

The central objective in this section is to test equation (5). However, a necessary preliminary is to proxy the term structure of exchange rate expectations. Proxying the level of the expected exchange rate at some undetermined date in the future presents enough problems in its own right. Therefore, attempting to proxy the term structure of exchange rate expectations may be overly ambitious. Nevertheless, a number of possible approaches are suggested and tried.

Unfortunately we cannot adopt the approach of Porter [16] who argues that the term structure of exchange rate expectations is implicit in the term structure of uncovered interest rate differentials. This option is not open to us because it assumes away what we seek to test insofar as the Porter approach takes the interest parity conditions for granted. Beenstock [2, chap. 8] has confronted this issue before when modeling the term structure of forward exchange rates in which context it was necessary to specify the determination of the term structure of exchange rate expectations. On that occasion the exchange rate was assumed to adjust over time to maintain purchasing power parity according to

$$S_t = \sum_{i=0}^{M} w_i RP_{t-i} + u_t, \tag{8}$$

where RP denotes an appropriate relative price index and u_t is a stochastic term that is white noise. If equation (8) represents the appropriate model of the exchange rate, then the rational expectation of the difference between the expected spot rate k periods out and the expected spot rate j periods ($k>j$) out is

$$S^e_{t+k} - S^e_{t+j} = E_t(S_{t+k} \mid I_t) - E_t(S_{t+j} \mid I_t), \tag{9}$$

where, for example, $E_t(S_{t+k} \mid I_t)$ is the expected value of the exchange k periods out conditional on the current information set I_t. Substituting equation (8) into (9) implies

$$S^e_{t+k} - S^e_{t+j} = \left(\sum_{i=1}^{k} w_i - \sum_{i=1}^{j} w_i \right) RP_t + \sum_{i=k+1}^{M} w_i RP_{t+k-i} - \sum_{i=j+1}^{M} w_i RP_{t+j-i} \tag{10}$$

assuming for simplicity that *RP* is not expected to change in the future and $M>k$.

The main shortcoming of this approach is that it is difficult to apply since it entails numerous restrictions on the distributed lag function with respect to *RP* as is evidenced by Beenstock [2, pp. 132–34]. Therefore in what follows some simpler procedures are suggested.

Recalling equation (5) our basic objective is to proxy $(S_s^e - S)/S$ and $(S_L^e - S)/S$. One possibility, following McCallum [13], is to proxy the former term using the relevant future spot rate itself. Thus

$$(S_s^e - S)/S = (S_{t+j} - S_t)/S_t, \tag{11}$$

and as McCallum argues, this form of rational expectations model requires the use of instrumental variables with respect to S_{t+j}. Assuming k is sufficiently large (in fact k is ten years in the fitted model) it seems appropriate to assume that S_L^e will equal the long run equilibrium exchange rate. One candidate for this long-run value is based on the monetary theory of the exchange rate, for example, Ball, Burns, and Warburton [1], where the exchange rate adjusts to balance the supply and demand for money at home and abroad, or where

$$\ln S_L^e = \alpha_0 + \ln(M_w/M)_t + \alpha_1 t. \tag{12}$$

M_w represents the quantity of money abroad, M the domestic quantity of money, and t is a time trend that reflects relative rate of productivity growth and GDP growth as elaborated in Ball, Burns, and Warburton. From equation (12) we may proxy

$$(S_L^e - S)/S = \alpha_0 + \ln(M_w/MS)_t + \alpha_1 t. \tag{13}$$

Substituting equations (13) and (11) into equation (5) yields the following estimable equation:

$$\begin{aligned} Y_t = \delta - \gamma_2\alpha_0 + X_t + \gamma_1 \ln S_{t+j}/S_t \\ - \gamma_2 \ln(M_w/MS)_t - \gamma_2\alpha_1 t + v_{1t}, \end{aligned} \tag{14}$$

where δ is a factor reflecting the possibility that, for example, international differences in tax regimes will drive a wedge between the domestic and foreign term structures, where v_{1t} is a disturbance term and where $Y = RL\text{-}RS$ and $X = RL_w - RS_w$.

A second and even simpler approach derives from equation (12)—if the exchange rate is expected to adjust to its long run value according to equation (15)—

$$\Delta \ln S_{t+1} = \lambda \ln S_t/S_L^e. \tag{15}$$

Substituting from equation (12) into (15) and substituting the result into equation (14) assuming $j=1$ implies the following estimable equation:

$$Y_t = \pi_0 + \pi_1 X_t + \pi_2 \ln(M_w/MS)_t + \pi_3 t + v_{2t}, \tag{16}$$

where

$$\begin{aligned} \pi_0 &= \delta + \alpha_0(\gamma_1\lambda - \gamma_2) \\ \pi_1 &= 1 \\ \pi_2 &= \gamma_1\lambda - \gamma_2 \\ \pi_3 &= \gamma_1\lambda\alpha_2 - \gamma_2\alpha_1, \end{aligned} \tag{17}$$

and where v_{2t} is a disturbance term. The signs of π_0, π_2, and π_3 are indeterminate. However, if the exchange market is expected to equilibrate slowly, λ will be small and π_2 could be negative. If as in our case below k is ten years out and j is three months out, γ_1 should equal 4 and γ_2 should equal 0.1. On this basis $\pi_2 \lesseqgtr 0$ as $\lambda \lesseqgtr ^{1/40}$. The restriction that $\pi_1 = 1$ is referred to below as the proportionality requirement.

Estimation Methodology

The estimation procedure that has been applied is based upon the methodology given in Mizon [14] and Davidson et al. [5]. The central issue in this context is that equations (14) and (16) are long run relationships that may not be satisfied in the short run reflecting inter alia costs of international portfolio adjustment. Therefore shifts in the foreign term structure might not be immediately paralleled by shifts in the domestic term structure, and the outstanding discrepancies might be eliminated over time.

For example, if the model we wish to estimate is

$$Y_t = \pi_0 + \pi_1 X_t, \tag{18}$$

it may be appropriate to specify derivative and proportional error correction mechanisms such as

$$\Delta Y_t = h_0 + h_1 \Delta X_t - h_2(Y-X)_{t-1} + h_3 X_{t-1} \tag{19}$$

where h_1 represents derivative corrections and h_2 proportional corrections. To test the restriction that $\pi_1 = 1$ h_3 is included, as given by equation (17), since the steady-state solution of equation (19) is

$$Y = \frac{h_0}{h_2} + \frac{h_2 + h_3}{h_2} X. \tag{20}$$

If $\hat{h}_3$ is not significant we may infer that $\pi_1 = 1$. The focus in much of what follows is how to identify from the data the appropriate form of equation (19). In this context the structure of the disturbance terms may be taken as an indication of the overall validity of the restrictions that one places on the data. The selected nested equations we report were subjected to a variety of tests, both for the presence of autocorrelation in the estimated residuals and the predictive stability of the model. The initial estimation period is 1969Q1 to 1978Q1: the equations were then used to predict to 1979Q1. Equations that passed these tests were subsequently fitted over the entire sample period.

We begin by abstracting from the term structure of exchange rate expectations.

The Basic Relationship

The basic relationship to be tested is given by equation (18). Details of the data used are provided in the appendix. The reason for representing *RL* by a ten-year rate is that the average maturity of British government stock is 10 years. Shorts are represented by the 3-month maturity and unless otherwise stated the reported results refer to the period 1969Q1 to 1978Q1.

Figure 1 shows the time profile of the U.K. and world term structure over the estimation period. The U.K. term structure has been consistently steeper than that of the world over the major part of the 1970s. According to the theory in section 2, this implies that the expected long-term rate of depreciation of sterling was greater than its expected short-term rate of depreciation; on the other hand, it might also reflect tax differentials, etc. The temporary reversal of this feature in 1976 was the result of the collapse of sterling and the accompanying rapid rise in short-term interest rates. However, the main feature of Figure 1 is that the marginal relationship between the two time series is apparently quite strong.

We began by attempting to fit an instantaneous model such as equation (18), but the result gave rise to severe serial correlation suggesting that the model may be dynamically misspecified as may be seen from equation (21).

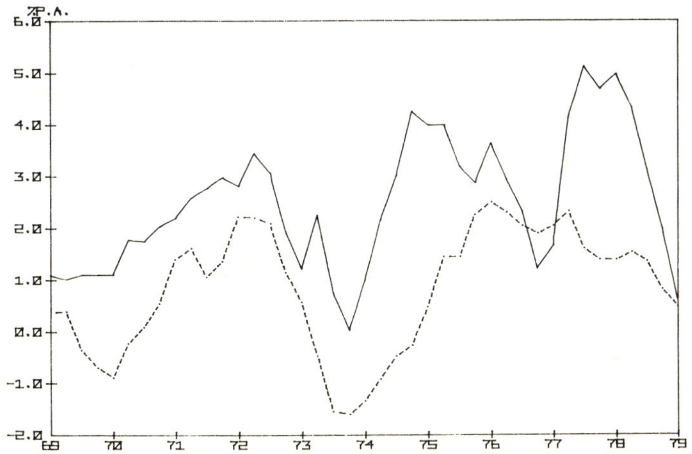

FIG. 1. Comparison of U.K. and World Term Structures, 1969–1979 (Y = ———; X = ----)

$$Y_t = \underset{(0.15)}{0.58}\, X_t + \underset{(0.002)}{0.02}, \tag{21}$$

$$\bar{R}^2 = 0.29,\ S = 0.01079.$$

$$Z_1(4) = 4.50,\ Z_2(4,35) = 1.11,\ Z_3(4) = 19.24,\ Z_4(12) = 48.57.$$

Standard errors are in parentheses. S is the standard deviation of the residuals. Z_1 is a chi-square test for post sample parameter stability,[1] Z_2 and Z_3 are the Chow test of parameter consistency and the Lagrange Multiplier Test [9] for the randomness of the autocorrelation profile of the residuals, respectively. Z_4 is the Box and Pierce [3] "Q" statistic for the randomness of the residual correlogram with an adjustment for sample size. (See [6].) (The numbers in brackets refer to the degrees of freedom.) The high values for Z_3 and Z_4 suggest possible dynamic misspecification. Nevertheless, equation (21) indicates that X has a significant effect on Y, and the hypothesis of parameter stability cannot be rejected.

Following Mizon [14], we then proceeded to estimate an unrestricted version of equation (18) using up to five lagged values of X and Y, which provided $\bar{R}^2 = 0.70$, $S = 0.00708$, and $Z_3(5) = 20.60$ suggesting that the relationship remains dynamically misspecified (see Table 1).

After careful experimentation (details of which will be provided on request) we were led to the following equation:

$$\begin{aligned}\Delta Y_t = {} & \underset{(0.25)}{0.42}\, \Delta X_t + \underset{(0.24)}{0.76}\Delta X_{t-1} - \underset{(0.14)}{0.45}(\Delta_3 X_{t-2} - \Delta X_{t-3}) \\ & - \underset{(0.11)}{0.28}(Y-X)_{t-2} + \underset{(0.002)}{0.005},\end{aligned} \tag{22}$$

$$\bar{R}^2 = 0.35,\ S = 0.00618.$$

$$Z_1(4) = 6.11,\ Z_2(4,32) = 1.13,\ Z_3(5) = 7.08,\ Z_4(10) = 14.21.$$

The steady state solution of equation (22) is

$$Y_t = 1.0\, X + 0.02, \tag{23}$$

which suggests that $\pi_1 = 1$. Attempts to test this restriction by including X_{t-2} as an additional term produced a significantly higher value for S and a standard error on the parameter of X_{t-2} seven times the value of its coefficient. Nevertheless, it is possible to derive alternative models where $\pi_1 < 1$ and where statistical performance

[1] $Z_1(m)$ is distributed in large samples as $\chi^2(m)$ under the null hypothesis of constant parameters and homoscedastic variance. It is calculated as

$$Z_1(m) = \sum_{t=n+1}^{n+m} (e_t/\hat{S})^2,$$

where m is the number of periods forecast, e_t is the post sample residual for the tth observation, and S the estimated standard error of the equation.

TABLE 1

ESTIMATED COEFFICIENTS ON THE UNRESTRICTED FORM OF THE BASIC TERM STRUCTURE EQUATION

i	0	1	2	3	4	5		
Y_{t-i}	−1	1.1 (0.20)	−0.45 (0.30)	0.18 (0.31)	−0.12 (0.29)	0.04 (0.21)	$\sum_{i=0}^{5}$	= − 0.25
X_{t-i}	0.42 (0.29)	0.27 (0.49)	−0.89 (0.50)	0.50 (0.53)	−0.49 (0.53)	0.44 (0.34)	$\sum_{i=0}^{5}$	= 0.25

$K_0 = 0.005$
(0.004)

$\bar{R}^2 = 0.70$, $S = 0.00708$

$Z_1(4) = 4.26$, $Z_2(4,25) = 0.46$, $Z_3(5) = 20.60$, $Z_4(7) = 14.95$

SOLVED COEFFICIENTS FOR EQUATION (22)

i	0	1	2	3	4	5
Y_{t-i}	−1	1	−0.28			
X_{t-i}	0.42	0.34	−0.93	0.45	−0.45	0.45

$K_0 = 0.005$

is very similar to that of the reported equation. Such an equation is shown as equation (24):

$$\Delta Y_t = \underset{(0.15)}{0.50\Delta_2 X_t} - \underset{(0.11)}{0.38\ Y_{t-2}} + \underset{(0.13)}{0.21\ X_{t-3}} + \underset{(0.002)}{0.008}, \tag{24}$$

$$\bar{R}^2 = 0.31,\ S = 0.00652.$$

$$Z_1(4) = 2.2,\ Z_2(4.33) = 0.46,\ Z_3(5) = 2.70,\ Z_4(3) = 2.41.$$

The steady state of this equation is

$$Y = 0.55X + 0.02, \tag{25}$$

a result very similar to that reported in equation (21). In this instance the data rejected the proportionality requirement. Attempts to impose $\pi_1 = 1$ produced a higher value of S, and an additional levels term in X_{t-3} was found to be significant.

Clearly the foreign term structure has an important bearing upon the domestic term structure. However, the quandary remains that the data seems to support two conflicting models without providing statistically significant criteria for distinguishing between them. In view of the widespread evidence, for example [7], supporting the Efficient Markets Hypothesis especially in financial markets, our strategy has been to test models based on equation (22) rather than to build ad hoc models such as equation (24).

The Role of Exchange Rate Expectations

Considerable difficulty was encountered in estimating equation (14) since we were unable to derive proxies for the short-term expected rate of appreciation that provided sensible coefficients. Since these proxies were based on the approach suggested in equation (15) it is possible that this reflects colinearity between the short and long run expected rates of appreciation. Moreover, the results thus obtained failed the parameter consistency test (Z_1).

We therefore sought estimates of equation (16) where the short- and long-term expected rates of appreciation are proxied by a single variable, as described in section 2. In doing so our starting point was the model suggested in equation (22). Our preferred model is

$$\Delta Y_t = \underset{(0.25)}{0.52\ \Delta X_t} + \underset{(0.24)}{0.76\ \Delta X_{t-1}} - \underset{(0.14)}{0.43}\ (\Delta_3 X_{t-2} - \Delta X_{t-3})$$

$$-\underset{(0.14)}{0.45}(Y - X)_{t-2} - \underset{(0.017)}{0.023}\ \ln\left(\frac{M_w}{MS}\right)_t + \underset{(0.002)}{0.0005T} - \underset{(0.02)}{0.026}, \tag{26}$$

$$\bar{R}^2 = 0.39,\ S = 0.006010.$$

$$Z_1(4) = 7.9,\ Z_2(4.30) = 1.27,\ Z_3(4) = 2.70,\ Z_4(10) = 11.89.$$

The steady state version of this equation is

$$Y = 1.0X - 0.05 \ln\left(\frac{M_w}{MS}\right) + 0.001\,T - 0.06, \tag{27}$$

which indicates that $\pi_2 < 0$. If we assume as described in section 2 that $\gamma_1 = 4$ and $\gamma_2 = 0.01$, the implicit value of λ is 0.015, which suggests a slow convergence (of 1.5 percent per quarter) of the exchange rate towards its equilibrium value.

Once again we find $\pi_1 = 1$: when we tested this restriction by specifying an additional term X_{t-2}, the standard error of the estimate rose but not significantly suggesting that the restriction cannot be rejected. The inclusion of expectational considerations constitutes a mild improvement in the model.

Figure 2 shows the impulse response upon Y when X rises on a sustained basis by one percentage point in the first quarter. The profile shown is based on equation (26) and the broken line represents the steady state response as calculated from equation (27). The graph indicates that Y instantly overshoots its equilibrium value by a slight amount. However, in Q4 and Q5 Y temporarily falls before cycling around the new equilibrium value in a damped fashion. By Q12 Y lies very close to its steady state value of 1.0. The impulse response derived from equation (22) has a very similar pattern up to Q8, after which the equilibrium reached in a mildly oscillatory fashion.

The puzzling feature about these profiles is the reaction in Q4 and Q5, although this is explicable in terms of short-term market reactions and uncertainty. For example, the initial rise in interest rates might not be expected to persist in the belief

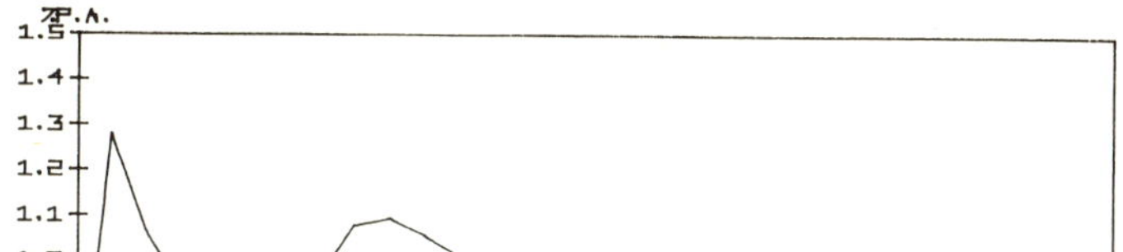

FIG. 2. Long Run Equilibrium Response for Y of a One Percent Increase in X (Equation 26) (Y = ————)

that the authorities will seek to stabilize interest rates. But such expectations are short-lived, and the model suggests that after about a year the new structure of interest rates will tend to emerge.

The Level of Interest Rates

As an additional test of equation (26) we attempted to estimate the separate relationships for shorts and longs given by equations (3) and (4) and which underpin equation (26).

Using the model fitting methodology described above we were lead to the following equation for the long term rate of interest:

$$\Delta RL_t - \underset{(0.25)}{0.75}\, \Delta_2 RLw_t - \underset{(0.10)}{0.20}(RL - RL_w)_{t-2} - \underset{(0.01)}{0.02} \ln\left(\frac{M_w}{MS}\right)_t$$

$$+\underset{(0.0002)}{0.0005}T - \underset{(0.02)}{0.03}, \tag{28}$$

$$\bar{R}^2 = 0.30,\ S = 0.00665.$$

$$Z_1(4) = 2.1,\ Z_2(4{,}32) = 0.45,\ Z_3(4) = 5.5,\ Z_4(4) = 1.92.$$

The steady state solution from this equation is

$$R_L = 1.0 RLw - 0.10 \ln\left(\frac{M_w}{MS}\right) + 0.0003\,T - 0.015. \tag{29}$$

In the case of the short interest rate, attempts to incorporate the influence of the expected short-term exchange rate met with little success. The result we present therefore is for the basic relationship that abstracts from exchange rate expectations.

$$\Delta RS_t = \underset{(0.15)}{0.25}\Delta RS_{t-1} - \underset{(0.09)}{0.11}\Delta_2 RS_{t+2} + \underset{(0.16)}{0.49}(\Delta_2 RSw_t - \Delta RSw_{t-2})$$

$$- \underset{(0.09)}{0.17}(RS - RSw)_{t-2} + \underset{(0.002)}{0.003}, \tag{30}$$

$$\bar{R}^2 = 0.31,\ S = 0.01015.$$

$$Z_1(4) = 0.55,\ Z_2(4{,}32) = 0.69,\ Z_3(4) = 2.65,\ Z_4(4) = 0.82.$$

The steady state solution of equation (30) is

$$RS = 1.0\ RSw + 0.02. \tag{31}$$

The proportionality requirement was accepted by the data in each case. Also when considered together the two equations show a pattern of dynamic adjustment similar to that identified in equation (26).

4. CONCLUSIONS

The principal conclusion is that the international term structure has an important bearing on the U.K. term structure as measured by the differential between the rate of interest on ten-year and three-month government liability in the U.K. As such the international theory of the term structure as developed in section 2 serves as a new and important alternative to the existing theories.

The data did not reject the hypothesis of proportionality ($\pi_1 = 1$) although it was possible to generate alternative models in which $\pi_1 = 0.5$. Such negative corroboration suggests that when the external term structure alters by one percentage point so does the domestic term structure.

However, the relationship between the domestic and foreign term structures does not seem to be instantaneous. In fact the lags are often protracted although the change in the U.K. term structure is contemporaneously affected by the first difference in the foreign term structure.

Perhaps not surprisingly, relatively little progress was made in integrating the term structure of exchange rate expectations into the empirical analysis. A simple rational expectations model of the term structure of exchange rate expectations was suggested that mildly improved the basic model.

No attempt has been made in this paper to test empirically the international theory against its traditional counterparts. Alternatively it might be possible to integrate the international theory with the other main theories concerning the term structure of interest rates.

DATA APPENDIX

U.K. Data

RL = Redemption yield on medium dated U.K. government stocks, percent per annum. Source: Bank of England Quarterly Bulletin.

RS = Rate of interest on U.K. 91 day Treasury Bills, percent per annum. Source: Financial Statistics.

M = Index of sterling M3 (1975=100). Source: Financial Statistics.

S = Effective exchange rate index for sterling (1975=100). Source: Bank of England Quarterly Bulletin.

World Data

M_w = Index of world money stock (1975=100), which is a weighted average of money supply for seventeen industrialized countries measured in terms of world currency as described by T. Burns and B. Robinson in *Exchange Rate Outlook,* Gower Press. Sources: International Financial Statistics, IMF. Consistent time series for overseas interest rates are more elusive. The world short rate is therefore defined as

$$RS_w = 0.55RS_{us} + 0.21RS_g + 0.12RS_f + 0.12RS_j,$$

where

RS_{us} = Rate of interest on 91 day Treasury Bills in the U.S., percent p.a.
RS_g = 3 month interbank rate in West Germany, percent p.a.
RS_f = Unconditional call money rate in France, percent p.a.
RS_j = Rate on day-to-day loans against private bills in Japan, percent p.a.
Source: Financial Statistics, OECD.

The weighting pattern reflects the considerations set out in "Special Drawing Rights: Some Recent Developments." Bank of England Quarterly Bulletin, June 1979.

The definition of the world long-term rate of interest is

$$RL_w = 0.55RL_{us} + 0.21RL_g + 0.12RL_f + 0.12RL_j,$$

where

RL_{us} = Secondary market yield of U.S. government bonds of maturity $\geqslant$ ten years, percent p.a.
RL_g = Secondary market yield of West German public sector bonds of maturity $\geqslant$ four years, percent p.a.
RL_f = Secondary market yield of French public and semipublic sector bonds of maturity $\geqslant$ ten years.
RL_j = Secondary market yield of Nippon Telegraph and Telephone bonds (Japan) of maturity $\geqslant$ ten years.
Source: Financial Statistics, OECD.

LITERATURE CITED

1. Ball, R. James, Terry Burns, and Peter J. Warburton. "The London Business School Model of the UK Economy: An Exercise in International Monetarism." In *Modelling the UK Economy,* edited by Paul Ormerod, pp. 86–114. London: Heinemann, 1980.
2. Beenstock, Michael C. *The Foreign Exchanges: Theory, Modelling and Policy*. New York: St. Martin's, 1978.
3. Box, George E. P., and David A. Pierce. "Distribution of Residual Autocorrelations in Autoregressive-Integrated Moving Average Time Series Models." *Journal of the American Statistical Association,* 65 (December 1970), 1509-26.
4. Branson, William H. *Financial Capital Flows in the US Balance of Payments*. Amsterdam: North-Holland, 1968.
5. Davidson, James E. H., David F. Hendry, Frank Srba, and Stephen Yeo. "Econometric Modelling of the Aggregate Time Series Relationship between Consumers Expenditure and Income in the United Kingdom." *Economic Journal,* 88 (December 1978), 661-92.
6. Davies, N., C. M. Triggs, and P. Newbold. "Significance Levels of the Box-Pierce Portmanteau Statistic in Finite Samples." *Biometrika,* 64 (December 1977), 517–22.

7. Fama, Eugene. "Efficient Capital Markets: A Review of Theory and Empirical Work." *Journal of Finance,* 25 (May 1970), 383-417.

8. Frankel, Jeffrey A. "On the Mark: A Theory of Floating Exchange Rates Based on Real Interest Differentials." *American Economic Review,* 69 (September 1979), 610-22.

9. Godfrey, Leslie G. "Testing for Higher Order Serial Correlation in Regression Equations when the Regressors Include Lagged Dependent Variables." *Econometrica,* 46 (November 1978), 1303-10.

10. Hicks, John R. *Value and Capital; An Inquiry into Some Fundamental Principles of Economic Theory.* Oxford: Clarendon Press, 1939.

11. Hodjera, Zoran. "International Short Term Capital Movements: A Survey of Theory and Empirical Analysis." *I.M.F. Staff Papers,* 20 (November 1973), 683-740.

12. Lutz, Frederick A. "The Structure of Interest Rates." *Quarterly Journal of Economics,* 55 (November 1940), 636-63.

13. McCallum, Bennett T. "The Role of Speculation in the Canadian Forward Exchange Market: Some Estimates Assuming Rational Expectations." *Review of Economics and Statistics,* 59 (May 1977), 145-51.

14. Mizon, Grayham E. "Model Selection Procedures." In *Studies in Modern Economic Analysis,* edited by Michael J. Artis and A. Robert Nobay, pp. 97-120. Oxford: Basil Blackwell, 1977.

15. Modigliani, Franco, and Richard Sutch. "Innovations in Interest Rate Policy." *American Economic Review,* 56 (May 1966), 178-97.

16. Porter, Michael G. "A Theoretical and Empirical Framework for Analyzing the Term Structure of Exchange Rate Expectations." *I.M.F. Staff Papers,* 18 (November 1971), 613-45.

JESS B. YAWITZ
WILLIAM J. MARSHALL*

Measuring the Effect of Callability on Bond Yields

1. INTRODUCTION

Most CORPORATE AND MANY government bond issues contain call provisions. Since both buyer and seller are concerned with the effect that the terms of call provisions ought to have on yields, considerable effort has been devoted to developing models of the relationship between yields and callability. Also of interest are the benefits from optimal design[1] and exercise of the call. In addition, researchers concerned with the impact on yields of credit risk, issue size, and other bond characteristics have had to make some provision in empirical models for callability. Generally, empirical models of the effect of callability have not controlled for the other factors determining yields. Neither have studies of other yield determinants attempted to construct sophisticated measures to represent callability.

In this paper we develop a theoretically sound model of the effect on yield spreads of callability and test that specification within the context of a comprehensive empirical model of yield spreads first estimated by Cook and Hendershott [3] (henceforth, C-H). C-H provide for the effects of taxes, default risk, relative security supply, and, through a simple proxy, for callability. Substituting our more sophisticated measure of the effect of call, we are able to test our model against the

*The authors wish to acknowledge the helpful comments from Timothy Cook, Patric Hendershott, and two referees of this journal.
[1]See our paper, "Optimal Terms of the Call Provision on a Corporate Bond" [12], on this point.

JESS B. YAWITZ *is professor of finance and business economics, and* WILLIAM J. MARSHALL *is associate professor of finance, Washington University, St. Louis.*

0022-2879/81/0281-0060$00.50/0
JOURNAL OF MONEY, CREDIT, AND BANKING, vol. 13, no. 1 (February 1981)

standard of their earlier work, provide estimates of the yield compensation for callability under various conditions, and investigate the impact of their use of a less refined proxy on their conclusions about the effects of other factors on yield spreads.

The remainder of our paper is organized as follows. In section 2 we discuss those factors other than callability that have been hypothesized to have an effect on yield spreads. Since the majority of this material is drawn from C-H, this section is brief. We present in section 3 a description of our model for the effect of callability on yield spreads and derive a suitable specification for empirical testing. Then, in section 4 we compare the C-H results with those obtained using their data with our measure for callability. We conclude in section 5 with an evaluation of the C-H conclusions in light of our respecification.

2. FACTORS OTHER THAN CALLABILITY AFFECTING THE CORPORATE-U.S. YIELD SPREAD

While the primary purpose of the C-H paper was to study the effects of default risk, relative security supplies, and callability on yield spreads, a major contribution of their work is the adjustment of the reported Treasury yield series to account for various technical factors influencing these yields during the 1961–75 period. Their adjustment to the Treasury yield data is designed to purge this series of the effect of a tax bias introduced from two sources. First, as a result of the rising level of interest rates and the fact that no new U.S. bonds with a maturity of twenty years or greater were issued from May, 1963, through January, 1973, all outstanding U.S. bonds in that maturity range sold at a discount. An adjustment was made in the yield data to account for the fact that coupon income is taxed as ordinary income while the difference between purchase price and redemption value (for discount bonds) is taxed at the lower long-term capital gains rate. A second adjustment to the government yield series was made to account for another tax effect: virtually all U.S. bonds issued prior to 1971 are redeemable at par for estate tax purposes. In addition to the tax biases, C-H make a further adjustment for the decline in the average maturity of those bonds included in the reported government yield series. The adjusted series, the New Issues-Equivalent U.S. Bond Yield Series, is used in their empirical work.

C-H propose that several factors other than callability exert an influence on the corporate-U.S. yield spread. First, C-H observed that the spread between the Salomon Brothers' Aa deferred-call utility yield series and the U.S. yield series increased dramatically during the second quarter of 1974 when Con Edison failed to pay a dividend. As they discuss in their paper [3, p. 1179], C-H make a direct adjustment to the yield series from that date forward in order to account for the market's increased concerns over default. This augmented utility yield series is denoted as RAa.

The second impact of default risk is attributable to the relationship between the business cycle and the compensation in yield required for the possibility of default.

C-H propose two proxies in an attempt to capture the impact of cyclical risk on the premium between the utility yield series and their new-issue equivalent, tax-adjusted, U.S. bond series (RUS). The first is MOOD, a measure of consumer sentiment constructed by Fair [5] from data collected by the University of Michigan Research Center. The second proxy is the employment pressure index (EPI) developed by William Cullison [4] to measure labor market pressure. This index is supposed to measure excess demand or supply in the labor market.

C-H also employ the new issue equivalent U.S. bond series as a third variable in order to measure the effect on the spread when yields rise with risk held constant. The authors derive an explicit model for the effect of default risk on the magnitude of the yield spread. This model is consistent with the theoretical models of default risk premiums developed by Bierman and Hass [1] and Yawitz [9].

C-H derive a proxy intended to capture the impact of relative security supplies (RSS) on yield spreads. They define this proxy as the difference between the book values of corporate bonds and long-term Treasury debt, adjusting both for foreign holdings and the latter for Federal Reserve holdings.

3. THE EFFECT OF CALLABILITY ON YIELD SPREADS

The literature has suggested that the general level of interest rates exerts a direct effect on the compensation in yield required for the inclusion of a call provision.[2] The basic argument is that when rates are at an historically high level, there is a greater than normal probability that rates will have fallen some time after call protection expires, and that the firm will exercise its option to refinance the debt at more favorable terms. In order to compensate bondholders fully for this possibility when rates are high, a substantial yield premium is required.

From the preceeding discussion it should be evident that the effect of the level of yields on the compensation for callability is due to the hypothesized link between the current level of yields and expectations as to the level of yields that will prevail in the future. More properly, C-H attempt to model anticipated yield movements directly. They use the spread between either the three and five-year or four and seven-year Treasury yields as their proxy for interest rate expectations (EXP).

An Alternative Approach

For the purpose of our analysis, we employ a fairly simple approach to model the call provision. It has been shown that, without taxes, the callable bond is actually a hybrid financial instrument composed of (1) a noncallable bond with the same total coupon, maturity, and par value as the callable issue, and (2) a call option on this noncallable bond [11]. From the perspective of the firm issuing the callable bond, the call has value because it grants the firm the option to refinance in the future if interest rates have fallen. Conceptually, this refunding operation is analogous to the

[2]See Van Horne [8, pp. 180–81] for a discussion of the relationship between the level of yields and the value of the call feature.

firm exercising a call option to purchase the noncallable bond at a striking price that is below the market value at the time of the call. As a result, the bondholder will require compensation, in the form of a reduced price at purchase, for bearing the contingent liability that accompanies the inclusion of the call provision.[3]

Our approach is to relate the size of the contingent liability, and hence the compensation in yield, to the expected movement in the *price* of the underlying bond (the equal coupon noncallable issue) from the date it is issued until the call date. Yawitz and Anderson [10] demonstrate that the price of a noncallable bond having the same total coupon, par value, and remaining maturity as the callable bond determines the gain (or loss) to the firm (and hence, to the bondholder) from exercising the call option. Just as in the case of an equity call option, the writer of the option (in this instance the bondholder) incurs a greater loss the greater the price of the underlying security at call date. Therefore, the value of the contingent liability will vary directly with the magnitude of the expected price change on the underlying bond.

In order to develop a workable measure of the value of the option to call, we begin by modeling a simplified call provision for a default-free bond. We assume that the call is the European type that can only be exercised exactly M years into the life of an N year bond: that is, the call protection is M years and the option expires instantaneously if not exercised.[4] We also assume that market participants are expected return maximizers. Therefore, the terms of the callable bond must be such that the investor has the same expected wealth at the time the call comes due from either of the following alternatives: purchase only a noncallable bond or, purchase an otherwise identical callable bond at a lower price and invest the difference elsewhere.

The following notation is used throughout the analysis:

- r is the yield to maturity on N year noncallable debt.
- $100r$ is the coupon on a noncallable bond priced to sell at par ($100).
- δ is the coupon premium sufficient to permit a callable bond to be priced to sell at par.
- $100+\Delta$ is the price of a noncallable bond offering a coupon of $100r + \delta$ and a par value of $100.
- N is the initial maturity (years) of the callable and noncallable bonds.
- M is the number of years of call protection.
- P is the uncertain price in M years of a noncallable bond offering a coupon of $100r + \delta$ and having N-M years remaining until maturity.
- P_c is the call price.

[3]Alternatively, and equivalently, one could say that the compensation comes in the form of a higher coupon on the callable bond for equal initial dollar outlays.

[4]Our use of "years" rather than periods is for expository ease.

$E(P|\text{event})$ is the expected value of P conditional on the occurrence of "event."

γ is the probability of call = $\text{Prob}(P > P_c)$.

The contingent payoffs in year M for equal initial dollar investments in callable (including investing the extra cash) and noncallable instruments are detailed in Table 1. A bond with an annual coupon of $100r + \delta$ can be purchased for either \$100 in a callable bond or, from the definition of Δ, $\$100 + \Delta$ in a noncallable bond. Thus, we can express the initial price difference between the two bonds as the present value of the incremental coupon on the callable security, discounted at the noncallable yield.

$$\Delta = \frac{\delta}{r}\left[\frac{(1+r)^N - 1}{(1+r)^N}\right] \tag{1}$$

The purchaser of a callable bond has available $\$\Delta$ at the time of purchase that can be invested to provide an accumulated value of $\Delta(1 + r)^M$, M years hence. The accumulated value M years hence, of coupons received and reinvested, is the same under both alternatives. Therefore, the difference between the expected payoffs is simply

$$\gamma[E(P|\text{Call}) - P_c] - (1 + r)^M\Delta = 0 \tag{2}$$

and is set equal to zero to satisfy the requirement of investor indifference. Combining and rearranging equations (1) and (2), one obtains an explicit expression for the incremental coupon (remembering that δ depends on Δ),

$$\delta = \left\{\frac{\gamma[E(P|\text{Call}) - P_c]}{(1+r)^M}\right\}\left\{\frac{r(1+r)^N}{(1+r)^N - 1}\right\}. \tag{3}$$

The first term in major brackets on the RHS of equation (3) is the present value of the expected loss from call. The second major brackets contain a factor that converts the expected loss to a coupon equivalent for an N period bond.

An additional insight into the derivation of our model for the compensation for callability can be obtained by rearranging equation (3) into (3a).

$$\frac{\delta}{r}\left[1 - \frac{1}{(1+r)^N}\right] = \frac{\gamma[E(P|\text{Call}) - P_c]}{(1+r)^M} \tag{3a}$$

The LHS is the present value of an N year annual annuity of $\$\delta$. This is the compensation to the bondholder for the inclusion of the call feature. The RHS is the present value of the contingent liability inherent in the call. Investor indifference requires that the equality in equation (3a) be satisfied.

TABLE 1

TABLE OF PAYOFFS IN YEAR M FROM THE PURCHASE OF A CALLABLE OR NONCALLABLE BOND

	Payoff‡	
Investment Alternative*,§	Call (Prob = γ)	No Call (Prob = $(1-\gamma)$)
Callable†	Accumulated Coupons§ $+ P_c$ $+ \Delta(1+r)^M$	Accumulated Coupons§ $+ E(P\vert\text{No Call})$ $+ \Delta(1+r)^M$
Noncallable	Accumulated Coupons§ $+ E(P\vert\text{Call})$	Accumulated Coupons§ $+ E(P\vert\text{No Call})$

*Equal expenditures of $100+\Delta$ at time 0.
†Investment of Δ in a default-free pure discount instrument at a rate of r.
‡All values expressed in year M dollars.
§Equal coupons are provided by the callable and noncallable positions and are assumed to be reinvested at the rate r. Hence, in order to compare the two alternatives, we need not compute this amount.

To derive an observable proxy for δ from equation (3), values for M and N must be chosen, a decision must be made as to the rate series to use for r, and some means of estimating $E(P|\text{Call})$ must be developed. We use $M = 10$ and $N = 30$ and replace r by two different rates depending on whether the indicated maturity is ten or thirty years. The rates R_{10} and R_{30} are yields on Treasury bonds reported by Salomon Brothers. With these substitutions, equation (3) becomes

$$\delta = \gamma[E(P|\text{Call}) - P_c]\frac{R_{30}\ (1 + R_{30})^{30}}{(1 + R_{10})^{10}\ [(1 + R_{30})^{30} - 1]} \tag{4}$$

The choice of a maturity of thirty years is dictated by the data used for rates on callable issues, an index rate on new issue corporate bonds reported by Salomon Brothers. The maturity of those issues underlying the composite rates tends to be about thirty years.

The call protection of the issues reported by Salomon Brothers is generally five years. However, there is no reason to assume that the call will be exercised immediately after the call protection expires since, as with equity options, the intrinsic value of the option can exceed the difference between the market price of the underlying security and call price. This result follows from the fact that the holder of the option benefits from all subsequent price increases but stands to lose at most an amount equal to the current difference between the market and the call prices. Since it is unlikely that the optimal time to call is immediately upon expiration of call protection, we choose, somewhat arbitrarily, ten years after issuance (on average, five years after expiration of the call protection) as the point in time to evaluate the two alternatives. At that point, the average corporate bond represented by our data has a remaining life of twenty years. We did experiment with alternative evaluation times and obtained similar empirical results.

It is apparent from the theoretical development of our model of the call premium that the rates used to determine δ should correspond to noncallable bonds. Noncallable corporates are extremely rare; so, we use instead Treasury bond rates of the appropriate maturities.[5] Since the C-H tax-adjusted series is available only for the longer-term rate, we use the unadjusted yields provided by Salomon Brothers in order that the ten and thirty-year rates will be comparable. Note that δ is an increasing function of R_{30} but a decreasing function of R_{10}, and the biases introduced will to some extent offset.

Since $E(P|\text{Call}) - P_c$ is unobservable, we assume the following relationship to be true:

$$E(P|\text{Call}) - P_c = C + \alpha[\hat{P} - 100], \tag{5}$$

where α and C are parameters to be estimated and $\hat{P}$, discussed in detail later, is a measure of $E(P)$, the unconditioned expectation of P. The contingent liability is assumed to be linearly related to the difference between $E(P)$ and the par value of the bond. The constant C causes some inconvenience, but will be seen to be important conceptually. Substitution from equation (5) into equation (4) gives the empirical model of δ to be used:

$$\delta = \alpha\gamma[\hat{P} - 100]\left[\frac{R_{30}(1 + R_{30})^{30}}{(1 + R_{10})^{10}[(1 + R_{30})^{30} - 1]}\right] + C\gamma\left[\frac{R_{30}(1 + R_{30})^{30}}{(1 + R_{10})^{10}[(1 + R_{30})^{30} - 1]}\right], \tag{6}$$

which we simplify to

$$\delta = \beta_1 y + \beta_2 K,$$

where

$$\beta_1 = \alpha\gamma$$

$$\beta_2 = C\gamma$$

$$y = [\hat{P} - 100]\left[\frac{R_{30}(1 + R_{30})^{30}}{(1 + R_{10})^{10}[(1 + R_{30})^{30} - 1]}\right]$$

$$K = y/(\hat{P} - 100)$$

[5]While the level of Treasury rates is obviously below corporates, the bias introduced should be small since we compare expected future rates to current yields for the purpose of computing expected future bond prices. So long as maturity exerts a similar effect on corporate and Treasury yields our procedure will be appropriate.

Clearly, both γ and α should be positive. Hence, β_1 should be positive. The equation is underidentified, however, in the sense that some assumption about the magnitude of α must be made if a direct estimate of γ is to be obtained.

Another problem is that $[\hat{P} - 100]$ can be negative while $[E(P|\text{Call}) - P_c]$ cannot.[6] The inclusion of a constant in the expression describing the proxy permits $[E(P|\text{Call}) - P_c]$ to remain positive even when $[E(P) - 100]$ is not. In estimation, K appears as a separate independent variable as a result of the constant in the proxy expression. The coefficient β_2 provides an estimate of $C\gamma$ and should be positive if negative values of $(\hat{P} - 100)$ are to be consistent with positive values of $[E(P|\text{Call}) - P_c]$. Some diagnostic information on the adequacy of the proxy expression will be obtained by estimating the relationship for a subset of the data where $\hat{P} > 100$ and then comparing estimated coefficients.

Another potential source of difficulty is that the difference between $E(P|\text{Call})$ and $E(P)$ will be greater, the greater is the variance of the subjective distribution of future prices. That variance cannot be measured directly, but the variance of the proxy for $E(P)$ would seem to be an appropriate alternative measure. Thus, we will examine whether the observable variance for subperiods within the sample provides for the possibility of changes in β_1 between subperiods.

Finally, $\hat{P}$ is calculated as

$$\hat{P} = \frac{100\, R_{30}}{E_{20}} \left[1 - \frac{1}{(1 + E_{20})^{20}} \right] + \frac{100}{(1 + E_{20})^{20}} , \qquad (7)$$

where E_{20} is the twenty-year Treasury yield expected ten years hence. Conceptually, the expression in equation (7) prices the initial coupon bond at the future yield (E_{20}) inferred from the yield curve at time 0 for a twenty-year bond, ten years hence. Our procedure for decomposing the yield curve to produce E_{20} from R_{30} and R_{10} corrects for coupon effects.

In summary, by formally modeling the relationship determining δ, the coupon premium, we expect to improve significantly on the explanatory power of the empirical model estimated by C-H. Conceptually, their approach to modeling the impact of callability on yield spreads is inferior to ours in that (1) the point in time at which expectations are measured is inconsistent with typical call provisions; (2) the forward rate they measure corresponds to an instrument whose maturity is too short; and (3) their measure of the forward rate is crude (the difference between three and five, or four and seven-year yields) and serves as an indication of the slope of the yield curve rather than a true forward rate. In addition to enabling better predictions of the yield spread that will result from any set of bond characteristics, our model produces estimated coefficients that have theoretical meaning and empirical interpretation.

[6]C-H experience a similar problem with their yield spread proxy for interest rate expectation. See [3, note 17] for their discussion of this problem.

4. EMPIRICAL RESULTS

The Data

Following C-H, our data cover the period from the beginning of 1961 through the end of 1975. C-H generously provided their data for our tests. Those data are supplemented by the yield series for ten, twenty, and thirty-year government securities reported by Salomon Brothers. Since the C-H data is quarterly and the government series are monthly, the middle month of each quarter is taken as the relevant point of observation for the values of R_{10}, R_{20}, and R_{30}. Each time series consists of sixty observations spanning the period 1961–75. Table 2 identifies the abbreviated variable names used in reporting the results of estimation and the source of each variable.

TABLE 2

DESCRIPTION AND SOURCE OF VARIABLES USED IN YIELD SPREAD REGRESSIONS

Variable	Source	Description
δ = RAa-RUS	C-H	The yield spread between callable corporate and noncallable government bonds
MOOD	C-H	Consumer sentiment measure
EPI	C-H	Employment pressure index
EXP	C-H	Interest rate expectation measure
y	Y-M	Joint proxies for the impact of callability
K	Y-M	See text
RUS	C-H	Tax-corrected treasury bond yield
RSS	C-H	Relative security supplies

NOTE: C-H denotes from Cook-Hendershott; Y-M from Yawitz-Marshall.

The Estimation Procedure

The equations estimated by C-H displayed significant autocorrelation of the error terms. Since the sample size is such that a corrective procedure is desirable,[7] we choose to employ a generalized least squares technique based on the method of estimation of the autocorrelation coefficient proposed by Cochrane and Orchutt [2] as described fully by Gallant and Goebel [6]. The technique we use differs from C-H in that only one iteration is used in the estimation of the autocorrelation coefficient. Multiple iteration is not always desirable,[8] and the results of our replication of the C-H equations suggest that the differences are trivial in the case at hand.

Before reporting the results of our empirical analysis, a comment on the interpretation of statistics seems appropriate. Reported statistics for autoregressive relationships can be deceptive. The R^2s reported for the quasi-differenced equations provide the basis for valid statistical comparisons of alternative specifications, but do not necessarily reflect the predictive abilities of the models when subsequently applied to levels rather than differences of the variables. This is because the ability to predict levels is generally improved as the degree of autocorrelation increases, while

[7]See Maddala [7, pp. 278–83] on this point.
[8]See Gallant and Goebel [6].

the R^2 of a quasi-differenced equation is generally reduced as the differencing coefficient increases (in absolute value) to reflect greater autocorrelation. Thus, we choose to report R^2s for the quasi-differenced models and mean-square-errors (MSE) of predictions for each model transformed to levels form. Direct comparison of R^2s, we feel, should be limited to models with similar error structures. In our opinion, the MSEs are the more valid basis of comparison.

Regression Results

Table 3 reports the empirical results obtained when we estimate the C-H "best" specification and several versions using our proxy for callability. A pair-wise comparison of equations (C-H) and (Y-M1) indicates the following results. The equation (Y-M1), which contains only the MOOD and callability variables, has an R^2 of 0.652 versus 0.376 obtained for equation (C-H) that includes the EXP and RSS variables in addition to MOOD and the C-H callability measure. We found that the addition of the labor pressure variable (EPI) added nothing to the explanatory power of our equation. Our specification reduces the mean square error of the equation by 9.2 percent for increased degrees of freedom. The overall measures of performance indicate that (Y-M1) is definitely superior.

Moreover, the correlation among the error terms is reduced by more than one-half with our specification, indicating that an explanatory variable was "left out" in the C-H equation. A common explanation of autocorrelation of errors is the exclusion of a relevant explanatory variable that is itself autocorrelated. By exclusion, that variable becomes incorporated in the error. As noted earlier, the variables relevant

TABLE 3

COMPARATIVE REGRESSION RESULTS FOR THE COOK-HENDERSHOTT AND YAWITZ-MARSHALL YIELD SPREAD MODELS

	Equations				
Variable	C-H	Y-M1	Y-M2	Y-M3	Y-M4
Intercept	8.28	−5.42	−0.89	−1.55	−4.80
	(1.74)	(2.28)	(0.131)	(0.267)	(1.17)
MOOD	−0.009	−0.012	−0.011	−0.011	−0.012
	(1.92)	(2.91)	(2.47)	(2.55)	(2.82)
EPI	−0.071				
	(1.56)				
EXP	−0.571				
	(2.69)				
y		4.077	2.58	2.86	4.50
		(5.39)	(0.820)	(1.05)	(2.69)
K		176.4	50.86	68.40	160.0
		(3.40)	(0.281)	(0.438)	(1.56)
RUS	0.062		0.065	0.065	
	(1.50)		(0.731)	(0.737)	
RSS			0.0002		0.0002
			(0.195)		(0.187)
R^2 (differences)	0.376	0.6523	0.6512	0.6509	0.6526
MSE (levels)	0.02264	0.02055	0.02033	0.02034	0.02054
ρ	0.562	0.267	0.275	0.275	0.267

NOTE: Dependent variable: δ.

to this study all exhibit high degrees of autocorrelation. Because of the nature of the autoregressive estimation procedure, one could argue that the improvement in the mean square error using our call measure *understates* the true improvement in the model. This conclusion follows directly from the fact that the autoregressive technique estimates a value for the autoregressive term that, in conjunction with the contemporaneous values of the independent variables, results in the greatest explanatory power. Generally speaking, for a given MSE, the higher is the autocorrelation of the error terms, the smaller is the contribution to explanatory power from the independent variables. As a result, the conventional measures of performance overstate explanatory power when the equation is not specified properly. This point has added importance in our study, since there is no sound theoretical argument for an autoregressive model in determining yield spreads. In fact, autoregressive errors might be interpreted to imply market inefficiency with respect to information processing.

Turning now to the individual variables in equation (Y-M1), we obtained highly significant t-statistics (5.39 and 3.40) for each of the variables that jointly capture the effect of callability on yield spreads. The coefficient on y provides an estimate of the size of the increase in coupon required on a callable bond as compensation for a \$1 increase in the expected price of the underlying noncallable bond, ten years hence. From equation (6), we can derive the following expression for $\partial\delta/\partial\hat{P}$:

$$\frac{\partial\delta}{\partial\hat{P}} = \frac{\beta_1\,[R_{30}\,(1 + R_{30})^{30}]}{(1 + R_{10})^{10}\,[(1 + R_{30})^{30} - 1]}\,, \tag{8}$$

which, for a 7 percent level of yields, takes on the value \$0.16. The inference is that \$0.16 additional coupon is required as compensation for a \$1 increase in the expected price of the underlying security at the time the call may be exercised.

Equations (Y-M2) and (Y-M3) report on the additional empirical tests that were conducted using our call specification and other variables suggested by C-H as possibly influencing the yield spread. As indicated, the addition of either RSS or RUS to equation (Y-M1) leads to negligible improvement in the R^2 and the mean square error. While the high degree of correlation between our K term and RSS makes it impossible to make a definitive statistical judgment, our findings must be viewed as supportive of the C-H conclusion that relative security supply does not seem to be an important factor in determining yield spreads.

5. CONCLUSION

The conclusion as to the primary purpose of our paper is obvious: the proxy for the effect of callability on yield spreads developed herein is preferable to that of C-H. This finding is not surprising since C-H endeavor to obtain a proxy for the effect of interest rate expectations on future prices while we measure the variable directly.

The empirical analysis of the factors, other than callability, that were examined by C-H indicates that, consistent with C-H, the MOOD variable is statistically significant in each equation estimated. In addition, the value of the coefficient obtained was nearly identical in every format. Our conclusion is that the MOOD variable serves as a meaningful proxy for the impact of cyclical influences on the yield compensation for default. The "performance" of the MOOD variable explains in part why we devoted little attention to the labor pressure variable (EPI) that was also hypothesized to proxy cyclical influences. The near zero *t*-statistic, obtained for EPI, differs from C-H who found this variable to be significant at a 10 percent level.

LITERATURE CITED

1. Bierman, Harold Jr., and Jerome E. Hass. "An Analytic Model of Bond Risk Differentials." *Journal of Financial and Quantitative Analysis,* 10 (December 1975), 757-73.
2. Cochrane, Donald, and Guy H. Orcutt. "Application of Least Square Regression to Relationships Containing Autocorrelated Error Terms." *Journal of the American Statistical Society,* (1949), 32-61.
3. Cook, Timothy Q., and Patric H. Hendershott. "The Impact of Taxes, Risk, and Relative Security Supplies on Interest Rate Differentials." *Journal of Finance,* 33 (September 1978), 1173-86.
4. Cullison, William E. "An Employment Pressure Index as an Alternative Measure of Labor Market Conditions." *Review of Economics and Statistics,* 57 (February 1975), 115-21.
5. Fair, Ray C. *A Short-run Forecasting Model of the United States Economy.* Lexington, Mass.: D. C. Heath, 1971.
6. Gallant, A. Ronald, and J. Jeffrey Goebel. "Nonlinear Regression with Autoregressive Errors." *Journal of the American Statistical Association,* 71 (1976), 961-67.
7. Maddala, G. S. *Econometrics.* New York: McGraw-Hill, 1977.
8. Van Horne, James C. *Financial Market Rates and Flows.* Englewood Cliffs, N.J.: Prentice-Hall, 1978.
9. Yawitz, Jess B. "An Analytical Model of Interest Rate Differentials and Different Default Recoveries." *Journal of Financial and Quantitative Analysis,* (September 1977), 481-90.
10. Yawitz, Jess B., and James A. Anderson. "The Effect of Bond Refunding on Shareholder Wealth." *Journal of Finance,* 32 (December 1977), 1738-46.
11. Yawitz, Jess B., and William J. Marshall. "Why Firms Issue Callable Debt: A Bias in the Tax Laws." Working Paper, Washington University, 1978.
12. ______. "Optimal Terms of the Call Provision on a Corporate Bond." *Journal of Financial Research,* in press.

ENRIQUE R. ARZAC
ROBERT A. SCHWARTZ
DAVID K. WHITCOMB

The Leverage Structure of Interest Rates

WHILE IT SEEMS INTUITIVELY CLEAR that competitive credit markets should generate an increasing leverage structure of interest rates, and while Fisher's [7] classic study of bond yields gives empirical evidence of a significant leverage premium, the theoretical literature contains only fragmentary development of conditions for a leverage structure. The purpose of this paper is to present sufficient lender supply and borrower demand conditions for a leverage structure to characterize equilibrium in competitive markets. The model allows for default, and assumes that lenders and borrowers are price takers, that they maximize concave utility functions, that they face an institutional regime of limited liability, and that they can invest both in a competitively available risk asset yielding stochastic constant returns and in a risk-free asset. Our framework is more general than mean-variance analysis; the latter would not be desirable in any event due to its inability to deal with a non-zero default probability under general utility assumptions.[1]

[1]Some of the early mean-variance literature may be read to imply a leverage structue of interest rates, but only under very restrictive utility assumptions. Tobin's [17] result that a risk averse investor demands a higher interest rate on consols as the variance of capital gains rises can be extended directly to loans having positive default probability (and hence a truncated distribution) only by assuming quadratic utility. Mossin [12] allows for default, but only in the special case of an independent two-point distribution of terminal wealth, and he implicitly assumes the case of quadratic utility plus the CAPM assumption of riskless lending and borrowing. His utility assumption cannot be relaxed by alternatively assuming, e.g., a normal distribution, because of the truncation of the lender's returns distribution induced by the possibility of default.

ENRIQUE R. ARZAC *is professor of economics and finance, Graduate School of Business, Columbia University.* ROBERT A. SCHWARTZ *is professor of economics, Graduate School of Business Administration, New York University.* DAVID K. WHITCOMB *is professor of finance, Graduate School of Business Administration, Rutgers University.*

0022-2879/81/0281-0072$00.50/0
JOURNAL OF MONEY, CREDIT, AND BANKING, vol. 13, no. 1 (February 1981)

Earlier works that have in passing stated supply side conditions for an increasing leverage structure are an example of Boness [6] and Barro's [5] elegant model of interest rate determination on collateral loans in the presence of default costs. Both assume lender risk neutrality (which yields the special case result that the lender's expected return on a leveraged loan is constant with respect to the leverage ratio, although the contractual interest rate rises) and neither states demand side conditions for support of a leverage structure. Baltensperger [4] and Stapleton [16] assume a positive leverage structure of interest rates in their contributions to the literature of credit rationing and the leverage structure of the firm, respectively. A leverage structure of interest rates is particularly important for the issue of credit rationing since it would substitute price rationing for quantity rationing and would be Pareto efficient [see the Smith [15] and Baltensperger [4] exchange]. However, since institutional constraints on interest rates commonly exist, the seminal Jaffee and Modigliani [9] contribution is a natural approach to the study of the effects of regulation or imperfect competition in credit markets. We consider lender behavior under a flat structure in another paper [3].

Section 1 of this paper presents a model of the credit transaction between individuals embedded in a competitive credit market. Section 2 obtains conditions for the optimal supply of leverage by price-taking lenders and derives restrictions on the leverage structure of the contractual interest rate and the risk premium. Section 3 shows that differences in borrower wealth or risk aversion are sufficient conditions for borrower support of an increasing leverage structure. Section 4 then presents an arbitrage proof of the necessity of an increasing leverage structure for competitive credit market equilibrium; we do not, however, undertake the considerably more formidable task of developing a proof of the existence of equilibrium under a leverage structure of interest rates. Section 5 contains our conclusions.

1. A MODEL OF COMPETITIVE CREDIT BEHAVIOR UNDER UNCERTAINTY

This section presents a model of the credit transaction between individuals embedded in a competitive credit market. In this model, the individual has to decide on the optimal allocation of his initial investible capital K, among a risk asset with random rate of return R-1 available to all investors, a riskless asset with return s-1, and lending to or borrowing from another individual. Short sales of the risk asset are not permitted.[2]

The amount of the loan is denoted by $|L|$, with $L > 0$ denoting a lender and $L < 0$ denoting a borrower. Individuals who borrow an amount $|L|$ to invest in the risk asset put up their entire investment in the risk asset as collateral. The borrower has limited liability in that if he defaults, he retains the portion of his capital M invested in the riskless asset; the remainder of his capital, C $(=K\text{-}M)$, is at risk.

[2]We note that all the results of this paper hold with trivial modifications if the individual also receives an exogenously-determined random "wage" income. Since inclusion of this variable would add no insight into credit behavior, it has been deleted to simplify the exposition.

The quality of the loan is measured by the leverage ratio

$$V = \frac{|L|}{C + |L|} .$$

Investors are assumed to be price takers, that is, to take as given whatever contractual interest rate, $r(V) - 1$, may be determined in the market.[3] Like any price takers, lenders can choose the size (L) and the quality (V) of the loan, but must take the corresponding market price. Under limited liability, the random interest rate on the loan is

$$\tilde{r} = \begin{cases} r & \text{if } R \geqslant R^* \ (= rV) \\ R/V & \text{if } R < R^* . \end{cases}$$

R^* is the default rate of return on the risk asset; any return below R^* is insufficient to repay the loan in full.

With this notation and our assumptions, the individual's terminal wealth can be written

$$W = (K - M - L)R + L\tilde{r} + Ms .$$

Assuming the investor has a differentiable subjective probability distribution of returns on the risk asset $F(R)$, with density $f(R)$ and $F(0) = 0$,[4] and a twice differentiable utility function $U(W)$, his expected utility may be written

$$E(U) = \int_0^{R^*} U[(K - M + C)R + Ms]dF(R)$$

$$+ \int_{R^*}^{\infty} U[(K - M - L)R + Lr + Ms]dF(R),$$

$$L \geqslant 0 \text{ (lender)}, \tag{1}$$

$$E(U) = U(Ms)F(R^*) + \int_{R^*}^{\infty} U[(K - M - L)R + Lr + Ms]dF(R),$$

$$L < 0 \text{ (borrower)} . \tag{2}$$

Any given individual can decide to be a lender or a borrower depending on his preferences and probability beliefs. The first order conditions for optimal lending

[3]We take r to be a differentiable function of V; sufficient conditions for $r'(V) > 0$ will be shown later, but we make no assumption as to the slope of $r(V)$ at this point.

[4]The probability beliefs of borrowers and lenders are not assumed to be homogeneous in this paper. However, we do not deal with the implications of heterogeneity. If individuals take informational asymmetry into account, their optima as well as the resulting market equilibrium are likely to be affected as a consequence. See [10] and [11].

and investment are derived by differentiating (1) with respect to L, M, and C using Leibniz' Rule:[5]

$$\int_{R^*}^{\infty} U'[(K - M - L)R + Lr + Ms]\left(r + L\frac{\partial r}{\partial L} - R\right)dF(R) = 0, \tag{3}$$

$$\int_{0}^{\infty} U'(W)(s - R)dF(R) = 0, \tag{4}$$

$$\int_{0}^{R^*} U'[(K - M + C)R + Ms]RdF(R) + \int_{R^*}^{\infty} U'[(K - M - L)R + Lr + Ms]\,L\frac{\partial r}{\partial C}dF(R) = 0\,. \tag{5}$$

The conditions for optimal borrowing and investment follow from differentiating (2) with respect to L and M. The condition for optimal L is formally identical to (3).[6] The condition for optimal M is now

$$U'(Ms)sF(R^*) + \int_{R^*}^{\infty} U'[(K - M - L)R + Lr + Ms]\left(s - R + L\frac{\partial r}{\partial M}\right)dF(R) = 0\,. \tag{6}$$

Example: This simple example illustrates how the model can generate borrowing and lending solutions. Assume that no riskless asset is available for investment (i.e., $M = 0$ above) and let $U(W) = -exp\,(cW)$, $c < 0$, and $f(R) = \alpha\ exp\,(-\alpha R)$, $\alpha > 0$, for $R \geqslant 0$. Substituting U and f into (3) yields

$$L = K + \frac{1}{c}\left[\frac{1}{(1 - V)\,r + L\dfrac{\partial r}{\partial L}} - \frac{1}{E(R)}\right],$$

which gives $L < 0$ for sufficiently small $|c|$ (absolute risk aversion) and r, and sufficiently large $E(R)$, and $L > 0$ vice versa.

Some Properties of the Optimum

Condition (3), which applies to both lending and borrowing, can be written

$$\frac{E_{R^*}^{\infty}[U'(W)R]}{E_{R^*}^{\infty}[U'(W)]} = r + L\frac{\partial r}{\partial L}, \tag{3'}$$

[5]In deriving (3), we have made use of the following equality:

$$(K - M + C)R^* = (K - M - L)R^* + Lr, \qquad \text{for } L > 0.$$

A statement of Leibniz' rule may be found in [1, p. 220], for example. Note that by taking the derivative with respect to L and C (the borrower's equity in the risk asset) the lender effectively chooses among borrowers so as to obtain optimal L and V. In the borrower's decision, below, choice of L and M determines C.

[6]In deriving (3) for borrowing, note that $(K - M - L)R^* + Lr = 0$ when $L < 0$.

where E_{R*}^{∞} is the partial expectation operator over $[R^*, \infty)$. That is, at the optimum, the return on the risk asset weighted by the marginal utility of terminal wealth over $[R^*, \infty)$ should equal the marginal gross interest rate on the loan.

From (4) we obtain

$$\frac{E[U'(W)R]}{E[U'(W)]} = s, \tag{4'}$$

which is the well-known condition for the optimal portfolio of a risky and a riskless asset [2, pp. 99–100]. In the next section we show that, as one might expect, (3′) and (4′) are intimately related.[7]

One can show (see app. A) that conditions (3)–(6) satisfy the first-order conditions for a Pareto efficient allocation of claims between a borrower and a lender constrained only by the structure of returns (including the leverage structure) and by limited liability.

The Pareto efficiency of credit markets operating under a leverage structure was demonstrated by Baltensperger [4] for a more restrictive model. Earlier, Smith [15] found that, under a flat structure, the borrower's capital acts as an external economy to the borrower. The next section formalizes the notion, put forward in various ways by Boness [6], Baltensperger [4], and Barro [5], that lenders will require higher interest rates in order to supply higher leverage loans.

2. THE SUPPLY OF LEVERAGE

Examination of (5) reveals that when $Pr[R \geqslant R^*] = 1$ (zero probability of default), the first term equals zero and the condition requires (for $L > 0$)

$$\frac{dr}{dC} = -\frac{V^2}{L} r'(V) = 0, \qquad \text{or } r'(V) = \frac{dr}{dV} = 0 .$$

Furthermore, the left-hand sides of (3′) and (4′) are identical and the two conditions can be simultaneously satisfied only if

$$r = s, \text{ for } Pr[R \geqslant R^*] = 1 .$$

That is, the interest rate on a default-free loan should equal the riskless interest rate.

More interesting is the case where $Pr[R \geqslant R^*] < 1$ (positive probability of default). In this case (5) implies

$$r'(V) = \frac{\int^{R^*} U'(W)R\,dF(R)}{V^2 \int_{R^*}^{\infty} U'(W)\,dF(R)} > 0, \tag{7}$$

[7]Condition (6) also leads to a similar expression, but the random return on the risk asset appearing in the numerator now is s for $R \in [0,R^*)$ and $R - L\,\partial r/\partial M$ for $R \in [R^*, \infty)$.

since $L\, \partial r / \partial C = -V^2 r'(V)$. Hence we can state:

PROPOSITION 1. *A competitive lender's leverage supply function must be such that:*

$$r'(V) = 0, \qquad r = s, \text{ for } V \text{ such that } Pr\,[R \geqslant R^*] = 1,$$
$$r'(V) > 0, \qquad r > s, \text{ for } V \text{ such that } Pr\,[R \geqslant R^*] < 1\,.$$

Note that (7) and proposition 1 do not depend on the sign of U'' and are, therefore, valid also for risk indifference or risk seeking. Moreover, they do not depend on the assumption that lenders can invest in the same risk asset as borrowers. Denoting by Q the return on the asset available to the lender, the following trivial changes apply to (7): $F = F(R,Q)$, and the domains of integration in numerator and denominator become $[0,R^*] \times [0,\infty)$ and $[R^*,\infty) \times [0,\infty)$, respectively. In particular, no risk asset need be available to the lender.

Barro [5] derives a result equivalent to our (7) for the case of a risk neutral lender unable to invest in the risk asset (but with the additional feature of explicit default costs).[8] The Boness and Barro assumption of lender risk neutrality implies that the lender's *expected* rate of interest on the loan equals the risk-free rate and is therefore constant with respect to leverage. This is, of course, the case with our model. Note that

$$E(\tilde{r}) = \int_0^{R^*} \frac{R}{V}\, dF(R) + \int_{R^*}^{\infty} r\, dF(R)$$

and

$$\frac{d}{dV} E(\tilde{r}) = -\int_0^{R^*} \frac{R}{V^2}\, dF(R) + \int_{R^*}^{\infty} r'\, dF(R),$$

which is precisely the form taken by condition (5) for the lender's optimum under risk neutrality and, therefore, equals zero.

Under lender risk aversion, it can be shown that the *expected* rate of interest on the loan rises with leverage. In order to establish this result we first prove the following:

LEMMA 1. *Consider the functions* $h(R)$, $k(R)$, *and* $F(R)$ *defined on* $[R_1, R_2]$ *such that* $h(R) \gtreqless 0$ *as* $R \gtreqless R^\circ$, $\int_{R_1}^{R_2} h(R)\, dF(R) = 0$, *$k(R)$ is positive and monotonic and $F(R)$ is positive and increasing on* $[R_1, R_2]$. *Then* $sgn \int_{R_1}^{R_2} k(R) h(R)\, dF(R) = sgn[k(R_2) - k(R_1)]$.

Proof.

$$\int_{R_1}^{R_2} k(R) h(R)\, dF(R) \gtreqless \int_{R_1}^{R^\circ} k(R^\circ) h(R)\, dF(R) + \int_{R^\circ}^{R_2} k(R^\circ) h(R)\, dF(R)$$

[8]See Barro [5, eq. (14), p. 449].

$$\left[= k(R^{\circ}) \int_{R_1}^{R_2} h(R)dF(R) = 0 \right] \text{ as } k(R_2) - k(R_1) \gtreqless 0 . \qquad \text{Q.E.D.}$$

Let us define

$$\theta = \begin{cases} -R/V^2, & \text{for } R \in [0,R^*) \\ r', & \text{for } R \in [R^*, \infty); \end{cases}$$

hence we can write

$$\frac{d}{dV}E(\tilde{r}) = E(\Theta) .$$

Likewise, condition (5) becomes

$$E(U'\theta) = 0 . \tag{5'}$$

Risk neutrality gives $E(\theta) = 0$ as stated above. In order to sign $E(\theta)$ under risk aversion ($U' > 0$, $U'' < 0$), we apply lemma 1 with $k(R) = 1/U'$ and $h(R) = U'\theta$, and write $E(\theta) = E(hk)$. Note that $k(R)$ is continuous and $k'(R) = -(1/U'')(dW/dR) > 0$ for $R \neq R^*$, hence $k(R)$ is increasing. Moreover, $h(R) \gtreqless 0$ as $R \gtreqless R^*$, and from (5′), $E(h) = E(U'\ \theta) = 0$. Applying lemma 1 we conclude that $E(\theta) = E(hk) > 0$. Hence, we have proved the following:

PROPOSITION 2. *Under risk aversion the lender's expected rate of interest on the loan is an increasing function of leverage.*

This means that the risk premium $E(\tilde{r}) - s$ increases with leverage under risk aversion. If that were not the case, and $E(\theta) = 0$, lemma 1 then implies that $E(U'\theta) < 0$ for $U'' < 0$, which, in the terminology introduced by Rothschild and Stiglitz [14], means that higher leverage would produce a mean-preserving increase in risk rejected by every risk averter.

3. THE DEMAND FOR LEVERAGE

Turning to the demand side, it is not obvious that borrowers will support an increasing leverage structure by demanding loans at more than one point on the structure. In this section we show that differences in wealth and degree of risk aversion are alternative sufficient conditions to produce demand for loans of different leverage in the presence of an increasing leverage structure of interest rates.

Response to Change in Wealth

In order to study the demand for leverage as a function of wealth, we need to derive the comparative statics responses of the optimal solution for the borrower.

Given the form of the expected utility function, the analysis is cumbersome if we consider simultaneously the responses of L and M to a change in wealth. Hence, we shall consider the simpler case where the investment in the riskless asset is not subject to decision, specifically where there is an equal proportional change in the two forms of wealth, that is:[9]

$$dK = dC + dM, \qquad \text{where } dM = (M/C)\, dC\,. \tag{8}$$

Since no decision concerning M has to be made, only condition (3) applies.

We now prove:

PROPOSITION 3. *For dC as in (8), the demand for loans satisfies*

$$sgn\, \frac{dV}{dK} = -\, sgn\, \frac{d\rho_R}{dW},$$

where $\rho_R = -\, U''(W)W/U'(W)$ *is the Arrow* [2] *and Pratt* [13] *relative risk aversion measure.*

Proposition 3 is claimed for any arbitrary (market determined) structure $r(V)$, and in particular for $r'(V) > 0$. We first note that (see app. B)

$$sgn\, \frac{dV}{dK} = -\, sgn\, C\, \frac{\partial^2 E(U)}{\partial C \partial L} + L\, \frac{\partial^2 E(U)}{\partial L^2}, \tag{9}$$

where $C = K - M$.

Furthermore, it is shown in Appendix (C) that taking the derivatives of (3) with respect to K and L and substituting into the right hand side of (9) yields

$$sgn\, \frac{dV}{dK} = -\, sgn \int_{R^*}^{\infty} \rho(W) U'(W) \left[R - \left(R + L\, \frac{\partial r}{\partial L} \right) \right] dF(R)\,. \tag{10}$$

Finally, letting

$$\rho(W) = k(R), \text{ and } U'(W) \left[R - \left(r + L\, \frac{\partial r}{\partial L} \right) \right] = h(R)$$

in (10), and applying lemma 1, completes the proof of proposition 3.

We have thus established that for the case of an equal proportional change in wealth invested in risky and riskless assets, the demand for higher leverage loans decreases (increases) with wealth for increasing (decreasing) relative risk aversion. Hence, since proposition 3 holds for $r'(V) > 0$, and since borrowers generally differ in wealth levels, some borrowers will be willing to pay the higher r required by lenders in order to obtain higher leverage.

[9]A more general case is considered in app. D.

Proposition 3 can be expressed in terms of the wealth elasticity of the demand for loans. Let $\eta = (K/L)(dL/dK) = (C/L)(dL/dC)$. Then

$$\frac{dV}{dC} = -\frac{L}{(C\text{-}L)^2}(\eta - 1)$$

(see exp. (A8) in app. B). Hence, since $L < 0$ and $dV/dK = (C/K)dV/dC$, we have the following:

COROLLARY. *For dC as in (8), the demand for loans satisfies* $sgn\,(\eta - 1) = -\,sgn\,\frac{d\rho}{dW}$.

It is trivial to verify that proposition 3 also holds in the particular case in which no riskless asset is available and $M = 0$.

Response to Changes in Attitude Toward Risk

We now consider the effect on L and V of changes in the borrower's attitude toward risk under the assumption of predetermined investment in the riskless asset. Consider the case of constant nonunitary relative risk aversion utilities:

$$U(W) = \frac{1}{\gamma}W^{\gamma}, \qquad \gamma \neq 0, < 1, \tag{11}$$

where $\gamma = 1 - \rho_R(W)$. Differentiating (3) (for $L < 0$) totally with respect to γ gives the borrower's optimal response to a decrease in the degree of relative risk aversion:

$$sgn\,\frac{dL}{d\gamma} = sgn\,\frac{E(U)}{\partial\gamma\partial L}.$$

Substituting (11) into (2) and differentiating with respect to L and γ one obtains

$$\frac{\partial^2 E(U)}{\partial\gamma\partial L} = -\int_{R^*}^{\infty}(\log W)W^{\gamma-1}\left[R - \left(r + L\frac{\partial r}{\partial L}\right)\right]dF(R). \tag{12}$$

Finally, letting $\log W = k(R)$ and $W^{\gamma-1}(r + L(\partial r/\partial L) - R) = h(R)$ in (12), and applying lemma 1, gives $dL/d\gamma < 0$.

A similar result can be established for the class of constant absolute risk aversion utilities $U(W) = -\,exp\,(cW)$, $c < 0$. Therefore, recalling that $L < 0$ for the borrower, we have proved:

PROPOSITION 4. *Borrowers with different constant relative or absolute risk aversion utilities will,* ceteris paribus, *demand higher leverage loans the lower their degree of risk aversion, even when the leverage structure of interest rates is increasing.*

Propositions 3 and 4 constitute a set of reasonably general diversity conditions sufficient to guarantee that borrowers will demand loans of different leverage in the presence of an increasing leverage structure of interest rates.

4. AN ARBITRAGE PROOF THAT COMPETITIVE EQUILIBRIUM IS CHARACTERIZED BY AN INCREASING LEVERAGE STRUCTURE OF INTEREST RATES

The results we have shown thus far apply to individual lenders and borrowers. These results do not immediately imply that across all lenders and loan sizes a nonincreasing leverage structure could not characterize equilibrium. We now prove the more powerful result:

PROPOSITION 5. *A nonincreasing leverage structure of interest rates is incompatible with equilibrium in a competitive credit market in the sense that it would permit the realization of pure arbitrage profits.*

To prove this proposition we have to extend the scope of our model to allow for the possibility of financial intermediaries. The proof will consist of showing that a nonincreasing leverage structure would enable intermediaries to realize pure arbitrage profits.

Proof. Let $r'(V) \leqslant 0$ and consider an intermediary who borrows L_I, offering the lender collateral $L_I + C_I$, and lends a borrower $L_B = L_I$, obtaining collateral $L_B + C_B > L_I + C_I$. That is, the intermediary uses only part of the collateral pledged by the borrower to cover his loan, and hence $V_B < V_I$. With $r'(V) \leqslant 0$, we have $r(V_B) \geqslant r(V_I)$ so the intermediary need pay no interest rate penalty for withholding part of the borrower's collateral from his pledge to the lender. There are three distinct ranges of R (the return on the underlying risk asset) to be considered. Each range with its corresponding default characterization and expression for final wealth is given in Table 1. The first inequality in the last column of this table follows from $C_B > C_I$. The second inequality follows from the default conditions $R < r(V_I)V_I$ and from $r'(V) \leqslant 0$, which imply $R < r(V_B)V_I = r(V_B)L_I/(C_I + L_I)$, or $L_I r(V_B) > (C_I + L_I)R$. Finally, the third inequality follows from $r'(V) \leqslant 0$.

Intermediation increases wealth over $[0, rV_I)$ and increases (for $r'(V) < 0$) or maintains (for $r'(V) = 0$) wealth over $[rV_I, \infty)$. Hence, the intermediary has succeded in constructing a probability distribution of terminal wealth that absolutely dominates the previous distribution for any increasing utility function [8], and interme-

TABLE 1

ARBITRAGE—INTERMEDIATION OUTCOMES

Range of Risk Asset Return	Loans Defaulted	Final Wealth Generated by Intermediation
$[0, r(V_B)V_B)$	L_I, L_B	$(C_B - C_I)R > 0$
$[r(V_B)V_B, r(V_I)V_I)$	L_I	$L_I r(V_B) - (C_I + L_I)R > 0$
$[r(V_I)V_I, \infty)$	none	$L_I[r(V_L) - r(V_I)] \geq 0$

diation is unambiguously profitable. A similar argument rules out the possibility of loans of different size following a nonincreasing leverage structure.[10]

In attempting to induce borrowers to accept more low leverage loans, intermediaries would bid down the interest rate on such loans. So long as the supply curve of loans is not so backward bending as to drive interest rates for high loans down faster, intermediation will not have an explosive impact and will produce a positive leverage structure across all V.[11] In other words, if a competitive equilibrium exists, it must be characterized by a positive leverage structure of interest rates.

5. CONCLUSION

The focus of this paper has been the effect of leverage on interest rates. While we have not attempted to state conditions for the existence of a competitive equilibrium characterized by a leverage structure of interest rates, we have shown that if a competitive equilibrium exists, it will exhibit an increasing leverage structure of interest rates.

On the supply side, positive marginal utility of wealth is the only restriction required to make an increasing leverage structure necessary for an interior maximum of the lender's utility function. On the demand side, risk averse borrowers will support an increasing leverage structure by demanding loans at more than one point on the structure if, besides some other mild assumptions, there are differences in wealth among borrowers or differences in the degree of absolute or relative risk aversion.

By allowing for the possibility of arbitrage intermediation, we also derive an arbitrage proof that rules out a nonincreasing leverage structure in a competitive market.

No statement of demand side conditions for support of an increasing leverage structure by borrowers appears in the literature, and Barro's [5] supply side conditions are stated for the special case of a risk neutral lender unable to invest in the risk asset (although, as we see here, they may be extended a fortiori to risk aversion). To our knowledge, the arbitrage proof and its use of stochastic dominance are also new. We have also proved that the risk premium on loans (i.e., the difference between the *expected* interest rate and the riskless rate) will be an increasing function of leverage.

Our work, taken together with the Baltensperger [4] and Barro [5] contributions, serves to clarify the relationship between the leverage structure of interest rates and

[10]Suppose $r(V_1) \leq r(V_2)$ for some $V_1 > V_2$ when $L_1 > L_2$. Then the intermediary can realize pure arbitrage profits by borrowing L_1 with leverage V_1 and making two loans: L_2 and L_3 ($= L_1 - L_2$), each with leverage $V_2 = V_3$. We note that $C_2 + C_3 > C_1$. That is, the collaterals pledged to the intermediary exceed his collateral pledge.

[11]One can show the present model admits a backward bending supply of loans. See Jaffee and Modigliani [9] and Smith [15] for detailed analyses of this property in models that are specific instances of ours. Explosive intermediation would occur only with a negatively inclined supply curve that never intersects demand from above as loan quantity increases. Demonstration of the existence and stability of equilibrium are beyond the scope of this paper.

credit rationing: when a competitive equilibrium is allowed to and does occur, it will (at least under the conditions we have assumed here) be characterized by an increasing leverage structure of interest rates, and there will not be credit rationing in the accepted meaning (i.e., there will be price, instead of quantity rationing). When a flat leverage structure is imposed, leverage will be rationed as in the models of Jaffe and Modigliani [9] and Smith [15].

APPENDIX

A. Pareto Efficiency

We shall establish that conditions (3)-(6) satisfy the first-order conditions for a Pareto efficient allocation of claims. Let X_1 and $C + l$ denote the lender's and the borrower's investment in the risk asset, respectively (l denotes the amount of the loan). The Lagrangian of the Pareto optimization problem then is

$$\phi = \int_0^{R^*} U_1\,[(X_1 + C + l)R + M_1 s]dF_1(R) + \int_{R^*}^{\infty} U_1[X_1R + lr + M_1s]$$

$$dF_1(R) + \lambda\left[U_2(M_2s)F_2(R^*) + \int_{R^*}^{\infty} U_2[(C + l)R - lr + M_2s]\right.$$

$$\left.dF_2(R)\right] + \mu(K_1 + K_2 - X_1 - C - l - M_1 - M_2),$$

where λ is an arbitrary welfare weight and μ is the multiplier of the planner's budget constraint.

Differentiating ϕ with respect to X_1, M_1, l, C, and M_2, respectively, yields

$$\int_0^{\infty} U_1'\, RdF_1(R) - \mu = 0, \tag{A1}$$

$$\int_0^{\infty} U_1's\, dF_1(R) - \mu = 0, \tag{A2}$$

$$\int_0^{R^*} U_1'\, RdF_1(R) + \int_{R^*}^{\infty} U_1'\left(r + l\frac{\partial r}{\partial L}\right)dF_1(R) +$$

$$\lambda \int_{R^*}^{\infty} U_2'\left(R - r - l\frac{\partial r}{\partial L}\right)dF_2(R) - \mu = 0, \tag{A3}$$

$$\int_0^{R^*} U_1'\, RdF_1(R) + \int_{R^*}^{\infty} U_1'\, l\frac{\partial r}{\partial C}dF_1(R) +$$

$$\lambda \int_{\infty}^{R^*} U_2'\left(R - l\frac{\partial r}{\partial C}\right)dF_2(R) - \mu = 0, \tag{A4}$$

$$U_2' (M_2 s) dF_2(R) + \int_{R^*}^{\infty} U_2' \, s dF_2 (R) - \frac{\mu}{\lambda} = 0 \, . \tag{A5}$$

Eliminating μ from (A1) and (A2) gives (4). Eliminating μ from (A1) and (A3) yields

$$\int_{R^*}^{\infty} U_1' \left(r + l\frac{\partial r}{\partial L} \right) dF_1(R) + \lambda \int_{R^*}^{\infty} U_2' \left(R - r - l\frac{\partial r}{\partial L} \right) dF_2(R) = 0, \tag{A6}$$

which is satisfied by (3), since each of the first and second integrals of (A6) equals zero by condition (3) for the lender and the borrower, respectively. Finally, the sum of the first two integrals in (A4) equal zero by (5). Hence,

$$-\frac{\mu}{\lambda} = \int_{R^*}^{\infty} U_2' \left(- R + l\frac{\partial r}{\partial C} - \mathrm{R} \right) dF_2(R) = 0, \tag{A7}$$

which, upon substitution into (A5), yields (6). (Note that $l \; \partial r / \partial C$ in (A7) equals $L \partial \mathrm{r} / \partial M$ in (6).)

B. Derivation of Expression (9)

Differentiating $V = -L/(C - L)$ yields

$$\frac{dV}{dC} = - \frac{dL}{dC} \frac{C}{(C - L)^2} + \frac{L}{(C - L^2} \tag{A8}$$

but, from the total differential of (3) w.r.t. C one obtains

$$\frac{dL}{dC} = - \frac{\partial^2 E(U)/\partial C \partial L}{\partial^2 E(U)/\partial L^2} \, , \tag{A9}$$

where $\partial^2 E(U)/\partial L^2 < 0$ by the second-order condition. Substituting (A9) into (A8) yields

$$\frac{dV}{dC} = \frac{L}{(C - L)^2} \left[- \frac{C}{L} \frac{\partial^2 E(U)/\partial K \partial L}{\partial^2 E(U)/\partial L^2} + 1 \right],$$

which implies (9), since $L < 0$ and $dV/dK = (C/K) dV/dC$.

C. Derivation of Expression (10)

Substituting the derivatives of (3) w.r.t. C ($= K - M$) and L into the left-hand side of (9) yields

$$C\left[\int_{R^*}^{\infty} U''(W)\left(R + L\frac{\partial r}{\partial C} + s\frac{dM}{dC}\right)\left(r + L\frac{\partial r}{\partial L} - R\right)dF(R)\right.$$

$$+ \int_{R^*}^{\infty} U'(W)\left(\frac{\partial r}{\partial C} + L\frac{\partial^2 \mathrm{r}}{\partial C \partial L}\right)dF(R) - U'(Ms)$$

$$\left.\left(r + L\frac{\partial r}{\partial L} - R^*\right) f(R^*)\frac{\partial R^*}{\partial C}\right] + L\left[\int_{R^*}^{\infty} U''(W)\right.$$

$$\left(r + L\frac{\partial r}{\partial L} - R\right)^2 dF(R) + \int_{R^*}^{\infty} U'(W)\left(2\frac{\partial r}{\partial L} + L\frac{\partial^2 r}{\partial L^2}\right)$$

$$\left. dF(R) - U'(Ms)\left(r + L\frac{\partial r}{\partial L} - R^*\right) f(R^*)\frac{\partial R^*}{\partial L}{}_2\right]. \tag{A10}$$

Next, differentiation of $R^* = rV$, $r = r(V)$, $V = -L/(C - L)$ shows that

$$C\frac{\partial Z}{\partial C} + L\frac{\partial Z}{\partial L} = 0, \qquad \text{for } Z = V, R^*, r\,. \tag{A11}$$

Hence the terms involving $U'(Ms)$ cancel and one term involving $\partial r/\partial C$ and $\partial r/\partial L$ in each of the U'' and U' expression also cancels. Now, substituting $dM/dC = M/C$ from (8) and recognizing that $CR - LR + Lr + Ms = W$, (A10) becomes

$$\int_{R^*}^{\infty} U''(W)W\left(r + L\frac{\partial r}{\partial C} - R\right) dF(R) + \int_{R^*}^{\infty} U'(W)L$$

$$\left(C\frac{\partial^2 r}{\partial C \partial L} + L\frac{\partial^2 r}{\partial L^2} + \frac{\partial r}{\partial L}\right) dF(R)\,. \tag{A12}$$

Finally, note that

$$\frac{\partial^2 r}{\partial C \partial L} = \frac{\partial}{\partial C}\left(\frac{dr}{dV}\frac{\partial V}{\partial L}\right) = \frac{d^2 r}{dV^2}\frac{\partial V}{\partial W}\frac{\partial V}{\partial L} + \frac{dr}{dV}\frac{\partial^2 V}{\partial C \partial L},$$

and

$$\frac{\partial^2 r}{\partial L^2} = \frac{d^2 r}{dV^2}\left(\frac{\partial V}{\partial L}\right)^2 + \frac{dr}{dV}\frac{\partial^2 V}{\partial L^2}\,.$$

Then, by (A11)

$$C\frac{\partial^2 r}{\partial C \partial L} + L\frac{\partial^2 r}{\partial L^2} = \frac{dr}{dV}\left(C\frac{\partial^2 V}{\partial C \partial L} + L\frac{\partial^2 v}{\partial L^2}\right) = -\frac{C}{(C - L)^2}\frac{dr}{dV}\,. \tag{A13}$$

But, since

$$\frac{\partial r}{\partial L} = \frac{dr}{dV}\frac{C}{(C - L)^2}, \tag{A14}$$

(A13) equals $-\partial r/\partial L$ and the second term in (A12) equals zero. Multiplying the integral of the remaining term in (A12) by $U'(W)/U'(W)$ gives the right-hand side of (10).

D. Generalization of Proposition 3

We now derive dV/dK, where (8) is replaced by the milder assumption $dC/dK > 0$. That is, we assume that some of the increase in wealth is allocated to the risk asset. Note that Arrow's proposition [2, app. to essay 3] (that favorable risk assets exhibiting stochastic constant returns to scale are superior under decreasing absolute risk aversion) does not permit us to conclude that $dC/dK > 0$. C is only a fraction of the individual's total investment in the risk asset, and borrowing under limited liability destroys the stochastic constant returns to scale property of the risk asset.

The following additional notation is needed: $\psi = \rho W$ for the Arrow and Pratt absolute risk aversion measure, and $\chi = (C/M)\, dM/dC$ for the elasticity of investment in the riskless asset with respect to the individual's equity in the risk asset. We now prove:

PROPOSITION 3′.

Decreasing absolute risk aversion and $dC/dK > 0$ imply

$$\frac{dV}{dK} < 0, \qquad \text{if } \frac{d\rho}{dW} \geqslant 0, \text{ and } \chi < 1$$

$$\frac{dV}{dK} \gtreqless 0, \qquad \text{as } \frac{d\rho}{dW} \gtreqless 0, \text{ if } \chi = 1$$

$$\frac{dV}{dK} > 0, \qquad \text{if } \frac{d\rho}{dW} \leqslant 0, \text{ and } \chi > 0 .$$

dV/dK is undefined, otherwise.

Proof. Proceeding as in (B) we obtain

$$sgn\,\frac{dV}{dK} = -\,sgn\left(C\frac{\partial^2 E(U)}{\partial C \partial L} + L\frac{\partial^2 E(U)}{\partial L^2} + C\frac{\partial^2 E(U)}{\partial M \partial L}\frac{dM}{dC}\right)\frac{dc}{dK}\,. \tag{A15}$$

Substituting the derivatives of (3) w.r.t. C,L, and M into the left-hand side of (A15), and using (A11), (A13), and (A14) as in (C) yields

$$\int_{R^*}^{\infty} U''(W)(CR + Lr)\left(r + L\frac{\partial r}{\partial L} - R\right) dF(R)$$

$$+ C\frac{dM}{dC} s \int_{R^*}^{\infty} U''(W)\left(r + L\frac{\partial r}{\partial L} - R\right)dF(R) .$$

Finally, multiplying the second term of this expression by M/M, adding and subtracting

$$Ms \int_{R^*}^{\infty} U''(W)\left(r + L\frac{\partial r}{\partial L} - R\right)dF(R),$$

and taking into account the definitions of W, ρ, ψ, and χ yields

$$\int_{R^*}^{\infty} \rho(W)U'(W) \left[R - \left(r + L\frac{\partial r}{\partial L}\right)\right] dF(R)$$

$$+ (\chi - 1)Ms \int_{R^*}^{\infty} \rho (W)U'(W) \left[R - \left(r + L\frac{\partial r}{\partial L}\right)\right] dF(R) . \qquad \text{(A16)}$$

Applying lemma 1 to each term of (A16) gives proposition 3′.

LITERATURE CITED

1. Apostol, Tom. *Mathematical Analysis*. Reading, Mass.: Addison-Wesley, 1957.
2. Arrow, Kenneth J. *Essays in the Theory of Risk Bearing*. Chicago: Markham, 1971.
3. Arzac, Enrique R., Robert A. Schwartz, and David K. Whitcomb. "A Theory and Test of Credit Rationing: Some Further Results." Working Paper, 1979.
4. Baltensperger, Ernst. "The Borrower-Lender Relationship, Competitive Equilibrium, and the Theory of Hedonic Prices." *American Economic Review*, 66 (June 1976), 401–405.
5. Barro, Robert J. "The Loan Market, Collateral, and Rates of Interest." *Journal of Money, Credit, and Banking*, 8 (1976), 439–56.
6. Boness, A. James. "A Pedagogic Note on the Cost of Capital." *Journal of Finance*, 19 (March 1964), 99–106.
7. Fisher, Lawrence. "Determinants of Risk Premiums on Corporate Bonds." *Journal of Political Economy*, 67 (June 1959), 217–37.
8. Hadar, Josef, and William R. Russell. "Rules for Ordering Uncertain Prospects." *American Economic Review*, 59 (March 1969), 25–34.
9. Jaffee, Dwight M., and Franco Modigliani. "A Theory and Test of Credit Rationing." *American Economic Review*, 59 (December 1969), 850–72.
10. Jaffee, Dwight M., and Thomas Russell. "Imperfect Information, Uncertainty, and Credit Rationing." *Quarterly Journal of Economics*, 90 (1976), 651–66.
11. Leland, Hayne L., and David H. Pyle. "Informational Asymmetries, Financial Structure and Financial Intermediation." *Journal of Finance*, 32 (May 1977), 371–87.
12. Mossin, Jan. *Theory of Financial Markets*. Englewood Cliffs, N.J.: Prentice-Hall, 1973.

13. Pratt, John W. "Risk Aversion in the Small and in the Large." *Econometrica,* 32 (1964), 122–36.

14. Rothschild, Michael, and Joseph E. Stiglitz. "Increasing Risk: I. A Definition." *Journal of Economic Theory,* 2 (September 1970), 225–43.

15. Smith, Vernon L. "A Theory and Test of Credit Rationing, Some Generalizations." *American Economic Review,* 62 (June 1972), 477–83.

16. Stapleton, Richard C. "A Note on Default Risk, Leverage, and the MM Theorem." *Journal of Financial Economics,* 2 (1975), 377–81.

17. Tobin, James. "Liquidity Preference as Behavior Towards Risk." *Review of Economic Studies,* 25 (February 1958), 65–86.

NOTES, COMMENTS, REPLIES

A Tribute to Clark Warburton, 1896–1979

*A Note by Thomas F. Cargill**

Clark Warburton died on September 18, 1979, at the age of 83 after a long and productive career. His productive effort reached a peak in the late 1940s and early 1950s and was at variance with the views of an overwhelming majority of the profession. His numerous papers and presentations were essentially ignored for years. Yet, when we look back at his efforts today, it is clear that he anticipated much of the current discussion of money and monetary policy by a generation. He may not have coined the word monetarism, but he was the first monetarist of the post-World War II period.

Clark Warburton received his baccalaureate and master's degrees from Cornell in 1921 and 1928, and his Ph.D. from Columbia in 1932. His dissertation "The Economic Results of Prohibition" showed the inductive and logical empiricism that was to characterize his later work. He had a short teaching career with several positions in the United States and India, but his comparative advantage was in research. He was associated with the Brookings Institution from 1932 to 1934 where he worked on the national income accounts. In 1934, he joined the new Federal Deposit Insurance Corporation (FDIC) as a research economist and continued there until 1966 when he retired as chief of the Banking and Business Section of the Division of Research and Statistics. It was during the first years at the FDIC that he began to formulate a monetary interpretation of the Great Depression and the concept of monetary disequilibrium.

These are the basic facts of Clark Warburton's career, but to understand his work, we must consider it in relationship to the major monetary issues of the last two decades which have witnessed the reemergence of the Quantity Theory in the Keynesian-monetarist debate. There is no longer any disagreement about the importance of monetary factors, and the debate has now shifted to broader questions of

*This paper was written while the author was a visiting scholar, Banking Research and Economic Analysis, Comptroller of the Currency. The author expresses appreciation to Leland Bach, Gillian Garcia, Homer Jones, and Paul Trescott for comments though they should not be held responsible for any of the views.

THOMAS F. CARGILL *is professor of economics, University of Nevada, Reno.*

0022-2879/81/0281-0089$00.50/0

philosophy about the right and responsibility of government in a market oriented system.[1]

Though much of Clark Warburton's work has been vindicated, it was paid little attention when first presented despite the fact that the majority of papers appeared in well-known journals. The editors of the American Economic Association's *Readings in Monetary Theory,* published in 1951 [12], chose to include one of his more important papers. By the early 1960s, a few individuals began to emphasize the significance of his accomplishments. Richard Selden [7] drew attention to his contributions on the lag in the effect of monetary policy and the monetary growth rule. Milton Friedman and Anna J. Schwartz acknowledged his role as a precursor for many of their ideas in the preface to their *A Monetary History:*

> We owe an especially heavy debt to Clark Warburton. His detailed and valuable comments on several drafts have importantly affected the final version. In addition, time and again, as we come to some conclusion that seemed to us novel and original we found that he had been there before. [4, p. xxii]

Recently, Michael Bordo and Anna J. Schwartz [1], Thomas F. Cargill [2], Thomas M. Humphrey [5], Richard Selden [8], George S. Tavlas [9], and Paul Trescott [10] have recounted his remarkable accomplishments.

I met Clark Warburton in 1966, during my graduate education at the University of California at Davis. He had just retired from the FDIC and was invited as a visiting professor to UCD where, through Professor Thomas Mayer's efforts, Warburton's name was well recognized.

He did not have a dynamic personality and was not comfortable in a classroom environment. Poor health prevented him from assuming a full teaching load. He instead offered a small seminar that was attended by two other students and me. Once a week, for three hours, we would listen to Clark Warburton recount what it was like to be a monetarist during the Keynesian Revolution. It was a memorable experience.

Two events stand out. The first occurred during a discussion of the empirical findings of Friedman and Schwartz. To my suggestion that he must be pleased that the Friedman and Schwartz evidence was being seriously debated in the profession, he responded with utter frustration because he had argued many of the same points during the 1940s and early 1950s and had been ignored.

The second occurred several weeks later during a faculty seminar in which Clark presented an updated version of his empirical work. Summarizing many of his arguments made fifteen years earlier, he stood at the podium and with a determined expression described himself as "having stood alone against the profession."

[1]Franco Modigliani recently emphasized the philosophical differences between the Keynesian (which he referred to as nonmonetarist) and the monetarist views in his 1976 Presidential Address to the American Economic Association. "In reality the distinguishing feature of the monetarist school and the real issues of disagreement with nonmonetarists is not monetarism, but rather the role that should probably be assigned to stabilization policies. Nonmonetarist accept . . . the fundamental practical message of *The General Theory:* that a private enterprise economy using an intangible money *needs* to be stabilized, *can* be stabilized, and therefore *should* be stabilized by appropriate monetary and fiscal policies" [6, p. 1].

Clark Warburton regarded himself as "standing alone" primarily because he had challenged the profession repeatedly to substantiate their antimonetary interpretation of economic activity with empirical evidence, and, yet, his published research received little recognition.[2] This does not mean that he was alone in criticizing the Keynesian view or presenting the monetarist view. Carl Snyder, Lionel Edie, Lauchlin Currie, James Angell, Arthur Marget, and others have been classified as forerunners of monetarism. Clark Warburton was aware of their contributions and regarded his own work as simply a continuation of the classical tradition of eighteenth and nineteenth century views modified to place greater emphasis on empirical verification. At the same time, he clearly stands out among the early forerunners in a number of areas [2, pp. 428–31]. He is the only forerunner to extensively publish during the height of the Keynesian Revolution and discuss most of the essential elements of the current monetarist view.

During the period from 1943 through 1953, Clark Warburton published over thirty papers, many in leading journals, and made numerous presentations. His productivity was remarkable as he worked at the FDIC when research was not emphasized. He had no graduate students and little access to the interactions of an academic institution. There is no question about the quantity of his productive effort, and the quality is attested to by the degree by which he predated most of the important issues and empirical findings of modern monetarism.

His work is reflected in present day monetarism in several important respects. (1) Clark Warburton emphasized the importance of empirical verification of competing theories. This methodology characterizes the work of Friedman and Schwartz, Friedman and David Meiselman, and many others. (2) He developed extensive empirical evidence to support the hypothesis that changes in the money supply were both necessary and sufficient to produce major changes in economic activity. As part of this evidence, he showed that the lag in effect of monetary policy was both long and variable; however, he did not extend the long and variable lag to an indictment against discretionary policy. (3) He questioned the common argument that deficit spending would increase the level of economic activity and emphasized the need to consider the monetary effect of a given fiscal action, predating the later discussion over "crowding out." (4) He believed that market forces would ensure a long run, full employment equilibrium and that the appropriate monetary policy was to provide a steady growth of the money supply defined as M2; however, he argued for a more flexible version of the growth rule than Friedman did. (5) He was very critical of the Fed's lack of understanding of the economy and how monetary policy influenced economic activity. He argued that Keynesians had misinterpreted the role of the Fed in the Great Depression. Rather than pursuing an expansionary policy by allowing interest rates to remain low, the Fed had pursued a tight monetary policy throughout much of the 1930s, and the depression was evidence of the importance of stable monetary growth rather than an example that money did not matter. (6) He emphasized the direct links between money and economic activity

[2]Warburton made one of his most direct attacks on the profession in 1948 [11]. A response by Rendigs Fels [3] represents one of the few attempts to deal with his work.

rather than the Keynesian indirect mechanism. Emphasis on the indirect mechanism and the use of interest rates as guides to monetary policy led to erroneous conclusions about monetary policy and unstable changes in the money supply. These are only the main elements of Clark Warburton's work that foreshadowed discussions in the 1960s when an increasing number argued that changes in the money supply exerted an independent and important influence on economic activity. In addition, he anticipated the profession on a number of other ideas.

His 1943–44 papers on wartime inflation clearly show an awareness of the relationship between money and inflation, which he reemphasized in 1966 in the collected papers volume [13, pp. 11–12]. These papers also show that he anticipated the Friedman and Meiselman work on the relative importance of monetary and Keynesian variables in the consumption function [10]. He suggested that profit maximizing behavior of banks made them focus on their reserve position rather than passively respond to the demand for loans. And he continually emphasized the disequilibrium adjustment to changes in the money supply and though he did not spell out the transmission process in any detail, modern discussion has also been subject to the "black box" criticism.

Apparently, in 1953 he received pressure from the Treasury to cease publishing and making presentations, marking a sudden stop to his productivity. Despite the feelings of frustration, Clark continued working for the next two decades. He again began publishing papers in 1958, providing testimony to Congress,[3] and attending conferences. He had just finished a paper entitled "Monetary Disequilibrium Theory in the First Half of the Twentieth Century" several months before his death. To my knowledge it was his last paper.[4]

Why was he ignored? This is a difficult question that I have discussed elsewhere [2, pp. 442–47]. There are several points worth emphasizing. First, there are particular characteristics of his work that may have prevented professional recognition. The equation of exchange framework turned off readers schooled in the interactive market general equilibrium framework of the Keynesian model, which so dominated the profession that arguments couched in the framework of the equation of exchange were considered silly. Second, the profession failed to grasp the need for detailed empirical verification and comparison between the Quantity Theory and the Keynesian model when the Great Depression and the performance of the Fed had convinced most everyone that "money does not matter" and monetary policy is like "pushing on a string." Third, his writing and method of argument often turned his typewriter into a flamethrower. He was a hypersensitive person who would heatedly argue about minor technical and definitional issues. Fourth, he was not part of an academic institutional framework with graduate students that would further develop and market his ideas. His was a one-man show. Last and most important, the times were simply not conducive to an examination of the role of money within the framework of the Quantity Theory. He was out of step with the times. It was not

[3]Warburton's contribution to the congressional supervision of monetary policy has been noted by Robert W. Weintraub [14, p. 342].

[4]This paper will be published in the near future by the *History of Political Economy*.

until the early 1960s that the monetarist view was seriously debated. By then, Clark Warburton's major research efforts were a decade old and did not reflect the quantitative and econometric standards of the more recent efforts. He was again out of step with the profession.

Monetarism has reemerged and now forms a significant focal point of professional debate. A lot that looks new today appears in the pages of Clark Warburton, who kept alive, if he did not create, many of its most fundamental concepts.

LITERATURE CITED

1. Bordo, Michael, and Anna J. Schwartz. "Clark Warburton: Pioneer Monetarist." *Journal of Monetary Economics,* 5 (January 1979), 43-65.

2. Cargill, Thomas F. "Clark Warburton and the Development of Monetarism Since the Great Depression." *History of Political Economy,* 11 (Fall 1979), 425-49.

3. Fels, Rendigs. "Warburton vs. Hansen and Keynes." *American Economic Review,* 39 (September 1949), 923-29.

4. Friedman, Milton, and Anna Jacobson Schwartz. *A Monetary History of the United States: 1867-1960.* Princeton, N.J.: Princeton University Press, 1963.

5. Humphrey, Thomas M. "Role of Non-Chicago Economists in the Evolution of the Quantity Theory in America 1930-1950." *Southern Economic Journal,* 38 (July 1971), 12-18.

6. Modigliani, Franco. "The Monetarist Controversy or Should We Forsake Stabilization Policies?" *American Economic Review,* 67 (March 1977), 1-19.

7. Selden, Richard. "Stable Money Growth." In *In Search of a Monetary Constitution,* edited by Leland Yeager, pp. 253-74. Cambridge, Mass.: Harvard University Press, 1962.

8. ______. "Monetarism." In *Modern Economic Thought,* edited by Sidney Weintraub, pp. 253-74. Philadelphia: University of Pennsylvania Press, 1977.

9. Tavlas, George S. "Some Further Observations on the Monetary Economics of Chicagoans and Non-Chicagoans." *Southern Economic Journal,* 42 (April 1976), 685-92.

10. Trescott, Paul B. "Discovery of the Money Income Relationship In the United States: 1921-1944." *History of Political Economy,* in press.

11. Warburton, Clark. "Hansen and Fellner on Full Employment Policies." *American Economic Review,* 38 (March 1948), 128-34.

12. ______. "The Misplaced Emphasis in Contemporary Business Fluctuation Theory." In *Readings in Monetary Theory,* pp. 284-318. Philadelphia: Blakiston, 1951.

13. ______. *Depression, Inflation, and Monetary Policy: Selected Papers, 1945-1953.* Baltimore: Johns Hopkins Press, 1966.

14. Weintraub, Robert E. "Congressional Supervision of Monetary Policy." *Journal of Monetary Economics,* 4 (April 1978), 341-62.

Sluggish Price Adjustments and the Effectiveness of Monetary Policy Under Rational Expectations

*A Comment by Roman Frydman**

1. Introduction

The question of the effectiveness of monetary policy has become one of the most controversial issues in macroeconomics in recent years. Sargent and Wallace [16] demonstrated that, in a model in which prices are assumed to adjust to clear markets each period,[1] output behaves according to the Lucas [9] supply function and expectations are formed according to the rational expectations hypothesis, any systematic monetary policy will be ineffective. (This proposition will be referred to, in this paper, as the Lucas-Sargent Proposition, the LSP.) Fischer [6] showed, however, that if wages are assumed to adjust sluggishly systematic monetary policy can be effective. The same conclusion was also reached by Phelps and Taylor [15], who assumed that the prices set by the firms are based on the expected price level and are sticky. The assumption of perfect price flexibility appeared to be crucial for the validity of the LSP. Since the empirical relevance of perfect price flexibility has long been seriously questioned,[2] the practical importance of LSP seemed to be undermined. Thus, Modigliani [13] in his presidential address to the American Economic Association explicitly rejected the importance of the LSP and argued for an active stabilization policy.

McCallum [10] has introduced price level stickiness into a model similar to the one used by Sargent and Wallace. He concluded that ''recognition of price level stickiness does not, in and of itself, negate the Lucas-Sargent Proposition.'' In a recent paper in this journal, McCallum [11] has ''attempted to establish the basic compatibility of sluggish price adjustments and the LSP.'' In another paper he modified and extended this analysis to include the effects of oligopolistic pricing behavior on the validity of the LSP [12]. He again concluded that the failure of the LSP ''does not result because of markup pricing and sluggish adjustments.'' These

*I am grateful to Edmund Phelps for his invaluable help in the preparation of this paper. I would like to thank Professors Blinder and Taylor for most helpful comments. I am also indebted to Professor Blinder for suggesting a clear exposition of the argument in section 2. All remaining errors are mine. Professor McCallum's kind response to this paper is appreciated.

[1]This price adjustment behavior will be called the perfect price flexibility.

[2]For some recent examples, see Nordhaus [14], Gordon [8], and Modigliani [13].

ROMAN FRYDMAN *is assistant professor of economics, New York University.*

0022-2879/81/0281-0094$00.50/0
JOURNAL OF MONEY, CREDIT, AND BANKING, vol. 13, no. 1 (February 1981)

results, if correct, would restore the practical significance of the LSP by eliminating the importance of the perfectly flexible price adjustments for the validity of the LSP.

It is clear that McCallum's surprising conclusions have to be reconciled with the earlier contrary conclusions of Fischer and Phelps and Taylor.

In this paper I show that McCallum's conclusions concerning the compatibility of the LSP with sluggish price adjustments are incorrect because either his arguments in [10] and [11] implicitly employ an unacceptable assumption regarding the producers' supply behavior, or his method of analysis in [12] is applicable only to models characterized by perfectly flexible prices.

The order of our presentation is as follows: In section 2 a simplified version of McCallum's model is formulated and his conclusions in [11] and [10] are criticized; in section 3 McCallum's [12] analysis is discussed; finally, section 4 contains concluding remarks.

2. *Sluggish Price Adjustments and the LSP*

In this section I formulate a simplified version of a model used by McCallum [11]. This model focuses on the essential elements required for my criticism of his conclusions.

The model is as follows:

$$x_t = \alpha_1 + \alpha_2(p_t - E_{t-1}p_t) + u_t \tag{1}$$

$$d_t = \beta(m_t - p_t) + v_t \tag{2}$$

$$p_t - p_{t-1} = \lambda(p_t^* - p_{t-1}), \qquad 0 < \lambda < 1, \tag{3}$$

where x_t = real output; p_t = logarithm of the actual price level prevailing in period t; d_t = real aggregate demand; m_t = logarithm of the money stock; p_t^* = logarithm of the market clearing price in period t; E_{t-1} = mathematical conditional expectation operator, given information up to the beginning of period t; u_t, v_t = serially uncorrelated disturbance terms with mean zero; and α_1, α_2, β = positive constants.

Equation (1) is the output determination equation (see [9]). Equation (2) represents the demand side of the model. Equation (3) incorporates sluggish price adjustments.

I will now analyze[3] the validity of the LSP in the model (1)–(3). Since we define p_t^* as that p_t which equates $x_t(p_t)$ in (1) to $d_t(p_t)$ in (2), we can solve (1) and (2) for p_t^*. Using the result for p_t^* in (3) gives

$$p_t = (1 - \lambda)p_{t-1} - \delta_1\alpha_1 + \delta_1\beta m_t + \delta_1\alpha_2 E_{t-1}p_t + \delta_1(v_t - u_t), \tag{4}$$

where $\delta_1 = \lambda/(\alpha_2 + \beta)$. Assuming $E_{t-1}m_t = m_t$ and using (4) to solve for $E_{t-1}p_t$, we obtain

[3]McCallum uses the method of solution suggested by Lucas in [9]. My model allows a simple and straightforward solution.

$$p_t = \delta_2 p_{t-1} - \delta_3\alpha_1 + \delta_3\beta m_t + \delta_1(v_t - u_t), \tag{5}$$

where $\delta_2 = (1 - \lambda)/(1 - \delta_1\alpha_2)$, $\delta_3 = \delta_1/(1 - \delta_1\alpha_2)$. Using (5) in (1) and (2) yields

$$x_t = \alpha_1 + \alpha_2\delta_1(v_t - u_t) + u_t \tag{6}$$

$$d_t = \beta(\delta_2 m_t - \delta_2 p_{t-1} + \delta_3\alpha_1) + v_t - \beta\delta_1(v_t - u_t). \tag{7}$$

McCallum concluded that (6) "illustrates vividly" the LSP.[4]

In the remainder of this section I will analyze the validity of this conclusion. McCallum considers a model in which the price level does not move instantly to equate aggregate demand and supply each period. The two most common possibilities in such a situation are as follows: (a) sales are at the minimum of supply and demand; or (b) demand is always met and inventories fill the (positive or negative) gap between supply and demand. For simplicity, I will assume that producers maintain a sufficient stock of inventory and demand is always met (case(b)).[5]

As noted above, in McCallum's model, the price level p_t adjusts sluggishly to the market clearing price p_t^*. This means that producers will generally experience a discrepancy between aggregate demand and supply. This discrepancy will manifest itself in an inventory accumulation or decumulation. It is obvious that these inventory changes are a *necessary* outcome of sluggish price adjustments. The output determination equation (1) implicitly assumes that producers do not respond to the inventory changes. Consequently, the Lucas supply function does not seem to be a reasonable output determination equation when prices are assumed to adjust sluggishly. A more natural and plausible assumption is to suppose that when prices do not move to market clearing levels each period, producers will also adjust output.

The simplest way to introduce this effect is to modify equation (1) in the following way:

$$x_t = \alpha_1 + \alpha_2(p_t - E_{t-1}p_t) - \alpha_3(N_{t-1} - N^*) + u_t. \tag{8}$$

In (8) output supplied is negatively related to the difference between the stock of inventory at the end of the previous period N_{t-1} and the optimal stock of inventory N^*.[6,7] For simplicity we assume N^* to be a constant in the short run.[8]

[4]McCallum's equation (15), p. 425, is basically the same as equation (6).

[5]It should be emphasized that as long as producers adjust output in response to the discrepancy between aggregate demand and supply, my criticism of McCallum's conclusions would be valid.

[6]After I had written this paper, the paper by Blinder and Fischer [3] was brought to my attention. They modify the Lucas supply function in the same way and provide microfoundations. Their model, however, assumes perfectly flexible prices.

[7]For a related discussion of the supply behavior in a different context, see Blinder [1].

[8]N^* is optimal in the sense that it can be derived from the firms' profit maximization (see Blinder [2]). N^* would depend on a number of variables, but the empirical results of Feldstein and Auerbach [5] suggest that N^* changes very slowly. Analytically N^* could be subsumed in α_1 without changing any of the conclusions.

To close a model I assume that quantity sold each period is equal to demand and inventories adjust passively according to

$$N_t = N_{t-1} + x_t - d_t. \tag{9}$$

Following our derivation it is easy to see that the modified model implies the following equations in place of (6) and (7):

$$x_t = \alpha_1 - \alpha_3(N_{t-1} - N^*) + \alpha_2\delta_1(v_t - u_t) + u_t \tag{10}$$

$$d_t = \beta[\delta_2 m_t - \delta_2 p_{t-1} + \delta_3\alpha_1 - \delta_3\alpha_3(N_{t-1} - N^*)] + v_t - \beta\delta_1(v_t - u_t). \tag{11}$$

We observe that the evolution of aggregate demand d_t depends on the parameters of the monetary rule. Since the price level is assumed to adjust sluggishly to the market clearing price, aggregate demand differs from aggregate supply in the short run. This implies that the time path of the stock of inventory depends on the parameters of the monetary rule. Finally, equation (10) implies that the evolution of output depends on the monetary rule. The LSP is *not valid* in this model.

We conclude that once a more reasonable output determination equation is adopted, McCallum's conclusion concerning "the basic compatibility of sluggish price adjustments and the LSP" would not be valid.

Finally, I will briefly discuss McCallum's [10] criticism of the Phelps and Taylor [15] results. Phelps and Taylor introduced an effect of inventory changes into an output equation in a model with sticky prices. McCallum [10] introduces an inessential modification of price level stickiness. He also recognizes that carrying of the inventory stock involves costs and introduces an inventory demand function. Surprisingly, he does not recognize that whenever producers are faced with unexpected inventory accumulation (or decumulation) they will usually make some output adjustment in order to bring their inventory stock to the desired level. Consequently, he does not introduce any effect of inventories on output and he again claims that "the Lucas-Sargent result would hold."

According to the previous discussion in this section, McCallum's criticism of Phelps and Taylor's results does not appear to be valid.[9]

3. *Oligopolistic Pricing and the LSP*

Modigliani [13], in his presidential address to the American Economic Association, seriously questioned the relevance of the model used by the rational expectations theorists "as a useful formalization of present day Western economies." One

[9]The validity of McCallum's arguments does not seem to have been generally questioned. For example, Blinder and Fischer [3] state that McCallum has demonstrated in [10] that "some types of nonmarket clearing still do not permit any role for monetary policy in affecting output." The only exception that I am aware of appears to be an independent argument presented by Gordon in [8]. Gordon was the first to argue that the Lucas supply function is incompatible with sluggish price adjustments and he criticized McCallum's arguments in [10].

of his most serious objections was to the "modeling of the commodity market as a perfectly competitive one." He suggested that the empirical evidence can "instead, be accounted for by the oligopolistic pricing model."

McCallum [11] discussed briefly the question of compatibility of the LSP with the oligopolistic pricing behavior. This discussion is extended and modified in McCallum [12], where Modigliani's objection to the LSP is analyzed by means of a model in which prices are purported to be set in accordance with the "basic principles of the oligopolistic pricing theory described by Modigliani: prices adjusting with lags to levels specified by markups (reflecting entry preventing consideration) on long run minimum average cost values, with the markups changing in response to current market conditions." McCallum developed his version of the FR-MIT-PENN (MPS) model and concluded that "failure of the LSP in the MPS model does not result because of markup pricing or sluggish adjustments. . . . Instead, the failure results from the joint appearance or 'mixing' of real and nominal variables in the pricing equation." McCallum added that "this conclusion is not specific to the MPS model" and cited in this connection the models of Eckstein and Brinner [4], Tobin [18], and Gordon [7]. Thus, McCallum ascribed a high degree of generality to his conclusions.

In order to discuss McCallum's analysis I will reformulate a model used in the previous section. This model focuses on the essential elements required for my criticism of his analysis.

My version of the model is as follows:

$$p_t^* = w_t + \alpha_1 + \alpha_2 x_t + u_t \tag{12}$$

$$w_t = E_{t-1} p_t + \gamma \tag{13}$$

$$d_t = \beta(m_t - p_t) + v_t , \tag{14}$$

where in addition to the variables defined in section 1, we define p_t^* = logarithm of the "desired" price (which is not necessarily equal to the market clearing price) associated with the desired markup in period t, and w_t = logarithm of the money wage in period t.

Following McCallum I introduce pricing with or without sluggishness by appending[10] to (12)-(14) either the adjustment equation

$$p_t - p_{t-1} = \lambda_1(p_t^* - p_{t-1}) , \tag{15}$$

or the alternative equation

$$(p_t - w_t) - (p_{t-1} - w_{t-1}) = \lambda_2[(p_t^* - w_t) - (p_{t-1} - w_{t-1})]. \tag{16}$$

[10]For a detailed discussion of these equations, see McCallum [12].

It should be noted that the price level is assumed to adjust here to the "desired" price p_t^*. According to McCallum, this aspect of the model is supposed to represent oligopolistic pricing behavior.

McCallum considers the following cases depending on whether (15) or (16) is appended to (12)-(14): (1) $\lambda_1 = 1$; (2) $0 < \lambda_1 < 1$; (3) $0 < \lambda_2 \leq 1$. The logic of McCallum's argument appears to be as follows:

I. He demonstrates that *the LSP does not hold* in case (2). The reason for this result is that (2) does not imply the Lucas supply function[11] as the output equation.

II. He argues that *the LSP is valid* in case (1). He shows that (1) leads to the Lucas supply function. Then, he invokes the Sargent and Wallace result and claims that the LSP holds.

III. Finally, he again argues that case (3) implies the Lucas supply function and *the LSP is valid*.

Having "demonstrated" I, II, and III, McCallum notes that the price adjustment equations corresponding to cases (1), (2), and (3) "are not obviously inconsistent with basic principles of the oligopolistic pricing theory as described by Modigliani." Since McCallum considers all of the cases of pricing behavior ((1), (2), and (3)) to be compatible with oligopolistic pricing, but finds the LSP to be valid in some cases ((1) and (3)) but not in others (2), he concludes that nonneutrality of the monetary policy "does not result because of markup pricing or sluggish adjustments."

In the remainder of this section I show that whenever McCallum [12] finds the LSP to be valid, he implicitly treats prices prevailing in a given period as market clearing prices. Since McCallum's model and my simple version of the model lead to the Lucas supply function in such cases, McCallum's result is entirely expected. It *is not* a demonstration that the LSP holds in a model with oligopolistic prices. McCallum's result is simply *the same* as the conclusion obtained by Sargent and Wallace [16] in a model with perfectly flexible prices.

I will now demonstrate that McCallum's analysis of the model (12)-(14) and (16) is applicable only when *prices are assumed to be perfectly flexible.* I will just consider the case of $\lambda_2 < 1$, which ostensibly represents sluggish adjustments of the actual markups to their desired values. My argument can easily be seen to follow when $\lambda_2 = 1$ or equivalently $\lambda_1 = 1$. This will cover cases (1) and (3) above. McCallum claimed that the LSP is valid in those cases.

Combining (12) and (16) and solving for $p_t - w_t$ gives

$$p_t - w_t = \lambda_2\alpha_1 + \lambda_2\alpha_2 \sum_{i=0}^{\infty} (1-\lambda_2)^i x_{t-i} + \lambda_2 \sum_{i=0}^{\infty} (1-\lambda_2)^i u_{t-i}. \qquad (17)$$

[11]It can be easily shown, but it will not be done here, that the "mixing" in the Lucas supply function invalidates the LSP even in the models with perfectly flexible prices. This point is logically distinct from the question of the effects of sluggish prices on the validity of the LSP. The issue of sensitivity of the LSP with respect to the form of the supply function has been discussed by Shiller [17].

Plugging (13) into (17) and rearranging, we obtain

$$x_t = \delta_1(p_t - E_{t-1}p_t) - \delta_2 - \sum_{i=0}^{\infty}(1-\lambda_2)^i x_{t-i} - \delta_3 \sum_{i=1}^{\infty}(1-\lambda_2)^i u_{t-i}, \tag{18}$$

where $\delta_1 = 1/\lambda_2\alpha_2$; $\delta_2 = (\lambda_2\alpha_1 + \gamma)\delta_1$; $\delta_3 = 1/\alpha_2$.

At this point McCallum argues that (18) "is similar in form to the supply function used by Sargent and Wallace [16], so *it is evident* that the LSP will hold"[12] [12, p. 65, emphasis added]. According to McCallum this can formally be shown by solving the following equation:[13]

$$x_t(p_t) = d_t(p_t) \tag{19}$$

for p_t, and then deriving the expression for the expectational error. This procedure in my model gives

$$p_t - E_{t-1}p_t = \frac{1}{\beta + \delta_1}(\delta_3 u_t + v_t). \tag{20}$$

McCallum concluded that "the distribution of the expectational error is independent of the monetary policy rule": the LSP "is valid."

We observe that p_t, which is a solution of (19), is a market clearing price. The crucial point here is that once markup pricing and sluggish adjustments are assumed by McCallum to lead to market clearing prices each period, any analytical distinction between sluggish and perfectly flexible price adjustments disappears. Since a model leads to the version of the Lucas supply function it is not surprising that the LSP is found to be valid.

What is the role of the "markup price" p_t^* in this model? It is obvious that equation (16) is not *a behavioral equation* representing the adjustment of the actual markup $p_t - w_t$ to the "desired" markup $p_t^* - w_t$. Equation (16) is simply an arbitrary definition of the "desired" markup. The model *is solved*, by McCallum, for the market clearing price p_t. Equation (13) determines the corresponding w_t. Then $p_t^* - w_t$ is *defined* by equation (16) to be as follows:

$$p_t^* - w_t = \frac{1}{\lambda_2}[(p_t - w_t) - (p_{t-1} - w_{t-1})] + (p_{t-1} - w_{t-1}). \tag{21}$$

Clearly, $p_t^* - w_t$ does not play the intended role in McCallum's method of analysis. The price level prevailing, p_t, *is not* determined by markup considera-

[12]To avoid confusion, it should be noted that McCallum invokes the Sargent and Wallace result in connection with his analysis of case (1). In case (3), which we are considering here, he simply shows that his model yields the Lucas supply function. Then, he appeals to the formal analogy between cases (1) and (3). I have chosen to analyze case (3) because it represents sluggishly adjusting markup prices and, therefore, most strikingly illustrates my criticism. Obviously, my criticism applies to case (1) as well, where markup prices are also treated by McCallum as market clearing prices.

[13]McCallum's equations (10) and (16) correspond to my equations (14) and (18).

tions, but is simply the market clearing price level. The market clearing price level together with the Lucas supply function imply the validity of the LSP.

In summary, my argument demonstrates that unless we are willing to assume that markup pricing and sluggish adjustments always result in the market clearing prices, McCallum's analysis is inconsistent with oligopolistic pricing behavior and is irrelevant for whatever implications Modigliani's oligopolistic pricing theory may have for the effectiveness of monetary policy in macro-models.

4. Concluding Remarks

In this paper I discussed the question of the effectiveness of monetary policy in models with sluggish price adjustments. I presented an argument that monetary policy can be expected to affect output in such models. This conclusion contrasts sharply with the results recently obtained by McCallum, who argued thát sluggish price adjustments are basically compatible with the short run neutrality of money. Thus, the fundamental point about the LSP implied by Modigliani in his presidential address, that market clearing prices are crucial to the proposition, appears to be valid.

LITERATURE CITED

1. Blinder, Alan S. "A Difficulty with Keynesian Models of Aggregate Demand." In *Natural Resources, Uncertainty and General Equilibrium Systems,* edited by Alan S. Blinder and Phillip Friedman, pp. 125–36. New York: Academic Press, 1977.
2. ______. "Inventories and the Demand for Labor." Unpublished manuscript, March 1978.
3. Blinder, Alan S., and Stanley Fischer. "Inventories, Rational Expectations and the Business Cycle." MIT Working Paper, June 1978.
4. Eckstein, Otto, and Roger Brinner. "The Inflation Process in the United States." A study prepared for the Joint Economic Committee, 92nd Congress of the United States. Washington, D.C.: U.S. Government Printing Office, 1972.
5. Feldstein, Martin S., and Alan Auerbach. "Inventory Behavior in Durable Goods Manufacturing: The Target Adjustment Model." *Brookings Papers on Economic Activity,* 2 (1976), 351–96.
6. Fischer, Stanley. "Long-Term Contracts, Rational Expectations, and the Optimal Money Supply Rule." *Journal of Political Economy,* 85 (February 1977), 191–205.
7. Gordon, Robert J. "Can the Inflation of the 1970's Be Explained?" *Brookings Papers on Economic Activity,* 1 (1977), 253–77.
8. ______. "The Theory of Domestic Inflation." *American Economic Review,* 67 (February 1977), 128–34.
9. Lucas, Robert E., Jr. "Some International Evidence on Output-Inflation Tradeoffs." *American Economic Review,* 63 (June 1973), 326–34.
10. McCallum, Bennett T. "Price-Level Stickiness and the Feasibility of Monetary Stabilization Policy with Rational Expectations." *Journal of Political Economy,* 85 (June 1977), 627–34.
11. ______. "Price Level Adjustments and the Rational Expectations Approach to Mac-

roeconomic Stabilization Policy." *Journal of Money, Credit, and Banking,* 10 (November 1978), 418-36.

12. ______. "Monetarism, Rational Expectations, Oligopolistic Pricing, and the MPS Econometric Model." *Journal of Political Economy,* 87 (February 1979), 57-74.

13. Modigliani, Franco. "The Monetarist Controversy or Should We Forsake Stabilization Policies?" *American Economic Review,* 67 (March 1977), 1-19.

14. Nordhaus, William D. "Inflation Theory and Policy." *American Economic Review,* 66 (May 1976), 59-64.

15. Phelps, Edmund S., and John B. Taylor. "Stabilizing Properties of Monetary Policy under Rational Expectations." *Journal of Political Economy,* 84 (February 1977), 163-90.

16. Sargent, Thomas J., and Neil Wallace. " 'Rational Expectations,' the Optimal Monetary Instrument, and the Optimal Money Supply Rule." *Journal of Political Economy,* 83 (April 1975), 241-54.

17. Shiller, Robert J. "Rational Expectations and the Dynamic Structure of Macroeconomic Models: A Critical Review." *Journal of Monetary Economics,* 4 (1978), 1-44.

18. Tobin, James. "The Wage-Price Mechanism: Overview of the Conference." In *The Economics of Price Determination,* edited by Otto Eckstein. Washington, D.C.: Board of Governors of the Federal Reserve System, 1972.

Sluggish Price Adjustments and the Effectiveness of Monetary Policy Under Rational Expectations

*A Reply by Bennett T. McCallum**

Section 1 of Frydman's note [1] offers a worthwhile criticism of the models used in my papers [3] and [4], namely, that they assume inventory-output relationships that are somewhat implausible. But this criticism is insufficient to overturn my basic claim, which is that the Lucas-Sargent Proposition (LSP) is not automatically negated by the existence of price level stickiness. In fact, the validity of this claim has recently been demonstrated in a framework that is not open to Frydman's objections and in which prices are sticky in a stronger sense than in the models of [3] and [4]. More specifically, it is shown in [6] that the LSP holds in a model[1] in which prices are set in advance of the period in which they prevail, so that the price level fails entirely to respond to current conditions of excess supply or demand. Since these prices are preset by rational agents whose expectations for a period are based on observations of relevant variables up through the previous period, and since no additional information is available to the monetary authority,[2] the output effects of systematic policy actions can be precisely offset by the price setting behavior of the private agents. Furthermore, it is argued in [7] that the assumed behavior will be optimal for these agents—in particular, for worker-firm combinations—when prices must be preset, and it is shown that the model is consistent with several of the more prominent facts of business cycle experience. Consequently, [1] provides no reason to alter my previous conclusion that the "recognition of price level stickiness does not, in and of itself, negate the Lucas-Sargent Proposition" [3, p. 633].

Frydman's section 2 is concerned with my paper [5] on the relationship between oligopolistic pricing behavior—as represented in the MPS econometric model—and the LSP. Frydman contends that "unless we are willing to assume that markup pricing and sluggish adjustments always result in the market clearing prices, McCallum's analysis is inconsistent with oligopolistic pricing behavior and is irrelevant

*I am indebted to Alan Blinder and Bill Dewald for useful criticisms of an earlier draft and to the National Science Foundation (SES 79-15353) for financial support.

[1]The model is one in which inventories do not appear, but an extension could be carried out without affecting the validity of the LSP. Haraf [2] and Sheffrin [8] have also indicated that the LSP can hold in plausible models with inventories and preset prices.

[2]Which is assumed, as usual, to utilize a policy feedback rule.

BENNETT T. MCCALLUM *is visiting professor, Graduate School of Industrial Administration, Carnegie-Mellon University and professor, University of Virginia.*

0022-2879/81/0281-0103$00.50/0
JOURNAL OF MONEY, CREDIT, AND BANKING, vol. 13, no. 1 (February 1981)

for . . . Modigliani's pricing theory. . . ." [2, p. 11]. The basis for this claim is that the model under discussion—which is accurately characterized by equations (12), (13), (14), and (16) in his paper—is one in which output equals quantity demanded in each period.[3] But this feature, $x_t = d_t$ for all t, also holds in the model (12), (13), (14), and (15) in his paper, even in the case in which $\lambda_1 < 1$. Thus that model too, according to his argument, must be "inconsistent with oligopolistic pricing behavior," etc. But that set of equations is precisely the one that represents the simplified version of the MPS model developed in [5], and the MPS specification is itself an operational manifestation of Modigliani's oligopolistic pricing theory. Consequently, since Frydman does not question the accuracy of my representation, his discussion can have no bearing on my argument.[4] If there is any validity to Frydman's discussion, it is awkward for the MPS specification, not for my analysis.

Finally, consider Frydman's contention that my equation (16) "is simply an arbitrary definition of the 'desired' markup" in the model (12), (13), (14), and (16), so that "the price level prevailing, p_t, *is not* determined by markup considerations" [2, pp. 10–11]. What this suggests is that it is possible to solve the model for p_t without using equation (16), but that is simply incorrect. Equations (12), (14), and (16) must be solved simultaneously for p_t, p_t^*, and $x_t = d_t$.

LITERATURE CITED

1. Frydman, Roman. "Sluggish Price Adjustments and the Effectiveness of Monetary Policy under Rational Expectations: A Comment." *Journal of Money, Credit, and Banking,* 13 (February 1981), 94–102.
2. Haraf, William. "Tests of a Natural Rate Model with Persistent Effects of Aggregate Demand Shocks." Brown University (January 1980).
3. McCallum, Bennett T. "Price-Level Stickiness and the Feasibility of Monetary Stabilization Policy with Rational Expectations." *Journal of Political Economy,* 85 (June 1977), 627–34.
4. ———. "Price Level Adjustments and the Rational Expectations Approach to Macroeconomic Stabilization Policy." *Journal of Money, Credit, and Banking,* 10 (November 1978), 418–36.
5. ———. "Monetarism, Rational Expectations, Oligopolistic Pricing, and the MPS Econometric Model." *Journal of Political Economy,* 87 (February 1979), 57–73.
6. ———. "A Monetary Policy Ineffectiveness Result in a Model with a Predetermined Price Level." *Economics Letters,* 3 (1979), 1–4.
7. ———. "Rational Expectations and Macroeconomic Stabilization Policy: An Overview." *Journal of Money, Credit, and Banking,* 12 (November 1980, Part 2), 716–46.
8. Sheffrin, Steven M. "Unanticipated Money Growth and Output Fluctuations." *Economic Inquiry,* 17 (January 1979), 1–13.

[3]See [1, eq. (19)].

[4]One cannot logically claim that model A is unlike model B *because* A has a certain property, when B has the same property.

A Possible Error in the Expectations Theory

A Comment by Frans J. Ballendux and Marius J. L. Jonkhart

Looking at the market place we can observe a current spot rate of R_n for a n period discount bond and of R_{n-1} for a $n-1$ period discount bond. Implied in these two spot rates is a forward rate f_n for a loan during the nth period. According to the expectations theory, this forward rate is an unbiased estimate of the expected future one period spot rate r_n (which in itself is a random variable), that is, $f_n = E[r_n]$.

Recently Amihud [1] argued that although the foregoing is correct, if investors are risk neutral and if they seek to maximize their expected terminal wealth, it is not if they seek to maximize the expected present value or, equivalently, the expected rate of return of their holdings. Instead, he claims that in the latter two cases forward rates would be downward biased estimates of the expected future spot rates.

The basic proposition of this comment is that $E[r_n] \neq f_n$ is inconsistent with an equilibrium in a perfect capital market where discount bonds of different maturities are traded by risk neutral investors. Even if investors seek to maximize the expected present value or the expected rate of return of their holdings, the no arbitrage condition of capital market equilibrium requires that $E\ [r_n] = f_n$.

Amihud starts his argument by presenting the so-called Hicks equality [3, p. 145], which states that in equilibrium

$$(1+R_n)^n = (1+R_{n-1})^{n-1}\,(1+E[r_n]) = (1+R_{n-1})^{n-1}\,(1+f_n). \qquad (1)$$

It follows straightforwardly from equation (1) that $E[r_n]=f_n$. Amihud agrees with this result provided that investors maximize the expected terminal value of their investments. On the other hand, he argues that if investors maximize the expected present value of their holdings, then[1]

$$\begin{aligned}(1 + R_n)^{-n} &= E[\{(1 + R_{n-1})^{n-1}\,(1 + r_n)\}^{-1}] \\ &= \{(1 + R_{n-1})^{n-1}\,(1 + f_n)\}^{-1}. \qquad (2)\end{aligned}$$

[1]Amihud [1, eq. (2)]; note that there is a printing error in Amihud's equation (2): $(1+R_{n-1})^{-1}$ should be read as $(1+R_{n-1})^{n-1}$.

Frans J. Ballendux *and* Marius J. L. Jonkhart *are assistant professors, Department of Business Finance, Erasmus University, Rotterdam.*

0022-2879/81/0281-0105$00.50/0
Journal of Money, Credit, and Banking, vol. 13, no. 1 (February 1981)

Applying Jensen's inequality[2], it is claimed that now $E[r_n] > f_n$. However, this does not follow conclusively. Since Jensen's inequality is not strict, all we may conclude from (2) is that this equation does not necessarily imply that $E[r_n] = f_n$. Whether or not $E[r_n] = f_n$ depends on the particular content of r_n in (2).

From (1) it follows that

$$1+E[r_n] = (1+R_n)^n (1+R_{n-1})^{1-n} , \qquad (1')$$

and from (2) that

$$E[(1+r_n)^{-1}]^{-1} = (1+R_n)^n (1+R_{n-1})^{1-n}. \qquad (2')$$

Note that we started this comment by stating that we *observe* a R_n and a R_{n-1}. Hence R_n and R_{n-1} must be the same in both approaches, and therefore the right-hand sides of (1′) and (2′) are equal. So, given the fact that a proper comparison requires that both approaches are based on the same set of beliefs regarding the one period future spot rates, it follows that the left-hand side of (2′) cannot but equal $1+E[r_n]$. Hence, even if investors seek to maximize expected present values, the implied forward rate f_n must be an unbiased estimate of $E[r_n]$.

One is apt to forget that there is *economic reasoning* behind the mathematics. If $E[r_n] > f_n$, then

$$(1+R_n)^n = (1+R_{n-1})^{n-1}(1+f_n) < (1+R_{n-1})^{n-1}(1+E[r_n]). \qquad (3)$$

A "greedy" investor will now have an incentive to trade. In particular, he will issue (or: sell) n period bonds and buy $n-1$ period bonds, reinvest the proceeds after $n-1$ periods at the then prevailing one period spot rate, and make an expected profit of $(1+R_{n-1})^{n-1}(1+E[r_n]) - (1+R_n)^n$. This arbitrage possibility will only be eliminated if $E[r_n] = f_n$. Note that contrary to Amihud's claim, the investor's exact objective is not crucial; "greediness" is sufficient.

In summary, we feel that Amihud has not shown the expectations theory to be incorrect. Instead, his note highlights the basic economic reasoning behind this theory, which argues that if investors are risk neutral, there can only be a capital market equilibrium if $E[r_n] = f_n$.

LITERATURE CITED

1. Amihud, Yakov. "A Possible Error in the Expectations Theory." *Journal of Money, Credit, and Banking,* 11 (May 1979), 243–45.
2. Feller, William. *An Introduction to Probability Theory and Its Applications,* Vol. II. Second edition. New York: Wiley, 1971.
3. Hicks, John R. *Value and Capital: An Inquiry into Some Fundamental Principles of Economic Theory*. Oxford: Clarendon Press, 1939.

[2]According to Jensen's inequality $E[(1+r_n)^{-1}] \geqslant (1+E[r_n])^{-1}$. For an explanation, see for instance [2, pp. 153–54].

A Possible Error in the Expectations Theory

A Rejoinder by Yakov Amihud

In their comment, Ballendux and Jonkhart (B & J) [2] question my proposition that under some assumptions on investors' behavior, the forward interest rate is smaller than the expected future one period spot rate

$$f_n < E(r_n). \tag{1}$$

They base their doubt on a claim that Jensen's inequality in the case under consideration is not strict, thus (1) may be an equality. Then they develop an economic rationale to show that the proposed inequality may never hold.

The first argument of B & J and their footnote 2 hardly needs a rejoinder. It is well known that Jensen's inequality is *strict* when applied to a *strictly* convex function, such as $1/(1 + r)$, and when the underlying variable is nondeterministic as I assumed.[1]

The second argument of B & J doubts the economic rationale behind my result and suggests that the investors' "greed" will lead to an equality in (1).[2] To demonstrate my point, assume a "greedy" investor who buys from B & J's investor the n period bond and sells him the $n-1$ period bond. By the end of the $n-1$ period, having to redeem the shorter-term bond, he will sell his n period bond (or issue an additional one-period bond) for a price of $E(1+r_n)^{-1}$. Clearly, equilibrium will be attained when

$$(1+R_{n-1})^{-(n-1)} E(1+r_n)^{-1} = (1+R_n)^{-n}, \tag{2}$$

which leads to (1). Had (1) been an equality, as B & J suggest, then $(1+R_{n-1})^{-(n-1)}$ $E(1+r_n)^{-1} > (1+R_n)^{-n}$, which leads to expected profit opportunities by issuing $n-1$ period bonds and buying n period ones. As a result, the price of the former will fall and that of the latter will rise, until (2) is restored, leading to (1).

[1]Proof: Let $u(x)$ be a strictly convex function, $u''(x)>0$. Then, applying the Taylor theorem and taking expectations, we obtain $E(u(x)) = u(E(x)) + (1/2)u''(\xi)\, E(x-E(x))^2$ where $\xi = f(x)$. Then for $E(x-E(x))^2 > 0$, $E(u(x)) > u(E(x))$. The quotation of B & J from Fellers' book fails to recognize that he referred to a weakly convex function, $u''\geqslant 0$, while the function $(1+r)^{-1}$ is strictly convex.

[2]The example that they use, which deals with a maximizer of expected future value $(1-R_{n-1})^{n-1}$ $(1+E(r_n)) = (1+R_n)^n$, replicates my (1) in [1], and clearly leads to $E(r_n) = f_n$.

YAKOV AMIHUD *is on the Faculty of Management, Tel-Aviv University, and the Graduate School of Business Administration, New York University.*

0022-2879/81/0281-0107$00.50/0
JOURNAL OF MONEY, CREDIT, AND BANKING, vol. 13, no. 1 (February 1981)

Perhaps a numerical example will clarify the issue: Let $R_2=0.15$, $r_3=0.25$ or 0.05 with probability of 1/2($\bar{r}_3=0.15$), and (by B & J) $R_3=0.15$. The price of a \$1 discount bond for 2- and 3-periods is $P_2=\$0.75614$ and $P_3=\$0.65752$, and $E(1/(1+r_3)) = \$0.87619 > \$0.86957 = 1/1.15$. If the investor buys a bond for P_3, he can sell it by the end of period 2 and expect to obtain then \$0.87619. He could then issue a 2-period discount bond with a face value of \$0.87619 for a price of P_2, obtaining \$0.66252 ($=P_2 \times 0.87619$), buy a 3-period bond for a price of $P_3 = \$0.65752$, and end up with an expected profit of \$0.005 (=0.66252 − 0.65752). Only if the long rates change such that $(1+R_3)^3/(1+R_2)^2-1 \equiv f_3=[E(1+r_3)^{-1}]^{-1} -1 =0.141<0.15 =\bar{r}_3$, will this profit opportunity vanish.

LITERATURE CITED

1. Amihud, Yakov. "A Possible Error in the Expectations Theory." *Journal of Money, Credit, and Banking,* 11 (May 1979), 243–45.
2. Ballendux, Frans J., and Marius J. L. Jonkhart. "A Possible Error in the Expectations Hypothesis, A Comment." *Journal of Money, Credit, and Banking,* 13 (February 1981), 105–6.

The Bank Failures of 1930–31

A Comment by Robert F. Stauffer

Introduction

Peter Temin [4] has provided empirical evidence that the bank failures of the early years of the depression were induced by falling farm incomes. He therefore argues that bank failures and related monetary disturbances were not an independent cause of the depression, but rather a mechanism by which the money supply was equilibrated to a rapidly falling money demand. This analysis is an important building block in Temin's "spending hypothesis" which is offered as an alternative to the "monetary hypothesis" of Friedman and Schwartz.

The Friedman and Schwartz [2, pp. 308–12, 355] explanation of the 1930–31 bank failures emphasizes the role of bank panics and Federal Reserve passivity, along with a suggestion that poor loans and investments made in the 1920s could be a factor. Cagan [1, pp. 223–29, 265–68], after a general historical review of bank panics and business contractions, concludes the inexplicable nature of bank panics is of most importance while the contractions themselves have not been a major factor. The purpose of this comment is to present the results of additional empirical tests on bank failure causation in 1930–31.

Were the Failures of 1930–31 Unique?

In order to demonstrate that the bank failures of 1930–31 were entirely a result of the depression, it is first necessary to disassociate them from the failure trends of the 1920s, thereby eliminating the myriad banking problems of that decade as possible significant causes. Temin [4, pp. 88–90] accomplishes this by using state cross section regression analysis. More specifically, he regresses the state failure rate for the combined 1921–29 period against the single year failure rates for 1930 and 1931. There is no significant relationship on a state-by-state basis between the single years of the 1930s and the nine-year period of the 1920s. However, I performed additional tests that indicate significant relationships do exist on a state-by-

ROBERT F. STAUFFER *is assistant professor, Department of Economics and Business Administration, Roanoke College.*

0022-2879/81/0281-0109$00.50/0
JOURNAL OF MONEY, CREDIT, AND BANKING, vol. 13, no. 1 (February 1981)

state basis between single year bank failure rates for 1930–31 and single year rates for the 1920s.[1]

Perhaps there is a process at work here that contributes to the development of short run trends in bank failures. Problems such as bad management and customer distrust may take their toll for a few years, and then instilled caution on the part of management and survival of the stronger banks allow the failure rate to recede, only to be followed by increasing problems as new banks arrive on the scene and old lessons are forgotten. Whatever the explanation, it is clear that the bank failure trends of 1928 and 1929 did carry over into the early 1930s to some extent.

It is also worth noting that the bank failure trends of the late 1920s continued into the 1930s in respect to broad geographical groupings and the type of banks involved. Table 1 indicates that the incidence of bank failures was higher in the agricultural states for the entire period from 1927 to 1933. Moreover, from 1928 to 1930 the incidence of bank failures in agricultural regions was constant, considering the region's share of total banks (both the incidence of failures and the share of banks fell by 1 percent per year from 1928–30). In addition, Table 1 indicates that the trend of high failure rates among nonmember banks in the late 1920s continued into the early 1930s.

TABLE 1

THE INCIDENCE OF BANK FAILURES ACCORDING TO BROAD GEOGRAPHICAL GROUPINGS AND TYPE OF BANK, 1927–33.

Year	Agricultural Regions		Other Regions		+All States	
	Percent of Total Failures	Percent of Total Banks	Percent of Total Failures	Percent of Total Banks	Failed Nonmember Banks / Total Failed Banks	Total Nonmember Banks / Total Banks
1927	0.92	0.75	0.08	0.25	0.82	0.65
1928	0.96	0.75	0.04	0.25	0.85	0.65
1929	0.95	0.74	0.05	0.26	0.88	0.64
1930	0.94	0.73	0.06	0.27	0.86	0.64
1931	0.83	0.73	0.17	0.27	0.78	0.63
1932	0.83	0.73	0.17	0.27	0.77	0.62
1933	0.81	0.70	0.19	0.30	0.68	0.58

NOTES: Included in the agricultural grouping are the following regions as defined in the 1932 *Statistical Abstract of the United States:* East North Central, West North Central, South Atlantic, East South Central, and West South Central. These regions accounted for about 78 percent of the value of total crop production in 1929, while the other regions (New England, Middle Atlantic, Mountain, and Pacific) accounted for the remaining 22 percent.

The data for the columns under "All States" are from *Banking and Monetary Statistics*, pp. 283, 19, and 23. Private banks are included.

Bank Failures and Declining Farm Incomes

Temin's cross section regression analysis also indicates a consistent and highly significant relationship between bank failures by state and the level of cotton sales

[1]If the ratio of failed deposits to total deposits is used, the correlation coefficient between 1930 and 1929 failures is 0.38, and the coefficient for 1930 and 1928 is 0.41. When failures are measured by the ratio of the number of failures-to-total banks, the correlation coefficient between 1930 and 1929 is 0.42, and the coefficient for 1931 and 1929 is 0.31. With a sample size of 48, we can reject the hypothesis of no correlation at the 0.05 significance level if the coefficient is greater than 0.29. All data on bank failures are from *Banking and Monetary Statistics* (Board of Governors of the Federal Reserve System, 1943), pp. 284–85.

by state for 1930 and 1931.[2] The declines in cotton prices and sales were severe, but the question remains as to whether this demonstrates causation or merely association, since most of the thirty-two states with no recorded cotton income also experienced low bank failure rates in this period. A state-by-state investigation of changes in cotton income relative to bank failures in just the major cotton producing states may shed some light on this issue.

It is also possible that other rural related variables may have contributed to bank failure problems or actually induced failures. Examples of such variables could be characteristics of rural banking structure—namely, the prevalence of small banks and of nonmember banks. These types of banks would be more prone to poor management, depositer mistrust, and inadequate liquidity.

To investigate the importance of declining cotton sales relative to weaknesses in bank structure I selected the eleven states where changes in cotton income were the largest (greater than 2 percent of personal income).[3] I then selected the following variables:

1. Measures of bank failures—the ratio of failed deposits by state-to-total deposits (RD), and the ratio of the number of failed banks by state-to-total banks (RN).
2. Measures of farm income—the ratio of the change in total cotton sales-to-state personal income (CS/PI), and the ratio of the change in all crop sales-to-state personal income (AS/PI).
3. Measures of banking system weakness—the ratio of nonmember deposits-to-total deposits (NMD/D), and the ratio of deposits at country national banks-to-deposits at all national banks (CNB/ANB).[4]

Higher values for the bank structure variables are assumed to reflect greater weakness in a state's banking system. Nonmember banks were generally smaller and operated under lower banking standards, while country national banks were generally much smaller than reserve city banks (data were not available for country banks with state bank charters).

Due to the small sample size and multicollinearity among the variables, regression analysis was not feasible. I therefore ranked all variables from high to low values and calculated Spearman rank correlation coefficients by pairing each of the bank failure measures with each of the "explanatory" variables. These coefficients

[2]The other farm income variables used by Temin [4, pp. 88-89] were the levels of wheat sales and levels of all other farm sales. The wheat sales variable was consistently insignificant, while the other farm sales variable had a significant coefficient in a few regressions, depending on the year, the exact specification of the regression, and the way in which bank failure incidence was measured.

[3]The eleven states are Alabama, Arizona, Arkansas, Georgia, Louisiana, Mississippi, North Carolina, Oklahoma, South Carolina, Tennessee, and Texas.

[4]The data sources are: (1) bank failures—see footnote 1; (2) farm sales—from *Statistical Abstract of the United States* (Department of Commerce, 1932), pp. 627, 637-39, and personal income—from *Personal Income by States Since 1929* (Commerce Department, Schwartz and Graham, 1956); (3) nonmember deposits—from *Banking and Monetary Statistics,* pp. 25-33, and national bank deposit data—compiled from the *Annual Report of the Comptroller of the Currency* (data on state member banks not available).

are presented in Table 2. The results here strongly support the hypothesis that bank structure was a crucial determinant of bank failures in these states. All the bank structure coefficients are significant, while only one income coefficient is significant (AS/PI for 1931). Of equal importance is the fact that the ranked income variables perform very poorly for the crucial year of 1930 when the banking system first began to crumble.[5] This result lends support to Cagan's [1, p. 226] observation that business conditions generally have little impact on bank failures in the early stages of a downturn.

TABLE 2

THE RELATIONSHIP BETWEEN BANK FAILURES, GROSS FARM INCOME CHANGES, AND BANK STRUCTURE VARIABLES FOR ELEVEN COTTON PRODUCING STATES, 1930–31, AS MEASURED BY SPEARMAN RANK CORRELATION COEFFICIENTS

Bank Failure Variable	Explanatory Variables			
	CS 29–30 / PI 29	AS 29–30 / PI 29	NMD 29 / D 29	CNB 30 / ANB 30
RD_{30}	0.027	0.064	0.691*	0.650*
RN_{30}	0.109	−0.091	0.727*	0.782**
	CS 30–31 / PI 30	AS 30–31 / PI 30	†NMD 29 / D 29	CNB 31 / ANB 31
RD_{31}	0.345	0.409	0.591*	0.664*
RN_{31}	0.445	0.527*	0.700*	0.800**

*Significant at the 0.05 level of significance, using a one-tailed test—see *Nonparametric Statistics for the Behavioral Sciences*, by Sidney Siegel. New York: McGraw-Hill, 1956.

**Significant at the 0.01 level, using a one-tailed test.

†State data for 1930 and 1931 are not available.

Another piece of evidence on the relation between farm incomes and bank failures can be found in Table 1 of the previous section. Temin's hypothesis implies that the incidence of bank failure in 1930 and 1931 should have risen in agricultural areas. Yet Table 1 indicates that the failure incidence for agricultural regions was constant for 1928–1930 (when adjusted for the share of total banks), and it dropped swiftly in 1931.

These results indicate that bank failures were not just the result of inexorable declines in farm incomes. A major part of the explanation lies in the weaknesses in the banking systems of rural states. Such weaknesses are measured rather imprecisely here by the bank structure variables, but these variables still perform remarkably well.

There are other possible institutional causes of bank failures. They may be of even greater importance, but they are virtually impossible to quantify. The lack of deposit insurance, the role played by rumor and panic, and the failure of the Federal

[5]The ranked income variables do very poorly in 1930 mainly because farm income changes in North Carolina, Oklahoma, and Texas were not closely related to bank failure variables. North Carolina was ranked second with both bank failure variables, last in respect to both cotton and all crop sales declines, and third and fifth in respect to weakness in her bank structure. Oklahoma and Texas had the least serious bank failures, income declines that were ranked from third to fifth in severity, and bank structures that were ranked the strongest (from ninth to eleventh).

Reserve to take any meaningful actions are all factors that could greatly exacerbate the weaknesses of any banking system.

Conclusion

The major conclusions of this study are:

1. The origins of the bank failures of 1930 and 1931 cannot be found solely in the events of those same years. The problems and weaknesses of the banking system of the 1920's did continue into the early 1930's.
2. Declining farm incomes, at the very most, can attain the status of a necessary, but not a sufficient condition for inducing bank failures. Certainly, falling farm prices and incomes were part of the problem. But even in the case of cotton production where price and income declines were particularly severe, the explanatory power of falling incomes is limited.

The results here are compatible with the work of Friedman and Schwartz [2] and Phillip Cagan [1]. Little support is found for Temin's ''spending hypothesis'' [4]. However, perhaps as Gandolfi and Lothian [3, p. 690] suggest, the most fruitful approach to the depression's causes is to investigate the interrelationships between real and monetary factors, instead of using a dichotomous approach that attempts to justify either a monetary or spending hypothesis.

LITERATURE CITED

1. Cagan, Phillip. *Determinants and Effects of Changes in the Stock of Money, 1875-1960.* New York: Columbia University Press, 1965.
2. Friedman, Milton, and Anna J. Schwartz. *A Monetary History of the United States, 1867-1960.* Princeton, N.J.: Princeton University Press, 1963.
3. Gandolfi, Arthur E., and James R. Lothian. ''Review of 'Did Monetary Forces Cause The Great Depression?' '' *Journal of Money, Credit, and Banking,* 9 (November 1977), 679-91.
4. Temin, Peter. *Did Monetary Forces Cause The Great Depression?* New York: Norton, 1976.

BOOK REVIEWS

Financing Black Economic Development, by Timothy Bates and William Bradford. New York: Academic Press, 1979. 198 pp. $16.00

Financial institutions operating in limited income areas have been the subject of considerable study over the past decade. The earlier work concentrated primarily on black-owned banks and dealt with problems of bank viability and social responsibility. Professor Bradford has extended this body of work to include black-owned savings and loan associations and has found that many of the same problems and circumstances that confront the banks are also faced by the S&Ls. The co-authorship of a volume with Professor Bates is appropriate since they have worked on similar projects in the past and have co-authored other papers. Here, to Bradford's continuing work on S&Ls is added Bates' research on black businesses.

Together Bates and Bradford present a compilation of their earlier efforts, which is a valuable contribution especially to those who are unfamiliar with their previous efforts. As such, *Financing Black Economic Development* provides the reader with an introduction to the role of black enterprise in limited income communities.

Unfortunately there are several omissions that perhaps will be considered by the authors in subsequent writings. First, the important issue of redlining is raised and is assumed to be pervasive without recognition of demand factors, the risk-return tradeoff, and a careful delineation of the difference between redlining (geographic discrimination) and discrimination on legally prohibited bases. Not included is reference to the growing body of literature that carefully and scientifically addresses these issues and their implications for communities and the institutions that serve their residents. Second, the authors do not relate their individual contributions in such a manner to illustrate the role that banks and S&Ls can play in financing venture capital and seed money to black businesses. Third, the role of other financial institutions such as finance companies and credit unions is not discussed.

In particular, credit unions play a vital role in many disadvantaged communities. A casual sampling by this writer reveals at least seven hundred black credit unions. Although most of these are associational, some are residential. Recently, the National Credit Union Administration and the Community Services Administration have implemented a demonstration project to provide seed capital and technical assistance to strengthen a limited number of community development credit unions. The anticipation is that the loans will enable the credit unions to deliver improved services and aid in the revitalization and economic development of their communities.

Thus, credit unions should be considered in the financing of black economic development. Recent legislation has enabled credit unions to provide more services to their members. Credit unions can offer home mortgages, home improvement loans, and share drafts, which allow members to write third party transfers on deposits. Credit unions offer counseling services and many provide food stamp services to their members. However, these institutions, being constrained to lend to their members, cannot make commercial loans to businesses. Nevertheless, if the owner of a small business is a member of a credit union, the institution can make a personal loan to that individual. Credit unions provide for capital accumulation within a community, teach financial responsibility, and importantly retain the funds for use within the community. If one is concerned with the question of financial disinvestment, then these institutions should not be ignored as a vehicle for community development.

Consequently, this volume by Professors Bates and Bradford should be viewed as having addressed only part of the issue. Obviously, more can be said on the role of institutions other than banks and S&Ls. More could also be said on the role of private lenders and of participation in secondary markets. What Bates and Bradford have done is to wet the palate. Presumably, the main course will soon follow.

HAROLD BLACK

National Credit Union Administration

The International Monetary Tangle: Myths and Realities, by Guillaume Guindey. White Plains, N.Y.: M. E. Sharpe, 1977. 128 pp. $10.00

This is a revised and updated version of the author's *Mythes et Réalités de la Crise Monetaire,* published in 1973 in Paris. It might be considered one view of recent international monetary history by an insider, since the author is said to have taken part in most international financial negotiations from 1944 to 1965 in various capacities, part of that time being in the French Ministry of Finance and part as director general of the Bank for International Settlements. He has also held various positions in French and foreign business firms. Indeed it is the author's varied background that makes his comments on the international monetary scene of special interest. In the first part of the book he reviews international monetary cooperation from 1943 to 1976. In the second part he indicates what he considers to be the lessons to be learned from that experience. The length of the book makes it clear that this is not an attempt to provide either an adequate history of the international monetary developments during the period or a systematic analysis of international monetary problems. It does provide numerous comments on both events and problems that should interest readers with some backgrounding in both. It can be considered a "balanced" presentation, giving, for example, good grades to the IMF in general despite specific criticisms. It is not narrowly French nationalist in viewpoint, but after giving the U.S. ample credit for some policies, it is highly critical of others and blames much recently on U.S. "egocentrism."

Three periods of international monetary cooperation are distinguished: from Bretton Woods to 1958, from 1958 to 1971, and since 1971. There is an elementary review of the conditions Bretton Woods was intended to correct and of the mechanisms chosen for that purpose, but not of the alternatives rejected at Bretton Woods. It is duly noted that some matters were not resolved or dealt with clearly or adequately. Brief attention is then given to some subsequent developments. The author is critical of U.S. pressure for premature convertibility of the pound sterling in 1947, and of methods used in the 1949 devaluations. That the BIS did not die as scheduled but played a useful role is indicated, and allowing the EPU to die is deplored as indicative of insufficient attention to the need to develop instruments of cooperation among countries concerned about international capital movements.

There is a brief description of U.S., British, and Continental cooperation during the 1958–1971 period in the BIS, OECD, gold pool, and Committee of Ten. A sketchy account is given of the different views eventuating in the creation of SDRs. The dilatory attitude toward the Eurodollar problem is deplored as is the 1971 U.S. solution of its balance of payments problem of long standing by unilateral measures, thereby destroying the Bretton Woods system instead of subjecting itself to an IMF solution.

After 1971, the behavior of dollar exchange rates led in due course to more "managed floating" and, along with oil crises, to new U.S. interest in monetary collaboration with Europe. Reform of the international monetary system proved impossible under the circumstances prevailing, however. Even the European "snake" had a hard time, given the divergent behavior of European economies. The dollar and the Eurodollar dominate the present international "regime" or nonsystem.

The second part of the book starts by contending that some people have learned the wrong lessons from all this experience, have oversimplified and created myths. The author argues that general condemnation of the Bretton Woods system is unwarranted—monetary and gold market disorder was caused by various policies rather than by the role allotted to gold in the system; the trouble was not largely due to the sins of creditor nations, since their responsibilities do not extend to matching the inflation of deficit countries; the gold exchange standard is not pernicious but that it was abused, primarily for the benefit of the U.S.; and if parities were too rigid it is the fault of governments, not of the IMF, which should not take initiatives in that area. The concept of free floating is characterized as a mere intellectual game; the real problems relate to cooperation in "managing floating." Central among these problems is coordination of policies and mutual financial support among "financial market countries" that are subject to large and sudden movements of short- and long-term capital. The fund could handle current account problems, but for any system to work, more progress on these capital account problems must be made. The author does not do more than hint at substantive steps that may be involved, but suggests the framework might well be the OECD operating outside, in liason rather than in conflict with, the IMF. It is suggested that the U.S. deficit during the 1960s should have been financed by Europe extending long-term credits rather than by purchase of dollars and inflation of money supplies. There is no mention of the objection that deGaulle and others would have had to this, nor the question as to how long the U.S. might have continued to enjoy the advantages of an overvalued currency. Guindey does object to efforts to demonetize gold, contending it can still have a useful role. He fears excess SDR creation, especially if the Third World dominates such decisions. More immediately, the danger is lack of control of Eurodollar creation, important though its function is. Inflation control in general is a fundamental problem for the international picture as well as the domestic. The developing countries are said to require much larger assistance programs as well as short-term credits to handle oil price increases.

The book ends with a note of concern over whether the U.S. will overcome its ''egocentric'' attitude in international monetary matters and be willing to enter into forms of cooperation that entail, along with other nations, committments, financial obligations, and risks, or whether the U.S. will expect others to take the risks of stabilizing the dollar and meeting U.S. needs while the U.S. remains unilaterally free to take any action it chooses.

HARLAN M. SMITH
University of Minnesota

Bankruptcy Risk in Financial Depository Intermediaries, by Michael F. Koehn. Lexington, Mass.: Lexington Books, D.C. Heath, 1979. xii + 156 pp. $19.95

An appropriate and more exciting title would have been ''How government regulation increases the bankruptcy risk of financial intermediaries.'' The book might become a really hot item if the dustcover, which it does not have, mentioned that according to the author regulators accept that a commercial bank may go bankrupt within three months, with a probability of 0.0005. This may be low enough to put a depositor at ease, but the implication is that one should expect a few scores of bank failures in the U.S. each year. There is no ambiguity about the author's conclusion: ''Therefore, regulators appear to be moving away from their objective of ensuring the solidity of the depository intermediary system.'' The argument leading to this conclusion requires many steps, but it is carried through with impeccable logic.

The author considers four classes of intermediaries: Commercial Banks, Mutual Savings Banks, Savings and Loan Institutions, and Credit Unions. These are in different ways subject to three kinds of solvency regulations: Portfolio Restrictions, Capital Adequacy Requirements, and Regulation Q Restrictions (ceilings on interest paid on various classes of deposits). The regulation will restrict the sets of investment portfolios from which the intermediaries make their choice. To study the effect of these restrictions the author constructs a model of a market with twenty-five classes of securities, ranging from U.S. government discount bills to the Standard and Poor's Industrial equity index. For each class he computes quarterly return for the years 1969–1977. From the thirty-six observations, expectations and covariances are estimated, and these are used to compute the efficient portfolios by the usual method of minimizing the variance for a required expected rate of return. The computations are carried out without restrictions, and with the particular sets of regulatory restrictions that apply to the four types of intermediaries. Optimal portfolios are also computed for some changes in the restrictions actually in force.

The restrictions increase the risk the institutions must accept in order to obtain the desired expected return, and in general they will increase the risk of bankruptcy. With the author's definition, bankruptcy occurs if in a quarter investment income plus equity capital is insufficient to pay the interest due to depositors. An upper limit of the probability of this event is then found from Chebychev's inequality. These limits are of course extremely conservative, and it is a little surprising that the author just mentions in a footnote that one can obtain ''much more precision'' if the variables can be assumed to be normally distributed. This is really an understatement, since the difference can be dramatic. A deviation from the expectation greater than 6.1 times the standard deviation will, according to the Chebychev condition, have a probability smaller than 0.027. If normality is assumed the probability will be below 10^{-9}.

The portfolio model, based on mean-variance analysis, really assumes that returns are normally distributed. The author is well aware of this, and carries out a standard test, which indicates that it is reasonably safe to assume normality and apply the model. This does not necessarily mean that the normality assumption holds at the tail of the distribution, and can be used to compute the probability of bankruptcy. The Chebychev condition, however, holds for any distribution, and it should be possible to make some reasonable assumptions about the shape of the distribution of returns, which would give much lower limits for probability of bankruptcy.

The author's conclusion that regulation can only increase the bankruptcy risk is certainly correct under his assumptions, but the increase may well be infinitesimal.

The purpose of regulation is presumably to force the intermediary to behave as a prudent risk averse investor. Koehn assumes that the intermediaries use the portfolio model, and this implies in a sense that most of the need for regulation is assumed away. For instance, restrictions that limit investments in securities issued by a single corporation will in general be unnecessary, if the investor seeks an optimal diversified portfolio. Only if the intermediary shows too little risk aversion will it be necessary to lay down some restrictions to prevent all the eggs from being put in one basket. If the intermediary wants to diversify in any case, as Koehn assumes, additional restrictions, if they have any effect at all, can only increase the risk of bankruptcy.

The book is written in a clear and engaging style, and the computations are easy to follow, through a series of well-designed tables. The results are illustrated by a number of graphs, which also serve as a basis for the author's arguments. There is some deficiencies in the generality of these geometric consideration, and some readers may have preferred analytic proofs. This is, however, a minor objection. The book should be useful to anybody interested in applied portfolio models, and it will be read with pleasure by those who suspect that much of the current regulatory activity is counterproductive.

KARL H. BORCH
Norwegian School of Business

An Unformalized Forecasting Model, by Aleksander Markowski. Stockholm; National Institute of Economic Research, 1979. 119 pp.

There is a considerable tension in macroeconomics between the use of formal mathematical models of the economy and the reliance upon subjective informed opinion. This conflict surfaces in debates over theory, policy, and forecasting. It has been called the battle of the models versus the mystics.

Model builders argue that the explicit construction of a model compels the revelation of one's behavioral assumptions and thought processes, and makes economics scientific in that forecasts can then be mechanically replicated by others. Thus, Samuelson wrote that

> science is public knowledge, reproducible knowledge. When Robert Adams wrote an MIT thesis on the accuracy of different forecasting methods, he found that 'being Sumner Slichter' was apparently one of the best methods known at that time. This was a scientific fact, but a *sad* scientific fact. For Slichter could not and did not pass on his art to an assistant or to a new generation of economists. It died with him, if indeed it did not slightly predecease him. What we hope to get by scientific breakthrough is a way of substituting for men of genius men of talent and even just run-of-the-mill men. That is the sense in which science is public, reproducible knowledge. [2, p. 8]

However, in practice most modelers are also subject to this indictment in that their parameter estimation involves subjective nonreplicable model alterations. In addition, when actually using their models for forecasting, the parameters or models are adjusted to obtain forecasts that are in accord with their own informed judgements.[1] This is true, for example, of Lawrence Klein's very successful Wharton Model, which Samuelson has compared to the chess playing automaton that baffled the crowned heads of the world in the late eighteenth and early nineteenth centuries [2]. Hidden inside the machine was an expert chess player who only lost when he wasn't quite sober. Similarly, inside the Wharton Model one can find Lawrence Klein making subjective forecasts. And when he retires, the performance of the Wharton Model will surely suffer.

Model builders argue that the economy is too complicated to be successfully analyzed by mental gymnastics alone. A complex detailed model and a computer are needed to organize one's thoughts and to keep track of all the linkages, indirect effects, and feedbacks, Judgmentalists respond that the models are mathematically sophisticated but theoretically crude. Too much attention is paid to convenience and too little to realism. Too many equations are assumed to be linear. Too many variables are dropped because their parameters cannot be accurately estimated. Too many factors are ignored because they have not or cannot be measured. Too much time is spent with computers and too little time with people. Economic decisions are made by humans in very nonmechanical ways. These decisions are critically dependent upon individual perceptions and interpretations ("animal spirits") that we do not understand and cannot quantify. Similarly, the judgments of informed observers will not be easily described by mechanical equations. Economics is indeed an art and not a science.

Since the early 1960s the National Institute of Economic Research in Stockholm has been regularly publishing forecasts for the Swedish economy based upon a blend of data, models, and subjective judgment. The book reviewed here describes some of their procedures. Although rather sparse, it does serve to illustrate the strengths and weaknesses of both models and mysticism.

The institute's informal "KI model" is aimed at short-term projections. Annual forecasts for a given year are published the preceding October and in January, May, and October of that year. Formal econometric relations are estimated for many sectors of the economy, and their implied predictions serve as a base for the final

[1]The Fair Model [1] is one of the few that makes wholly mechanical forecasts.

forecasts. There is a heavy reliance on survey data and subjective interpretations of recent historical experience.

This book describes many of the specific factors taken into account. There is an imperfectly related Keynesian demand side and input-output supply side. Interest rates and financial markets play a very minor role. The hourly wage rate depends upon vacancies and an exogenous negotiated wage increase. Prices depend upon input costs and world prices.

The construction of consumption predictions is discussed in some detail. The institute's predictions of private consumption (C) are influenced by forecasts of personal disposable income (Y), consumer prices (P), lagged consumption, and lagged retail sales. The consumption forecasts are "made on a purely judgmental basis, though several formal equations are consulted" (p. 28). A chapter is devoted to investigating the extent to which the actual forecasts can ex post be formally explained by an explicit model. This exercise is useful and the results are interesting.

The following regressions are reported:

$$\dot{C} = a_1 + b_1\dot{Y} + c_1\dot{P} \tag{1}$$

$$C = a_2 + b_2Y + c_2\dot{P}Y_{-1} + d_2Y_{-1} + e_2C_{-1}, \tag{2}$$

where $\dot{X}$ signifies the percentage change in X, and various combinations of the parameters other than a_i and b_i are set equal to zero. In one set of regressions all of the data are forecast values; in the second set actual values are used.

It turns out that the institute's forecasts can be fairly well, albeit imperfectly, explained by these equations. These specific relations also indicate the value of explicitly revealing the factors that influence judgmental forecasts. First, such a revelation discloses the different assumptions that cause dissimilar forecasts. A choice between competing forecasts can then be based upon assumption preferences. Second, there can be criticism and possibly improvement in one's judgment. Here many would question the presence of an intercept in the rate of change equation (1). In both the forecast and actual data, the estimates of a_1 range between one and a half and three. Apparently there are nonlinearities or undisclosed factors that have exerted a continuing upward pressure on both forecast and actual consumption. Many observers would also inquire about the simultaneous presence of $\dot{P}$ in both the C and $\dot{C}$ relations. Does this reflect Pigou or Wicksell effects, or seemingly the former in (1) and the latter in (2)? Besides the confusion and the possible need for both price level and rate of change effects, the equations immediately suggest interest rates and the market value of wealth as possible additional influences. It may well be that the institute's researchers have a plausible rationale for their forecasts. But it is surely useful to expose that rationale to critical scrutiny.

The other side of that coin is that their forecasts are undoubtedly quite sophisticated and complex, both in functional form and in the number of influences taken into account, and consequently cannot be perfectly described by simple mechanical formulas. It is interesting though that there are smaller standard errors here for the equations using forecast rather than actual data. This suggests the existence of important additional influences on consumption that were not in fact taken into account by the institute's forecasters. In addition, their forecasts are found to be more sensitive to income and much less influenced by inflation (and often with the opposite sign) than are actual consumption data. These kinds of exercises may be helpful in evaluating and improving forecasts. Reportedly, the efforts by Lars Jacobsson in the late 1960s to construct a formal econometric version of the institute's judgmental methods has in fact "affected the methods employed for the judgmental forecast" (p. 66).

The institute's forecasts of consumption, as well as other selected variables, are recorded in an addendum.[2] In the annual January forecasts[3] of $\dot{C}$ for 1964–77, the root mean squared error (RMSE) is 1.85. For comparison the benchmark naive model using average $\dot{C}$ up until the year preceding the forecast has a RMSE of 2.01. In 1971 there is a revision break in the data such that actual $\dot{C}$ is not really comparable with the forecasts. With 1971 excluded the RMSEs are 1.68 for the institute and 1.67 for the naive model. It would be very interesting to also compare the institute's judgmental forecasts with those from a formal model such as (1).

There is a chapter comparing the cyclical patterns in the forecasts with actual data for various variables. With the forecasts made in October of the preceding year and in January, the degree of correspondence with the actual data is disappointing. As might be expected, the May and October same year forecasts are closer to actual experience.

A major inadequacy of an informal judgmental model is that one cannot examine its implied predictions in hypothetical (perhaps policy) simulations. This is particularly true when as here there is a heavy reliance on survey data. This book is consequently of interest mainly to other model builders who want to compare notes.

LITERATURE CITED

1. Fair, Ray C. *A Model of Macroeconomic Activity,* Vols. I and II. Cambridge, Mass.: Ballinger, 1976.
2. Samuelson, Paul A. "The Art and Science of Macro Models Over 50 Years." In *The Brookings Model: Perspective and Recent Developments,* edited by Gary Fromm and Lawrence Klein, pp. 2–10. Amsterdam: North-Holland, 1975.

GARY SMITH

University of Houston

Substitution Effects, Speculation and Exchange Rate Stability, by Patrick Minford. Amsterdam: North-Holland, 1978. x +222 pp. $36.75

Throughout the 1950s and 1960s substitution effects were of minor importance in theories of the balance of payments. Analysis of the trade account focused on income effects although a devaluation was recognized as an expenditure switching

[2]I examined the consumption forecasts because of their emphasis in the text. A reasonable comprehensive evaluation of all the institute's predictions is difficult, since the addendum contains more explanatory footnotes than forecasts.

[3]In the four years where multiple forecasts are given, a simple average was used. In three of the years it was necessary to ignore the qualification "just over" or "just under."

mechanism whose effects were thought to be perverse by elasticity pessimists. Substitution effects were unimportant in determining the capital account predominantly because of prohibitive government regulations that lead to the assumption of imperfect or zero capital mobility in theoretical models. Even as the regulations were relaxed, economists modeled capital flows as a function of the interest differential between two countries implying low substitutability between the assets. Subsequent research in the balance of payments theory has recognized the importance of substitution effects to the extent that purchasing power parity and interest rate parity are now primary building blocks of most international financial theories.

What the profession wishes to know now is the empirical importance of the intertemporal substitution and expectational effects that have arisen in asset market theories of open economies. The bulk of Patrick Minford's book addresses this question, but, in this reader's view, far from successfully. Minford's main thesis is that the dynamic movement of the economy is best modeled as a disequilibrium phenomenon. He recognizes that the predictions of structural models of the balance of payments that explain individual accounts are often in conflict with models in the tradition of the monetary approach, and he sees his work focusing "on disequilibrium behavior, an area where neither has staked out at all definite claims." Whether a dynamic equilibrium or disequilibrium approach eventually will be most successful in explaining the behavior of the balance of payments is certainly an open issue. I find fault with Minford, not so much for adopting a disequilibrium methodology, but rather for ignoring the microeconomic foundations of his aggregate models and estimating equations.

Chapter 3 provides a good example of the problems that I have in this regard. The chapter discusses and estimates an econometric model of U.K. manufactured exports. The demand for exports is thought to depend on long distributed lags of relative prices and a world business cycle index. The distributed lags are postulated as arising from order-delivery lags, information search costs, costs of adjustment for factors of production, and expectations of the future. The supply of exports depends on a time trend and distributed lags of the relative price and U.K. domestic expenditure. Minford at first specifies relatively simple behavioral equations, but then justifies his rejection of an equilibrium model by noting that since the simple demand curve is shifted by world real income and the simple supply curve is shifted by domestic real income, "unless there is synchronization of home and world cycles to a certain rather exact degree, it is likely that often market-clearing in the standard sense will not be possible without violent swings in relative export prices" (p. 69). The relative price, however, does not fluctuate violently, so Minford argues that markets don't clear and that the price is set in some other fashion. A model is developed in which the price of U.K. exports is determined by equality of long-run supply and demand. This notion motivates an estimating equation in which the price of exports is regressed on a time trend and distributed lags in world and domestic prices. Since prices are determined independently from quantities, the quantity equation is estimated using a modification of the technique of switching-regression.

By not explicitly considering the dynamic problems facing demanders and suppliers of exports, Minford is unable to place restrictions on the length of the lag distributions or the cross equation time series properties of the data. In this regard it should be noted that the switching regression framework destroys the continuity of the data and hence its time series properties, making the determination of the influence of expectations of the future exceedingly difficult if not impossible.

Again in chapter 4, inadequate microeconomic foundations cause me to be suspect of the conclusions. Chapter 4 presents a model of the three-month and one-year U.K. forward exchange rates and the short-term and long-term capital accounts from 1963 to 1971. Minford notes that modern portfolio theory suggests that capital flows, since they are changes in wealth holdings, are simultaneously determined with changes in rates of return on assets. Rather than test this specification, however, he asserts that short-term capital flows are related to the change in the short-term interest rate differential while long-term capital flows are related to a distributed lag in the level of the long-term interest differential. Minford justifies this procedure by arguing that costs of adjustment increase with the maturity of the asset and that the interest differential determines desired asset holdings to which actual holdings adjust with a lag. My assertion is that explicit consideration of the portfolio optimization problem under rational expectations, subject to the costs of adjustment, would place very strong cross equation restrictions on the capital flow and interest rate data, which would be very different from the general distributed lag framework.

A related problem that is ignored is the potential instability of the coefficients of "structural" equations when policy regimes change. This possibility was first noted by Lucas [2] and arises when models are not based on maximizing behavior. Minford is aware that changes in the exchange rate regime from Bretton Woods to the managed float changed the nature of uncertainty in the system. In particular, the discussion in chapter 7 demonstrates how to assess the change in the nature of uncertainty facing speculators as the regime changes. Under fixed rates the speculator is assumed to know the size of a potential devaluation, although a revaluation of equal percent is also given slight probability. Under flexible rates the expected future exchange rate is taken to be symmetrically distributed around the current spot rate. Using this framework Minford finds in chapter 8 that the elasticity of capital flows with respect to changes in the expected future exchange rate increases under flexible rates. There is no denying that this result is plausible. Nonetheless, the expected utility model, which is used to derive the results, also implies that the parameter is actually a function of the expected return and hence is unlikely to be constant in either regime.

In chapter 4, the long-term forward rate is postulated to be determined by "semi-rational" expectations. In theory, this imaginative idea is that speculators have a popular economic model in their minds when they form expectations of future variables. The speculators' model, however, is different from that of the econometrician since he uses better or newer economic theory. In practice Minford merely regresses the one-year forward rate (expressed as a percentage deviation from parity) on fourteen lags of the visible balance of the current account. This idea, as well as much of the rest of the specification of the model in chapter 4, draws heavily on Hutton [1].

In chapter 5, simulations of a simultaneous model of the determination of the current account, the capital account, and the exchange rate demonstrate that the "semi-rational" expectations (which Minford thinks may be representative of the way the world worked during the "teething-period" at the beginning of the flexible exchange rate era) may lead to dynamic instability. The model specifies that the current account depends only on a twenty-four quarter lag of the actual exchange rate, the capital account depends only on five quarter lags of the expected and realized exchange rates, and the expected exchange rate depends only on a fifteen quarter lag of the current account. With such a model is it surprising that there is dynamic instability?

Instability problems are examined in detail in chapter 6. As before, Minford postulates simple behavioral models and checks them for instability. A good deal of effort is devoted to developing ad hoc arguments to rule out unstable roots of difference equations rather than to examining the microeconomic plausibility of the behavior implied by the model.

In summary, I should note that Minford has done the profession a service by emphasizing the effects of substitution and expectations in an empirical investigation of a small open economy. Similarly, he is correct in noting that costly adjustment, order-delivery lags, search costs and imperfect information, and expectations of the future cause the simplest of monetary models to be inconsistent with the data. The major shortcoming of this volume is his failure to investigate these issues at the microeconomic level. As a consequence, his empirical results are unconvincing.

LITERATURE CITED

1. Hutton, John P. "A Model of Short-Term Capital Movements, the Foreign Exchange Market and Official Intervention in the U.K., 1963-1970." *Review of Economic Studies*, 44 (February 1977), 31–41.
2. Lucas, Robert E., Jr. "Econometric Policy Evaluation: A Critique." In *The Phillips Curve and Labor Markets*, edited by Karl Brunner and Allan H. Meltzer, Carnegie-Rochester Conference Series, 1. Amsterdam: North-Holland, 1976.

ROBERT J. HODRICK

Carnegie-Mellon University

On the Generality of Keynesian Economics, by Jukka Pekkarinen. Helsinki: Commentationes Scientiarium Socialium, 1979. 166 pp.

This book will bring relief to those who have tired of discussions of what Keynes "really meant"; rather it provides a "Hicksian" critique of the currently dominant IS-LM approach to "Keynesian" macrotheory. It also represents the first book by a committed disciple of *John* Hicks, and a first step towards the formation of a modern "Hicksian" approach to macroeconomics.

Basing himself on Hicks's most recent work, Pekkarinen uses the concept of "Fundist Plutology" as the "standard of appraisal" of the "generality" of "Keynesian" economics in "conditions in which the under-utilization of resources is not uniform and in which inflation is a problem" (p. 157). The identification of "(1) the effective demand hypothesis, an outcome of the multiplier theory which states that quantities react to changes in demand and that prices remain passive, and . . . (2) that Portfolio Approach, an outcome of the liquidity preference theory," which holds that changes in the supply of money affect investment by altering the terms under which economic agents are willing to hold the existing stock of wealth as the "central characteristics" of Keynesian theory, implies the conclusion that the theory is not general and not appropriate to short run analysis (p. 103).

It should be evident that by "Keynesian," Pekkarinen refers to the macrotheory that has grown up around the IS-LM analysis proposed by Hicks in 1937 [1], his subsequent *Value and Capital* [2], and "the further elaborations at the hands of Samuelson, of Debreu and of so many others" [6], which Hicks himself feels he has "outgrown" and which fails to capture the essential problems of economic analysis because of its static equilibrium nature. It would serve no purpose to delineate how this theory, as it is presented in Pekkarinen's book, bears no resemblance to that found in Keynes's *General Theory,* its recent interpretation by post-Keynesian theorists, or the extent to which Keynes did explicitly consider those very factors whose absence from "Keynesian" theory causes Pekkarinen to judge the theory as without "general validity." Rather, the book can be better understood as the use of Hicks's later views as a vehicle for criticism of the dominant IS-LM theory.

In recent years Hicks has become increasingly preoccupied with the question of time in economics. This has led him to criticize the further developments of the IS-LM approach because of its static nature—because it is not "in time"—as well as to propose a reappraisal of the Austrian theories [3] as a potential remedy to this defect. From this work comes Hicks's distinction between the post-Keynesian and neoclassical approaches to capital and growth theory in terms of "fundists" and "materialists" [4], and the distinction between approaches concerned primarily with production or exchange aspects (plutologic or catallactic) of economic systems [5]. It is from these later Hicksian sources that Pekkarinen constructs his "standard of appraisal": "the flow of production . . . is at the center of Fundist Plutology. This mode of analysis is flow-based and conceives of production being made up of flows spread over time in a specific manner" (p. 43). With these Hicksian tools the basic weakness of the IS-LM approach is identified as (1) lack of analysis of supply factors, in particular those due to market imperfections; (2) lack of an analysis of price formation, in particular the difference between fix- and flex-price markets; and (3) lack of recognition that liquidity (or flexibility) is a characteristic of time-related sequences that is based on "borrowing power" and functions through the cost of borrowing, rather than the basis for a simplified demand for money function which determines the rate of interest, which sets the limit to investment. The absence of analysis of these factors leads to the conclusion that IS-LM Keynesianism is not general and cannot be extended to the analysis of present day conditions. Therefore, it should be replaced by "Fund" analysis, which does recognize the importance of these factors.

At only one point does Pekkarinen differ markedly from Hicks's analysis: when he states his "contention" that the IS-LM theory he is criticizing "has to a large extent preserved the analytical structure of the *General Theory.*" Hicks suggests that it represents only "one of the elements in what Keynes said" [6, p. viii] and eliminates the most important because it "reduces the *General Theory* to equilibrium economics" [6].

To do justice to Keynes's approach and escape the static framework, "one must assume that the people in one's models do not know what is going to happen, and know that they do not know what is going to happen. As in history!" [6].

Thus expectations must play a crucial role. In Pekkarinen's analysis this aspect is reflected in the concept of "liquidity . . . the degree of flexibility which economic agents possess with respect to the temporal structure of the economic process . . . which in the Fundist approach refers to an interconnected sequence of inputs and outputs over time." Thus, "the short run cannot be discussed separately from the entire sequence 'making up' the fund. The fixed time profile of a fund links consecutive periods together. . . . As a result expectations enter the picture'' (p. 72). But this seems to be a rather different approach than that suggested by Hicks for it links expectations, not to the ''human predicament'' aspect of time stressed by, for example, Shackle and Lachmann in which the future results of present actions cannot be known, but rather to the ''sequence'' aspect of time in which all future time paths are known, but once one is chosen it cannot be changed without both loss and the passage of time. This latter method also suggested recently by Hahn seems more appropriate to what Lowe, in his definitive work on the subject [7], called prescriptive or ''instrumental'' analysis. To the extent that knowledge of an ''interconnected sequence of inputs and outputs over time'' is implicit in the Fundist approach, it does not seem a likely vehicle for that ''elusive element'' in Keynes's approach which went beyond statics.

As a critical vehicle, however, the Fundist approach may provide a useful method for analyzing alternative specifications of the role of expectations. For example, in the ''rational'' expectations approach individuals are presumed to take decisions on the basis of expectations formed from existing, available information. Unanticipated changes in demand then have effects on nominal expenditure and prices. But such changes cannot persist because rationality implies that individuals will rapidly recognize them to be inconsistent with their existing expectations of output. To paraphrase, this approach leads to an ''effective demand hypothesis'' in which prices may react to changes in demand but quantities remain passive—just the opposite of the traditional ''Keynesian'' position outlined by Pekkarinen. The Fundist approach suggests, however, that the ''rationality'' of expectations will depend on the flexibility or liquidity of the individual. The maintenance of rational expectations in the face of unanticipated events would require complete flexibility over the sequence of future inputs. With less than perfect liquidity even ''irrational'' expectations may be ''rational'' given the degree of flexibility available. To the extent that this implies the assumption of perfectly functioning financial markets in the rational expectations approach neither can it be considered as having ''general validity'' in Pekkarinen's sense. Drawing attention to the importance of money and financial market behavior in modern macroeconomic analysis is perhaps of sufficient importance to merit further exploration of the Fundist approach.

LITERATURE CITED

1. Hicks, John R. ''Mr. Keynes and the Classics.'' *Econometrica*, (April 1937).
2. ———. *Value and Capital; An Inquiry into Some Fundamental Principles of Economic Theory*. Oxford: Clarendon Press, 1939.
3. ———. *Capital and Time: A Neo-Austrian Theory*. Oxford: Clarendon Press, 1973.
4. ———. ''Capital Controversies: Ancient and Modern.'' *American Economic Review*, Papers and Proceedings, May 1974.
5. ———. *The Crisis in Keynesian Economics*. Oxford: Blackwell, 1974.
6. ———. *Economic Perspectives: Further Essays on Money and Growth*. Oxford: Clarendon Press, 1977.
7. Lowe, Adolf. *The Path of Economic Growth*. New York: Cambridge University Press, 1976.

J. A. KREGEL
Livingston College, Rutgers University
Rijksuniversiteit te Groningen

The U.S. Balance of Payments and the Sinking Dollar, by Wilson E. Schmidt. New York: New York University Press, 1979. xii + 157 pp. $10.00 (cloth); $4.95 (paper)

This little book on the ''monetary'' aspects of international economics is intended to be a companion volume to Melvyn Krauss' book on the new protectionism (*The New Protectionism: The Welfare State and International Trade*). Both are published for the International Center for Economic Policy Studies, an institute recently (1977) founded with the aim ''to provide readable, though analytical publications, which improve public understanding of economic problems and the market process.''

Accordingly, this is not a book that seeks to add to economic knowledge or to develop new and more elegant techniques of its presentation. It is addressed to the general public, who—in the opinion of the author—is inadequately informed and even misled by the media in balance of payments and exchange rate matters. The importance of informing the intelligent layman is seen in the fact ''that policymakers' perceptions of what the electorate thinks about the balance of payments are important in determining events'' (p. 3).

A short introduction to the issues is followed by a chapter explaining composition (structure) and mechanics of the balance of payments with two rather lengthy appendixes comprising the ''Explanatory Notes for the U.S. Balance of Payments'' of the U.S. Treasury Balance of Payments Division and the IMF's ''Concepts of Balances.'' The author rightly warns against fixing the attention on the balance of trade or—for that matter—on any other specific set of transactions. He also argues against the common practice of selecting specific currencies (the yen, the Swiss franc, and the German mark) in evaluating the change in the value of the dollar, and points out that with the use of effective rates, the devaluation of the U.S. dollar is far less spectacular, or, in specific time spans, nonexistent. One could perhaps argue that in trying to counterbalance the exaggerated weight often placed on the trade balance, the author makes a little too much of the balancing properties of a double entry bookkeeping system. One also wonders whether a stronger reliance on the concept of real exchange rate changes from the start would not have helped in destroying common misconceptions. Although such advice admittedly might easily lead to a less readable, less transparent, and hence pedagogically less valuable text than the present one.

The central chapters of the book pose two questions: ''Does the Balance of Payments Matter?'' and ''Do Exchange Rate Fluctuations Matter?''. The author's answers to the first question are that the balance of payments does not matter very much, because the dollar is a reserve currency and many currencies are floating against the dollar, that inflationary effects of dollar depreciations on the U.S. are very small (as compared to internal sources of inflation), and that exchange rate adjustments and capital inflows will correct potential negative employment effects of deficits in the balance of goods and services. Since in the view of the author, liquid assets of foreigners held in the U.S. are ''locked in,'' and therefore, the U.S. need not worry about borrowing abroad, in balance of payments matters ''there is nothing to fear but fear itself'' because fear could bring about costly controls and restrictions, and market distorting export subsidies might be granted by the U.S. government (p. 101).

The second central question of the book (Do exchange rate fluctuations matter?)

is answered in a more roundabout way. The author first argues quite correctly, I believe, that a reestablishment of fixed exchange rates is not feasible at the moment, and that, if reestablished, such a system would not be credible. He goes on to the (somewhat academic) exercise of defining the optimum exchange rate and to show that it is desirable to have exchange rates fluctuate.

The author even addressed the difficult question of excessive fluctuations. Here he tries to show (perhaps unnecessarily) that the movements of the dollar exchange rate have been within the permissible band agreed upon at the Smithsonian conference in December 1971. In his demonstration, however, he uses effective exchange rates, which is hardly what the participants of the Smithsonian conference had in mind. But apart from this, the author makes it sufficiently clear that it is next to impossible to determine in advance the optimum exchange rate by showing the different influences on the exchange rate and stressing interest differentials, expectations, and the resulting short-term capital movements as well as the influence of statements of government officials. He then includes a section on public speculation, which in a book like this is invaluable since there is an unexplainably strong inclination in the general public to believe there is perfect wisdom and information concentrated somewhere at the top, especially in economic affairs. He argues that there is no evidence that central bank intervention has improved the performance of the market and that the authorities seem to have no more information than the market (which is, perhaps, an overstatement, with the exception of the information on their own actions, if these are not according to preannounced rules).

In the conclusion of the book, which is written in the tradition of the monetary approach to the balance of payments, the author maintains that the balance of payments does not matter as long as the exchange rates are floating freely and that the only dangers remaining are government interventions. The author rightly warns that these interventions, should they take the form of operations in the foreign exchange market or of controls, are likely to have high costs either to the taxpayer or in the form of gains from trade and capital movements foregone.

For a reviewer, whose predilections are usually very close to those argued in the book, it is difficult to say something critical. All in all, this is a very readable and extremely useful little book, lucidly written in an argumentative style, and it will go far to educate the reader in balance of payments and exchange rate matters, correcting misconceptions, and thus eliminating unfounded fears. But, of course, there are differences in emphasis. One cannot help feeling that the author's views on the dollar problem are too sanguine and complacent. The author, I believe, tends to make too much of the fact that the dollar is the reserve currency and that it is difficult to see it dethroned. This keeps him from stressing the problems caused by changing currency areas both for "internal" monetary policies (in the U.S. and elsewhere) as well as for the thereby aggravated adjustment problems in trade. (Not to mention the increasing problems encountered in explaining to OPEC countries why they should exchange their oil with a high commodity own rate of interest against a U.S. dollar that is constantly losing value). There are advantages for a reserve currency (as, for instance, seignorage), but there are also problems, especially when the trust in the reserve currency is diminishing, as can be learned from the history of the pound sterling.

From a European point of view, the treatment of the dollar reserves ("overhang") at times is somewhat irritating. The argument is that foreign countries get good interest on their dollar reserves and therefore are, or at least should be, content with holding large amounts of it. Two questions arise in connection with this much debated issue. Why did considerable pressure of a political nature have to be brought to bear on partner countries to keep their dollar reserves if the real interest on these currency reserves has been and is so attractive? Is the U.S. government paying less for its debt because of the interest-lowering effect of dollar reserves invested in government securities and (additionally) because it is offering special low interest rates to reserve holders? Sometimes, the author seems to be inclined to concede to the media that the interest paid by the U.S. government for these reserves is a burden. But this is a question of the reference system: without these reserves held in short-term government assets, would not the U.S. government have to pay considerably more interest for its debt? However, the author is correct in pointing out that central banks outside the U.S. have intervened in favor of the dollar and are still doing so because they are trying to help their own countries' export industries.

A question the author does not pose is whether in the context of the emerging international division of labor the U.S. should be an importer of capital. Should it not run, like Japan and West Germany have done before the latest domestic rises in oil prices, an export surplus and—on balance—be an exporter of capital? The commonly held view that—apart from the oil problem—the central international "imbalance" to be corrected lies mainly between the two surplus countries Japan and Germany on one side, and the U.S. on the other, is perhaps mistaken: should not all three of them, after having adapted to the energy situation, be major exporters of capital to the developing world? Admittedly, this is a question which transcends the scope of the book and there is always a price to be paid for compartmentalization.

Overall, this is a highly welcome and very useful contribution towards informing the public in matters of international monetary economics. The author has admirably solved the task he set for himself, and he is to be congratulated on his great pedagogic skills. The fact that he might have taken upon himself the additional task of educating the American public to a more "internationalistic" point of view detracts little from the merits of the book.

HUBERTUS MÜLLER-GROELING

Institut für Weltwirtschaft an der Universität Kiel

The Equity Funding Papers, by Lee J. Seidler, Frederick Andrews, and Marc J. Epstein. New York: Wiley, 1977. ii + 578 pp. $14.95

As the 1980s begin, a look back at one of the most dramatic financial stories of the past decade is a valuable, although disquieting, experience. The reader of *The Equity Funding Papers,* by Seidler, Andrews, and Epstein, will find an exciting analysis of a widely acclaimed business success story of almost ten years that was revealed in 1973 to be the multi-billion dollar fraud of the century.

Earlier books [2, 4] and other accounts of the rise and fall of the Equity Funding Corporation of America were too premature to sort out coherently the complex and confusing ramifications of this gigantic white-collar crime. More amazing than the mere size of the swindle is the fact that it was perpetrated over a period of five years or more by nearly 100 employees who deceived nationally prominent lawyers, auditors, bankers, financial analysts, stock exchanges, the Securities Exchange Commission, and other regulators.

The authors use the lengthy and excellent 1974 report of the bankruptcy trustee, Robert M. Loeffler, as the foundation for their story. Included in its entirety, the report encompasses 150 pages as the central part of the book. Earlier chapters set the stage with glowing progress reports from Equity Funding executives, press releases extolling the earnings that were fictitiously tripled over actual returns, the first auditor reports that almost found the fraud, and the rumors and revelations prompted by a disgruntled employee, Ron Secrist, which exposed the financial mess in April 1973. The trustee's report is seen as "a fascinating document," as "it unravels complexity within complexity, first laying out what Equity Funding's business proported to be, no simple task, and then showing how that web was corrupted into a tangle of fraud" (p. 5).

Interestingly, several points are documented that contradicted the public's view of the scandal as one which was a sophisticated insurance fraud based upon computer-age wizards. Instead, it is shown to be (1) primarily a *securities* fraud (using bogus insurance policies sold to duped reinsurers to sustain "profits" that pushed stock prices from below $10 in 1965 to more than $90 three years later); (2) mostly based on *nonexisting assets* rather than embezzlement or theft of real assets; and (3) simply a *pencil* fraud that inflated accounting entries on commission income and earnings with virtually no support, accomplished with the help of glaring failures by the company auditors.

The major criticism that the authors (a financial analyst, a financial editor for the *New York Times,* and an accounting professor) offer for the trustee's report is the incredible lack of answers for the question: "Why didn't anybody tell?" That so many persons were involved in carrying out the fraud for so long intrigues the authors throughout the last six chapters of the book, as they relate the sequence of auditor's reports, clues of impending trouble in the financial history of Equity Funding, conviction of fraud for many of the company officers and auditors, and postevaluation by the accounting profession itself as to how the entire fraud remained undetected for many years.

General "moral blindness' is refuted as a sufficient explanation for the many diverse and human reasons that employees and outsiders gave as rationale for their participation. Financially, only a relatively few top executives had financial gain, through fat salaries and stock options or purchases, as a valid reason for their part in the fraud. Many others merely went along with the bogus reports, either to protect their jobs or by looking at the fraud as an amusing game. Most employees did not apparently recognize the staggering magnitude of the fraud, and merely downgraded their wrongdoing as a temporary financial ploy that could only hurt the big reinsurers and other companies rather than thousands of innocent stockholders.

In retrospect, the glaring discrepancies on the accounting statements of Equity Funding Corporation of America were overlooked continually not by one or a few financial experts, but by all of the many business firms and regulators who had access to voluminous public reports and prospectuses issued as required for a huge publicly held conglomerate listed on the national stock exchanges. Established underwriting firms were involved repeatedly in new shares and debt issues, the Internal Revenue Service verified falsified revenues, and several Big Eight accounting firms audited various subsidiary firms. The Securities and Exchange Commission approved the merger of the Wolfson, Weiner auditing firm into the prominent Seidman and Seidman accounting firm in spite of many unanswered questions about the adequacy and accuracy of the audits in progress. Then the fraud continued, and a consortium of large banks gave EFCA a line of credit of over $100 million only nine months before the fraud broke.

Five experienced insurance companies reinsured about $1.2 billion of life insurance policies, as insurance regulators in California, New York, and Illinois periodically examined the Equity Funding Life Insurance Corporation. In spite of the fact that real life insurance policyholders suffered no losses in the fraud, the fictitious sales not discovered resulted in the reinsurers paying for policies on nonexistent policyholders. One of the most ludicrous episodes of the escalating fraud in the accounts was the ''killing off'' of selected phony policyholders by computer programming that alleviated any reinsurers' suspicions of the coming debacle.

The reader of *The Equity Funding Papers* may occasionally be discouraged by the sheer volume of the information presented. The general organization, however, is commendable. An excellent introduction of less than twenty pages helps by giving an overview of the sequence of related events before the 1973 bankruptcy proceedings began, how the fraud worked, and how it was discovered and later analyzed by the bankruptcy trustee and accounting firms. Much of the detail is separately presented in the final two hundred pages which offer full or excerpted financial statements, prospectuses, and quarterly reports. The introductory sections of each chapter are particularly worth close reading. For example, the summary section ''The Accounting Profession Examines Itself'' gives the authors' opinions as to the succeeding special committee report of the American Institute of Certified Public Accountants. The public accounting professions' dilemma, obligations, and mistakes are well explained. Important lessons to be learned are critically but fairly presented.

As supplementary reflections to the book, observers of the total scandal during the latter part of the decade will appreciate more fully the new items which tell the results that followed. Orion Capital Corporation emerged in 1976 as the successor to EFCA, whose stockholders received about 12 cents of Orion stock for each $1 of EFCA stock. In 1978 Ray Dirks, a key figure in the exposé, did well in coauthoring *The Great Wall Street Scandal* [2]. However, he also was later suspended by the SEC for the use of inside information in advising clients without proper disclosure to the public, and four investment companies were censured at the same time [3]. A class action suit against four accounting firms was settled in 1978 for a total of $62 million, one of the largest settlements ever for such a case.

Innumerable other lawsuits, and convictions against most of the top executives who were indicted, are all part of the sorry saga. Aptly chronicled in this book, the events leading to all these parts of the aftermath of the ''crime of the century'' are imperative reading for students of banking, insurance, and finance. The subtitle chosen by the authors, ''An Anatomy of a Fraud,'' is well chosen, and the dissection is a fascinating work.

LITERATURE CITED

1. ''Blowing the Whistle Ends in Book, Movie, and $500,000 a Year.'' *The Wall Street Journal,* February 15, 1978, 1.

2. Dirks, Raymond L., and Leonard Gross. *The Great Wall Street Scandal.* New York: McGraw-Hill, 1974.

3. "Equity Funding Scandal Rulings Set Aside by SEC Aide." *The Wall Street Journal,* September 8, 1978, 3.

4. Soble, Ronald L., and Robert E. Dallos. *The Impossible Dream: The Equity Funding Story.* New York: G. P. Putnam, 1974.

DAVID L. BICKELHAUPT

Ohio State University

The Pay Board's Progress: Wage Controls in Phase II, by Arnold R. Weber and Daneil J. B. Mitchell. Washington, D.C.: Brookings Institution, 1978. xvi + 454 pp. $12.95

This book, one of the Brookings Institution's studies in wage-price policy, examines wage controls during Phase II of the U.S. Economic Stabilization Program. Both authors were wage controllers in Phase II: Weber was a member of the Pay Board, and Mitchell was the board's chief economist. This experience has enabled them to describe completely the Pay Board, its organization, and its operation, but it has not benefited their analysis of the effects of Phase II wage controls. In this respect, *The Pay Board's Progress* is similar to other price controllers' books and essays about the 1971-74 controls. It contributes to the historical record of those controls, but it adds little if anything to our understanding of how price and wage controls work.

Recall that Phase II spanned the 14-month period from November 1971 to January 1973; supervision of the price and wage controls was handled by the Cost of Living Council; prices were regulated by the Price Commission; wages and other forms of labor compensation were regulated by the Pay Board. So Weber and Mitchell focus on just one component of the Economic Stabilization Program, and devote three-fourths of their book (some three hundred pages) to describing the Pay Board and its policies. The detail is excruciating. We are told how the name "Pay Board" was selected for the wage control agency. There are about fifteen accounts of George Meany's antics. Five wage control cases from the beginning of Phase II are set out at length to show how the board's policies developed. One chapter discusses the original, short-lived tripartite (business, union, and public) composition of the Pay Board and how it was counterproductive to controlling wages.

The most interesting institutional chapters describe the formulation, coverage, and enforcement of Phase II wage controls. The basis for the Pay Board's 5.5 percent ceiling on wage increases was that a 5.5 percent increase in aggregate income together with a predicted 3 percent productivity increase is consistent with a goal of a 2 to 3 percent increase in the general price level. Changes in relative wages were not considered explicitly—not surprising, perhaps, since the idea of price controls denies importance of the relative price system—although allowances were made implicitly in a variety of exclusions, special exceptions, and rules for computing pay increases. For example, the ceiling applied to an employer's total wage bill, so pay increases could be distributed disproportionately as long as the total was within the ceiling. Phase II wage controls covered all workers except federal government employees; yet, the Pay Board concentrated its regulatory efforts on units of five thousand or more employees, about 10 percent of the covered workers. Rhetoric about fighting inflation notwithstanding, one would expect this kind of policy from wage controllers with a budget constraint who wanted maximum impact on the index used to measure aggregate wages. The wage controls were enforced by the Internal Revenue Service, but enforcement decisions involved the Pay Board, the Cost of Living Council, and the Justice Department, too. IRS records show some twenty-four thousand checks for wage control compliance during Phase II, but they report no statistics on how many violations were found or what action was taken. According to Weber and Mitchell, the Pay Board often found that what seemed to be a violation merited an exception to the rules (p. 239). Very few violations resulted in court cases (the number, it seems, is four), and the authors conclude that "[t]he risk of violating the rules may have appeared greater than was actually the case, at least for a while" (p. 252).

The analytical chapters consider the effects of Phase II controls on wages, labor shortages, income distribution, and industrial relations (contracts, unionization, strikes, etc.). These are interesting questions. We know that controls can suppress but cannot cure inflation; but we do not know much about the way controls differ across industries, who benefits and who loses from controls, and how firms and workers adjust to avoid or reduce the impact of controls. Unfortunately, Weber and Mitchell provide no insights. They take for granted that inflation is a problem of cost-push due to administered prices and wages—a notion with neither theoretical nor empirical support—and dwell on anti-inflation aspects of wage controls. Moreover, their empirical analysis is superficial, so it does not even show what the effects were.

Did the controls hold wages down? Weber and Mitchell think so—especially wages in new union contracts—but their arguments are unpersuasive because they have no estimates of the wage increases that would have occurred in the absence of controls. They simply compare the Phase II rate of change in an aggregate wage index to rates prior to controls (pp. 283-88). They examine differences across industries by comparing average characteristics (unionization, unemployment, etc.) for industries above and below the median wage increase (pp. 288-98). In both cases multiple regression analysis would have been appropriate. Several previous studies estimated the rates of wage change that would have prevailed without controls by substituting control period explanatory variables in a wage equation that was fitted to precontrol data, and concluded that Phase II wage controls were ineffective because actual wage changes exceeded the estimates. Weber and Mitchell claim that those tests are wrong. (Although the wage estimates can be challenged on econometric grounds, they ignore that line of attack.) In their view, wage equation estimates are "normal" (desirable) wage behavior, differences between the actual and estimated rates reflect wage-push inflation, and effective controls reduce that (positive) residual (p. 308). To make any sense of this notion, one has to remember that Weber and Mitchell see wages as being administered rather than market determined. They try several wage equation estimates, and for some find that average residuals during controls are less than precontrol residuals (pp. 309-12). Even if their results were consistent, and even if their wage equations were econometrically sound, there is no theoretical basis for their interpretation of the estimates. All in all, Weber and Mitchell's wage evidence is inadequate to support any conclusion about the effects of Phase II.

The rest of the analysis is even less diligent. They conclude there were no labor shortages because the aggregate quit rate was no higher than expected, the aggregate wage index did not accelerate at the start of Phase III, and the Pay Board found no evidence of shortages (pp. 315–17). As far as income distribution, they refer to two studies that show decreases in profits' share during Phase II. If anything, these results would suggest that the wage controls were ineffective. However, the Pay Board focused on large union bargaining units, so any impact that the controls had would be more likely to show up in cross-sectional analysis. Weber and Mitchell claim that the controls' effects are obscured in aggregate data (p. 383), but they do not explain why they ignored the appropriate analytical approach.

A researcher who is investigating Phase II price and wage controls may find *The Pay Board's Progress* is to be a useful source of institutional information. A general reader will not benefit from wading through this book, though—he will learn more than he wants to know about the Pay Board without learning anything essential about the control of wages and prices.

CHARLES C. COX

Texas A & M University

Ohio State
University Press

May
1981

Journal of Money, Credit and Banking

US ISSN 0022-2879

JOURNAL OF MONEY, CREDIT AND BANKING

ISSN 0022-2879.

JOURNAL OF MONEY, CREDIT AND BANKING

VOLUME XIII NUMBER 2 MAY 1981

ARTICLES

International Currency Substitution and the Apparent Instability of Velocity in Some Western European Economies and in the United States *Bruce Brittain* 135

Monetary Policy and Foreign Price Disturbances Under Flexible Exchange Rates: A Stochastic Approach *Stephen J. Turnovsky* 156

Measurement of the Real Rate of Interest and Related Problems in a World of Uncertainty *Stuart M. Turnbull* 177

The Effects of the Banking Acts of 1933 and 1935 on Capital Investment in Commercial Banking *Gerald P. Dwyer, Jr.* 192

Risk Premia and the Sources of Inflation *Yoram Landskroner and Nissan Liviatan* 205

NOTES, COMMENTS, REPLIES

A Reexamination of the Role of Stocks in the Consumption Function and the Transmission Mechanism *A Note by Geoffrey Woglom* 215

A Dynamic Analysis of the Impact of Fiscal Policy on the Money Supply *A Note by W. Douglas McMillin* 221

Purchasing Power Parity and the Equilibrium Exchange Rate *A Note by Richard N. Barrett* 227

Exchange Market Pressure During the 1970s in Argentina: An Application of the Girton-Roper Monetary Model *A Note by Nelson C. Modeste* 234

Describing Bank Equity Returns: The Year-by-Year Record *A Note by William L. Beedles and Nancy K. Buschmann* 241

(*Continued*)

BOOK REVIEWS

Rational Expectations and Economic Policy, edited by Stanley Fischer
A Review Essay by Stephen A. McCafferty 248

Composite Reserve Assets in the International Monetary System, by Jacob S. Dreyer
Reviewed by Peter B. Clark 254

Corporate Growth and Common Stock Risk, by David R. Fewings
Reviewed by James Ang 257

Inflation: Global, International and National Aspects, by Assar Lindbeck
Reviewed by James M. Boughton 259

Trade and Payments Adjustment Under Flexible Exchange Rates, edited by John P. Martin and Alasdair Smith *Reviewed by Leonard M. Dudley* 262

Bank Credit Cards for EFTS: A Cost Benefit Analysis, by Robert W. McLeod
Reviewed by Lewis Mandell 264

City Lights, by E. Victor Morgan, Richard A. Brealey, Basil S. Yamey, and Paul Bareau *Reviewed by Gordon A. Fletcher* 265

Die deutsche Währung in der Weltwirtschaftskrise 1929–1933 (The German Currency in the World Depression 1929–1933), by Jürgen Schiemann
Reviewed by Walther P. Michael 267

Inflation and the Personal Income Tax: An International Perspective, by Vito Tanzi *Reviewed by Oswald H. Brownlee* 269

Correction: Figures 1 and 2 in "Credit Rationing and Implicit Contract Theory" by Joel Fried and Peter Howitt, in the August 1980 issue, were inadvertently reversed. The figure captioned "Equilibrium Contracts with No Credit Rationing" should have been captioned "The Supply of Credit."

JOURNAL OF MONEY, CREDIT, AND BANKING (ISSN 0022-2879). Published quarterly in February, May, August, and November by the Ohio State University Press, 2070 Neil Avenue, Columbus, Ohio 43210. Richard C. Rose, Managing Editor; Kummi Ranjit, Production Editor; Lisa Satterfield, Assistant Editor; Lois Fausnaugh, Subscriptions Manager; Jeanette White, Secretary to the Editor, Department of Economics, Ohio State University. Second-class postage paid at Columbus, Ohio, and at additional mailing offices.

SUBSCRIPTIONS. Individual: U.S.$20.00 per year; library: U.S.$25.00; student: U.S.$16.00; additional subscriptions to the same address: U.S.$16.00 per subscription. Postage outside the United States: add $3.00 per year. Sustaining Subscriptions: U.S.$5.00 per year. Supporting Subscriptions: U.S.$100 per year. Claims for missing issues must be made within four months of the date of publication. Allow six weeks for address change. Checks should be made payable to the Ohio State University Press, 2070 Neil Avenue, Columbus, Ohio 43210.

MANUSCRIPTS. Manuscripts are to be submitted in triplicate to the Editor, *Journal of Money, Credit, and Banking,* Department of Economics, Ohio State University, 1775 College Road, Columbus, Ohio 43210. Submission fee: individual subscribers U.S.$15; nonsubscribers U.S.$25. Checks are to be made payable to the Journal of Money, Credit, and Banking and enclosed with submitted manuscripts. Complete instructions for preparing text and illustrations may be obtained from the editor.

BRUCE BRITTAIN*

International Currency Substitution and the Apparent Instability of Velocity in Some Western European Economies and in the United States

1. INTRODUCTION

THE PURPOSE OF THIS PAPER is to describe and interpret some empirical regularities in the movements of money's income velocity of circulation in major industrial countries. These movements have tended to be closely coincident, particularly since the beginning of the period of floating exchange rates. These two facts suggest that anomalous velocity movements in any one country may be related to the anomalous velocity movements in the others. Furthermore, all of these movements considered together may have something to do with the shift to flexible exchange rates.

Countries of principal concern in this discussion are the United States and Germany. In the United States unexpectedly low levels of velocity in the early 1970s and unexpectedly high values after 1975 have been one of the main reasons for the monetary authorities' skepticism regarding the advisability of monetary targeting. Attention has focused on the period after mid-1974. Since that time, money-demand forecasts based on equations such as those estimated by Enzler, Johnson, and Paulus [1] significantly overpredict the growth of money demand or underpredict money's income velocity of circulation. (Money in those studies was narrowly defined U.S. money, or M1.) Hamburger [2] has clarified the issue by showing that the prediction errors can, to a large degree, be eliminated by adopting a more general form of the money-demand function. The more general form includes rates

*William A. Allen, Peter Isard, and Warren D. McClam made extensive and useful comments on earlier drafts, as did two anonymous referees. I am responsible for any remaining errors.

BRUCE BRITTAIN *is vice-president, Salomon Brothers, New York.*

0022-2879/81/0581-0135$00.50/0
JOURNAL OF MONEY, CREDIT, AND BANKING, vol. 13, no. 2 (May 1981)

of return on long rather than short-dated government bonds and the price-earnings ratio for equities.

While Hamburger's explanation is compelling—movement in rates of return on U.S. dollar-denominated substitutes for U.S. currency seems to be a reasonable source of change in the behavior of U.S. money—it is interesting to note a coincidence of monetary policy problems and velocity movements in the United States and other countries. Unexpected velocity movements in Switzerland, Germany, Italy, and the United Kingdom have been problematic from the point of view of monetary targeting. Furthermore, velocity movements in these countries have been coincident with movements in the United States. In Switzerland and Germany, for example, money's income velocity of circulation has been unexpectedly low since early 1977, while the U.S. M1 velocity measure has been high. Conversely, the Swiss and German measures were high prior to 1977, when the U.S. measure was low. In addition, anomalous velocity movements can be observed in the United Kingdom and Italy and these, too, follow the pattern of the U.S. movements closely. The German case is particularly interesting since a substantial overshooting of the monetary target in 1978 was attributed to diversification out of dollars and into Deutsche marks.

As I implied in the first paragraph, these empirical regularities would seem to suggest certain limits on any potential explanation of velocity's behavior. First, the factors invoked to explain movements in the United States ought to be admissible as an explanation of movements in Germany, Switzerland, Italy, and the United Kingdom. Second, as coincidental movements of velocity in these five countries have been observed principally since the breakdown of the Bretton Woods fixed exchange rate agreements, they ought to be in some way connected with floating exchange rates. In part 2 of this paper, I shall describe the empirical regularities that justify this line of argument.

In the subsequent section, I shall discuss potential explanations as to why these regularities may have occurred. One possible explanation is that demand for any single national currency may reflect a demand for money to be held in a diversified currency portfolio. Rules for optimal currency diversification could be imposed on this portfolio, so that one might expect to see the proportions of various currencies in the portfolio—as well, therefore, as conventional measures of velocity—varying with the risk and expected rates of return of the specific currencies in the portfolio.

Work by Kouri and Braga de Macedo [4] would seem potentially fruitful in this regard. Based on their model of currency portfolio behavior, I would expect the relevant measures of risk and rate of return to involve the levels and variability of the spot and forward exchange rates as well as the variability of the difference between national inflation rates and interest rates on financial instruments denominated in the domestic currency. Such arguments would be of interest because, on the one hand, they could imply that the porportions of various currencies in the portfolio, and therefore measures of velocity's circulation, might be more stable with greater exchange rate stability. On the other hand, they are interesting because they contrast sharply with others that rely on purely domestic variables to explain velocity's recent behavior.

In part 4 of the paper, I shall present estimates of money-demand functions for the pound sterling, the deutsche mark, and the U.S. dollar. In each case the money-demand formulations reflect the influence of portfolio variables. The estimates are an attempt to test specific forms of the more general portfolio model suggested by the empirical regularities described in the second section of this paper.

The statistical results offer support for the portfolio view. The German equations are most convincing: the portfolio variables are not only significant and of the expected sign, but they are also important in eliminating the bulk of the unexplained increase in German money demand since the end of 1976.

The U.S. equations perform well, with the portfolio variables contributing significantly to the behavior of money demand. The variables do not, however, fully explain the problematic shifts in U.S. money demand after 1971. In the U.S. case, the portfolio approach adds modestly to an understanding of movements in money demand, whereas in the German case the contribution is substantially greater.

The U.K. equations perform worse than either the German or the U.S. equations. While they provide modest support for the hypothesis, the U.K. equations are best evaluated remembering that British exchange control explicitly limited individual attempts at portfolio diversification during the sample period.

2. THE PROBLEMS OF EXPLAINING RECENT VELOCITY MOVEMENTS IN THE UNITED STATES AND GERMANY

There are a number of reasons for being concerned about the behavior of money's income velocity of circulation. The reason that interests me is that velocity's instability has been used to justify a lack of urgency in attempts to target the money stock in a number of different countries. Successful targeting would lower the average money-stock growth rate, reduce its variability and inevitably, and it is to be hoped, bring down the inflation rate.

This tendency to discount the desirability of stable monetary aggregates appears to have a certain justification. As regards the United States, velocity often strays from trend and may do so because the demand for money rather than conditions involving its supply are changing. Indeed, based on simple logarithmic trend calculations for the period 1955 to 1979, between the middle of 1969 and the middle of 1975 velocity moved from a level near 5 percent above its trend value to a level more than 4 percent below. That movement was unexpectedly reversed between end-1975 and late 1978, as the velocity of M1 rose from 4 percent below trend to almost 7 percent above. Is this behavior of U.S. M1 velocity unexplainable?

Hamburger [2] has told us that it is not. By including rates of return on equity and on long-term bonds in simple money-demand functions, he succeeds statistically in explaining a good part of U.S. velocity's unexplained variability. While the argument is attractive as far as it goes, the issue may not yet be closed. My principal concern is that velocity instability in the United States has been an implicit excuse—possibly quite adequate—for exceeding monetary targets in Germany and for dropping them for a time in Switzerland. The German and Swiss explanations of why their own velocity measures dropped so sharply in 1977 and 1978 are that there were shifts out of U.S. dollars and into Swiss francs and deutsche marks. These shifts imply that U.S. money's income velocity of circulation should have risen more than would have been predicted on the basis of purely domestic considerations. The Hamburger explanation has neither explicitly been made consistent with these arguments nor shown them to be incorrect. In addition the Hamburger approach predicts no coincident transnational movements in velocity.

To show why the portfolio shift arguments may be important, I shall consider for a moment the simple correlation coefficients relating the deviations of the log of velocity from trend in the United States, Germany, Italy, Switzerland, and the United Kingdom. The construction of the trends is described in Table 1. The correlation coefficients are reported in Table 2.

There is a strong negative correlation between deviations in Switzerland and Germany, on the one hand, and the United States, Italy, and the United Kingdom, on the other. There are also strong positive correlations within each group. The simple correlation coefficients seem consistent with the idea that individuals favor the deutsche mark and the Swiss franc whenever they disfavor the Italian lira, the pound sterling, and the U.S. dollar, and vice versa.

TABLE 1

CALCULATION OF VELOCITY TRENDS

	Constant	Time	$\bar{R}^2$	D-W	SEE	Frequency	Period
LN(VUK)	7.807 (174.8)	−6.38* (−0.141)	−0.0156	0.165	0.068	Q	1959.I–79.I
LN(VUS)	0.857 (123.1)	0.0072 (89.71)	0.988	0.168	0.023	Q	1955.I–79.II
LN(VIT)	0.718 (27.94)	−0.0057 (−20.67)	0.850	0.444	0.053	Q	1960.I–78.IV
LN(VCH)	−8.682 (−205.3)	0.0021 (4.637)	0.212	0.473	0.088	Q	1960.I–79.I
LN(VDE)	2.300 (174.9)	−2.9† (−2.090)	0.043	0.317	0.027	Q	1960.I–79.I
LN(VUS)	0.851 (65.52)	0.029 (47.7)	0.990	0.517	0.020	A	1955–78
LN(VIT)	0.723 (14.89)	−0.023 (−11.05)	0.871	0.413	0.049	A	1960–78
LN(VDE)	2.294 (92.95)	−9.6† (−0.919)	−0.009	0.806	0.025	A	1960–78

NOTE: *t*-statistics in brackets.
* $\times 10^{-5}$
† $\times 10^{-4}$

TABLE 2

CORRELATION COEFFICIENTS BETWEEN DEVIATIONS OF MONEY'S INCOME VELOCITY OF CIRCULATION FROM TREND FOR FIVE COUNTRIES

	United States	Germany	Italy	Switzerland	United Kingdom
United States	1.0				
Germany	−0.695	1.0			
Italy	0.504	−0.252	1.0		
Switzerland	−0.443	0.447	−0.417	1.0	
United Kingdom	0.516	−0.351	0.532	−0.506	1.0

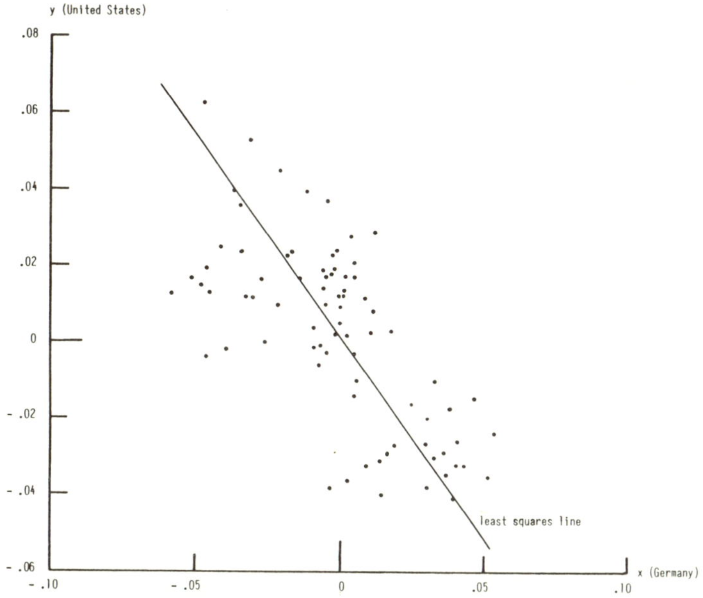

FIG. 1. Deviation of U.S. M1 Velocity of Circulation from Trend versus Deviation of German Central-bank Money from Trend.

As another partial illustration of these points, I have included Figure 1, which is a scattergram relating the deviations of U.S. velocity from trend to the deviation of German velocity from trend. A least-squares line is plotted through the scatter.

These crude statistical measures seem to imply systematic interdependence among deviations of velocity from trend in Italy, the United Kingdom, Germany, Switzerland, and the United States. A worthwhile question is whether this interdependence is useful in explaining any of the particularly sharp, anomalous movements in velocity in the countries concerned, or whether the interdependence reflects coincident movements of a less interesting nature. Is this dependence useful in explaining the tendency for U.S. velocity, for example, to be below trend between 1971 and 1975 and above trend thereafter?

To give a rough answer to this question, I have regressed the log of U.S. M1's income velocity of circulation against time and against various combinations of deviation of other countries' velocity from trend. The results are presented in Table 3. Because of the high degree of collinearity between the Italian and the U.K. variables and between those for Germany and Switzerland, I have excluded the U.K. and Swiss variables from among the list of potential explanatory variables. German and Italian variables are highly correlated, so when the two would have been included together in any regression equation I have subtracted the Italian from the German deviation. The regression results for both annual and quarterly data are presented in Table 3.

The deviation of foreign velocities from trend, as the earlier correlation coeffi-

TABLE 3

REGRESSIONS WITH THE LOG OF U.S. NARROWLY DEFINED MONEY'S INCOME VELOCITY OF CIRCULATION AS THE DEPENDENT VARIABLE

	Explanatory Variables									
Equation	Constant	Time	(X) ERRORDE	(Y) ERRORIT	(X − Y)	$\bar{R}^2$	D-W	SEE	Frequency	Time period
1	0.884	0.0069	−0.324		−0.155	0.992	0.730	0.014	Q	1960.I–78.IV
	(131.3)	(96.12)	(−4.30)		(−4.95)					
2	0.886	0.0069		0.211		0.986	0.326	0.019	Q	1960.I–78.IV
	(97.89)	(71.23)		(5.15)						
3	0.880	0.0070	−0.592			0.989	0.513	0.016	Q	1960.I–79.I
	(111.8)	(83.02)	(−8.55)							
4	0.875	0.028	−0.359		−0.174	0.994	1.981	0.012	A	1960–78
	(74.16)	(55.49)	(−2.33)		(−2.79)					
5	0.875	0.028		0.261		0.987	0.871	0.017	A	1960–78
	(50.88)	(38.07)		(3.034)						
6	0.875	0.028	−0.643			0.992	1.533	0.014	A	1960–78
	(62.14)	(46.50)	(−4.65)							
1′	0.835	0.0004	−0.010		−0.132	0.404	0.510	0.014	Q	1960.I–78.IV
	(121.2)	(5.30)	(−0.13)		(−4.16)					
2′	0.836	0.0004		0.147		0.372	0.470	0.015	Q	1960.I–78.IV
	(118.3)	(5.02)		(4.60)						
3′	0.825	0.0005	−0.287			0.364	0.302	0.018	Q	1960.I–79.II
	(95.6)	(5.69)	(−3.69)							

NOTE: t-statistics in brackets
ERRORDE = error term from quarterly German velocity equation, Table 1.
ERRORIT = error term from quarterly Italian velocity equation, Table 1.

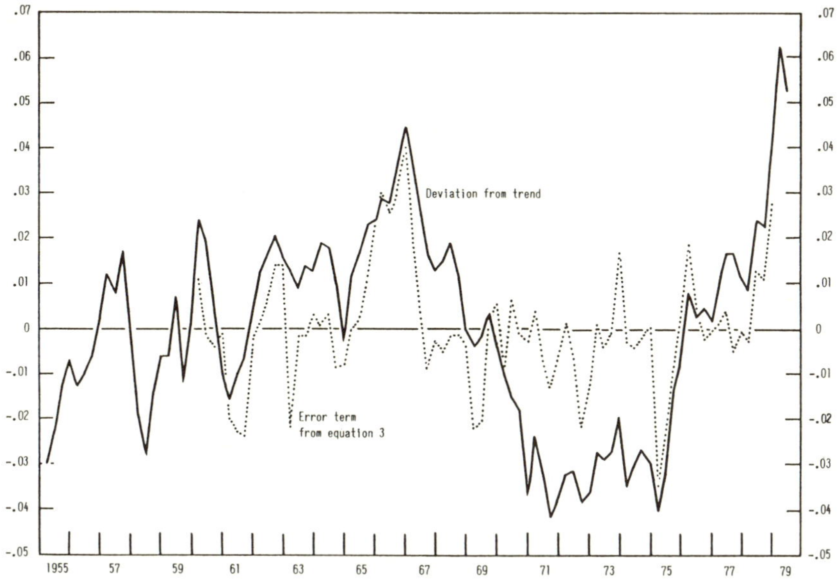

FIG. 2. Deviation of M1 Velocity of Circulation from Trend and Error Term from equation (3) of Table 3.

cients implied they would, significantly improve the explanation of U.S. velocity's behavior, particularly in the turbulent period after 1971. Perhaps the best way of demonstrating the nature of the improvement is to examine the deviations of U.S velocity from trend and the error terms from the regression equations reported in Table 3 and which include velocity as a dependent variable. Figure 2 includes plots of residuals from the equation with both German and Italian variables included, estimated using quarterly data.

In Figure 2 the residuals from equation (1) are compared with the simple deviation of velocity from trend—the trend being derived from the results in Table 1. The first set of residuals appear similar in both the pre- and post-1971 periods. The deviations from trend, by contrast, appear more marked after 1971. In addition, the substantial "unexplained" undershooting of velocity between 1971 and 1975 disappears, as does the current overshooting.[1]

I have argued that U.S. velocity behavior is consistent with, and can be partly explained by, shifting composition of the international money portfolio. Nonetheless, a better argument based on these results is that the behavior of velocity in Germany, Switzerland, Italy, the United Kingdom, and the United States is *jointly* consistent with this shifting composition. To see the implications of this point,

[1]These results were based on an examination of velocity measures calculated using the monetary aggregate that is most closely targeted by the monetary authority in question and thus on M1 for the United States. I have recalculated regressions (1), (2), and (3) reported in Table 3 using U.S. M2. The results are reported as equations (1′), (2′), and (3′) in Table 3.

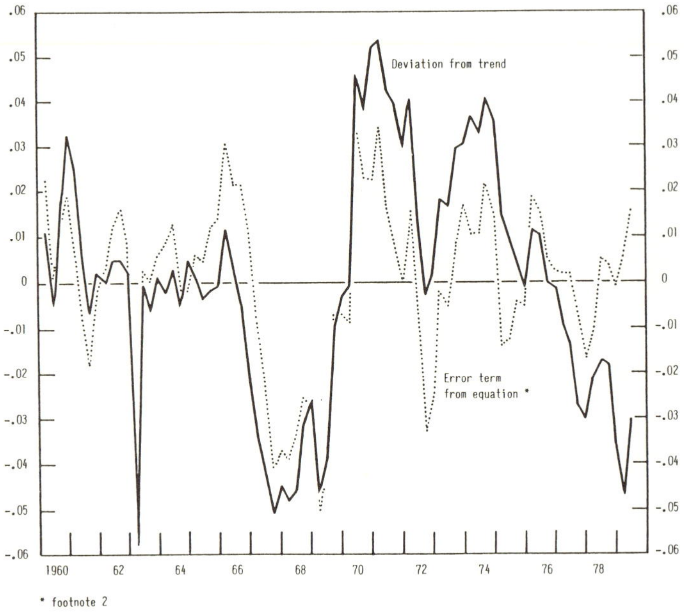

FIG. 3. Deviation of German Central-bank Money Velocity from Trend and Error Term from German Velocity Equation.

consider Figure 3, which includes plots of the residuals of a regression of the log of German velocity on time and the residuals from a regression using time and the U.S. velocity residual as explanatory values.[2] The portfolio argument seems particularly useful in explaining the anomalous movement in German velocity after 1977. Thus, the standard error of the regression of the German velocity equation is reduced from 0.027 to 0.020 by inclusion of the deviation of U.S. velocity from trend. The U.S. velocity equation standard error is reduced from 0.023 to 0.016 by the inclusion of the German error term.

On the basis of these rough comparisons, undertaking further empirical study of international shifts in currency portfolios would seem worthwhile. On the surface of it, unexplained velocity movements in the United States seem related to similar movements in Italy and the United Kingdom, and to opposite movements in Switzerland and Germany. All seem related to exchange rate flexibility. Whether these movements reflect systematic shifts into and out of the Swiss franc and the deutsche mark at the expense of the U.S. dollar, the Italian lira, and the pound sterling or whether they are due to factors unrelated to portfolio shifts is the question taken up in the remainder of the paper.

[2]The actual regression results were:

$$\ln(\text{VDE}) = \underset{(244.6)}{2.31} \; \underset{(-4.17)}{-0.004^{*}\,\text{TIME}} \; \underset{(-8.23)}{-0.775^{*}\,\text{ERRORUS}}$$

$\bar{R}^2 = 0.489$; D-W $= 0.671$; SEE $= 0.0196$.

3. IMPLICATIONS OF MULTICURRENCY PORTFOLIO MODELS FOR THE ESTIMATION OF MONEY-DEMAND FUNCTIONS

The argument of the preceding section established only the coincidence of movements in the velocity of circulation of several major currencies. Although that coincidence suggests that similar factors may have simultaneously influenced velocity in different countries, it does not establish that the movements are behaviorally related and, if they are, what form the relationship might have. This section is an initial attempt at explaining how the coincident movements might have occurred.

An immediately plausible explanation for the transnational similarities in velocity movements is that currencies should be considered elements of internationally diversified portfolios. The theoretical groundwork for this suggestion has been laid by Kouri and Braga de Macedo [4]. There is, of course, ample indirect support for the view among "realists" who explain recent swings in the U.S. dollar in terms of changes in confidence and the rearrangement of currency portfolios.

A potentially useful way of formulating the money-demand function to take account of these portfolio considerations is equation (1):

$$M_i = a + B.R.' + C.V.C' + D.Y', \tag{1}$$

where M_i is the nominal quantity demanded of currency i, one of n currencies, a is a constant term, B, C, and D are $(1 \times n)$ row vectors of coefficients, R is a $(1 \times n)$ row vector of expected opportunity costs of holding the various currencies, V is an $(n \times n)$ variance-covariance matrix of expected opportunity costs, Y is a $(1 \times n)$ row vector of income in the various countries under consideration.

The derivation of a money-demand function incorporating currency portfolio assumptions is presented in the first technical appendix hereto. When there is only one currency, equation (1) very closely approximates the estimating form of standard money-demand functions (cf. [2]). The only difference is that standard forms exclude the variance of the expected return on money—an exclusion that seems unexceptionable in practice if not in theory.

When there are several currencies, the exclusions implied by this simple formulation are somewhat less acceptable. When there are two currencies, this point is easily made. Let us look at the demand, M_C, for country C's currency.

$$M_c = a + b_C^1 \cdot r_C + b_C^2 r_{US} + \sum_{i=1}^{2} \sum_{j=1}^{2} c_{ij} \sigma_i \sigma_j + d_C^1 Y_C + d_C^2 Y_{US};\ i,j = US, C. \tag{2}$$

With regard to the effect that changes in U.S. income might have on M_c, let us suppose that C is a trading partner of the U.S., that trade between C and the U.S. (partly denominated in C's currency) accounts for a significant proportion of U.S.

trade, and that the proportion of U.S. trade to income in C is quite large. An increase in U.S. income could, therefore, produce a measurable increase in the demand for C's currency. The increased demand would be a demand to finance a greater volume of transactions and would be related to the growth of trade. To exclude U.S. income from C's money-demand equation would be to misspecify the function.

Consider now the effects that changes in variances and covariances of expected returns might have on the demand for C's currency. Should σ_C^2 rise relative to σ_{US}^2—perhaps because U.S. inflation is expected to be less variable than C's—then holders of C's currency might be expected to substitute U.S. currency for their own. This effect might be measurable if, for example, residents in C already found it convenient to hold relatively large quantities of U.S. currency for transaction purposes or to finance trade. Similar arguments could be advanced concerning $\sigma_C\ \sigma_{US}$, the covariance of expected returns.

As a final point regarding the importance of the variance and covariance terms in the multicurrency model, σ_C^2 would, for all practical purposes, equal σ_{US}^2, and $\sigma_C\ \sigma_{US}$ would equal unity as long as the exchange rate between the two currencies was expected to remain fixed. Thus, a move to flexible exchange rates would free σ_C^2 and σ_{US}^2 from one another, and $\sigma_C\ \sigma_{US}$ from unity, producing shifts in the demand for C's currency.

Lastly, let us examine the effect that expected rates of return might have on the demand for C's currency. Since increases in r_C represent increases in the opportunity cost of holding C's currency, they should cause a decline in M_c. By contrast, an increase in r_{US} represents an increase in the opportunity cost of holding U.S. currency and should induce an increase in the demand for that of C.

The following objection can be made to this argument. Because differences in the interest rates on assets with similar risk characteristics denominated in different currencies equal the forward exchange agio—by arbitrage—the expected rates of return on investments denominated in various currencies are all equal. Thus, if wealth holders were to attempt to diversify out of domestic currency—say because inflation is expected to rise—domestic interest rates will rise and the exchange rate will fall so that the incentive for diversification is removed. I have, nonetheless, used the uncovered differential in my calculations. I did so for three reasons. The first is that the forward rate may be a biased predictor of the future spot rate. The second is that interest rate levels may be a proxy for the expected variability of prices. The third is that central banks have tended systematically to intervene in foreign exchange markets, tending thereby to inhibit the elimination of incentives to diversity.

As is widely argued [3], the forward exchange rate tends to underestimate the increase in the spot exchange rate when the exchange rate is rising, and to underestimate the decline in the spot exchange rate when it is falling. This possible systematic forecasting error implies that the foreward exchange rate need not equal the expected future spot rate. If this were so, the uncovered differential could be taken as an indicator of the expected opportunity costs of holding a particular currency. Thus if the uncovered interest differential between dollar and deutsche mark instruments rose with an increase in U.S. interest rates, individuals might think the opportunity cost of holding dollars relative to deutsche marks had risen. They would thus diversify out of dollars into deutsche marks.

The second argument for including the uncovered differential is that it approximates the difference in expected variances in the rate of return on two different assets. If the nominal interest rate reflects inflationary expectations and if inflation rates are more variable when they are high, the level of interest rates may also serve to represent the expected variability of the opportunity cost of holding the relevant money. The interest differential may then reflect divergence between the variance of two expected rates of return. Again, as the interest differential widened "in favor" of a particular currency, individuals could be expected to diversify out of that currency because the widening spread may reflect an increase in the riskiness of that currency in their portfolios.

The third argument is that many central banks, particularly the Deutsche Bundesbank during late 1977 and 1978, intervened directly in the foreign exchange markets to minimize fluctuations in the currency. In the German case, exchange market intervention was supported by alterations in the domestic availability of lombard and discount credits. The domestic operations of the Deutsche Bundesbank tended particularly to distort the domestic interest rate structure. Interest rates were held lower than market forces would have dictated when the currency was tending to appreciate and were forced higher during periods of exchange rate weakness. This distortion of market interest rates is another reason why the uncovered interest differential may be taken as an indicator of opportunity costs and thus an appropriate representation of the portfolio diversification variable.

4. ESTIMATING THE PORTFOLIO MODEL

Table 4 presents estimates of demand functions for the U.S. monetary base, U.S. M1, U.S. M2, the German central-bank money stock, German M1, German M3, U.K. M1, and U.K. sterling M3. The estimates are based on quarterly data for the period 1960. I to 1979. II for the United States and Germany, and for the period 1963. I to 1979. II for the United Kingdom. Equation estimates for both stock equilibrium and partial stock adjustment models are described. To parallel Hamburger's article, I have presented a subset of the full regression results that are consistent with his estimating form. Thus estimates of equation (1) are reported in the form (1′):

$$Y/M = a + b.(Y/M)_{t-1} + c.r_d + d.(r_f - r_d), \qquad (1')$$

where $r_f - r_d$ is a foreign less a domestic interest rate.

As I have indicated, the results presented here are a subset of a larger group that are fully set out in Appendix 2 and that are summarized on its first page. To explore the sensitivity of the results to various factors I have estimated models using both annual and quarterly data, various measures of the money stock (described above), stock equilibrium and partial stock adjustment assumptions, and two different measures of the portfolio variable—the one, an interest differential, the other, the absolute value of a foreign interest rate. The summary table and detailed results exclude estimates based on annual data since the outcomes are essentially similar to those based on quarterly data. In addition, I have estimated models using values of the money stock deflated both by nominal income and and by the relevant GNP or GDP deflator.

I undertook to estimate the model in these various forms because statistical problems, common to all money-demand estimates, arose as I estimated these functions. Serial correlation of error terms is a problem in stock equilibrium models estimated using quarterly data. I therefore estimated partial adjustment models using quarterly data and equilibrium models using annual data. Correlation of the portfolio variable with real income was a problem for models in which the endogenous variable was the money stock deflated by the price level. This was another reason for estimating models for which the money stock variable was deflated by the value of gross national or gross domestic product.

As can be seen from Table 4 and from the summary page for Appendix 2, the regression results generally support the portfolio hypothesis: in most instances, the portfolio variable is of the anticipated sign and it is frequently significant. It is most often significant in the German case and in the U.S. case when the models are

TABLE 4

SELECTED REGRESSION RESULTS

Dependent Variable	Constant	Lagged Dependent Variable	Domestic Interest Rate	Portfolio Variable	$\bar{R}^2$	D-W
Germany						
VCBM	0.700	0.688	0.003	−0.003	0.76	2.22
	(4.35)	(9.75)	(−2.89)	(−2.60)		
VM1	0.496	0.713	0.010	−0.002	0.90	2.21
	(5.70)	(14.61)	(5.88)	(−1.98)		
VM3	0.098	0.933	−0.000	−0.003	0.93	1.84
	(1.32)	(19.26)	(−0.15)	(−1.61)		
United States						
VM1	0.002	1.004	−0.001	−0.001	0.99	1.86
	(1.40)	(62.0)	(−0.62)	(−1.68)		
VMBASE	0.010	0.999	0.001	−0.002	0.99	2.18
	(−0.20)	(56.19)	(1.27)	(−2.19)		
VM2	0.096	0.883	0.001	−0.002	0.87	1.76
	(2.04)	(15.83)	(1.21)	(−2.50)		
United Kingdom						
VM3	−0.668	0.915	0.002	−0.002	0.84	1.67
	(−1.42)	(15.29)	(0.53)	(−1.01)		
VM3	−7.922		0.027	−0.022	0.25	0.24
	(−289.3)		(4.79)	(−3.85)		
VM1	−1.47	0.873	−0.008	0.002	0.97	2.74
	(−3.38)	(27.03)	(−3.33)	(0.62)		
VM1	−1.29		−0.034	−0.009	0.57	0.289
	(−30.97)		(−4.02)	(−0.99)		

NOTE: t-statistics in brackets; quarterly data, 1960.I to 1979.II except for the United Kingdom, 1963.I to 1979.II.

estimated using quarterly data. The hypothesis is less strongly supported by the U.K. results. Generally speaking, estimation of partial stock adjustment models eliminates the problems of serial correlation of error terms but lowers the calculated values of t-statistics on the portfolio variables. The signs of the portfolio variable coefficients are, broadly speaking, unaltered by choice of estimating form, frequency of data, or form of the portfolio variable.

Anomalies arose, however, and it may be best to deal with them on a country-by-country basis. Strongest support comes from the German case in which all models estimated in stock equilibrium form give coefficients of the correct sign and in which only a small minority are statistically insignificant. Correcting for serial correlation of error terms by estimating stock adjustment models reduces the significance of the coefficients only somewhat, as does correction by estimation with annual data.

The case of the United States provides substantial support for the hypothesis as well—at least on the basis of estimates in which the dependent variables are measures of velocity. Results are unclear for equations in which the dependent variables are values of the money stock divided by the price level—these equations consistently display significant serial correlation of error terms despite changes in the estimating form and in the frequency of the data.

U.K. money-demand estimates provide the least support for the portfolio hypothesis. While all estimates involving the stock equilibrium assumption—on both quarterly and annual data and on all estimating forms—produce coefficients of the correct sign and of which half are significant, the estimating equations' error terms show high degrees of serial correlation. All attempts to correct for this substantially reduce the significance of the coefficient estimates and in some cases actually reverse their sign. Sterling M3 based models generally perform better than models based on M1. I attribute the superiority of the M3 models to the extreme interest sensitivity of M1 to movements of domestic interest rates. A possible reason for the relative inferiority of the British results is the existence of British exchange controls. Comparison of British interest levels with those in Germany show that there was a systematic trend in the two that should have induced diversification out of sterling and into Deutsche marks over the sample period. Virtually all sterling balances are held by residents of the United Kingdom, however, and until recently, they have been severely restricted in their access to foreign currency balances. Systematic regulation of the markets which prevents portfolio diversification is one reason why the portfolio hypothesis is only weakly supported by the U.K. evidence. Tightly enforced exchange controls would have to have been violated for the hypothesis to have been supported.

While the German results are the strongest evidence of international currency portfolio diversification, the U.S. results are also suggestive since explanations of U.S. velocity are improved by considering changes in the financial conditions obtaining in the markets for foreign currencies. To explore how much foreign developments may contribute to explaining the behavior of U.S. velocity, it may be useful to see how the Hamburger [2] equation changes when a foreign interest rate

TABLE 5

ESTIMATED U.S. M1 VELOCITY EQUATIONS AUGMENTED BY PORTFOLIO VARIABLES (quarterly data, 1960.II to 1979.II)

Constant	Lagged Dependent Variable	DP	RGL	RCB	RUS	RDE	RD	$\bar{R}^2$	D-W
0.805		−0.042	0.026	0.113			−0.011	0.96	0.32
(27.58)		(−1.50)	(3.11)	(10.57)			(−4.16)		
0.032	0.965	−0.001	0	0.006			−0.001	0.99	1.84
(1.19)	(29.77)	(−0.10)	(−0.01)	(1.26)			(−1.84)		
0.817		−0.012	0.025	0.114		0.011		0.96	0.32
(34.76)		(−1.67)	(3.03)	(10.63)		(−4.00)			
0.042	0.954	0.002	0.003	0.007		−0.002		0.99	1.81
(1.48)	(28.44)	(0.22)	(0.98)	(1.42)		(−2.17)			
0.942		−0.288			0.038		−0.021	0.73	0.29
(13.46)		(−4.66)			(5.12)		(−2.80)		
0.002	1.005	0.001			−0.001		−0.001	0.99	1.86
(0.15)	(83.75)	(0.13)			(−0.62)		(−1.67)		
0.942		−0.288			0.060	−0.021		0.73	0.29
(13.46)		(−4.66)			(8.14)	(−2.80)			
0.002	1.005	0.001			0.001	−0.001		0.99	1.86
(0.15)	(83.75)	(0.13)			(0.78)	(−1.67)			

NOTE: Where DP is the price dividend ratio on common stocks, RGL is the long-term government bond yield, RCP is the interest rate paid on passbook accounts at commercial banks, RUS is the 90-day US Treasury bill rate, RDE is the 90-day German Treasury bill rate, and RD is RDE-RUS; *t*-statistics in parentheses.

or a covered interest differential is added. Likewise, it may be useful to see how the demand equation for U.S. dollars, viewed as one component of an internationally diversified portfolio, behaves when the price dividend ratio for common stocks suggested by Hamburger is added.

Table 5 includes the results of estimating the equation suggested by Hamburger augmented by either the uncovered interest differential between U.S. interest rates and German interest rates or by the German interest rate. Likewise, the table includes results of the equation suggested by international portfolio diversification considerations augmented by the dividend price ratio. I have used Hamburger's naming convention so that DP is the price dividend ratio for common stocks, RGL is the rate of return on long-term government bonds, and RCB is the interest rate on pass-book savings accounts at commercial banks.

I have not reported the results of estimating the exact equation suggested by Hamburger since the price dividend ratio performed more poorly than in those reported here. Rather than taking the logs of the domestic interest rate variables, I included them as they were. The results show quite clearly that both the covered interest differential and the German interest rate contribute significantly to improving the explanatory power of the equation suggested by Hamburger. Conversely, the dividend price ratio contributes significantly to the explanatory power of equations suggested by currency portfolio diversification considerations when these are estimated in stock equilibrium form (although in these cases, the estimates exhibit significant serial correlation of error terms). When the equations are estimated in stock adjustment form, the price-dividend's contribution falls significantly.

5. CONCLUSION

These results and the recent behavior of short-term interest rates in the United States and Germany suggest that basic supply conditions expressed in terms of relative opportunity costs and variances of expected rates of return on U.S. dollars and on deutsche marks have since 1970 grown slowly to favor the deutsche mark. Since 1976 that shift has speeded up drastically. U.S. M1 velocity movements, while clearly influenced by factors suggested by Hamburger [2], have nonetheless been significantly affected by shorter-term fluctuations in the variables inducing these international portfolio shifts. The various measures of Germany's velocity of circulation have been even more significantly affected, and particularly in the period since 1976. During that period increases in the opportunity cost and in the risk associated with holding dollars have argued strongly in favor of a shift in currency demand toward the deutsche mark.

APPENDIX 1

The purpose of this appendix is explicitly to derive a variant of the demand-for-money function, estimates of which are discussed in the main body of the text. I have made the assumption that the individual portfolio holder's motive is to minimize the expected opportunity cost on his currency portfolio, subject to his attitudes towards risk and to the cost of holding transaction balances denominated in various currencies.

The derivation of money-demand functions relying on cost minimization in a situation of uncertainty is equivalent to the problem of maximizing the value of a portfolio of risky securities over time, so I shall not go into detail on that aspect of the problem. I would, however, like to discuss the role of the income variables in the estimating equations. According to equation (1) in the text, the demand function for any particular currency should, in principle, include the levels of income in all countries. I would like to discuss one simple reason as to why that may be so.

Assuming the portfolio owner to be engaged in international trade, it may be reasonable to suppose that, in addition to the cost-minimizing-subject-to-risk aspect of his demand for cash, he will also distinguish among currencies for transaction purposes. He will find it convenient to hold individual currencies as some function of his transactions denominated in that currency. If this is the case, then the costs associated with the various transactions technologies in the areas concerned might be expected to determine optimal—or cost-minimizing—shares of various currencies in his portfolio. These shares will have certain values when the variances and covariances of expected returns are all zero, and I shall define these proportions as being the row vector $\mathbf{A}$ in the following discussion. Costs may be thought of as rising whenever one of the individual components of A, the actual shares, diverge from $\mathbf{A}$. I assume that these costs rise by amounts that are independent of the sign of the deviation of a_i from $\mathbf{a}_i$ and of the currency under consideration.

I assume that the cost function is of the form:

$$C = A.R' - 0.5BAVA' - 0.5GA\mathbf{A}', \tag{A1}$$

where: A, R, V, and $\mathbf{A}$ have already been defined; B is a measure of risk aversion; and G is a measure of the costs associated with deviations of the portfolio shares from their zero risk values. The problem is to derive an expression for A, which I do by maximizing equation (A1) subject to the construction that Ae', the sum of the portfolio shares, equals unity (e is a $(1 \times n)$ vector of ones). Thus, I differentiate the Lagrangian function (A2) with respect to A and to L, and set the partial derivatives to zero.

$$M = AR' - 0.5BAVA' - 0.5GA'A - L(Ae' - 1) \tag{A2}$$

$$\partial M/\partial A = R' - BVA' - G\mathbf{A} = Le' \tag{A3}$$

$$\partial M/\partial L = Ae' - 1 = 0. \tag{A4}$$

Equations (A3) and (A4) imply (A5).

$$\begin{pmatrix} A' \\ -L \end{pmatrix} = \begin{pmatrix} -BV & -e' \\ e & O \end{pmatrix}^{-1} \cdot \begin{pmatrix} R' - G\mathbf{A} \\ 1 \end{pmatrix}. \tag{A5}$$

It is easily verified that equation (A5) has the properties of the model described by Kouri and Braga de Macedo [4], for the last column vector on the right-hand side of the equation.

Equation (A5) implies that a currency's share in the portfolio should rise as the result of a decline in its opportunity cost, a decline in the variance of its own expected returns, an increase in the variance of the other country's opportunity cost, or a decrease in its expected opportunity cost. Similarly, an increase in income in Y_i will increase the share of M_i depending on how intensively M_i is used in transactions denominated in terms of the currency of country i.

APPENDIX 2

List of Variables (Sources: OECD, Main Economic Indicators, and Data Resources, Inc.)

Variables relating to U.K. money-demand functions

- VM1, VM3 = narrowly defined U.K. money stock "M1," and "sterling M3" divided by U.K. nominal gross domestic product
- RM1, RM3 = U.K. "M1" and "sterling M3" divided by the gross domestic product deflator
- RY = real gross domestic product
- RF = rate of return on 90-day German Treasury bills
- RUK = rate of return on 90-day U.K. Government Treasury bills
- RD = RUK less RF

Variables relating to U.S. money-demand functions

- VM1, VM2, VMB = narrowly defined U.S. money "M1," broadly defined U.S. money "M2," and the U.S. monetary base divided by U.S. nominal gross national product
- RM1, RM2, RMB = "M1," "M2" and the monetary base divided by the gross national product deflator
- RY = real gross national product
- RUS = rate of return on 90-day U.S. Government Treasury bills
- RF = rate of return on 90-day German Government Treasury bills
- RD = RUS less RF

Variables relating to German money-demand equations

- VMCB, VM1, VM3 = German "central-bank money stock," narrowly defined money "M1," and broadly defined money "M3" divided by German nominal gross national product
- RMCB, RM1, RM3 = "central-bank money stock," "M1," and "M3" divided by the gross national product deflator
- RDE = rate of return on 90-day German Government Treasury bills
- RF = rate of return on 90-day U.S. Government Treasury bills
- RD = RDE less RF

APPENDIX 2.1

SUMMARY OF REGRESSION RESULTS: SIGN AND SIGNIFICANCE OF THE CURRENCY SUBSTITUTION VARIABLE'S COEFFICIENT

Portfolio Variable:	Uncovered Differential		Foreign Interest Rate	
Frequency:	Quarterly		Quarterly	
Lagged Dependent Variable:	Present	Absent	Present	Absent
Dependent variable and country				
United Kingdom				
VM3	S	SS	S	SS
VM1	*O*	S	*O*	S
RM3	S	SS	S	SS
RM1	*O*	S	*O*	S
United States				
VM1	*SS*	SS	*SS*	SS
VMB	*SS*	SS	*SS*	SS
VM2	*SS*	SS	*SS*	SS
RM1	X	X	X	SS
RMB	*O*	SS	*O*	SS
RM2	*O*	SS	O	SS
Germany				
VM	*SS*	SS	*SS*	SS
VM1	*SS*	SS	*SS*	SS
VM3	*SS*	SS	*SS*	SS
RM	*SS*	SS	*X*	S
RM1	*SS*	SS	*SS*	SS
RM3	*S*	SS	*S*	SS

NOTES: S indicates coefficient of correct sign; SS indicates correct sign and significant at the 5 percent level; O indicates wrong sign; X indicates wrong sign and significant at the 5 percent level; italicized letter (e.g., *SS*) indicates that the equation from which the coefficient is drawn shows no significant serial correlation of error terms.

APPENDIX 2.2

THE UNITED KINGDOM (quarterly data, 1963.I to 1979.II)

	Constant	Lagged Dependent Variable	RY	RUK	RD	$\bar{R}^2$	D-W
VM3	−7.922			0.027	−0.022	0.25	0.240
	(−289.3)			(4.79)	(−3.85)		
VM3	−0.688	0.915		0.002	−0.002	0.84	1.670
	(−1.41)	(15.29)		(0.53)	(−1.01)		
VM1	−1.290			−0.034	−0.009	0.57	0.289
	(−30.97)			(−4.02)	(−0.99)		
VM1	−0.147	0.873		−0.008	0.002	0.97	2.744
	(−3.38)	(27.03)		(−3.33)	(0.62)		
RM3	−5.756		0.805	0.032	−0.021	0.82	0.266
	(−5.58)		(8.96)	(5.37)	(−3.86)		
RM3	−0.736	0.959	0.080	−0.002	−0.002	0.97	1.315
	(−1.41)	(17.16)	(1.39)	(−0.76)	(−0.60)		
RM1	9.66		0.014	−0.004	−0.006	0.19	0.330
	(13.06)		(0.22)	(−0.93)	(−1.41)		
RM1	0.599	0.837	0.093	−0.009	0.002	0.81	2.530
	(0.80)	(14.12)	(2.76)	(−4.10)	(0.89)		

APPENDIX 2.3

THE UNITED KINGDOM (quarterly data, 1963.I to 1979.II)

	Constant	Lagged Dependent Variable	RY	RUK	RDE	$\bar{R}^2$	D-W
VM3	−0.668	0.915		−0.001	0.003	0.84	1.67
	(−1.41)	(15.29)		(−1.41)	(1.01)		
VM3	−7.922			0.005	0.022	0.24	0.24
	(−289.3)			(1.54)	(3.85)		
VM1	−0.147	0.873		−0.007	−0.002	0.96	2.74
	(−3.33)	(27.00)		(−3.79)	(−0.62)		
VM1	−1.290			−0.042	0.009	0.57	0.29
	(−30.97)			(−9.11)	(0.99)		
RM3	−0.736	0.959	0.080	−0.004	0.002	0.97	1.31
	(−1.41)	(17.16)	(1.39)	(−2.05)	(0.60)		
RM3	−5.756		0.805	0.011	0.021	0.82	0.27
	(−5.76)		(8.96)	(2.65)	(3.86)		
RM1	0.599	0.837	0.093	−0.007	−0.002	0.81	2.53
	(0.80)	(14.12)	(2.76)	(−4.73)	(−0.89)		
RM1	9.666		0.067	−0.010	0.006	0.19	0.33
	(13.06)		(0.22)	(−3.10)	(1.41)		

APPENDIX 2.4

THE UNITED STATES (quarterly data, 1960.II to 1979.II)

	Constant	Lagged Dependent Variable	RY	RUS	RD	$\bar{R}^2$	D-W
VM1	0.002	1.004		−0.001	−0.001	0.99	1.86
	(0.15)	(96.16)		(−0.62)	(−1.68)		
VM1	1.233			0.050	−0.298	0.66	0.34
	(34.70)			(6.32)	(−3.55)		
VMB	0.010	0.999		−0.001	−0.002	0.99	2.18
	(0.20)	(50.19)		(−1.27)	(−2.19)		
VMB	2.420			0.033	−0.012	0.70	0.39
	(130.3)			(7.91)	(−2.77)		
VM2	0.096	0.883		0.001	−0.002	0.87	1.76
	(2.04)	(15.83)		(1.21)	(−2.50)		
VM2	0.842			0.005	−0.004	0.42	0.41
	(128.9)			(3.48)	(−2.59)		
RM1	−0.378	1.076	−0.001	−0.005	−0.002	0.98	1.45
	(−2.91)	(37.06)	(−0.16)	(−5.79)	(−2.74)		
RM1	4.145		0.181	−0.003	0.129	0.63	0.17
	(20.50)		(5.88)	(−0.96)	(4.76)		
RMB	0.013	0.869	0.082	−0.003	−0.000	0.99	1.69
	(0.25)	(12.16)	(2.07)	(−4.05)	(−0.76)		
RMB	0.466		0.560	−0.001	0.003	0.99	0.54
	(7.15)		(56.53)	(−0.79)	(3.01)		
RM2	−0.166	0.937	0.084	−0.005	−0.000	0.99	1.33
	(−2.88)	(20.46)	(1.85)	(−6.85)	(−0.63)		
RM2	−0.850		1.001	−0.005	0.004	0.99	0.41
	(−7.01)		(54.33)	(−2.60)	(2.51)		

APPENDIX 2.5

THE UNITED STATES (quarterly data, 1960.II to 1979.II)

	Constant	Lagged Dependent Variable	RY	RUS	RDE	$\bar{R}^2$	D-W
VM1	0.002	1.004		0.001	−0.001	0.99	1.86
	(0.15)	(96.16)		(0.78)	(−1.68)		
VM1	1.233			0.080	−0.030	0.66	0.34
	(34.70)			(12.03)	(−3.55)		
VMB	0.010	0.999		0.000	−0.001	0.99	2.18
	(0.20)	(50.19)		(0.41)	(−2.19)		
VMB	2.42			0.045	−0.012	0.70	0.39
	(130.3)			(12.95)	(−2.77)		
VM2	0.096	0.883		0.003	−0.002	0.87	1.76
	(2.04)	(15.83)		(3.93)	(−2.50)		
VM2	0.842			0.009	−0.004	0.42	0.41
	(128.9)			(7.42)	(−2.59)		
RM1	−0.378	1.076	−0.001	−0.003	−0.002	0.98	1.45
	(−2.91)	(37.06)	(−0.16)	(−3.59)	(−2.74)		
RM1	0.842			0.009	−0.003	0.42	0.41
	(128.9)			(7.43)	(−2.59)		
RMB	0.013	0.869	0.082	−0.002	−0.000	0.99	1.69
	(0.25)	(12.16)	(2.07)	(−3.20)	(−0.76)		
RMB	0.466		0.560	−0.003	0.002	0.99	0.54
	(7.15)		(56.53)	(−2.99)	(3.01)		
RM2	−0.165	0.937	0.084	−0.005	−0.000	0.99	1.33
	(−2.88)	(20.46)	(1.85)	(−5.71)	(−0.63)		
RM2	−0.850		1.001	−0.009	0.004	0.99	0.41
	(−7.01)		(54.33)	(−4.31)	(2.51)		

APPENDIX 2.6

GERMANY (quarterly data, 1960.II to 1979.II)

	Constant	Lagged Dependent Variable	RY	RDE	RD	$\bar{R}^2$	D-W
VCBM	0.700	0.688		0.003	−0.003	0.76	2.22
	(4.35)	(9.75)		(2.89)	(−2.60)		
VCBM	2.27			0.005	−0.009	0.46	0.71
	(295.2)			(2.82)	(−6.23)		
VM1	0.496	0.713		0.010	−0.002	0.90	2.21
	(5.70)	(14.61)		(5.88)	(−1.98)		
VM1	1.765			0.025	−0.005	0.62	0.55
	(150.70)			(9.38)	(−2.46)		
VM3	1.531			−0.021	−0.027	0.57	0.32
	(102.4)			(−6.30)	(−9.72)		
VM3	0.098	0.933		−0.000	−0.003	0.93	1.84
	(1.32)	(19.26)		(−0.15)	(−1.61)		
RCBM	−0.026	0.952	0.040	−0.004	0.002	0.99	1.53
	(−0.391)	(39. 02)	(1.61)	(−4.12)	(2.20)		
RCBM	−1.930		0.959	0.001	0.003	0.97	0.18
	(−9.40)		(28.07)	(0.311)	(0.664)		
RM1	−0.309	0.784	0.233	−0.008	0.004	0.99	2.29
	(−3.58)	(14.71)	(5.13)	(−5.29)	(2.16)		
RM1	−1.033		0.878	−0.014	0.017	0.98	0.80
	(−7.325)		(37.44)	(−4.69)	(5.83)		
RM3	−0.372	0.845	0.180	−0.001	0.002	0.99	1.46
	(−2.63)	(17.27)	(3.16)	(0.47)	(1.26)		
RM3	−2.345		1.136	0.009	0.014	0.98	0.28
	(−12.48)		(36.36)	(2.35)	(3.495)		

APPENDIX 2.7

GERMANY (quarterly data, 1960.II to 1979.II)

	Constant	Lagged Dependent Variable	RY	RDE	RUS	$\bar{R}^2$	D-W
VCBM	0.700	0.688		0.006	−0.003	0.76	2.22
	(4.35)	(9.75)		(4.40)	(−2.60)		
VCBM	2.266			0.014	−0.009	0.46	0.71
	(295.2)			(7.64)	(−6.23)		
VM1	0.496	0.713		0.012	−0.002	0.90	2.21
	(5.70)	(14.61)		(6.49)	(−1.98)		
VM1	1.765			0.030	−0.005	0.62	0.55
	(150.70)			(10.87)	(−2.46)		
VM3	0.098	0.932		0.002	−0.003	0.93	1.84
	(1.32)	(19.26)		(1.72)	(−1.61)		
VM3	1.53			0.006	−0.027	0.57	0.32
	(102.4)			(1.73)	(−9.72)		
RCBM	−0.026	0.952	0.040	−0.002	−0.002	0.99	1.53
	(−0.391)	(39.02)	(1.61)	(−2.506)	(−2.20)		
RCBM	−1.930		0.959	−0.001	0.002	0.97	0.18
	(−9.40)		(28.07)	(−0.43)	(0.66)		
RM1	−0.309	0.748	0.233	−0.012	0.004	0.99	2.29
	(−3.58)	(14.71)	(5.134)	(−6.79)	(2.16)		
RM1	−1.033		0.878	−0.032	0.017	0.98	0.80
	(−7.33)		(37.44)	(−13.19)	(5.83)		
RM3	−0.372	0.844	0.180	−0.003	0.002	0.99	1.46
	(−2.63)	(17.27)	(3.16)	(−2.30)	(1.26)		
RM3	−2.345		1.136	−0.004	0.014	0.98	0.28
	(−12.48)		(36.36)	(−1.38)	(3.50)		

LITERATURE CITED

1. Enzler, Jared, Lewis Johnson, and John Paulus. "Some Problems of Money Demand." *Brookings Papers on Economic Activity I* (1976), 261-80.

2. Hamburger, Michael J. "Behaviour of the Money Stock: Is There a Puzzle?" *Journal of Monetary Economics,* 3 (1977), 265-88.

3. Isard, Peter. "Exchange Rate Determination: A Survey of Popular Views and Recent Models." *Princeton Studies in International Finance,* 42 (1978), 12–14.

4. Kouri, Pentti J. K., and Jorge Braga de Macedo. "Exchange Rates and the International Adjustment Process." *Brookings Papers on Economic Activity I* (1978), 111-50.

STEPHEN J. TURNOVSKY*

Monetary Policy and Foreign Price Disturbances Under Flexible Exchange Rates

A Stochastic Approach

1. INTRODUCTION

THE ANALYSIS OF MONETARY POLICY under flexible exchange rates has received extensive treatment during recent years. Particular attention has been devoted to the role of exchange rate expectations, with a general conclusion being that many of the propositions of the traditional static Fleming-Mundell model (see Fleming [8] and Mundell [19]) require substantial modification once such expectations are taken into account (see [5, 21, 24]). With few exceptions, the analysis has been carried out in a deterministic framework. The usual assumption made is that any monetary expansion that is introduced is initially (ex ante) unanticipated, but having taken place, it is then (ex post) expected to be permanent. This assumption underlies, for example, the recent contribution by Dornbusch [5] and much of the subsequent work that stems from it.[1]

This assumption, while very natural, is also a polar one. In practice, agents in the economy may attempt to anticipate monetary policy and the policies themselves

*I am grateful for helpful comments received from members of seminars at the University of Minnesota, Virginia Polytechnic Institute, and Duke University.

[1]This statement refers to the bulk of the literature that deals with *unannounced* monetary expansions. Recently, some authors have analyzed the effects of a *preannounced* monetary expansion [14, 26]. Obviously this is anticipated by the time it actually takes place.

STEPHEN J. TURNOVSKY *is professor of economics, Australian National University.*

0022-2879/81/0581-0156$00.50/0
JOURNAL OF MONEY, CREDIT, AND BANKING, vol. 13, no. 2 (May 1981)

may, and may be expected to, vary in their permanency. It is intuitively clear that the effects of monetary policy—and for that matter any other policy—will vary substantially, depending upon the extent to which it is predicted and the permanence with which it is expected to continue. This view would seem to be one of the central messages to emerge from the current rational expectations literature.

The prime objective of the present paper is to analyze the effects of monetary policy under flexible exchange rates, allowing for more general assumptions regarding these kinds of expectational issues. To do so, it is desirable to develop the analysis within a stochastic framework. But having constructed the framework, it is then straightforward to use it to investigate similar kinds of issues with respect to other exogenous disturbances. Of these, one of the more interesting concerns foreign price disturbances. This has also been receiving increased attention recently, with economists investigating the extent to which flexible exchange rates insulate the domestic economy against such disturbances (see [10, 15, 16, 25]). Yet precisely the same limitation characterizes the existing literature in this area; it deals with ex ante unanticipated, but ex post expected permanent, changes in the foreign price level. Thus a secondary objective of the paper is to generalize these kinds of assumptions about foreign price changes.

Like much of the current work on exchange rate determination, expectations play a central role in our analysis. The expectations of the endogenous variables appearing in the model (the one period expectations of the exchange rate and the cost of living) are assumed to be consistent with the structure of the model and conditional on the predictions of the exogenous variables (the money supply and foreign price level). Through this process the predictions of all future exogenous variables impinge on the current state of the economy. Such a rational expectations framework is attractive and natural for analyzing the kinds of expectational issues we have noted, enabling us to distinguish explicitly between actual and anticipated changes on the one hand, and permanent and temporary changes on the other. Indeed the application to exchange rate determination is not new. This framework has been employed recently by Frenkel [11], Mussa [20], Barro [1], and Cox [4], among others, and the present paper can be viewed as an extension of this work. In particular, more attention is devoted to analyzing the response of the complete system to alternative forms of monetary disturbances.[2]

The rest of the paper proceeds as follows. Section 2 details the model and reduces it to a form convenient for further analysis. In order to determine the short-run equilibrium, it is first necessary to solve the system for the endogenously determined rational expectations, and this is undertaken in section 3. After summarizing the short-run equilibrium in section 4, the following section analyzes the effects of a variety of anticipated and actual monetary disturbances. Section 6 briefly deals with the effects of foreign price disturbances, while our main conclusions are summarized in the final section.

[2]In some respects our analysis parallels Fischer's [7] recent paper analyzing the neutrality of monetary disturbances in a closed economy.

2. STOCHASTIC MODEL OF AN OPEN ECONOMY UNDER FLEXIBLE EXCHANGE RATES

The model we shall develop shares much in common with the recent models emphasizing the monetary approach to exchange rate determination (see [1, 5, 14, 22]).[3] Two general features we wish to stress at the outset are the following. First, the country is assumed to produce a single (composite) commodity, part of which is consumed domestically, the remainder of which is exported. The price of this commodity is determined in the market for domestic output, so that the price of exports is endogenously determined. On the other hand, we assume that the country is sufficiently competitive in the market for its imports to take the (foreign) price of imports as given. Second, the domestic bond market is assumed to be perfectly integrated with that in the rest of the world. Thus the model is described by the following five equations:

$$Y_t = d_1 Y_t - d_2[r_t - (C^*_{t+1,t} - C_t)] + d_3[Q_t + E_t - P_t],$$
$$0 < d_1 < 1,\ d_2 > 0,\ d_3 > 0 \tag{1a}$$

$$C_t = \delta P_t + (1-\delta)(Q_t + E_t) \tag{1b}$$

$$M_t - C_t = \alpha_1 Y_t - \alpha_2 r_t, \qquad \alpha_1 > 0,\ \alpha_2 > 0 \tag{1c}$$

$$r_t = \rho + E^*_{t+1,t} - E_t \tag{1d}$$

$$Y_t = \alpha + \gamma_1[P_t - C^*_{t,t-1}] + \gamma_2[P_t - P^*_{t,t-1}],\ \gamma_1 > 0,\ \gamma_2 > 0 \tag{1e}$$

where

Y_t = real domestic output at time t, expressed in logarithms
r_t = domestic nominal interest rate at time t
ρ = the foreign nominal interest rate, taken to be exogenous and fixed
P_t = price of domestically produced good (in terms of domestic currency), expressed in logarithms
Q_t = price of imported good (in terms of foreign currency), expressed in logarithms
E_t = logarithm of the current exchange rate (measured in units of the domestic currency per unit of foreign currency)
C_t = domestic cost of living (measured in domestic currency), expressed in logarithms
M_t = domestic nominal supply expressed in logarithms
$E^*_{t+s,t}$ = expectations of E for time $t+s$, held at time t; $s = 1,2,\ldots$, all t

[3]It is worth noting that these models vary considerably with respect to their detailed specification. Some (e.g., [5]) assume sticky prices with goods market disequilibrium; others, including the present analysis, assume that the domestic goods market clears each period; still others (e.g., [1]) assume that the domestic goods market is perfectly integrated with that in the rest of the world. Not surprisingly, these differences in assumptions account to some extent for the differences in implications, particularly with respect to exchange rate overshooting.

$C^*_{t+s,t}$ = expectation of C for time $t+s$, held at time t; $s = 1,2,\ldots$, all t
$P^*_{t+s,i}$ = expectation of P for time $t+s$, held at time t; $s = 1,2,\ldots$, all t.

Before proceeding further, the following points regarding the formulation should be noted. First, the specification of some variables in terms of logarithms is purely for convenience, enabling us to avoid problems of linearization, which would otherwise be necessary. Second, as our concern is with the distinction between actual and anticipated components of the money supply and foreign price level, the only random disturbances we need consider are embodied in these variables. Additive random variables could be appended to each of these relationships, but these would be of no relevance for the issues we wish to discuss.

Equation (1a) describes the domestic economy's *IS* curve. The demand for domestic output varies positively with domestic income and the relative price of foreign to domestic goods.[4] It varies inversely with the real rate of interest, which is defined to be the domestic nominal rate, less the expected rate of inflation of the domestic CPI. Equation (1b) defines the domestic CPI to be a multiplicatively weighted average of the price of domestic goods and the domestic price of foreign goods. While we choose this form primarily for convenience, it does have some theoretical merit. It is the "true" cost of living index if the domestic residents' utility function, defined with domestic goods and foreign goods as arguments, is Cobb-Douglas (see [23]). The relative weight δ can be used to parameterize the degree of openness of the economy; the larger δ, the less open the economy and vice versa.

The monetary sector is summarized in equations (1c) and (1d). The first of these equations describes the domestic *LM* curve, making the usual assumption that all domestic money is held by domestic residents who also hold no foreign currency.[5] Note that the domestic stock of money is deflated by the overall CPI, reflecting the fact that part of the transactions demand for money is for imports. The specification of the real transactions variable by Y follows convention, though it is at best only a proxy. A more accurate measure of real transactions would involve some weighted average of the consumption of imports plus domestic goods. But this would be intractable, since these components of aggregate consumption are themselves endogenous.[6] The assumption of perfect capital market integration is embodied in the interest rate parity condition, equation (1d). The domestic nominal interest rate r_t equals the exogenous world rate ρ plus the expected rate of exchange depreciation.

Finally, the supply of domestic output is governed by equation (1e). This resembles a Lucas [17] supply function, although as Flood [9] has argued, with both international and intranational trading, this rationale is inappropriate. Rather, it may be justified in terms of the wage determinaion model of Gray [13] and Fischer [6].

[4]We abstract from wealth effects, which are difficult to incorporate adequately in a log-linear framework, due to the fact that wealth is an *arithmetic* sum of separate components.

[5]This means that we are abstracting from the possibility of "currency substitution," an issue that is receiving increasing attention in the international monetary literature [12, 18, 2].

[6]In any event, our general conclusions are reasonably robust with respect to alternative specifications of the money demand function.

We assume that the nominal wage contract (the logarithm of the money wage) is set with the goal of equating the expected supply of labor to the expected demand. Assuming that workers are concerned with their real wages in terms of the CPI, their expected supply of labor, $N^{s*}_{t,t-1}$, is described by

$$N^{s*}_{t,t-1} = a + b[W_t - C^{*}_{t,t-1}], \qquad a > 0, b > 0. \tag{2a}$$

Assuming further a production function linking the logarithm of output and employment of the form

$$Y_t = \epsilon N_t, \qquad 0 < \epsilon < 1, \tag{2b}$$

it follows that the expected demand for labor is determined by the marginal product condition

$$ln\ \epsilon + (\epsilon - 1)N^{d*}_{t,t-1} = W_t - P^{*}_{t,t-1}, \tag{2c}$$

where firms evaluate real wages in terms of the price of their product (domestic output). In order to ensure that the labor market is expected to clear, W_t must be set to equate the expected demands and supply appearing in equations (2a) and (2c), namely

$$W_t = \frac{ln\ \epsilon + (\epsilon - 1)a + (1-\epsilon)bC^{*}_{t,t-1} + P^{*}_{t,t-1}}{1 + b(1-\epsilon)}, \tag{2d}$$

so that W_t increases with the respective price expectations of both workers and firms. Actual employment, however, is assumed to depend inversely upon the realized real wage in accordance with the firm's marginal product schedule

$$ln\ \epsilon + (\epsilon - 1)N_t = W_t - P_t. \tag{2c$'$}$$

combining equations (2b), (2c′), and (2d) yields

$$Y_t = \frac{\epsilon[a + bln\ \epsilon]}{1 + b(1-\epsilon)} + \frac{\epsilon}{1-\epsilon}\left[\frac{(1-\epsilon)b(P - C^{*}_{t,t-1}) + (P_t - P^{*}_{t,t-1})}{1 + b(1-\epsilon)}\right], \tag{2e}$$

which is of the form (1e).[7]

The two key exogenous variables in the model upon which we wish to focus are M_t and Q_t. The endogenous variables to be determined by the system include Y_t, r_t, E_t, P_t, and C_t. These are determined on the assumption that expectations are rational in the sense that expectations of the endogenous variables $C^{*}_{t,t-1}$, etc., are

[7]Note that equation (1e) reduces to an exact analogue of the Lucas function when $\delta = 1$. The general conclusions of our analysis continue to hold if equation (1e) is replaced by an expectations augmented Phillips curve, though in this case the lags embodied in the price adjustment process will introduce additional lags into the system.

equal to the predictions yielded by the model, conditional upon the expectations of the exogenous variables held at the same time. These latter expectations, since they pertain to variables exogenous to the model, can themselves be taken to be exogenous.

In order to simplify notation, it is convenient to define initial base levels of the exogenous variables, $\bar{M}$ and $\bar{Q}$, and to consider subsequent changes in the system relative to the base level so defined. Thus we may express the system in deviation form about an initial equilibrium as

$$(1-d_1)y_t = -d_2[(e^*_{t+1,t}-e_t) - (c^*_{t+1,t}-c_t)] + d_3[e_t + q_t - p_t] \tag{3a}$$

$$c_t = \delta p_t + (1-\delta)(q_t + e_t) \tag{3b}$$

$$m_t - c_t = \alpha_1 y_t - \alpha_2[e^*_{t+1,t} - e_t] \tag{3c}$$

$$r_t - \bar{r} = e^*_{t+1,t} - e_t \tag{3d}$$

$$y_t = \gamma[p_t - c^*_{t,t-1}] + \gamma_2[p_t - p^*_{t,t-1}], \tag{3e}$$

where lower-case letters denote deviations; that is, $m_t = M_t - \bar{M}$, etc. The advantage of defining the system about its initial equilibrium is that it enables us to incorporate the constants and exogenous parameters of the system (such as ρ) in the initial equilibrium solution.

The basic scenario we shall analyze is a situation in which prior to some initial time period, $t = 0$, say, the economy is in stationary equilibrium. Then at time 0, for a variety of reasons, individuals may begin to expect the exogenous variables to change over subsequent periods. These changes in expectations may come about through announcements, "leaks in information," observation of events taking place or expected to take place at home and abroad, etc. The details of what generate the changes in these expectations of exogenous variables are themselves exogenous to the model and need not concern us. Our task is to trace through the effects of changes in these expectations, as well as the effects of change in the actual variable (when and if they actually occur), on the endogenous variables of the economy.

To solve the model it is further convenient to eliminate $(r_t - \bar{r})$, c_t, $c^*_{t,t-1}$, and $c^*_{t+1,t-1}$ from equations (3a), (3c), and (3d). This may be done by first taking conditional expectations of (3b) at time $t-1$:

$$c^*_{t,t-1} = \delta p^*_{t,t-1} + (1-\delta)(q^*_{t,t-1} + e^*_{t,t-1}). \tag{4}$$

Then substituting from (3b), (3d), and (4) we obtain

$$(1-d_1)y_t = -d_2[\delta(e^*_{t+1,t} - e_t) - \delta(p^*_{t+1,t} - p_t) - (1-\delta)(q^*_{t+1,t} - q_t)] + d_3[e_t + q_t - p_t] \tag{5a}$$

$$y_t = \gamma_1[p_t - \delta p^*_{t,t-1} - (1-\delta)(q^*_{t,t-1} + e^*_{t,t-1})] + \gamma_2[p_t - p^*_{t,t-1}] \tag{5b}$$

$$m_t = \delta p_t + (1-\delta)(q_t+e_t) + \alpha_1 y_t - \alpha_2[e^*_{t+1,t}-e_t]. \tag{5c}$$

Equations (5a), (5b), and (5c) yield three stochastic difference equations in domestic output y_t, the price of the domestic good p_t and its expectations, the exchange rate e_t and its expectations, together with the exogenous variables m_t and q_t and their expectations.

3. SOLUTION FOR EXPECTATIONS

In order to determine the solutions for y_t, p_t, and e_t, it is first necessary to solve for the expectations of the endogenous variables appearing in equations (5a)–(5c). To do this, we take conditional expectations of (5a)–(5c) for an arbitrary date i, held at the initial time 0:

$$(1-d_1)y^*_{i,0} = -d_2[\delta(e^*_{i+1,0} - e^*_{i,0}) - \delta(p^*_{i+1,0} - p^*_{i,0}) - (1-\delta)(q^*_{i+1,0} - q^*_{i,0})] + d_3[e^*_{i,0}+q^*_{i,0}-p^*_{i,0}] \tag{6a}$$

$$y^*_{i,0} = \gamma_1(1-\delta)[p^*_{i,0} - e^*_{i,0} - q^*_{i,0}] \tag{6b}$$

$$m^*_{i,0} = \delta p^*_{i,0} + (1-\delta)(e^*_{i,0} + q^*_{i,0}) + \alpha_1 y^*_{i,0} - \alpha_2[e^*_{i+1,0}-e^*_{i,0}], \tag{6c}$$

where for any variable X, say, $X^*_{t+1,t}$ denotes the prediction formed at time t ($t = 0, 1, \ldots$) for time $t+i$ ($i = 0, 1, \ldots$). In forming these expectations, we are using the familiar property of conditional expectations operators

$$\xi_{t-1}[\xi_t(X_{t+i})] = \xi_{t-1}[X_{t+i}] = X^*_{t+i,t-1}, \tag{7}$$

and we define $X^*_{t,t} = X_t$. This last assumption merely asserts that the prediction of the current value of a variable is the actual current value and is another way of saying that the variable is instantly observable.

The most convenient procedure for solving for the expectations of the endogenous variables is as follows. First, let us define the relative price of domestic to foreign goods at time 0, say,

$$z_0 \equiv p_0 - q_0 - e_0, \tag{8}$$

so that the expectation of the relative price formed at time 0 for time i, say, is

$$z^*_{i,0} = p^*_{i,0} - q^*_{i,0} - e^*_{i,0}. \tag{8'}$$

Substituting for $y^*_{i,0}$ from equation (6b) into (6a) and using the definition (8′) yields the following first order difference equation in $z^*_{i,0}$:

$$d_2\delta z^*_{i+1,0} - [d_2\delta+\gamma_1(1-d_1)(1-\delta) + d_3]z^*_{i,0} = -d_2[q^*_{i+1,0}-q^*_{i,0}]. \tag{9}$$

The general solution to this equation is

$$z^*_{i,0} = A(1/\mu)^i + \frac{\mu}{\delta}\sum_{j=1}^{\infty} [q^*_{i+j,0} - q^*_{i+j-1,0}]\mu^{j-1}, \tag{10}$$

where A is an arbitrary constant and

$$\mu = \frac{d_2\delta}{d_2\delta + \gamma_1(1-d_1)(1-\delta) + d_3} < 1.$$

Since $1/\mu > 1$, as long as $A \neq 0$, the expectations of the relative price held at time 0 over lengthening forecast horizons (i.e., as $i \to \infty$) will diverge. In order to rule out such behavior and thus ensure that $z^*_{i,0}$ remains bounded we set $A = 0$. This procedure, typical of rational expectations models, is often justified on the grounds that the instability that would otherwise occur would be inconsistent with observed behavior. Alternatively it may be justified more formally by appealing to transversality conditions from appropriate optimizing models, which, provided the underlying utility function satisfies suitable restrictions, ensure that the expected price movements remain bounded (see [3]). Thus setting $A = 0$, the solution reduces to

$$z^*_{i,0} = \frac{1}{\delta}\sum_{j=1}^{\infty} (\Delta q^*_{i+j,0})\,\mu^j, \tag{11}$$

where

$$\Delta q^*_{i+j,0} \equiv q^*_{i+j,0} - q^*_{i+j-1,0}.$$

Substituting the solution for $z^*_{i,0}$ into equation (6b), the corresponding solution for the expected value of real output $y^*_{i,0}$ is given by

$$y^*_{i,0} = \frac{\gamma_1(1-\delta)}{\delta}\sum_{j=1}^{\infty} (\Delta q^*_{i+j,0})\mu^j. \tag{12}$$

From equations (11) and (12) it is observed that the expectations $z^*_{i,0}$ and $y^*_{i,0}$ of the *real* variables are independent of expectations about the nominal money supply $m^*_{j,0}$. They are also independent of any sustained uniform increase in the foreign price level that is expected to occur at or before time i. On the other hand, any increase in the foreign price level that is expected to occur after period i will influence these expectations. For example, a once and for all increase in the foreign price level that is expected to occur in period $i + J$ will generate a reduction in the expected real rate of interest for period $(i+J)$, thereby stimulating the expected demand and expected output for that period and forcing up the expected relative price of domestic output. These effects taper off as $J \rightarrow \infty$.

To determine the solutions for the expectations of the nominal variables $e^*_{i,0}$ and $p^*_{i,0}$, we note equation (8′) and substitute for $z^*_{i,0}$ and $y^*_{i,0}$ into equation (6c). This yields the following equation in $e^*_{i,0}$:

$$\alpha_2 e^*_{i+1,0} - (1 + \alpha_2)e^*_{i,0} = \left[1 + \frac{\alpha_1 \gamma_1 (1 - \delta)}{\delta} \right] \sum_{j=1}^{\infty} (\Delta q^*_{i+j,0})\mu^j + q^*_{i,0} - m^*_{i,0} \tag{13}$$

With $\alpha_2 > 0$, the complementary function for this equation implies an unbounded solution for $e^*_{i,0}$. Thus in order to ensure stability, its coefficient in the general solution must be set to zero, yielding the following solution for $e^*_{i,0}$:

$$e^*_{i,0} = \frac{1}{1 + \alpha_2} \left[\sum_{k=0}^{\infty} (m^*_{i+k,0} - q^*_{i+k,0})\lambda^k \right] - \frac{1}{1 + \alpha_2} \left[1 + \frac{\alpha_1 \gamma_1 (1 - \delta)}{\delta} \right] \left[\sum_{k=0}^{\infty} \lambda^k \sum_{j=1}^{\infty} (\Delta q^*_{i+j+k,0})\mu^j \right], \tag{14}$$

where

$$\lambda = \frac{\alpha_2}{1 + \alpha_2} < 1.$$

The expectation of the exchange rate held at time 0 for time i, say, depends upon the time profile of the expectations of the money supply and foreign price level for all time periods beginning at time i and extending indefinitely into the future. For example, if the money supply is expected to undergo an increase dm^* beginning at time $i + J$, say, and if this increase is expected to continue permanently, the exchange rate at time i will be expected to devalue by an amount

$$\frac{\partial e^*_{i,0}}{\partial m^*} = \lambda^J. \tag{15}$$

If $J = 0$ and the increase is expected to occur immediately, the percentage expected devaluation will be equal to the expected percentage increase in the money supply. Otherwise, the expected devaluation will be less than proportional and, indeed as $J \rightarrow \infty$, the effect will dampen out. The effects of an expected future increase in the foreign price level on currently held expectations of the exchange rate can be similarly analyzed, though the expression is somewhat more complex due to the expected real interest rate effect it generates.

Finally, substituting the solution for $e^*_{i,0}$ into equation (11), and using (8′), we obtain the following solution for the expected price of domestic output:

$$p^*_{i,0} = q^*_{i,0} + \frac{1}{1+\alpha_2}\sum_{k=0}^{\infty}[m^*_{i+k,0} - q^*_{i+k,0}]\lambda^k + \frac{1}{\delta}\sum_{j=1}^{\infty}(\Delta q^*_{i+j,0})\mu^j \tag{16}$$
$$- \frac{1}{1+\alpha_2}\left[1 + \frac{\alpha_1\gamma_1(1-\delta)}{\delta}\right]\left[\sum_{k=0}^{\infty}\lambda^k\sum_{j=1}^{\infty}(\Delta q^*_{i+j+k,0})\mu^j\right].$$

From this equation the effects of expected future increases in the domestic money supply and foreign price level on currently held expectations of the price level can be calculated.

4. SHORT-RUN EQUILIBRIUM OF SYSTEM

The short-run solutions for the endogenous variables y_t, p_t, and e_t obtained from equations (5a), (5b), and (5c) can be expressed in terms of the conditional expectations $e^*_{t+1,t}$, $e^*_{t,t-1}$, $z^*_{t+1,t}$, and $z^*_{t,t-1}$. It is clear that the choice of conditioning date 0 in section 3 was made for notational convenience and that analogous expressions to equations (11), (12), (14), and (16) hold with respect to expectations formed at any arbitrary time t for any arbitrary time $t + i$. Specifically,

$$z^*_{t+i,t} = \frac{1}{\delta}\sum_{j=1}^{\infty}(\Delta q^*_{t+i+j,t})\mu^j \tag{12'}$$

$$e^*_{t+i,t} = \frac{1}{1+\alpha_2}\sum_{k=0}^{\infty}[m^*_{t+i+k,t} - q^*_{t+i+k,t}]\lambda^k \tag{14'}$$
$$- \frac{1}{1+\alpha_2}\left[1 + \frac{\alpha_1\gamma_1(1-\delta)}{\delta}\right]\left[\sum_{k=0}^{\infty}\lambda^k\sum_{j=1}^{\infty}\Delta q^*_{t+i+j+k,t}\mu^j\right].$$

Thus the solutions for y_t, p_t, and e_t can be expressed most conveniently by writing equations (5a)–(5c) as the matrix equation

$$\begin{pmatrix} (1-d_1) & (d_3 + d_2\delta) & -(d_3 + d_2\delta) \\ -1 & \gamma & 0 \\ \alpha_1 & \delta & 1 - \delta + \alpha_2 \end{pmatrix}\begin{pmatrix} y_t \\ p_t \\ e_t \end{pmatrix}$$
$$= \begin{pmatrix} d_2\delta z^*_{t+1,t} + d_2(q^*_{t+1,t} - q_t) \\ (\gamma_1\delta + \delta_2)z^*_{t,t-1} + \gamma(q^*_{t,t-1} + e^*_{t,t-1}) \\ m_t + \alpha_2 e^*_{t+1,t} - (1-\delta)q_t \end{pmatrix} \tag{17}$$

where $\gamma \equiv \gamma_1 + \gamma_2$, $q^*_{t+1,t}$ and $q^*_{t,t-1}$ are exogenous, and $z^*_{t+1,t}$, $z^*_{t,t-1}$, and $e^*_{t+1,t}$ are obtained by setting $i = 1$ in equations (12′) and (14′). Through these latter variables, the solutions for y_t, p_t, and e_t depend upon the expectations of all future values of the exogenous variables (as formed at times $t-1$ and t), an aspect that is a central feature of rational expectations models.

Our concern will be to analyze the effects of actual and anticipated changes in the money supply and the level of foreign prices on the endogenous variables of the system. We shall interpret such changes in m as reflecting actual and anticipated autonomous policy changes. However, one could also postulate the money supply to be generated by some feedback control law, in which case it would follow some stochastic process. In this case, the anticipated change would be derived by calculating conditional expectations of the stochastic process embodied in the control law.[8] This approach constrains the possible range of policy changes, and for our purposes it is more convenient to leave the specification of the domestic monetary process rather general. Finally, we could allow q to be generated by some specific stochastic process, but here too we find it useful to keep the specification of actual and foreign price changes quite open.

5. DOMESTIC MONETARY EXPANSION

It will be recalled that all variables in equation (17) have been measured as deviations about an initial deterministic equilibrium. To analyze the effects of actual and anticipated monetary expansions it is convenient to assume that the foreign price level remains fixed, and is expected to remain fixed, at its initial level $\bar{Q}$. Hence we may set $q^*_{t+i,t} = q_t = 0$. The solutions for the (deviations of) domestic output, price level, and the exchange rate can be expressed in a variety of equivalent ways, probably the simplest and most easily interpreted being the following:

$$y_t = \frac{\gamma(d_3 + d_2\delta)}{J}\left[(m_t - m^*_{t,t-1}) + \sum_{k=1}^{\infty}(m^*_{t+k,t} - m^*_{t+k,t-1})\lambda^k\right] \quad (18a)$$

$$p_t = \frac{(d_3 + d_2\delta)}{J}\left[(m_t - m^*_{t,t-1}) + \sum_{k=1}^{\infty}(m^*_{t+k,t} - m^*_{t+k,t-1})\lambda^k\right] + \frac{1}{1+\alpha_2}\sum_{k=0}^{\infty} m^*_{t+k,t-1}\lambda^k \quad (18b)$$

$$e_t = \frac{[(1-d_1)\gamma + (d_3 + d_2\delta)]}{J}\left[(m_t - m^*_{t,t-1})\right.$$

[8]For example, if the money supply is generated by the feedback rule

$$m_t = \rho_1 m_{t-1} + \rho_2 y_{t-1} + \rho_3 p_{t-1} + \rho_4 e_{t-1},$$

then the expectation of the money supply must satisfy

$$m^*_{t+i+1,t-1} = \rho_1 m^*_{t+i,t-1} + \rho_2 y^*_{t+i,t-1} + \rho_3 p^*_{t+i,t-1} + \rho_4 e^*_{t+i,t-1}$$

In order to determine the conditional expectations $y^*_{t+i,t-1}$, the procedure outlined in section 3 must now take into account the conditional expectations of the control law itself.

$$+ \sum_{k=1}^{\infty} (m^*_{t+k,t} - m^*_{t+k,t-1})\lambda^k \Big] + \frac{1}{1+\alpha_2} \sum_{k=0}^{\infty} m^*_{t+k,t-1}\lambda^k, \qquad (18c)$$

where

$$J = \gamma(1-d_1)(1-\delta+d_2) + (d_3+d_2\delta)(1+\alpha_2+\alpha_1\delta) > 0. \qquad (19)$$

Two critical factors appearing throughout these expressions are $(m_t - m^*_{t,t-1})$ and $(m^*_{t+k,t} - m^*_{t+k,t-1})$, $k = 1,2,\ldots$. The first of these is simply the unanticipated component of the actual money supply at time t, relative to what was anticipated at time $t-1$. The second term measures the amount by which the forecast of the money supply for time $t+k$ is revised between times $t-1$ and t, presumably on the basis of new information acquired during period t.

From equations (18) we can draw the following general conclusions. The level of domestic output, its price, and the rate of exchange all vary positively with the unanticipated component of the money supply at time t. They also vary positively with the discounted sum of the amounts by which the forecasts for all future periods are revised between time $t-1$ and time t. In addition, the monetary variables p_t and e_t depend upon the discounted sum (weighted average) of the expected money supplies for all future periods (as perceived at time $t-1$), with the weights summing to unity.

Using equations (18) enables us to determine the effects of a multitude of types of actual and anticipated monetary disturbances on the economy. For obvious reasons, we restrict ourselves to just a few examples that are convenient to categorize as follows: (a) partial expectations effects, (b) actual monetary expansions, and (c) announcement effects.

A. Partial Expectations Effects

1. The anticipation at time $t-1$ of an increase in the money supply for the *single* period $t+K$, which ex post at time t is no longer expected to occur (i.e., $dm^*_{t+K,t-1} > 0$, $dm^*_{t+k,t-1} = 0$, $k \neq K$; $dm^*_{t+k,t} = 0$, all k), will cause the price of domestic output to rise and the level of domestic output to fall. The reason is that the expectation of the increase in the money supply will increase the expected price of domestic goods (see eq. (16)). This leads to an upward shift in the domestic supply function for period t, forcing the actual price of domestic goods to increase during the period, thereby reducing the demand for these goods and causing domestic output to fall. Both responses are proportional to λ^K, and so tend to zero as $K \to \infty$.

The effect on the exchange rate is indeterminate, being given by the expression

$$\frac{\partial e_t}{\partial m^*_{t+K,t-1}} = \frac{\gamma[\alpha_1(d_3 + d_2\delta) - (1 - d_1)\delta]\lambda^K}{J(1+\alpha_2)}. \qquad (20)$$

On the one hand, the endogenous increase in p_t will raise the demand for money; on the other hand, the decrease in y_t will reduce the demand for money. The net effect of these two offsetting influences can be shown to *decrease* the demand for money by an amount proportional to $[\alpha_1(d_3+d_2\delta) - (1-d_1)\delta]$.[9] Thus, in the event that this term is positive, the demand for money will decrease. At the same time, the net effect of an increase in e_t, taking into account both its effect on the cost of living and its effect on the domestic interest rate, is to raise the demand for money.[10] Hence if $[\alpha_1(d_3+d_2\delta) - (1-d_1)\delta] > 0$, the domestic exchange rate must increase (depreciate) in order to increase the demand for money and maintain equilibrium with the exogenously given fixed nominal supply. The opposite argument applies if the sign of this term is reversed.

The changes in the variables y_t, p_t, and e_t are only transitory. In period $t+1$, when expectations are revised back down, these variables will return to their original levels. We may also observe that essentially the same adjustment applies if the initial increase in expectations occurring in period $t-1$ is expected to apply uniformly to all periods beyond $t+K$. The responses are simply scaled by a factor $1/(1-\lambda) = 1 + \alpha_2$.

2. The anticipation of an expansion in the money supply, initially expected in period t to take place in the single period $t+K$ ($dm^*_{t+k,t-1} = 0$, all k; $dm^*_{t+K,t} > 0$, $dm^*_{t+k,t} = 0$, $k \neq K$), will raise all three variables—the real domestic output, the price of domestic goods, and the exchange rate—during period t. The reason is that the immediate effect of the increase in $m^*_{t+K,t}$ is to raise both $p^*_{t+1,t}$ and $e^*_{t+1,t}$ proportionately. The domestic nominal interest rate will rise, reducing the demand for money, though the domestic real interest rate will remain unchanged. With the nominal money supply fixed, the demand for money will have to be increased, and this can occur through increases in y_t, e_t, or p_t. Assuming that the most rapid adjustment is in e_t, this will put an upward pressure on domestic prices, stimulating output. If in period $t+1$ expectations are revised back down to their original levels, y_{t+1}, p_{t+1}, and e_{t+1} will respond as in case (1). In period $t+2$, they will be back to their original levels.

3. Combining (1) and (2) we see that an anticipation of an expansion in the money supply for the single period $t + K$ initially formed at time $t-1$ and maintained at time t ($dm^*_{t+K,t-1} = dm^*_{t+K,t} > 0$) will have no effect on real income during period t, which we noted above responds to the rate of forecast revision. The current price of domestic output and the exchange rate will both rise by the same amount, leaving the relative price of domestic output unaffected.

[9]The net effect on the demand for money (m^d) resulting from the changes in p_t and y_t is

$$\frac{\partial m_t^d}{\partial m^*_{t+K,t-1}} = \frac{\delta \partial p_t}{\partial m^*_{t+K,t-1}} + \frac{\alpha_1 \partial y_t}{\partial m^*_{t+K,t-1}}.$$

Calculating the appropriate partial derivatives from equations (18a) and (18b), and substituting, yields

$$\frac{\partial m_t^d}{\partial m^*_{t+K,t-1}} = \frac{-\gamma(1 - \delta + \alpha_2)[\alpha_1(d_3 + d_2\delta) - (1 - d_1)\delta]}{J(1 + \alpha_2)}.$$

[10]The net effect of an increase in e_t on the demand for money is

$$\frac{\partial m_t^d}{\partial e_t} = 1 - \delta + \alpha_2 > 0.$$

B. Actual Monetary Expansions

1. A purely unanticipated random increase in the level of the domestic money supply, which is not expected to continue beyond the current period ($dm^*_{t+k,t-1} = dm^*_{t+k,t} = 0$, all k, $dm_t > 0$), has an expansionary effect on domestic output and leads to an increase in the domestic price level, coupled with a depreciation of the domestic currency. With expectations unchanged, the adjustment is quite conventional and accords with traditional analyses of monetary policy for flexible rate systems under perfect capital mobility and static expectations (see [8, 19]).

2. One of the most interesting disturbances to consider is that of an increase in the domestic money supply that is initially unanticipated, but having occurred, is then expected to continue permanently ($dm^*_{t+k,t-1} = 0$, for all k; $dm_t = dm^*_{t+k,t} > 0$, for $k = 1, 2, \ldots$). This is precisely the monetary disturbance analyzed by Dornbusch [5] and subsequent authors, and it has been shown in some cases to be associated with "overshooting" of the short-run exchange rate in relation to its long-run equilibrium proportionate response. In the present context such a disturbance leads to an unambiguous increase in the three variables—the domestic output, the price of domestic output, and the exchange rate. The short-run percentage increase in the price of domestic output is less than that of the money supply, so that p_t undershoots its long-run proportionate response, just as it does in these other models [11] Rewriting equation (18c) we can show

$$\frac{de_t}{dm_t} = 1 + \frac{\gamma[\delta(1 - d_1) - \alpha_1(d_3 + d_2\delta)]}{J}. \tag{21}$$

Hence, whether or not the exchange rate overshoots its ultimate proportionate response depends upon $\delta(1-d_1) - \alpha_1(d_3 + d_2\delta)$. If $\delta(1-d_1) - \alpha_1(d_3 + d_2\delta) > 0$, it is clear from equation (21) that $de_t/dm_t > 1$ and that short-run overshooting occurs; if $\delta(1-d_1)-\alpha_1(d_3+d_2\delta) < 0$, $de_t/dm_t < 1$, the short-run exchange rate adjusts only partially towards its equilibrium.

To understand the response of the exchange rate further, it is convenient to write the third equation appearing in (17) in the form

$$\alpha_1 y_t + \delta z_t = (1 + \alpha_2)(m_t - e_t). \tag{22}$$

To derive equation (22) we have set $q_t = 0$; in addition, equation (14′) in conjunction with the expectational assumption enables us to set $e^*_{t+1,t} = m_t$. The expression on the left-hand side is the net effect on the demand for money resulting from changes in the real variables income y_t and the relative price z_t. Given the increase in y_t associated with this monetary disturbance, the relative price z_t must fall in order to stimulate demand and maintain product market equilibrium. Thus the net effect of these two changes on the demand for money is ambiguous and turns out to

[11]In other words, an unanticipated permanent change in the money supply is not neutral. The same conclusion, arising for the same reason, is obtained in the Fischer model when supply is assumed to be generated by a Lucas supply function (see [7, p. 246]).

be proportional to $\alpha_1(d_3 + d_2\delta) - \delta(1-d_1)$.[12] If this term is negative, say, then these two components generate a net fall in the demand for money. In this case it follows from equation (22) that in order to generate sufficient additional demand to absorb the increased supply, $de_t/dm_t > 1$.

Hence the likelihood of overshooting decreases with d_1, d_2, d_3, and α_1 and will increase or decrease with δ accordingly as $\alpha_1 d_2 - (1-d_1) \lesseqgtr 0$. This is perfectly consistent with Dornbusch [5], who takes $\delta = 1$ and throughout most of his analysis assumes output is fixed, which is equivalent to setting $\alpha_1 = 0$. Overshooting is then inevitable. With endogenous income and $\alpha_1 > 0$ the possibility of undershooting arises. In effect, the larger α_1, the more the burden of adjustment to an increase in the money supply is undertaken by income and the less need be borne by the exchange rate, reducing the likelihood of overshoot. In the limiting case when $\delta = 0$, undershooting will always occur.

To conclude this case, two further points should be made. First, our propositions regarding overshooting or undershooting, while developed for an initially totally unexpected increase in the money supply, continue to hold as long as the initial disturbance is underpredicted ($dm_t > dm^*_{t,t-1}$). Second, assuming that the increase in the money supply undertaken at time t is still expected at time $t+1$ to continue permanently (i.e., $dm^*_{t+k,t+1} = dm_t$), we immediately see that $dy_{t+1} = 0$, $dp_{t+1} = de_{t+1} = dm_t$. The economy adjusts to its new equilibrium in just *one* period. The contrast with Dornbusch in this respect arises simply because of our different choice of supply function, which is the source of the gradual adjustment in his analysis.

We turn now briefly to three other disturbances.

3. An anticipated increase in the money supply, which ex ante is expected to be permanent, but which ex post is expected to be only transitory ($dm^*_{t+k,t-1} = dm_t$, $k = 0,1,\ldots$; $dm^*_{t+k,t} = 0$, $k = 1,\ldots$), has a contractionary effect on income. It also leads to short-run increases in both p_t and e_t, though in both cases the percentage increase will be less than that of the money supply. This is because the contractionary effect of a given expected increase in the money supply more than outweighs the expansionary effect resulting from the actual increase. The fall in output must be met by a rise in the relative price z_t in order to maintain product market equilibrium. Thus p_t must rise by more than e_t, and since with $dm^*_{t+k,t}$ the response of p_t is necessarily less than that of m_t (this can be shown from eq. (18b)), the same must be true of e_t.

4. A fully anticipated increase in the money supply, which both ex ante and ex post is expected to be only transitory ($dm^*_{t,t-1} = dm_t$; $dm^*_{t+k,t-1} = dm^*_{t+k,t} = 0$, $k = 1,\ldots$), will have *no* effect on real output, and as in case (3) will lead to partial increases in both p_t and e_t.

[12] In this case we have

$$\delta \frac{\partial z_t}{\partial m_t} + \alpha_1 \frac{\partial y_t}{\partial m_t} = \frac{-\delta\gamma(1-\alpha_1)(1+\alpha_2) + \gamma\alpha_1(d_3 + d_2\delta)(1+\alpha_2)}{J}$$

$$= \frac{\gamma(1+\alpha_2)[\alpha_1(d_3 + d_2\delta) - (1-d_1)\delta]}{J}.$$

5. Finally, a fully anticipated increase in the money supply, which both ex ante and ex post is expected to be permanent ($dm^*_{t+k,t-1} = dm^*_{t+k,t} = dm_t$, all k), will have no effect on real output. Both the price of domestic output and the exchange rate will rise immediately by the full amount of the monetary increase.

C. Announcement Effects

The effect of an announcement of a future monetary expansion on the current exchange rate has been investigated in the context of the Dornbusch model in two recent papers by Gray and Turnovsky [14] and Wilson [26]. These authors demonstrate that the announcement at time 0, say, of a monetary expansion to take effect at a future time T, will lead to an upward jump in the exchange rate at time 0. Thereafter, the exchange rate will continue to rise in a continuous exponential manner until the stable arm of the saddle is reached, which is then followed towards the new equilibrium.[13] The announcement moderates the initial jump, and indeed with sufficient lead time, the initial overshooting may no longer occur. In this case a lesser degree of overshooting will take place at some point before the monetary expansion actually takes effect.

The solution we have given in equation (18) can easily be used to analyze announcement effects in the present context. Suppose that the monetary authority announces at time 0 a monetary expansion of dm to be introduced at time T. Assuming this is believed by the public, we may write

$$\begin{aligned} dm^*_{t',t} &= 0 && t' = 1, \ldots, T-1, \text{ all } t < t' \\ &= dm && t' = T, T+1, \ldots \\ dm_t &= 0 && t = 1, \ldots, T-1 \\ &= dm && t = T, T+1, \ldots . \end{aligned} \tag{23}$$

Now substituting these values into equations (18a)–(18c) we obtain the following solutions for the changes in the three endogenous variables:

$$\begin{aligned} dy_t &= 0 && t = 1, \ldots, T-1 \\ &= 0 && t = T, \ldots \end{aligned} \tag{24a}$$

$$\begin{aligned} dp_t &= \lambda^{T-t} dm && t = 1, \ldots, T-1 \\ &= dm && t = T, \ldots \end{aligned} \tag{24b}$$

$$\begin{aligned} de_t &= \lambda^{T-t} dm && t = 1, \ldots, T-1 \\ &= dm && t = T, \ldots . \end{aligned} \tag{24c}$$

[13]Because of the lagged price adjustment embodied in the Phillips curve, the dynamics of the systems considered by these authors is second order, having one stable and one unstable root, thus exhibiting saddle-point type instability.

The behavior of the economy is very simple. In the period following the announcement both the price of domestic output and the exchange rate will rise by an amount λ^{T-1}. Thereafter, they will both increase monotonically at the rate (per period) $1/\alpha_2$ until time T when the monetary expansion takes place, when they will have risen by the full amount of the monetary expansion dm.[14] In contrast to the Gray and Turnovsky [14] and Wilson [26] analyses, there is no overshoot of the exchange rate. The reason for the difference is that we do not take the price level to be fixed in the short run, thereby allowing it to bear some of the necessary adjustment. Note that if $T = 1$, the adjustment is completed within one period; the present analysis essentially reduces to case B(5) discussed above.

The other feature to observe is that real output remains fixed throughout the entire adjustment process. The reason for this is evident from equation (18a), where we have commented that real output responds to forecast errors and to the revision of forecasts for future periods. But with the future monetary expansion announced, neither of these phenomena occur. The monetary expansion at time T is perfectly foreseen. Also, during the transition (i.e., before time T) there is no reason to update forecasts. Thus while the announcement of the monetary expansion leads to immediate responses in the nominal variables p_t and e_t, these adjustments turn out to be identical, leaving the *real* variables, such as the relative price and the level of output, unaffected. The only instant at which the real variables will be affected is at time 0, the announcement date itself, when previously held expectations are revised. These effects prevail for only one period, with output immediately returning to its equilibrium level and the nominal variables following the transitional paths described above.

6. CHANGES IN FOREIGN PRICE LEVEL

With $e^*_{t+1,t}$ in particular being a rather complex function of the expected foreign price level for all future periods (see eq. (14′)), a detailed analysis of the effects of future expected price disturbances on the current behavior of the system becomes rather tedious. We shall therefore restrict our attention to the case where these expectations formed at time t are held uniformly for all future periods. That is,

$$q^*_{t+k,t} = q^*_t, \qquad k = 1, \ldots, ; \text{ all } t, \tag{25}$$

where q^*_t denotes the uniformly held expectation at time t. It is also convenient to assume that the money supply remains, and is expected to remain, at its original equilibrium level $\bar{M}$, enabling us to set $m_t = m^*_{t+k,t} = 0$. With these assumptions, the two critical expectations, equations (12′) and (14′), simplify drastically to

$$z^*_{t+1,t} = 0 \tag{12″}$$

[14]The rate of change per unit period = $(1-\lambda)/\lambda = 1/\alpha_2$.

$$e^*_{t+1,t} = -q^*_t. \tag{14''}$$

Substituting equations (12″) and (14″) into the matrix equation (17), the solutions for y_t, p_t, and e_t are

$$y_t = \frac{\gamma}{J}[d_3\alpha_2 - d_2(1 - \delta)(1 + d_2)](q_t - q^*_t) \tag{26a}$$

$$p_t = \frac{1}{J}[d_3\alpha_2 - d_2(1 - \delta)(1 + d_2)](q_t - q^*_t) \tag{26b}$$

$$e_t = -q_t + \eta(q_t - q^*_t), \tag{26c}$$

where

$$\eta = (1/J)[[(1-d_1)\gamma + d_3 + d_2\delta]\alpha_2 + (\delta + \alpha_1\gamma)d_2] > 0.$$

With the assumption of uniformity of expectations, the initially held expectations of q (i.e., those formed at time $t-1$) play no role. The reason is that any increase in q^*_{t-1} that would influence the system through the domestic supply function is exactly offset by a decrease in $e^*_{t,t-1}$ (see eq. (14″)), leaving the supply function and the system unaffected. Indeed the critical factor determining the behavior of the system is the term $(q_t - q^*_t)$. This measures the extent to which q_t is expected to change uniformly during subsequent periods. It therefore describes the *expected transitory* component of the current foreign price level (relative to the future). If the current foreign price level is expected to continue permanently, then $q_t = q^*_t$; if the current level is expected to be a purely transitory positive deviation from $\bar{Q}$, then $q_t > 0$, $q^*_t = 0$.

From equations (26a)–(26c) we find that any increase in the foreign price level q_t, which at time t is expected to be permanent ($dq^*_t = dq_t$), will have no effect on both real domestic output and its price.[15] The exchange rate will appreciate equally, leaving the relative price z_t also unchanged. By contrast, an increase in q_t that is expected to be at least partly temporary ($dq_t - dq^*_t$) will have an impact on both y_t and p_t. However, these effects are ambiguous and depend upon the sign of the expression $[d_3\alpha_2 - d_2(1-\delta)(1+\alpha_2)]$. The sources of the indeterminacy are primarily the real ($r_{e,t}$) and nominal (r_t) interest rates, which using equation (14″) can be written, respectively, as

$$r_{e,t} = \delta z_t + (q_t - q^*_t)$$

$$r_t = z_t - p_t + (q_t - q^*_t).$$

[15]Strictly speaking, our analysis of foreign price disturbances is incomplete. In practice q_t is an endogenous variable in the rest of the world, as is the foreign interest rate ρ. Thus any stochastic shift in q_t is likely to be accompanied by a stochastic change in ρ, as both variables respond to the common random influence. The degree of correlation between these two foreign variables will vary, depending upon the source of the foreign disturbance. By ignoring accompanying changes in the interest rate, we are making a special assumption about the nature of the underlying disturbance.

For given values of z_t and p_t, an increase in $(q_t - q_t^*)$ will lead to corresponding increases in both the real and nominal rate. The first of these will tend to reduce the demand for domestic goods, causing its price and hence supply to fall. This is reflected in the term, $-d_2(1-\delta + \alpha_2)$. At the same time the increase in the nominal rate will reduce the demand for money. With the supply of money fixed, output and the price level will have to increase in order to restore demand and maintain money market equilibrium. This is reflected in the term $(d_3 + d_2\delta)\alpha_2$. Finally, the response of the exchange rate given in equation (26c) implies that $de_t/dq_t > -1$; that is, the exchange rate will appreciate by less than the amount of the foreign price increase.

7. CONCLUSIONS

In this paper we have developed a stochastic model of a small open economy operating under a flexible exchange rate, and we have considered its response to two types of exogenous disturbances, namely, a domestic monetary expansion and a foreign price increase. With respect to the former, we have shown that the level of domestic output, its price, and the exchange rate at a given time all vary positively with: (1) the unanticipated component of the money supply during that period; and (2) the discounted sum of the amounts by which the forecasts for all future money supplies are revised during that period, from what they were in the previous period. In addition, the latter two variables depend upon the discounted sum (with weights adding to unity) of the expected money supplies for all future periods, as perceived at the end of the previous period.[16] When these factors are all taken into account, any given monetary disturbance can generate a variety of short-run effects, depending upon the accuracy with which it is predicted and how it causes expectations to be revised. It may be associated with overshooting or undershooting of the exchange rate, depending in part upon how accurately it is predicted, and may even have perverse short-run effects on output.[17] Such will be the case if the monetary expansion is initially perceived as being permanent, but having taken place, it is then expected to be only temporary.

In equilibrium, the model possesses the usual monetary neutrality properties in that a 1 percent increase in the money supply will have no effect on real output and will raise the price level and exchange rate proportionately. The transitional dynamics to a given monetary disturbance can take various forms, depending particularly upon how rapidly expectations of future money supplies adjust and the time period between the announcement (if any) of the policy and its implementation. In

[16]We have restricted our attention to the price of domestic output. The response of the overall domestic CPI can be easily derived using equation (3b) from that of the price of domestic output and the exchange rate. Indeed it is just an average of that of p_t and $(q_t + e_t)$ and for that reason is not discussed separately.

[17]The reason for the possible perverse short-run effect of a monetary expansion on output in the present analysis is quite different from the reason for the similar result obtained in Niehans's [21] paper. In our case it results from expectational errors; a monetary expansion that is initially perceived as being permanent turns out only to be transitory. Niehans's result on the other hand arises if an increase in the exchange rate leads to a substantial deterioration in the balance of trade; in effect it occurs if the Marshall-Lerner conditions are strongly violated.

contrast to previous analyses, the announcement of a future monetary expansion eliminates the overshooting of the exchange rate. And while it will give rise to immediate adjustments in the nominal variables, with the exception of the instant at which the announcement is made, it will leave the real behavior of the system unaffected.

The responses to a foreign price change may be most usefully summarized by relating them to the discussion concerning the insulation properties of flexible exchange rates against such disturbances, as mentioned in section 1. As noted there, this literature is conducted in a deterministic framework and has focused on initially unanticipated permanent increases in the foreign price level. Much of the emphasis has been on the role of domestic resident's wealth held in domestic and foreign denominated currencies. A principal conclusion is that flexible rates will provide only partial insulation against a foreign price increase as long as domestic residents hold some foreign securities in their portfolios. Unfortunately, to include wealth effects in a log-linear framework such as this is not easily accomplished, so that our analysis does not incorporate this aspect. Under the assumptions of the present model, the existing literature draws the conclusion that flexible exchange rates will provide complete insulation against foreign price disturbances.

The analysis of section 6 has shown that in the absence of wealth effects in the asset demand functions, flexible exchange rates will provide perfect insulation against increases in the foreign price level that are *expected* to be permanent (they need not actually be, however). Moreover, this proposition is true irrespective of the accuracy with which the foreign price level is initially anticipated. This latter proposition depends upon the uniformity assumption upon which section 6 is based and need not hold if expectations vary between the various future periods. On the other hand, even abstracting from wealth effects, a flexible rate does not provide complete insulation against a foreign price disturbance that ex post is expected to be only transitory. Indeed the more transitory it is expected to be, the less the insulation. This raises the question of what the optimal exchange rate regime—or what the optimal intervention policy in the face of such disturbances—ought to be. But this is a subject for future research.

LITERATURE CITED

1. Barro, Robert J. "A Stochastic Equilibrium Model of an Open Economy Under Flexible Exchange Rates." *Quarterly Journal of Economics,* 92 (February 1978), 149–64.
2. Bilson, John F. O. "Recent Developments in Monetary Models of Exchange Rate Determination." *IMF Staff Papers,* 26 (June 1979), 201–23.
3. Brock, William A. "Money and Growth: The Case of Long-Run Perfect Foresight." *International Economics Review,* 15 (October 1974), 750–77.
4. Cox, W. Michael. "Unanticipated Money, Output, and Prices in the Small Economy." *Journal of Monetary Economics,* 6 (July 1980), 359–84.
5. Dornbusch, Rudiger. "Exchange Rate Expectations and Monetary Policy." *Journal of Political Economy,* 84 (December 1976), 1161–76.

6. Fischer, Stanley. "Wage Indexation and Macroeconomic Stability." In *Stabilization of the Domestic and International Economy,* edited by Karl Brunner and Allan Meltzer, pp. 107-47. Amsterdam: North-Holland, 1977.

7. ______. "Anticipations and the Nonneutrality of Money." *Journal of Political Economy,* 87 (April 1979), 225-52.

8. Fleming, J. Marcus. "Domestic Financial Policies under Fixed and Floating Exchange Rates." *IMF Staff Papers,* 9 (November 1962), 369-79.

9. Flood, Robert. "Capital Mobility and the Choice of Exchange Rate System." *International Economic Review,* 20 (June 1979), 405-16.

10. Floyd, John E. "The Asset Market Theory of the Exchange Rate: A Comment." *Scandinavian Journal of Economics,* 80 (February 1978), 100-103.

11. Frenkel, Jacob A. "A Monetary Approach to the Exchange Rate: Doctrinal Aspects and Empirical Evidence." *Scandinavian Journal of Economics,* 78 (May 1976), 200-224.

12. Girton, Lance, and Don Roper. "Theory and Implications of Currency Substitution." Board of Governors, Federal Reserve System, 1976.

13. Gray, Jo Anna. "Wage Indexation: A Macroeconomic Approach." *Journal of Monetary Economics,* 2 (April 1976), 221-35.

14. Gray, Malcolm R., and Stephen J. Turnovsky. "The Stability of Exchange Rate Dynamics Under Perfect Myopic Foresight." *International Economic Review,* 20 (October 1979), 643-60.

15. Kouri, Pentti J. K. "The Exchange Rate and the Balance of Payments in the Short Run and in the Long Run: A Monetary Approach." *Scandinavian Journal of Economics,* 78 (May 1976), 280-304.

16. Laidler, David. "Expectations and the Behaviour of Prices and Output Under Flexible Exchange Rates." *Economica,* 44 (November 1977), 327-36.

17. Lucas, Robert E., Jr. "Some International Evidence on Output-Inflation Tradeoffs." *American Economic Review,* 63 (June 1973), 326-34.

18. Miles, Marc A. "Currency Substitution, Flexible Exchange Rates and Monetary Independence." *American Economic Review,* 68 (June 1978), 428-36.

19. Mundell, Robert A. *International Economics.* New York: Macmillan, 1968.

20. Mussa, Michael. "The Exchange Rate, the Balance of Payments and Monetary and Fiscal Policy under a Regime of Controlled Floating." *Scandinavian Journal of Economics,* 78 (May 1976), 229-48.

21. Niehans, Jürg. "Some Doubts about the Efficacy of Monetary Policy Under Flexible Exchange Rates." *Journal of International Economics,* 5 (August 1975), 275-81.

22. Parkin, J. Michael. "A Comparison of Alternative Techniques of Monetary Control Under Rational Expectations." *Manchester School.* 46 (September 1978), 252-87.

23. Samuelson, Paul A., and Subramanian Swamy. "Invariant Economic Index Numbers and Canonical Duality: Survey and Synthesis." *American Economic Review,* 64 (September 1974), 566-93.

24. Turnovsky, Stephen J. *Macroeconomic Analysis and Stabilization Policy.* Cambridge, England: Cambridge University Press, 1977.

25. ______. "On the Insulation Properties of Flexible Exchange Rates." *Revue Economique,* 30 (July 1979), 719-46.

26. Wilson, Charles A. "Anticipated Shocks and Exchange Rate Dynamics." *Journal of Political Economy,* 87 (June 1979), 639-47.

STUART M. TURNBULL*

Measurement of the Real Rate of Interest and Related Problems in a World of Uncertainty

1. INTRODUCTION

THIS PAPER IS CONCERNED WITH two distinct though closely related issues. The first issue is the use of the expected real rate of return on the nominal discount bond. The real rate of return on such a bond is risky if the rate of inflation across different future states of nature is uncertain. In equilibrium the expected real rate of return on the nominal riskless discount bond will be composed of a risk premium that will depend upon the distribution of the real pay-off of the bond and the distribution of the marginal rates of substitution between initial consumption and consumption in the future states of nature (see [23]). Consequently, if for some reason the distribution of the rate of inflation across different states of nature changes, while the distribution of the marginal rate of substitution remains unchanged, then this will affect the risk premium and the expected real rate of return.

In a world of perfect certainty, the real rate of interest is determined by the marginal rate of substitution between present and future consumption, and in equilibrium this equals the marginal rate of technical substitution, assuming a production-exchange economy. In a world of uncertainty where claims are traded in

*The comments of Michael Brennan, Stephen Buser, Jack Carr, Andrew Chen, David Fehr, Paul Halpern, Gailen Hite, and James Pesando are gratefully acknowledged. An earlier version of this paper was presented at the finance workshop, Ohio State University, and at the American Finance Association meetings, Atlanta, December 1979. Responsibility for errors remains with the author.

STUART M. TURNBULL *is associate professor, Institute for Policy Analysis, University of Toronto.*

0022-2879/81/0581-0177$00.50/0
JOURNAL OF MONEY, CREDIT, AND BANKING, vol. 13, no. 2 (May 1981)

real terms, the real rate of interest can be defined to equal the expected marginal rate of substitution between present and future consumption across different states of nature, and this equals the average (across different states of nature) of the marginal rates of technical substitution [14, chap. 9]. If claims are traded in nominal terms, the expected real rate of return on the nominal riskless discount bond will not in general equal the real rate of interest. To the economist trained to interpret changes in the expected real rate of return on the nominal riskless bond as changes in the expected marginal productivity of capital,[1] it is argued that such an interpretation can be misleading; the expected real rate of return on the nominal riskless bond can change when in real terms nothing in the economy has changed.

Apart from the theoretical implications, this has potentially important empirical ramifications. The actual magnitude and practical significance of this error and related biases are empirical questions. Due to data limitations, empirical evidence about these issues is not presented in this paper. However, to illustrate some of the empirical problems that might arise, hypothetical data are used. It is shown that even if the real and monetary sectors of the economy are independent, changes in the expected rate of inflation, caused by a change in the distribution of the rate of inflation across different states of nature, need not necessarily cause an equal change in the nominal riskless rate of interest. In testing whether the real rate of interest is in part determined by the expected rate of inflation, as hypothesized by Mundell [16], Hess and Bicksler [13] use the real rate of return on the nominal riskless discount bond to empirically argue that a negative relationship exists. It is theoretically demonstrated that serious error might occur if causal observation of changes in the real rate of return on the nominal riskless discount bond and the rate of inflation is used to make inferences about the correlation between the real and monetary sectors of the economy.

The second issue is to examine the effect of personal taxation upon the structure of asset prices and the estimation of marginal tax rates.[2] Estimation of the marginal tax rate derived by comparing the yields on taxable and nontaxable bonds will in general be biased. The price of the taxable bond is determined by the present value of the after tax payments across all states of nature. If the marginal tax rate differs across different states of nature due to the heterogeneity of investors' wealth and individual tax rates, then this gives rise to the existence of a risk premium. A direct comparison between the yields on the taxable and nontaxable bonds, which does not take account of the risk premium, will result in a possible biased estimation of the marginal tax rate. In the testing of the term structure of interest rates, the term premia are usually estimated neglecting the effects of personal taxation (see [6, 17, 19]). It is demonstrated that the neglect of taxation can cause spurious results.

The model is described in section 2. The estimation of the real rate of interest is given in section 3 as well as the empirical implications. The effects of personal

[1]This is the implicit interpretation used by Fama and Schwert [8, p. 116]. See also [21, 2, 3].

[2]While Robichek and Niebuhr [21] have demonstrated that personal taxation can cause substantial bias in yield to maturity estimates if constructed from quotations on bonds selling below par, they do not attempt to describe the exact nature of the bias upon the term structure of interest rates, forward rates of interest, or the estimation of the real rate of interest. See also [15].

taxation are described in section 4. The model is extended to a multi-period framework in section 5. Section 6 summarizes the conclusions of the paper.

2. REAL AND NOMINAL INTEREST RATES IN A TWO-DATE PARADIGM

It is assumed that individuals act to maximize the expected utility of current consumption at date $t = 0$ and future consumpion at date $t = 1$. Given initial wealth of W_0 dollars, the individual must decide how much should be allocated for present consumption and how much invested for future consumption. It is assumed that the investment decisions of firms are fixed, implying that social endowments are exogenous to the model. Money is introduced in an artificial manner by assuming that all claims are traded in terms of dollars and that the money supply is exogenous.[3] Individuals can trade in state contingent claims that pay one dollar iff a particular state of nature occurs. At date $t = 1$ individuals must pay taxes on total wealth.[4] In keeping with the artificial nature of money in this model, it is assumed that government destroys (at zero cost) all tax revenue.

The state at date $t = 0$ is known with certainty, at date $t = 1$ any one of $E(e = 1, 2, \ldots, E)$ states can occur. Each individual at date $t = 0$ allocates positive present dollar wealth W_0 among present consumption $(\theta_0 C_0)$ and E state contingent claims to future dollar wealth W_e at date $t = 1$, where θ_0 is the price per unit of consumption at date $t = 0$, and C_0 is the quantity of consumption. Let P_e denote the date $t = 0$ present value of one dollar received at date $t = 1$ iff state e occurs. The budget constraint facing the individual is of the form $W_0 = \theta_0 C_0 + \Sigma_e P_e W_e$. Let $\pi_e > 0$ denote the subjective probability the individual attaches to state e and $U(C_0) + \rho\, \Sigma_e \pi_e U(C_e)$ denote the individual's additively, separable expected utility function over present and future consumption, where ρ is a positive constant measuring patience; and U is a function such that $U' > 0$ and $U'' < 0$.

The decision problem facing the individual can be represented as

$$\text{Max } U(C_0) + \rho\, \Sigma_e \pi_e\, U(C_e), \tag{1}$$

subject to the constraints

$$W_0 = \theta_0 C_0 + \Sigma_e P_e W_e \tag{2}$$

and

$$W_e (1 - \Gamma_e) = \theta_e C_e, \qquad \text{(all } e\text{)}, \tag{3}$$

where θ_e is the dollar price per unit of consumption good in state e at date $t = 1$; W_e

[3]In this model money is not a desired good and does not enter the utility function of the individual. See [14, chap. 5] for a discussion on this issue.

[4]The effects of an income tax are considered later in the paper.

is the number of state e contingent claims that are purchased; and Γ_e is the personal tax rate in state e. If state e occurs, the individual uses the after tax wealth of $W_e(1-\Gamma_e)$ to purchase the consumption good.[5]

The necessary and sufficient conditions for a unique optimum are

$$P_e\, U'(C_0)\,/\,\theta_0 = \rho\, \pi_e\, (1 - \Gamma_e)\, U'(C_e)\,/\,\theta_e \tag{4}$$

$$e = 1, \ldots, E$$

and

$$W_0 = \theta_0 C_0 + \Sigma\, P_e W_e .$$

To provide for the endogenous determination of security prices, take the aggregate production decisions across dates and states as given

$$C_0^m = \Sigma_i C_0^i \tag{5}$$

$$C_e^m = \Sigma_i C_e^i, \qquad (\text{all } e), \tag{6}$$

and taking the money supply as given

$$M_0^s \equiv \Sigma_i \theta_0 C_0^i \tag{7}$$

and

$$M_e^s \equiv \Sigma_i \theta_e C_e^i, \qquad (\text{all } e), \tag{8}$$

where the population of the economy is $I(i=1, \ldots, I)$. Equations (7) and (8) describe a simple quantity theory of money, with the velocity of money being unity.

A nominal risk free bond is defined as a security paying one dollar in every state of nature. The rate of return on such a bond is given by

$$(1 + R_f)^{-1} = \Sigma_e P_e = N, \tag{9}$$

where N is the dollar price of the bond at date $t = 0$. The real rate of return from investing in such a bond is not riskless. If state e occurs at date $t = 1$, the individual receives one dollar and can purchase $\$1/\theta_e$ units of the consumption good. The expected real rate of return is

$$\begin{aligned} 1 + \bar{r}_f &= \Sigma_e \pi_e\, (1/\theta_e)/(N/\theta_0) \\ &= (1 + R_f)\, \Sigma_e \pi_e\, (1 + \gamma_e)^{-1}, \end{aligned} \tag{10}$$

where γ_e is the rate of inflation in state e and is defined by $\theta_e = \theta_0(1 + \gamma_e)$, for all e.

[5]For simplicity, it is assumed that there is only one consumption good.

3. THE REAL RATE OF INTEREST

For the purpose of the present section all taxes will be ignored. If claims are traded in real terms, the price of a bond at date $t = 0$ paying one unit of the consumption good in every state of nature at date $t = 1$ would be

$$(1+r_f)^{-1} = \Sigma_e \rho\pi_e\, U'(C_e)/U'(C_0), \tag{11}$$

where r_f is the real risk free rate of interest; and it is assumed that all individuals are identical, U being the utility function of a representative individual.[6] Define $Y_e = \rho U'(C_e)/U'(C_0)$, which, apart from a minus sign, is the marginal rate of substitution between consumption at date $t=0$ and consumption in state e at date $t=1$; then equation (11) can be written in the form

$$(1+r_f)^{-1} = E(\tilde{Y}), \tag{11$'$}$$

where E is the expectation operator, and the tilde denotes a random variable. The real rate of interest is determined by the expected value of the marginal rate of substitution across different states of nature.[7]

For empirical studies if claims are not traded in real terms and if an index bond does not exist, then the real rate of interest cannot be observed and thus must be estimated using the expected real rate of return on the nominal riskless bond (see [3, 4, 19]). If equation (11) is interpreted as defining the unobservable real rate of interest, it remains to show the relationship between equations (10) and (11).

Equations (9) and (10) can be rewritten in the form, using equation (4):

$$(1+R_f)^{-1} = E(\tilde{Y}\tilde{X}) \tag{9$'$}$$

and

$$(1+\bar{r}_f)^{-1} = E(\tilde{Y}\tilde{X})/E(\tilde{X}), \tag{10$'$}$$

where $X_e = (1+\gamma_e)^{-1}$, the inverse of one plus the rate of inflation if state e occurs. Using equations (10′) and (11′), then

$$(1+\bar{r}_f)^{-1} = (1+r_f)^{-1} + \text{cov}(\tilde{Y},\tilde{X})/E(\tilde{X}), \tag{12}$$

where $\text{cov}(\tilde{Y},\tilde{X})$ is the covariance between the marginal rate of substitution and the inverse of the rate of inflation. Thus the expected real rate of return on the nominal riskless bond is a biased estimator of the unobservable real rate of interest. If the covariance is positive (negative), then $\bar{r}_f < (>) r_f$, assuming $E(\tilde{X})$ to be positive. Clearly, the expected real rate of return will be an unbiased estimator if the marginal

[6]While this assumption can be relaxed—see [22]—it saves having to discuss distributional problems that are not pertinent to the main theme of the paper.

[7]In the economy described in section 2 individuals can construct their own forms of index bond by purchasing claims $\{1+\gamma_e\}$, $e = 1, \ldots, E$. The real rate of return on the index bond will equal $(1+r_f)$.

rate of substitution and the inverse of the rate of inflation are uncorrelated. This will occur if there is no endowment risk, in the sense that all states are equally well endowed, or if the rate of inflation is constant across all states of nature.[8]

This bias arises not because of any form of approximation used in calculating the expected real rate return,[9] nor does it result due to any form of wealth redistribution that might be caused by inflation.[10] The reason for this result is that the real return on the nominal riskless bond is risky, so that in equilibrium the expected real rate of return at $t = 0$ contains a risk premium, which depends upon the real return $1/\theta_e$ (proportional to X_e) and the marginal rate of substitution between current and future consumption: Y_e, $e = 1, \dots, E$. Thus, if there is uncertainty about the future social endowment and the rate of inflation, then this gives rise to the possibility of the existence of a risk premium and the expected real rate of return will be a biased estimator of the unobservable real rate of interest.

While equation (12) gives a formal expression for the bias, its magnitude at any point in time can only be determined empirically. A priori, equation (12) provides little, if any, intuitive insight as to the magnitude or sign of the bias. Given that the bias depends upon the covariance between the inverse of the rate of inflation and the marginal rate of substitution, a quantity that is unobservable, direct measurement of the bias is not possible. If an index bond existed, then $1+r_f$ could be measured and equation (12) used to estimate the bias. However, in practice there could still be difficulty depending upon the price index used for the bond in a many commodity economy. In the absence of empirical data, two hypothetical sets of data are used to illustrate the types of errors that might result. Whether in practice these errors are ''serious'' is, of course, an empirical question.

The effect of social endowment risk is demonstrated in Table 1. It is assumed that in both cases the money supply grows at a constant rate of 20 percent across all states. Case 1 describes a world of perfect certainty, as the social endowment and money supply are the same in both states. The rate of inflation is 9.09 percent. The real rate of return on the nominal riskless bond equals the real rate of interest, which is 10 percent. In case 2 there is endowment risk; if state one occurs there is no real growth in the economy. The nominal rate of interest remains the same at 20 percent, while the expected real rate of inflation increases to 14.55 percent. The deduced expected real rate of return on the nominal bond decreases to 5 percent. This overestimates the real rate of interest, which is now 4.76 percent.

Anticipated changes in the money supply, keeping real social endowments fixed, should have no effect upon the real rate of interest; in real terms nothing has changed. However, this will not be the case if equation (10) or (10′) is used to estimate the unobservable real rate of interest, as demonstrated in Table 2. It is assumed that in both cases the social endowment remains fixed. The real rate of interest is −5.27 percent which, as social endowments are fixed, does not change

[8]This will also be the case if, as advocated by Friedman [12], the growth in the money supply is identical to the growth in social endowments; that is, if the growth rate, G_e, in social endowments is defined by $C_e^m = C_0^m(1+G_e)$, for all e, then money supply in state e is given by $M_0^s(1+G_e)$.

[9]A demonstration of some of the possible errors that might arise is given in Fischer [10, p. 513].

[10]It should be recalled that it is assumed that all individuals are identical.

TABLE 1

CHANGES IN REAL ENDOWMENTS

Money Supply		Social Endowments					
		Case 1			Case 2		
$t = 0$	$t = 1$	$t = 0$		$t = 1$	$t = 0$		$t = 1$
$M^s{}_0 = 50$	$M^s{}_1 = 60$ $M^s{}_2 = 60$	$C^m{}_0 = 50$		$C^m{}_1 = 55$ $C^m{}_2 = 55$	$C^m{}_0 = 50$		$C^m{}_1 = 50$ $C^m{}_2 = 55$
1. $E(1 + \tilde{\gamma})$		12/11	=	1.0909	63/55	=	1.1455
2. $E(\tilde{X})$		11/12	=	0.9167	7/8	=	0.875
3. $1 + R_f$		6/5	=	1.2	6/5	=	1.2
4. $1 + \bar{r}_f$		11/10	=	1.1	21/20	=	1.05
5. $1 + r_f$		11/10	=	1.1	22/21	=	1.0476

NOTE: Assumptions: (1) Economy of representative individuals with utility functions of the form $U(C_0,C_1) = \ln(C_0) + \ln(C_1)$; (2) Two possible states of nature at date $t = 1$; $\pi_1 = \pi_2 = 1/2$.

TABLE 2

CHANGES IN THE MONEY SUPPLY

Social Endowments		Money Supply					
		Case 1			Case 2		
$t = 0$	$t = 1$	$t = 0$		$t = 1$	$t = 0$		$t = 1$
$C^m{}_0 = 50$	$C^m{}_1 = 45$ $C^m{}_2 = 50$	$M^s{}_0 = 50$		$M^s{}_1 = 50$ $M^s{}_2 = 55$	$M^s{}_0 = 50$		$M^s{}_1 = 50$ $M^s{}_2 = 60$
1. $E(1 + \tilde{\gamma})$		199/180	=	1.1056	52/45	=	1.1556
2. $E(\tilde{X})$		199/220	=	0.9045	52/60	=	0.8667
3. $1 + R_f$		22/21	=	1.0476	12/11	=	1.0909
4. $1 + \bar{r}_f$		199/210	=	0.9476	52/55	=	0.9454
5. $1 + r_f$		18/19	=	0.9473	18/19	=	0.9473

NOTE: Assumptions: (1) Economy of representative individuals with utility functions of the form $U(C_0,C_1) = \ln(C_0) + \ln(C_1)$; (2) Two possible states of nature at date $t = 1$; $\pi_1 = \pi_2 = 1/2$.

for the two cases. In case 1 the nominal riskless rate of interest is 4.76 percent, and the expected rate of inflation is 10.56 percent. The expected real rate of return on the nominal bond is −5.24 percent. In case 2 the money supply is increased in the relatively well-endowed state two. The expected rate of inflation increases to 15.56 percent and the nominal rate of interest to 9.09 percent. The expected real rate of return on the nominal bond *decreases* from −5.24 percent to −5.45 percent. It should also be observed that in case 1 the expected real rate of return on the nominal bond overestimates the real rate of interest, while in case 2 underestimation occurs.[11]

[11]As expected from equation (12), increased uncertainty about the rate of inflation will have an ambiguous effect on the expected real rate of return on the nominal riskless discount bond. In case 1, Table 2, the variance of the rate of inflation $\text{var}(1 + \tilde{\gamma}) = 0.00003087$. Suppose that the distribution of the money supply changes, so that $\theta'_1 = \theta_1 - \epsilon$ and $\theta'_2 = \theta_2 + \epsilon$, implying that the expected rate of inflation $E(1+\tilde{\gamma})$ remains constant. Let $\epsilon = 0.1$, so that $\text{var}(1+\gamma') = 0.0089$, then $1 + R_f' = 1.035$ and $1 + \bar{r}_f' = 199/211 < 1 + \bar{r}_f$. If $\epsilon = -0.1$ so that $\text{var}(1 + \tilde{\gamma}') = 0.0111$, then $1 + R_f' = 1.043$ and $1 + \bar{r}_f' = 199/209 > 1 + \bar{r}_f$.

The above results have potentially important empirical implications. Observed changes in the expected real rate of return could be interpreted as changes in the expected marginal productivity of capital—see Carlson [2]. From Table 2 it is clear that such an interpretation can be misleading, for in real terms nothing has changed. When testing the hypothesis that the expected real rate of return is constant, a regression equation of the form $R = \alpha + \beta E(\gamma)$ is usually used, where α and β are constants. The null hypothesis is that $\beta = 1$, implying that all changes in the expected rate of inflation are reflected in the nominal riskless rate of interest [1]. It is also consistent with the hypothesis that the expected real rate of return and the expected rate of inflation are uncorrelated. Fama and Schwert [8] interpreted this as implying that the real and monetary sectors of the economy are independent. Using the results given in Table 2 to calculate α and β, it is found that $\alpha = -0.0438$ and $\beta = 0.866$. Given the absence of measurement error, it is clear that the null hypothesis would have to be rejected, yet in real terms nothing in this economy has changed. From Table 2 it is observed that as the expected rate of inflation increases from 10.56 to 15.56 percent, the expected real rate of return decreases from −5.24 to −5.46 percent. This could be interpreted as providing support for the Mundell hypothesis [16]. Yet given the pure exchange nature of the model, such an interpretation is incorrect.

4. TAXATION

The presence of personal taxation implies that the prices of contingent claims, as given by equation (4), will in general depend upon the marginal tax rate. The normal riskless rate of interest, ${}_{\Gamma}R_f$, using equation (9), is given by

$$(1+{}_{\Gamma}R_f)^{-1} = E[\tilde{Y}\tilde{X}(1 - \tilde{\Gamma})], \tag{13}$$

where it is again assumed that all individuals are identical and have the same marginal tax rate, Γ, which is assumed to be state dependent.[12] The expected real rate of return on the nominal riskless bond is

$$(1+{}_{\Gamma}\bar{r}_f)^{-1} = E[\tilde{Y}\tilde{X}(1 - \tilde{\Gamma})]/E(\tilde{X}). \tag{14}$$

Estimation of the expected marginal tax rate can be obtained by comparing the prices of taxable and nontaxable nominal bonds [20]. Let A_e be the price of a contingent claim that pays one dollar iff state e occurs and the holder of the claim is not taxed on the proceeds of such a claim. Individuals are free to choose between the tax free and taxable claims implying that prices will adjust so that at the margin an investor will be indifferent between the two types of claims. For the marginal

[12] A similar form of expression as equation (12) can be derived in a more general model with individuals differing in wealth and having different personal tax rates. However, even if the individual tax rates are state independent, the average marginal tax rate, $\bar{\Gamma}$, defined by $(1-\bar{\Gamma}_e)\Sigma_j U_j'(C_e^j) = \Sigma_j(1-\Gamma^j) U'(C_e^j)$, will be in general state dependent.

investor with tax rate Γ_e, $P_e = A_e(1-\Gamma_e)$. Extending the analysis used to derive equation (4), it can be shown that nominal riskless rate of interest for the tax free bond is

$$(1+R_f)^{-1} = \Sigma_e A_e = E(\tilde{Y}\tilde{X}). \tag{15}$$

To facilitate interpretation of these results, equation (13) can be written in the form[13]

$$(1+{}_\Gamma R_f)^{-1} = (1+R_f)^{-1}\, E(1 - \tilde{\Gamma}) + \mathrm{cov}(-\tilde{Y}\tilde{X},\, \tilde{\Gamma}). \tag{16}$$

In general, one might expect $\mathrm{cov}(-\tilde{Y}\tilde{X}, \tilde{\Gamma})$ to be positive—poorly endowed states (high Y_e) to be accompanied with low marginal tax rates, though the actual sign of the covariance term is dependent upon the distribution of the rate of inflation. If $\mathrm{cov}(-\tilde{Y}\tilde{X}, \tilde{\Gamma}) > 0$, then $(1 + R_f) \geqslant (1 + {}_\Gamma R_f)\, E(1 - \tilde{\Gamma})$, which suggests that if the expected marginal tax rate is estimated neglecting the covariance term in equation (16), it will be underestimated.

Apart from a general wealth tax, it is of interest to consider the effects of other forms of taxation upon the structure of asset prices. Suppose that income from investment is taxed. Consider a bond with market value B that pays one dollar before tax in every state of nature. If a particular state e occurs, the after tax wealth of an individual owning the bond is $\$[1-\Gamma_e(1-B)]$, where it is again assumed that all individuals have the same state dependent tax rate. Clearly, for a discount bond this is equivalent to taxing the implicit interest or yield on the bond. The market value of the bond is determined by

$$\Sigma_e\, \pi_e\, Y_e X_e[1-\Gamma_e(1-B)] = B, \tag{17}$$

which can be written in the form

$$E(\tilde{Y}\tilde{X}) - B = E(\tilde{Y}\tilde{X}\tilde{\Gamma})\ (1-B). \tag{18}$$

The left-hand side of equation (18) can be interpreted as the difference in price between a tax free bond and the taxable bond, B, and the right-hand side as the present value of the tax paid on the taxable bond.

[13]In a more general model with individuals differing in wealth and tax rates, individuals in different tax brackets will then have a preference for either the taxable or tax free bond. Consequently, an additional term must be added to equation (15), which reflects differences in the average marginal rates of substitution for the two groups. Define two sets I_{1e}, I_{2e}, such that individual $i \epsilon I_{1e}$ if $P_e/(1-\Gamma_e{}^i) < B_e$ and individual $K \epsilon I_{2e}$ if $P_e/(1-\Gamma_e{}^K) \geqslant B_e$ then

$$(1+{}_\Gamma R_f)^{-1} = (1+R_f)^{-1}\, E(1 - \tilde{\Gamma}) + \mathrm{cov}[\tilde{Y}\tilde{X}, (1 - \tilde{\Gamma})] + E(\tilde{\eta}\tilde{X})\, E(1 - \tilde{\Gamma}),$$

where

$$Y_e = \rho \sum_{i \epsilon I_{1e}} U'(C_e{}^i) \Big/ \sum_{i \epsilon I_{1e}} U'(C_0{}^i)$$

$$Y_{1e} = \rho \sum_{K \epsilon I_{2e}} U'(C^k{}_e) \Big/ \sum_{K \epsilon I_{2e}} U'(C^k{}_0)$$

$$\tilde{Y} = \tilde{Y}_1 + \tilde{\eta}.$$

The relationship between the nominal rates of return on the taxable and nontaxable bonds is given by, using equation (18),

$$_{B}R_{f}\,[1 - E(\tilde{\Gamma})] = R_{f} + {}_{B}R_{f}\,(1 + R_{f})\,\mathrm{cov}(\tilde{Y}\tilde{X},\,\tilde{\Gamma}), \tag{19}$$

where $(1+{}_{B}R_{f})^{-1} = B$, and R_{f} is the nominal riskless rate of interest on the tax free bond, $(1+R_{f})^{-1} = E(\tilde{Y}\tilde{X})$. If the marginal tax rate is not state dependent then equation (19) would reduce to the expression used by McCulloch [15] and Scott [24]. The presence of the extra covariance term arises because if individuals have different wealth and tax rates, as is usually the case, the average marginal tax rate will be state dependent even though individual tax rates could be state independent. This implies that estimation of the marginal tax rate neglecting this extra covariance term will be biased. If the covariance term is negative, as previously argued, then the marginal tax rate will tend to be underestimated.[14]

The taxation of investment income provides a general description of the tax treatment accorded to treasury bills, if held to maturity. In many empirical studies treasury bill data are used to make inferences about the real rate of interest (see [6, 19]). As taxation is usually neglected, it is instructive to compare the estimates of the expected real rate of return on the taxable bond with the real rate of interest using the data given in Table 2. The expected real rate of return on the taxable bond is given by

$$1+{}_{B}\bar{r}_{f} = (1+{}_{B}R_{f})\,E(\tilde{X}). \tag{20}$$

In Table 2, case 1, the nominal rate of interest on the taxable bond is 6.8 percent, assuming a state independent marginal tax rate of 30 percent. The expected real rate of return is -3.39 percent, given that the expected rate of inflation is 10.56 percent. In case 2, the expected rate of inflation is 15.56 percent and the nominal rate of interest on the taxable bond is 12.98 percent.[15] The expected real rate of return is -2.07 percent. Again it is seen that even though social endowments remain fixed in the two cases, the expected real rate of return changes. Furthermore, when the two estimates are compared to the real rate of interest, which is -5.27 percent, it is observed that in the presence of taxation substantial bias can result.

It should also be observed that now in the presence of taxation there is a positive relationship between changes in the expected real rate of return on the nominal risk-free taxable bond and changes in the expected rate of inflation, instead of the negative relationship that was observed in section 3.[16] While these results indicate the possible serious nature of the biases that can occur when returns are subject to personal taxation, most empirical studies completely ignore the effects of taxation.[17]

[14]In attempting to estimate marginal tax rates McCulloch [15] neglects such a term.

[15]Again, it is seen that the ordinary Fisher relationship does not hold. A 4.33 percent increase in the expected rate of inflation causes a 6.18 percent increase in the nominal rate of interest on the taxable bond.

[16]While Nelson and Schwert [18] express some awareness of the possible pitfalls of neglecting taxation, they ignore this and present evidence of a negative relationship between the expected real rate of return and the expected rate of inflation.

[17]See, e.g., [3, 4, 7, 19]. Numerous other references could be given.

5. MULTI-PERIOD PRICING

To extend the analysis to a multi-period framework, consider a three date ($t = 0, 1, 2$) economy. At date $t = 0$ an individual acts to maximize the expected utility of present and future consumption:

$$\text{Max } U(C_0) + \rho_1 \Sigma_e \pi_e U(C_e) + \rho_1 \rho_2 \Sigma_e \pi_e \Sigma_s \pi_{s.e} U(C_{s.e}),$$

subject to the constraints

$$\begin{aligned} W_0 &= C_0\theta_0 + \Sigma_e P_e W_e + \Sigma_e P_e \Sigma_s P_{s.e} W_{s.e} \\ C_e\theta_e &= W_e(1-\Gamma_e) \\ C_{s.e}\theta_{s.e} &= W_{s.e}(1-\Gamma_{s.e}), \end{aligned}$$

where at date $t = 2$ any one of S ($s = 1, 2, \ldots, S$) states can occur; $\pi_{s.e}$ denotes the state e conditional subjective probability attached to state s; $P_{s.e}$ denotes the state e conditional date $t = 1$ present value of one dollar received at date $t = 2$ iff state s occurs; ρ_2 measures patience between dates $t = 1$ and $t = 2$; $\theta_{s.e}$ denotes the state e conditional dollar price per unit of consumption good in state s at date $t = 2$; $C_{s.e}$ denotes the state e conditional quantity of consumption in state s at date $t = 2$; $\Gamma_{s.e}$ is the state e conditional personal tax rate in state s at date $t = 2$; and $W_{s.e}$ is the number of purchased state e conditional claims that pay one dollar iff state s occurs at date $t = 2$.

The necessary and sufficient conditions for a unique optimum are

$$\begin{aligned} P_e U'(C_0)/\theta_0 &= \rho_1 \pi_e (1-\Gamma_e) U'(C_e)/\theta_e \\ P_{s.e}(1-\Gamma_e) U'(C_e)/\theta_e &= \rho_2 \pi_{s.e}(1-\Gamma_{s.e}) U'(C_{s.e})/\theta_{s.e}, \end{aligned} \tag{21}$$

plus the budget constraint. To provide for the endogenous determination of security prices, aggregate production decisions across dates and states are given—see equations (5), (6), and

$$C^M_{s.e} = \Sigma_i C^i_{s.e}, \tag{22}$$

and the money supply in each state is given—see equations (7), (8), and

$$M^s_{s.e} = \Sigma_i C^i_{s.e} \theta_{s.e}. \tag{23}$$

While tax rates may differ over states, assume for simplicity that all individuals have the same tax rate. From equation (21) the nominal riskless rate of interest on one and two period discount bonds is respectively given by

$$(1+{}_\Gamma R_{f1})^{-1} = E[\tilde{Y}_1 \tilde{X}_1 (1-\tilde{\Gamma}_1)] \tag{24}$$

and

$$(1+{}_{\Gamma}R_{f2})^{-2} = E[\tilde{Y}_1\tilde{X}_1\tilde{Y}_2\tilde{X}_2(1-\tilde{\Gamma}_2)], \tag{25}$$

where $X_{ie} = (1 + \gamma_e)^{-1}$; $X_{2s.e} = (1 + \gamma_{s.e})^{-1}$; $Y_{ie} = \Sigma_i\rho_1 U_i'(C_e^i)/\Sigma_i U_i'(C_0^i)$; $Y_{2s.e} = \Sigma_i\rho_2 U_i'(C_{s.e}^i)/\Sigma_i U_i'(C_e^i)$; $1 - \Gamma_{1e} = 1 - \Gamma_e$; and $1 - \Gamma_{2s.e} = 1-\Gamma_{s.e}$. The effect of taxation upon the term structure can be demonstrated by comparing the interest rates on one and two period nontaxable discount bonds:

$$(1 + R_{f1})^{-1} = E(\tilde{Y}_1\tilde{X}_1), \tag{26}$$

and

$$(1 + R_{f2})^{-2} = E(\tilde{Y}_1\tilde{X}_1\tilde{Y}_2\tilde{X}_2). \tag{27}$$

Thus

$$(1 + {}_{\Gamma}R_{f1})^{-1} = (1 + R_{f1})^{-1}\, E(1-\tilde{\Gamma}_1) + \text{cov}\,(\tilde{Y}_1\tilde{X}_1,\ 1-\tilde{\Gamma}_1), \tag{28}$$

and

$$(1 + {}_{\Gamma}R_{f2})^{-2} = (1 + R_{f2})^{-2}\, E(1-\tilde{\Gamma}_2) + \text{cov}\,(\tilde{Y}_1\tilde{X}_1\tilde{Y}_2\tilde{X}_2,\ 1-\tilde{\Gamma}_2). \tag{29}$$

If personal tax rates are not state dependent then the covariance terms in equations (28) and (29) are zero implying a direct linear relationship between prices. However, if rates of return on a per period basis are used, this introduces a nonlinearity of the form

$$(1 + R_{fn}) = (1 - \Gamma_n)^{1/n}(1 + {}_{\Gamma}R_{fn}). \tag{30}$$

For large value of n (maturity) the difference between the two rates will be small. Using equation (30), the relationship between the forward rates of interest for the taxable and nontaxable bonds is

$$(1 + {}_{t+1}f^{\Gamma}_{1,t}) = (1 + {}_{t+1}f_{1,t})(1-\Gamma_1)/(1-\Gamma_2), \tag{31}$$

where ${}_{t+1}f^{\Gamma}_{1,t}$ is the forward rate for the taxable bonds and ${}_{t+1}f_{1,t}$ is the forward rate for the nontaxable bonds. The form of equation (31) suggests that the bias will, in general, be negligible.

This type of result explicitly depends upon the form of tax considered. Instead of a general wealth tax, suppose that investment income is taxed. Consider a bond with market value B_2 that pays one dollar, before tax, in every state of nature at date $t = 2$. Generalizing equation (17) the market value of the bond is given by

$$E(\tilde{Y}_1\tilde{X}_1\tilde{Y}_2\tilde{X}_2) - B_2 = E(\tilde{Y}_1\tilde{X}_1\tilde{Y}_2\tilde{X}_2\tilde{\Gamma}_2)(1-B_2), \tag{32}$$

which can be interpreted in the same way as equation (18). If tax rates are not state dependent, then equation (32) reduces to the form

$$(1 + {}_BR_{f2})^2 = (1 + R_{f2})^2/(1 - \Gamma_2) - \Gamma_2/(1 - \Gamma_2). \tag{33}$$

where $(1 + {}_BR_{f2})^{-2} = B_2$, and R_{f2} is the nominal riskless rate of interest for the two period tax free discount bond. The forward rates of interest implied by the taxable and nontaxable bonds are related by

$$1 + {}_{t+1}f^B_{1,t} = \left(\frac{1 - \Gamma_1}{1 - \Gamma_2}\right)\left[1 + {}_{t+1}f_{1,t} - \frac{\Gamma_2}{1 + R_{f1}}\right] \Big/ \left[1 - \Gamma_1/(1 + R_{f1})\right], \tag{34}$$

using equations (19) and (33). The difference between the two forward rates can be quite large. For example, if the nominal risk free rates of interest on one and two period tax free bonds are 7.7 percent and 8.54 percent, respectively, implying a forward rate of 9.39 percent, then the rates of interest on the one and two period taxable bonds are 11.0 percent and 12.0, respectively, assuming a marginal tax rate of 30 percent. The forward rate of interest is 13.0 percent. Given the use of taxable bond data in empirical studies, the size and nonsystematic nature of the bias can induce spurious results.[18]

6. IMPLICATIONS AND CONCLUSIONS

It has been shown that even in the absence of personal taxation, the expected real rate of return on the nominal riskless discount bond is a biased estimator of the real rate of interest. This might induce spurious results in empirical studies examining the determinants of the real rate of interest, the stationarity of real rate of interest, and the correlation between the real rate of interest and the rate of inflation.

The introduction of personal taxation affects the structure of asset prices and might cause substantial bias in the estimation of the real rate of interest and forward rates of interest, though the magnitude of the bias is sensitive to the form of taxation. For empirical studies examining the determinants of term premia, the tax induced bias in the estimation of the forward rates of interest can cause spurious results. Estimation of the expected marginal tax rate derived by comparing the yields on taxable and nontaxable bonds will also, in general, be biased.

Hypothetical data has been used to demonstrate some of the empirical implications of the problems raised in this paper. For the empirical researcher, the results of this paper indicate possible pitfalls in methodology and interpretation of results. Whether these results are "serious" or of second order is an empirical question, which remains to be answered.

[18]Fama [6], in examining the use of forward rates of predictors of future spot rates, completely neglects the effects of personal taxation.

LITERATURE CITED

1. Cargill, Thomas F., and Robert A. Meyer. "Intertemporal Stability of the Relationship Between Interest Rates and Price Changes." *Journal of Finance,* 32 (September 1977), 1001-15.
2. Carlson, John A. "Short-Term Interest Rates as Predictors of Inflation: Comment." *American Economic Review,* 67 (June 1977), 469-75.
3. Elliott, Jan W. "Measuring the Expected Real Rate of Interest: An Exploration of Macroeconomic Alternatives." *American Economic Review,* 67 (June 1977). 429-44.
4. Fama, Eugene. "Short Term Interest Rates as Predictors of Inflation." *American Economic Review,* 65 (June 1975), 269-82.
5. ______. "Inflation Uncertainty and Expected Returns on Treasury Bills." *Journal of Political Economy,* 84 (June 1976), 427-48.
6. ______. "Forward Rates as Predictors of Future Spot Rates." *Journal of Financial Economics,* 3 (October 1976), 361-78.
7. ______. "Interest Rates and Inflation: The Message in the Entrails." *American Economic Review,* 67 (June 1977), 487-96.
8. Fama, Eugene, and G. William Schwert. "Asset Returns and Inflation." *Journal of Financial Economics,* 5 (November 1977), 115-46.
9. Feldstein, Martin. "Inflation, Income Taxes, and the Rate of Interest: A Theoretical Analysis." *American Economic Review,* 66 (December 1976), 809-20.
10. Fischer, Stanley. "The Demand for Index Bonds." *Journal of Political Economy,* 83 (June 1975), 509-34.
11. Fisher, Irving. *The Theory of Interest as Determined by Impatience to Spend Income and Opportunity to Invest It.* New York: Macmillan, 1930.
12. Friedman, Milton. "The Quantity Theory of Money—A Restatement." *In Studies in the Quantity Theory of Money,* edited by Milton Friedman. Chicago: University of Chicago Press, 1956.
13. Hess, Patrick J., and James I. Bicksler. "Capital Asset Prices Versus Time Series Models as Predictors of Inflation: The Expected Real Rate of Interest and Market Efficiency." *Journal of Financial Economics,* 2 (December 1975), 341-60.
14. Hirshleifer, Jack. *Investment, Interest, and Capital.* Englewood Cliffs, N.J.: Prentice-Hall, 1970.
15. McCulloch, J. Huston. "The Tax-Adjusted Yield Curve." *Journal of Finance,* 30 (June 1975), 811-30.
16. Mundell, Robert A. "Inflation and Real Interest." *Journal of Political Economy,* 71 (June 1963), 280-83.
17. Nelson, Charles R. "Estimation of Term Premiums From Average Yield Differentials in the Term Structure of Interest Rates." *Econometrica,* 40 (March 1972), 277-87.
18. Nelson, Charles R., and G. William Schwert. "Short Term Interest Rates as Predictors of Inflation: On Testing the Hypothesis that the Real Rate of Interest is Constant." *American Economic Review,* 67 (June 1977), 478-86.
19. Pesando, James. "Determinants of Term Premiums in the Market for United States Treasury Bills." *Journal of Finance,* 30 (December 1975), 1317-27.
20. Pye, Gordon. "On the Tax Structure of Interest Rates." *Quarterly Journal of Economics,* 83 (November 1969), 562-79.
21. Robichek, Alexander A., and W. David Niebuhr. "Tax-Induced Bias in Reported Treasury Yields." *Journal of Finance,* 25 (December 1970), 1081-90.

22. Rubinstein, Mark. "An Aggregation Theorem for Securities Markets." *Journal of Financial Economics,* 1 (September 1974), 225–44.

23. ———. "The Valuation of Uncertain Income Streams and the Pricing of Options." *Bell Journal of Economics,* 7 (Autumn 1976), 407–25.

24. Scott, James. "The Valuation of Nominal Cash Flows with Risk Adjusted Discount Rates and Market Certainty Equivalents." Working Paper, Columbia University, December 1977.

GERALD P. DWYER, JR.*

The Effects of the Banking Acts of 1933 and 1935 on Capital Investment in Commercial Banking

1. INTRODUCTION

FOLLOWING THE BANKING CRISIS of the early 1930s, a temporary deposit-insurance plan administered by the Federal Deposit Insurance Corporation (FDIC) was begun by the Banking Act of 1933 and became effective on January 1, 1934.[1] This temporary system was extended by Congress until a permanent system was established by the Banking Act of 1935. The maximum value of any person's total deposits in a commercial bank that is insured has been increased over time, but other than these changes the system has changed little over the years. The rapid and virtually complete acceptance of federal deposit insurance suggests that it is an inexpensive substitute for other forms of insurance. By the middle of 1934, about 90 percent of all commercial banks with 97 percent of deposits had been approved for insurance; in 1974, slightly over 98 percent of all commercial banks with 99 percent of deposits were covered.

Because the insurance charges are not designed to prevent substitution, commercial banks have an incentive to substitute deposit insurance for the forms of insur-

*The Federal Reserve Bank of Chicago generously supported this research during my stay there, and the members of a research department seminar, especially Larry Mote, provided several helpful comments. Nonetheless, the analysis and conclusions should not necessarily be attributed to any employee or any part of the Federal Reserve System. Fellowships from the Earhart Foundation and Intercollegiate Studies Institute also supported parts of this research. Several stimulating discussions with Sam Peltzman have significantly improved the paper. Members of the Money and Banking Workshop at the University of Chicago and the Money Workshop at Texas A&M also provided several helpful comments. The referees' comments led to a substantial sharpening of the empirical results.

[1]For a more detailed discussion of federal deposit insurance, see [4; 3, pp. 434–42].

GERALD P. DWYER, JR., *is assistant professor of economics, Texas A&M University.*

0022-2879/81/0581-0192$00.50/0
JOURNAL OF MONEY, CREDIT, AND BANKING, vol. 13, no. 2 (May 1981)

ance used prior to 1933—most pertinently, bank capital. Besides holdings of low-risk assets, equity capital is an important form of insurance. Depositors losses are less for a given loss on loans if equity capital is greater relative to deposits. The emergence of deposit insurance, however, has made the size of equity capital immaterial for covered depositors, except for a possible restriction of their deposit accounts for a day or two after bankruptcy.

Nonetheless, the assumption of insurance by the FDIC implies that the level of equity capital is not a matter of indifference to that institution. If the FDIC wishes to limit its losses, as is generally supposed, then the prior concern of depositors has been transferred to the FDIC. Depositors previously expressed and enforced their judgments by their choice of banks, thereby affecting the earnings of bank owners. FDIC charges are not based on the level of capital; therefore, there is no direct impact on owners' earnings. Instead, the FDIC has tried to enforce its judgment of asset portfolios and "capital adequacy" by persuasion based upon examinations with powerful and seldom-used penalties available.

Cross-section studies suggest that banks have substituted deposit insurance for capital; a single time-series study by Adrian W. Throop [11] suggests that they have not. Sam Peltzman's [8] cross-section estimates suggest that bank regulators have not prevented the substitution of deposit insurance for bank capital, and that deposit insurance explains all of the decline of the capital-deposit ratio since 1935. A study by John J. Mingo [6], using cross-section data and a model similar to Peltzman's, also indicates that banks have substituted deposit insurance for bank capital.

This contrast in results is particularly disturbing because the use of cross-section results to establish a counterfactual historical proposition is fraught with difficulty. Moreover, since one of the variables included in the cross-section regressions is the return to investors in banks, arbitrage in banking implicitly is assumed to be imperfect across state lines [8] or even across banks within the same local areas [6]. Explicitly, Peltzman and Mingo each assume that opportunity costs do not differ across their observations.

The purpose of this paper is to estimate a model explaining bank capital investment and to examine the effects of the Banking Acts on bank capital using the time-series data. A model of capital supply developed by Peltzman [7] has been the basis of all of the previous empirical work.[2] In section 2, a model of capital investment based on both demand and supply is formulated. Empirical estimates then are presented.

2. THE MARKET FOR BANKING CAPITAL

The model of capital investment presented in this section is based upon the idea that bank capital is an input into the production of banking services.[3] Not only is

[2]Throop [11] attempts to differentiate his model from Peltzman's, but it is also based on capital supply alone.

[3]The definition of banking output has been a subject of substantial controversy, but no particular definition is necessary for the present problem. For a detailed discussion of the functions of banking capital, see [8, pp. 1–2].

bank capital an input because it is used to purchase assets, but more importantly because it provides insurance to depositors against a decline in the value of bank's assets. Investors in bank stock are suppliers of capital and managers of their portfolios. Operators of banks are demanders of capital, or, at one remove, depositors are the demanders of capital.

If this much is granted, then the general formulation of the market for bank capital naturally suggests itself. After presenting the model of capital investment, I discuss briefly the relationship between entry and the capital investment model. Competition is assumed throughout this section, except where the contrary is explicitly stated.

A Supply and Demand Model of Capital Investment

A simple version of a model including demand factors is based on the flow supply of capital $(dc/dt)^s$ and the stock demand for capital c^d (lower-case italic letters denote the logarithms of variables). The quantity of capital demanded declines as the cost of capital paid by a bank, π, increases, because a bank can adjust to a higher cost of capital by increasing the pecuniary and nonpecuniary rates that it pays to depositors, reducing the probability of capital losses by decreasing the riskiness of its loan portfolio, and reducing its assets to adjust to a higher cost of capital. The quantity of capital supplied per unit of time rises as π increases relative to the alternative rate of return, π_a, due to adjustment and search costs borne by investors and implies that, despite an infinitely elastic long-run supply of capital at π_a, the rate of return received by investors in banking is not always equal to π_a.[4]

The workings of the model can be illustrated graphically (see Fig. 1). Initially the stock of capital is $0A$ and demand is c^d, which implies that $\pi = \pi_a$ and the flow of capital supplied is zero (or, more generally, the expected growth rate). Suppose that demand unexpectedly increases from c^d to $c^{d'}$, due to an unexpected increase in the demand for banking services.[5] With the existing stock $0A$, π increases to π_1 and the flow supplied increases from zero to $0a$. Over time the stock increases to $0B$, which implies that π falls to π_2 and the flow supplied falls to $0b$. Thus, the model represents a return to stock-flow equilibrium over time with the flow of capital supplied to banking returning to zero and π declining to π_a.

This model can be augmented by a stock supply of capital that has a finite elasticity with respect to π.[6] The upward slope of the stock-supply curve is due to

[4]Of course π less marginal adjustment cost equals π_a.

[5]If deposits are viewed as an output of banks, it is plausible that an increase of deposits will result in an increase in the demand for banking capital because an increase of deposits desired by customers can be viewed as an implicit increase of the demand for capital services. If deposits are viewed as an input, then the reader should think of an increase of the demand for loans with deposits and capital complements in the production of loan services.

[6]The flow supply of capital combined with a finite-elasticity stock supply is the basis of the model proposed by Peltzman [7]. This model, however, is an amalgamation of supply and demand in which an increase of deposits increases the *supply* of capital to banks by investors.

Both Peltzman's model and the one presented here are special cases of the model discussed in detail by Friedman [2, chap. 17], which includes finite-elasticity flow and stock demands as well as supplies. Empirical results not reported are consistent with a hypothesis of infinitely elastic flow demand; therefore, this elaboration is not pursued.

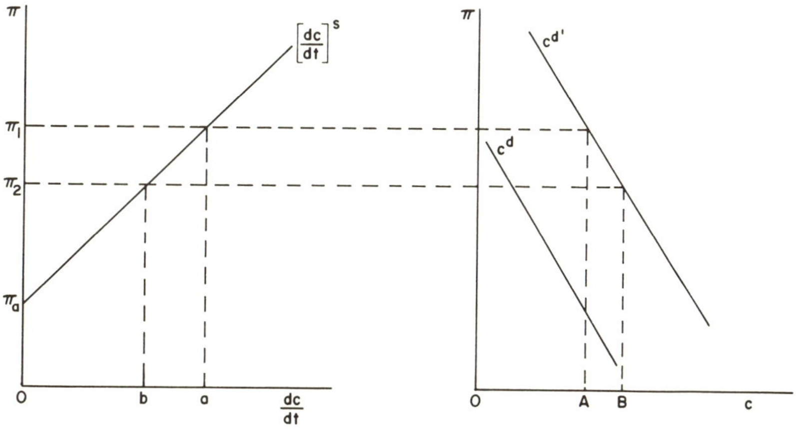

FIG. 1. The Bank Capital Market.

risk aversion and an increase of the risk associated with portfolios as larger proportions of them are invested in a single industry.[7] As can be verified, the only difference between the simple model in Figure 1 and one with a finite elasticity of stock supply is that π is not necessarily equal to π_a in long-run equilibrium.[8]

This analysis can be summarized compactly in two equations. The logarithm of the quantity of capital demanded by an individual bank j, c_j^d, is a function of the cost of capital, π, and other variables. This can be written

$$c_j^d = \underset{(-)}{f(\pi, \ldots)},$$

where the sign in parentheses indicates the sign of the variable's partial derivative. Aggregating over all banks and assuming that the quantity of capital demanded is homogenous of degree one in the number of banks, the aggregate equation is

$$(c-n)^d = \underset{(-)}{f(\pi, \ldots)}, \qquad (1)$$

where n is the number of banks. The flow supply of bank capital is a function of the rate of return in banking, π, the level of capital in banking relative to the level of real capital in alternative employments C_a, and other variables. Presumably this function should reflect aggregation over investors as equation (1) reflects aggregation over banks, but I ignore this for lack of data and suppose that the rate of change of investors is constant. Therefore, the flow supply of capital can be written

[7]This line of argument was suggested by Sam Peltzman in conversation.

[8]Throop's argument [11, pp. 194–96] that competitive supply of bank capital implies no effect of deposit insurance on the rate of return to investors can be interpreted as an attempt to impose this long-run market equilibrium result on a structural equation.

$$\frac{dc^s}{dt} = \underset{(+)}{g(\pi}, \underset{(-)}{c^s - c_a}, \ldots). \tag{2}$$

If deposit insurance is an effective substitute for bank capital and bank regulators have not prevented banks from substituting the insurance for capital, then an increase of deposit insurance shifts the demand for capital to the left, decreases the level of capital, and may decrease the marginal rate of return to investors. If the stock supply of capital is infinitely elastic (as in Fig. 1), then the marginal rate of return will temporarily fall and eventually return to equality with the alternative rate of return, with the fall of the equilibrium capital stock equal to the decrease of the demand for capital. If the stock stupply has a finite elasticity, then the marginal rate of return to investors declines and the capital stock falls less than the full amount of the decrease in demand. Therefore, inclusion of a deposit-insurance variable in the stock demand for capital permits a test of the hypothesis that banks have substituted deposit insurance for bank capital.

Other variables in addition to the proportion of deposits insured, *INSR*, affect the level of demand for banking services and the allocation of assets. I assume that the demand for capital is proportional to the level of total deposits per bank, *D/N*, other variables in the model constant. Because capital plus deposits is approximately equal to total liabilities, the level of total assets is fixed. Given total assets, the capital desired by banks is a decreasing function of cash assets, that is, those assets that are currency or have low costs of trading into currency and a low probability of loss. Except for required reserves, cash assets are endogenous to banks' decisions and are inversely related to interest rates on loans and investments. I include the short-term commercial paper rate, *CPR*, as a determinant of the return on loans and investments and therefore the level of nonrequired cash assets. In addition, the required reserve ratio, *RRR*, is included in the equation as an exogenous determinant of cash assets. In linear form the demand equation is

$$(c-n)^d = a_1 + \underset{(-)}{b_{11}\pi} + \underset{(+)}{b_{12}(d-n)} + \underset{(+)}{b_{13}\, CPR} + \underset{(-)}{b_{14}\, RRR} + \underset{(-)}{b_{15}\, INSR}. \tag{3}$$

The equation for the supply of capital is completed by adding rates of return from alternative allocations of investment. It is also desirable to correct the measured rate of return for losses, which is accomplished by including the failure rate F.[9] The rate of return on alternative equity investments, π_a, and the rate of return on commodities, dp/dt, are included as measures of rates of return on alternative investments. The supply equation in linear form with these variables included is

$$\frac{dc^s}{dt} = a_2 + \underset{(+)}{b_{21}\pi} + \underset{(-)}{b_{22}F} + \underset{(-)}{b_{23}(c^s - c_a)} + \underset{(-)}{b_{24}\pi_a} + \underset{(-)}{b_{25}\left[\frac{dp}{dt}\right]}. \tag{4}$$

[9]The rate of return paid by any bank in operation is π. The average rate of return received by owners is less than this, π adjusted for failures.

Including the return of commodities as a short-term return rather than as the expected rate of change of prices over a long period is better than ignoring the nominal character of the other yields in the equation. Nonetheless, the variable's short horizon suggests that taking the difference between the long-term rates of return and the current rate of change of prices is likely to be a poor approximation of the real long-term rates of return.

In this continuous time version, the model is closed by the fixity of the level of capital at any point in time, and the equality of quantities demanded and quantities supplied. Superscripts "s" and "d" disappear in equations (3) and (4), and a new equation, $c = \bar{c}$, the fixed level of capital, is added. Thus, there are three equations in the three endogenous variables, c, dc/dt, and π, and the system of equations is complete.

The Effect of Entry Restriction on the Model

There is one important effect of the Banking Acts of 1933 and 1935 on the bank-charter market that could complicate estimation of the capital-investment model. It is possible the rate of return to owners, which is calculated as a long-term interest rate times the ratio of the market value of bank stock to the book value, reflects rents received by organizers of banks. This calculated yield is an average yield, not the marginal return for capital invested in existing banks.

An increase of economic rents due to entry restriction would be reflected in an increase of the measured rate of return and, consequently, a seeming decrease in the supply of capital to banking and a seeming increase in the demand. At first glance this appears paradoxical but the effects are quite straightforward. It is simplest to examine the problem in the simple model of Figure 1 with an infinitely elastic stock supply. The economic rents force a divergence between the measured rate of return and the marginal return available to investors. If π is interpreted as the average return, this divergence is reflected in an upward shift of the flow supply in the $\pi - dc/dt$ plane. Similarly, banks are paying the marginal return, not the average; therefore, the quantity demanded as a function of average return shifts up. These vertical shifts are equal because the divergence between the average and marginal rates are the same for both investors and banks.

It is likely that the most important empirical confounding of changes of economic rents and the effects of deposit insurance is a result of the introduction of deposit insurance in the 1930s and the simultaneous regulation of deposit interest rates and restriction of entry. The rapid acceptance of deposit insurance suggests that deposit insurance generates rents for commercial banks. In addition, although alternative interpretations are possible, there is some evidence that the regulation of interest rates paid on deposits by commercial banks have reduced the rates paid [1; 3, pp. 434–45; 9; 5]. These restrictions were applied to member banks in the Banking Act of 1933 and to all insured banks in the Banking Act of 1935. Combined with an effective restriction of entry, some economic rents to commercial banks, which were capitalized in their market value, may have ensued. If the divergence between the average and marginal rate has not changed since 1935, a dummy variable in both the demand and supply equations suffices to estimate this effect on the average rate of return used in the regressions. The essential assumption for the estimated capital investment model is that, for practical purposes, changes in the divergence are unrelated to the variables in the model.[10]

If the divergence between the average and marginal rates of return is adequately represented as being constant, then the relationship of the coefficients of the capital demand and supply equations can be derived. With a subscript m to denote the marginal rate of return, the marginal rate of return is

$$\pi_m = \pi - R, \tag{5}$$

where R is the part of the rate of return that is rent and is not collected by investors in existing banks. If a dummy variable DV equals one if the divergence is R, and zero if the divergence is zero, then the coefficients of the dummy variable, b_{16} and b_{26}, with the average rate of return, π, in equations (3) and (4) are

$$\begin{aligned} b_{16} &= -b_{11} R \\ b_{26} &= -b_{21} R. \end{aligned} \tag{6}$$

I assume that the divergence between average and marginal returns due to the Banking Acts began in 1936, one year after the Banking Act of 1935 codified a "convenience-and-needs" criteria for federal charters, Federal Reserve membership of new banks, and deposit insurance. This is the same date Peltzman [7, pp. 11–13] uses.

3. EMPIRICAL ESTIMATES OF THE ACTS' EFFECTS ON BANK CAPITAL

In the first part of this section, the continuous-time model is reduced to a discrete-time counterpart. Empirical estimates of this model are presented with tests of hypotheses concerning the effects of the banking acts and deposit insurance.[11]

The set of continuous-time equations, (3) and (4) with (6), are approximated by measuring the levels of variables either at the middle of years or by annual averages. Rates of change are calculated from the beginning to the end of the year. As a consequence, the level of capital is no longer fixed but is endogenous. If the rate of change of capital in the first half of the year is a stable linear function of the rate of change over the whole year, then the equation

$$(c - c_{-\frac{1}{2}}) = a_3 + b_{31} \, \Delta c \tag{7}$$

[10]This is not as implausible as it seems at first. The restriction of entry by regulators may have been reflected more in the nonreplacement of banks that failed from 1929 through 1934 than in a subsequent decrease in the number of banks. The number of banks fell by almost 40 percent from 1929 to 1934. The number of commercial banks reached a minimum in 1962 and has risen since. The decline from 1934 to 1962 was about 13 percent, or a compounded annual rate of decrease of one-half percentage point per year.

[11]A discussion of the empirical definitions of the variables is presented in a data appendix available from the author.

can be used to determine the mid-year level, where $c_{-\frac{1}{2}}$ is the logarithm of the exogenous beginning-of-the-year level and Δc is the rate of change from the beginning to the end of the year.[12]

The simultaneous-equations estimation technique used to estimate the model—three-stage least squares—requires that a different endogenous variable be specified on the left-hand side of each equation in the model. The demand equation (3) is renormalized with the rate of return in banking, π, on the left-hand side and capital on the right-hand side, which has no effect on the demand equation specified other than to divide all coefficients and the error term by $-(1/b_{11})$.[13] Even though this change may be a minor disadvantage of the technique, three-stage least squares is useful for implementing tests of hypotheses across equations and for valid tests of restrictions on the coefficients.

The estimated coefficients of the supply and demand equations are presented in Table 1.[14] In the demand equation, capital's coefficient is constrained to equal the negative of deposit's coefficient, because a test indicates that this hypothesis is consistent with the data. All of the estimated coefficients have the correct signs except the coefficient of the rate of return in alternative uses of capital, which is not statistically significant.[15] The evidence on the substitution of deposit insurance for bank capital in these data is extracted before discussing the estimated elasticities of supply and demand.

The hypothesis that the Banking Acts of 1933 and 1935 have had no direct effect on the demand for bank capital and the supply of bank capital marginally cannot be rejected. The joint hypothesis that the dummy variable's and the insurance variable's coefficients are zero cannot be rejected; these restrictions yield an F-ratio of 2.51 with 3 and 144 degrees of freedom, less than the 5 percent significance value of 2.67. The hypothesis that the insurance variable's estimated coefficient is zero marginally cannot be rejected at the 5 percent significance level; the variable's t-ratio is -1.93. A test of the hypothesis that both of the dummy variable's estimated coefficients are zero has an F-ratio of 3.75 with 2 and 144 degrees of freedom. This has a marginal significance level of about 2.5 percent. These results are consistent with the hypothesis of no substitution, though not strikingly so.

The hypothesis that coefficients are zero, while usual, is not necessarily the appropriate null hypothesis. It is the appropriate null hypothesis if one's prior belief is that the Banking Acts had no direct effect on bank owner's rents and capital investment. On the other hand, if one's prior belief is that the Banking Acts did

[12]Estimates of equation (7) are not presented with the estimated supply and demand equations because they are of no intrinsic interest.

[13]The estimated coefficients from two- or three-stage least squares are not independent of the normalization. For example, if the demand equation were estimated with the capital-deposit ratio on the left and π on the right, and the supply equation were estimated with π on the left and the rate of change of bank capital on the right, the estimated coefficients would not be the same as those obtained by taking the coefficients actually estimated and calculating the coefficients of these transformed equations.

The particular normalization chosen is based on initial two-stage least squares estimates, which suggests that this normalization minimizes the problem of serial correlation of residuals in the sample.

[14]As in [7], the year 1933 is excluded from the sample for reasons discussed in the data appendix available from the author.

[15]This result for π_a is consistent with the evidence in [7]. The closeness of the coefficient of Δp to one is suspicious, but initial tests suggest that the results are not sensitive to the deletion of Δp.

TABLE 1

ESTIMATED SUPPLY AND DEMAND REGRESSIONS (1921–74)

Normalized Endogenous Variables	Right-hand Side Variables and Estimated Coefficients							Standard Error of Residuals
	Constant	*c-d*	*CPR*	*RRR*	*INSR*	*DV*		
π†	0.0535 (3.73)*	−0.0050 (−0.71)	0.3911 (4.16)	−0.3534 (−4.59)	−0.0184 (−1.93)	0.0233 (2.57)		0.0093
	Constant	π	*F*	$c\text{-}c_a$	π_a	Δp	*DV*	
Δc	−0.4335 (−5.23)	1.3699 (2.17)	−1.2501 (−7.11)	−0.0677 (−4.63)	0.4238 (1.16)	−0.9401 (−8.64)	−0.0256 (−1.83)	0.0201
	Rent Component of π Equal to 2 Percent							
	Constant	*c-d*	*CPR*	*RRR*	*INSR*	*DV*		
π	0.0505 (4.35)	−0.0059 (−0.91)	0.4026 (4.49)	−0.3394 (−5.26)	−0.0156 (−2.42)	0.0200		0.0093
	Constant	π	*F*	$c\text{-}c_a$	π_a	Δp	*DV*	
Δc	−0.4269 (−7.67)	1.3116 (4.55)	−1.2340 (−7.40)	−0.0670 (−8.04)	0.4357 (3.21)	−0.9306 (−10.00)	−0.0262 (−4.55)	0.0198

*Estimated *t*-ratios are in parentheses.

†The variables are π, the rate of return in banking; Δc, the change of the logarithm of bank capital; *c-d*, the logarithm of the capital-deposit ratio; *CPR*, the commercial paper rate; *RRR*, the ratio of required reserves to total deposits; *INSR*, the fraction of deposits insured; *DV*, a dummy variable equal to zero before 1936 and one subsequently; *F*, the failure rate; $c\text{-}c_a$, the logarithm of the ratio of bank capital to capital in the economy; π_a, the rate of return on equity capital in alternative uses; and Δp, the change of the logarithm of the price level.

increase rents to bank owners, then the appropriate test is a different one. The alternative question to be asked of the data is: Can we reject the hypothesis that rents were created by deposit insurance and, conditional on acceptance of this hypothesis, was deposit insurance substituted for bank capital?

Conditional on the hypothesis that the average rate of return was raised 2 percentage points per year (0.02 as the variable is actually measured), the hypothesis that deposit insurance has not been substituted for bank capital can be rejected. A test of this hypothesis is implemented by imposing the increased rent per dollar of capital, performing an F-test of the implied restrictions on the coefficients of the dummy variables, and performing a t-test on the estimated coefficient of *INSR*. The divergence of 2 percentage points per year between the measured return and the marginal returns to investors is estimated from the initial three-stage least squares estimates in Table 1.[16] The F-ratio for the restriction on the dummy variable's coefficients is 0.13 with 1 and 144 degrees of freedom. The estimates (in Table 1) subject to the restrictions on the dummy variable's coefficients also yield a t-ratio of −2.42 for the fraction of deposits insured. Therefore, it cannot be said that the data are inconsistent with the hypothesis that the Banking Acts of 1933 and 1935 have created rents in the banking industry and that, conditional on acceptance of this hypothesis, deposit insurance has been substituted for bank capital.[17]

TABLE 2

ESTIMATED CORRELATION MATRIX (1921–74)

	c-d	*INSR*	*DV*	Time
c-d	1.00			
INSR	−0.80	1.00		
DV	−0.83	0.92	1.00	
Time	−0.71	0.89	0.77	1.00

The inability to reject either hypothesis can be explained by multicollinearity. Consider the correlation matrix in Table 2. With the exception of time, these variables are on the right-hand side of the demand equation when allowance is made for the posited effects of the banking acts. These high correlations are consistent with the hypothesis that deposit insurance has affected the level of capital in banking. The introduction of deposit insurance and the restriction of entry were virtually simultaneous; the fraction of deposits insured rose from 0 to 60 percent in 1935. Therefore, the fraction of deposits insured has a substantial jump that results in a

[16]Two percentage points per year is an approximation to the implied rents in the estimated supply and demand equations if the restrictions are to be satisfied. A maximum-likelihood procedure could be used to fit the model with the restrictions (6) and simultaneously obtain an estimate of that part of the rate of return due to rents. Such estimates would not, however, be very different than the rough 2 percentage points obtained from the unrestricted estimates in Table 1. From equation (6), the restriction tested is that $(b_{11}/b_{16}) = (b_{21}/b_{26})$.

[17]The block of F-tests in this paragraph and above produce the same conclusion when the estimates are altered by: (i) not constraining the coefficients of c and d in the supply equation to be equal in absolute value; (ii) not constraining the coefficients of c and c_a in the demand equation to be equal in absolute value in addition to (i); and (iii) deleting 1932 and 1934, years with questionable data. The F-ratios generally are smaller for all tests. The point estimates of coefficients are little different than those in Table 1.

high positive correlation with the dummy variable. If deposit insurance has the hypothesized effect, then the capital-deposit ratio would be expected to fall noticeably within a few years. In fact, it did fall: the capital deposit ratio fell from 18 percent in 1931 to 16 percent in 1935 and 14 percent in 1936; the capital-deposit ratio has not been as high as 10 percent since 1942.[18]

While the decline of the capital-deposit ratio is consistent with the hypothesis that deposit insurance reduced the demand for capital, which thereby explains the multicollinearity, these observations are no substitute for statistical evidence that the alternative hypothesis of no effect can be rejected.[19] These estimates from the time-series data do not, however, provide such evidence. In addition, because of the imprecision of the estimated elasticity of demand, it is not possible to get a very precise estimate of the reduced-form effect of deposit insurance.

The estimated structural parameters in Table 1, nonetheless, can be used to estimate characteristics of the bank-capital market. It makes little difference, but I will base the estimates of market characteristics on the restricted model at the bottom of Table 1.

The point estimate of the elasticity of demand is quite high. Measured at the mean of the rate of return in banking, about 5 percentage points per year, the estimated elasticity of demand is -8.5. The large asymptotic standard error of the estimated coefficient of the stock of capital implies that this estimate is very imprecise. Evidence from other sources, probably cross-section data, will be necessary to reduce the imprecision of this estimate.

The long-run elasticity of supply is greater than the short-run elasticity but is far from infinitely elastic. The estimated coefficient of the stock of capital in banking relative to alternative uses is easily significant; therefore, the hypothesis that the long-run, or stock, supply is infinitely elastic can be rejected. Peltzman's intuition that the stock supply has a finite elasticity appears to be confirmed. The point estimate of the long-run elasticity of supply is about 0.98. The point estimate of the short-run, or flow, elasticity is about 0.07.

The final characteristic of the bank capital market of general interest is the average lag between changes in the desired stock of capital and changes in the actual stock. For this purpose, it is useful to view the estimated equations as the set of differential equations that they are intended to approximate.[20] To estimate the average lag, it is important that the system be stable, which it is. The median lag—the length of time that passes before 50 percent of adjustment to a change is completed—is about nine years for the system as a whole. This is remarkably close to the estimate of eleven years obtained by Peltzman from cross-section data [8, p. 19].

[18]The decline in the average value is not just the result of a trend in the two sample periods. The correlation of *c-d* with time is -0.02 from 1921 through 1931 and -0.30 from June 1935 through 1974. The correlation of *INSR* and time is 0.93 from 1935 through 1974.

[19]One possible statistical fixup to generate such evidence would be to estimate the model in first-difference form. This, however, can have adverse effects on residuals. More importantly, the primary interest is in the long-run effects of the banking acts. As Sims points out [10, p. 173], a first-difference filter emphasizes the short-run or high-frequency movements in the data, which gives more weight to these short-run movements in the estimated coefficients and less weight to the long-run movements.

[20]It makes little difference if they are treated as difference equations.

4. SUMMARY AND CONCLUSIONS

The explicit introduction of the demand for bank capital clarifies the relationship between the bank capital and bank charter markets. With a demand and a supply equation, the natural result is that the marginal return to investors is determined in the capital market. Nonetheless, if rents to existing banks and returns to organizers of banks are posited, these rents and returns are determined in the bank-charter market and appear in the calculated average return. Thus, the markets for bank capital and bank charters jointly determine the measured average rate of return in banking.

In addition, an explicit demand for bank capital permits a test of Peltzman's [8] hypothesis that the supply of bank capital has a finite elasticity in the long run. The hypothesis that the supply is infinitely elastic is indeed rejected. It is, however, better to have an empirical basis for this proposition instead of positing it.

The empirical results also resolve a conflict of cross-section and time-series evidence concerning the substitution of deposit insurance for bank capital. There is no conflict. As Throop [11] found, these estimates indicate that the time-series data are consistent with the hypothesis that banks have not substituted deposit insurance for bank capital. Conditional on the hypothesis that the banking acts created rents captured by owners of banks, the estimates in this paper are consistent with the hypothesis that deposit insurance has been substituted for bank capital. The time-series data do not contain enough information to distinguish between these hypotheses. By default, cross-section evidence on the effects of deposit insurance is decisive.

Two highly pertinent issues remain unresolved. Because of multicollinearity, the estimated coefficients of the demand equation are imprecise. Cross-section estimates of the demand for capital by commercial banks should be very useful for increasing the precision of these estimates. In addition, the estimates presented in this paper provide no evidence on either the preferences of bank regulators concerning the substitution of deposit insurance for bank capital or on the extent to which substitution desired by banks has been prevented by bank regulators.

LITERATURE CITED

1. Cox, Albert H., Jr. *Regulation of Interest Rates on Bank Deposits*. Michigan Business Studies, Volume 17, Number 4. Ann Arbor, Mich.: University of Michigan, 1966.
2. Friedman, Milton. *Price Theory*. Chicago: Aldine, 1976.
3. Friedman, Milton, and Anna J. Schwartz. *A Monetary History of the United States, 1867–1960*. Princeton, N.J.: Princeton University Press, 1963.
4. Golembe, Carter H. "The Deposit Insurance Legislation of 1933: An Examination of its Antecedents and its Purposes." *Political Science Quarterly*, 75 (June 1960), 181–200.
5. Klein, Benjamin. "Competitive Interest Payments on Bank Deposits and the Long-Run Demand for Money." *American Economic Review*, 64 (December 1974), 931–49.
6. Mingo, John J. "Regulatory Influence on Bank Capital Investment." *Journal of Finance*, 30 (September 1975). 1, 111–21.

7. Peltzman, Sam. "Entry in Commercial Banking." *Journal of Law and Economics,* 8 (October 1965), 11-60.

8. ______. "Capital Investment in Commercial Banking and Its Relationship to Portfolio Regulation." *Journal of Political Economy,* 78 (January/February 1970), 1-26.

9. Ruebling, Charlotte E. "The Administration of Regulation Q." *Federal Reserve Bank of St. Louis Review,* 52 (February 1970), 29-40.

10. Sims, Christopher A. "The Role of Approximate Prior Restrictions in Distributed Lag Estimation." *Journal of the American Statistical Association,* 67 (March 1972), 169-75.

11. Throop, Adrian W. "Capital Investment and Entry in Commercial Banking: A Complete Model." *Journal of Money, Credit, and Banking,* 7 (May 1975), 193-214.

YORAM LANDSKRONER
NISSAN LIVIATAN

Risk Premia and the Sources of Inflation

1. INTRODUCTION

THE PROCESS OF INFLATION is associated not only with a rising general price level, but also with *uncertainty* about its rate of change. It is the latter aspect of inflation that may give rise to risk premia on nominal assets as compared with a real safe asset. A possible framework for analyzing the structure of risk premia under inflationary conditions is the well-known Capital Asset Pricing Model (CAPM) developed by Sharpe and Lintner. Indeed, a number of papers have recently dealt with these risk premia by means of the CAPM framework or some close variety of it. We may mention the works of Roll [9], Sarnat [10], Fischer [4], Chen and Boness [1], and Friend, Landskroner, and Losq [5].[1]

The CAPM and its extentions to conditions of inflation use a microeconomic approach in a partial equilibrium analysis of the risk premia. A basic feature of the foregoing literature is the implicit treatment of inflation as exogenous. Alternatively, there is no theory to relate the real return on money (to be denoted π) to the other variables in the CAPM formulation. This leads to two important shortcomings. First, the covariance of π with the rates of return appears as completely arbitrary. Second, since π was considered as exogenous, the authors did not consider the need to include in their models the government's nominal transfer pay-

[1]Chen and Boness [1] and Friend, Landskroner, and Losq [5] derive models of capital asset pricing under uncertain inflation. Sarnat [10], Fischer [4], and to some extent also Roll [9] concentrate on the effects of indexed bonds on financial equilibrium. In the latter study money balances are included.

YORAM LANDSKRONER *is lecturer, School of Business Administration, and* NISSAN LIVIATAN *is professor of economics, Hebrew University of Jerusalem.*

0022-2879/81/0581-0205$00.50/0
JOURNAL OF MONEY, CREDIT, AND BANKING, vol. 13, no. 2 (May 1981)

ments to the public, which are often the main source of inflation. These shortcomings limit severely the conclusions one can draw from the analysis.

It may be noted that the lack of attention to the macroeconomic aspects of inflation led most of the writers to omit money completely from the list of assets in the CAPM. Some of the writers who do include money assume explicitly, as Fama and Farber [3], or implicitly that the government does not make any payments to individuals, which means, in the present context, that we have inflationary uncertainty with a fixed money supply. This implies that the inflationary uncertainty is caused only by "real" disturbances (such as technological changes or varying "weather" conditions). We know, however, that monetary factors which lead to changes in the money supply are often the more important causes of inflation.

Why is it important to inquire into the sources of inflation when one analyzes risk premia? The answer is that information about the origins of inflation provides additional information about the covariances among some important rates of return and especially about the covariance of transfer payments made by government and returns from assets. These covariance terms in turn are among the main determinants of the risk premia.

An attempt to use macroeconomic constraints to analyze risk premia on nominal bonds was made by Levhari and Liviatan [6, 7]. However, their analysis has not been formulated in terms of the familiar CAPM approach. They do not deal with risky equity or stocks and do not consider the case where we have both monetary and real disturbances simultaneously.

The purpose of the present paper is to integrate the two approaches mentioned above. Thus, we shall still use the CAPM approach as the microeconomic basis of the analysis, but we shall impose on it the macroeconomic constraints relating to the sources of inflation. In particular, we shall have to state explicitly the relation between output, transfer payments, and prices on the aggregative level to supplement the individual's optimization problem. By integrating micro and macro aspects of the analysis, we shall be able to derive some new conclusions about the effects of inflation uncertainty on the risk premia.

2. EQUILIBRIUM MODEL OF CAPITAL ASSET PRICING UNDER INFLATION INCLUDING THE GOVERNMENT SECTOR

We consider an economy with the following attributes. (1) Capital markets are perfectly competitive, thus there are no transaction costs and investors are price-takers. (2) Individuals have homogeneous expectations about future rates of return on risky securities and changes in the general price level. (3) Individuals (hereafter investors or households) are risk averse, with a planning horizon of two periods. They are assumed to maximize the sum of utility of current (first period's) consumption (including consumption of liquidity services) and expected utility of end of (first) period wealth (second period's consumption) In addition. we assume the existence of two sectors in the economy—the private sector consisting of investors (households) and firms producing a single commodity, and the government sector that collects taxes from households and transfers some payments to households.

Following this structure of the economy, we assume two types of capital assets. The first type is marketable securities of the private sector consisting of stocks, nominal bonds, and real bonds, which are bonds whose return is linked to commodity prices. The second type of assets is a nonmarketable monetary one issued by the government—these are the nominal net transfer payments of the government to the households, that is, transfer payments minus personal tax payments. Our treatment of transfer payment is similar to that of corporate dividends, in the sense that their *probability distribution* but not the specific outcome is known in advance. In our model individual investors are distinguished from firms in that only individuals issue nominal bonds and are subject to taxation and transfer payments. This definition of the economy and assets represents a fundamental expansion over the traditional models of financial equilibrium in which analysis is limited to a single sector economy (only private sector), which usually deals only with marketable assets, excluding money from the analysis.

The notation used in the subsequent analysis follows:

S_i = the market value of the ith stock
S_{ih} = the market value of the hth investor's holding of the ith stock
B_{nh} = the market value of the hth investor's holdings of the nominal bond
B_{fh} = the market value of the hth investor's holdings of the real (linked) bond
π = the random real return on money, i.e., $\pi = (1/p_2)/(1/p_1)$, where P_1 and P_2 are the prices of the commodity at the beginning and end of the first period (first period and second period), respectively. Setting $P_1 = 1, \pi$ becomes the purchasing power of money in the second period.
R_i = the random real return on the ith stock (one plus the real [net] rate of return)
R_n = the random real return on the nominal bond, where $R_n = r_n \pi$, and r_n is the nonrandom nominal return
R_f = the nonrandom real return on the real riskless bond
t_h = the random nominal *net* transfer payment received by the hth investor divided by P_1
c_h = real consumption of the hth investor
m_h = the nominal money balances of the hth investor divided by P_1.

Using the above notation the budget constraint (initial wealth) of the hth investor can be written as

$$V_h = c_h + m_h + \sum_i S_{ih} + B_{fh} + B_{nh}. \tag{1}$$

The investor's end of first period (and beginning of second period) real wealth can then be expressed as

$$W_h = m_h\pi + \sum_i S_{ih}R_i + B_{nh}R_n + B_{fh}R_f + t_h\pi$$

or

$$W_h = \sum_i S_{ih}(R_i - R_f) + B^*_{nh}(R_n - R_f)$$

$$+ \left(V_h - c_h - \frac{(r_n - 1)m_h}{r_n} \right) R_f + t_h\pi, \quad (2)$$

where $B^*_{nh} = (B_{nh} + (m_h/r_n))$ are his nominal "bond" holdings and $(V_h - c_h - ((r_n - 1)m_h/r_n))$ can be considered to be the "investable" wealth of the household. Thus, in our analysis, money balances, m, are partitioned into two components: $((r_n - 1)m_h/r_n)$ represents consumption of liquidity services and a second component (m_h/r_n) represents an investment that is equivalent to an investment in a nominal bond. For this reason, one may combine the two, that is, (m_h/r_n) and B_n, into a new variable B^*_n as in equation (2).[2] In the subsequent analysis subscripts h for households will be dropped except where required for clarity. The investor's expected utility can be expressed as

$$F = J(c, m) + E\,[U(W)], \quad (3)$$

where $J(c, m)$ and $U(W)$ are strictly concave utility functions of consumption and wealth, respectively. The investors maximize expected utility in equation (3) subject to the budget constraint of equation (2). This maximization yields the first order conditions with respect to (c, m, S_i, B^*_n).

In order to obtain explicit demand relations, we have to assume specific forms of the utility functions of the investor. In this paper we are mainly interested in financial equilibrium relations and therefore will only specify parameters of a utility function of wealth. We assume a quadratic utility function of end of period wealth of the following form:

$$U_h(W_h) = \alpha_h W_h - \beta_h W_h^2, \quad (4)$$

where by construction $\beta > 0$ and $\alpha > 2\beta W$ in order to be consistent with the assumptions of risk aversion and positive marginal utility. The derivation of the following equilibrium results is based on the standard procedure of the traditional CAPM. Because of space limitations we will not present the explicit calculations in the present paper but only the final results. Summing the first-order condition for stock i over all investors yields a return equilibrium relation for the ith stock:[3]

$$A[E(R_i) - R_f] = [S\,\mathrm{cov}(R_i, R_m) + B^*_n\,\mathrm{cov}(R_i, R_n) + \mathrm{cov}(R_i, t\pi)],$$
$$(\text{all } i), \quad (5)$$

[2]This useful interpretation of money balances was provided by Fama and Farber [3].

[3]It has been shown by Mayers [9] and can also be shown here that the introduction of nonmarketable assets in the opportunity set of investors will result in investors no longer having the same portfolio of risky assets. Thus, the separation theorem of the traditional CAPM will not hold.

where

$S = \sum_i \sum_h S_{ih}$ is the aggregate market value of all stocks

R_m = the weighted return on all stocks in the market

B_n^* = the aggregate market value of all "nominal" bonds, $B_n^* = \sum_h B_{nh}^* = (1/r_n)\sum_h m_h = m/r_n$, since by the clearing condition $\sum_h B_{nh} = 0$, i.e., borrowing cancels out lending in the market as a whole

$t = \sum_h t_h$ is total nominal value of government transfer payments

$[A = \sum_h \frac{\alpha}{2\beta} - \sum_h E(W)] > 0$, since marginal utility of wealth is positive.

Summing equation (5) over assets yields:

$$A[E(R_m) - R_f] = S \text{ var}(R_m) + B_n^* \text{ cov}(R_m, R_n) + \text{cov}(R_m, t\pi). \tag{6}$$

where $A^{-1} \equiv \gamma$ is a market risk aversion factor, it is equal to the market price of risk that is a measure of market compensation in terms of return per unit of market risk.

In a similar way, we can derive the equilibrium return differential for the nominal bond:

$$A[E(R_n) - R_f] = [B_n^* \text{ var}(R_n) + S \text{ cov}(R_m, R_n) + \text{cov}(R_n, t\pi)]. \tag{7}$$

Results (5) to (7) in their general form are similar to those obtained in the traditional CAPM.

3. INFLATION SOURCES AND ASSET PRICING

Let us now introduce explicitly the sources of inflationary uncertainty. The monetary shocks will be represented by the variability of the transfer payments that are assumed to be provided to the population by printing new money (this includes taxation as negative transfer payments). The "real" shocks will be associated with "technological uncertainty"[4] on the production side. Each firm (i) is assumed to produce a random output y_i of a uniform commodity ("wheat"). For the sake of simplicity we shall consider the distribution of y_i as given, as will be the case in the very short run, where all inputs are fixed.

In view of the foregoing assumption, we may interpret the returns on stocks as

$$R_i = \frac{y_i}{S_i}, \text{and } R_m = \frac{y}{S} = \sum \left(\frac{S_i}{S}\right) R_i,$$

where $y = \sum y_i$ is the aggregate output in the economy.

We may now relate the monetary and real variables to the general price level by means of the "quantity theory of money" equation, which states that for the economy as a whole

[4]For a discussion of technological uncertainty, see Diamond [2].

$$(M + T) = kP_2y. \tag{8}$$

Thus, next period's money supply (consisting of this period's nominal money stock M plus next period's nominal transfer payments) is proportional to the nominal value of next period's output. Alternatively, we may write equation (8) as

$$\pi(m + t) = ky, \tag{9}$$

where $\pi = (P_1/P_2)$, $m = (M/P_1)$, and $t = (T/P_1)$. The main assumption concerning equations (8) and (9) is that k is a positive constant, the famous "Cambridge k." This means that possible variations in next period's k are considered to be of little consequence. While this assumption greatly simplifies the analysis, it does not alter qualitatively our results with respect to "monetary inflation," as will be explained below (see n. 5).

The expressions for the risk premia on stocks and on the nominal bond as given by equations (5)-(7) can be expressed alternatively as

$$A[E(R_n) - R_f] = \text{cov}(R_n, W) \tag{10}$$

$$A[E(R_m) - R_f] = \text{cov}(R_m, W) \tag{11}$$

$$A[E(R_i) - R_f] = \text{cov}(R_i, W), \tag{12}$$

where $W = \Sigma_h W_h = SR_m + B_n^* R_n + t\pi$. Using the appropriate definitions and equation (9), we can express W as

$$W = y + m\pi + t\pi = y(1 + k). \tag{13}$$

we may then rewrite equations (10)-(12) as follows:

$$A[E(R_n) - R_f] = (1 + k)r_n\text{cov}(\pi, y) \tag{14}$$

$$A[E(R_m) - R_f] = (1 + k)\frac{1}{S}\text{var}(y) \tag{15}$$

$$A[E(R_i) - R_f] = (1 + k)\frac{1}{S_i}\text{cov}(y_i, y). \tag{16}$$

A. Monetary Inflation

Let us consider first the extreme case where all the variation in the purchasing power of money, π, originates from the monetary side. In this case we assume for *aggregate* output $\text{var}(y) = 0$, although we permit random variability of individual outputs y_i. Since in this case y is a constant and all the risk premia in equation (14)-(16) are zero, we have a unique expected real return

$$R = R_f = E(R_n) = E(R_m) = E(R_i), \qquad \text{(all } i\text{)}. \tag{17}$$

Thus in the case of "monetary inflation" we obtain the classic Fisher equation, $R_f = r_n E(\pi)$, in terms of expected values.[5]

The elimination of the risk premium for the nominal bond requires some comment. Following equations (7) and (10) we have

$$A[E(R_n) - R_f] = r_n[m \operatorname{var}(\pi) + \operatorname{cov}(\pi, t\pi)].$$

The first term in the brackets on the RHS of the equation, $m \operatorname{var}(\pi)$, indicates the positive effect of uncertainty about the purchasing power of money on the risk premium. However, the second term on the RHS reminds us that we have also to take into account the compensating effect of the transfer payments. In fact, since $t\pi = ky - m\pi$, we have $\operatorname{cov}(\pi, t\pi) = -m \operatorname{var}(\pi)$, which shows that the compensating variation in $t\pi$ offsets completely the effect of the first term of the risk premium.

At this point the reader may wonder why should anyone wish to hold a *positive* amount of nominal bonds if it does not command a premium over the safe indexed bond (holdings of nominal *liabilities* are easily explained as a hedge against inflationary variation in real balances). Since $B_{nh}\pi$ is subject to uncertainty, the investor must receive some compensation to make him hold B_{nh} willingly. The compensation that he gets is related to the variation in transfer payments, the real value of which is $t_h\pi$. For the average investor $t_h\pi$ must vary inversely to $B_{nh}\pi$, since we know from our earlier discussion that $\operatorname{cov}(\pi, t\pi) = -m \operatorname{var}(\pi)$. It follows that for all investors who have a negative covariance between π and $t\pi$, the asset $B_{nh}\pi$ serves as a hedge against the variability of $t_h\pi$. It is this hedging property of nominal bonds that constitutes an implicit compensation.

B. Real Inflation

The other extreme case is where all the variability of π originates from real factors, that is, from y, so that t equals a constant that can be taken to be zero, $\operatorname{var}(t) \equiv 0$, and $\operatorname{var}(y) > 0$. We shall refer to this case as "real inflation." Using equation (9), which in this case reduces to $m\pi = ky$, equation (14) becomes

$$A[E(R_n) - R_f] = (1 + k)\frac{k}{m} r_n \operatorname{var}(y), \tag{18}$$

while equations (15) and (16) remain unchanged.

We thus find that under "real inflation" there are positive risk premia on the market portfolio of stocks and on nominal bonds, and these premia are related to

[5]It may be worthwhile at this stage to relax the assumption of the constancy of k. Suppose that when more money is being injected into the economy, through t, the nominal interest rate falls and hence k rises. Thus $\operatorname{cov}(t, k) > 0$. Since an increase in t will be associated with a decline in π (as p_2 rises), we have $\operatorname{cov}(\pi, k) < 0$. Applying this result to equation (11) we still find that $E(R_m) = R_f$, that is, no risk premium on the stock market expected return. However, from equation (10) we obtain $\operatorname{cov}(R_n, W) = r_n y \operatorname{cov}(\pi, k) < 0$, which implies $E(R_n) < R_f$. This is an interesting result, which may explain why we often do find that the inflation adjusted nominal rate (R_n) tends to be very low or even negative. Thus if k is allowed to vary then the positive risk premium on nominal bonds is not simply eliminated but may even become negative.

var(y). Thus in order to create a wedge between the return on the safe asset and the expected return on foregoing risky ones, we need to have variability of aggregate output. As for the risk premia on individual stocks, we find, as expected, that they are related to cov(y_i, y).

C. The Basic Theorem on Risk Premia Under Independence of Monetary and Real Shocks

The two cases considered above belong to a broader class in which we have simultaneously both monetary and real disturbances that are statistically independent. We may refer to these disturbances as "mixed and independent inflationary shocks." Letting variation in t and y represent the two types of disturbances, we consider the cases where $E[g(t)f(y)] = E[g(t)]E[f(y)]$, where g and f are any functions of t and y.

From equation (9) we have

$$\pi = \frac{k}{m} y\tau; \qquad \tau \equiv \frac{1}{1 + \frac{t}{m}}. \tag{19}$$

We may then state that τ and y are independent. This implies that $E(\pi) = (k/m)E(\tau)E(y)$. The case of monetary inflation is one where cov(τ, y) = 0, because y is constant, and a special case of real inflation is where $\tau \equiv 1$ (since $t \equiv 0$). The more general case is one of mixed (real and monetary) shocks that are statistically independent.

The formulas for risk premia in equations (15) and (16) remain unchanged for the most general case, that is, even when y and τ are not independent. As for the nominal bond in the latter case, the risk premium $E(R_n - R_f)$ can be expressed, using equation (19), as

$$E(R_n - R_f) = (1 + k)k\frac{r_n}{m}\text{cov}(\tau y, y)\gamma. \tag{20}$$

However, in the case of mixed and *independent* inflationary shocks we have $\text{cov}(\tau y, y) = (E\tau)\,\text{var}(y)$ so that we may express equation (20) as

$$E(R_n - R_f) = (1 + k)k\frac{r_n}{m}(E\tau)\ \text{var}(y)\gamma. \tag{21}$$

Thus under independence the risk premium on nominal bonds is necessarily positive (when var(y) $\rightarrow$ 0 the premium tends to zero as it should be under a monetary inflation).

Thus it has been shown that under the independence assumption, the market awards a positive risk premium for nominal bonds and for the market portfolios of stocks. There is, however, a much stronger relation between these risk premia. Specifically, under the independence assumption $E(R_n)$ and $E(R_m)$ must be exactly equal.

This basic theorem can be proved as follows. Substituting in equation (21) equation (15), we obtain (provided var(y) > 0)

$$E(R_n - R_f) = k\frac{r_n}{m}E(\tau)S[E(R_m) - R_f]. \tag{22}$$

However, under the independence assumption equation (19) implies $E(\tau) = (E(\pi)/E(y))(m/k)$. Substituting the latter expression in equation (21) and using the definition $E(R_n) = r_nE(\pi)$ and $E(y)/S = E(R_m)$ yields

$$E(R_n - R_f) = \frac{E(R_n)}{E(R_m)}E(R_m - R_f),$$

which implies $E(R_n) = E(R_m)$.

This result is rather surprising since it otherwise may be thought that the risk premium on stocks is determined by risks associated with the real factors of the economy, while the risk premium on nominal bonds is associated with the variability of the purchasing power of money, which is related to monetary factors. Our result shows, however, that if the real and monetary shocks are independent, then the macro constraint (equation (19)) imposes an equality of risk premia on stocks (in general) and nominal bonds.

An intuitive interpretation of this result may run as follows. We have seen in the case of a "monetary inflation" that the variability of the real transfer payments offsets the risk arising from the variability of the purchasing power of money. It seems that under independence of monetary and real shocks one may eliminate the risk arising from the monetary shocks in a similar way. We are then left only with influence of real shocks on the inflationary risk. However, under "real inflation" we have $\pi = (k/m)y$, that is, π is proportional to y. Recall that π is the source of risk on nominal assets while y (through $R_m = (y/S)$) is the source of risk of stocks. The proportionality of π and y implies therefore that the risk on nominal assets (B_n^*) and on stocks is essentially the same risk (through the macroeconomic constraint). Consequently, the risk premia must also be the same.

The assumption of independence is of course crucial in the derivation of the foregoing result. This may be illustrated by an extreme example. Suppose that the government is expected to follow a price-stabilizing policy by varying t so as to keep $(y/m+t)$ constant. We can then see from equation (14) that $E(R_n - R_f) = 0$ while by equation (15), $E(R_m - R_f) > 0$. This is the case when monetary policy stabilizes π completely so that nominal and indexed bonds become identical, and we are back at the usual capital asset pricing model with a single risk free bond.

LITERATURE CITED

1. Chen, Andrew H., and A. James Boness. "Effects of Uncertain Inflation on the Investment and Financing Decisions of a Firm." *Journal of Finance,* 30 (May 1975), 469–83.

2. Diamond, Peter A. "The Role of a Stock Market in a General Equilibrium Model with Technological Uncertainty." *American Economic Review,* 57 (September 1967), 759–76.

3. Fama, Eugene F., and André Farber. "Money, Bonds, and Foreign Exchange." *American Economic Review,* 69 (September 1979), 639–49.

4. Fischer, Stanley. "The Demand for Index Bonds." *Journal of Political Economy,* 83 (June 1975), 509–34.

5. Friend, Irwin, Yoram Landskroner, and Etienne Losq. "The Demand for Risky Assets Under Uncertain Inflation." *Journal of Finance,* 31 (December 1976), 1287–97.

6. Levhari, David, and Nissan Liviatan. "Government Intermediation in the Indexed Bonds Market." *American Economic Review Papers and Proceedings,* 66 (May 1976), 186–92.

7. Liviatan, Nissan, and David Levhari. "Risk and the Theory of Indexed Bonds." *American Economic Review,* 67 (June 1977), 366–75.

8. Mayers, David. "Nonmarketable Assets and Capital Market Equilibrium Under Uncertainty." In *Studies in the Theory of Capital Markets,* edited by Michael C. Jensen. New York: Praeger, 1972.

9. Roll, Richard. "Assets, Money, and Commodity Price Inflation Under Uncertainty Demand Theory." *Journal of Money, Credit, and Banking,* 5 (November 1973), 902–23.

10. Sarnat, Marshall. "Purchasing Power Risk, Portfolio Analysis, and the Case for Index-Linked Bonds." *Journal of Money, Credit, and Banking,* 5 (August 1973), 836–45.

NOTES, COMMENTS, REPLIES

A Reexamination of the Role of Stocks in the Consumption Function and the Transmission Mechanism

*A Note by Geoffrey Woglom**

''Money matters'' is a phrase that would spark little debate among economists today, in contrast to twenty-five years ago. There is much more debate, however, about the transmission mechanism of monetary effects. For example, most macroeconometric models show large monetary policy multipliers but contain very different transmission mechanisms (see [3]).

This paper examines one part of the transmission mechanism, the effect of stock prices on consumption, in the FMP Quarterly Model. The transmission mechanism in this model is particularly interesting because the model was designed to ''examine the influence of monetary policy actions on economic activity'' [4]. Franco Modigliani, in an article describing the transmission mechanism of the FMP model, highlighted the importance of the stock-price effect on consumption:

> In real terms, we see that, if we ignore the wealth effect, the money multiplier, . . . , is modest and slow; it reaches a peak of just about two, after two years, and tends to remain at that level one year later. By contrast when we allow for the wealth effect . . . the peak effect is reached in the fifth quarter and that peak is just over 3. By that quarter, the *wealth effect via consumption accounts for nearly half of the total.* (emphasis in the original) [7, pp. 48–49]

It should be emphasized that the wealth effect referred to is the wealth effect due solely to changes in stock prices.[1]

The large stock-price effect on consumption in the FMP model has been criticized both on theoretical and empirical grounds. On the theoretical level it has been

*Most of the research reported in this paper was done while I was at the Federal Reserve Bank of Boston. I would like to thank my colleagues at the Federal Reserve Bank, Stephen McNees and Richard Kopcke, for help and advice. The views expressed are my own and may not represent Federal Reserve opinion.

[1]The stock-price effect in the FMP consumption function is the only wealth effect that includes capital gains. Changes in capital values on all other household financial assets and liabilities are not included.

GEOFFREY WOGLOM *is associate professor of economics, Amherst College.*

0022-2879/81/0581-0215$00.50/0
JOURNAL OF MONEY, CREDIT, AND BANKING, vol. 13, no. 2 (May 1981)

pointed out that the life-cycle hypothesis underlying the FMP consumption function implies that changes in stock prices affect consumption through income and substitution effects [8]. Very little success, however, has been achieved at empirically separating out these income and substitution effects. This calls into question whether the empirically estimated consumption function is really consistent with the underlying theoretical model.

On more purely empirical grounds some have argued that the observed correlation between stock prices and consumption is neither a wealth effect nor a causal relationship. These critics argue that the pure stock-wealth effect on consumption will be small or zero because of the highly skewed distribution of stock ownership. The main function stock prices play in the consumption function is as a proxy, albeit a poor one, for consumer sentiment. These critics point to the fact that the size of the stock-price effect depends crucially on the estimation period and definition of variables (see [2, 5]).

If stock prices affect consumption because they serve as a proxy for consumer sentiment, the transmission mechanism through the stock-price effect is overstated in the FMP model. Monetary policy undoubtedly affects consumer sentiment and therefore stock prices, but monetary policy also affects stock prices directly by determining (at least in the short run) interest rates on competing financial instruments. Thus monetary policy is probably more powerful in affecting stock prices than consumer sentiment.

These arguments imply that there may be at least two roles for stocks in the consumption function: (1) the role of stocks as a component of household net worth; (2) the role of stock values as an implicit measure of consumers' expectations of future earnings. The observed instability of the stock-price effect on consumption in FMP-type equations may be the result of lumping the two roles of stock prices together. The two roles of stocks in the consumption function can be illustrated in the following simplified model that ignores lags and other complications of the estimated equations.

$$C = aYD + bVKN + cFVST + eRVST + u, \tag{1}$$

and $VST = FVST + RVST$; $FVST = f(\mathbf{Z})$; $RVST = g(\mathbf{X})$. C is consumption. YD is disposable income. VKN is the value of nonstock, household net worth. VST is the value of stocks. $FVST$ is the value of stocks due to quantifiable factors, the vector $\mathbf{Z}$. $RVST$ is the value of stocks due to nonquantifiable factors, the vector $\mathbf{X}$, which is comprised of unobservable variables reflecting investor confidence. A disturbance term is u. The FMP model imposes the restrictions $b = c = e$. The hypothesis that the nonquantifiable value of stocks reflects expectations of future income as well as being a component of net worth implies $e > c$. The hypothesis that the pure wealth effect of stocks is small or zero implies $b > c \geq 0$.

A test of the latter hypothesis is straightforward. A test of the former hypothesis is more difficult because of the nonlinearity of $f(\cdot)$. One test can be derived by regressing VST on the nonlinear function $f(\mathbf{Z})$, treating $RVST$ as a residual. Equation (1) is then estimated using the fitted values of $f(\mathbf{Z})$ as *FVST* and the residuals as *RVST*. The restriction that $c = e$ is the null hypothesis tested. There is no bias toward rejecting the null hypothesis when it is in fact correct.[2] Regressing *VST* on $f(\mathbf{Z})$ suffers from a misspecification problem, the omitted variable, $g(\mathbf{X})$. This will tend to increase the residual variance when the hypothesis $c > e$ is correct, causing a bias against rejecting the null hypothesis.

The first step in performing the tests is to derive an estimate of *FVST*. The theory of stock-price determination [6] suggests the quantifiable factors should be measures of the investors' discount rate and the quantifiable determinants of expected future earnings. Estimates of the current rental costs of producers' durables and structures are used to capture the effects of depreciation rates and tax laws on the present value of the returns to capital.[3] The monetary base and productive capacity of the business sector are used to capture the effects of quantifiable factors on expected future earnings. The effects of monetary policy on stock prices are accounted for in two ways: directly by the monetary base and indirectly by the corporate bond rate in the rental costs. By including these two measures of monetary effects, the major systematic impact of monetary policy on stock values should be accounted for.

Equation (2) is the regression used to identify *FVST* and *RVST*; the estimation period is 1960. I to 1977. III.

$$\begin{aligned}\log VST = \; & \underset{(-0.2)}{-0.9} + \underset{(3.8)}{2.7} \log MB + \underset{(1.4)}{1.9} \log (1 + RTPD) \\ & \underset{(-6.2)}{-7.5} \log (1 + RTPS) - \underset{(-0.4)}{0.4} \log XBC,\end{aligned} \tag{2}$$

$$\bar{R}^2 = 0.97,\ \rho = 0.78,\ \text{SEE} = 0.05,\ \text{D-W} = 1.3.$$

MB is the adjusted monetary base from the St. Louis Federal Reserve Bank. *RTPD* and *RTPS* are estimates of the current dollar rents on producers' durables and structures, respectively. *XBC* is productive capacity for business output. The coefficients on *MB* and *RTPS* enter with the expected signs and are statistically significant. *RTPD* and *XBC* have the wrong signs but are insignificant. The quantifiable value of stocks, *FVST*, is taken to be the antilog of the right-hand side of equation (2) plus one-half the estimated variance of the residuals.[4] The nonquantifiable value

[2]To the extent that *VST* is measured with error there may be a bias in favor of rejecting the null hypothesis in favor of an alternative that $c > e$. Presumably, the quantifiable factors are uncorrelated with measurement errors so that in regressing *VST* on $f(\mathbf{Z})$ the residuals *RVST* contain the measurement errors. As will be apparent from the results, the null hypothesis of $c = e$ is never rejected where the estimated value of $e < c$.

[3]In the FMP model the interest rate used in calculating the rental costs, however, is twice the dividend-price ratio. To avoid explaining stock prices with stock prices, the rental costs have been recalculated using the corporate bond rate as the competing financial interest rate. I wish to thank Douglas Battenberg of the Federal Reserve Board for providing these data.

[4]This adjustment is accurate only for the sample means. An alternative procedure involves a separate adjustment factor for each observation. This laborious procedure was not employed, because any inaccuracy in the identification of the quantifiable value of stocks biases against rejecting the null hypothesis when the alternative is correct.

TABLE 1

TESTS OF THE TWO ROLES OF STOCKS IN THE CONSUMPTION FUNCTION

Equation No.	*YD*	*U·YD*	*VKN*		*VST*	*FVST*	*RVST*	$\bar{R}^2$	SEE	ρ	D-W	End of Estimation	Restriction Tests
3	0.593	0.502	93.1		−0.6			0.999	0.0121	0.81	1.86	1977.III	$b = c$ $F(1,51) = 4.86$
	(9.0)	(2.3)	(4.0)		(−0.0)								
4	0.673	0.849		46.6				0.999	0.0126	0.88	1.72		
	(9.7)	(4.0)		(3.2)									
5	0.704	0.138	65.6		−3.8			0.999	0.0101	0.81	2.08	1972.IV	$b = c$ $F(1,32) = 1.39$
	(10.1)	(0.5)	(2.4)		(−0.0)								
6	0.757	0.149		34.5				0.998	0.0102	0.84	1.73		
	(11.9)	(0.5)		(2.6)									
7	0.694	−0.073	84.5			−38.6	32.2	0.999	0.0115	0.61	1.77	1977.III	$c = e$ $F(2,49) = 3.78$
	(18.7)	(−0.4)	(6.3)			(−2.1)	(1.4)						
8	0.644	0.394	78.7				45.7	0.999	0.0117	0.79	1.88		$c = e$ $F(2,30) = 10.98$
	(11.5)	(3.4)	(4.6)				(2.0)						
9	0.744	−0.041	81.9			−75.5	6.6	0.999	0.0079	0.30	2.17	1972.IV	$c = 0$ $F(2,49) = 1.82$
	(39.8)	(−0.3)	(8.8)			(−3.3)	(0.4)						
10	0.735	0.249	53.8				52.7	0.999	0.0090	0.49	1.93		$c = 0$ $F(2,30) = 5.85$
	(30.6)	(2.5)	(7.4)				(3.7)						

NOTE: All estimations start in 1963.I. Numbers in parentheses are *t*-statistics. *U* is a measure of the unemployment rate. *VKN* is a measure of real nonstock household net worth adjusted for capital gains on housing. *VST* is calculated by dividing a measure of corporate dividends by the S&P 500 dividend-price ratio.

The coefficients on *YD*, *U·YD*, and *VST* are the sum of the lag coefficients on second-degree polynomial. Almon lags tied at the tail. The lags on income terms are 9 period and the lags on stock wealth are 7 periods. These lags were selected to conform to those in the May 1977 writeup of the FMP Quarterly Model. Also, as in the FMP model the consumption function was estimated in per capita terms. The data come from the FMP Model File, and the May 1977 writeup contains a more detailed description of the variables and adjustments.

of stocks, *RVST,* is just the difference between *VST* and *FVST*. The exponentiation of equation (2) does not preserve the orthoganality of the fitted values and the residuals, but the correlation coefficient between fitted *FVST* and *RVST* is only 0.1.

Table 1 presents regressions of the FMP restrictions. Given the criticism expressed by Hymans [5] that the stock-price effect is sensitive to the estimation period, tests are performed with the full data set and with the data up to the 1973–1974 recession.

The results support Hymans's criticism. It is disconcerting that in neither equations (3) nor (5) does the coefficient on the stock-price variable enter with a significantly positive sign. Over the shorter estimation period, however, imposing the restriction b is equal to c does not hurt the explanatory power of the equation. Both equations (4) and (6) look similar to other estimations of the FMP specification (see [1; 2, p. 261]), though the estimation periods are different.

Equations (7) and (9) test the restriction $e > c$. The null hypothesis that the coefficients on the two measures of stocks are the same can be rejected for both estimation periods. In neither case, however, are the coefficients of the nonquantifiable value of stocks statistically significant, though they have the correct signs. More puzzling are the negative signs on *FVST* and the signs on $U \cdot YD$. It should be noted that while the sum of the lag coefficients of the latter term are not significantly different from zero, this is the result of summing significantly positive and negative lag coefficients. The coefficients of the $U \cdot YD$ terms are presumably meant to capture the marginal propensity to consume out of transitory income. While all the lag coefficients could conceivably be zero, none of the lag coefficients should be negative. Equations (7) and (9) while not supporting the alternative hypothesis appear to be suffering from other problems.[5]

Equations (8) and (10) attempt to solve the inappropriate sign on $U \cdot YD$ by dropping *FVST*.[6] None of the nine lag coefficients of $U \cdot YD$ is negative in equation (8) and only the first two are negative in equation (10), though neither of these two

[5]An alternative test of $c = e$ is to substitute *VST* and the vector **Z** for the stock terms in equation (1). The null hypothesis implies the coefficient on **Z** should be zero. Given $f(\cdot)$ is nonlinear this test is also biased. The test was tried with *MB* and *RTPS* as the elements of **Z**, with results similar to those reported in Table 1.

[6]Other methods were tried to solve the problem of the significantly negative coefficients on some of the lag terms of $U \cdot YD$. Equations (7) and (9) were estimated excluding *RVST* instead of *FVST* as in equations (8) and (10). This did not solve the problem. Additionally the sum of the lag coefficients of *FVST* continued to enter the equations with significantly negative signs in both estimation periods.

Equations (7) and (9) were also estimated excluding $U \cdot YD$ instead of either stock variable. In this regression the sum of the lag coefficients on *RVST* was 59.8 for the longer period and 53.1 for the shorter period, and both were statistically significant. The sum of the lag coefficients on *FVST* drops in absolute value from what it is in equations (7) and (9), falling to −20.1 and −10.7, respectively, with only the former statistically significant.

Finally, equations (7) and (9) were estimated with no lag terms of *FVST*. If *FVST* affects consumption solely as a component of net work, it is not clear it should enter the regression any differently than *VKN*. This equation also solves the problem; only the first two lag coefficients of $U \cdot YD$ in the regression with the shorter estimation period are negative, but they are insignificant. The coefficient on *FVST* is positive in one regression and negative in the other, in neither case statistically significant. The sum of the lag coefficients on *RVST* is 57.6 for the longer estimation period and 40.1 for the shorter period, both statistically significant.

Thus in any regression that avoids the anomalous, significantly negative coefficients on $U \cdot YD$ lag terms, the sum of the lag coefficients on *RVST* is of the correct a priori sign and statistically significant in both estimation periods.

coefficients is statistically significant. The sum of the lag coefficients of *RVST* are larger and are now statistically significant. The *F* statistics in the last column of Table 1 test the restriction that the coefficients of *FVST* are zero. Only in the longer estimation period does this hypothesis fail to be rejected. Thus imposing the restriction that the wealth effect of stocks is zero solves some of the problems of equations (7) and (9), provides support for the alternative hypothesis of nonquantifiable stocks as an expectational variable, but does hurt the explanatory power of the regression particularly in the shorter estimation period.

In none of the regressions was the FMP specification of the stock-price effect on consumption supported. There is modest support for the view that some changes in stock prices reflect expectation of future income. But over the estimation periods studied, it is difficult to reject the hypothesis that stocks do not belong in the consumption function.

LITERATURE CITED

1. Board of Governors of the Federal Reserve System. "The FMP Quarterly Model." Unpublished, May 1977.
2. Bosworth, Barry. "The Stock Market and the Economy." *Brookings Papers on Economic Activity,* 2 (1975), 257-300.
3. Christ, Carl. "Judging the Performance of Econometric Models of the U.S. Economy." In *Econometric Model Performance Compared,* edited by Lawrence R. Klein and Edwin Burmeister. Philadelphia: University of Pennsylvania Press, 1976.
4. Fromm, Gary. "Implications to and from Economic Theory in Models of Complex Systems." *American Journal of Agricultural Economics,* 55 (May 1973), 259–71.
5. Hymans, Saul H. "Comments and Discussion on Bosworth's Paper." *Brookings Papers on Economic Activity,* 2 (1975), 291-93.
6. Keran, Michael. "Expectations, Money, and the Stock Market." *Federal Reserve Bank of St. Louis Review,* 53 (January 1971), 16–31.
7. Modigliani, Franco. "Monetary Policy and Consumption." In *Consumer Spending and Monetary Policy: The Linkages,* pp. 9–85. Boston: Federal Reserve Bank of Boston, Conference Series No. 5, June 1971.
8. Tobin, James, and Walter Dolde. "Wealth, Liquidity and Consumption." In *Consumer Spending and Monetary Policy: The Linkages,* pp. 99–147. Boston: Federal Reserve Bank of Boston, Conference Series No. 5, June 1971.

A Dynamic Analysis of the Impact of Fiscal Policy on the Money Supply

*A Note by W. Douglas McMillin**

1. Introduction

Although a positive (accommodative) fiscal policy-money supply relationship is frequently suggested [3, 5], often because of an hypothesized overriding concern by the Federal Reserve with stabilizing interest rates, the available empirical evidence is mixed.[1] With the exception of [4], the empirical studies have provided estimates of the impact multipliers for various fiscal variables on alternative monetary variables, but they have not addressed the question of the impact of a sustained change in a fiscal variable upon the money supply over time. In a world in which fiscal variables affect financial and product sector variables with a lag, the examination of only the impact multipliers may give an incomplete and/or misleading picture. Thus, the aim of this paper is to extend the analysis to a dynamic setting in which the impact of the fiscal variables upon the time path of M1 is examined within the context of a small macroeconomic model. In particular, dynamic multipliers for the money supply are derived and analyzed.

2. Discussion of the Federal Reserve Reaction Function

The structural model employed is similar to that used in an earlier paper by McMillin and Beard [10]. It is a linear variant of the *IS-LM* model that incorporates endogenous taxes, an endogenous wealth variable, and inflationary expectations. The model is estimated by iterative three-stage least squares from nominal seasonally adjusted quarterly data beginning in 1953.I and ending in 1976.IV. Since the model is of a standard nature, the estimates of the structural model will not be presented here, but are available from the author upon request.

*The bulk of the simulations were performed while the author was research fellow at the Brookings Institution. The author thanks the Brookings Institution for the use of its facilities, and Thomas R. Beard, G. Randolph Rice, James A. Richardson, the editor, and two anonymous referees of the *Journal* for their many valuable comments.

[1]Some evidence of a positive relationship is found in [1, 2, 7, 10, 11]. Some evidence of a nonaccommodating relationship is found in [4, 6, 9, 12]. It should be noted, however, that with the exception of [2, 4, 10,11], the chief aim of these studies was not the investigation of the fiscal policy-money supply relationship. In many cases, the evidence is weak and/or the conclusions ambiguous.

W. Douglas McMillin *is assistant professor of economics, University of Kentucky.*

0022-2879/81/0581-0221$00.50/0
Journal of Money, Credit, and Banking, vol. 13, no. 2 (May 1981)

An essential element of the analysis is the treatment of Federal Reserve behavior as endogenous. The Federal Reserve is viewed as acting as though it minimizes a quadratic loss function subject to its perception of the structure of the economy. The loss function is given by

$$l = w_1(y_t - y_t^*)^2 + w_2(\dot{P}_t - \dot{P}_t^*)^2 + w_3(BT_t - BT_t^*)^2 + w_4(i_{m,t} - i_{m,t}^*)^2 . \quad (1)$$

It thus contains as arguments the weighted squared deviations of actual from desired (indicated by the *) values for real output (y_t), the inflation rate ($\dot{P}_t$), the balance of trade (BT_t), and the short-term interest rate ($i_{m,t}$). The first three arguments are measures of macroeconomic stabilization goals, and the last argument is a proxy for Federal Reserve concern for financial market stability.

Minimization of l subject to the structural model leads to specification of a reaction function that relates the Federal Reserve's policy variable—assumed to be unborrowed reserves adjusted for reserve requirement changes (UBR)—to the lagged endogenous and exogenous variables of the structural model (which include fiscal policy variables) and to the desired values of the arguments in the loss function.[2] The coefficients of this function are complex mixtures of the loss-function weights and the structural parameters. This reaction function contains twenty-two explanatory variables. However, to avoid undesirably reducing the degrees of freedom for the estimation, nominal output lagged one period (Y_{t-1}) is employed as a proxy for all lagged endogenous and exogenous variables other than exogenous Federal purchases of goods and services (G_t^F) and exogenous Federal net tax receipts ($T_t^{F,EX}$). The estimated reaction function is (t-statistics are in parentheses)[3]

$$\begin{aligned} UBR = {} & \underset{(6.21)}{2.57} + \underset{(4.02)}{0.026}G_t^F - \underset{(-2.38)}{0.027}T_t^{F,EX} + \underset{(19.73)}{0.015}Y_{t-1} + \underset{(6.88)}{0.007}y_t^* \\ & + \underset{(3.27)}{0.133}\dot{P}_t^* - \underset{(-13.31)}{0.583}i_{m,t}^* + \underset{(2.51)}{0.075}IRTBL, \end{aligned} \quad (2)$$

$$\bar{R}^2 = 0.998, \; SEE = 0.124.$$

All explanatory variables are statistically significant at the 5 percent level.

The estimated coefficients on the fiscal variables, G_t^F (0.026) and $T_t^{F,EX}$ (−0.027), indicate that the Federal Reserve accommodates expansionary fiscal policies within the same quarter. Within the theoretical framework of this paper, these coefficient signs are expected when the Federal Reserve weights financial market stability more heavily than its macrostabilization goals.[4]

[2]The reaction function is formally derived in the appendix to [10].

[3]It was assumed that BT_t^* was neither surplus nor deficit, so BT_t^* does not appear in the estimated reaction function.

[4]From [10], the coefficient on G_t^F is $(1/D)[-w_1j_1h_{12}-w_2j_2h_{22}-w_3j_3h_{32}-w_4j_4h_{42}]$ and the coefficient on $T_t^{F,EX}$ is $(1/D)[-w_1j_1h_{13}-w_2j_2h_{23}-w_3j_3h_{33}-w_4j_4h_{43}]$, where $D = (w_1j_1^2+w_2j_2^2+w_3j_3^2+w_4j_4^2)$ and

The coefficient on y_t^* (measured by high-employment real GNP) is positive. A positive coefficient on y_t^* suggests the existence of counter-cyclical policy concerns since it implies that the weight on $(y_t - y_t^*)^2$ in the loss function is greater than zero.[5]

Based upon the assumption that the Federal Reserve does not want to induce large quarter-to-quarter fluctuations in the inflation rate, $\dot{P}_t^*$ is defined as a four-quarter moving average of actual inflation rates. As expected, the coefficient on $\dot{P}_t^*$ is positive and provides further evidence of the existence of counter-cyclical policy concerns.[6]

The desired short-term interest rate, $i_{m,t}^*$, is defined as $i_{m,t-1}$. This measure is consistent with defining financial market stability as the absence of large quarter-to-quarter movements in the short-term interest rate. The estimated coefficient on $i_{m,t}^*$ is negative (-0.583), as expected.[7] An interaction dummy variable, *IRTBL*, is added to test the proposition that Federal Reserve response to $i_{m,t}^*$ shifted with its announced increased emphasis upon controlling monetary aggregates in mid-1970. *IRTBL* consists of $i_{m,t}^*$ from 1970.III to 1976.IV and zeros elsewhere. The estimated coefficient on *IRTBL* is positive.

In summary, the estimated coefficients on G_t^F and $T_t^{F,EX}$ are anticipated when the Federal Reserve weights financial market stability more heavily than its macroeconomic stabilization goals. At the same time, the estimated coefficients on y_t^* and P_t^* are consistent with Federal Reserve counter-cyclical policy concerns. This conclusion is reinforced by the positive coefficient on Y_{t-1}.[8]

3. *Predictive Properties of the Model*

Although the $\bar{R}^2$s indicate good fits to the data for the individual equations, the predictive ability of the model is not adequately evaluated by examining the $\bar{R}^2$s. Several additional tests of the predictive ability of the model are performed. An historical sixty-four-quarter dynamic simulation of the model was run for the period

---

$w_i, i = 1 \ldots, 4$ = loss function weights in text equation (1). $j_i, h_{i2}, h_{i3}, i = 1, \ldots, 4$ are the coefficients on UBR_t, G_t^F, $T_t^{F,EX}$ in the reduced-form equations (from the structural model) for y_t, P_t, BT_t, and $i_{m,t}$, respectively. For example, j_1, h_{12}, h_{13} are the coefficients on UBR_t, G_t^F, and $T_t^{F,EX}$ in the equation for y_t. Standard theory leads to the expectation that $j_1, j_2, h_{12}, h_{22}, h_{42}, h_{33} > 0$ and $j_3, j_4, h_{32}, h_{13}, h_{23}, h_{43} < 0$. Thus if w_4 (the weight on the financial-market stability proxy) exceeds the weighted sum of the stabilization goal weights, the expected signs on G_t^F and $T_t^{F,EX}$ are positive and negative, respectively. For example, if $w_4 > [w_1(j_1h_{12}/j_4h_{42}) + w_2(j_2h_{22}/j_4h_{42}) + w_3(j_3h_{32}/j_4h_{42})]$, the expected sign of G_t^F is positive.

[5]From [10], the coefficient on y_t^* is $(1/D)[w_1j_1]$. As noted in note 4, D and $j_1 > 0$. Thus the coefficient is expected to be > 0 if $w_1 > 0$.

[6]Alternative measures of P_t^* are discussed in [10]. From [10], the coefficient on P_t^* is $(1/D)[w_2j_2]$. As noted in note 4, D and $j_2 > 0$. Thus, if $w_2 > 0$, the coefficient is expected to be > 0.

[7]From [10], the coefficient on $i_{m,t}^*$ is $(1/D)[w_4j_4]$. Since $D > 0$ and $j_4 < 0$ (note 4), if $w_4 > 0$, then the coefficient is expected to be < 0.

[8]To test whether Federal Reserve response to y^* and P^* varied with changes in presidential administrations, several interaction dummy variables were added to the reaction function. The use of interaction dummy variables is a crude way of testing for structural shifts. It was felt that this was preferable to splitting the sample into three subsets of thirty-two observations and estimating the *entire* system with only thirty-two observations. The estimated coefficients on these variables provide some evidence of shifts in Federal Reserve behavior, although not all are significant at the 5 percent level. However, there are no statistically significant changes in the estimated coefficients on G^F and $T^{F,EX}$ or any basic changes in the dynamic multipliers when these variables are added; therefore, the simpler formulation is used in the text. The coefficient and dynamic multiplier estimates are available upon request from the author.

1961.I to 1976.IV. The simulation is dynamic in the sense that the values of the lagged endogenous variables in quarters subsequent to 1961.I are their predicted values, not their historical values. Actual values of exogenous variables are employed in the simulation, and no adjustments are made to any of the behavioral equations in the model. The results of this simulation are compared with the results from an historical dynamic simulation of a naive forecasting model[9] and with the results from an out-of-sample dynamic simulation of the structural model for the period 1977.I to 1978.IV.

The Theil U statistic for the historical simulation of the structural model is 0.04. The percent root mean square errors (percent RMSEs) for M1 from the historical simulations of the structural and autoregressive models are 0.60 percent and 3.33 percent, respectively. The percent RMSE for the out-of-sample simulation is 1.48 percent. The simple correlation coefficient for the actual and predicted values for the historical simulation for M1 is 0.989, and 92 percent of all turning points in M1 are correctly predicted. Based upon these results, the model's ability to track M1 is quite good.

4. *Dynamic Multipliers for M1*

The impact of fiscal policy upon the time path of the money supply can be evaluated by computing dynamic multipliers for M1 for changes in the exogenous fiscal policy variables. The dynamic multipliers are calculated from the differences in the time paths of M1 from the historical dynamic simulation and dynamic simulations from 1961.I to 1976.IV for a sustained \$1 billion increase in G^F, a sustained \$1 billion decrease in $T^{F,EX}$, and a sustained \$1 billion increase in the federal deficit. For purposes of comparison, dynamic multipliers for exogenous Federal Reserve behavior were calculated from simulations of the model with the reaction function suppressed. All changes in the fiscal variables are from their historical values.

Both dynamic multipliers and cumulative dynamic multipliers (which give the total change in M1 in response to a change in a fiscal variable over both the current and all previous periods) are shown in Table 1. From Table 1, we see that the dynamic multipliers decline over time, though there is some oscillation in their movements. After four years, the cumulative change in G^F ($T^{F,EX}$)(Federal deficit) is \$4 billion (−\$4 billion)(\$4 billion), and the cumulative change in M1** (endogenous Federal Reserve) is \$0.687 billion (\$0.603 billion)(\$0.703 billion). The elasticities of M1** at the end of four years with respect to the fiscal variables are not very large; for example, the elasticity of M1** with respect to G^F evaluated at the simulation period means is 0.074. Both sets of multipliers vary considerably depending upon the assumption about Federal Reserve behavior. The multipliers for M1* (exogenous Federal Reserve) reflect only private sector response to fiscal

[9]The equation used is (t-statistics are in parentheses)

$$\underset{}{M1_t} = \underset{(-2.5)}{-1.3} + \underset{(13.96)}{1.5M1_{t-1}} - \underset{(-3.40)}{0.67M1_{t-2}} + \underset{(1.60)}{0.32M1_{t-3}} - \underset{(-1.20)}{0.14\,M1_{t-4}}.$$

changes and are much smaller than the multipliers for M1**, which reflect both private sector and Federal Reserve response to fiscal changes.

TABLE 1

DYNAMIC MULTIPLIERS FOR M1

	$1 Billion Increase in G^F		$1 Billion Decrease in $T^{F,EX}$		$1 Billion Increase in Federal Deficit
Period	M1*	M1**	M1*	M1**	M1**
0	0.055	0.192	0.012	0.153	0.213
1	0.014	0.115	0.012	0.078	0.110
2	0.012	0.065	0.012	0.049	0.062
3	0.013	0.044	0.012	0.037	0.043
	(0.094)	(0.416)	(0.048)	(0.317)	(0.428)
4	0.012	0.036	0.012	0.035	0.038
5	0.012	0.030	0.012	0.030	0.031
6	0.012	0.029	0.012	0.029	0.029
7	0.010	0.027	0.011	0.028	0.028
	(0.140)	(0.538)	(0.095)	(0.439)	(0.554)
8	0.007	0.028	0.009	0.030	0.029
9	0.008	0.026	0.009	0.027	0.027
10	0.008	0.025	0.009	0.027	0.025
11	0.008	0.027	0.009	0.028	0.028
	(0.171)	(0.644)	(0.131)	(0.551)	(0.663)
15	0.004	−0.028	0.006	−0.025	−0.028
	(0.200)	(0.687)	(0.166)	(0.603)	(0.703)

NOTE: Cumulative dynamic multipliers are in parentheses.
*Federal Reserve behavior exogenous (UBR exogenous).
**Federal Reserve behavior endogenous (UBR endogenous).

5. *Summary and Conclusions*

The purpose of this paper is to estimate the impact of changes in several fiscal policy variables upon the time path of the narrowly defined money supply. The magnitude of the dynamic multipliers varies substantially according to the assumption about Federal Reserve behavior. The considerably smaller multipliers for exogenous Federal Reserve behavior suggest that failure to model Federal Reserve response to fiscal policy will lead to underestimates of the effect of fiscal actions on the money supply and also provide empirical support for the Goldfeld and Blinder [8] argument that model multipliers will be biased if policymakers react systematically to the state of the economy and this systematic reaction is not explicitly accounted for in the model.

LITERATURE CITED

1. Barro, Robert J. "Unanticipated Money Growth and Unemployment in the United States." *American Economic Review,* 67 (March 1977), 101–15.
2. ———. "Comment from an Unreconstructed Ricardian." *Journal of Monetary Economics,* 4 (August 1978), 569–81.

3. Buchanan, James A., and Robert E. Wagner. *Democracy in Deficit: The Political Legacy of Lord Keynes*. New York: Academic Press, 1977.

4. Cacy, James A. "Budget Deficits and the Money Supply." *Federal Reserve Bank of Kansas City Monthly Review,* June 1975, 3–9.

5. Francis, Darryl R. "How and Why Fiscal Actions Matter to a Monetarist." *Federal Reserve Bank of St. Louis Review,* 56 (May 1974), 2–7.

6. Friedlaender, Ann F. "Macro Policy Goals in the Postwar Period: A Study in Revealed Preference." *Quarterly Journal of Economics,* 87 (February 1973), 25–43.

7. Froyen, Richard T. "A Test of the Endogeneity of Monetary Policy." *Journal of Econometrics,* 2 (July 1974), 175–88.

8. Goldfeld, Stephen M., and Alan S. Blinder. "Some Implications of Endogenous Stabilization Policy." *Brookings Papers on Economic Activity,* 3 (1972), 585–640.

9. Gordon, Robert J. "World Inflation and Monetary Accommodation in Eight Countries." *Brookings Papers on Economic Activity,* 2 (1977), 409–68.

10. McMillin, W. Douglas, and Thomas R. Beard. "The Short-Run Impact of Fiscal Policy on the Money Supply." *Southern Economic Journal,* 47 (July 1980), 122–35.

11. Niskanen, William A. "Deficits, Government Spending, and Inflation." *Journal of Monetary Economics,* 4 (August 1978), 591–602.

12. Wood, John H. "A Model of Federal Reserve Behavior." In *Monetary Process and Policy: A Symposium,* edited by George Horwich, pp. 135–66. Homewood, Ill.: Irwin, 1967.

Purchasing Power Parity and the Equilibrium Exchange Rate

*A Note by Richard N. Barrett**

1. Introduction

According to the relative version of purchasing power parity theory, the equilibrium exchange rate, E, expressed in units of domestic currency per unit of foreign currency, equals the ratio of domestic prices, P^d, to foreign prices, P^w, where all three variables are measured as indices with the same base period, that is,

$$E = P^d/P^w. \tag{1}$$

Because both traded and nontraded goods are included in the relevant price indices, this relationship holds only if two conditions simultaneously hold: (a) internationally traded goods have the same prices at home and abroad (in one or another currency); and (b) there is constancy over time, both at home and abroad, in the ratio of tradables prices to nontradables prices.

This paper considers the circumstances under which the theory may be properly applied in the conduct of exchange rate policy. Purchasing power parity is typically used to measure overvaluation of the domestic currency or, equivalently, the devaluation needed to restore external equilibrium in economies experiencing deficits in the balance of payments.[1] Since equation (1) cannot hold both before and after devaluation occurs, this application of parity apparently requires that the domestic price level take on its postdevaluation value prior to the occurrence of devaluation itself.[2]

To determine whether this apparently implausible condition can be met, we develop a model analyzing the relationship between purchasing power parity and the

*Much of this paper was written while the author was senior researcher at the Latin American Monetary Studies Center, Mexico City. That institution's support is gratefully acknowledged.

[1]Although the discussion is framed in terms of deficits, it is applicable symmetrically to surpluses.

[2]It is taken for granted that equation (1) must hold *after* devaluation, that is, when the exchange rate is in fact in equilibrium. This is inherent in the rationale for the equation given in the text. It is also assumed that devaluation will have no effect on the foreign price level.

RICHARD N. BARRETT *is associate professor of economics, University of Montana.*

0022-2879/81/0581-0227$00.50/0

JOURNAL OF MONEY, CREDIT, AND BANKING, vol. 13, no. 2 (May 1981)

exchange rate under disequilibrium conditions. We find that, in general, when the balance of payments is initially in deficit, parity understates the true equilibrium value of the exchange rate but may nevertheless be a reasonable approximation to it under certain conditions relevant to policymaking.

2. *A Model of Parity and the Exchange Rate*

Consider an economy at full employment that produces two types of products—tradables and nontradables. The country is small so that the absolute prices of tradables are exogenous to it. Assume moreover that the exchange rate is fixed, the world inflation rate is zero, the economy is initially in complete equilibrium, and that the supply of productive factors does not grow during the period of analysis.[3]

Suppose, now, that the supply of money increases due to an expansion of domestic credit by the monetary authorities. Since the determinants of the demand for money are constant, the expansion of credit produces an ex ante excess supply of money with a corresponding excess demand for real output.

Under the conditions postulated, two adjustment mechanisms will operate. First, the price of nontradables, and hence the price level, will rise. Second, a deficit in the balance of payments will develop. In what follows it will be assumed that the impact on the money supply of the resulting loss of reserves is sterilized. This means that the ex ante excess supply of money is not automatically eliminated. It is reduced by the rise in prices, but sterilization implies that the balance of payments adjustment mechanism is inoperative. This is because the excess supply of money is maintained by increasing the domestic credit component of the money supply at a rate that just offsets the reduction in the international reserve component.

Suppose now that the monetary authority wishes to devalue in order to restore complete internal and external equilibrium. It is evident, given the assumed situation, that the increase in the price of foreign exchange required to restore equilibrium is equal to the increase in the money supply (both expressed as percentages of their original values).[4] It can be concluded, therefore, that if the monetary authority adjusts the exchange rate in accordance with purchasing power parity, the devaluation will be of the correct magnitude only if the elasticity of the price level (as measured by the authority's index) with respect to the money supply equals unity.

But note that if this elasticity, denoted by $e_{p,m}$, in fact equals unity (its upper theoretical bound, as shown below), no devaluation is necessary. For then the whole ex ante excess money supply would have been eliminated by the rise in the price level without any effect on the balance of payments. Under these circumstances, devaluation will merely return internal relative prices to their initial position. In general, however, $e_{p,m}$ will be less than unity and purchasing power parity will

[3]This model follows to some extent one developed in a different context by Dornbusch [2].

[4]To restore equilibrium, the real money stock must return to its original value. Thus the price level and the nominal stock must rise by the same percentage. If, moreover, money is neutral in the sense that *in complete equilibrium* relative prices of tradables and nontradables are invariant with respect to the nominal money stock, *all* prices, and hence the exchange rate, must rise by this same percentage of their original values. In the short run, prior to devaluation, money is not neutral in this sense. Increases in the money supply increase the price of nontradables but not tradables.

understate the devaluation needed to restore equilibrium. These results may be demonstrated and clarified with the following model.

Let the subscripts N and T apply to nontradable and tradable goods, respectively. Let α be the price of nontradables relative to tradables. Without loss of generality all absolute prices and hence the price level and α may originally be set at unity. The equations of the model are as follows:

$$X_i = X_i(\alpha), \qquad i = N,T. \tag{2}$$

The production (X) of both goods depends only on relative prices. Changes in these outputs correspond to movements along the production frontier.

$$D_i = D_i(\alpha, Z), \qquad i = N,T. \tag{3}$$

The demand (D) for both goods depends on relative prices and the real level of expenditure, Z.

$$X_N = D_N. \tag{4}$$

The excess demand for nontraded goods is zero.

$$B = X_T - D_T. \tag{5}$$

The balance of payments, in terms of tradable goods, is equal to the excess supply of these goods. The balance of payments is consequently defined to equal the trade balance and excludes capital movements.

$$Y = p_T X_T + p_N X_N. \tag{6}$$

Nominal income equals the nominal value (pX) of tradables and nontradables production. Since p_T is initially unity and does not vary prior to devaluation, equation (6) may be rewritten as

$$Y = X_T + \alpha X_N \tag{6'}$$

$$M_d = kY. \tag{7}$$

The demand for nominal balances is a constant proportion, k, of nominal income.

$$M_s = \bar{M}_s. \tag{8}$$

The nominal money stock is exogenous. As noted above, this requires that the monetary authority sterilize the impact of international reserve movements on the money supply during the period of analysis.

$$H = \gamma[M_d - M_s]. \tag{9}$$

Hoarding, H, the amount by which nominal income exceeds expenditure, is a proportion, γ, of the stock excess demand for money. H equals the nominal value of the balance of payments, and, since p_T equals one, also equals its real value in terms of tradables, that is,

$$B = H. \tag{10}$$

Given the model represented by equations (2) to (10), and assuming that the weight, W_N, given to nontraded goods in the calculation of the price level can be approximated by X_N/Y,[5] the elasticity of the price level with respect to the money supply, $e_{p,m}$, is given by equation (11)[6]

$$e_{p,m} = \frac{(W_N \gamma M_S)}{(W_N \gamma M_S) - X_T\ (S^X_{T,N} - S^D_{T,N})} \tag{11}$$

where $S^X_{T,N}$ and $S^D_{T,N}$ are the elasticities of substitution of traded for nontraded goods in production and consumption, respectively; $S^X_{T,N}$ is negative and $S^D_{T,N}$ is positive.

As equation (11) shows, $e_{p,m}$ approaches unity only for very small absolute values of the substitution elasticities and/or X_T.[7] The principal conclusion to be reached from this analysis is therefore that purchasing power parity underestimates the equilibrium exchange rate under conditions of excess external demand of monetary origin, and that this understatement is least severe in economies with relatively small traded goods sectors or with small elasticities of substitution between traded and nontraded goods in both consumption and production.[8] Since these elasticities are smaller (in absolute value) in the short run than in the long run, purchasing

[5]In fact, W_N will vary with the price index selected and will be higher in the consumer than wholesale price index, given the greater importance of the prices of services in the calculation of the latter.

[6]Equation (11) is derived in the Appendix.

[7]If the substitution elasticities are zero, $e_{p,m}$ equals unity. This is the somewhat peculiar case referred to above in which the price of nontradables rises sufficiently to entirely eliminate the excess supply of money. The balance of payments is unaffected. Notice that money in this case is not neutral in the long run. Given the zero elasticities of subsitution between tradables and nontradables, the price of nontradables may rise to restore equilibrium in the money market without affecting the original equilibria in the markets for both goods. The only impact of a devaluation under these circumstances will be to lower real balances. The resulting reduction of expenditure will cause the price of nontradables to fall, restoring the original equilibrium relative price.

[8]More formally, substituting $(1-W_T)$ for W_N and W_TY for X_T in equation (11) yields

$$e_{p,m} = \frac{(1 - W_T)\gamma M_s}{(1 - W_T)M_s - W_T\, Y(S^X_{T,N} - S^D_{T,N})}$$

The derivative of this expression with respect to W_T is

$$\frac{\partial e_{p,m}}{\partial W_T} = \frac{\gamma Ms\, Y(S^X_{T,N} - S^D_{T,N})}{[(1 - W_T)Ms - W_T\, Y(S^X_{T,N} - S^D_{T,N}]^2} < 0,$$

that is, as the relative size of the trade sector grows, $e_{p,m}$ falls.

power parity may be an approximately correct measure of the equilibrium rate under crawling peg regimes. However, if the monetary authority is to undertake a large devaluation in response to a disequilibrium that has persisted for some time in the past, purchasing power parity may greatly underestimate its correct value.[9]

A second implication is that the rate of growth of the money stock rather than the price level is the appropriate measure of the equilibrium rate of devaluation. In a more realistic, nonstatic context, however, the appropriate measure becomes the rate of growth in the ex ante excess supply of money. In practice the short run behavior of the ex ante excess supply may be difficult to evaluate because measures of the determinants of money demand are unavailable. These conditions may require the use of purchasing power parity as a "rule of thumb" measure of the equilibrium exchange rate, and it is under these short-run conditions that the rule of thumb is most likely to approximate the correct result.[10]

Appendix

The elasticity of the price level with respect to the nominal money stock, is defined as follows:

$$e_{p,m} = \frac{dP}{dM}\cdot\frac{M}{P}. \tag{A1}$$

P, the price level, is given by

$$P = p_T(W_N\alpha + W_T), \tag{A2}$$

where p_T, α, W_N, and W_T are the price of tradables, the relative price of nontradables, and the price index weights, respectively. Since all prices and thus P may be initially set at unity and p_T is constant prior to devaluation, equation (A1) may be written

$$e_{p,m} = \frac{d\alpha}{dM}\cdot W_N\cdot M. \tag{A3}$$

To derive the value of $d\alpha/dM$, substitute from equations (2) and (3) into (4) and (5) and from (7), (8), and (10) into (9). The model in this form becomes

$$X_N(\alpha) = D_N(\alpha, Z) \tag{A4}$$

[9]This conclusion may be subject to significant qualifications when the dynamics of the adjustment process are taken into account. For example, suppose that the existence of an excess supply of money leads to increased expenditure on both traded and nontraded goods and, *with some delay,* a rise in the price of the latter. In the short run, before this process has run its course, the economy may experience a deficit, with parity as yet unaffected. Only after a longer period will the value of parity rise. How much it rises will still presumably depend on the substitution elasticities.

[10]However, parity will be an acceptable short-term measure of the equilibrium exchange rate only when the payments deficit is of monetary origin. It has no clear relevance to exchange rate adjustments that are made necessary by significant shifts in the external terms of trade.

$$B = X_T(\alpha) - D_T(\alpha, Z) \tag{A5}$$

$$Y = X_T + \alpha X_N \tag{A6}$$

$$B = \gamma[kY - M_s]. \tag{A7}$$

Differentiating this set of equations,

$$\frac{dX_N}{d\alpha} d\alpha = \frac{\partial D_N}{\partial \alpha} d\alpha + \frac{\partial D_N}{\partial Z} dZ \tag{A8}$$

$$dB = \left[\frac{dX_T}{d\alpha} - \frac{\partial D_T}{\partial \alpha} \right] d\alpha - \frac{\partial D_T}{\partial Z} dZ \tag{A9}$$

$$dY = \left[\frac{dX_T}{d\alpha} + \alpha \frac{dX_N}{d\alpha} + X_N \right] d\alpha \tag{A10}$$

$$dB = \gamma k dY - \gamma dM_s \tag{A11}$$

are obtained. Equations (A8) and (A9) may be solved for dB in terms of $d\alpha$, yielding

$$dB = \left[\frac{dX_T}{d\alpha} - \frac{\partial D_T}{\partial \alpha} - \frac{(\partial D_T/\partial Z)}{(\partial D_N/\partial Z)} \left(\frac{dX_N}{d\alpha} - \frac{\partial D_N}{\partial \alpha} \right) \right] d\alpha. \tag{A12}$$

Let $e_{i,j}$ be the elasticity of i with respect to j. Then equation (A12) can be written as

$$dB = \left[\frac{X_T}{\alpha} e_{XT,\alpha} - \frac{D_T}{\alpha} e_{DT,\alpha} - \frac{(D_T/Z)e_{DT,Z}}{(D_N/Z)e_{DN,Z}} \left(\frac{X_N}{\alpha} e_{XN,\alpha} - \frac{D_N}{\alpha} e_{DN,\alpha} \right) \right] d\alpha. \tag{A12$'$}$$

Since $X_N = D_N$ and $X_T = D_T$ (initially) and assuming homothetic preferences so that $e_{DT,Z} = e_{DN,Z}$, equation (A12′) simplifies to

$$dB = (X_T/\alpha)[e_{XT,\alpha} - e_{DT,\alpha} - e_{XN,\alpha} + e_{DN,\alpha}]d\alpha. \tag{A13}$$

Then, since $e_{XT,\alpha} - e_{XN,\alpha} = S^X_{T,N}$, the elasticity of substitution of tradables for nontradables in production and $e_{DT,\alpha} - e_{DN,\alpha} = S^D_{T,N}$, the analogous elasticity of substitution in consumption, equation (A13) may be written

$$dB = \frac{X_T}{\alpha}(S^X_{T,N} - S^D_{T,N})\, d\alpha. \tag{A14}$$

Now, dividing both sides of equation (A10) by $(dX_T/d\alpha)$

$$\frac{dY}{(dX_T/d\alpha)} = \left[1 + \alpha\frac{(dX_N/d\alpha)}{(dX_T/d\alpha)} + \frac{X_N}{(dX_T/d\alpha)} \right] d\alpha. \qquad \text{(A15)}$$

The equilibrium condition in production requires that the marginal rate of substitution of traded for nontraded goods equal $-\alpha$, that is,

$$\frac{dX_T}{dX_N} = -\alpha. \qquad \text{(A16)}$$

Therefore, the term $(dX_N/d\alpha)/(dX_T/d\alpha)$ in equation (A15) equals $-(1/\alpha)$ and

$$dY = X_N d\alpha. \qquad \text{(A17)}$$

Substituting this result into equation (A11) yields

$$dB = \gamma k X_N d\alpha - \gamma dM_s. \qquad \text{(A18)}$$

Solving equations (A18) and (A14) for $(d\alpha/dM_s)$ yields

$$\frac{d\alpha}{dM_s} = \frac{\gamma}{\gamma k X_N - \frac{X_T}{\alpha}(S^X_{T,N} - S^D_{T,N})}. \qquad \text{(A19)}$$

The term $\gamma k X_N$ in equation (A19) may be written as $\gamma M_s W_N$ if W_N is taken to be equal to (X_N/Y) and since M_s equals $k\,Y$. Making this replacement and substituting equation (A19) into (A3) and recalling that α equals one yields

$$e_{p,m} = \frac{W_N \gamma M_s}{W_N \gamma M_s - X_T(S^X_{T,N} - S^D_{T,N})}. \qquad \text{(A20)}$$

LITERATURE CITED

1. Balassa, Bela. "The Purchasing-Power Parity Doctrine: A Reappraisal." *Journal of Political Economy,* 72 (December 1964), 584–96.
2. Dornbusch, Rudiger. "Real and Monetary Aspects of the Effects of Exchange Rate Changes." In *National Monetary Policies and the International Financial System,* edited by Robert Aliber, pp. 64–81. Chicago: University of Chicago Press, 1974.
3. Frenkel, Jacob A. "A Monetary Approach to the Exchange Rate: Doctrinal Aspects and Empirical Evidence." *Scandanavian Journal of Economics,* 78 (May 1976), 200–224.
4. Holmes, James M. "The Purchasing-Power-Parity Theory: In Defense of Gustav Cassel as a Modern Theorist." *Journal of Political Economy,* 75 (October 1967), 686–95.
5. Officer, Lawrence H. "The Purchasing Power Parity Theory of Exchange Rates: A Review Article." *I.M.F. Staff Papers,* 23 (March 1976), 1–60.

Exchange Market Pressure During the 1970s in Argentina: An Application of the Girton-Roper Monetary Model

*A Note by Nelson C. Modeste**

This paper examines the external imbalance of Argentina under a managed float system for the period 1972–78. The basic hypothesis that is being tested is that under a system of managed float, and in accordance with the monetary approach to balance of payments theory and exchange rate determination, an excess demand for money will cause a combination of currency appreciation and/or an inflow of international reserves. It is felt that this theory is particularly applicable to Argentina for two reasons. First, because a large proportion of the exchange market pressure (EMP) in the 1970s was absorbed by depreciating the Argentine peso. Second, because according to Diaz Alejandro [4], the Argentine economy can be regarded as a small, open economy, in the sense that world monetary conditions and world prices for goods, services, and capital are considered to be given. As a result of this, it is therefore possible to use the Michael Connolly and José Dantas da Silveira (C-S) [2] version of the Lance Girton and Don Roper (G-R) [6] model of EMP to explain the monetary experience of Argentina in the 1970s.

The paper is organized into three sections. The first section briefly outlines the basic framework of the monetary model of EMP. In the second section the results generated from estimating the EMP equation, with quarterly data for Argentina over the period 1972–78, will be presented. Finally, the third section of the paper will summarize the main conclusions of the paper.

1. A Simple Monetary Model of Exchange Market Pressure

In a small, open economy under a system of managed flexibility in the exchange rate, the combined variations in the balance of payments and the exchange rate represent another very important mechanism for attaining and maintaining equilibrium in the monetary sector. For example, if there is an excess supply of money then persons will attempt to restore equilibrium in their portfolios by increasing their expenditures on goods and services and nonmoney assets. As a result, part of the adjustment process would involve domestic residents exchanging their local money

*I would like to thank William G. Dewald, Michael Connolly, and an anonymous referee for their suggestions for improving this paper.

NELSON C. MODESTE *is assistant professor of economics, University of Tennessee.*

0022-2879/81/0581-0234$00.50/0
JOURNAL OF MONEY, CREDIT, AND BANKING, vol. 13, no. 2 (May 1981)

for foreign currency and thereby reducing the supply of money. Moreover, this demand for foreign currency results in a depreciation of the exchange rate, which subsequently leads to an increase in the domestic price level and thereby increases the community's demand for money (see [3, 7]). Equilibrium in the monetary sector is therefore restored by an increase in the demand for money and/or a reduction in the supply of money.

The formal monetary model based on [2, 6, 7] centers around (1) a money demand function with the Cambridge k being constant, (see [5]); (2) the process of money creation as specified by Mundell [9]; (3) purchasing power parity; and (4) the equilibrium condition for the monetary sector. The model can be expressed in terms of the following equations:

$$L = kPY \tag{1}$$

$$M \equiv R + D \tag{2}$$

$$P = EP^* \tag{3}$$

$$L = M, \tag{4}$$

where L is the demand for money; k is the fraction of income people hold in the form of money balances; P is the domestic prices; Y is the real income; M is the money supply; R is the net holdings of international reserves by the central bank and the commercial banks measured in domestic currency and valued at their purchase price; D is the net domestic assets of central bank and commercial banks measured in domestic currency; E is the exchange rate, expressed in terms of number of units of domestic currency per unit of foreign currency; and, P^* is the foreign prices.

By replacing P with EP^* in equation (1), substituting equations (1) and (2) in (4), and differentiating (4) logarithmically, the following equation, which measures exchange market pressure in percentage changes, is obtained:

$$r + e = -d + p^* + y. \tag{5}$$

From equation (5) one obtains three important propositions: (a) an increase in the rate of growth in domestic assets will result in a proportional, combined, depreciation in the exchange rate and an outflow of foreign reserves; (b) an increase in real income will result in a proportional, combined, appreciation in the exchange rate and an inflow of foreign reserves; (c) an increase in the world price level will result in a proportional, combined, appreciation in the exchange rate and an inflow of foreign reserves. These propositions are of great interest because unlike the propositions derived from the standard model of balance-of-payments theory and exchange rate analysis, they suggest that an imbalance in the external sector could be alleviated by changes in foreign reserves and/or the exchange rate, rather than by changes in only reserves or the exchange rate (see [1, 7]).

2. *Empirical Analysis*

Throughout the 1960s and the early 1970s all exchange transactions in Argentina were channeled through a single official foreign exchange market. On occasions the exchange rate in this market was allowed to fluctuate, while at other times the exchange rate, though pegged, was nevertheless frequently adjusted by small amounts whenever necessary. In September 1971, this single official foreign exchange market was abolished and a dual exchange rate system was established. As part of this system a commercial market was established for channeling most traded goods and services at a fixed rate of exchange. All other transactions that could not be channeled through the commercial market had to be channeled through the financial market at a fluctuating rate of exchange. In August 1975, following a number of ''mini-devaluations'' in the exchange rate, a special financial market was created for channeling the receipts and payments for invisible items as well as for certain types of foreign capital. For the remainder of 1975 and until March 1976, when a new official market in conjunction with a freely fluctuating market was established, the Argentine peso continued to be constantly depreciated. Finally, in November 1977 a single free foreign exchange market was introduced and has remained in operation up to the present time.[1]

For empirical testing it is felt that the frequent and continuous depreciation of the Argentine peso since 1972 would provide another good opportunity for testing the monetary model of exchange market pressure. The first test to be performed is designed to determine whether EMP is independent of its composition. In this definition, $r+e$, of EMP, it is implied, with equal weights being given to r and e, that the trade-off between r and e is one-to-one.[2] As a result it is hypothesized that the magnitude of market pressure, defined as $r+e$, is independent of whether the authorities absorb EMP in their exchange rate or in their foreign reserves. Following the studies by C-S and G-R, this notion is tested for Argentina by introducing another independent variable, $Q = (e-1)/(r-1)$, into equation (5). The results as reported in Table 1 indicate that the variable Q is statistically insignificant. This finding is similar to that reported by G-R for Canada and by C-S for Brazil in their models of EMP.

The empirical estimates for equation (5) are reported in Table 1. The results indicate that all the estimated coefficients have the correct sign and are close to their hypothesized values of minus one for d, and plus one for y and p^*, respectively. The evidence also indicates that the estimated coefficients for d and y are significantly different from zero at the 5 percent confidence level. The estimated coefficient for p^* is, however, insignificantly different from zero. In spite of this an F-value of 9.41 indicates that the three variables together are useful in explaining the combined variation in the balance of payments and the exchange rate. The

[1]For a discussion of the Argentine exchange rate system see [4, 8].

[2]Roper and Turnovsky in a recent study have formulated another measure of EMP that does not require r and e to be given equal weights [10]. This measure is particularly useful in those instances where the trade-off between r and e is not consistent with the assumption of neutrality.

TABLE 1

THE ESTIMATED COEFFICIENTS FOR THE MODEL OF EXCHANGE MARKET PRESSURE

Regression Equation	Technique	Period	Dependent Variable	Estimated Coefficients for the Independent Variables					
				d	p^*	y	Q	R^2	D-W
1	OLS	1972.II–1978.III	$r + e$	−1.18	10.78	0.65	−0.18	0.60	1.67
				(−3.23)	(1.59)	(1.38)	(−1.65)		
2	OLS	1972.II–1978.III	$r + e$	−1.46	1.10	0.87		0.55	1.60
				(−4.38)	(0.32)	(1.86)			
3	OLS	1972.II–1978.III	r	−0.27	3.94	0.11		0.37	1.07
				(−2.68)	(3.64)	(0.77)			
3-A	CORC	1972.II–1978.III	r	−0.33	−0.60	0.16		0.36	
				(−3.46)	(−0.23)	(1.49)			
4	OLS	1972.II–1978.III	e	−1.18	−2.84	0.75		0.54	1.47
				(−3.60)	(−0.83)	(1.64)			

SOURCE: The empirical results reported here are based on quarterly data for the period between 1972 and 1978. In the empirical analysis a five-period moving average was used only for Q. The data for all of the dependent variables as well as for d, p^*, and y were not adjusted. All of the quarterly data for the variables used in this analysis were obtained from the International Financial Statistics.

NOTES: $r = \Delta R/M$; $e = \Delta(1/E)/(1/E)$; $d = \Delta D/M$; P^* = U.S. consumer price index; $p^* = \Delta P^*/P^*$; Y = index of manufacturing production; $y = \Delta Y/Y$; R^2 = coefficient of determination; D-W = Durbin-Watson statistic; and CORC = Iterated Cochrane-Orcutt. The t-values are reported in parentheses below the estimated coefficients.

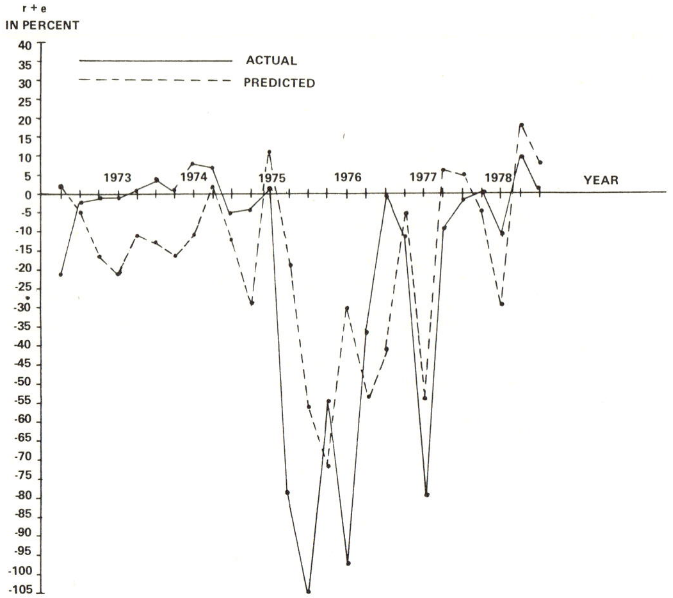

FIG. 1. Argentina's Exchange Market Pressure, 1972.II–1978.III

explanatory power of the model is illustrated in Figure 1, where the actual and predicted movements in $r+e$ are compared.

To further test the efficacy of the monetary model of exchange market pressure, it is now essential to determine whether using (r) as the sole dependent variable instead of the sum of $(r+e)$, would yield a better general fit. Following [2, 11], equation (6) is estimated by ordinary least squares

$$r = -d + p^* + y. \tag{6}$$

The results for that equation, when compared to the results that are obtained from using the sum of r and e as the dependent variable, are notably very poor (see Table 1). In fact, once allowance is made for serial correlation, only the estimated coefficient for the domestic credit variable is significantly different from zero. In addition to this, the estimated coefficient for the variable, p^*, has the wrong sign.

As most of the pressure in Argentina was absorbed by changes in the exchange rate, it is also interesting to determine whether the movements in e are consistent with the monetary approach to exchange rate determination. To perform this test, the following equation

$$e = -d + p^* + y \tag{7}$$

was estimated. The results as reported in Table 1 indicate that using e as the sole dependent variable provides results that are also inferior to those that are obtained from the EMP equation. Indeed the evidence shows that the estimated coefficients for y and p^* are insignificantly different from zero. These results also indicate that the estimated coefficient for p^* has the wrong sign.[3]

3. Conclusions

The empirical analysis suggests that the experience of Argentina during the 1970s provides another good example of a country that alleviated imbalances in their external sector by combining changes in their reserves with changes in their exchange rate. In addition to this, the evidence indicates quite strongly that the monetary model of EMP is superior to those models that emphasize changes only in foreign reserves or the exchange rate, but do not include as an explanatory variable the behavior of the monetary authorities as measured by the variable, Q.

LITERATURE CITED

1. Bilson, John F. O. "The Current Experience with Floating Exchange Rate: An Appraisal of the Monetary Approach." *American Economic Review,* 68 (May 1978), 392–97.
2. Connolly, Michael, and José Dantas Da Silveira. "Exchange Market Pressure to Postwar Brazil: An Application of the Girton-Roper Monetary Model." *American Economic Review,* 69 (June 1979), 448–54.
3. Connolly, Michael, and Dean Taylor. "Testing the Monetary Approach to Devaluation in Developing Countries." *Journal of Political Economy,* 84 (August 1976), 849–59.
4. Diaz Alejandro, Carlos F. *Exchange Rate Devaluation in a Semi-Industrialized Country: The Experience of Argentina 1955–1961.* Cambridge, Mass.: MIT Press, 1965.
5. Diz, Adolfo C. "Money and Prices in Argentina, 1935–1962." In *Varieties of Monetary Experience,* edited by David Meiselman, pp. 71–162. Chicago: University of Chicago Press, 1970.

[3]When inflationary expectations, ρ, were introduced into the analysis, via the demand for money function, the following results were obtained for the EMP equation:

$$r+e = \underset{(-2.83)}{-3.40\Delta\rho} - \underset{(-2.60)}{0.89d} + \underset{(1.47)}{9.02p^*} + \underset{(1.24)}{0.54y} - \underset{(-1.67)}{0.17Q},$$

$$R^2 = 0.71,\ \text{D-W} = 1.84.$$

$$r+e = \underset{(-2.71)}{-3.39\Delta\rho} - \underset{(-3.67)}{1.16d} + \underset{(0.05)}{0.14p^*} + \underset{(1.83)}{0.78y},$$

$$R^2 = 0.67,\ \text{D-W} = 1.75.$$

Moreover, when $(r+e)$ is replaced by (r) or (e) as the dependent variable, the empirical analysis again indicates that the monetary model of EMP provides better results than the monetary model for the balance-of-payments or the monetary model for determining the exchange rate. For the above results, the t-values are reported in parentheses below the estimated coefficient. An interesting aspect of these results is that the estimated coefficient for $\Delta\rho$ not only has the correct sign but also is significant at the 5 percent confidence level. The inflationary expectations variable was constructed, according to the following scheme: $\rho_t = \delta \dot{P}_t + (1-\delta)\rho_{t-1}$, where $\dot{P}$ is the rate of inflation and δ is a given constant. In this study a value of 0.3 was used for δ. In addition, the above empirical results are for the period between 1972.III and 1978.III.

6. Girton, Lance, and Don Roper. "A Monetary Model of Exchange Market Pressure Applied to the Postwar Canadian Experience." *American Economic Review,* 67 (September 1977), 537–48.

7. Johnson, Harry. "The Monetary Approach to Balance-of-Payments Theory." *Journal of Financial and Quantitative Analysis,* 7 (March 1972), 1555–71.

8. Mallon, Richard D. "Exchange Policy-Argentina." In *Development Policy-Theory and Practice,* edited by Gustav F. Papanek, pp. 175–206. Cambridge, Mass.: Harvard University Press, 1968.

9. Mundell, Robert. *Monetary Theory.* Pacific Palisades, Calif.: Goodyear, 1971.

10. Roper, Don, and Stephen J. Turnovsky. "Optimal Exchange Market Intervention in a Simple Stochastic Macro Model." *Canadian Journal of Economics,* 13 (May 1980), 296–309.

11. Sargen, Nicholas. "An Empirical Analysis of a Monetary Model of Exchange Rate and Reserve Fluctuations." Unpublished paper, Federal Reserve Bank, San Francisco, 1975.

Describing Bank Equity Returns: The Year-by-Year Record

*A Note by William L. Beedles and Nancy K. Buschmann**

1. Introduction

The market model of Sharpe [11] is widely embraced by both the professional and academic communities as the premier characterization of the return generating mechanism for common stocks. The present study is focused upon an allegation that appears in the intermediation folklore and literature, namely, that banks' stock returns are produced by a regime different from that of typical listed equities and hence do not subscribe to the market model paradigm. Such a prospect is of critical importance since it impinges upon the equity financing decisions of bankers and supervision of bank capital adequacy by regulators.

The conventional wisdom and past empirical investigations are overviewed in section 2. Section 3 includes descriptions of the statistical procedures employed and results of the tests. As a summary of the substantive results, conventional wisdom is for the most part rebutted. The evidence suggests that the market model is consistently a slightly *better* characterization of bank equity returns than industrials.

2. Review of Folklore and Literature

The contention that banks operate in a substantially different setting than industrials has been supported on at least four fronts. First, bank stocks have been conspicuous by their absence from organized exchanges. Historically most banks were able to satisfy their ongoing equity capital needs through earnings retention. As a consequence, only five bank stocks were listed on the New York Stock Exchange prior to 1968. By 1978 about fifty bank stocks were listed on national and major regional exchanges. Second, while the ultimate risk of industrials is essentially borne by the stockholders, bank owners share some degree of risk [6, 8, 9] with large depositors, the central bank, and the Federal Deposit Insurance Corporation.

A third alleged distinguishing characteristic is the homogeneity and interdependence of banks relative to industrials. Many banks have the same customers, face

*The research leading to the paper was partially supported by the University of Kansas General Research Fund grant 3029-0038.

WILLIAM L. BEEDLES *is associate professor of business administration, and* NANCY K. BUSCHMANN *is assistant professor of business administration, University of Kansas.*

0022-2879/81/0581-0241$00.50/0
JOURNAL OF MONEY, CREDIT, AND BANKING, vol. 13, no. 2 (May 1981)

the same marginal cost of funds, and participate in the network of interbank lending and deposit relationships. These interrelationships among banks and between banks and their corporate customers may create important default risks not captured by the market model.

Finally, virtually without exception banks are more highly leveraged than industrial firms. This observation has prompted the hypothesis that bank equity returns may be more sensitive to interest rate fluctuations than are the returns of nonfinancial firms. This possibility has been the thesis most carefully scrutinized by other investigators.

Martin and Keown [5] found some "group" effect that was shared by four industries, including banks, and hypothesized that this effect might be attributed to the high leverage, and hence interest rate sensitivity of these industries. However, in tests conducted by Lloyd and Shick [4] using Stone's [12] two index model, both the equity and interest rate parameters were typically insignificant at the 5 percent level for their bank sample. Lloyd and Shick inferred that bank returns are not more sensitive than industrials to interest rate fluctuations and, furthermore, that bank returns are poorly characterized by both one and two index models.

While the belief may therefore be embraced by many that bank equities are somehow "different" than industrials, tests to date have not provided strong support for this thesis. Consequently, the present investigation has been designed to focus *directly* on the allegation by assessing the *comparative* adequacy of the single index market model.

3. *Empirical Investigation*

The sample employed for this investigation includes all banks whose equities were traded on the New York Stock Exchange at the end of 1978 and hence for whom *daily* return information was available from the University of Chicago's Center for Research in Security Prices (CRSP) data base. The use of daily data is important since it permits an investigation of the time-series properties of the returns.

As a first step, two versions of the single-index model were estimated, the first being the standard market model, which may be stated as

$$\tilde{R}_{i_t} = \hat{a}_i + \hat{b}_i \tilde{R}_{m_t} + \tilde{v}_{i_t}, \qquad (1)$$

where $\tilde{R}_{i_t}$ and $\tilde{R}_{m_t}$ are the stochastic (denoted with the tildes) returns of investment i and a market proxy, respectively, in period t; $\hat{a}_i$ and $\hat{b}_i$ are estimated (denoted with the circumflexes) explainable firm-unique and systematic return components; and $\tilde{v}_{i_t}$ is an unexplained firm-unique residual return.

Following the lead of Scholes and Williams [10] whose results suggest the existence of nonstationarity, a time-series dummy-variable version of the model was also estimated [1, pp. 192–207]:

$$\tilde{R}_{i_t} = \hat{c}_2 + \hat{d}_2 \tilde{R}_{m_t} + \sum_{j \geq 1}^{15} + \hat{e}_{i_j} D_j + \sum_{j \geq 1}^{15} \hat{f}_{i_j} D_j \tilde{R}_{m_t} + \tilde{g}_{i_t}. \qquad (2)$$

For equation (2), the left-hand side term and the first two and last right-hand side terms are interpreted as in equation (1). D_j is a dummy variable that takes on a value of unity for year *j*, zero otherwise. For example, D_1 corresponds to the first year's data, so $\hat{e}_{i_1}$ reflects firm-specific explainable influences (i.e., intercept values) that are uniquely characteristic of the year 1963. By the same token, the $\hat{f}_{i_j}$ values are year-unique slopes. Not all of the sample banks have data for the entire period, so the index *j* often does not begin until after 1963. The results of estimation of equations (1) and (2) are summarized in Table 1.

Focusing initially on the estimates of equation (1), the first striking feature is the small magnitude of the estimated slopes. Noting the cross-sectional standard deviation of 0.220, the average of the bank $\hat{b}_i$ values is significantly smaller than the population value of unity.

TABLE 1

ESTIMATES OF STANDARD AND DUMMY-VARIABLE VERSIONS OF MARKET MODEL

	Equation (1)				Equation (2)			
Name	$\hat{b}_i$	R^2	F	D-W	R^2	Number of D	Number of $t(\hat{e}) > 2.0$	Number of $t(\hat{f}) > 2.0$
Bank of New York*	0.371	0.037	88.792	1.944	0.037	8	0	0
Bankers Trust*	0.419	0.035	83.331	1.840	0.042	8	0	0
Charter New York*	0.793	0.143	420.404	2.119	0.150	9	0	4
Chase Manhattan*	0.991	0.178	706.194	1.905	0.196	12	0	6
Chemical Bank*	0.465	0.042	100.232	1.872	0.042	8	0	0
Citicorp*	1.178	0.197	618.400	1.687	0.218	9	1	3
Continental Illinois*	0.627	0.058	78.181	1.614	0.064	4	0	0
First Chicago*	0.707	0.048	89.159	1.732	0.059	6	0	2
First National Boston*	0.494	0.036	67.210	1.811	0.041	6	0	0
J.P. Morgan*	0.446	0.040	95.939	1.624	0.048	8	0	2
Bancal Tri-State	0.287	0.009	18.982	2.012	0.008	7	0	0
Bank of Virginia	0.417	0.019	34.868	2.032	0.022	6	0	0
Bankamerica	0.603	0.038	30.815	1.860	0.039	1	0	0
Equimark	0.498	0.034	63.888	2.218	0.035	6	0	0
Fidelity Union	0.193	0.016	29.424	1.969	0.018	6	0	0
First International	0.499	0.046	61.793	1.694	0.044	4	0	0
First Pennsylvania	0.525	0.029	46.379	1.927	0.032	5	0	0
General Bancshares	0.464	0.025	104.519	2.400	0.025	15	0	3
Industrial National	0.684	0.066	179.904	1.984	0.075	9	0	0
Marine Midland	0.826	0.083	363.865	2.128	0.087	15	1	4
National Detroit	0.358	0.038	50.223	1.987	0.036	4	0	0
Northwest Bancorporation	0.628	0.074	321.148	1.946	0.080	15	0	1
Republic of Texas	0.461	0.043	23.748	1.847	0.046	1	0	0
Southeast Banking	0.403	0.014	21.918	2.085	0.014	5	1	0
Texas Commerce	0.361	0.025	26.913	2.020	0.022	3	0	0
Union Bancorporation	0.562	0.013	14.453	2.211	0.011	3	0	0
Union Commercial	0.435	0.013	20.411	2.061	0.012	5	0	0
United Jersey Banks	0.278	0.009	19.957	2.373	0.008	7	0	0
Western Bancorporation	0.920	0.139	648.362	1.901	0.150	15	0	7
Average:	0.548				Total:	210	3	32
Standard Deviation:	0.220				Proportion:		0.014	0.152

*Denotes money-center bank

A second noteworthy attribute is the extremely small magnitudes of the coefficients of determination. On average, only about 6 percent of the variance of the equity returns of the banks is explained by the market proxy. While these values are much smaller than those found in previous studies [3], the magnitudes are not troubling. Most past works have employed monthly data and have focused on estimates for portfolios. The results at hand for individual firms, estimated with daily data, simply reflect the facts that "fit" and differencing interval are closely related [3] and that portfolios have comparatively less residual risk. The small magnitudes notwithstanding, all of the F-statistics indicate significance of the R^2 values far beyond the 1 percent level.

In somewhat the same vein, autocorrelation is more prevalent with daily data than with longer differencing intervals, a fact previously noted by Scholes and Williams [10]. Of the twenty-nine Durbin-Watson (D-W) statistics, four (for Continental Illinois, J. P. Morgan, General Bancshares, and United Jersey Banks) are significant at the 0.05 level.

The last characteristic of equation (1) deserving emphasis concerns the differences between money-center and non-money-center banks. The average $\hat{b}_i$ of the former is nearly 20 percent larger than the latter; R^2 values are nearly twice as large.

Shifting attention to the summary of the estimates of equation (2), Citicorp will serve as a convenient illustration. Return data covering 1969–78 were available for this firm, so a total of eighteen dummy variable parameters were estimated (nine intercepts and nine slopes, covering 1969–77). One dummy-intercept and three dummy-slopes were significantly different than zero at the 5 percent level.

For the entire sample, a very small proportion of the intercepts were significant. However, slightly over 15 percent of the slopes were significantly different than zero, over three times the number expected by chance alone.

To summarize, the results to this point suggest three steps that must be followed in order to assess the comparative adequacy of the market model as a characterization of equity returns. First. the apparent nonstationarity of the slopes mandates year-by-year analyses rather than a total-period investigation. Second, since R^2 values are related to the levels of $\hat{b}_i$ [2], and since the slopes of banks are smaller than the population, adjustment for the cross-sectional bias is needed. And finally, money-center and non-money-center banks must be distinguished.

These adjustments are accomplished by a matched-sampling procedure, where for each year each bank is matched to the industrial firm (from a random sample of five hundred) with the most similar $\hat{b}$ value. The result is two groups of firms, one of banks and the other of industrials, with essentially identical distributions of slopes. Relevant summary data, in the form of group averages, are presented in Table 2.

The data for the banks, which are reported in the first six columns of the table, are first of all interesting in an absolute sense. Relative to the other years in the sample period, the average slopes are large in 1969, 1974, and 1975, which were years of record high interest rates. The result was narrowed short-run profit margins for the large banks, which depended heavily on purchased liabilities. In addition, 1974 and

TABLE 2

YEAR-BY-YEAR MARKET MODEL ESTIMATES, AVERAGES, AND TESTS OF FIT FOR MONEY-CENTER (MC), NONMONEY-CENTER (NMC), AND $\hat{b}$-EQUIVALENT (bE) GROUPS

Year	Money-Center Banks			Nonmoney-Center Banks			$\overline{R}^2$; $\hat{b}$-Equivalents		$\overline{R}^2$ t-Statistics		
	Sample Size	$\bar{b}$	$\overline{R^2}$	Sample Size	$\bar{b}$	$\overline{R^2}$	MC	NMC	MC-NMC	MC-bE	NMC-bE
1963	0			4	0.745	0.051		0.041			0.44
1964	0			4	0.608	0.021		0.023			−0.22
1965	0			4	0.425	0.029		0.014			1.31
1966	1			4	0.528	0.052		0.034			1.33
1967	1			4	0.570	0.045		0.040			0.31
1968	1			4	0.543	0.038		0.013			2.07
1969	3	0.973	0.177	5	0.846	0.126	0.094	0.110	1.38	2.12	0.43
1970	7	0.566	0.132	5	0.648	0.113	0.052	0.063	0.38	1.69	1.43
1971	7	0.365	0.041	7	0.351	0.029	0.020	0.023	0.89	1.43	0.46
1972	9	0.205	0.011	10	0.262	0.012	0.006	0.011	−0.15	0.80	−0.20
1973	9	0.451	0.068	13	0.379	0.053	0.037	0.018	0.50	1.11	1.75
1974	10	0.884	0.120	15	0.611	0.071	0.107	0.034	1.48	0.30	1.68
1975	10	0.887	0.113	17	0.644	0.061	0.092	0.033	1.94	0.59	1.75
1976	10	0.671	0.069	17	0.417	0.027	0.053	0.017	2.30	0.54	1.39
1977	10	0.711	0.073	19	0.464	0.019	0.024	0.014	1.97	1.68	0.84
1978	10	0.727	0.115	19	0.485	0.048	0.055	0.041	2.17	1.86	0.42
Averages		0.644	0.092		0.533	0.050	0.054	0.032			

Since comparisons of means are made, data are reported only when the sample size exceeds one.

1975 reflect the shock waves resulting from the Franklin National Bank failure and the highly publicized risk exposure from third world and REIT loans. In contrast to folklore allegations, these data are consistent with the thesis that the market *does* perceive and evaluate the interdependence among banks and between banks and other industries.

The major focus here, however, is on the *comparative* accuracy of the characterization, which is reflected in the R^2 values between groups. First, comparing the data of the third and sixth columns of Table 2, note that the market model fit is better for the money-center than for the non-money-center banks, which would be expected given the difference in average slopes noted in Table 1. Moreover, the data are amenable to more precise comparison by utilizing a t-test [13, p. 214]. Reading from the ninth column of Table 2, nine of the ten t-statistics are positive, and three of them significantly so at the 5 percent level.

Of much greater import here are the differences between the R^2 averages of the banks and their $\hat{b}$-equivalent nonbank brethren shown in the last two columns of Table 2. While the t-statistics are small in magnitude (only two values exceed 2.0), thirty-four of the thirty-six values are positive. In sum then, the market model is an habitually superior characterization of the return mechanism for bank stocks than for typical firms, but the superiority is only slight. Importantly though, *any* superiority runs counter to the canon! The folklore and literature of the intermediation field support the inference that the fit should be *worse* for banks, so these empirical results should probably be interpreted as *strong* rebuttal of the conventional wisdom.

4. *Conclusion*

That the stocks of banks are somehow "different" than those of industrial firms is a thesis supported by the distinct operating, financial, and regulatory structure within which banks are cast. This study has been designed to investigate this allegation by comparing the equities of banks and industrials using the premier return generating characterization. In contrast to some previous works, the results at hand clearly appear to rebutt the belief. Bank stock returns are described by the market model *at least* as well as typical securities.

LITERATURE CITED

1. Johnston, John. *Econometric Methods*. Second edition. New York: McGraw-Hill, 1972.
2. Klemkosky, Robert C., and John D. Martin. "The Effect of Market Risk on Portfolio Diversification." *Journal of Finance*, 30 (March 1975), 147–54.
3. Levy, Haim. "Equilibrium in an Imperfect Market: A Constraint on the Number of Securities in the Portfolio." *American Economic Review*, 68 (September 1978), 643–58.
4. Lloyd, William P., and Richard A. Shick. "A Test of Stone's Two-Index Model of Returns." *Journal of Financial and Quantitative Analysis*, 12 (September 1977), 363–76.
5. Martin, John D., and Arthur J. Keown. "Interest Rate Sensitivity and Portfolio Risk." *Journal of Financial and Quantitative Analysis*, 12 (June 1977), 181–95.

6. Mason, John M. *Financial Management of Commercial Banks*. Boston: Warren, Gorham & Lamont, 1979.

7. McEnally, Richard W. "A Note on the Return Behavior of High Risk Common Stocks." *Journal of Finance*, 29 (March 1974), 199–202.

8. Orgler, Yair E., and Benjamin Wolkowitz. *Bank Capital*. New York: Van Nostrand Reinhold, 1976.

9. Reed, Edward W., Richard V. Cotter, Edward K. Gill, and Richard K. Smith. *Commercial Banking*. Englewood Cliffs, N.J.: Prentice-Hall, 1980.

10. Scholes, Myron, and Joseph Williams. "Estimating Betas from Nonsynchronous Data." *Journal of Financial Economics*, 5 (1977), 309–27.

11. Sharpe, William F. "A Simplified Model for Portfolio Analysis." *Management Science*, 9 (January 1963), 277–93.

12. Stone, Bernell K. "Systematic Interest-Rate Risk in a Two-Index Model of Returns." *Journal of Financial and Quantitative Analysis*, 9 (November 1974), 709–21.

13. Wonnacott, Thomas H., and Ronald J. Wonnacott. *Introductory Statistics*. Third edition. New York: Wiley, 1977.

BOOK REVIEWS

Rational Expectations and Economic Policy

Edited by Stanley Fischer. Chicago: University of Chicago Press, 1980. ix + 293 pp. $22.00

A Review Essay by Stephen A. McCafferty

This volume contains the proceedings of a conference, sponsored by the National Bureau of Economic Research, which was held at Bald Peak Colony Club, New Hampshire, October 1978. Participants included forty of the most distinguished scholars in the field of business cycle research, representing a broad range of views on the subject. As such, this volume represents an important contribution to the literature, if for no other reason than the quality of the debate and the interchange of ideas apparent in the comments on and discussions of the papers. Beyond this, the individual papers themselves make important contributions to our understanding of business cycle behavior and the extent to which government policy could, or should, attempt to alter the characteristics of these business cycle fluctuations.

As an overview of the proceedings, it is perhaps best to first try to summarize the points of agreement and disagreement among the conference participants.

The major points of agreement are: (1) rational expectations represents the proper expectational assumption and (2) the Lucas critique of econometric policy evaluations is valid. Expectations are rational if they incorporate all information available to the economic agent forming them. In macroeconomic model building this means that economic agents' expectational schemes must be endogenously determined. Behavior based on an expectations scheme must be consistent with the same scheme generating the mathematical expectation of the variable in question. Five or ten years ago this notion was quite controversial. However, to deny it demands the acceptance of the proposition that individuals systematically ignore information at their disposal.

Closely allied to this concept is the idea, first advanced by Robert E. Lucas, Jr., that econometric forecasting of alternative policy regimes will not generally yield accurate policy prescriptions unless the impact of the policy change on private economic behavior is properly accounted for. One natural implication is that alternative policy regimes will change the way individuals form expectations. However, there is also the possibility that policy shifts may cause other changes in economic interrelationships.

STEPHEN A. MCCAFFERTY *is assistant professor of economics, Ohio State University.*

0022-2879/81/0581-0248$00.50/0
JOURNAL OF MONEY, CREDIT, AND BANKING, vol. 13, no. 2 (May 1981)

Beyond these two points. the conference participants show considerable disagreement in a number of vital areas. The major point of contention centers around the ultimate cause of fluctuations in the level of aggregate economic activity.

The major competing hypotheses here include:

1. Confusion of local and aggregate disturbances
2. Intertemporal substitution of leisure
3. Implicit labor contracts
4. Wage and price rigidities.

Among these competing hypotheses, different participants significantly split with each favoring his own particular source, or combination of sources, of business cycle fluctuations. This controversy is heightened by the fact that at least (1) and (2) in combination with rational expectations generally imply the irrelevance of systematic monetary policy.

A substantial number of the participants feel that wages and prices continuously clear markets and therefore genuinely reflect the perceived terms of trade available to market participants. Even among this group there is disagreement about the exact mechanism by which business cycles are propagated. One group emphasizes the possibility that economic agents mistakenly (though rationally) confuse aggregate nominal disturbances with changes in relative prices and therefore react with quantity variations that they, ex post, regret. This explanation of cyclical upturns depends upon a shared misperception that current real wages are higher than they really are.

Another group of participants stresses the possibility that wage and price fluctuations over time may cause labor suppliers to work more intensively when wages are viewed as higher than average and less intensively when wages are lower than average. This explanation of cyclical upturns is based on the possibility that workers may correctly believe that current real wages are higher than future real wages. This belief may be based on the possibility that technological factors make current production more efficient than usual. This explanation is therefore logically separate from questions of imperfect information.

While somewhat similar in terms of their view of market forces and the economic responses of labor suppliers, these two explanations of business cycles vary substantially in terms of their policy implications. Those subscribing to the first explanation view policy actions as an attempt to trick economic agents into supplying and demanding differing quantities than they would under full and perfect information. On the other hand, those favoring the intertemporal substitution of leisure might feel that some smoothing of production and consumption behavior could improve economic welfare.

The main other set of conference participants favor explanations of fluctuations in aggregate economic activity based upon the assumption that prevailing wages and prices often do not satisfy market-clearing conditions. Some of these researchers simply point to empirical evidence on the apparent sluggish response of wages and prices to exogenous disturbances. They argue that, in the interim, quantities transacted will be the lesser of the quantities supplied and demanded. Others would argue that risk-shifting and risk-pooling arrangements result in implicit contracts that predetermine nominal wages and prices. Within this group some contend that such contracts, although characterized by sticky wages and prices, are still fully contingent upon all new developments. They argue that quantities transacted under such contracts satisfy productive efficiency conditions and therefore precisely replicate the auction market outcome. Others contend that costs of information gathering and contract writing and enforcement preclude such contracts. They argue that the quantities transacted under such contracts will more closely replicate the quantities that would be transacted in a disequilibrium market transacting at the prearranged wage-price vector.

While each of these explanations is logically consistent and conforms to some empirical regularities of historical business cycles, all seem a little preposterous when pushed to their logical extreme. With rapid publication and dissemination of data on money supplies and prices, is it really believable that workers could long remain confused about the true values of their real wage rate? If fluctuations represent optimal intertemporal allocations of time, why should this pattern be sensitive to monetary disturbances? While implicit labor contracts can explain wage rigidity, they must rely on one of the other three mechanisms to provide a source of employment fluctuations. Finally, to rely on wage and price stickiness demands that we assume that employees and workers stubbornly refuse to exhaust mutually perceived gains to trade.

With this basic backdrop of differing research strategies, there is also considerable debate about which of these business cycle scenarios is best supported by existing empirical evidence. Unfortunately, this debate seems far from convincingly settled. About all that can be completely agreed upon is that no empirical test has yet been devised that can successfully discriminate among the competing hypotheses. Some empirical evidence is presented, or referred to, in favor of each explanation, but no empirical consensus emerged. In fact, if any fault can be found with the conference proceedings it would be with its failure to finally put this question to rest empirically.

With the lack of clear empirical evidence on the basic source of business cycles, discussion of the proper role of economic policy occasionally lapses into a reliance on conjectures based on prior beliefs and casual empiricism. This is meant not as a criticism of the proceedings, but rather as a sober reflection on the current state of economic expertise. In fact, probably the most controversial issue associated with rational expectations is the issue of whether systematic government monetary and fiscal policies can affect the time pattern of economic activity. While the ineffectiveness of systematic policy is the natural outcome of incomplete information, intertemporal substitution of leisure, and efficient labor contracts models that incorporate rational expectations, this result is in conflict with the gut feelings of a substantial number of macroeconomists. While many of these scholars either dispute that economic agents behave rationally or that they refuse to exhaust exchanges viewed as mutually beneficial, it is not clear that either attack can be very persuasive. Yet many times we see specific government policy moves that do in fact appear to affect the economy. How do we reconcile these conflicting ideas? Does this mean that all such policy moves were unanticipated and/or unperceived? More importantly, what basis do we have for making real world policy recommendations? These seem to be the most important questions left unanswered at the conference.

The introductory paper by Herschel I. Grossman, entitled "Rational Expectations, Business Cycles and Government Behavior," discusses the present state of economic knowledge about business cycle behavior and gives a brief summary of the remaining papers in the volume. A main point of the paper is that the recent past has dramatically changed our basic approach to business cycle behavior and the role of government. The natural rate hypothesis has completely replaced the belief in the possibility of a stable, exploitable Phillip's Curve trade off between inflation and unemployment, and we have lost much of our faith in the idea of government as a benevolent doctor trying to cure a sick economy. Grossman questions whether the key implications of the incomplete information paradigm—that anticipated policies are neutral while unanticipated and unperceived policies are not neutral—are logically and empirically consistent. On the other hand, he also questions the existence of transaction and contracting costs needed to explain non-market-clearing behavior and the consequent nonneutrality of anticipated policy.

The paper by Robert J. Barro and Mark Rush, entitled "Unanticipated Money and Economic Activity," represents an extension of some earlier work by Barro that attempts to obtain separate estimates of the effects of anticipated versus unanticipated movements in the money supply on the level of economic activity. As in Barro's earlier work, Barro and Rush find that unanticipated movements in the money supply affect aggregate output while anticipated movements in money only affect the level of prices. This result was found to be robust in that it held up with both annual and quarterly data.

This research has been highly imaginative and represents an important advance in an attempt to apply the theoretical concept of rational expectations to empirical investigations. The main problem with the approach is that the authors can only estimate reduced forms rather than structural equations. As might be expected this aspect of the paper left it subject to a wide variety of interpretations by different conference participants. Barro and Rush implicitly seem to interpret the results as meaning that systematic monetary policy will have no effect on the behavior of real economic magnitudes. Others, most notably Stanley Fischer and Alan Blinder, point out that Barro's results are almost impossible to discriminate from models in which policy does matter. Apparently, at least on this important point, more empirical analysis is still needed.

The paper by Olivier J. Blanchard extends an earlier work by Blanchard and Wyplosz. It provides an estimation of a model of aggregate demand that implicitly assumes that agents form expectations rationally. This aggregate demand model is then combined with an assumed aggregate supply model, and a number of policy simulations are carried out. An important advance here is that the analysis is immune to the Lucas critique argument.

The result shows that with sufficiently sluggish price adjustment, even perfectly anticipated changes in the money supply affect real economic variables. However, these effects seem to be smaller the further in advance the monetary change is anticipated. The main problem with the paper is that Blanchard could not estimate the aggregate supply schedule and therefore had to assume it. This is unfortunate because the effect of policy in the model seems to depend crucially on the specification of aggregate supply. The paper is a very important one in that it provides a good example of the kind of econometric technique needed to fit models employing the assumption of rational expectations. This has proved to be a difficult problem.

Robert J. Shiller studies the question "Can the Fed Control Real Interest Rates?" Much of the efficient market's literature might suggest that the rationally expected real interest rate might be invariant with respect to Federal Reserve policy—at least if this policy is known sufficiently far in advance. Shiller imaginatively evaluates evidence bearing on this point. Emphasizing what he believed were two instances in which a policy regime was clearly changed—the founding of the Fed in 1913 and the Accord of 1951—Shiller presents evidence that the Fed can, within limits, alter the time pattern of the rationally expected real rate of interest. However, as he himself noted, this proposition is in fact difficult to verify empirically. Beyond this, Shiller was unable to bring evidence to bear on the key neutrality-nonneutrality issues.

Finn Kydland and Edward C. Prescott's paper, "A Competitive Theory of Fluctuations and the Feasibility and Desirability of Stabilization Policy," presents an argument against the use of fiscal policy for stabilization purposes. The authors present a model in which monetary shocks and shocks to productivity create fluctuations in employment because individual labor supplies fluctuate due to the possibility of intertemporal substitution of leisure. The model then generates momentum, or serial correlation, to the economy by assuming that investment plans take a number of periods to complete. Within this framework, such fluctuations are consistent with Pareto optimality. The authors then use the tools of modern public finance theory to bear on whether a time pattern of taxation that would reduce fluctuations in output would be relatively efficient. To reduce such fluctuations requires a tax on the production of capital goods that fluctuates over time. However, because capital goods produced at different times are close substitutes, their demand elasticity is high. Therefore, the loss in consumer surplus from such a tax is high and therefore it is a costly form of stabilization policy.

This analysis by Kydland and Prescott raises the level of discussion about fiscal policy considerably. Most notable is their recognition of the potential importance of the effects of fiscal policy on relative prices. However, the main problem with the paper is that their interpretation rests entirely on the assumption that business cycle fluctuations originate with workers' intertemporal substitution of leisure. Other possibilities, such as the possibility of confusion of local and aggregate disturbances or failure of markets to clear would generate completely different results. Again we come to the problem of our failure to understand the basic cause of business cycle fluctuations.

The paper by Robert E. Lucas, Jr., "Rules, Discretion, and the Role of the Economic Advisor," and the paper by Stanley Fischer, "On Activitist Monetary Policy with Rational Expectations," debate the wisdom and feasibility of monetary stabilization policy. Fischer favors some policy activism, while Lucas argues for Milton Friedman's proposal of a fixed rate of growth in the money supply. The authors' conclusions are closely related to their ideas about the source of business cycle fluctuations. Lucas leans toward the idea of confusion between local and aggregate disturbances as the source of fluctuations and therefore opposes activism on the grounds that it is likely to compound the signal extraction problem. However, while leaning toward this as the source of fluctuations, he also candidly admits to some doubts. His view is that the state of our understanding about business cycle dynamics is still rather backward. Therefore, he doubts that we can confidently recommend a specific policy rule that will outperform the constant growth rate rule.

Fischer argues that there is a proper role for policy activism. He views the business cycle as resulting from implicit and explicit contractual arrangements. However, costs of contract writing, monitoring, and enforcement preclude the existence of contracts that fully protect both parties from the potentially ill effects of all future contingencies. Therefore, unforeseen events may, due to the fixed terms of the contract, preclude the exhaustion of all perceived, mutually advantageous transactions. The role of policy is then to try to mitigate the effects of disturbances that might create such inefficiencies. Fischer views the Federal Reserve as having a comparative advantage over private contract writers in the identification of aggregate disturbances and the mitigation of their potentially harmful effects. In this view, economic policy becomes a cooperative venture between the government and the private sector, which can help reduce overall contracting costs.

While Fischer presents a case for policy activism, he also recognizes the practical problems involved. In particular, he notes a lack of precise knowledge of how policy works and the potential for the political system to dictate destabilizing policies. Therefore, in principle he comes close to accepting the constant growth rate rule. However, he would not want to have the hands of policymakers tied by legislating this policy. Instead he would favor discretion in the case of significant actual or anticipated economic disturbances, with the requirement for ex post legislative review of the particular deviation from the constant growth rate rule.

The final two papers, "What to Do (Macroeconomically) When OPEC Comes," by Robert M. Solow, and "Macroeconomic Policy 1971–75: An Appraisal," by William Poole, both deal with economic policy preceding the 1974–75 recession. Solow believes that policy erred by not sufficiently accommodating the supply shock of the 1974 OPEC oil price increase. This resulted in a contraction of aggregate demand, which then induced the recession. While Solow recognizes that the OPEC oil price increase necessarily caused a reduction in real GNP below what it would have been otherwise, he feels that the reduction was intensified by the lack of a sufficiently rapid increase in the money supply.

Poole views the issue of the appropriateness of Fed policy in a different light. He feels that the policies of 1973–75 cannot be studied independently of the policies pursued in 1971–72, including wage and price controls. While he does concede that monetary policy had a destabilizing effect over this entire period, he feels that it would have been difficult for the Fed to have done much better than it did. Political forces constrained the Fed to a policy of too much money growth in 1972 in order to keep the economy prosperous during the period of wage and price controls. Poole also points to political forces that made the Fed wary of appearing overly stimulating during the 1974 congressional elections. While he favors policy rules, and possibly the need for a constant growth rate rule, he also feels that rules have to be consistent with the political environment and should be flexible enough to adjust over time as our knowledge about how monetary policy works improves and institutional arrangements evolve.

In my view this volume is an important contribution. It is representative of the broadest spectrum of economic thinking with respect to weaknesses in current approaches to macroeconomic theory and policy. It is suggestive of many areas of important future research. The authors and discussants can be congratulated for the quality of their work and the editor and sponsors for bringing them together.

Composite Reserve Assets in the International Monetary System, by Jacob S. Dreyer. Greenwich, Conn.: JAI Press, 1977. xvi + 191 pp. $21.50

Recent discussions of the Substitution Account proposal (the exchange of officially held dollars for SDR-denominated claims) have generated renewed interest in the features of composite reserve assets in general, and the characteristics of the SDR in particular. Although the IMF Interim Committee decided in the spring of 1980 not to set up a Substitution Account, questions regarding the role, value, and return on SDRs will no doubt be with us for some time, so that Dreyer's book will still be relevant.

Written as a Ph.D. dissertation in the mid-1970s, this monograph first focuses on the implications of alternative techniques of valuation of the SDR both for reserve composition and management and for the operation of the SDR as a "pivot." It then describes the conditions for stability of the composition of reserve portfolios in a two-asset model, including the effects of changes in the yield on SDRs and in their quantity. Two of the major conclusions reached in the study are (1) that it would be preferable to have an explicit technique for maintaining the currency value of the SDR, rather than define the SDR so that its currency value can fluctuate, as is currently the case with the "standard basket" definition of the SDR, and (2) changing the stock of SDRs, rather than their rate of return, is the preferable method for achieving a stable composition of assets in countries' reserve portfolios.

The first substantive chapter deals with alternative methods of valuation of the SDR. It describes the current "standard basket" SDR in which the number of currency units is kept constant, but because of exchange rate changes the currency value of the SDR is variable. It compares this method of valuation to other techniques, some of which maintain the currency value of the SDR through either variations in the quantities or par values of currencies in the basket to offset changes in the value of the SDR resulting from exchange rate changes. This chapter and the accompanying appendix provide a lucid description of how these valuation techniques work and their different implications for the value of the SDR. For example, in the current "standard basket" SDR the number of units of each currency in the basket is fixed but the weights of each currency vary in response to exchange rate changes. As a result, currencies depreciating relative to other currencies will have a declining weight in the basket, although, as Dreyer points out, there may be no reduction in the importance of these currencies in international trade and finance. On the other hand, it is possible that as a result of currency substitution, there could be a shift from depreciating to appreciating currencies in international payments, in which case variable weights in the SDR basket would be appropriate.

Since the work of the Committee of Twenty and the shift on July 1, 1974, from valuing the SDR in terms of gold to valuing it in terms of a basket of currencies, there has been little further discussion of alternative techniques for determining the value of the SDR in transactions against currencies. However, this issue could receive renewed attention in connection with examination by the IMF of the possibility of making the SDR and interest rate baskets identical, as requested by the Interim Committee in their communique issued on April 25, 1980 [2]. In this case Dreyer's monograph would provide useful background reading.

The following chapter is on the use of the SDR as a pivot point for the adjustment of exchange rates, that is, the point on a scale of exchange rate changes separating depreciating from appreciating currencies. This topic is of less interest now than when Dreyer wrote his book. The reason for this is that under the current system of managed floating, exchange rates move primarily in response to market forces; there is little sentiment for adjusting exchange rates in either a discrete or continuous manner as required for the operation of a pivot. Nevertheless, Dreyer does make a number of useful points about the SDR as a pivot, for example, that the location of the standard basket version of the SDR as a pivot on the scale of rates of inflation of the currencies in the basket will shift down over time as a result of the increasing weight given to low-inflation countries.

The second half of Dreyer's book provides an analysis of the stability of the composition of reserve portfolios under an SDR-exchange standard. The vehicle for this analysis is a model with two assets, dollar-denominated claims and SDRs, two endogenous variables, the interest rate on dollar-denominated claims, and a risk factor (y, the ratio of dollar claims held by nonkey currency countries, F, to SDRs held by the United States, C_u), and two agents, the United States monetary authorities and those of nonkey currency countries. The model is based on the assumptions of fixed par values and asset convertibility: that is, the United States has an obligation to exchange dollars for SDRs at the prevailing par value. Since liabilities to official foreign holders may exceed the U.S. stock of SDRs, there is a risk (measured by y) that the United States will not be able to meet its convertibility obligation. In the basic version of this model, the higher this risk, the greater the demand for SDRs. Since the demand for SDRs is inversely related to the interest rate on dollar claims, the primary focus of the analysis is on the combination of interest rates and risk factors that will be consistent with a stable composition of reserve assets. One basic conclusion of the anlysis is that the system will be dynamically unstable when U.S. official liabilities exceed U.S. SDR holdings ($y>1$). If U.S. official liabilities are less than the stock of U.S.-held SDRs ($y<1$), then stability requires that U.S. monetary policy be directed towards eliminating the excess demand for dollars. that is, the United States must refrain from using monetary policy for domestic purposes.

Unfortunately, the usefulness of this model would appear to be vitiated by a number of difficulties. First, in the static model the definition of the risk factor is not included as part of the system. While the markets for money and SDRs determine the interest rate and risk factor that clear these markets, apparently there is no constraint on the values that y can assume. However, $y = F/C_u$, and the comparative static exercise is to examine the effects of a switch from dollars to SDRs on the part of nonkey currency countries, that is, $dC_u = dF$. The nature of the experiment and the definition of y therefore determine the *change* in y. Consequently there appears to be an inconsistency between the market-clearing risk factor and the value of y given by $dC_u = dF$. (In the dynamic specification of the model (p. 100), the definition of y is used as part of the system.)

Second, in part of the model (p. 92) Dreyer imposes the constraint that $dC_u = dF$, but then proceeds to derive comparative static results (dy/dF, dy/dC_u, di/dF and di/dC_u) on the assumption that F and C_u can be varied independently. These comparative static results are plausible; for example, $di/dF > 0$ on the assumption that foreign central banks hold noninterest bearing dollar deposits, and $di/dC_u < 0$ on the assumption that the Federal Reserve varies the money supply in the same direction as changes in its holdings of SDRs. However, given the built-in constraint that $dC_u = dF$ (eqq. IV.7 and IV.5a on p. 92), it is not clear how meaningful these results are.

Third, the assumptions underlying the model mentioned above are rather unrealistic. U.S. liabilities to foreign official institutions are concentrated in U.S. Treasury securities and other interest-bearing U.S. liabilities. Consequently it would have been preferable to specify the asset switch as between U.S. bonds and SDRs, rather than between U.S. money and SDRs. With regard to the response of the Federal Reserve to a loss in SDRs, it would be more realistic to assume that the Federal Reserve does not adjust the monetary base whenever there is a change in its holdings of SDRs. Nevertheless, Dreyer's model is interesting in that it shows that if the U.S. monetary base is insulated from fluctuations in the U.S. stock of SDRs, then the system becomes unstable.

Perhaps because Dreyer found this instability property unappealing, he explores a variant of the basic model in which the interdependence between the actions of reserve holders and the reaction of the reserve center is recognized. As a result of this "mutual interdependence recognized," the peripheral countries are assumed to have a stake in the continuation of the system and temper their conversion of dollars into SDRs. Not surprisingly, this enhances the stability of the system. Part of the novel treatment of this topic is Dreyer's analysis of the extent to which different techniques of value maintenance of the SDR in transactions against currencies (discussed in earlier chapters of his book) affect the peripheral countries' conversion decisions. However, Dreyer's analysis of self-restraint regarding the conversion of officially held dollars would have been more informative for the reader if he had compared his results with those in the literature (e.g., [3, 4]).

In the penultimate chapter Dreyer analyzes two methods for promoting a stable composition of reserve portfolios: changing the interest rate on SDRs and manipulating the available stock of SDRs. He argues that the latter method of reducing excess demand for SDRs involves fewer distortions than adjusting the interest rate on SDRs. The basis for this conclusion is not clear: since an excess supply of one asset, for example, SDRs, must be matched by an excess demand for other reserve assets on the given assumption of an unchanged *aggregate* demand for reserve assets, changing the rate of return on SDRs would appear to involve less of a disruption of the aggregate demand for reserves than changing the stock of SDRs, which clearly will affect aggregate reserve holdings. A more formal analysis would have been helpful here; it would have been fairly easy to construct a two-asset portfolio model and compute the change in the rate of return on SDRs needed to eliminate any excess supply. Also, reference to the literature on the relationship between the rate of return on reserves and adjustment would have been helpful (e.g., [1]).

In summary, Dreyer's book provides a systematic analysis of the effects of changes in the attractiveness and quantity of SDRs on the composition of reserve portfolios. In particular, his examination of alternative techniques of valuation of the SDR provides a useful addition to the literature. However, his analysis is couched in terms of reserve asset convertibility and a par value system, and consequently is not as directly relevant as one might desire for current discussion of the value and return on SDRs in the present world of managed floating. For example, Dreyer does not deal with the possibility that the interest rate on the SDR, defined as a weighted average of interest rates on the currencies in the basket, could adjust to offset exchange rate changes, that is, higher nominal interest rates would tend to be associated with depreciating currencies. Also, it would have been helpful if some attention had been given to the implications of different properties of the SDR for switches between reserve currencies, since the problem of reserve diversification has become more acute. Finally, an extension of the analysis to include an examination of the Substitution Account proposal (which is limited to pp. 177–78 in the book) would have been welcome, but one cannot blame Dreyer for failure to predict the resurgence of interest in this topic when he wrote his book in the mid-1970s.

LITERATURE CITED

1. Clark, Peter. "Interest Payments and the Rate of Return on International Fiat Currency." *Weltwirtschaftliches Archiv,* 108 (1972), 537-64.
2. IMF Interim Committee. *IMF Survey.* May 5, 1980, p. 132.
3. Makin, John. "On the Success of the Reserve Currency System in the Crisis Zone." *Journal of International Economics,* 2 (February 1972), 77-85.
4. ______. "The Problem of Coexistence of SDRs and a Reserve Currency." *Journal of Money, Credit, and Banking,* 6 (August 1972), 509-28.

PETER B. CLARK

Board of Governors, Federal Reserve System

Corporate Growth and Common Stock Risk, by David R. Fewings. Greenwich, Conn.: JAI Press, 1979. xvi + 146 pp. $23.50

In the last ten years, there have been considerable advances made in the direction of capital asset pricing in a multiperiod framework. There are presently two alternative approaches to this problem. One is the general equilibrium intertemporal asset pricing model as exemplified by the works of Merton, Cox, Ingersoll and Ross, and others. The other approach attempts to modify the single-period model by incorporating some proxy of the multiperiod world. This book takes the latter approach. Specifically, an expected growth rate for the firm was used to approximate its stochastic investment opportunity sets over time. The book then proceeds to examine, theoretically and empirically, the effect of expected corporate growth rate on the riskiness and thus expected return of an underlying common stock.

The book is organized into three parts. The first part, three chapters, includes the introduction and the literature review. The theoretical development is contained in the second part (chaps. 4 and 5). The last part, four chapters, reviews past empirical research and presents some new Canadian and U.S. results.

Chapter 2 reviews the traditional stock valuation theories based on discounting future dividend streams. The author argues against the validity of Modigliani and Miller's original and others supporting work. Two arguments based on previous work are cited as the intuitive basis for justifying the theme of this book. The first is the well-known "bird in the hand" argument where the risk-adjusted discount rate increases with time. The second involves the analogy of the effect of duration on bond prices to the effect of growth duration on common stock prices.

Chapter 3 surveys empirical studies on the corporate dividend decision, including various versions of partial adjustment, adaptive expectations, and information content models.

In chapters 4 and 5, the theory relating growth and capitalization risk is derived. It consists of substituting Gordon's constant perpetual growth model for stock prices, and Miller and Modigliani's definition for growth, into the one period definition of the holding period return. The positive relationship between total capitalization risk and growth is inferred from the partial derivative with respect to growth of the elasticity of the modified one period holding return. To infer the same relationship between systematic capitalization risk (beta) and growth, the modified expressions for the holding period returns for both the firm and the market portfolio are substituted into the one period capital asset pricing model. Specifically, a covariance term is calculated and the partial derivative with respect to the growth rate is taken.

Although I sympathize with Professor Fewings's attempt to avoid the technically more difficult alternative of investigating this topic in the framework of the intertemporal capital asset pricing model, his approach has several major shortcomings. Mixing the infinite period constant dividend growth model with the one period holding return and covariances introduces both conceptual and technical difficulties. For instance, Fewings points out that the expression for the covariance term with stochastic earnings in chapter 5 has an ambiguous relationship with growth. (In my opinion, the use of the term stochastic earnings is probably a misnomer since there is no error or innovations component in the formulation.) Furthermore, he even attempts to differentiate between the growth rate of earnings and the growth rate of dividends in a perpetual constant growth model, and to include the effect of outside equity on growth. (Since growth opportunities are options at exercise, it does not matter how they are financed, with debt or outside equity; the gain to the existing equity holder is the same in a frictionless world.)

These difficulties could be circumvented. If the objective is to obtain the qualitative statement that the total or systematic risk of the equity is a positive function of expected growth for the purpose of empirical testing, then a less cumbersome approach can be used. For instance, Professor Stewart Myers makes an interesting argument that arrives at the same result. He argues that growth opportunities are options, and since options are generally more risky than existing assets, firms with a greater proportion of growth opportunities, that is, growth firms, should be expected to have higher capitalization risks.

The remaining portion of the book examines empirical work. Chapter 6 reviews previous studies of the determinants of systematic risk in a firm. It presents an interesting critique of the methodologies used in these studies. The qualitative hypothesis that there is a positive relationship between the beta of a stock and the expected growth of that firm is tested in chapters 7 and 8. Chapter 7 investigates this relationship in sixty-five Canadian firms in two subperiods; 1960–66 and 1967–73.

Using annual data, the following variables are used in a multiple regression against the market beta: accounting earnings' beta, retention proportion of equity financing, debt equity ratio based on book value, and three different proxies for growth (earnings and dividends, earnings, and total assets). In chapter 8, an equivalent regression is run on 325 U.S. firms taken from the Compustat file over the period 1966–75. Monthly prices are used to approximate the market beta and quarterly data are used to determine the other variables. The first two growth variables are found to be significant in most cases.

Although Fewings has not overcome the still intractable problems of estimating growth and growth duration, the empirical work is the most important part of the book. It is one of the very few instances where we are given an opportunity to study "comparative finance." Given that we do not have a very high degree of segmentation between these two capital markets, it would be helpful if Fewings would have explained in greater detail the difference between the two results, for example, the contribution of growth to R^2 (from 0.06 to 0.23) in the Canadian case versus the U.S. case (from 0.001 to 0.04), and on the other hand, why the rest of the explanatory variables are often more significant in the U.S. than the Canadian case.

Overall, the book is well organized and fairly readable. Although it fails to accomplish its stated objective of studying the effect on the riskiness of the stock of "unexpected revisions in investor assessments of future profit potential or from changes in the general equilibrium rates of time preference, risk premium requirements and inflation outlook," it does, however, add some interesting comparative Canadian versus U.S. results with respect to the effect of corporate growth on the systematic risk of common stock.

JAMES ANG
Purdue University

Inflation: Global, International and National Aspects, by Assar Lindbeck. Leuven, Belgium: Leuven University Press, 1980. 117 pp. 340 Belgian francs

This is a gem of a book, in which Lindbeck synthesizes his "Swedish model" of the inflation process with a variety of competing views. The resulting stew will not be palatable to every taste, but almost all of us—and American economists in particular—will find some intriguing arguments to challenge our entrenched opinions about both the causes and cures of recent inflationary pressures.

The text comprises four lectures that Lindbeck delivered at the Katholieke Universiteit in Leuven, Belgium during March 1979. The first presents a view of inflation as a global phenomenon with origins that arc partly national and partly supranational. This distinction then is pursued in the second lecture, which examines the extent of national autonomy and the nature of the international transmission process. Lecture 3 argues that the concept of "cost inflation" is important, is empirically differentiable from demand inflation, and gives rise to unique problems with respect to anti-inflationary policy. Lecture 4 evaluates the various options available for controlling inflation, concluding with a brief, blunt dismissal of incomes policy.

Much of the discussion will be familiar ground to Lindbeckians. We enter a world peopled by "endogenous" politicians seeking to occupy optimum positions on the Phillips curve, especially as elections approach; by "Scandinavian" wage-earners seeking higher wages until they are at the brink of job loss; and by "unilateral" businesses setting prices primarily by standard markups over costs. In this world, the task of the inflation fighter is to dominate, subvert, or control these troublesome impulses as much as it is to limit the growth of aggregate demand. For example, Lindbeck endorses a rather fanciful proposal to desynchronize elections between major countries in order to reduce the cyclical impacts resulting from the tendency to inflate money income prior to elections. He suggests that governments announce in advance that wage increases will not be accommodated through expansionary demand policies, in order to throw the responsibility for subsequent unemployment onto the labor leadership. And he suggests that the effects of markup pricing could be mitigated through national efforts to promote free trade and break up cartels. Clearly, Lindbeck has aligned himself with the structuralists in all of these areas.

And yet, in spite of Lindbeck's disclaimers, the underlying model is firmly founded on a demand-pull base. At the most general, global level, the fundamental determinant of inflation is the rate of "capacity utilization of real resources." Still at the global level, neither wage changes nor price markups exert an exogenous influence on inflation, as both are in turn determined by excess demand for labor and products, respectively. Only when Lindbeck turns to "additional factors" do the structural elements intrude. In a summary statement of the inflation model, these elements include (1) the dispersion of capacity utilization among commodities and among nations, (2) cost-push variables in product and labor markets, (3) the "global money stock" via its effects on asset valuation, and (4) the "inflation trend" via its effect on expectations. Lindbeck emphasizes that none of these "additional" or secondary factors can produce a sustained inflation without accommodating demand policies. The essential difference, then, between a pure demand inflation (generated by high rates of capacity utilization) and cost inflation (initiated by the secondary factors and perpetuated by accommodation) is that the latter cannot be cured solely by demand management without generating politically unacceptable levels of unemployed resources.

The central role of capacity utilization rates (CU) in this model bears closer scrutiny. Lindbeck devotes very little attention to the sources of variation in CU, beyond noting that it depends on both monetary and fiscal policies. There is little comfort here for those—if there are any left in the 1980s—who adhere to the money-causes-inflation-end-of-explanation school. But the role of fiscal policy is asserted rather than argued, so these lectures contribute little to that aspect of the debate. Of greater interest is Lindbeck's view of the transmission process from CU to inflation. Building on his 1975 Richard T. Ely lecture, Lindbeck argues that, unless exchange rates are freely floating, national labor markets generally are more autonomous than are national product markets. Therefore inflation in a single country is more likely to follow from excess demand for labor than from excess product demand. Only at the global level is it valid to view excess demand for output as an autonomous source of inflation. Thus there exist circumstances in which the inflationary process runs from, say, fiscal expansion to wage inflation to commodity price inflation; Lindbeck appears to view most of the late-sixties inflation as fitting this paradigm. By the early 1970s, global expansion of money stocks and international reserves were pushing output markets out of shape and generating a far more pervasive form of inflationary pressure.

Another major difference between Lindbeck's economy and that of either the monetarists or the structuralists is that Lindbeck combines his belief in the importance of structural factors with a view that governments can control inflation only by pursuing demand policies aimed at nonaccommodation of inflationary impulses. Moreover, the purpose of nonaccommodation is not (as most monetarists would have it) to reduce inflation directly by reducing output demand, but rather in the first instance to shift the burden for employment onto the private sector, especially the trade unions. That is, if labor can be persuaded that monetary growth will be held to an announced ceiling regardless of the outcomes of wage-setting decisions, and if they can be persuaded that nominal wage increases will therefore reduce employment opportunities, they will then be less likely to inflate the wage level. Lindbeck admits, however, that the evidence for such optimism is limited to open economies with centralized bargaining: Scandinavia and West Germany in particular. American economists might well wonder why private bargainers who have been unmoved by the obvious depressant effect of nominal wage increases on real wages over the past several years would react so differently if threatened by the possibility of employment declines. It seems more probable that the U.S. labor market is sufficiently atomistic that macroeconomic consequences simply do not feed back to the basic micro level.

Lindbeck is at his weakest when he attempts to evaluate the empirical content of his model. He has a disdain for econometric models and prefers to rely upon what he calls "eye econometrics": plotting data series over time and searching for major episodic correlations. But his cornea frequently leads him astray, as he is forced by it to emphasize large irregular shocks at the expense of smaller but more regular relationships. That inflation depends on the rate of change of CU as well as its level is deduced from the single episode of 1972–73; can one infer that a threshold was then crossed, or is there a more persistent relationship? It is difficult to develop sympathy with this vantage. At one point Lindbeck claims that certain "theoretical specifications as well as the statistics," are "too shaky" to support econometric estimation (p. 35n.). At another he laments that the "complexity of the issue is perhaps too great for formalized econometric studies to make sense" (p. 109). Perhaps so, but these complexities also make the raw data that much less amenable to visual interpretation. Lindbeck makes an excellent case for the specification of his list of determinants of inflation, but the task of sorting out their relative importance remains to be completed.

If inflation is an eclectic problem, what can governments do to alleviate it? In the final lecture, Lindbeck offers some interesting solutions. First, he notes that the major causes of post–World War II inflation have been mistakes in government policies. It follows that a *de*synchronization of national policies, perhaps by staggering the scheduling of major elections, would reduce the amplitude of international cycles and thereby attenuate inflationary pressures. This conclusion may seem odd to those who place sufficient confidence in national policymaking to believe that international coordination would be preferable to a plan promoting offsetting errors. Indeed, the OECD "McCracken Report," to which Professor Lindbeck was a major contributor, is curiously ambivalent on this issue: calling at once for desynchronization and "better coordination" of demand management policies (*Towards Full Employment and Price Stability,* Paul McCracken et al. [Paris: OECD, 1977], pp. 235–37). One is left with the impression that neither Lindbeck nor his colleagues have quite worked out the practicalities of the program.

To Lindbeck the crucial component in any anti-inflationary program is "to prevent organizations with strong market power, in particular labor unions, from exploiting these powers" (p. 100). But neither direct controls nor selective tax policies are reliable medicine, because both distort relative prices and prevent required market corrections. Only if policymakers publicly abandon all concern with employment can they have any hope of reducing the presently high levels of inflation. At the close of these lectures, Lindbeck admits to some doubts about the general applicability of these solutions. But if the only feasible alternatives, as he claims, are a permanently low level of capacity utilization or a distortive incomes policy, then one is forced to agree with him in his final but weak conclusion that it "is perhaps at least worth trying" (p. 113).

JAMES M. BOUGHTON
Indiana University

Trade and Payments Adjustment Under Flexible Exchange Rates, edited by John P. Martin and Alasdair Smith. New York: Holmes & Meier, 1979. xxiv + 250 pp. $48.50

The widening of the differences among national rates of inflation that occurred in the late 1960s had two consequences that in retrospect appear inevitable. First came the abandonment of the system of fixed exchange rates among major currencies. Second and somewhat later came an outpouring of research on the implications of the resulting system of flexible rates. The nine papers in this volume were presented at the University of Sussex in September 1977. They belong to an initial wave of such studies, prepared at a time when the importance of the change in institutions was recognized but no consensus as to its consequences had yet begun to emerge. Since the studies consist of reports on quite specialized topics rather than surveys of broad areas, it is convenient to group them into four categories.

In a first group are two theoretical papers that analyze the implications of flexible exchange rates for national stabilization policy. An elegant paper by Willem Buiter opens the Sargent-Wallace [3] model to include international trade and financial flows within a rational-expectations setting. The author assumes what might be called the *strong* version of purchasing power parity (PPP); namely, that the "law of one price" holds at all times between countries. He then considers the impact of alternative exchange-market strategies on an objective function whose arguments are output, reserves, and prices. That the policy rule chosen has no effect on real output comes as no surprise. However, it is worth noting that a managed float is preferable to either a fixed or freely-floating rate if price stability is an objective.

Brian Hindley discusses this same question of the choice of exchange regime from a quite different methodological standpoint; namely, in a static Keynesian model with rigid real (rather than nominal) wages. His basic point is not unreasonable: in the presence of both traded and nontraded goods, devaluation can be a useful supplement to fiscal policy in maintaining full employment. However, the presentation is sufficiently confusing that it is not always clear what question is being asked. Moreover, the author makes no reference to the existing literature on two-sector balance of payments models such as Dornbusch [1].

A second group of papers attempts to explain observed movements in exchange rates. William Branson and Hannu Halttunen present a version of their portfolio-balance model in which the emphasis is on asset-market equilibrium. In the short run movements in the exchange rate are determined by investors' decisions to reallocate their portfolios among fixed stocks of money and domestic and foreign securities, while in the long run the stock of foreign assets itself increases with the current account surplus. The model is then used to explain monthly observations of six exchange rates from 1971 to 1976. While most coefficients have the expected sign, a significant degree of first-order autocorrelation in the residuals suggests that the model may not be properly specified.

Part of the problem may lie in the authors' assumption that money supplies are exogenous with respect to the exchange rate. In a companion paper Malcolm Knight and Donald Mathieson present evidence that in both the fixed and flexible-rate periods the monetary effects of changes in reserves were in fact not sterilized. Their macroeconomic model of an open economy is built around a *weak* version of PPP in which changes in (rather than the level of) a country's effective exchange rate are explained in part by divergences from the law of one price. With the exception of the U.K., their estimates indicate that the responsiveness of the exchange rate to changes in relative prices is generally quite sluggish.

A third group of papers examines some of the microeconomic implications of flexible rates at the level of the firm or industry. Stephen Magee provides further evidence against the strong version of PPP in a comparison of American and Japanese wholesale-price data for tires, plywood, steel, and autos. The data indicate substantial and prolonged departures from PPP. American goods were apparently undervalued in the late 1950s and early 1960s and overvalued in the late 1960s. Under flexible rates in the 1970s, international differences in prices actually increased, although the average amount of time they lasted declined. In another study, Stephen Carse and Geoffrey Wood confirm Grassman's [2] results concerning the currency of invoicing: 79.5 percent of a sample of British exports and 72.1 percent of a sample of British imports were invoiced in the exporter's currency. Moreover they find that the use of forward cover was limited primarily to imports but that only a quarter of total imports were so covered. The authors then proceed to offer a plausible argument for the *J*-curve based on this evidence.

A study by Alan Deardorff, Robert Stern, and Mark Greene on the output and employment effects of exchange rate changes is somewhat disappointing. This paper reports on simulations from a large, disaggregated (eighteen countries, twenty-nine sectors) model of trade and production. However, so few details are provided as to the structure of the model, the data base, the period of estimation, and the assumptions underlying the simulations that the results are difficult to assess. Not only are many of the reported exchange-rate elasticities of output large, but also they vary greatly among countries with similar degrees of openness and industrialization. As the authors themselves note, if these elasticities are to be believed the exchange-rate changes in the 1973–77 period should have caused greater disruptions in output and employment than actually occurred. The authors' failure to endogenize exchange rates may help explain this discrepancy.

The final two papers discuss the implications of flexible exchange rates for reforms in the international system of trade and payments. Alec Chrystal questions the need for centrally created reserves such as the IMF's Special Drawing Rights. His argument is essentially that an international money cannot adequately fulfil the store-of-value function as a reserve currency unless it also serves the medium-of-exchange function as a vehicle currency. In reply, one might note that at the moment both gold and the ecu are limited essentially to the former role. Moreover, even if one accepts his argument as it stands, an appropriate response would be to devise means to increase the use of international money as a medium of exchange.

Richard Blackhurst makes the familiar point that flexible exchange rates eliminate the balance-of-payments motive for tariffs and should therefore facilitate further rounds of negotiations to lower trade barriers. What he perhaps overlooks is that the chronic current-account disequilibria, a feature of the Bretton Woods system, were perhaps an important factor in bringing countries together to negotiate reductions in trade barriers.

While is is difficult to cover all aspects of a subject such as exchange rates in a single volume, this reviewer regrets the omission of such topics as the monetary approach to the balance of payments, the efficiency of exchange markets, and the effect of the exchange regime on macroeconomic interdependence. In addition, since there was evidently considerable disagreement among the conference participants over methodology and assumptions, it would have been interesting to have a summary of the discussion that accompanied each paper.

In short, this book contains a sampling of some recent theoretical and empirical research—some of it preliminary—on the economic consequences of flexible exchange rates. While a few of the papers now appear somewhat dated, most of the contributions are recommended reading for the specialist in international economics.

LITERATURE CITED

1. Dornbusch, Rudiger. "Devaluation, Money and Nontraded Goods." *American Economic Review,* 63 (December 1973), 871–80.
2. Grassman, Sven. "A Fundamental Symmetry in International Payment Patterns." *Journal of International Economics,* 3 (May 1973), 105–16.
3. Sargent, Thomas, and Neil Wallace. " 'Rational' Expectations, the Optimal Monetary Instrument and the Optimal Money Supply Rule." *Journal of Political Economy,* 83 (April 1975), 241–54.

LEONARD M. DUDLEY
Université de Montréal

Bank Credit Cards for EFTS: A Cost Benefit Analysis, by Robert W. McLeod. Ann Arbor, Mich.: University Microfilms International, 1979. xiii + 142 pp. $23.95

Some dissertations are worthy of publication as books, Paul A. Samuelson's *Foundations of Economic Analysis* (Cambridge, Mass.: Harvard University Press, 1947) being perhaps the preeminent example. Most doctoral exercises do not merit this treatment, but recent advances in printing technology have made it possible for a number of firms to profitably publish dissertations with hot-sounding titles, which are sold to a limited audience at very high prices. This volume appears to be an example of the practice.

Unfortunately, the very topicality of the subject of electronic funds transfer, which may create demand for the book, means that almost any book published on the subject will be outdated by the time of publication. This book, which is based upon a dissertation that was accepted in 1977 (judging by the first copyright listed), is terribly out-of-date. The small bit of analysis that is included has largely been invalidated by recent developments including the Financial Institutions Deregulation and Monetary Control Act of 1980.

The book is also deficient as a history of either credit cards or electronic funds transfer. The small historical sections are based upon a few well-known books and articles and some undocumented interviews with "those individuals most directly involved with the development and implementation of electronic financial systems" (p. 3).

LEWIS MANDELL

University of Connecticut

City Lights, by E. Victor Morgan, Richard A. Brealey, Basil S. Yamey, and Paul Bareau. Islip, N.Y.: Transatlantic Arts, 1979. x + 70 pp. $5.50

The nineteenth in the Institute of Economic Affairs Readings series is intended as a reply to criticism of the financial institutions of the city of London. The volume draws together original contributions by four economists, each of whom examines a particular aspect of the financial process.

Criticism has recently centered on the question of the City's ability to provide the funds required for the "regeneration of British industry" and led directly to the setting up of the Committee to Review the Functioning of Financial Institutions (the Wilson Committee) by the Labour government in 1977. Professor E. Victor Morgan argues that the committee has concentrated too much on asking whether existing institutions will be able to cope with the flow of savings they are likely to receive and should instead have been asking why the U.K. has had so little net saving. He offers no explicit model of growth or of the saving-investment process but argues instead from the following premises: higher investment is a necessary but not sufficient condition for the achievement of a higher growth rate (p. 12) and "a low rate of saving has its counterpart in a low rate of investment" (p. 6).

Within the (low) rate for total saving the principal part is provided by personal sector saving, which plays a vital role in a market economy because of its flexibility in use and because it is processed through the financial system. Morgan suggests a number of reasons for the relatively low rate of household saving in the U.K., but finds that on the evidence available it is not possible to rank them in order of importance.

It is interesting to note that both the City's critics and Professor Morgan seem to be arguing that lack of investment is due primarily to a lack of finance, the critics pointing to inefficiency and the pursuit of short-sighted self-interested policies on the part of financial institutions and Morgan to an insufficient supply of savings available to efficient and properly functioning institutions. In view of this line of argument it is somewhat disconcerting to find Morgan concluding that "the low rate of investment in Britain must be attributed primarily to government or party policies that have undermined profitability and destroyed incentives" (pp. 17–18).

Professor R. A. Brealey attempts to answer criticism of the capital market mechanism by establishing consistent criteria for judging the performance of a capital market. As an element in this process the author makes clear the role of the secondary market as an integral part of a developed capital market. He explains that it is always possible to reconcile the demands of company investment policy with the disparate needs of individual investors, as long as each investor is able to adjust the risk and time pattern of his cash flows by way of transactions in the secondary market. On this basis Brealey is able to defeat criticism of secondary market activity, such as that it "syphons off funds" or that it encourages "socially wasteful gambling." However, his use of the device to justify retained earnings by companies brings him into conflict with Professor Morgan's assertion that "company saving impairs the freedom of shareholders . . . and is likely to distort the allocation of resources" (p. 14).

Professor B. S. Yamey provides an illuminating discussion of the economics of commodity futures markets, hedging, and speculation. As an alternative to hedging his position in a commodity by buying or selling the commodity forward, a trader can safeguard himself against adverse price movements by buying or selling an appropriate quantity of futures contracts. Futures contracts are highly standardized, abstracting from the details of quality, condition, delivery, etc., which would characterize a contract in "actuals." Therefore, transactions costs are lower and risk apart from price risk is largely excluded.

These conditions encourage the participation of specialist speculators whose activities, in turn, facilitate hedging operations and help to make prices more responsive to changes in market conditions. Yamey is able to quote empirical evidence which suggests that, contrary to popular belief, futures trading (including speculation) tends to reduce, not increase, price fluctuations.

International aspects of finance are represented by Paul Bareau's useful account of the origins and functions of the Eurocurrency markets. These international markets in offshore deposits arose out of the contrasting conditions produced by the partial dismantling of exchange control in 1958, when major currencies became freely convertible for nonresidents while remaining restricted in respect of residents' transactions.[1] The exploitation of the opportunities thus presented is seen as "proof of the creative dynamism of private enterprise" (p. 68).

In the oil-price crisis of 1973 onwards the markets played a major part in recycling the surpluses of the OPEC countries. This in turn relieved the burden on the intercentral bank intervention arrangements and thus mitigated the consequent monetary disturbance.

Overall this is a worthwhile collection, though suffering here and there from a lack of "polish" in presentation. It will be read with profit by those who keep an open mind on the question of state intervention in the financial system.

GORDON A. FLETCHER

University of Liverpool

[1]Exchange control for the U.K. was abolished in 1979, after Bareau wrote this essay.

Die deutsche Währung in der Weltwirtschaftskrise 1929–1933 (The German Currency in the World Depression 1929–1933), by Jürgen Schiemann. Bern, Switzerland: Paul Haupt, 1980. 385 pp. $27.00 (paper)

This study deals with the German economic policies during the depression, molded as they were by the constraints of the reparations agreements. Intertwined with this subject is the controversy over whether a devaluation of the mark would have been preferable to the exchange controls hastily introduced after the collapse of the German banking system in July 1931.

The circumstances were the following: under the Versailles treaty, Germany had to pay large reparations to the Allies, mainly France; on the other hand, the Allies had incurred war debts, mainly owed to the U.S. As far as the reparations were concerned, Keynes (*The Economic Consequences of the Peace, 1919,* reprinted in *Essays in Persuasion,* Part I, 1–3, by John M. Keynes [New York: W. W. Norton, 1963]) had warned that they would prove an impossible burden for the German economy, but the warning was somewhat premature since the transfer problem was solved for a time by capital flows—Americans (and others) lent Germany large amounts, which enabled the Germans to pay the reparations to the Allies, which enabled these to pay the war debts to America. This silly arrangement came to an end with the depression when first lending to Germany dried up and repatriations occurred; then the Hoover Moratorium suspended (July 1931) the war debt payments contingent upon suspension of the reparations, first for one year, then for two. Thus, the suspension of the reparation payments brought temporary relief. But, in addition to the expected resumption of these payments, Germany was now saddled with a large foreign debt.

The crucial policies fell to the Brüning government (March 1930–May 1932). The depression was deepening, but anticyclical policies were not understood at the time (pp. 123–24). Furthermore the problem was compounded by falling exports and dwindling reserves. It was for this reason that, after the devaluation of the pound sterling in September 1931, some advocated devaluation of the mark. In fact, the British themselves (after the U.S., Germany's largest creditor, whose credits had been frozen by the controls), as well as the Bank for International Settlements, suggested a 20 percent devaluation (the pound had depreciated by close to 30 percent). But the political and legal obstacles were formidable, and devaluation was really never seriously considered. Moreover, the balance of payments problem notwithstanding, the Brüning government saw an opportunity in the depression to end the reparations once and for all by convincing the Allies that the country was too poor to pay them, an opportunity that might never return once the economy had recovered (pp. 127, 175). An end to the reparations was now more and more demanded, particularly noisily by the growing Nazi party and the Communists. To achieve this aim it was considered imperative, until the cessation was successfully negotiated, not to take any unilateral action, such as a devaluation, which might trigger retaliatory measures (pp. 137, 207 ff.). The reparations were based on the gold parity of the mark, both by the Dawes Plan of 1924 and the renegotiated version of the Young Plan early in 1930. The French were therefore adamantly opposed to a German devaluation. In 1923, when Germany balked at further payments (which at that time had been made mainly in kind), the French occupied the Ruhr, which caused the last, most virulent, phase of the hyperinflation.[1] A similar

[1]The French tried to get the reparations in kind directly from the basic industries of the Ruhr, but the

intervention was feared (p. 199). The U.S. also objected, though the American loans were denominated in dollars, not in marks.

Domestically, the overwhelming opposition to devaluation was based on the fear of a new inflation (p. 226 ff.). The author could have made this reasoning more understandable if he had explained that during the German inflation the rate of inflation had not been measured by some index number, but by the rapidly falling exchange rate of the mark against the U.S. dollar, on which price increases were based. Thus, in a confusion of cause and effect, a fall in the exchange rate was seen as causing inflation directly. Reichsbank president Dr. Hans Luther also feared an inflationary impact, although his reasoning was more sophisticated (p. 214 ff.), and therefore thought devaluation inadvisable. Today, as the author points out, we would find this opinion hard to understand in view of the large unemployment at the time and the fact that the end of exchange restrictions would have tended to lower prices (pp. 220–22). But at the time it represented, of course, the state of the art of central banking. After all, the Federal Reserve, a few years later, obtained the power to raise reserve requirements because it was afraid that the gold-inflow-induced growing excess reserves of the member banks might cause inflation—in the midst of the depression! One also gets the impression from the many opinions quoted that there was a general obsession at home and abroad with the sanctity of the gold standard. It seems to have occurred to no one that exchange restrictions were just as much a departure from it as devaluation.

So, while the controls were maintained, Chancellor Brüning pursued a vigorous policy of deflation with two aims in mind. First, to increase exports—in which he failed in a world of rampant beggar-my-neighbor policies. Second, somewhat inconsistent with the first, to decrease income to a level that would still be politically acceptable, but low enough to demonstrate Germany's inability to resume reparation payments (p. 134). Politically acceptable it was not as it turned out, but an end to the reparations was eventually negotiated by Brüning's successor, von Papen, at the Lausanne Conference, July 1932.

The deflationary measures taken included among others a reduction *by decree* of all prices, wages, and salaries by 10 percent, and then a further 5 percent. If one looks for an economic model that might suggest the effects of such a policy, the Pigou effect comes to mind. In fact, as far as this reviewer knows, it is the only time that a government deliberately created the conditions for the Pigou effect. Of course, Brüning did not know it was the Pigou effect—he certainly did not have this effect in mind—nor did Pigou, who had not thought of it yet. Perhaps it is not a very good test case, however. The German middle class did not have much in the way of financial assets that could appreciate in real terms to stimulate expenditures, having lost them in the inflation. It lived on its current income, which kept shrinking. In any case, early in 1932, unemployment reached over one-third of the labor force, 44 percent of industrial labor with another 22 percent working only part-time (p. 303, Table 17). Two more short-lived governments were unable to improve the situation very much, and on January 30, 1933, aged President Hindenburg summoned Adolf Hitler to power. The rest, as the saying goes, is history.

As this reviewer sees it, and few I believe would disagree, three main elements brought Hitler to power with the terrible consequences for Germany and the world.

German workers refused to cooperate. The German government paid the workers, accelerating the printing presses, while the output of this key industrial district was lost to the economy.

First, there was the excessive and studied humiliation of the Versailles treaty (even according to the scaled-down version of the Young Plan, twelve years after the war, the reparations were to be paid till 1988!). Second, the inflation partially caused by the reparations, which wiped out all savings. And, third, the depression. But the first two, one might say, were necessary but not sufficient conditions. After the stabilization of the mark on November 15, 1923, the situation returned to normal. The public was resigned to its losses and the conditions of the treaty. For the next six or seven years the Weimar Republic was politically stable. Hitler and his Nazis were the lunatic fringe which were not heard from very much, and which nobody took very seriously. It was the depression that brought things to a head and generated policies that led to disaster. These policies, and the reasoning behind them, are very well presented by this study.

At the end of the book (pp. 252–92) the author attempts to calculate the possible balance of trade improvement by a devaluation of the suggested 20 percent, if devaluation had been politically feasible. (There was actually a large trade surplus at the time, but not large enough to offset the negative transfer and capital accounts that caused the deficit.) These calculations have their problems, however. There are a number of them, but the main problem is the method of calculation. The author proceeds from the percentage distribution of exports and imports by five classes of merchandise with respective demand elasticity estimates for each class. From this he calculates the percentage changes in exports and imports. Now, in spite of the labeling of some percentage figures as foreign currency changes and corresponding statements in the text, this calculation is obviously made in domestic currency, and the resulting percentage changes are shown in marks without any apparent allowance for the devaluation (p. 270). This may be useful to show the effect on domestic income, but not if the problem is foreign currency receipts and expenditures as it is here. Moreover, instead of converting the percentage changes into absolute changes in the import bill and export receipts to arrive at the net change, he nets out the percentage changes (in widely different absolute values) to arrive at the percentage improvement of the trade balance, which gives of course a meaningless result, even in marks. The author concludes that a much larger devaluation would have been necessary—and a rough recalculation using his data bears this out—but his kind of calculation cannot show it.

But this exercise is not the main contribution of the study, nor is it meant to be (p. 253). The reparations problem, the international aspects of the depression, have been treated in the literature and are known more or less in general outline. But the German policies during this period, the political and legal constraints under which they operated, and the motivations behind them are less well known. This amply documented study explains this subject very convincingly.

WALTHER P. MICHAEL

Ohio State University

Inflation and the Personal Income Tax: An International Perspective, by Vito Tanzi. New York: Cambridge University Press, 1980. xii + 176 pp. $27.50

This book by the assistant director, Tax Policy Division of the International Monetary Fund, consists of thirteen relatively short chapters dealing with various aspects of the way in which personal income taxation is affected by inflation, descriptions of how tax laws and regulations in some countries have been modified in response to inflation, and evaluations of the outcomes of these measures. That a tax system designed for an environment in which the general level of prices is expected to be stable will result in outcomes quite different than those intended by the persons formulating the laws, when the system is applied to an inflationary environment, is not a secret and has been written about in other books and journals. This book concentrates on the personal income tax and covers a broader range of topics than that to be found in an article or most books. It was written for policymakers concerned with tax problems, tax lawyers, and accountants as well as for economists, so the economic analysis of some of the topics is rather elementary. However, some chapters seem to be directed only toward professional economists.

A tax with nominal liabilities not homogeneous of degree one with respect to the nominal tax base will yield real liabilities that vary with the price level even though the real value of the base is a constant. The personal income tax usually (1) has marginal rates that increase as the tax base increases and (2) exempts some income from the tax base. Consequently the real tax liability rises with the price level. The tax could be made to vary proportionately with the price level by making the exemptions and the income brackets proportional to the price level. However, in the United States and many other countries, the personal income tax is not just a tax on income; the tax base includes "realized capital gains." Consequently, unless an adjustment is made in the net worth of the taxpayer as of the beginning of the taxing period to account for the change in the value of his assets due to inflation, the capital gains component of the tax is partially a tax on assets rather than a tax only on the increment in the value of one's initial assets.

These relationships between inflation and the income tax are well-known. Tanzi discusses some of the ways in which the real amount of tax could be made more nearly invariant with respect to the price level and describes briefly the experiences of some countries that have incorporated various schemes into their tax laws. As inflation has become more widespread and persistent more countries have adopted devices that make the tax structure a function of the price level. Latin American countries—particularly Argentina, Brazil, and Chile—have experienced chronic inflation. They have been among the group that first indexed taxes and would have most nearly made real personal income taxes independent of the price level were it not for the relatively long lag that exists between the assessment of the tax liability and the actual collection of the tax. With such a lag, inflation reduces the real value of tax payments. Tanzi incorporates the lag as one of the variables affecting the impact that inflation has upon the tax.

In spite of more than a decade of inflation, the United States still has not provided for automatically introducing more invariance between real personal tax burdens and inflation. Congress has adjusted the personal income tax structure several different times, generally keeping the average ratio of personal income taxes to income payments approximately a constant. This ratio is again at a high point because the unusually high rate of inflation during the past few years was not accompanied by a "cut" in personal income taxes. The tax "cuts" provided in the U.S. have been mostly of the kind that increase the size that income must achieve before any tax is paid, though there have been minor changes in the amounts of some other income exempted from the tax base. Achieving the tax "reductions" mostly through increasing the basic exemptions has made the personal income tax more progressive, that is, the ratio of real tax to real income increases more rapidly with real income than it did a decade ago. Marginal tax rates are now higher with respect to real income, and the elasticity of the tax yield to national income also has increased. The personal income tax became the source of unexpectedly large tax receipts, particularly for some state governments.

These outcomes are welcomed by those who believed that our initial tax structure was not sufficiently progressive and by those who favor higher ratios of government expenditure to national income. The fiscal "reform" they favor has been partially accomplished by inflation without any change in the tax statutes. Some legislators also seem to believe that the tax "cuts" that have been enacted are viewed by the taxpayer as genuine tax reductions, even though for those who pay the bulk of the taxes real tax burdens have increased. There has not been overwhelming support among economists nor strong support among politicians for indexing the U.S. tax structure.

Tanzi's discussion of indexing includes a brief analysis of super-indexation, that is, adjusting the structure for growth in real income as well as for inflation. The book also contains two chapters on the relationship of the rate of interest to inflation in an economy with a personal income tax like that of the U.S. and a chapter on "Inflation, Indexation, and the Wage-Tax Spiral." Tanzi states that according to Irving Fisher, the differential between the equilibrium money rate of interest and the equilibrium real rate of interest in a world without income taxes should be the expected rate of inflation. However, in a world with income taxes, the differential should be the expected rate of inflation divided by one minus the marginal tax rate. Thus, the adjustment of the price level to a given greater exogenous inflationary shock should be larger the larger the tax rate. Similarly, if wage income is subject to tax and real wages are to be held constant, the adjustment in money wages required to compensate for a given change in the price level will vary directly with the marginal tax rate.

Although taxation of business income is not discussed, the chapter dealing with capital gains provides the basis for understanding some of the most important adjustments in business income needed to make real business taxes more or less independent of inflation.

The book makes it apparent that patching up an income tax structure (such as that of the U.S.) to try to make it more neutral with respect to inflation is a costly operation that would redistribute some of the gains and losses and still would not satisfy some equity criteria. If we insist on financing such a large part of government expenditure with money issue that inflation results, perhaps the rest should be financed from an expenditures tax or an income tax with a constant rate and no personal exemptions.

OSWALD H. BROWNLEE

University of Minnesota

Programs of Graduate Study in Finance at The Ohio State University

Ohio State is the largest University in Ohio. It is a major center for graduate education, ranking eighth in the nation in doctoral degrees conferred. There are 350 masters students and 100 Ph.D. students pursuing advanced study in business administration.

Although the Business School is essentially self-contained, the size of its graduate program and the availability of other strong departments such as economics, statistics, and mathematics offer the graduate student considerable flexibility in developing a program of study.

Areas of Specialization. The Finance Faculty of twenty-one full-time professors combines a diversity of talents and interests to offer areas of specialization at the masters and doctoral levels in managerial finance, financial institutions, international finance, financial theory, and investments. Other closely related graduate programs are available in insurance and real estate.

Financial Aid. Four basic sources of financial aid are available: fellowships and teaching, research and administrative assistantships. The fellowships are competitively awarded and the teaching assistantships involve teaching one course per quarter. Continued financial support is normally available if a student is progressing satisfactorily in his graduate program.

Additional information may be obtained from: Director of Graduate Study, Faculty of Finance, The Ohio State University, 1775 College Road, Hagerty Hall, Columbus, Ohio 43210.

Back issues of the *Journal of Money, Credit, and Banking* are available from the Ohio State University Press. The following are in print:

1981 XIII, 1 (Feb)
1980 XII, 1-4 (Feb-Nov)
1979 XI, 1-4 (Feb-Nov)
1978 X, 1-4 (Feb-Nov)
1977 IX, 1 (Feb), 3 (Aug)
1976 VIII, 4 (Nov)
1975 VII, 2-3 (May-Aug)
1974 VI, 1 (Feb); 3-4 (Aug-Nov)
1973 V, 2 (May)
1970 II, 3-4 (Aug-Nov)
1969 I, 3 (Aug)

Price per copy: $6.00. Orders accompanied by payment are shipped postpaid in U.S.; outside U.S. add $.60 postage. Cash only on orders less than $10.00. Payment must be made in U.S. dollars and checks drawn on a U.S. bank. Address orders to Subscription Department, Ohio State University Press, 2070 Neil Avenue, Columbus, Ohio 43210.

Annual volume index published in November; indexes to I-XII supplied on request. Inquiries concerning reprinted or microfilm editions of out-of-print issues may be addressed to the Ohio State University Press.

Ohio State
University Press

August
1981

JOURNAL OF MONEY, CREDIT AND BANKING

US ISSN 0022-2879

JOURNAL OF MONEY, CREDIT AND BANKING

WILLIAM G. DEWALD, EDITOR
Ohio State University

ISSN 0022-2879.

JOURNAL OF MONEY, CREDIT AND BANKING

VOLUME XIII NUMBER 3 AUGUST 1981

ARTICLES

Temporal Variability of United States Consumer Price Index *William A. Gale* 273

Can the Reserves Approach to Monetary Control Really Work? *James M. Johannes and Robert H. Rasche* 298

Reserve Requirements, Deposit Insurance, and Monetary Control *Robert D. Laurent* 314

Optimal Portfolio of Foreign Currencies with Borrowing and Lending *Haim Levy* 325

Money, Income, and Causality in the United Kingdom: An Empirical Reexamination *John T. Cuddington* 342

FNMA Auction Results as a Forecaster of Residential Mortgage Yields *Herbert M. Kaufman and Don E. Schlagenhauf* 352

NOTES, COMMENTS, REPLIES

The Growth of Organizational Forms of Foreign Banks in the U.S. *A Note by Lawrence G. Goldberg and Anthony Saunders* 365

Organizational Form and Risk in Bank-Affiliated Mortgage Companies *A Note by John T. Rose and Roger D. Rutz* 375

Inflation Expectations and the Specification of Demand for Money Equations *A Note by Vittorio Corbo* 381

Indirect Evidence on the Efficacy of Selective Credit Controls: The Case of Consumer Credit *A Note by Brian A. Maris* 388

On the Revenue Maximizing Rate of Inflation *A Comment by David Chappell* 391

(*Continued*)

BOOK REVIEWS

Essays in Post-Keynesian Inflation, edited by James H. Gapinski and Charles E. Rockwood *A Review Essay by Preston J. Miller* 393

The Development of Economic Policy: Financial Institution Reform, by Sidney J. Jones *Reviewed by David W. Cole* 399

The Economics of the Eurocurrency System, by George W. McKenzie *Reviewed by John R. Hewson* 401

Rational Expectations and Monetary Policy, by Jac J. Sijben *Reviewed by Robert G. King and Charles I. Plosser* 404

Social Security Versus Private Saving, edited by George von Furstenberg *Reviewed by Michael R. Darby* 407

Journal of Money, Credit, and Banking (ISSN 0022-2879). Published quarterly in February, May, August, and November by the Ohio State University Press, 2070 Neil Avenue, Columbus, Ohio 43210. Richard C. Rose, Managing Editor; Kummi Ranjit, Production Editor; Lisa Satterfield, Assistant Editor; Lois Fausnaugh, Subscriptions Manager; Jeanette White, Secretary to the Editor, Department of Economics, Ohio State University. Second-class postage paid at Columbus, Ohio, and at additional mailing offices.

Subscriptions. Individual: U.S.$20.00 per year; library: U.S.$25.00; student: U.S.$16.00; additional subscriptions to the same address: U.S.$16.00 per subscription. Postage outside the United States: add $3.00 per year. Sustaining Subscriptions: U.S.$5.00 per year. Supporting Subscriptions: U.S.$100 per year. Claims for missing issues must be made within four months of the date of publication. Allow six weeks for address change. Checks should be made payable to the Ohio State University Press, 2070 Neil Avenue, Columbus, Ohio 43210.

Back Issues, Reprints, and Microfilm. Back issues in print are listed in the May and November issues and may be obtained from the Ohio State University Press. Microfilms of back volumes and reprints of articles and out-of-print issues may be obtained from University Microfilms International, 300 North Zeeb Road, Ann Arbor, Michigan 48106.

Manuscripts. Manuscripts are to be submitted in triplicate to the Editor, *Journal of Money, Credit, and Banking,* Department of Economics, Ohio State University, 1775 College Road, Columbus, Ohio 43210. Submission fee: individual subscribers U.S.$15; nonsubscribers U.S.$25. Checks are to be made payable to the Journal of Money, Credit, and Banking and enclosed with submitted manuscripts. Complete instructions for preparing text and illustrations may be obtained from the editor.

WILLIAM A. GALE*

Temporal Variability of United States Consumer Price Index

1. INTRODUCTION

WITH THE INCREASED LEVELS OF INFLATION in the United States in the 1970s has come an increased interest in the possible costs of inflation. It is generally agreed that if transaction costs are zero, if an inflation is fully anticipated, and if the inflation affects all goods and services equally, then there is no change in individual or aggregate welfare [23, chap. 9]. As an example of the thrust of the contention, an equitable contract for an income fixed in nominal terms can be drawn if the inflation rate is correctly anticipated. However, each of the conditions is violated in the real world, and some economists [1, 21] argue that there are in fact appreciable costs even for an anticipated inflation.

Suggested transaction costs that increase with anticipated inflation rates are greater costs from holding less money, the weakening of usefulness of past experience in repeated transactions for the same goods, and the corresponding diversion of managerial talent from production to procurement. There would be a large transaction cost, of course, to pay interest on cash holdings. Other costs are argued to increase with inflation because it is in fact difficult or impossible to make appropriate institutional arrangements. These include increasing the production of goods as opposed to services and avoidance of long-term contracts, with diversion of

*It has been a pleasure to make the statistical analyses, including the figures, in this work using the "S" Language and System for Data Analysis. I would also like to thank Robert McGill for assistance in reading a tape with the basic data for the study. Suggestions from Ramanathan Gnanadesikan led to distinguishing the post-1964 period. I thank John Carlson, Michael Darby, Milton Friedman, and Jeffrey Lagarias for comments on an earlier draft.

WILLIAM A. GALE *is a member of the technical staff, Bell Telephone Laboratories.*

0022-2879/81/0881-0273$00.50/0
JOURNAL OF MONEY, CREDIT, AND BANKING, vol. 13, no. 3 (August 1981)

managerial talent from production to speculation. Barro [3], among others, has built models of hyperinflation as the optimum rate of inflation to generate tax revenue by steady inflation.

Other costs arise from any *unpredictability* of the rate of inflation. These include discouragement of investment through additional uncertainty of the real rate of return and the exacerbation of each of the previously mentioned costs. Levi and Makin [16] provide data consistent with the hypothesis that the real rate of interest depends on the level of inflation through increased unpredictability. However, only if the variability of inflation *increases with* the level of inflation will these costs need to be accounted for in considering which level of inflation (including none) is optimal. This paper reviews and extends the evidence for such an increase of variability with an increase of level. Because there are several studies with divergent claims, a review is needed. Because their relevance to the United States is not certain, an extension is needed.

Finally, if the inflation affects different goods at different rates, then even if the average level can be anticipated, there will be a change in individual welfare levels and anticipatory expenses attempting to offset the effects. Logue and Sweeney [17] point out that increased relative price uncertainty makes a more difficult environment for the producer whose product may move differentially from his various supplies. Again, the question is how the individual differences among commodities vary with the inflation rate. However, Bach and Stephenson [2] have pointed out the difficulty of singling out any particular group of people that is hurt by relative price variations, because the categories of people that can be argued to be hurt are not the same for various effects. Other recent papers examining relative inflation have included a model based study by Parks [22] and a study by Vining and Elwertowski [25]. Relative inflation variability deserves a separate study, and it is not considered further here.

Various reasons have been advanced for the variability of inflation increasing with the level of inflation, though no formal models have been published. Okun [20] advanced the basic "stop and go" argument: "the brakes have been applied whenever inflation seemed to be a more serious problem . . . than idle resources." This argument is reinforced if policymakers normally stop trying to reduce inflation when it reaches zero or any positive value, for then the variability and average level will both be related to the maximum attained. Logue and Sweeney [17] point out that shocks to money demand are multiplied by the inverse of real cash balances, which are likely to be smaller with higher levels of inflation. Logue and Willett [18] make an instability argument: greater variability in investment can both lead to and be caused by greater variability in actual inflation rates. Friedman's Nobel lecture [7] noted that inflation tends to lower political cohesiveness through polarization of citizens differentially affected by inflation, reducing the capacity to govern and simultaneously calling for strong action.

Another possible reason for observing a relation between level and variability, but opposite in its impact on the interpretation of the results, is that measurement problems become worse at higher levels of inflation. For instance, the U.S. bureau of Labor Statistics "links in" goods with adjudged major quality changes, assuming that the goods in question had an inflation rate during the period equal to that for similar goods not changing in quality. This assumption is less defensible in times of high inflation.

A preliminary issue is to form operational definitions of *level of inflation* and *variability of inflation*. The rest of this introduction reviews definitions that have been used and their interpretations.

We denote a price index by p_t, with the period of the time index t not yet specified. The one period *inflation rate* is defined as

$$r_t = \frac{p_t - p_{t-1}}{p_{t-1}} .$$

Definitions of inflation level and variability are dependent on models of r_t. Two models in which the concept of level are meaningful are

$$r_t = \mu + u_t, \qquad u_t \sim N(O,\sigma^2), i.i.d. \tag{1}$$

$$r_t = \rho r_{t-1} + u_t, \qquad u_t \sim N(\mu(1 - \rho),\sigma^2),\ i.i.d. \tag{2}$$

In either model, we would identify μ as the level of inflation and estimate it by

$$\hat{\mu} = \frac{1}{T} \sum_{t=1}^{T} r_t .$$

If the model taken were

$$r_t = c_1 + c_2 t + u_t, \qquad u_t \sim N(O,\ \sigma^2),\ i.i.d., \tag{3}$$

then "level" would become a time dependent concept.

For any series of predictions r_t^* for r_t, we could use as measures of unpredictability or variability such quantities as

$$\frac{1}{T} \sum_{t=1}^{T} (r_t^* - r_t)^2$$

or its square root, or

$$\frac{1}{T} \sum_{t=1}^{T} |r_t^* - r_t| .$$

These variability measures compare some forecast to the actual result. The simplest kinds of forecasts are based on fitting models such as (1) and (2) above. For model (1) the best forecast is $r_t^* = \mu$, and an appropriate measure of variability would be $s = ((1/T - 1)\Sigma_{t=2}^{T}(\hat{\mu} - r_t{}^2)^{\frac{1}{2}}$. This estimate of σ is a reasonable measure of unpredictability if model (1) is valid, even though $\hat{\mu}$ is not available during $t=1, \ldots, T$, because prior data not available to the analyst would have informed citizens. For model (2) with $\rho = 1$, the best prediction is $r_t^* = r_{t-1}$, and an appropriate measure of variability would be

$$a = \frac{1}{T-1} \sum_{t=2}^{T} |r_{t-1} - r_t|.$$

I have called this measure *average acceleration* because the quantities summed are approximately second logarithmic differences of the price index. For model (2) with $\rho = 1$, there is not a meaningful definition of level of inflation. Prior work has still used the average rate of inflation as a measure of level when considering this definition of variability. The use of average acceleration overcomes the problem [11] that s can capture trend terms confounding them with unpredictable changes.

The interpretation of these two measures of variability, if model (2) holds, are of interest because positive autocorrelation has become common during the period of most of the studies considered. For the United States, from 1953 to 1978, the first-order autocorrelations for monthly, quarterly, and annual series were 0.57, 0.77, and 0.81. For model (2) the best one-period forecast is

$$\hat{r}_{t+1} = \rho r_t + \mu(1-\rho),$$

and the variance of the prediction error is σ^2. The optima long-term forecast is

$$\hat{r} = \mu$$

with variance $\sigma^2/(1-\rho^2)$.

Now consider what is measured by average acceleration and standard deviation over some period. Acceleration corresponds to the prediction $\hat{r}_{t+1} = r_t$ with error $(\rho-1)r_t + u_{t+1}$. The expected absolute value of this is $\sqrt{(2/\pi)}$ times the standard deviation of the error which is $\sqrt{(2\sigma^2/(1+\rho))}$, giving $2\sigma/\sqrt{(\pi(1+\rho))}$. The standard deviation calculated from T points has expected value (suppressing μ for clarity)

$$\begin{aligned} E(s_T^2) &= \frac{1}{T-1} E\left(\sum_{t=1}^{T} r_t^2 - \frac{1}{T}\left(\sum_{t=1}^{T} r_t \right)^2 \right) \\ &= \frac{1}{T-1} \left\{ \sum_{t=1}^{T} E(r_t^2) - \frac{1}{T} \left[\sum_{t=1}^{T} E(r_t^2) + 2 \sum_{u<t} E(r_u r_t) \right] \right\} \\ &= \frac{\sigma^2}{1-\rho^2} \left\{ 1 - \frac{2}{T-1} \left[\left(1 - \frac{1}{T} \right)\rho + \left(1 - \frac{2}{T} \right)\rho^2 + \ldots \right] \right\} . \end{aligned}$$

For small values of T, the standard deviation is a biased estimator of the long-run prediction variance. The bias is about 20 percent for $T = 6$ and $\rho = 0.5$. The acceleration is less intelligible, and the algebra omitted, but it is closer to a measure of short-run predictability. It is a biased measure of that. One might consider direct and unbiased measurement of the short- and long-term prediction variances. However, direct measures of ρ over short periods of time are highly variable. The six-year periods since 1945 gave −0.04, −0.14, 0.84, 0.98, and 0.29, for instance. Thus the biased measures appear to be better for short intervals such as are needed in the following study.

More advanced measures of variability rest on more advanced models. These might include more elaborate single series structure, or include predictive information from another series, such as money growth. This paper remains with single series models, but section 3 explores a definition of variability using an advanced model of trend and seasonal components.

2. REVIEW AND RECONCILIATION OF PREVIOUS STUDIES

Previous studies of temporal variability have concentrated on comparing a measure of variability of price changes across countries, using a price index compiled by each country. The likelihood of a lack of comparability of the concepts behind these various indexes is a caveat on this methodology. This section is a review in the sense that I have not gone behind the published measures of variability to the underlying data on international inflation. However, it will be clear that the divergent claims need some reconciliation. These cross-country studies have used two measures of variability. Define the price index for country i and time t as p_{it}, and the *inflation rate* as $r_{it} = (p_{it}/p_{it-1})-1$. Then the measures of variability that have been used are the standard deviation and the average acceleration, each being indexed by the country. The average rate of inflation has been used as a measure of level.

Okun [20] studied seventeen industrial countries for the period 1951–68. The measure of price index was the GNP deflator for each country as reported in OECD (Organization for Economic Cooperation and Development) data. He found that the correlation coefficient between r_i and s_i across countries was 0.78. The kind of result that he found can be seen by looking at Figure 1, which plots the values for s_i and r_i given by Logue and Willett [18] for the period 1950–70.[1] In Figure 1, the fifteen OECD countries that were among those considered by Okun have been plotted with the symbol "+." The relationship between s_i and r_i for the selected countries is evident.

Gordon [8], writing in the same volume, suggested that the Korean War aftermath had made prices behave strangely in the 1950s. Breaking the period 1951–68

[1]The points plotted by "+" in Figures 1 through 6 represent countries in the group Austria, Belgium, Canada, Denmark, Finland, France, Germany, Greece, Ireland, Italy, Japan, Netherlands, Norway, Sweden, Switzerland, United Kingdom, and United States. However, not all these countries are necessariliy in any one figure. Likewise, "L" represents countries in the group Bolivia, Chile, Colombia, Costa Rica, Dominican Republic, Equador, El Salvador, Guatemala, Mexico, Nicaragua, Panama, Peru, Uruguay, and Venezuela. The symbol "O" (other) represents countries from the group Australia, Ceylon, Iceland, Iran, Iraq, Israel, Korea, Morocco, New Zealand, Phillipines, Portugal, South Africa, Spain, and Thailand.

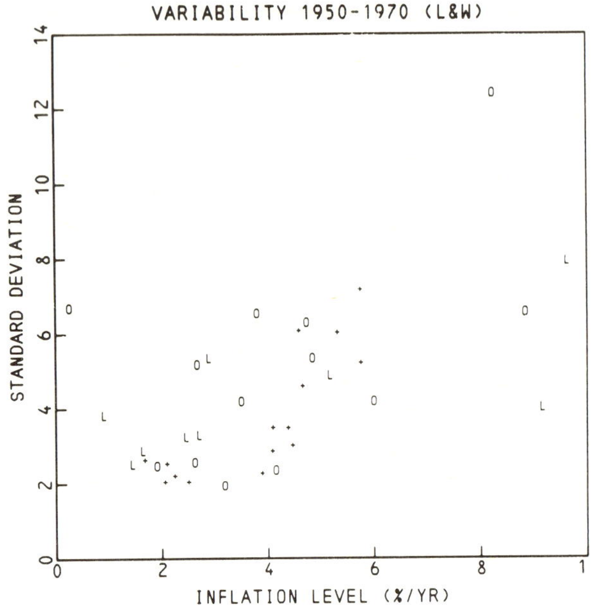

FIG. 1.

into subperiods 1951–60 and 1961–68, he found that the correlation across the same seventeen countries was 0.90 for the first subperiod and 0.40 for the second subperiod. Figure 2, also based on data of Logue and Willett, shows the kind of result that Gordon found. The figure again plots s_i versus r_i, but the time period is now 1960 to 1970. The selected OECD countries show little relationship between level and variability in this plot. Gordon also suggested that the countries with large variabilities were the countries with more open economies, and he pointed out a subset of twelve countries with a correlation close to zero for the 1960s. It is evident from Figures 1 and 2 that the countries emphasized had a different relationship between level and variability in the 1960s than they did for the two decades as a whole. This is discussed further after later findings are reviewed.

Logue and Willett [18] made a study of forty-one countries from 1950 to 1970 using consumer price indexes to measure price changes. It is the data from their Table 1 that appears in Figures 1 and 2. They made separate calculations for four subgroups of countries and for two subperiods. They reported that the correlation between s_i and r_i was significant overall, but not for the highly industrialized countries alone, and not for the group of the countries that had r_i in the lower half. They suggested that there might be a nonlinear relationship with "some range, near zero, over which higher rates of inflation carry with them little or no increase in variability." The work below will examine this suggestion, and we will refer to the point above that variability increases with inflation level as the *threshold inflation*

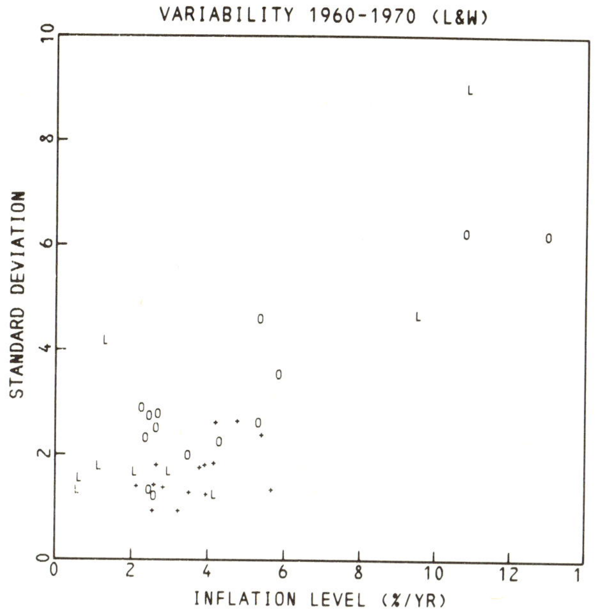

FIG. 2.

rate. With respect to the question of whether the 1960s gave a different result from the 1950s, Logue and Willett showed that for three groups of less-industrialized countries the correlations were somewhat lower in the 1960s than in the 1950s, and that the slopes were also lower. Thus, they found that a relationship still existed but was quantitatively weaker for the less-industrialized countries in their sample.

Foster [6] used a consumer price index from each of twenty-three industrialized countries and from seventeen Latin American countries. He first noted that effects possibly due to the Korean War could be seen through 1953 but not later. So he used data from 1954 onward. He found the correlation between average accelerations a_i and inflation level r_i to be 0.93 for the twenty-three industrialized countries for the time period 1954–75. He constructed various subsets of countries and subperiods of time in order to compare the Okun and Gordon findings. He found that the lowest correlation was for the twelve countries indicated by Gordon as relatively closed advanced economies, which showed a correlation of 0.76 for the time period 1961–75. This correlation he found to be significant at the 0.05 level. All other periods and sets of countries examined showed a higher correlation. This observation suggests that the atypical period was the 1960s rather than the 1950s. He found correlations in excess of 0.95 for the Latin American countries. The values of a_i and r_i for the industrialized countries from his Table 4 are plotted in Figure 3 along with those figures for Latin American countries from his Table 5 for which the inflation level lay within the range of the inflation levels of the industrial countries.

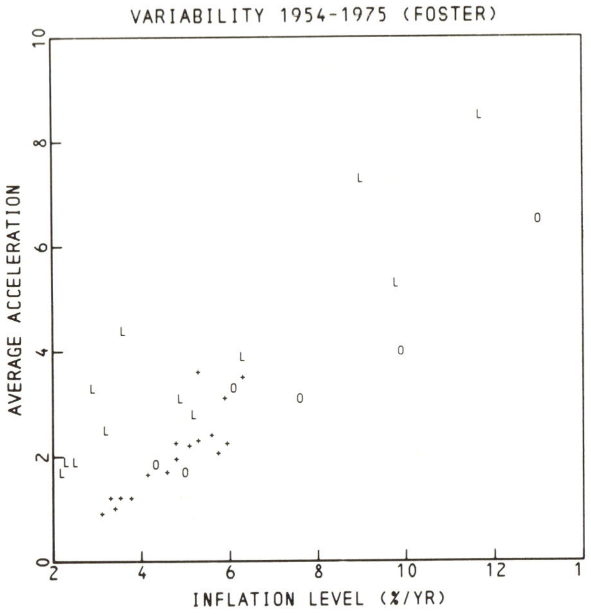

FIG. 3.

Notice that the Latin American countries are plotted with the letter "L." The figure shows clearly the relationship across the industrialized countries considered for the 1954 to 1975 time period. Foster concluded that "until a persuasive alternative explanation is offered [for the cross-country empirical results] we should recognize that choosing a more inflationary policy might carry the cost, not before recognized, of a more variable inflation."

While the findings of Foster and of Logue and Willett are different, there is a fairly simple reconciliation of the two studies. Both studies included tables of the values of variability and level as they measured them, and the Logue and Willett study includes twenty-one of the twenty-three advanced countries studied by Foster. (Italy and Ireland are not represented in the Logue and Willett study.)

We first consider the Logue and the Willett finding that the highly industrialized countries showed no relationship between level and variability of inflation. The finding is based on correlations shown in their Table 2 as 0.08, 0.76, and 0.07 for 1950–70, 1950–60, and 1960–70, respectively. The low correlation for the 1960–70 period for their highly industrialized countries is essentially the same observation as pointed out by Gordon, because their definition of highly industrialized countries includes only seven countries. The seven are not the highest in per capita income, but they are all included in the set plotted by "+" in Figures 1 through 6. The possible difference in the 1960s will be discussed further below. The low correlation for the highly industrialized countries for 1950–70 reported by Logue and Willett seems to be the result of a clerical error entering their calculations.[2] Using a revised value for Canada for 1950–70, the correlation is 0.87. Thus there is no conflict between the findings for the Logue and Willett highly industrialized countries, and for other small sets of OECD countries by others.

Second, Foster's data can be used to give the Logue and Willett result of no correlation for points in the lower half by magnitude of inflation level, by first combining the Latin American countries with the industrialized countries. The correlation between a_i and r_i for the twenty countries (half of 23 + 17) thus defined is 0.16. The reason can be seen clearly in Figure 3: the Latin American countries lie systematically above the industrialized countries. A hypothesis for the difference is that the developed countries have better mechanisms for the control of inflation rates, and thus a lower variability at any given inflation level. For instance, Harberger [10] notes in passing that the Banco de Brasil has the power to expand credit without discipline by the central bank, while apparently not believing that credit is inflationary. This hypothesis can be examined visually by making a partial residual plot. (See Larsen and McCleary [14] for a discussion of several kinds of partial residual plots.)

We will use the log of per capita income for 1972 from Urdang [24] as an estimate of level of development. Consider first the data from Logue and Willett on s_i and r_i for 1950–70. The partial residual of s_i is formed by taking the residuals from a regression of s_i on log of per capita income, and the partial residuals of r_i are similarly formed from the regression of r_i on log of per capita income. The regression coefficient for the r_i partial residuals in a regression of the s_i partial residuals on the r_i residuals is the same algebracially as the coefficient of r_i in a multiple regression of s_i on both r_i and log of per capita income. The value of the plot is that it allows one to see visually how the individual points appear and influence the regression coefficient. Figure 4 plots the s_i partial residuals against the r_i residuals for all the countries excepting the few with very large positive r_i residuals. It is clear that the lower half, or indeed any quarter of the data, continues to show a strong relationship between variability and level. It is quite clear that after considering level of development, there is no longer a suggestion of a threshold type nonlinear relationship. The biweight[3] correlation is 0.88, the equiweight correlation is 0.79. The slope calculated from the data shown is 0.92 ± 0.10.[4] A similar figure (Figure 5) results from using the average accelerations from the forty countries given by Foster. The slope for the points shown is 0.49 ± 0.02. If the r_t and r_{t-1} were independently normally distributed, with the same variances, we would expect to

[2]The standard deviations shown in their Table 1 for Canada are 0.2035, 0.0313, and 0.0133 for 1950–70, 1950–60, and 1960–70, respectively. It would appear that the first value is too large by a factor of ten. In using their data, I have used 0.0204 instead. Likewise, I have used numbers one order of magnitude smaller than given by their Table 1 for the 1950–60 inflation levels for Canada and Iceland, and I took the Dominican Repuglic figures for level as variability and vice versa.

[3]This is a robust counterpart of the correlation calculated with equal weights for all points. It is calculated as described in the Appendix.

[4]One standard deviation errors are stated unless otherwise noted.

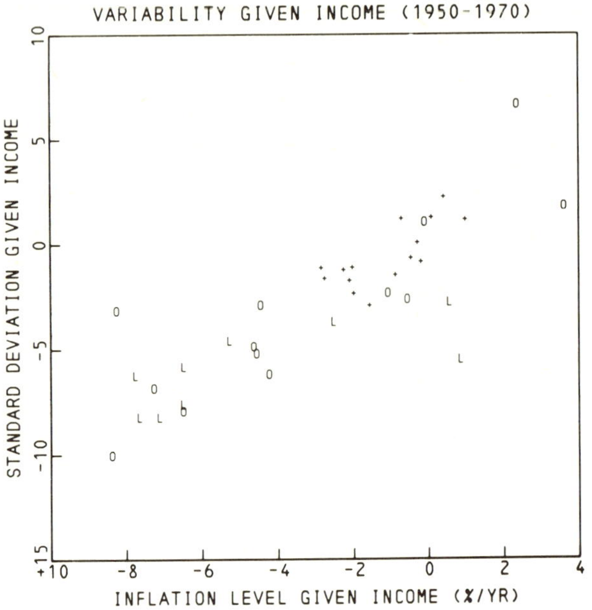
VARIABILITY GIVEN INCOME (1950-1970)
STANDARD DEVIATION GIVEN INCOME
INFLATION LEVEL GIVEN INCOME (%/YR)
10
5
0
-5
-10
-15
-10
-8
-6
-4
-2
0
2
4

Fig. 4.

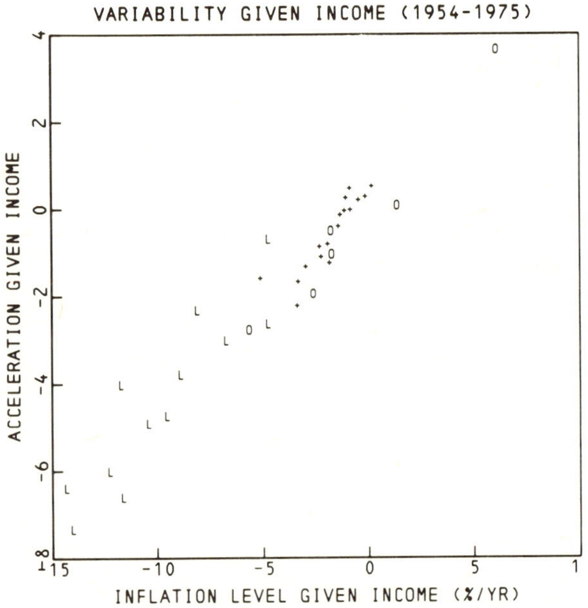
VARIABILITY GIVEN INCOME (1954-1975)
ACCELERATION GIVEN INCOME
INFLATION LEVEL GIVEN INCOME (%/YR)
4
2
0
-2
-4
-6
-8
-15
-10
-5
0
5

Fig. 5.

find this slope equal to $2/\sqrt{\pi} \approx 1.1$ times the slope calculated for the standard deviations. That it is less suggests that positive autocorrelation of inflation rates is usual among the countries studied. This was already pointed out in section 1.

Figure 6 makes an additional point about the variability-level relationship during the 1960s. It is the partial residual plot for the data of Figure 2. First, the relationship still seems to be strong when all the countries and not just the industrialized ones are considered. The slope estimated is 0.51 ± 0.05, which is in agreement with the Logue and Willett finding of a weaker relationship during the 1960s. Second, accounting for income levels has also pulled the OECD plotted by "+" countries toward the structure seen at other times. The equiweight and biweight correlations for those countries are 0.85 and 0.95, compared to correlations of about 0.25 before adjustment for income. Thus even with this group of advanced countries, the development levels have important differences. This raises the question of the relevance of results based on widely differing countries for policy in the United States. If the countries most similar to the United States are so similar that no real cross-sectional variation is seen, a cross-section study loses its power. Thus in proportion as the countries selected become more relevant, the power of the cross-section method declines. Therefore we turn shortly to examining evidence from the United States.

My impression from this review of the cross-country studies is that they clearly show an increase in the variability of inflation with the twenty (or more) year inflation level. The effect is approximately linear, with the increase in s_i approxi-

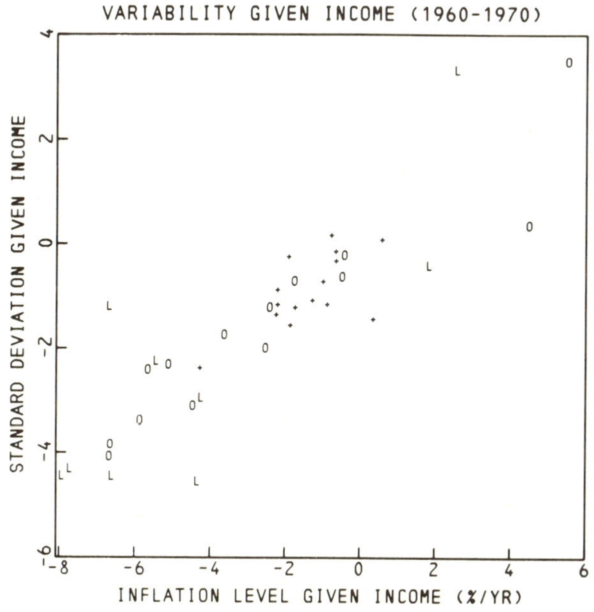

FIG. 6.

mately equal to the increase in r_i, the increase in a_i approximately half that. The amount of variability for very low levels of inflation depends on the development of the country, being almost zero for developed countries.

Two problems that arise in trying to study the annual inflation rates in a single country are (1) the definition of price must change greatly over the many years required and (2) there is considerable change in social and economic structure. Nevertheless, one worker, Benjamin Klein, has analyzed the annual variability of the United States price changes from 1870 to 1972. It should be noted that the period includes the gold standard period with a small government sector, two major wars, the great depression of the thirties, and the recent period with a large government sector and an increasing influence from other nations. Estimates of GNP deflator from three major different sources formed the price measure. He used two measures of variability, an annual measure (short term here) calculated as the six-term moving standard deviation of the annual rate of inflation, and a "long-term" measure calculated as the variance of a sum of six annual terms including the covariance from year to year. One paper [12] shows that the ratio of long-term to short-term variability changed from being roughly one-third in the gold standard period to being roughly two in the recent past. In another paper [13], he showed that the short-term variability was highly correlated with the moving average of the absolute annual rate of price change (ignoring sign). The recent period was an outlier with an unusually low short-term variability. This latter result was cited by Ackley [1] as evidence of the proposition that variability increased with average level of inflation. Unfortunately, the second measure, the moving average of absolute annual changes, confounds variability with level. For instance, if the average level in a period is zero, the measure is just of the variability in the period. If, on the other hand, the changes are all of one sign during some period, then the measure is just of level.

I have reviewed Klein's [12] data using definitions of variability and level suggested by the cross-country comparisons. The data for price, p_t, is from his Table 1 augmented with values for 1974–77. The use of a moving average does not give independent points, so I took seventeen six-year periods. The variability was estimated for each period by the standard deviation of the $r_t = p_t/p_{t-1} - 1$. The level was estimated by the absolute value of the means, $1/6|\Sigma_t r_t|$, rather than the mean of the absolute values, $1/6\Sigma_t|r_t|$, because as pointed out above the latter confounds variability with level. After considering the intervals selectable by varying the initial year, I selected an initial year that placed each world war in a single period.

Figure 7 shows the plot of the seventeen points, each representing a six-year period. The years printed for each point are the first years of the six-year periods. The correlation for these points is 0.56; however, we should be warned that the biweight correlation is only 0.10. It is clear that much depends on the interpretation of the experience during the two world wars. It might be argued that the uncertainty in inflation shown during these years was but a pale reflection of the many uncertainties occasioned by the wars. Yet clearly, these were times of both high inflation and high variability of inflation. Aside from the wartime periods, there is little

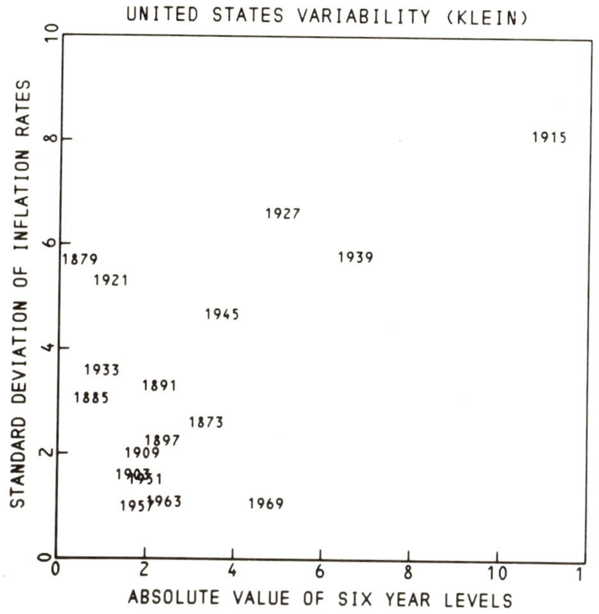

FIG. 7.

evidence of a level-variability relationship. Adding the log of per capita GNP to a regression to account for the development in the United States during the long time covered gives an estimated slope of 0.22 ± 0.38 in the peacetime data. In sum, the long-term evidence from the United States gives little support to the hypothesis of increased variability with increased level, but it is not such strong data as to be capable of refuting it. The study highlights the difficulties of drawing inferences from variables measured over a hundred-year period.

Another approach was put forward by Jaffee and Kleiman [11], who found the standard measure of variability unconvincing because it confounds trend with variability about trend. Regressing the standard deviations of groups of expected inflation rates determined by surveys against the means of the same expectations, they found a strongly significant result,

$$\Sigma = (1.38 \pm 0.09) + (0.31 \pm 0.03)E.$$

The surveys were quarterly from 1955.II to 1971.II. They raised methodological problems with this approach also.

3. RESULTS FOR UNITED STATES CONSUMER PRICE INDEX

This section complements the reviewed studies by a detailed examination of the United States Consumer Price Index (USCPI) in the recent period, together with subindexes of the USCPI by category of goods and city. The study uses analogues of both of the two measures of variability defined above in the cross-national studies, because they do seem to measure somewhat different aspects of variability. The following work also uses the biweight analogues of means, standard deviations, and average accelerations of inflation rates. These should be regarded as different measures rather than as possibly better measures. They provide information about the common occurrences, downweighting the unusual occurrences. But, if the data are reliable, the unusual occurrences have affected people and we want to know about them.

The data used are as follows. (1) The monthly USCPI for all cities and all covered goods. (2) The annual USCPI for the second level breakdown of goods.[5] (3) The annual USCPI for twenty-one U.S. cities.[6] These series are each used only since 1953, even though some are available before then. This is because the 1953 revision of the USCPI made substantial changes in the process of calculating the index. These changes resulted in considerable change to the variability characteristics of the index. (Some authors have omitted these years citing the Korean war as decreasing the validity of the price measurements.) The data were obtained from Data Resources, Inc., and spot checked against Bureau of Labor Statistics (BLS) published records. In each of the few hundred values checked, the data were exactly as published.

We first consider the variability of the USCPI by subperiods of time, measuring variability by monthly or quarterly fluctuations. The time between 1953 and 1978 is divided into T years or triennia, and means, standard deviations, and average accelerations are calculated: if

$$r_m = p_m/p_{m-1} - 1, \qquad m = 1, \ldots, 12*T$$

is the rate of inflation where m indexes the months of quarters and p_m is the corresponding price index, and if

$$R_t = \frac{1}{12} \sum_{12t-11}^{12t} r_m$$

is the average rate of price change during the year or triennium, then

$$s_t^2 = \frac{1}{11} \sum_{12t-11}^{12t} (r_m - R_t)^2, \qquad t = 1, \ldots, T$$

[5]These are defined as Cereal and Bakery Products FC, Meats, Poultry and Fish FM, Dairy Products FD, Fruits and Vegetables FF, Other Food at Home FX, Food away from Home FA, Shelter HS, Fuel and Utilities HU, Household Furnishings and Operation HF, Men's and Boy's Apparel AM, Women's and Girl's Apparel AW, Footwear AF, Private Transportation TV, Public Transportation TB, Medical Care SM, Personal Care SP, Reading and Recreation SR, and Other Goods and Services SX. These eighteen categories have data available since 1953. The abbreviations used in figures are shown. They are grouped by the first letter showing the major commodity class.

[6]Atlanta AT, Baltimore BL, Boston BS, Chicago CH, Cincinnati CN, Cleveland CL, Detroit DE, Houston HO, Kansas City KC, Los Angeles LA, Milwaukee ML, Minneapolis-St. Paul MN, New York NY, Philadelphia PH, Pittsburgh PT, Portland PR, St. Louis SL, San Francisco SF, Scranton SC, Seattle SE, Washington DC. The abbreviation used in the figures is shown with each name.

is the standard deviation of price changes in the year or triennium, and

$$a_t = \frac{1}{12} \sum_{12t-11}^{12t} |r_m - r_{m-1}|$$

is the average acceleration of price changes during the year or triennium. The corresponding biweighted quantities are also used.

Figure 8 shows the yearly standard deviations s_t plotted against the yearly mean inflation rates R_t. The year labels mark the biweighted quantities, while the line segments are drawn between the equiweighted quantities and the corresponding biweighted quantities. The figure shows in the first place that calculating the quantities with or without biweighting gives substantially the same results because the line segments are small with respect to the area in which the points lie. In some cases, including the high 1973 point, the equiweight and the biweight estimates coincide, showing that the estimate does not depend on an individual outlying month. Second, there is only a weak suggestion of relationship considering all the points shown. (The equiweight and biweight correlations for the labeled points are 0.58 and 0.38, respectively.) A simple regression line through all the biweighted points has slope 0.20 ± 0.07, which is significantly below the slope of approximately unity seen in the cross-national standard deviations of Logue and Willett. Alternatively, the figure could be interpreted as showing the kind of nonlinear effect suggested by Logue and Willett. In this case, the threshold inflation rate might be 6

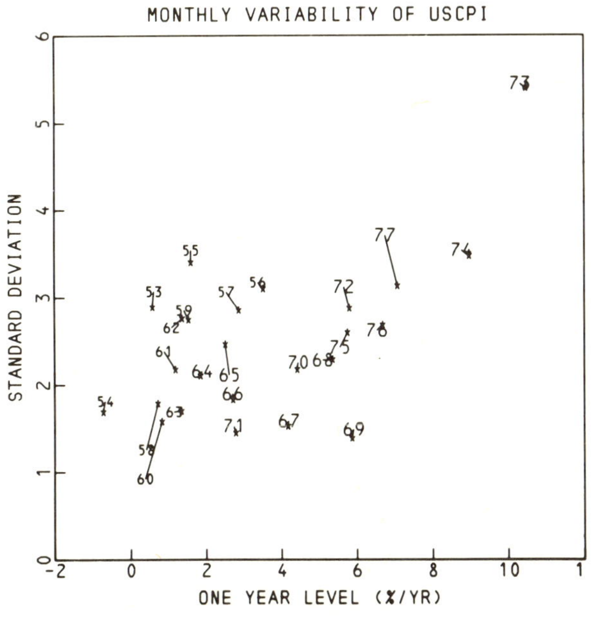

FIG. 8.

to 8 percent per year annual average inflation rate, a rough estimate of where the data appear to leave a horizontal pattern and begin rising.

However, notice that since 1964 there is a consistent relationship. (The points since 1964 are in slightly larger characters.) The points from before 1964 may also show a relationship, but the range of the mean inflation rates is restricted to 0 percent per year to 3 percent per year. In January 1964, there was a major redefinition of the USCPI. The selection of goods was reweighted, the set of cities measured was expanded, and more consumers (single-family households) were included. A change in interpolation was made that could lower monthly variability. A few cities are measured every month, while from 1953 through 1977 most cities were measured every three months. Before 1964 prices in the cities not measured in a given month were interpolated using those that were measured. After 1964 they were treated as if constant when not measured. Besides the possibility of a measurement-induced change, there is the possibility of some real change in the economy. In any case, the data from the most recent fourteen years suggest much more of a linear relationship between level and variability. The equiweight and biweight correlations are 0.80 and 0.71 for these years. The slope of an equiweight regression line among the labeled points is 0.36 ± 0.07, almost double the slope for all the points, but still below the slope of about unity seen cross-nationally over the entire postwar period.

Figure 9 plots the yearly average monthly accelerations a_t against the yearly mean inflation rates. The figure suggests somewhat less relationship between var-

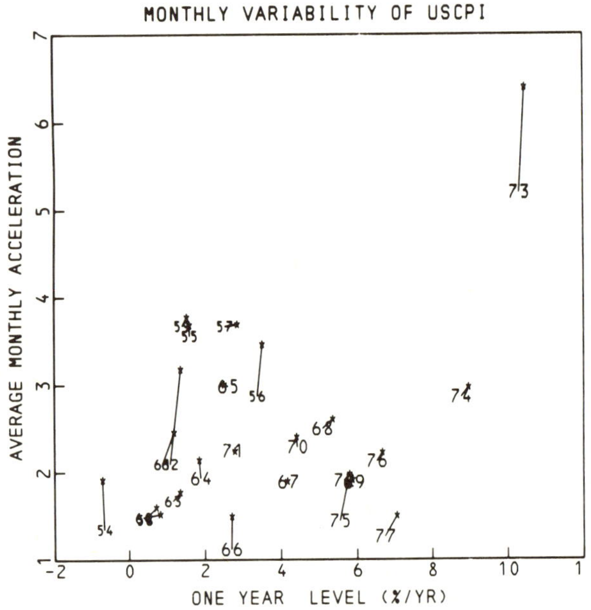

FIG. 9.

iability and level. The equiweight and biweight correlations among the labeled points are 0.34 and 0.05. The bulk of the points, excluding only 1973, show no increase of variability with level. The simple regression line among the biweighted points again has a slope (0.11 ± 0.07) significantly less than the slope of 0.49 ± 0.02 seen cross-nationally in Foster's collection of average accelerations. The difference between this figure and the previous one may be that the accelerations are measuring a short-term predictability while the standard deviations are measuring a longer-term predictability, as discussed in the Introduction.

Figures 10 and 11 show plots corresponding to Figures 8 and 9. However, the subscript *m* in the definitions above should be taken as referring to quarters, while the larger time periods over which averages are taken are triennia. In the plot, the triennia are labeled by the first year of the three. As a result of using triennia, there are only one-third as many data points, and conclusions are correspondingly less firm. The standard deviation measure of variability in Figure 10 shows one triennium (1954. III to 1957. III) that lies off a group of points in a fairly straight line. The five latest points (those since 1964) all show a clear relationship. Figure 11 showing accelerations is again less persuasive. The triennia starting in 1957 and 1960 have low average levels of inflation but have average accelerations almost as high as for those starting in 1972 and 1975. Considering the latest five points, however, there are a low group of three and a high group of two, with a positive slope between them. The time period for this prediction has increased somewhat from monthly accelerations, with perhaps a slight effect visible.

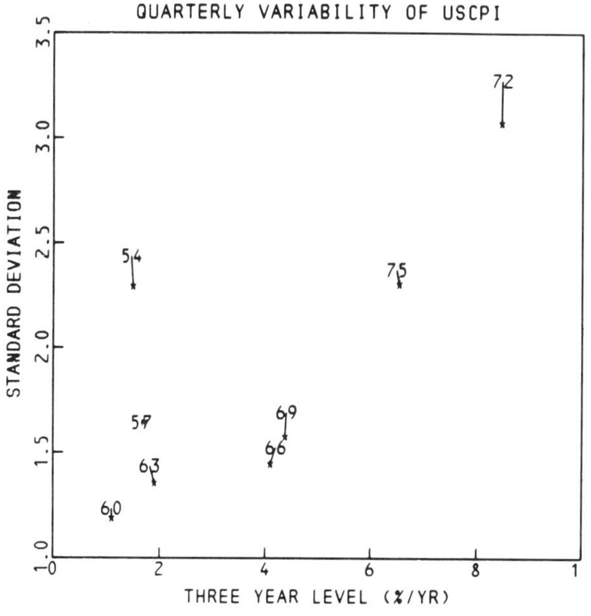

FIG. 10.

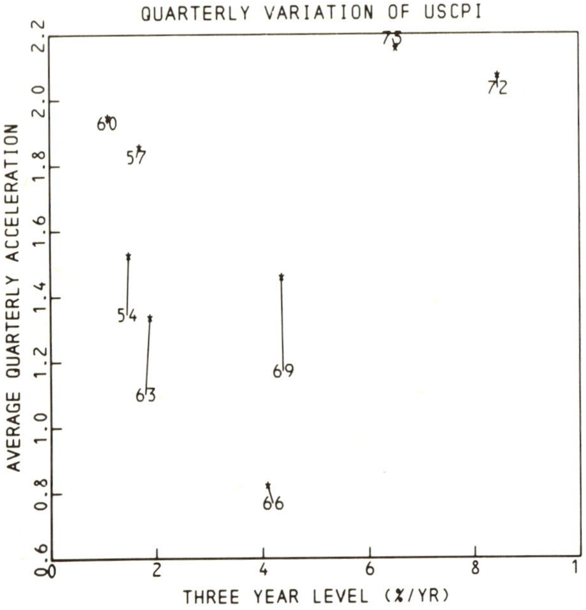
QUARTERLY VARIATION OF USCPI
AVERAGE QUARTERLY ACCELERATION
THREE YEAR LEVEL (%/YR)
0.6
0.8
1.0
1.2
1.4
1.6
1.8
2.0
2.2
0
2
4
6
8
1
60
57
54
63
69
66
75
72

FIG. 11.

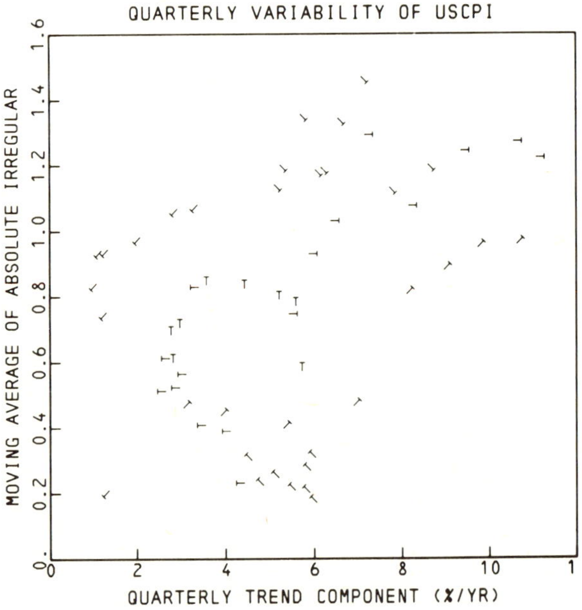
QUARTERLY VARIABILITY OF USCPI
MOVING AVERAGE OF ABSOLUTE IRREGULAR
QUARTERLY TREND COMPONENT (%/YR)
0.
0.2
0.4
0.6
0.8
1.0
1.2
1.4
1.6
0
2
4
6
8
10
1

FIG. 12.

Figure 12 shows an attempt to define a measure of variability that would not reflect seasonal or trend components to the inflation rate. In constructing this figure, the series of quarterly inflation rates, r_t, was decomposed into a *trend* component, a *seasonal* component, and an *irregular* component by the deseasonalization program SABL [4] described in the Appendix. The figure shows a scatter plot of a moving average of the absolute values of the irregular component against the trend component. The time period was divided into seven equal length subperiods and an "hour hand" used to plot the individual points, so that some information on the timing remains in the figure. That is, the first subperiod is plotted with the hand at 45 degrees ("1:30" on a clock) to the trend axis, and each subperiod after that rotates the hand another 45 degrees clockwise. A moving average of the absolute value of the irregular component is a measure of the variability of the series of price changes because moving averages of the irregular component are intentionally quite near zero. The moving average was taken as a 7 point equally weighted window.

The figure shows a loose but persuasive relationship. The equiweight and biweight correlations are virtually equal at 0.39 and 0.40, indicating that the interpretation is not dependent on outliers. However, the interpretation of this measure of variability needs some thought. The figure shows that the magnitude in percent per year of the measure is less than that of the standard deviation or the average acceleration. This is partly because more variance remains in the nonlinearly derived trend component than in a series of means for subperiods, partly because a seasonal component with variance 27 percent of the irregular component's variance has been removed, and partly because the underlying data have a high autocorrelation. Since the seasonal component can be predicted, it seems reasonable to consider variability with it removed. The remaining irregular component may be interpreted as an unpredictability for a quarter ahead after accounting for seasonal variability.

As pointed out above, the examination of annual changes for a single country from the aggregate series has several severe intrinsic difficulties. As compensation, a comparison of annual changes across commodities is possible within one country, whereas getting comparable definitions of categories of goods across countries would be extremely difficult. The notation for multiple goods is formally the same as that introduced above for multiple countries, with the index i indicating the $I = 18$ categories of goods previously mentioned. Figure 13 shows a plot of s_i versus r_i. As suggested by the previous graphs, this graph examines the period since 1964 with the longer-term measure of variability, the standard deviation. Goods with a high average (annual) standard deviation lie to the top of the figure, while goods with a high average inflation rate over the fourteen-year period lie to the right. Note that the range of levels is only 3.5 percent per year, smaller than in any previous plot. For most of the goods, the biweight mean and standard deviation are little different from the equiweight statistics. However, for three food categories, there are substantial differences. These three cases do not change conclusions about a relation between variability and level, however, because the movement from equiweight to biweight is similar to that of the relationship suggested by the rest of the data. With three exceptions, Shelter, Food Away from Home, and Medical Services, there is

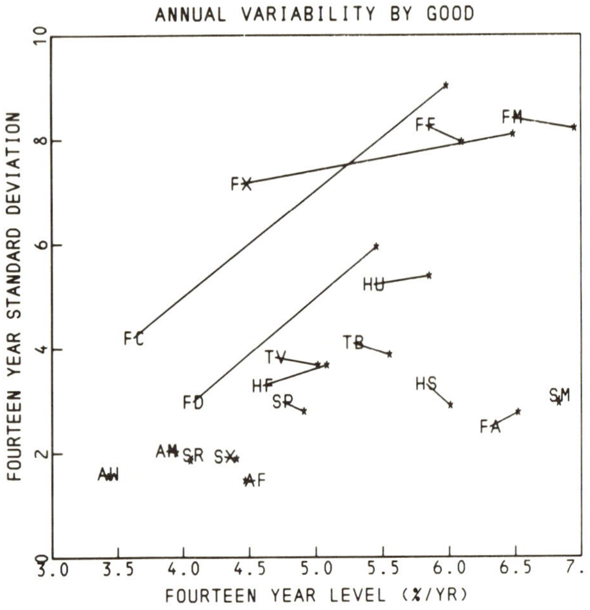

FIG. 13.

generally a higher variability for goods with higher levels. Shelter and Medical Services both have worse than average measurement problems. The equiweight and biweight correlations for the labeled (biweight statistics) points are 0.43 and 0.65, for the equiweight statistics they are 0.65 and 0.77. The slope of a regression among the biweight statistics is 0.91 ± 0.48, in good but uncertain agreement with cross-national data.

It is also possible to examine the inflation rates within the United States by city. The notation is again formally the same for multiple cities as for multiple countries, with the index i indicating cities and $I = 22$. The plot of s_i against r_i for 1964–78 in Figure 14 shows first that the mean yearly inflation rates by city are quite similar, the range of variation being about 1 percent per year. Nevertheless, the effect of biweighting is only moderate with respect to the differences shown. Second, there is a suggestion of a relationship even here. No cities lie in the upper-left-hand corner, and a relatively sparse group of three lies in the lower right. The equiweight and biweight correlations for the labeled points are 0.15 and 0.53. The difference is due to downweighting by the biweight of the cities in the lower right. For the purposes of estimating a general relationship between level and variability, we are on sounder ground to examine the relationship for the bulk of the points. The biweight regressions for the equiweight and biweight statistics give 1.15 ± 0.60[7] and 0.87 ± 0.52 for slopes.

[7]These are 95 percent confidence intervals calculated according to Gross's [8] method D4.

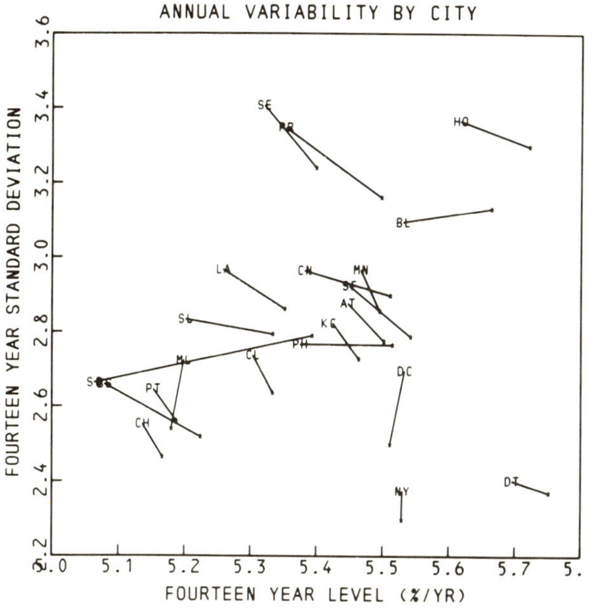

FIG. 14.

There seems to be a systematic difference between the slopes suggested by the time subperiod graphs and those suggested by various cross sections—goods, cities, or nations. Since the cross sections all refer to longer periods of time for the uncertainty, this is again consistent with the notion of a stronger relationship for longer-term predictions.

4. SUMMARY AND IMPLICATIONS

The examination of variability by subperiods of time has suggested a positive relationship between variability and level since 1964 in the United States. The relationship can be seen clearly in yearly data using the standard deviation of the monthly price changes as the measure of variability, and in the triennial data using the standard deviation of the quarterly price changes as the measure of variability. It is seen somewhat less clearly in the triennial data using average quarterly accelerations as the variability measure, and in the quarterly data using the deseasonalized, detrended residuals as a measure of variability. It is not evident in the yearly data using average monthly acceleration as the measure of variability. We have also seen that standard deviations refer to predictions of longer intervals for an autoregressive process. The effect is thus most clearly seen when the measure of variability refers to a longer prediction interval. The slopes of the standard deviation-level relationship suggested by these measures are roughly 0.4, which is considerably less than the approximate unity suggested by the cross-national studies.

The annual variability has been examined for categories of goods and for cities, using data since 1964. There has been a range of average annual inflation rates from 3 to 6 percent per year for goods categories. Across this range, there has been greater variability of goods with greater average annual inflation rates. The range of inflation rates across cities was only from 5 to 6 percent per year, yet within this range there has been, since 1964, greater variability for cities with greater average annual inflation levels. These two types of cross-sectional studies within the United States suggest slopes of roughly unity, being in rough agreement with the cross-national, cross-section studies.

The various cross-sectional studies—by nations, goods, or cities—may be measuring a longer-term relationship than the time subperiod studies. This would again be consistent with a stronger relationship for longer prediction intervals. The suggestion that the relationship is stronger for longer prediction intervals may be testable by considering explicit measures of predictability for various prediction intervals on data for the international, goods, and city cross sections.

These observations reinforce the multinational evidence that an increase in the level of inflation leads to an increase in its unpredictability. They also suggest that this relationship is stronger quantitatively for longer-range predictions. Since the unpredictability of inflation imposes real costs on the economy and leads to unpredictable redistributions of welfare, policy considerations of the desired level of inflation should account for the costs of increased uncertainty.

APPENDIX

Robust Statistical Estimators

The previous studies and the current one have dealt with relatively small amounts of data. The data may well be nonnormal in distribution because of the political processes in determining the inflation rate. The smallness of the samples means that a few percent contamination from nonnormal distributions would be hard to observe. Yet, just such small deviations from normality render the estimators that are optimal for normal distributions less efficient than many robust estimators [19]. In this case it is better practice to use robust estimators.

The robust counterpart of the mean that is used is a weighted mean. The weights are based on the data, with less weight given to points that lie far from the bulk of the others. The bisquare weighting was used in this study. These weights are given by

$$w = \begin{cases} (1 - u^2)^2 & |u| \leq 1 \\ 0 & otherwise , \end{cases}$$

where

$$u = (x - \overleftrightarrow{x})/ks$$

$\overleftrightarrow{x}$ = the median of the values of x
s = the median absolute deviation from the median
$k = 9$.

This choice of robust method was motivated by the need for a validated measure of spread. Lax [15] studied a variety of robust estimates of spread, comparing their efficiency in three different situations of data contamination. The one discussed in Mosteller and Tukey [19, p. 208] was one of three whose performance was not dominated by another. The equation used is

$$s_{bi}^2 = \frac{\sum w^2(x - \overleftrightarrow{x})}{n \sum w^{1/2}(1 - 5u^2)\left[-1 + \sum w^{1/2}(1 - 5u^2)\right]} .$$

This measure of scale is derived from the asymptotic variance of the biweighted mean given above, and may be called a biweight variance.

Given a robust estimate of spread, a robust estimate of a correlation coefficient can be calculated by the method of standardized sums and differences described by Devlin, Gnanadesikan, and Kettenring [5]. The calculation is

$$\frac{VS - VD}{VS + VD} ,$$

where VS and VD are variances of the sum of the two quantities to be correlated and of their difference. When equiweight variances are used, the ordinary correlation results. This study used biweight variances and called the result the biweight correlations.

SABL

SABL is a robust deseasonalization algorithm described by Cleveland, Dunn, and Terpenning [4]. In brief, it operates as follows: a first trend smooth is made using a window of length *nts* (with a suggested value three more than the periodicity); a first seasonal smooth is made on the series less the first trend smooth, using a window of length *nss* (with a suggested value one less than the periodicity); a second trend smooth is made on the series less the first seasonal smooth; then each time for N iterations, a resistant seasonal smooth is made from the series less the current trend smooth, and a resistant trend smooth is made from the series less the derived seasonal smooth; the irregular is the series less the final seasonal smooth less the final trend smooth. In this application, the number of terms in the trend smooth used was the suggested three more than the monthly periodicity, $nts = 15$, and the number of terms in the seasonal smooth was one less, $nss = 11$. $N = 2$ iterations were used.

LITERATURE CITED

1. Ackley, Gardner. "The Costs of Inflation," *American Economic Reivew Papers and Proceedings,* 68 (1978), 149-54.
2. Bach, George L., and James. B. Stephenson. "Inflation and the Redistribution of Wealth," *Review of Economics and Statistics,* 56 (1974), 1-13.
3. Barro, Robert J. "Inflationary Finance and the Welfare Cost of Inflation," *Journal of Political Economy,* 80 (1972), 978-1001.
4. Cleveland, William S., Douglas M. Dunn, and Irma J. Terpenning. "SABL, A Resistant Seasonal Adjustment Procedure with Graphical Methods for Interpretation and Diagnosis." In *Seasonal Analysis of Economic Time Series,* NBER, forthcoming.
5. Devlin, Susan J., Ramanathan Gnanadesikan, and Jon R. Kettenring. "Robust Estimation and Outlier Detection with Correlation Coefficients," *Biometrika,* 62 (1975), 531-45.
6. Foster, Edward. "The Variability of Inflation," *Review of Economics and Statistics,* 61 (1979), 346-50.
7. Friedman, Milton. "Nobel Lecture: Inflation and Unemployment," *Journal of Political Economy,* 85 (1977), 451-72.
8. Gordon, Robert J. "Steady Anticipated Inflation: Mirage or Oasis?," *Brookings Papers on Economic Activity,* 2 (1971), 499-510.
9. Gross, Alan M. "Confidence Intervals for Bisquare Regression Estimates," *Journal of the American Statistical Association,* 72 (1977), 341-54.
10. Harberger, Arnold C. "A Primer on Inflation," *Journal of Money, Credit, and Banking,* 10 (November 1978), 505-21.
11. Jaffee, Dwight, and Ephraim Kleiman. "The Welfare Implications of Uneven Inflation." Paper presented at the I.E.A. Conference on Inflation Theory and Anti-Inflation Policy, Saltsjobaden, Sweden, 1975.
12. Klein, Benjamin. "Our New Monetary Standard: The Measurement and Effects of Price Uncertainty 1880-1973," *Economic Inquiry,* 13 (1975), 461-84.
13. ______. "The Social Costs of the Recent Inflation: The Mirage of Steady 'Anticipated' Inflation," *Journal of Monetary Economics,* supplemental series, 3 (1976), 185-212.
14. Larsen, Wayne A., and Susan J. McCleary. "The Use of Partial Residual Plots in Regression Analysis," *Technometrics,* 14 (1972), 781-90.
15. Lax, David A. "An Interim Report of A Monte Carlo Study of Robust Estimates of Width." Technical report 93, Department of Statistics, Princeton University, 1975.
16. Levi, Maurice D., and John H. Makin. "Fisher, Phillips, Friedman and the Measured Impact of Inflation on Interest," *Journal of Finance,* 34 (1979), 35-52.
17. Logue, Dennis E., and Richard J. Sweeny. "Inflation and Uncertainty: Some Empirical Results." Manuscript, 1979.
18. Logue, Dennis E., and Thomas D. Willett. "A Note on the Relation between the Rate and Variability of Inflation," *Economica,* 43 (1976), 151-58.
19. Mosteller, Fredrick, and John W. Tukey. *Data Analysis and Regression: Second Course in Statistics.* Reading, Mass.: Addison-Wesley, 1977.
20. Okun, Arthur M. "The Mirage of Steady Inflation," *Brookings Papers on Economic Activity,* 2 (1971), 485-98.
21. ______. "Efficient Disinflationary Policies," *American Economic Review Papers and Proceedings,* 68 (1978), 348-52.

22. Parks, Richard W. ''Inflation and Relative Price Variability,'' *Journal of Political Economy,* 86 (1978), 79–95.

23. Trevithick, James A., and Charles Mulvey. *The Economics of Inflation.* New York: Wiley, 1975.

24. Urdang, Laurence. *The Official Associated Press Almanac 1975.* Maplewood, N.J.: Hammond Almanac, 1975.

25. Vining, Daniel R., Jr., and Thomas C. Elwertowski. ''The Relationship between Relative Prices and the General Price Level,'' *American Economic Review,* 66 (1976), 699–708.

JAMES M. JOHANNES
ROBERT H. RASCHE*

Can the Reserves Approach to Monetary Control Really Work?

1. INTRODUCTION

ON OCTOBER 6, 1979, the Board of Governors (BOG) of the Federal Reserve System announced that the Federal Open Market Committee (FOMC) was abandoning its historical preoccupation with an interest rate approach to monetary control in favor of a reserve aggregate approach.[1] Underlying this new approach is the fact that, at time t, any money stock concept, M, is the product of a money multiplier, m, and a reserve aggregate, R; that is,

$$M_t = m_t R_t . \qquad (1)$$

The board also announced its choices for R. On a day-to-day basis open market operations are to be aimed at managing nonborrowed reserves because "nonborrowed reserves are more closely under the control of the System Account Manager for open-market operations" [13, p. 4] than other reserve aggregates. Over the longer run, total reserves are to be the principal reserve objective because "total reserves provide the basis for deposits and thereby are more closely related to [monetary] aggregates than nonborrowed reserves" [13, p. 4]. The monetary base

*Financial assistance from the Graduate School of Business Administration, Michigan State University, is gratefully acknowledged, as are the comments of several referees.
[1]See Pierce and Thomson [11] for a distinction.

JAMES M. JOHANNES *is assistant professor and* ROBERT H. RASCHE *is professor, Department of Economics, Michigan State University.*

0022-2879/81/0881-0298$00.50/0

and the net monetary base (as control aggregates) have not received much consideration by the board (see [13, p. 4] or [14, p. 13] for an explanation).[2]

The purpose of this paper is to assess the wisdom of the change in FOMC operating procedure and the FOMC's choice of a bank reserves target by examining how well the FOMC could have controlled the new monetary aggregates M1B and M2 over the period November 1978 to October 1980, had a reserve aggregate control procedure using the Johannes and Rasche [4] method for forecasting money multipliers been employed. Throughout the paper it is assumed that the desired targets for reserve aggregates could have been achieved and that the Johannes-Rasche forecasting models are not affected by the choice of operating procedure.

Several interesting results emerge. First, total or nonborrowed reserves are not the best short-run control aggregates. (The experience of 1980 seems to support this conclusion.) The monetary base and the net monetary base are better control aggregates. Second, acceptable tolerance limits for longer run average monetary growth should be achievable using any reserve aggregate. Third, it makes little difference as far as control is concerned whether the target reserve aggregates are those defined by the BOG or those defined by the St. Louis Federal Reserve Bank.[3]

The plan of the paper is as follows. Section 2 demonstrates that the Johannes and Rasche multiplier forecasting method is consistent with the multiplier forecasting method now used by the FOMC, and, therefore, amounts to a useful operational alternative to their as-yet-unpublished multiplier forecasting technique. Section 3 describes the results of experiments based on the Johannes and Rasche multiplier forecasts that shed light on the FOMC's ability to control monetary aggregates with a reserve aggregate control procedure. Section 4 compares the results presented in section 3 with those obtained by using St. Louis definitions of reserve aggregates instead of the BOG definitions. Section 5 shows why a monetary base target is superior to a reserve target, and finally a few conclusions and final comments are presented in section 6.

2. THE RELATIONSHIP BETWEEN THE FOMC'S NEW OPERATING PROCEDURE AND THE JOHANNES-RASCHE MULTIPLIER FORECASTING TECHNIQUE

The two left-hand columns of Table 1 display statements made by Chairman Volcker and Governor Wallich of the Federal Reserve System that describe the FOMC's new reserve aggregate operating procedure. The statements, which have been abstracted from speeches made by Chairman Volcker [13] and Governor Wallich [14], are quite consistent and suggest that the FOMC follows a four-step procedure for obtaining a target value for unborrowed reserves: (1) project the currency/deposit composition of the FOMC's desired money stock target; (2) project the amount of total bank reserves that is consistent with that money target; (3)

[2]These various control aggregates may or may not be adjusted for changes in reserve requirements, though most policy discussions center around the adjusted series. For a description of the alternative adjustment methods, see Burger [2].

[3]Burger [2] discusses the difference between the St. Louis and BOG definitions.

TABLE 1

NEW FEDERAL RESERVE OPERATING PROCEDURE

Step	Volcker [13] Description	Wallich [14] Description	J-R ARIMA Model Equivalent
1	"Establishment of the paths involves projecting how much of the targeted money growth is likely to take the form of currency, of deposits at nonmember institution, and of deposits at member institution" (p. 2)	"Public's projected demand for currency is subtracted from targeted path for money, giving an implied target for deposits" (p. 6)	$\hat{D}^* = \frac{M^*}{(1+\hat{k})}$ (i)
2	"After the objective for money supply growth is set, reserve paths expected to achieve such growth are established. Moreover, estimates are made of reserves likely to be absorbed by expansion in other bank liabilities subject to reserve requirements, such as large CD's" (pp. 2 and 3)	"The volume of required reserves is estimated separately for various reserve categories and type and size of bank. In arriving at total reserves allowance must be made for some reserves to be absorbed by excess reserves. . . . Allowance must also be made for the absorption of reserves by bank liabilities that do not enter the money supply" (p. 7)	$\hat{R}^* = \widehat{(r+1-v)}\,(1+\hat{t}_1+\hat{t}_2+\hat{g}+\hat{z})\hat{D}^*$ (ii)
3	"The projected mix of currency and deposits, given the reserve requirements for deposits and bank's excess reserves, yields an estimate of the increase in total reserves and the monetary targets. The amount of nonborrowed reserves—that is total reserves less member bank borrowing—is obtained by initially assuming a level of borrowing near that prevailing in the most recent period" (p. 3)	"Given expected total reserves, a decision must be made as to what part of these total reserves is to be supplied through open market operations and what part through discount window . . . assumed in order to arrive at an estimate of the needs for nonborrowed reserves. Typically an amount in line with the existing volume of borrowed reserves is plugged into the calculation" (pp. 7 and 8)	$\hat{B}^* = \hat{b}(1+\hat{t}_1+\hat{t}_2+\hat{g}+\hat{z})\hat{D}^*$ (iii)
4	"Thus, total reserves represents the principal overall reserve objective . . . [but] because nonborrowed reserves are more closely under control of the System Account Manager for open market operations . . . he would initially aim at a nonborrowed reserve target" (p. 4)	"The new procedure thus focuses upon a family of reserve concepts. Total reserves are most closely related to the monetary aggregates . . . nonborrowed reserves are less closely related to the aggregate because borrowed reserves can change. For that reason, however, total reserves are less easily controlled by the Federal Reserve in the short-run, whereas nonborrowed reserves are under its immediate control" (p. 9)	$\hat{UR}^* = \hat{R}^* - \hat{B}^*$ (iv)

project the part of total reserves that will be borrowed; (4) project the nonborrowed reserves that must be provided to hit the total reserves, and, ultimately, money stock targets. The input to this procedure is the desired money stock, M^* (or its growth rate), and the output is the intermediate target value for unborrowed reserves, UR^*.[4]

The last column of Table 1 highlights the fact that each of these four steps can be expressed algebraically in terms of the money multiplier components k, g, t_1, t_2, z, b, and $r + 1 - v$ (see Appendix A for the exact description of these components).[5] The important point to notice is that the FOMC's new procedure amounts to using nonborrowed reserves, UR, as the control aggregate, R, in equation (1); forecasting the money multiplier corresponding to nonborrowed reserves, m_{UR}; and then setting (following the general form of (1))

$$UR^* = \left(\frac{1}{\hat{m}_{UR}} \right) M^*. \tag{2}$$

To see this, substitute equations (ii) and (iii) in Table 1 into (iv) and factor $\hat{D}$ from all right-hand side terms in the resulting expression. Then substitute for $\hat{D}$ using (i). The resulting expression is

$$UR^* = \left[\frac{(\widehat{r + 1 - v} - \hat{b})(1 + \hat{t}_1 + \hat{t}_2 + \hat{g} + \hat{z})}{(1 + \hat{k})} \right] M^*, \tag{3}$$

which is equal to equation (2) because the nonborrowed reserve multiplier, m_{UR}, equals the reciprocal of the bracketed term.[6] Besides identifying the FOMC's operating procedure, this last exercise demonstrates that the Johannes-Rasche multiplier forecasting technique, which forecasts each of the components of the multiplier, provides an alternative to the unknown multiplier forecasting procedure used by the FOMC that is consistent with the FOMC's procedure.

3. FEASIBILITY OF MONETARY GROWTH OBJECTIVES UNDER THE NEW FOMC OPERATING PROCEDURE

In this section we investigate the degree of precision with which the FOMC could have achieved its desired monthly targets for M1B and M2 over the period November 1978 to October 1980, had it followed the procedure described in section 2 and had it been able to achieve the values of the target reserve aggregate dictated by that procedure. Several potential reserve aggregates are considered. They are

[4]For additional descriptions of the new operating procedure, see "Monetary Policy and Open Market Operations in 1979," Federal Reserve Bank of New York *Quarterly Review* (Summer 1979), 50–64, or Lang [8].

[5]The construction of money multipliers for the new monetary aggregates is conceptually identical to the procedure outlined by Jordan [7]. Multipliers for the new monetary aggregates are discussed in Johannes and Rasche [6].

[6]See Johannes and Rasche [5] for a derivation of m_{UR} for the old monetary aggregates. The derivation for the new aggregates follows the same steps except that the components are defined as in Appendix A.

total member bank reserves, nonborrowed member bank reserves, the monetary base, and the net monetary base. The BOG's definition of each of these reserve aggregates, not the St. Louis definition, is used in this section, and all aggregates are adjusted for reserve requirements by the BOG.

Because a forecast of the money multiplier corresponding to the target reserve aggregate is an integral part of the new procedure, some multiplier forecasting method must be adopted for purposes of this experiment to assess the feasibility of the new procedure. Ideally, of course, the correct multiplier forecasting procedure would be that of the FOMC itself. This has not been released, so, instead, we adopt the component approach to forecasting money multipliers suggested by Johannes and Rasche [4]. There are three reasons for adopting this approach. First, it is completely consistent with the multiplier forecasting technique used by the FOMC. Second, it has proven to be quite accurate over the period of these experiments (even though it requires little information to implement) and, therefore, it provides an ideal benchmark against which the actual FOMC technique or other techniques might be compared.[7] Third, it is based on forecasts of the individual components of the money multipliers, rather than the multipliers themselves, and, therefore, it allows one to forecast the multipliers for all the reserve aggregates of interest consistently for they are just different combinations of the same components.[8]

The component models used in this paper are the same as those used in Johannes and Rasche [6].[9] Since the sample period over which the models were estimated ends in December 1978, any experimental results presented here involving multiplier forecasts with a November-December 1978 origin are not truly ex ante.

Summary error statistics for one month ahead forecoasts of the M1B and M2 multipliers for the alternative control aggregates over the periods November 1978 to September 1979 and October 1979 to October 1980 are displayed in Tables 2 and 3, respectively. Before comparing the error statistics for alternative control aggregates, three general remarks are in order. First, as is apparent from the Theil inequality statistics displayed in the last three columns of each table, the multiplier forecasts for all the control aggregates are essentially unbiased (U^m), and, in most cases, the

[7]This comparison, however, will have to be performed within the Federal Reserve System since staff documents prepared for the FOMC are available only with a five-year lag (see Lombra and Moran [9]).

[8]The prediction error for the natural log of the multipliers corresponding to any reserve aggregate can be expressed as a Taylor Series expansion around the *predicted values* of the various component ratios. Applying the expectations operator conditional on information available through t-1 to these expressions for $(\ln m_t - \ln m_t^p)$ generates *exact* expressions for the moments of the percentage prediction error of the multipliers in terms of the moments of the percentages prediction errors of all of the component ratios. This has important implications for the comparative analysis of various reserve aggregates presented here. It is sometimes alleged that direct comparisons such as those presented here are inaccurate because only one such aggregate can be controlled at a particular time. In the approach developed here, such inaccuracies would result only if the moments of the component ratios change as control regime changes. This is the well-known Lucas [10] problem. Since the moments of the percentage prediction errors of the multiplier with different reserve aggregates weight the moments of the component prediction errors differently, there is no way to anticipate how such structural shifts might alter the comparisons presented here and means that the ARIMA models for the component ratios would not be invariant to the control regime.

[9]There are two exceptions. Since this paper focuses on the BOG definitions, the models for the reserve components of the multipliers that are sensitive to the different definitions had to be reestimated. These new models are available from the authors.

TABLE 2

M1B Multiplier Forecasts

Reserve Aggregate	Simulation Period	Mean Error	RMSE	First-Order Autocorrelation in Errors	Relative RMSE	Relative RMSE/$\sqrt{12}$	Theil Inequality Proportions U^m	U^s	U^c
BOG Adjusted* Reserves	Nov. 78–Sept. 79	−0.0027	0.1065	0.237	0.0119	0.0034	0.001	0.262	0.738
	Oct. 79–Oct. 80	0.0109	0.1370	0.453	0.0148	0.0043	0.006	0.047	0.947
	Nov. 78–Oct. 80	0.0047	0.1240	0.388	0.0136	0.0039	0.001	0.093	0.905
BOG Adjusted Nonborrowed Reserves	Nov. 78–Sept. 79	−0.0023	0.1129	0.486	0.0123	0.0036	0.001	0.248	0.751
	Oct. 79–Oct. 80	0.0114	0.1767	0.322	0.0184	0.0053	0.004	0.001	0.995
	Nov. 78–Oct. 80	0.0051	0.1508	0.366	0.0160	0.0046	0.001	0.031	0.968
BOG Adjusted Monetary Base	Nov. 78–Sept. 79	−0.0021	0.0169	0.002	0.0067	0.0019	0.016	0.006	0.978
	Oct. 79–Oct. 80	0.0003	0.0185	0.530	0.0074	0.0021	0.001	0.016	0.983
	Nov. 78–Oct. 80	−0.0008	0.0178	0.335	0.0071	0.0020	0.002	0.007	0.990
BOG Adjusted Net Monetary Base	Nov. 78–Sept. 79	−0.0021	0.0157	0.267	0.0061	0.0018	0.018	0.027	0.955
	Oct. 79–Oct. 80	0.0004	0.0218	0.505	0.0086	0.0025	0.001	0.010	0.989
	Nov. 78–Oct. 80	−0.0007	0.0192	0.445	0.0076	0.0022	0.001	0.011	0.988

Notes: RMSE is the root mean squared error. Relative root mean squared error is RMSE divided by mean of actual multiplier ($\bar{m}$).
*Adjusted for reserve requirement changes by BOG.

TABLE 3

M2 MULTIPLIER FORECASTS

Reserve Aggregate	Simulation Period	Mean Error	RMSE	First-Order Autocorrelation in Errors	Relative RMSE	Relative RMSE/$\sqrt{12}$	Theil Inequality Proportions U^m	U^s	U^c
BOG Adjusted Reserves	Nov. 78–Sept. 79	−0.0299	0.3642	0.536	0.0104	0.0030	0.007	0.433	0.560
	Oct. 79–Oct. 80	0.0382	0.5865	0.576	0.0158	0.0046	0.004	0.060	0.935
	Nov. 78–Oct. 80	0.0070	0.4971	0.567	0.0138	0.0040	0.000	0.116	0.884
BOG Adjusted Nonborrowed Reserves	Nov. 78–Sept. 79	−0.0301	0.4496	0.454	0.0125	0.0036	0.004	0.231	0.764
	Oct. 79–Oct. 80	0.0376	0.6467	0.342	0.0169	0.0049	0.003	0.000	0.996
	Nov. 78–Oct. 80	0.0066	0.5649	0.379	0.0152	0.0044	0.000	0.032	0.968
BOG Adjusted Monetary Base	Nov. 78–Sept. 79	−0.0146	0.0402	0.559	0.0041	0.0012	0.132	0.000	0.868
	Oct. 79–Oct. 80	−0.0011	0.0503	0.533	0.0050	0.0014	0.001	0.002	0.997
	Nov. 78–Oct. 80	−0.0073	0.0460	0.552	0.0046	0.0013	0.025	0.001	0.974
BOG Adjusted Net Monetary Base	Nov. 78–Sept. 79	−0.0147	0.0449	0.601	0.0045	0.0013	0.107	0.004	0.888
	Oct. 79–Oct. 80	−0.0007	0.0480	0.317	0.0047	0.0014	0.000	0.084	0.916
	Nov. 78–Oct. 80	−0.0071	0.0466	0.445	0.0046	0.0013	0.023	0.011	0.966

mean squared forecast error can be attributed primarily to unequal covariation between the forecasted and actual values (U^c). Second, there is little evidence of first-order autocorrelation in the forecast errors of any of the multipliers.[10] Third, the forecast error statistics are larger for the period October 1979 to October 1980 than for the period November 1978 to September 1979. This increase is explained in large part by a single error in April 1980, a month that coincides with the imposition of credit controls, and, therefore, should not be attributed to the alleged switch in monetary control regimes.

The error statistics for the forecasts of the multipliers for the BOG's principal control aggregates, total and nonborrowed member reserves, are displayed in the top half of each table. For the most part, the forecasting errors for the M1B total reserves multiplier in any given period are comparable to those of the M1B nonborrowed reserves multiplier for the same period. The same is true of the M2 multipliers. The important thing to notice is that the relative RMSE statistics indicate that a band, such as that proposed by Poole [12] of about 3 percent around the desired midrange growth path, should represent an achievable short-run monetary growth target using either a total or nonborrowed reserves control procedure.[11]

Much smaller bands are possible, however, if the monetary base or net monetary base are used as control aggregates. An examination of the error statistics for the multiplier forecasts of these control aggregates (see the bottom half of Tables 2 and 3) reveals the relative RMSE's of the M1B gross and net base multipliers are about one-half of the relative RMSE's of the M1B total and nonborrowed reserve multipliers, and the relative RMSE's of the M2 gross and net base multipliers are less than one-half of the relative RMSE's of their total and net reserves counterparts. This means that Poole bands of about 1.5 percent for M1B and 1 percent for M2 around the FOMC's desired money growth paths should be achievable short-run money targets if the gross or net base is used as the control aggregate. In other words, using the gross or net base as the control aggregate should enable the FOMC to set short-run target ranges for monetary growth that are one-half the target ranges it should expect to achieve using total or nonborrowed reserves as its control aggregate.[12]

This does not mean that there will never be large monthly errors. In any particular month, using either a base or reserves control procedure may result in a large deviation of the actual money stock (or its growth rate) from the desired money stock (or its growth rate). However, because multiplier forecast errors are indepen-

[10] While some of the first order autocorrelation coefficients appear large, their standard errors, which equal $1/\sqrt{t}$ where t is sample size, and also quite large (see [1, pp. 34–36]).

[11] This conclusion is based on the assumption that the standard error of the growth rate of the multiplier equals the relative RMSE. Consequently, two relative RMSE's represent a 95 percent confidence interval around the desired monetary growth path and, therefore, represent an achievable Poole band.

[12] Interestingly enough, in an earlier version of this paper, we found that the FOMC could have achieved its two-month targets for the old M1 and M2 over the period January 1978 to December 1979 about 50 to 60 percent of the time had it used the gross or net base as its control aggregate but only about 25 percent of the time had it used total or nonborrowed reserves. This particular experiment cannot be repeated in this paper because no short-run targets were ever set for the new monetary aggregates. Indeed, they did not exist until early 1980.

dent across time, these errors do not cumulate nor do they persist. Indeed, they systematically average out over the longer run. What this means is that over periods such as a year the deviation of the observed annual average growth rate of M1B or M2 from their desired midrange growth paths using a total or nonborrowed reserves control procedure should not exceed about 1 percent.[13] If the gross or net monetary base is used as the control aggregate, the comparable maximum deviation is about 0.5 percent for M1B and 0.25 percent for M2. Consequently, while tighter control over money can still be exerted through the monetary base, either a base or reserve control aggregate should enable the FOMC to control the money supply or its growth rate quite closely over the longer run if it so chooses.

4. ST. LOUIS AGGREGATES VERSUS BOG AGGREGATES

In this section we compare the results presented in the last section, which were based on reserve aggregates as defined by the BOG, with the results of identical experiments based on the St. Louis Federal Reserve Bank definitions of the same reserve aggregates. The multiplier forecasting error statistics for the alternative control aggregates as defined by the St. Louis Federal Reserve Bank are displayed in Tables 4 and 5. A comparison of Tables 4 and 5 with Tables 2 and 3 indicates that there is very little difference as far as multiplier forecasting is concerned between the BOG defined control aggregates and the St. Louis aggregates. Consequently, the conclusions drawn above for the BOG definitions hold for the St. Louis definitions as well.[14]

5. THE ROLE OF THE MONETARY BASE VIS-À-VIS RESERVES

The monetary base remains a source of controversy in current policy discussions, even though the Board of Governors has implemented the Bach committee recommendation and now publishes an official monetary base series.[15] Two issues seem to

[13]Assuming forecast errors, F, are independent with standard deviations σ,

$$\mathrm{VAR}\left(\frac{\sum_{i=1}^{12} F_i}{12}\right) = \frac{1}{144}\,\mathrm{VAR}\left(\sum_{i=1}^{12} F_i\right) = \sigma^2/12.$$

Consequently, the annual average standard deviation is $\sigma/\sqrt{12}$. This annual average standard deviation is displayed in the column immediately following the relative RMSE in Tables 2 and 3. The annual standard deviation for the M1B nonborrowed reserve multiplier ranges from 0.0036 to 0.0053 depending on time period, and the annual standard deviation for the M2 nonborrowed reserve multiplier ranges from 0.0036 to 0.0049. Consequently, a 95 percent confidence interval of 2σ is approximately 1 percent in either case.

[14]It should be noted, however, that because of the way the BOG adjusts its aggregates for changes in reserve requirement, it is necessary to reestimate the model for the reserve component of the multiplier every time reserve requirements change. The model need not be reestimated if the St. Louis reserve adjustment procedure is used.

[15]See Board of Governors of the Federal Reserve System, Report of the Advisory Committee on Monetary Statistics, 1976, p. 8.

TABLE 4

M1B MULTIPLIER FORECASTS

Reserve Aggregate	Simulation Period	Mean Error	RMSE	First-Order Autocorrelation in Errors	Relative RMSE	Relative RMSE/$\sqrt{12}$	Theil Inequality Proportions		
							U^m	U^s	U^c
St. Louis Adjusted Reserves	Nov. 78–Sept. 79	−0.0205	0.0822	−0.338	0.0092	0.0027	0.062	0.005	0.933
	Oct. 79–Oct. 80	0.0203	0.1316	−0.212	0.0149	0.0043	0.024	0.148	0.828
	Nov. 78–Oct. 80	0.0016	0.1117	−0.157	0.0126	0.0036	0.000	0.029	0.971
St. Louis Adjusted Nonborrowed Reserves	Nov. 78–Sept. 79	−0.0207	0.0974	0.040	0.0107	0.0031	0.045	0.005	0.950
	Oct. 79–Oct. 80	0.0245	0.1938	0.146	0.0212	0.0061	0.016	0.068	0.916
	Nov. 78–Oct. 80	0.0038	0.1571	0.166	0.0172	0.0050	0.001	0.039	0.960
St. Louis* Monetary Base	Nov. 78–Sept. 79	−0.0025	0.0148	−0.138	0.0058	0.0017	0.029	0.033	0.938
	Oct. 79–Oct. 80	0.0014	0.0195	0.302	0.0078	0.0023	0.005	0.329	0.665
	Nov. 78–Oct. 80	−0.0004	0.0175	0.192	0.0070	0.0020	0.001	0.049	0.950
St. Louis Net Monetary Base	Nov. 78–Sept. 79	−0.0025	0.0141	0.135	0.0055	0.0016	0.032	0.002	0.966
	Oct. 79–Oct. 80	0.0016	0.0233	0.360	0.0093	0.0027	0.005	0.211	0.784
	Nov. 78–Oct. 80	−0.0003	0.0196	0.332	0.0078	0.0023	0.000	0.065	0.935

*St. Louis monetary base and net monetary base are adjusted for reserve requirements by the St. Louis Fed.

TABLE 5

M2 Multiplier Forecasts

Reserve Aggregate	Simulation Period	Mean Error	RMSE	First-Order Autocorrelation in Errors	Relative RMSE	Relative RMSE/$\sqrt{12}$	Theil Inequality Proportions		
							U^m	U^s	U^c
St. Louis Adjusted Reserves	Nov. 78–Sept. 79	−0.1004	0.2349	−0.121	0.0067	0.0019	0.183	0.013	0.804
	Oct. 79–Oct. 80	0.0707	0.4604	−0.235	0.0130	0.0038	0.024	0.000	0.976
	Nov. 78–Oct. 80	−0.0078	0.3743	−0.112	0.0106	0.0031	0.000	0.014	0.986
St. Louis Adjusted Nonborrowed Reserves	Nov. 78–Sept. 79	−0.1033	0.3785	0.042	0.0106	0.0031	0.074	0.006	0.919
	Oct. 79–Oct. 80	0.0848	0.6439	0.033	0.0176	0.0051	0.017	0.001	0.982
	Nov. 78–Oct. 80	−0.0014	0.5387	0.085	0.0149	0.0043	0.000	0.006	0.994
St. Louis Monetary Base	Nov. 78–Sept. 79	−0.0161	0.0333	0.345	0.0034	0.0010	0.232	0.028	0.741
	Oct. 79–Oct. 80	0.0031	0.0487	0.293	0.0049	0.0014	0.003	0.000	0.996
	Nov. 78–Oct. 80	−0.0057	0.0424	0.353	0.0043	0.0012	0.018	0.001	0.981
St. Louis Net Monetary Base	Nov. 78–Sept. 79	−0.0161	0.0426	0.351	0.0043	0.0012	0.143	0.022	0.835
	Oct. 79–Oct. 80	0.0038	0.0523	0.190	0.0052	0.0015	0.005	0.020	0.975
	Nov. 78–Oct. 80	−0.0054	0.0481	0.282	0.0048	0.0014	0.012	0.006	0.982

be under discussion simultaneously, and they are often not distinguished. The first is the role of the monetary base as an ultimate target of monetary policy, that is, an alternative to various money stock concepts. The second issue is the use of the monetary base as the control variable in a reserve aggregate control procedure where a money stock variable is the ultimate target.

It would appear to us that the first issue is now obsolete. Some of those who advocated looking at the base as a policy target, such as the Shadow Open Market Committee, took that position only when it became evident that there were extreme measurement problems with the old M1 concept in the presence of rapidly evolving institutional structures. The new M1B concept should overcome these difficulties at least temporarily.

The second issue, that of nonborrowed reserves versus the monetary or net monetary base as the appropriate policy guide by which to control the money stock, is the issue that we have addressed here and elsewhere. Wallich [14] appears to argue that reserves are preferable in such a role because

> when the public's demand for currency increases, the Federal Reserve automatically offsets it, under a reserves operating target, by providing the banks with reserves sufficient to cover the shortfall of reserves on the unwithdrawn balance of their deposits. Using the base as a policy guide would require a massive contraction or expansion of deposits with any temporary or permanent change in the ratio of currency to deposits. (p. 4)

As stated, without qualification, this statement is at least partially inaccurate. It fails to distinguish between anticipated (i.e., correctly forecasted) and unanticipated changes in the currency-deposit ratio. Wallich's statement is incorrect for changes in the currency-deposit ratio that are correctly anticipated. Consider Christmas. There is a well-established positive seasonal factor in the currency-deposit ratio in December. Those advocating use of the monetary base as a policy guide would recognize that there would be a seasonal drop in the base multiplier at this time of year, and they would advocate an appropriate seasonal increase in the monetary base to keep the money stock from falling, or an even larger seasonal increase in the monetary base if it were judged desirable to maintain the historical seasonal factor in the money stock at this time of year. Thus the only issue involves circumstances in which changes in the currency-deposit ratio are unanticipated.

Contrary to the impression given by the Wallich statement quoted above, unanticipated changes in the currency-deposit ratio cause money stock fluctuations when either reserves or the monetary base are used as a policy guide. In the former case, this can be seen by reference to Table 1, step (i) of the current procedures as described by Wallich. If there is a forecasting error in the currency-deposit ratio, then that error will be reflected in the implied target for demand deposits. As such it will carry through the entire procedure and will be reflected in an erroneous estimate of the nonborrowed reserves consistent with the desired money stock. Alternatively stated, there will be a forecast error for the multiplier so that the realized money stock, the product of the realized value of the multiplier and nonborrowed reserves supplied, will differ from the desired money stock, the product of the predicted multiplier and nonborrowed reserves supplied.

There are two substantive differences in the impact of forecasting errors for the currency-deposit ratio under a reserves policy guide versus a monetary base policy guide. First, the sign of the money stock error will differ; under a reserves guide, underprediction of the currency-deposit ratio will lead to an overshoot of the money stock target. Exactly the opposite will result under a monetary base policy guide. Second, the absolute value of the money stock errors in response to a given forecast error for the currency-deposit ratio will differ under the two regimes, with the absolute value of the error larger when the monetary base is used as a policy guide. This can be seen by examining the elasticities of the various multipliers with respect to the currency-deposit ratio. It can be shown that

$$\left| \frac{\epsilon(m_{NB},k)}{\epsilon(m_{NR},k)} \right| = \left| 1 - m_{NB} \right| > 1, \tag{4}$$

where

$\epsilon(m_{NB},k)$ = the elasticity of the net monetary base multiplier with respect to the currency-deposit ratio

$\epsilon(m_{NR},k)$ = the elasticity of the nonborrowed reserves multiplier with respect to the currency-deposit ratio

m_{NB} = the net monetary base multiplier.

At current values of the net monetary base multiplier, the error in the money stock from a given prediction error in the currency-deposit ratio should be about 1.5 times as large under a net monetary base policy guide as under a nonborrowed reserves policy guide.

If this is the case, then what accounts for the smaller ex ante forecast percentage errors for the monetary base multiplier compared with the nonborrowed reserves multipliers reported above? The answer is that the currency-deposit ratio is only one of several items that must be forecast to predict the relationship between either of these aggregates and the money stock. To single out only one component for discussion is incomplete and potentially misleading. Unpredicted changes in the quantities of other reserve absorbing assets relative to demand deposits held by the nonbank public will also cause errors in computing the appropriate amount of reserves or monetary base for a particular money stock target. This can be clearly seen in the description of step (ii) of the present procedures, given in Table 1. More importantly forecasting errors in such variables will produce larger deviations from the desired money stock under a nonborrowed reserves policy guide than under a monetary base policy guide. It can be shown that

$$\left| \frac{\epsilon(m_{NB},x)}{\epsilon(m_{NR},x)} \right| = \frac{m_{NB}}{m_{UR}} < 1, \tag{5}$$

where

$\epsilon(m_{NB},x)$ = the elasticity of the net monetary base multiplier with respect to x
$\epsilon(m_{NR}, x)$ = the elasticity of the nonborrowed reserves multiplier with respect to x
x = any one of the ratios t_1, t_2, g, z, $r+1$, or $r+1-v$.

At present values of the net monetary base multiplier the error in the money stock from a given prediction error in any one of these ratios should be about 0.28 times as large as under a nonborrowed reserves policy guide. Since the relative sensitivity of the money stock varies from step to step of the forecasting procedures for the two policy guides, the question of the superiority or inferiority or either guide is a question that can only be answered empirically, given a particular forecasting technique. From the information presented above, it is clear that given our forecasting models the forecast errors at the various steps of the procedure are such that the monetary base is the dominant policy guide.

6. CONCLUSION

The conclusion to be drawn from this paper is that an operational reserve aggregate control procedure does exist that would allow the FOMC to achieve its target ranges for the growth of monetary aggregates. Narrower short-run target growth ranges can be set if the gross or net monetary base is used as the control aggregate rather than total or nonborrowed reserves. For longer run control it makes little difference which control aggregate is used because any of the alternative control aggregates discussed here should allow the FOMC to hit its target growth rate for monetary aggregates plus or minus 1 percent.

In arriving at these conclusions it was assumed that the FOMC can achieve the level of the controlled reserve aggregate that is consistent with its money targets, and that the Johannes-Rasche multiplier forecasting models would remain stable in a reserve aggregate control regime. As Davis's [3] work indicates, all reserve aggregates are not equally controllable. Consequently, if the FOMC had a harder time controlling the monetary base than reserves, for example, then the fact that monetary base multipliers are more predictable than reserve multipliers, and hence facilitate better monetary control, would not be sufficient to guarantee that a monetary base control procedure would be superior to a bank reserve control procedure. This is not a problem in the current context, however, because Davis's work suggests that the monetary base and total bank reserves are equally controllable, as are the net base and nonborrowed reserves, the latter two reserve aggregates being easier to control than the former two.

APPENDIX A

Multiplier Components

Let C = Currency in hands of public
D = Total checkable deposits at banks and thrifts
$TLTD$ = Total large denomination time deposits at banks and thrifts
G = Government deposits at commercial banks plus note balances at commercial banks and thrifts
Z = Demand deposits at banks due foreign commercial banks and foreign official institutions plus time and saving deposits due foreign commercial banks and official institutions
V = Nonmember vault cash plus change in member vault cash over past two weeks
$TRPS$ = Term RP's
B = Member Borrowing
SB = Source Base
RAM = Reserve Adjustment Magnitude.

Then,

$$
\begin{aligned}
k &= C/D \\
t_1 &= (M_2 - M_{1B})/D \\
t_2 &= (M_3 - M_2)/D \\
g &= G/D \\
z &= Z/D \\
b &= B/(M_2 - C + TLTD + TRPS + G + Z) \\
r+1 &= (SB + RAM - C)/(M_2 - C + TLTD + TRPS + G + Z) \\
r+1-v &= (SB + RAM - C - V)/(M_2 - C + TLTD + TRPS + G + Z).
\end{aligned}
$$

LITERATURE CITED

1. Box, George E. P., and Gwilym M. Jenkins. *Time Series Analysis, Forecasting and Control.* San Francisco: Holden-Day, 1976.
2. Burger, Albert E. "Alternative Measures of the Monetary Base." Federal Reserve Bank of St. Louis *Review,* (June 1979), 3-8.
3. Davis, Richard G. "Short-Run Targets for Open Market Operations." In *Open Market Policies and Operating Procedures-Staff Studies,* Board of Governors of the Federal Reserve System, pp. 37-70, 1971.
4. Johannes, James M., and Robert H. Rasche, "Predicting the Money Multiplier." *Journal of Monetary Economics,* 5 (July 1979), 301-25.
5. ______. "Monetary Control: The Implementation Experience, Retrospective and Prospective." In "A Symposium on the Federal Reserve and Its Public Accountability," edited by Karl Brunner. Center for Research on Government Policy and Business, Graduate School of Mangement, University of Rochester, 1980a.

6. ______, "The Construction and Forecasting of Money Multipliers for the New Monetary Aggregates." In "Shadow Open Market Committee Policy Statement and Position Papers." Paper PPS-80-4, Center for Research in Government Policy and Business, Graduate School of Management, University of Rochester, 1980b.

7. Jordon, Jerry L. "Elements of Money Stock Determination." Federal Reserve Bank of St. Louis *Review*, (October 1969), 10–19.

8. Lang, Richard W. "The FOMC in 1979: Introducing Reserve Targeting." Federal Reserve Bank of St. Louis *Review*, (March 1979), 2–25.

9. Lombra, Raymond, and Michael Moran. "Policy Advice and Policy-making at the Federal Reserve." Mimeographed. Paper presented at the Carnegie-Rochester Conference, Pittsburgh, November 1979.

10. Lucas, Robert E., Jr. "Econometric Policy Evaluation: A Critique." In *The Phillips Curve and Labor Market*, edited by Karl Brunner and Allan H. Meltzer, pp. 19–46. Carnegie-Rochester Conference Series, 1. Amsterdam: North Holland, 1976.

11. Pierce, James L., and Thomas D. Thomson. "Some Issues in Controlling the Stock of Money." In *Controlling Monetary Aggregates II: The Implementation*, pp. 115–36. Boston: Federal Reserve Bank of Boston Conference Series No. 9, 1972.

12. Poole, William. "Interpreting the Fed's Monetary Targets." *Brookings Papers on Economic Activity*, 1 (1976), 247–60.

13. Volcker, Paul A. "The New Federal Reserve Technical Procedure for Controlling Money," Mimeographed. Attached to a statement before the Committee on Banking, Housing and Urban Affairs, U.S. Senate, February 4, 1980.

14. Wallich, Henry C. "Techniques of Monetary Control." Mimeographed. Remarks before the Missouri Valley Economic Association, Memphis, March 1, 1980.

ROBERT D. LAURENT*

Reserve Requirements, Deposit Insurance and Monetary Control

RESERVE REQUIREMENTS ARE USUALLY JUSTIFIED on grounds that they enhance the monetary authority's control over a monetary aggregate. Using reserve requirements to control a monetary aggregate has long posed a problem for economists in devising an institutional structure in which to conduct monetary policy. Higher reserve requirements give more accurate control over a target monetary aggregate, but they also impose higher taxes on the monetary aggregate. These higher taxes lead to the use of lower reservable instruments as substitutes for deposits included in the monetary aggregate and thereby alter the significance of the target.

Building on a reserve computation system presented earlier in this journal [8], this paper proposes a change in institutional structure that essentially merges the monetary policy functions of the Federal Reserve (Fed) with the deposit insuring authority of the Federal Deposit Insurance Corporation (FDIC). This proposed system would provide accurate weekly control over the target monetary aggregate while completely eliminating present reserve requirements and the reserve requirement tax. It further improves monetary policy by helping insulate the target monetary aggregate from innovations that would substitute new financial instruments for components of the target monetary aggregate. The proposal would greatly simplify banks' portfolio and reserve management tasks. It would eliminate the need for a

*The views expressed are those of the author alone and do not necessarily represent the views of the Federal Reserve Bank of Chicago or the Federal Reserve System. The author has benefited from the comments of John B. Carlson, Jack A. Galbraith, Chayim Herzig-Marx, Larry Mote, Neil Pinsky, and an anonymous referee. The author is especially indebted to Carl Vander Wilt for his valuable insights.

ROBERT D. LAURENT *is economist, Federal Reserve Bank of Chicago.*

0022-2879/81/0881-0314$00.50/0
JOURNAL OF MONEY, CREDIT, AND BANKING, vol. 13, no. 3 (August 1981)

reserve for the deposit insuring agency while reducing economic volatility and the risk of bank failure. Finally the proposal would simplify (and provide a compelling economic rationale for) the role of government in the financial system. These benefits would be obtained without mandatory reserve requirements or other compulsory measures.

The paper is divided into four sections. The first reviews the problem of reserve requirements and monetary control. The second describes the proposal to deal with the problem. The third provides the economic rationale for the role of government in the proposed system. The final section describes bank techniques of reserve management under the proposed system.

1. THE PROBLEM

The use of reserve requirements to control a target monetary aggregate appears to be very straightforward. In principle, the monetary authority provides a level of reserves consistent with the desired stock of the target monetary aggregate. The banking system then creates a level of the target monetary aggregate such that required reserves match the level of reserves provided. Thus, by moving reserves, the monetary authority can control a monetary aggregate. The level of the monetary aggregate that the banking system can create out of a given amount of reserves depends on the level of reserve requirements. Reserve requirements of 10 percent mean that \$10 in deposits can be created out of every dollar in reserves while reserve requirements of 20 percent mean that \$5 in deposits can be created. If the process operated in just this straightforward way, it would make little difference to monetary control what the level of reserve requirements were. The fundamental problem of monetary control arises because banks may hold more reserves than required by their level of deposits. These excess reserves, to the extent that they produce unpredictable variability in the relationship between reserves and required reserves (money), are the major problem in using reserve requirements to control a target monetary aggregate.

The severity of the problem posed for monetary control by excess reserves depends critically upon the level of reserve requirements. The higher are reserve requirements, the more predictable the multiplier connecting reserves to deposits. Higher reserve requirements improve monetary control by reducing both the size of the disturbances (unanticipated changes in excess reserves) and the multiplier that magnifies changes in excess reserves into monetary disturbances.

Improved monetary control would seem to call for high reserve requirements.[1] But increasing reserve requirements increases the tax on banks and bank customers. It is the fractional reserve nature of banking that allows banks to pay depositors interest on their deposits. A bank can afford to pay interest on deposits, under a fractional reserve system, because it can lend out all but that fraction of the funds it

[1]There is, in fact, an extensive literature dealing with proposals for 100 percent reserves requirements [1, 3, 4, 13]. A survey of these proposals is given in [7].

obtains as deposits. Increasing the fraction of deposits that must be held as reserves reduces the interest rate that can be paid on deposits. Because of the lower interest rate, higher reserve requirements would cause depositors to reduce deposit holdings below optimal levels and seek alternative lower reservable means of transferring funds, which would alter the significance of the target monetary aggregate.

One solution to the dilemma posed by the deterioration of monetary control with low reserve requirements and the increase in the tax on deposits with high reserve requirements involves interest payments by government on required reserves. Reserve requirements would be raised to improve monetary control, but the tax increase would be offset by government interest payments on required reserves.[2] However, the changes involved in bank operations under high reserve requirements are apparently presently considered too drastic, even with interest payments on reserves. Consequently, interest payments on reserves are no longer advocated along with high reserve requirements, but rather as compensation for the present level of reserve requirements. The payment of interest on required reserves at the present level of reserve requirements has two problems. First, it is not clear how the payment of interest on required reserves at the current level of reserve requirements gives accurate monetary control. Second, for any level of reserve requirements, there is the difficulty of determining the appropriate level of interest to be paid on reserves.

2. THE PROPOSAL

This paper proposes a different solution to the problem of monetary control and reserve requirement taxes. This solution uses a reserve computation system presented by the author in an earlier article [8]. This system, referred to as the reverse lag, reverses the present system in which the required reserves a bank must meet are based on deposits two weeks earlier. Under the reverse lag, a bank matches required reserves based on deposits in the current week to its reserves in the previous week. By looking at the required reserves against its deposits entering the current week and its reserves in the previous week, the bank knows what change in its asset holdings will match its current week's required reserves to reserves in the previous week. The reverse lag computation system is designed to insulate, within the settlement week, a bank's required reserves from outside disturbances. By allowing each bank to easily match required reserves in the current week to its reserves in the previous week, the reverse lag has the same effect as eliminating excess reserves and stabilizing the multiplier between reserves and money. The reverse lag system allows the monetary authorities to accurately set weekly required reserves. Most importantly, it works no matter how low the level of reserve requirements.

The problem dealt with in this paper is to translate the reverse lag's control over

[2]The earliest instance, the author has been able to find, of such a proposal is [11]. Other proposals that include paying interest on reserves are [5, 10, 12, 14].

required reserves into a system giving accurate weekly control over a target monetary aggregate.[3] Aside from the necessity of setting appropriate reserve requirements,[4] there is the problem of deposits held at different banks with different reserve requirements. An obvious solution is somehow to force every bank to meet the same reserve requirements. The problem with simply imposing uniform reserve requirements is that this imposes a tax on banks. Granted, under the reverse lag, reserve requirements could be reduced quite sharply so that the tax would be minimal. But a much better solution is available.

The fundamental problem of monetary control and the reserve requirement tax is that banks receive no benefit from the imposition of the reserve requirements that allow the monetary authority to control the target monetary aggregate. What is needed is something to compensate banks for reserve requirements. Fortunately, there already exists a benefit that government is uniquely qualified to provide and for which there appears to be great demand on the part of banks. This benefit is deposit insurance, presently provided by the FDIC. It is proposed that the monetary policy functions of the Fed be merged with the deposit insuring authority of the FDIC. This would allow the complete elimination of the present reserve requirements and reserve requirement tax while effectively translating control over required reserves into control over a target monetary aggregate. Present reserve requirements can be eliminated because changing the form in which deposit insurance charges are collected allows deposit insurance to replace the reserve requirement tax in controlling the target monetary aggregate.

Presently, insured banks pay an annual premium of one-thirtieth of 1 percent of all deposits (not just insured deposits) for deposit insurance. This would be transformed into a reserve requirement level that yields the same deposit insurance charges. Thus, with interest rates of 10 percent, a reserve requirement of one-third of 1 percent would cost banks the same amount as the present premium for deposit insurance. Any bank presently paying for deposit insurance (and almost all do) would be willing instead to hold reserves in payment for deposit insurance.[5]

Monetary policy would be conducted through changes in reserves. Banks holding reserves would be purchasing deposit insurance for deposits with that level of required reserves. Under the reverse lag computation system, banks can easily match required reserves to their reserve level in the previous week. Since all insured banks are matching required reserves to reserves, required reserves for the entire banking system are under control. Given appropriate reserve requirements, control over required reserves is equivalent to control over the target monetary aggregate. This control has been achieved while completely eliminating the present mandatory

[3]This paper and the reverse lag paper [8] present only the basic framework of the proposed system. The complete system is described in detail in [9].

[4]That is, reserve requirements ought to be consistent with the target monetary aggregate. Control over M1 calls for the elimination of reserve requirements against time and savings deposits, while control over M2 calls for the same reserve requirements against all deposits.

[5]Reserve requirements could be adjusted periodically (e.g., annually) to offset the effect of changes in interest rate levels and maintain the same charge for deposit insurance.

reserve requirements and reserve requirement tax and without adding any new compulsory measures.

3. ROLE OF GOVERNMENT

Merging the government's money issuing and deposit insuring functions might seem strange at first. But, even aside from the benefit for monetary control and the elimination of the reserve requirement tax, there are a number of attractive aspects to the merger. Most important, the proposal is consistent with a compelling economic rationale for both improving and simplifying the role of government in the financial system.

Why are deposits insured? A facile answer would be that insurance protects deposit holders from losses in the event of bank failure. But there are many financial assets held by the public that are not insured by government—insurance policies, real estate, bond holdings, stock holdings and some pension funds, Keogh Plans, and IRAs. There is a compelling economic rationale for deposit insurance that uses the same reasoning as underlies reserve requirements. Reserve requirements are imposed to give the monetary authority control over a target monetary aggregate. Presumably, control over a monetary aggregate is related to macroeconomic goals of importance to the economy. It seems natural that deposits included in the target monetary aggregate be under deposit insurance, because deposits are insured not to protect individual deposit holders, but rather to prevent widespread bank failures and the effects of a monetary contraction on the economy.

Why does government provide deposit insurance? If every bank failure were an independent event, deposit insurance could probably be provided more efficiently by private institutions. However, the need for deposit insurance is most crucial in a situation of widespread bank failures, such as the Great Depression. Providing deposit insurance against such possibilities seems a service that only government could provide.

What characteristics should be possessed by the government agency insuring deposits? Certainly, the most critical requirement is that the deposit insuring agency be capable of reimbursing depositors in the event of a bank failure. Under the present arrangement, it appears likely that in a serious emergency, the government would provide additional money to the deposit insuring agency. Nevertheless, it is clear that concern over the adequacy of its reserves has been a factor in past actions of the deposit insuring agency. If this agency had the money creating powers of the monetary authority, such concerns—indeed the necessity for a reserve at all—would be eliminated.

What factors determine the risk in providing deposit insurance? Again, if every bank failure were an independent event, the risk of a bank failure would be determined solely by the characteristics of the individual bank. However, the prevention of widespread bank failures was a prime motive for the establishment of government deposit insurance. The periodic occurrence of widespread bank failures suggests that economic conditions play an important role in determining the risk of bank failure. This being the case, it seems reasonable to subject the monetary authority that is responsible at least in part, for economic conditions, to the effects on the deposit insuring agency.[6]

This section has argued that there are a number of attractive aspects to a merger of the money creating and deposit insuring functions of government. The same deposits whose control is thought important for monetary policy purposes because of their impact on economic activity should, for the same reasons, be protected by deposit insurance. Government has an advantage in providing deposit insurance, and the most important characteristic for the deposit insuring agency is the money-creating power of the monetary authority. Finally, because the behavior of the monetary authority is an important determinant of the risks involved in insuring deposits, it appears reasonable that it share in the costs and benefits.

The proposal presented here has another extremely important advantage for a monetary policy operating through control of a monetary aggreagte. Even if that monetary aggregate target were controlled accurately, a reserve requirement tax will act to erode the target's economic significance. For example, one potential target monetary aggregate (M1) was originally defined to include those assets readily exchangeable for goods and services. The appearance of NOW accounts, ATS accounts, money market mutual funds, and corporate repurchase agreements that can serve the same role as demand deposits has raised the question of how accurately M1 satisfies its original purpose. One result of the proliferation of new types of deposits and quasi-deposits has been an explosion in the number of different monetary aggregates published. Unquestionably, the principle reason for the proliferation of various surrogate deposits has been interest rate controls on various deposit categories, particularly the prohibition of explicit interest on demand deposits. Probably no single step would do as much to improve monetary policy as the total elimination of interest rate ceilings. Interest rate controls have been inequitable, inefficient, and ineffective, while introducing a great deal of uncertainty and confusion into monetary policy. But even if interest rate controls were removed, there remains a problem for monetary policy. There is always an incentive for the creation of an instrument that serves the same function as components of the target aggregate but has lower reserve requirements.[7] Linking reserve requirements to the purchase of deposit insurance eliminates the incentive to avoid the reserve requirement tax by removing the tax itself. Without interest rate ceilings and the reserve requirement tax all the new demand deposit substitutes and problems of defining money disappear.[8]

[6]This connection between the actions of the monetary authority and the impact of bank failures on the deposit insuring agency was noted by Gibson [6].

[7]It is conceivable that even with market interest rates paid on all deposits, such instruments as repurchases and money market mutual funds would still be attractive since they have the advantages of interest yielding demand deposits while effectively reducing the reserve requirements against demand deposits. This is particularly true at times of high interest rates.

[8]The problems interest rate ceilings and reserve requirements pose for monetary control are described more extensively in [2].

This paper deals exclusively with the form and ignores completely the appropriate level of charges for deposit insurance. It is possible that a set of optimal charges for deposit insurance, however determined, might not be consistent with control over the target monetary aggregate. It suffices to show that any set of optimal charges can easily be made consistent with monetary control. Since the reverse lag will work no matter how low reserve requirements, it is always possible to find an appropriate set of relative reserve requirements to control the target monetary aggregate, at levels low enough that the absolute cost of deposit insurance for any deposit is no higher than the optimal deposit insurance charge. Having achieved control over the target monetary aggregate, the charge for deposit insurance on any deposit is raised to the optimal level by imposing the appropriate insurance premium on the deposit. Thus, deposit insurance on some deposits could be purchased through both required reserves and premium payments.

4. RESERVE MANAGEMENT

One aspect of the reverse lag requires more explanation for a system with low reserve requirements like that proposed in this paper. If reserve requirements are very low (e.g., the one-third of 1 percent mentioned in this paper), it is quite possible that a bank with a severe deposit outflow at the end of the settlement week could end the week with negative average reserves. Since under the reverse lag a bank must match required reserves one week to its reserves the preceding week, negative reserves would appear to pose a grave problem for a bank. However, there are a number of solutions to this problem. Some of these solutions would improve interbank adjustment and reserve management.

First, notice that because banks could use federal funds transactions to eliminate negative reserve levels earlier in the settlement week, the problem of negative reserves would occur only at the end of the week. Notice also that reserves could not go negative for the entire banking system. These conditions suggest some solutions to the problem. One solution would allow banks to trade federal funds after the close of business at the end of the settlement week as a way of eliminating any negative reserves.

A different solution would seem even better. Banks could simply trade reserves held in previous weeks. Banks would be able to use the federal funds markets to trade reserves in the current week and reserves in previous weeks. A bank that has fewer reserves (perhaps even negative reserves) in the previous week than its required reserves entering the current week would be able to purchase reserves from banks that had more reserves in the previous week than their required reserves entering the current week. This interbank adjustment through past reserves helps bring both banks to equilibrium. Adjusting through transfers of past reserves has the advantage that adjustment can occur when banks have accurate knowledge of both their previous reserves and current required reserves.

Adjusting through transfers of past reserves has another advantage over interbank adjustment through transfers of current reserves as in the present federal funds market. At present, a federal funds transaction involves the transfer of current reserves through an unsecured loan. Lending banks are not indifferent to the credit worthiness of the borrowing bank and it is not surprising that there are lists of approved borrowing banks. Banks in financial difficulty are cut off from the federal funds market. Interbank adjustment through trading reserves in previous weeks provides an avenue of adjustment where the borrowing bank's credit worthiness can be essentially ignored. This is because in transferring past reserves the lending bank makes only an accounting adjustment and does not risk losing reserves. If the borrowing bank defaults, the lending bank loses, at most, its interest payment. Transferring reserves held in a previous week simplifies the adjustment process by removing the necessity of considering credit worthiness, and unlike the present federal funds market, rates do not depend on the identity of the bank reducing its deficiency.[9]

A remaining problem aggravated by the low level of reserve requirements is the risk involved for the clearing institution (whether the monetary authority or a private clearinghouse) in allowing negative reserves. The monetary authority presently discourages banks from ending the day with negative reserves, but they do allow a bank's intraday reserves to go negative. Ideally, a system should be designed to give banks the flexibility of negative reserves at the end of the day (especially since negative reserves do not inhibit control of the target monetary aggregate) and yet remove the risk to the clearing institution. One solution would be to allow banks to deposit acceptable securities, such as Treasury bills, as collateral against possible negative reserves. A bank would be allowed negative reserves only to the extent of the value of the securities it had deposited as collateral. This would protect the clearing institution against loss from bank failure, while allowing banks the flexibility of negative reserves.[10]

Allowing banks to cover negative reserve positions with acceptable collateral helps answer a question that may occur to the reader. The proposal in this paper describes a system with very low reserve requirements. Yet, banks would voluntarily hold reserves even in the absence of reserve requirements. Is it possible that, under the proposal, banks will choose to hold more reserves than required for deposit insurance and thereby disrupt control over the monetary aggregate? To see

[9]An exactly equivalent type of adjustment could occur through interbank deposits under the reverse lag system. In computing required reserves, both at present and under the reverse lag, banks subtract net interbank deposits ("due-from" minus "due-to") from demand deposits. A bank with fewer reserves in the previous week than required reserves entering the current week would pay a second bank in the reverse situation to write up deposits in its name on the second bank's books. These interbank deposits help both banks come to equilibrium by reducing the first bank's required reserves and increasing the second bank's required reserves. This interbank adjustment is an exact counterpart to adjustment through the transfer of reserves held in previous weeks and has the same advantages of allowing adjustment after reserve and required reserve positions are known and reducing the risk in interbank adjustment.

[10]The situation would be similar, in some ways, to that faced by a commodities futures exchange. The total value of trader's contracts do not change since the change in the value of the long positions must be offset by the change in the value of the short positions. The value of an individual's holdings may vary substantially, but the exchange is not concerned as long as the holders maintain margin through cash or collateral.

why this will not happen, consider why banks hold reserves. A bank holds reserves because it believes them the cheapest way to avoid a deficiency. Under the reverse lag system a bank knows both how to eliminate any reserve requirement deficiency at the beginning of the week and that outside factors cannot make it deficient within the week. So it has no incentive to hold any reserves against a deficiency in required reserves. Indeed, as noted above, it can even have negative reserves within the week and still come to equilibrium in the following week.

However, the deficiency against which a bank would voluntarily hold reserves in the absence of reserve requirements is of another type. Suppose a depositor wishes to withdraw currency or transfer funds by check from his account. His bank must be able to provide currency out of vault cash or provide funds through a clearing institution to the bank that receives his check. Failure to provide these funds is a more fundamental type of deficiency than failing to meet reserve requirements. Under the reverse lag, banks would set vault cash and deposit securities at the clearing institution to protect against this fundamental type of deficiency.

Though a bank's holdings of vault cash and security collateral will be unpredictable, under the reverse lag system these holdings would not affect the targeted monetary aggregate. In the reverse lag accounting system, vault cash does not count as reserves but as a subtraction from demand deposits in computing required reserves. Likewise, securities on deposit as collateral against a negative reserve position at the clearing institution are not reserves and have no effect on the target monetary aggregate. Banks would be free to set vault cash and collateral security levels anywhere they desired as protection against a fundamental deficiency without affecting reserves or the target monetary aggregate. In effect the proposal separates the two functions currently served by reserves—control over the target monetary aggregate and protection against deposit outflows. Additionally, the proposal allows banks to earn interest on protection held against clearing imbalances.

5. CONCLUSION

The merger of the monetary authority with the deposit insuring agency would simplify and rationalize the government's role in the financial structure. Monetary policy would be directed to changes in the target monetary aggregate and implemented entirely through open market operations. Under the reverse lag computation system, banks would accurately match required reserves in one week to reserves in the previous week. In doing this, banks would obtain deposit insurance on all reservable deposits in return for reserves held in the previous week.[11] By stabilizing the multiplier that connects the target monetary aggregate to reserves, this proposal would give accurate weekly control over the target monetary aggregate

[11]The proposal, as presented, implicitly extends insurance to all deposits on which charges are levied, irrespective of deposit size. If desired, insurance could be limited to deposits under $100,000, as is presently the case. This would not disturb monetary control.

without the necessity of compulsory reserve requirements or the reserve requirement tax. Voluntary deposit insurance would give accurate monetary control at the same costs as are presently charged for deposit insurance. However, the proposal neither requires nor depends upon any particular arrangement of either charges for deposit insurance or regulatory responsibilities and is compatible with any arrangement.[12]

The merger of the money issuing and deposit insuring agencies has a number of benefits. It gives the monetary authority accurate weekly control over the target monetary aggregate. It removes the necessity of their compensating banks for reserve requirements either by interest payments or the provision of banking services. Further, along with the elimination of Regulation Q, it would eliminate any incentive to introduce new financial instruments that serve as substitutes for components of the target monetary aggregate.

The proposal helps the deposit insuring agency by removing all questions of the agency's ability to meet its contingent liabilities. Indeed, it makes the question of the adequacy of reserves superfluous. The proposal does not change the agency's revenues from deposit insurance, only the method by which they are obtained. To the extent that more accurate control over a monetary aggregate reduces economic volatility, the deposit insuring agency benefits from the reduction in the risk of bank failure.

Banks benefit from the proposal, both from the reduction in the costs of portfolio and reserve management due to the adoption of the reverse lag and from the elimination of the reserve requirement tax. The public shares in the benefits to the economy of an improved monetary policy. Bank customers benefit from the passing on of the gains obtained from elimination of the reserve requirement tax.

The only loser would be the taxpayer. By reducing the size of the monetary authority's securities portfolio, the after-expenses proceeds of which are turned over to the Treasury, the proposal reduces Treasury tax receipts. Reserve requirements are, however, a relatively minor source of earnings for the monetary authority, compared to currency issuance.[13] Even so, there appears to be no justification for the reserve requirement tax other than the control it gives over the target monetary aggregate. There are three problems with the present mandatory reserve requirement system. First, it does not give the monetary authority accurate control over a target monetary aggregate. Second, it induces the public to underutilize those targeted financial instruments that have reserve requirements. Third, by inducing innovation in creating new financial instruments to replace components of the target aggregate, it impairs the integrity of the target monetary aggregate. The system proposed here gives accurate control over a target monetary aggregate without any reserve requirement tax.

[12]Although outside the topic of this paper, the proposal is ideally compatible with open entry into banking and confining government regulation to the granting of deposit insurance. Also, although the proposal is presented in terms of merging the Fed and the FDIC, this is not absolutely necessary. Almost the same effects are achieved if reserves at the Fed are required for deposit insurance and the Fed pays the proceeds to the FDIC.

[13]For example, if the new Depository Institution Deregulation and Monetary Control Act had been entirely implemented at the end of 1979, it is estimated that reserves required at the Federal Reserve would have been \$16.7 billion while Federal Reserve currency outstanding was \$125.9 billion.

LITERATURE CITED

1. Angell, James W. "The 100 Per Cent Reserve Plan." *Quarterly Journal of Economics,* 50 (November 1935), 1-35.

2. Cagan, Phillip. "Financial Developments and the Erosion of Monetary Controls." Washington, D.C.: Studies in Contemporary Economic Problems, American Enterprise Institute, 1979.

3. Currie, Laughlin B. *The Supply and Control of Money in the United States.* Cambridge, Mass.: Harvard University Press, 1934.

4. Fisher, Irving. *100% Money.* New York: Adelphia, 1935.

5. Friedman, Milton. *A Program for Monetary Stability.* Chapter 3. New York: Fordham University Press, 1960.

6. Gibson, William E. "Deposit Insurance in the United States: Evaluation and Reform." *Journal of Financial and Quantitative Analysis,* 7 (March 1972), 1575-94.

7. Hart, Albert G. "The 'Chicago Plan' of Banking Reform, I. A Proposal for Making Monetary Management Effective in the United States." *The Review of Economic Studies,* 2 (February 1935), 104-16.

8. Laurent, Robert D. "Reserve Requirements—Are they Lagged in the Wrong Direction?" *Journal of Money, Credit, and Banking,* 11 (August 1979), 301-10.

9. ______. "A Comprehensive Proposal for Accurate Monetary Control through Reserves." *Staff Memoranda,* 81-1, Federal Reserve Bank of Chicago.

10. Mints, Lloyd W. *Monetary Policy for Competitive Society.* Chapters 8 and 9. New York: McGraw-Hill, 1950.

11. Seltzer, Lawrence H. "The Problem of Our Excessive Banking Reserves." *Journal of the American Statistical Association,* 35 (March 1940), 24-36.

12. Simons, Henry C. "Debt Policy and Banking Policy." *The Review of Economic Statistics,* 28 (May 1946), 85-89.

13. ______. *Economic Policy for a Free Society.* Chapter 2. Chicago: University of Chicago Press, 1948.

14. Tolley, George S. "Providing for Growth of the Money Supply." *Journal of Political Economy,* 65 (December 1957), 465-85.

HAIM LEVY*

Optimal Portfolio of Foreign Currencies with Borrowing and Lending

1. INTRODUCTION

UNTIL THE LATE SIXTIES, most American corporations held their liquid assets in the form of cash, short-term government notes, and other highly liquid marketable securities. Since the early seventies, more and more firms have begun to hold their current assets in foreign currencies beyond what would be required to conduct normal foreign operations. In the last few years companies have accumulated and retained much more cash than they held in the past. In order to understand the magnitude of this issue, realize that at the end of 1977, cash and short-term securities held by International Business Machines amounted to $5.4 billion; by Exxon, $4.2 billion; and Ford and General Motors held well above $3 billion. Obviously, with this cash pile up, most companies devote much attention to cash management. Even a slight improvement in the management of these assets means a substantial profit, and firms have responded with highly trained staff, in particular, people familiar with the international money market and the investment opportunities available.

The change in attitude toward cash management may be summarized by the following quotation from a senior adviser to the J. Henry Schroder Bank and Trust Company: "Companies are no longer looking at a bank balance, they're looking at a

*The author acknowledges the insightful comments of Zvi Lerman and an anonymous referee of this journal.

HAIM LEVY *is professor of finance, School of Business Administration, Hebrew University of Jerusalem, and professor, Department of Finance, Insurance, and Real Estate, University of Florida, Gainesville.*

0022-2879/81/0881-0325$00.50/0
JOURNAL OF MONEY, CREDIT, AND BANKING, vol. 13, no. 3 (August 1981)

portfolio'' [1, p. 62]. Obviously, not all companies follow the same investment strategy or necessarily use portfolio analysis in their cash management, but there is no question that they apply the main principle of portfolio diversification implicitly or explicitly. For example, Litton Industries had (1978) one-third of its funds in deutsche marks and Swiss francs, one-third in other European currencies, and one-third in U.S. and Canadian dollars. National Cash Register Corporation, on the other hand, diversifies in more than 100 currencies with no more than $50 million in any single currency. Other firms employ a more aggressive technique of cash management by borrowing one currency and investing the proceeds in other currencies. Use of the forward market to hedge against currency fluctuations of money market investments in other countries varies widely depending on the risk preferences of the management. These few examples are sufficient to demonstrate the many investment combinations available to the international money market and the importance of the portfolio approach to cash management.

It is the purpose of this paper to show the potential gain from diversification in foreign currencies. Recently, Levy and Sarnat [5] have shown that the American investor can benefit from diversification in other currencies. In this paper we investigate other dimensions of this problem: (1) The change in investor welfare when short positions are allowed. Recall that a short position in our context merely means borrowing a given currency, a position that has already been taken by many firms. We shall analyze the investment strategy as well as the mean-variance efficient frontier with and without short positions in foreign currencies. (2) Since the assumption regarding the investment horizon is crucially important (see [3, 4]), we shall analyze the impact of change in the investment horizon on the optimal strategy. In other words, does a corporation which invests for one month differ in investment strategy from that adopted by a corporation which invests its cash for three months, or six months? (3) We analyze and compare the optimal diversification among different currencies from the points of view of investors based in different countries. (4) Additionally, we shall include the interest return on investments in foreign instruments as well as the capital gains from fluctuating exchange rates.

One word of caution is called for before we turn to the next section. In this paper the use of ex post data serves as a proxy for the potential gain from diversification. Note that by the construction of the mean-variance efficient frontier with ex post data, we have a sampling bias in favor of assets that are characterized by a low variance (or a high mean) in the sample. Thus, the results are not free from the bias of other empirical studies that use unadjusted ex post data. Nevertheless, we believe that the main conclusions of this paper are unaffected by this sampling bias. Obviously, for investment decisions, one should use ex ante predictions. Thus, the quantitative results do not necessarily determine the optimal investment policy for the future; they only indicate the potential gain from diversification. The investor can adjust the ex post data and find the optimal investment strategy with the new set of parameters.

In section 2, we review the sample data used and explain the two methods used in deriving the mean-variance efficient set. Section 3 is devoted to the empirical results that are computed from various points of view. Concluding remarks are given in section 4.

2. SAMPLE AND METHODOLOGY

A company or individual investor who holds a foreign currency receives interest on the deposit and a capital gain (or loss) from exchange rate fluctuations. To be specific, let $p_{ij,t}$ be the exchange rate between currencies i and j at time t, expressed in units of currency j per one unit of currency i. The first index i designates the investor's country of origin and the second j designates the foreign currency. For brevity's sake, we say "investor i" whenever we actually mean "investor domiciled in country i."

Now suppose that investor i decides to hold foreign currency j. One unit of currency i will purchase $p_{ij,t}$ units of currency j in period t. After one holding period the investor converts back to his domestic currency and receives $p_{ij,t}/p_{ij,t+1}$. Thus, the holding period return from exchange rate fluctuations is (c denotes capital gain or loss)

$$R^c_{ij,t} = \frac{p_{ij,t}/p_{ij,t+1}}{1} - 1 = \frac{p_{ij,t} - p_{ij,t+1}}{p_{ij,t+1}} \quad . \tag{1}$$

Assume that the original investment was one unit of currency. $R^c_{ij,t}$ denotes the exchange rate capital gain return while the investment of the unit of foreign currency returns $r_{j,t}$ (e.g., interest rate on currency j holdings) and will grow to $p_{ij,t}\ (1+r_{j,t})$ during the period (in terms of the foreign currency j). When the investor converts this end-of-period amount into his domestic currency i at the rate $p_{ij,t+1}$, he nets a *total* return (superscript T denotes total) of

$$\begin{aligned} R^T_{ij,t} &= \frac{p_{ij,t}\ (1 + r_{j,t})}{p_{ij,t+1}} - 1 = \left(\frac{p_{ij,t}}{p_{ij,t+1}} - 1 \right) (1 + r_{j,t}) + r_{j,t} \\ &= R^c_{ij,t}\ (1 + r_{j,t}) + r_{j,t} = R^c_{ij,t} + r_{j,t} + R^c_{ij,t}\ r_{j,t} . \end{aligned} \tag{2}$$

The total return is thus the sum of the exchange rate capital gains return $R^c_{ij,t}$, the currency j interest rate for the holding period $r_{j,t}$, and the cross product $R^c_{ij,t}\ r_{j,t}$ representing exchange rate gains (or loss) on interest income. Since the rest of the paper relates mainly to total return, we will henceforth suppress the "T" and denote it simply by $R_{ij,t}$.

Data

Rates of return for a sample of seventeen countries were calculated representing seventeen different investors' (by countries) viewpoints (index i taking values from 1 to 17) with each investor allowed to diversify among sixteen foreign currencies (index j taking values from 1 to 16). The data consisted of monthly exchange rates for the period 1970–78, as published regularly in the IMF *International Financial Statistics*. The published exchange rates are usually expressed in units of country j currency per U.S. $1. For three countries (Australia, South Africa, and the U.K.) the exchange rates are traditionally expressed in U.S. dollars per one domestic currency unit. A provision was made in the computer program to convert these exchange rates to a common dollar base with the rest. The basic data thus represented the exchange rates p_{US} applicable to a U.S. investor diversifying among sixteen foreign currencies. To change the investment viewpoint from the U.S. to any other base currency i, we made use of the relation:

$$p_{ij,t} = p_{US\ j,t} / p_{US\ i,t} .$$

Annual interest rates for the period for the seventeen sample countries were also obtained from the *International Financial Statistics*. The corresponding time series are presented in Table 1. Under "Description" in this table is indicated what particular interest rate was selected for the country. There is an unfortunate lack of homogeneity in the interest rate series published by the IMF, and an attempt was made to select those rates that best approximate market rates payable on domestic currency deposits in each country. The rationale for this choice is self-evident; we assume that the investor deposits his foreign currency holdings in a bank account at a rate of interest applicable to each currency.

The exchange rate capital gains and losses and the total returns were calculated using expressions (1) and (2) for investors i from the seventeen countries. To each investor i there were sixteen foreign currencies j available. A holding period of one month was assumed in these basic calculations. The basic monthly returns were then compounded to yield exchange rate capital gains and total returns for holding periods of three and six months (referred to as quarterly and semiannual returns throughout).

Table 2 lists the average foreign currency returns and interest rates for the period 1970–78 from the viewpoint of a U.S. investor with holding periods of one, three, and six months. The exchange rate capital gains and the total returns are given separately for each holding period. Although we will refer to this table while analyzing the optimal investment strategy, it is worth noting a few items in the table at this point.

First, looking at the available total return for each country we see that twelve of sixteen foreign countries had a higher total return than the U.S. rate on Treasury bills (0.48 percent per month) during this period. The same results hold for quarterly as well as semiannual data. Thus, the necessary condition for diversifying in foreign currency prevails. Second, note the importance of the inclusion of capital gain in the total return as well as interest rates. For example, the capital gain from holding the Danish krone is only sixth, yet when the interest earned on deposits is also included the krone yields the highest rate of return. As we shall see from using ex post data, Danish currency plays a central role in the American investor's optimal portfolio.

TABLE 1

INTEREST RATES ON VARIOUS CURRENCIES 1970–78 (PERCENTAGE PER YEAR)

	1970	1971	1972	1973	1974	1975	1976	1977	1978	Description
Australia	6.26	6.14	4.91	6.30	9.33	8.46	8.69	9.74	8.80	Government bond yield (short term)
Belgium	9.25	8.70	2.48	4.81	9.25	4.63	8.31	5.49	5.23	Call money rate
Brazil	26.03	26.03	26.03	24.03	24.03	24.03	34.03	36.03	36.30	Discount rate
Canada	5.99	3.56	3.56	5.47	7.83	7.40	8.87	7.33	8.67	Treasury bill rate
Denmark	10.57	10.67	10.37	11.08	14.55	13.10	13.21	14.06	14.06	Government bond yield
France	8.68	5.84	4.95	8.91	12.91	7.92	8.56	9.07	7.98	Call money rate
W. Germany	8.65	6.06	4.30	10.19	8.87	4.41	3.89	4.14	3.40	Call money rate
Israel	12.00	12.00	12.00	12.00	19.00	15.00	18.30	23.10	28.00	Bank rate on deposits
Italy	7.73	7.00	6.59	6.92	9.61	10.04	12.66	14.71	13.70	Government bond yield (medium term)
Japan	8.29	6.42	4.72	7.16	12.54	10.67	6.98	5.68	4.36	Call money rate
Netherlands	7.96	4.85	1.93	6.44	9.20	4.17	7.28	3.80	6.50	Call money rate
Norway	6.29	6.40	6.27	6.19	7.10	7.29	17.25	7.39	8.45	Government bond yield
S. Africa	4.39	5.38	5.30	3.18	5.43	6.12	7.44	7.87	7.53	Treasury bill rate
Sweden	7.39	7.23	7.29	7.39	7.79	8.79	9.28	9.74	8.60	Government bond yield
Switzerland	5.82	5.27	4.97	5.60	7.15	6.44	4.99	4.05	1.07	Government bond yield
U.K.	7.01	5.57	5.54	9.34	11.37	10.18	11.12	7.68	8.51	Treasury bill rate
U.S.A.	6.44	4.34	4.07	7.03	7.87	5.82	4.99	5.27	7.22	Treasury bill rate

SOURCE: [2]; Bank of Israel Examiner of the Banks report, various issues (Israel only).

TABLE 2

AVERAGE RETURN ON FOREIGN CURRENCY HOLDING: U.S. INVESTOR'S VIEWPOINT (IN PERCENT)

	Monthly			Quarterly			Seminannuai		
	Cap. Gains	Interest	Total	Cap. Gains	Interest	Total	Cap. Gains	Interest	Total
Australia	0.05	0.62	0.66	0.11	1.85	1.96	0.20	3.74	3.93
Belgium	0.53	0.52	1.06	1.64	1.57	3.25	3.31	3.17	6.60
Brazil	−1.80	2.11	0.27	−5.26	6.45	0.85	−10.44	13.34	1.45
Canada	−0.10	0.53	0.43	−0.30	1.59	1.29	−0.58	3.20	2.60
Denmark	0.39	0.98	1.37	1.19	2.96	4.20	2.41	6.02	8.58
France	0.28	0.67	0.95	0.86	2.01	2.89	1.78	4.07	5.94
W. Germany	0.68	0.48	1.17	2.11	1.46	3.61	4.29	2.95	7.39
Israel	−1.42	1.30	−0.14	−4.18	3.94	−0.43	−8.22	8.06	−0.95
Italy	−0.24	0.79	0.54	−0.68	2.38	1.68	−1.47	4.81	3.27
Japan	0.64	0.60	1.24	1.76	1.80	3.58	3.58	3.64	7.31
Netherlands	0.60	0.47	1.07	1.82	1.41	3.26	3.61	2.85	6.58
Norway	0.34	0.65	0.99	1.07	1.95	3.04	2.10	3.95	6.13
S. Africa	−0.15	0.47	0.32	−0.45	1.43	0.97	−0.88	2.88	1.96
Sweden	0.19	0.66	0.85	0.61	1.98	2.60	1.16	4.00	5.20
Switzerland	0.93	0.41	1.34	2.85	1.23	4.12	5.75	2.48	8.37
U.K.	−0.19	0.68	0.49	−0.54	2.05	1.50	−1.13	4.15	2.96
U.S.A.	0.0	0.48	0.48	0.0	1.44	1.44	0.0	2.90	2.90

NOTES: Cap. Gains = mean exchange rate capital gains $E(R)$; Interest = mean interest on deposits $E(RF)$; Total = mean total return $E(R + RF + R^*RF)$ including capital gains and interest.

There is a crucial assumption that is implicit throughout the paper. We assume that each investor is an atomistic competitor and cannot affect through his own actions the exchange rate. This is not realistic for small countries such as Denmark, but it is nonetheless crucial to our analysis just as it is in any portfolio problem concerning risky assets.

Using the basic total returns from the U.S. point of view,[1] we also calculated the standard deviation of each currency as well as the correlation matrix of the other sixteen countries. We report the standard deviations later in the text when we present the efficient frontier, while the correlation matrices for monthly, quarterly, and semiannual rates of return are given in the Appendix. We repeated all the calculations for all seventeen points of view, but, for the sake of brevity, we will give only a summary of the results and will not report the basic figures.

Methodology

The derivation of the optimal diversification strategy in foreign currencies is accomplished by the familiar mean-variance rule [7, 10]. The individual's risky portfolio can be represented by an n-dimensional vector $\mathbf{x}$ where the component x_i is the proportion invested in risky asset i. The mean-variance efficient portfolio yielding a mean return u_p is obtained by solving

$$\min \sigma_p^2 = \mathbf{x}' \, \Omega \, \mathbf{x}$$

subject to

$$u_p = \mathbf{x}' \, \mathbf{u}$$

and

$$\Sigma x_i = 1 = \mathbf{1}' \, \mathbf{x}.$$

Here, Ω is the n by n variance-covariance matrix of returns, $\mathbf{u}$ is the n-dimensional mean return vector, and $\mathbf{1}$ is the n-dimensional unit vector. This classical optimization problem does not restrict the signs of the x_i to be positive. The optimal strategy is

$$\mathbf{x} = \Omega^{-1} (\mathbf{u} \; \mathbf{1}) A^{-1} \begin{pmatrix} u_p \\ 1 \end{pmatrix} ,$$

where A is a 2×2 symmetric matrix given by

[1]It is assumed that "point of view" refers to the base currency being used exclusively by the investor. For example, if a U.S. investor consumes 20 percent of German imports and 80 percent U.S. goods, a new base, accounting for the German proportion, should be used as the "domestic" currency. We ignore this problem and assume that a U.S. investor exclusively uses dollars for consumption. Treatment of this could easily be handled, however.

$$A = (\mathbf{u}\ \mathbf{1})'\ \Omega^{-1}\ (\mathbf{u}\ \mathbf{1}) = \begin{pmatrix} \mathbf{u}'\ \Omega^{-1}\ \mathbf{u} & \mathbf{u}'\Omega^{-1}\mathbf{1} \\ \mathbf{u}'\ \Omega^{-1}\ \mathbf{1} & \mathbf{1}'\ \Omega^{-1}\ \mathbf{1} \end{pmatrix} .$$

By varying u_p we obtain the set of mean-variance efficient portfolios [8].

The efficient portfolio **x** contains positive and negative values which represent short sales, which in this context occur as borrowing the foreign currency to augment investment in the optimal combination of long (positive x_i) positions in other currencies. Exclusion of short sales requires the additional constraint that

$$\mathbf{x} \geq 0 \text{ or } x_i \geq 0\ i=1 \ldots n .$$

The solution to this problem consists of assets (generally very few) held long and zero proportions for all other assets. No borrowing of foreign currencies is allowed. As a result, the constraint $\Sigma x_i = 1$ implies that $0 \leq x_i \leq 1$ for all i and $x_i = 1$ can obtain for one asset only.

If in addition to n risky assets the individual may invest in a riskless asset yielding a return r_f, the entire set of mean-variance efficient portfolios is reduced, under certain well-known conditions (Sharpe [9], Lintner [6]) to a single optimal portfolio which in the mean return-standard deviation space is the tangency portfolio between the efficient set of risky portfolios and the ray emanating from the risk-free asset r_f.

In the next section this analytical approach is applied to the management of foreign currency balances both with and without short sales. It is obvious that most large companies are able to borrow in other countries, thus the inclusion of short sales is more realistic.

3. EMPIRICAL FINDINGS

It is obvious that the optimum diversification strategy is a function of the assumed risk-free interest rate paid on dollars in the U.S. If we consider only the capital gain return (with no borrowing), we obtain the optimal investment as holding 100 percent Swiss francs. This is true for all three horizons. However, if total return is considered, the optimal portfolio requires diversification among the currencies of Denmark, Japan, Canada, and Australia. Note that the Swiss franc with its high capital gain is eliminated from the efficient portfolio because of the low interest return and its high correlation with the Danish krone.

Short Positions Forbidden

Table 3 presents the optimal diversification strategy for one-, three-, and six-month horizons for different risk-free U.S. interest rates without short selling allowed. The ex post interest rates for the U.S. used were 0.48 percent per month, 1.44 percent per quarter, and 2.9 percent for semiannual horizons. The main results of this table are as follows.

TABLE 3

OPTIMAL INVESTMENT STRATEGIES FOR VARIOUS HORIZONS, U.S. VIEWPOINT, WITHOUT SHORT SALES (IN PERCENT)

Currency of:	1-Month (r_f = 0.48)	3-Month (r_f = 1.44)	6-Month (r_f = 2.9)
Australia			8.18
Canada			0.19
Denmark	88.60	71.27	65.00
Japan	9.34	28.73	26.63
Switzerland	2.06		
Total	100	100	100
Portfolio expected return	1.36	4.02	7.85
Portfolio standard deviation	2.77	1.42	7.2

1. In all cases, no more than four currencies are included in the optimal portfolio. The other currencies have $x_i = 0$ (no shorts allowed).
2. The optimal strategy is not invariant to the investment horizon. The one-month horizon ($r_f = 0.48$ percent) requires 88.6 percent in the Danish krone, 9.34 percent in the Japanese yen, and about 2 percent in Swiss francs. However, if the firm has a three-month horizon only two currencies appear in the efficient portfolio; 28.73 percent in the Japanese yen and 71.27 percent in the Danish krone. For the six-month horizon about 27 percent of the optimal portfolio is in Japanese yen, 65 percent in Danish krone, and the remainder in Australian and Canadian currencies. The difference in the portfolios results from the variation in value of the dollar over the longer time period, which affects the variance-covariance matrix and thus alters the optimal portfolio. It is interesting to note that in almost all cases the same currencies are included in the different portfolios.
3. The fact that the Swiss franc and German mark with relatively high total returns (1.34 percent and 1.17 percent per month, respectively) are not included in the optimal portfolios, while the yen with a 1.24 percent return appears significantly in all portfolios, is a result of the high correlation between the Danish krone and the mark (0.92) and Swiss franc (0.79) (see Appendix A). The yen is not highly correlated with the krone (0.38). This shows that the combination of yen and krone dominates any other combination of currencies.

These results point out the potential gain from diversification in foreign currencies for American investors since the returns are greater than what could be earned with the risk-free rate in the U.S.

Short Positions Allowed

Table 4 reports the optimal investment strategy when borrowing ("short position") of any foreign currency is allowed. Results are given for one-, three-, and six-month horizons. The main results of the table are as follows.

TABLE 4

OPTIMAL INVESTMENT STRATEGIES FOR VARIOUS HORIZONS, U.S. VIEWPOINT, WITH SHORT SALES

Currency of:	1-Month	3-Month	6-Month
Australia	−14.55	59.84	160.01
Belgium	−343.48	−162.97	−1415.23
Brazil	−8.94	−11.84	−92.53
Canada	108.34	115.90	−51.28
Denmark	1003.88	1133.11	682.06
France	−84.19	−151.96	−266.98
W. Germany	53.75	−33.28	−51.73
Israel	−25.58	−20.29	85.37
Italy	27.94	37.33	654.38
Japan	5.40	59.75	234.76
Netherlands	−142.50	−176.66	1486.89
Norway	19.24	−65.25	800.17
S. Africa	−89.88	−86.75	−695.65
Sweden	−414.58	−470.55	−960.92
Switzerland	76.78	−49.91	117.47
U.K.	−71.63	−76.50	−586.80
Total	100.0	99.97	99.99
Portfolio expected return	6.09	18.08	62.45
Portfolio standard deviation	9.25	14.80	28.98

NOTES: Initial portfolio = \$100. Amounts of currency in dollars. Total deviates slightly from \$100.00 due to rounding errors.

1. With short positions, all sixteen currencies are included in the portfolios with about half of the currencies being held short and the other half being held long.
2. The optimal portfolio is not invariant to the time horizon. For example, the Australian currency is held short for the one-month horizon while for the three- and six-month horizons it is held long. Similar results appear for the German mark.
3. The Danish krone and Japanese yen again comprise a large part of the long positions when short sales are allowed.
4. Because of its high correlation with other currencies (Appendix A) and in spite of its high total return, the German mark is held short in the three- and six-month horizon portfolios. Thus, we see that the ''diversification motive'' dominates the ''profitability motive.''
5. Comparison of the portfolio's expected return with and without short sales demonstrates that by borrowing one currency and lending another, the American investor can significantly increase the average return. This benefit from borrowing is illustrated in Figures 1a, 1b, and 1c. In all three cases the efficient frontier with short sales lies northwest to that without short sales. The vertical distance between the two frontiers indicates the potential additional profit from borrowing in the international money market without changing the portfolio's risk.

Figure 2 illustrates the relationship of the mean-variance efficient frontier for quarterly data when capital gains are the sole source of return and then with interest return included. The difference between the curves indicates the gravity of the error in deriving the efficient set without the interest return (see Levy and Sarnat [5]).

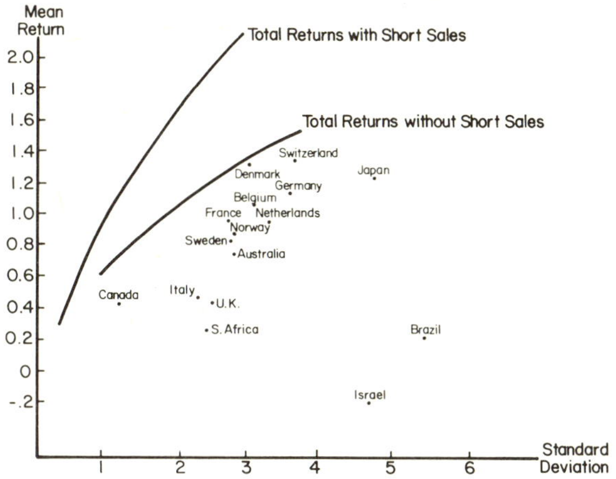

FIG. 1a. Mean-Variance Efficient Sets: Monthly Data.

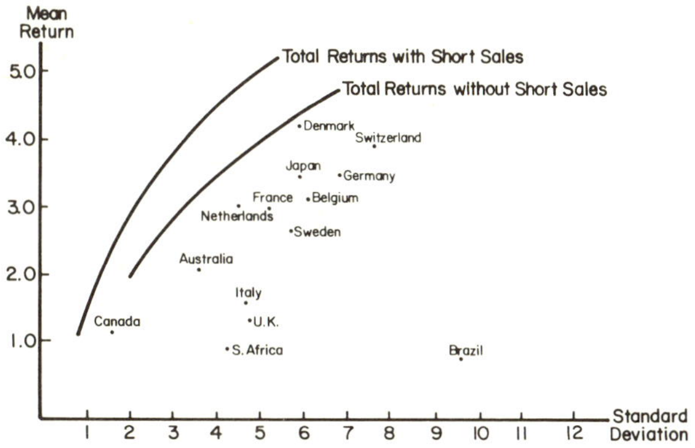

FIG. 1b. Mean-Variance Efficient Sets: Quarterly Data.

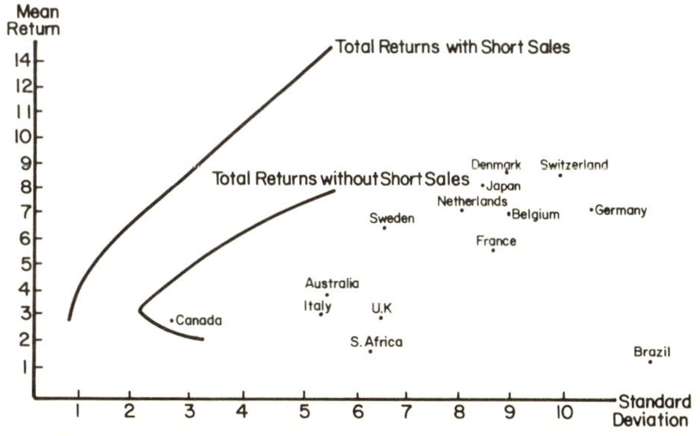

FIG. 1c. Mean-Variance Efficient Sets: Semiannual Data.

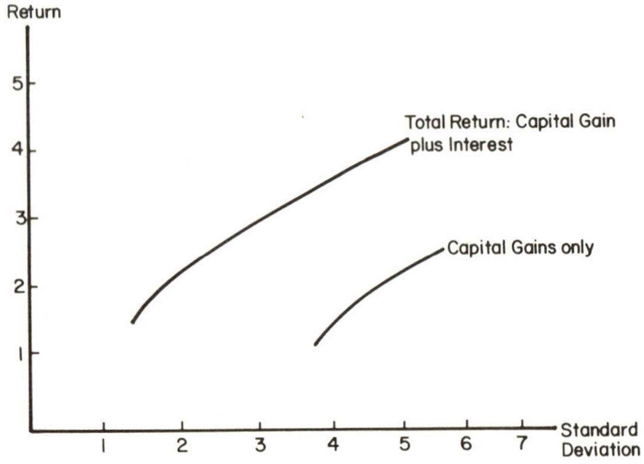

FIG. 2. Mean-Variance Efficient Sets for Capital Gains only and for Total Return: Quarterly Data, without Short Sales.

Other Points of View

So far the empirical results illustrate the potential gain from diversification to the American investor who holds foreign currencies. The same data have been used to calculate the expected returns, variances, and covariances from the point of view of the investors of each of the seventeen countries. The optimal portfolio for each point of view was calculated using the risk-free interest rate prevailing in the particular country. All three investment horizons were used, but for brevity we report in Table 5 only the results for quarterly investment horizon.

As can be seen in Table 5 the Danish krone is included in all portfolios and accounts for a significant proportion of the investment. With regard to other currencies, all investors would diversify in a very limited number of currencies. Since the German mark and the Dutch guilder appear in insignificant proportions, we do not

TABLE 5

THE COMPOSITION OF OPTIMAL PORTFOLIOS OF CURRENCIES FROM VARIOUS POINTS OF VIEW (WITHOUT SHORT SALES)

	Currencies Held (in percent)				
Investor Point of View	Danish krone	Japanese yen	Dutch guilder	Swiss franc	German mark
Australia	76.30	23.7			
Belgium	92.72		0.05	7.23	
Brazil	100.00				
Canada	73.91	26.09			
Denmark		5.49		93.75	0.76
France	88.97	11.03			
W. Germany	80.37		19.63		
Israel	99.72	0.28			
Italy	78.98	21.02			
Japan	98.26	1.74			
Netherlands	98.39				1.61
Norway	80.37			19.63	
S. Africa	80.73	19.27			
Sweden	100.00				
Switzerland	100.00				
U.K.	40.99	35.86		23.15	
U.S.A.	71.27	28.73			

hesitate to say, at least in an ex post sense, that only three currencies are relevant in choosing the optimal portfolio. These three currencies are the Danish krone, Swiss franc, and Japanese yen. While all investors agree to the central importance of the Danish krone, there is disagreement as to the importance of long positions in the yen and Swiss franc. For example, a Norwegian investor would hold about 80 percent of the portfolio in the Danish krone with 20 percent in Swiss francs, while a South African investor also would hold about 80 percent in krone yet put the other 20 percent in yen. Other relevant features of Table 5 are the following.

1. The Danish krone is the sole currency in seven of sixteen portfolios with almost no diversification in other currencies. This can be explained by the high return on the krone and its relatively low risk as compared to the other high return currencies. From the U.S. point of view, the krone returned 4.197 percent with standard deviation of 5.732 percent, while the Swiss franc returned 4.119 percent with a 6.835 percent standard deviation, and the yen returned 3.581 percent with a standard deviation of 5.5 percent. Also, since the Swiss franc is highly correlated with the krone, there is little motive for diversification.
2. The optimal portfolio is not invariant to the perspective taken by the investor. When we translate the returns to other points of view, different parameters for the optimization are generated thus giving different portfolios. A good illustration is the aforementioned discrepancy in the Norwegian and South African portfolios. The South African puts the remainder of the portfolio in yen while the Norwegian invests in Swiss francs. The explanation lies in the correlation of the return on the Danish krone (which comprises 80 percent of both portfolios) with the yen and Swiss franc. The correlation of the krone's return with the yen is 0.6 and with the Swiss franc is 0.85 from the South African point of view and 0.44 and 0.3, respectively, from the Norwegian investor's point of view. Thus, the changes in correlations from translating points of view induce heterogeneity in the portfolios.
3. The most diversified portfolio is of the British investor. This is due to similar high returns on many currencies relative to the pound, which is indicative of the pound's general decline during the period.

Table 5 represents only the portfolios constructed under the assumption of no borrowing. The results with borrowing for the seventeen different perspectives are similar to that obtained earlier for the U.S. investor. Returns are significantly increased and only four to six currencies are held long with all others being borrowed. In these portfolios, the Swiss franc becomes a short position in many portfolios while some currencies highly correlated with the franc are held long.

As was indicated before, investors may want to put a constraint on the proportion of the Danish currency in their portfolio since the market for this currency is small. Table 6 reports the optimal investment strategies (without short sales) for monthly time horizons with the Danish krone excluded from consideration. Ten different points of view were considered and virtually all investors concentrated their portfolios in three currencies: the mark, yen, and Swiss franc. In most cases, the mark and the franc constituted about 80 to 90 percent of the portfolio with the

TABLE 6

OPTIMAL PORTFOLIOS WITH DANISH KRONE EXCLUDED

Portfolio Components	Investor Viewpoint									
	U.S.	Australia	Belgium	Canada	France	Italy	South Africa	Netherlands	Sweden	U.K.
Australia										
Belgium										
Brazil										
Canada										
France										
W. Germany	11.6		49.3	18.6	19.9	11.7	21.6	49.8	54.0	28.8
Israel										
Italy										
Japan	20.9	17.0	4.5	19.6	7.2	11.0	15.0	3.3	6.7	12.6
Netherlands										
Norway									1.0	
S. Africa										
Sweden										
Switzerland	67.5	83.0	46.2	62.8	72.9	77.32	63.4	46.9	38.3	58.6
U.K.										
U.S.A.										
Total	100%	100%	100%	100%	100%	100%	100%	100%	100%	100%
Portfolio mean	1.3	1.33	0.72	1.40	1.03	1.57	1.48	0.66	1.05	1.49
Portfolio standard deviation	3.09	3.66	1.22	3.23	2.73	2.93	3.38	1.25	1.72	2.67

remainder in yen. Investors domiciled in Holland and Belgium invest almost equally in the franc and mark with a very small proportion going to the yen (3.3 percent and 4.5 percent, respectively). The American investor invests heavily in Swiss francs (67.5 percent) with 20.9 percent in yen and only 11.6 percent in marks.

The optimal portfolios for other points of view and different time horizons yielded the same results, namely that only three or four currencies were held. However, the proportions of currencies held in the portfolios are not the same when the time horizon is changed. The yen increases substantially with increase in the time horizon. For quarterly and semiannual horizons the yen constitutes 40–50 percent of an American investor's portfolio, whereas before it was only 20 percent. Similarly, the U.K. investor increases his holdings of yen to 24–48 percent. Thus, although the time horizon has little impact on which currencies are held, it does have a major impact on the optimal proportions.

4. CONCLUDING REMARKS

The last decade saw the fall of fixed exchange rates and the advent of fluctuating currency values, which have opened many investment opportunities for all investors, in particular, holders of large amounts of cash. Most large firms use these opportunities to increase the return from cash management and either implicitly or explicitly employ portfolio diversification techniques analyzed in this paper.

The potential gain from diversification in foreign currencies has been estimated for all points of view and for various assumed investment horizons. Aside from the extremely strong showing of the Danish krone in long positions, other currencies that appear as long positions are the yen, Swiss francs, and German marks. Substitution of the mark for the krone may be accomplished with little loss of return due to the high correlation between the two.

In spite of the fact that the same basic data are used, and even if we assume homogenous expectations, optimal portfolios would differ from country to country. This results from the fact that the basic data change as they are translated from perspective to perspective.

Finally, it is important to note that we have used ex post data to demonstrate the gain from diversification, whereas mean-variance analysis based on ex post data tends to systematically underestimate the variance of the efficient portfolio with a given mean because of selection bias in favor of securities with historically low variance. Clearly, decisions must be based on ex ante data, but the best estimates of correlations are probably those calculated from ex post data. Although return estimates may vary widely, the principal motive for diversification will remain, and the technique outlined in this paper can be used to derive the optimal portfolio of foreign currency holdings. As with ex post data, in employing ex ante data one would expect that the efficient portfolios generally depend on both "point of view" and the assumed "investment horizon," and some benefit from proper diversification among various currencies is expected.

APPENDIX A

CORRELATION MATRIX OF U.S. INVESTOR'S VIEWPOINT, TOTAL RETURNS

	Australia	Belgium	Brazil	Canada	Denmark	France	W. Germany
Monthly Data							
Australia	1.0000	0.3638	0.1244	0.3709	0.3628	0.3126	0.3463
Belgium	0.3638	1.0000	−0.0115	0.1372	0.9433	0.8202	0.9396
Brazil	0.1244	−0.0115	1.0000	−0.0277	0.0091	−0.0041	−0.0057
Canada	0.3709	0.1372	−0.0277	1.0000	0.1188	0.0378	0.1034
Denmark	0.3628	0.9433	0.0091	0.1188	1.0000	0.8362	0.9246
France	0.3126	0.8202	−0.0041	0.0378	0.8362	1.0000	0.8056
W. Germany	0.3463	0.9396	−0.0057	0.1034	0.9246	0.8056	1.0000
Israel	0.0072	−0.0021	−0.0012	−0.0394	0.0329	0.0392	−0.0298
Italy	0.1944	0.4945	0.0209	−0.1267	0.4957	0.5904	0.4628
Japan	0.2059	0.3534	−0.0069	−0.0054	0.3830	0.2953	0.3542
Netherlands	0.3758	0.9641	0.0045	0.1198	0.9292	0.8170	0.9466
Norway	0.3051	0.8790	0.0257	0.1204	0.8940	0.7798	0.8724
S. Africa	0.2757	0.3220	−0.0269	−0.0241	0.3242	0.2748	0.3553
Sweden	0.2776	0.8677	−0.0004	0.0966	0.9050	0.7697	0.8607
Switzerland	0.3338	0.7987	−0.0022	0.0250	0.7883	0.7184	0.8114
U.K.	0.2235	0.6145	−0.0303	0.0029	0.5871	0.5912	0.5656
Quarterly Data							
Australia	1.0000	0.3194	0.0688	0.0437	0.3067	0.3131	0.3310
Belgium	0.3194	1.0000	0.0358	0.0415	0.9591	0.7933	0.9320
Brazil	0.0688	0.0358	1.0000	−0.0842	0.0542	0.0705	0.0762
Canada	0.0437	0.0415	−0.0842	1.0000	0.0445	−0.1680	0.0535
Denmark	0.3067	0.9591	0.0542	0.0445	1.0000	0.8482	0.9418
France	0.3131	0.7933	0.0705	−0.1680	0.8482	1.0000	0.7864
W. Germany	0.3310	0.9320	0.0762	0.0535	0.9418	0.7864	1.0000
Israel	−0.1077	−0.2151	0.0091	−0.0802	−0.1915	−0.1406	−0.1735
Italy	0.2823	0.5219	0.0843	−0.2333	0.5160	0.5963	0.4638
Japan	0.4018	0.6038	0.0872	0.0226	0.6176	0.6403	0.5468
Netherlands	0.3339	0.9691	0.0604	0.0357	0.9533	0.7923	0.9375
Norway	0.3172	0.9262	0.0599	0.1368	0.9291	0.7013	0.9118
S. Africa	0.3839	0.3092	0.0374	−0.1658	0.2839	0.2405	0.3272
Sweden	0.2592	0.9229	0.0267	0.1674	0.9378	0.7846	0.8917
Switzerland	0.3641	0.8441	0.0501	0.0432	0.8582	0.7246	0.8700
U.K.	0.2386	0.6109	0.0213	−0.2046	0.5842	0.6418	0.5610
Semiannual Data							
Australia	1.0000	0.1127	0.1535	0.0280	0.1594	0.1702	0.2724
Belgium	0.1127	1.0000	0.0468	−0.1672	0.9458	0.8502	0.9096
Brazil	0.1535	0.0468	1.0000	−0.0874	0.1055	0.1098	0.1469
Canada	0.0280	−0.1672	−0.0874	1.0000	−0.1646	−0.1714	−0.1240
Denmark	0.1594	0.9458	0.1055	−0.1646	1.0000	0.9067	0.9359
France	0.1702	0.8502	0.1098	−0.1714	0.9067	1.0000	0.8591
W. Germany	0.2724	0.9096	0.1469	−0.1240	0.9359	0.8591	1.0000
Israel	0.2316	−0.2438	−0.0122	0.0909	−0.1416	−0.1414	−0.1214
Italy	0.1351	0.5917	−0.0298	−0.4304	0.5409	0.6572	0.4129
Japan	0.2971	0.4991	0.0943	−0.0704	0.5259	0.6472	0.4675
Netherlands	0.1387	0.9794	0.0894	−0.1670	0.9499	0.8499	0.9348
Norway	0.0351	0.9122	0.1111	−0.0849	0.9156	0.7494	0.9229
S. Africa	0.4116	0.4610	0.1061	−3049	0.5441	0.4260	0.6201
Sweden	−0.0060	0.8822	0.0489	−0.0354	0.9093	0.8677	0.8413
Switzerland	0.1966	0.8051	0.1432	−0.1089	0.8509	0.8114	0.8538
U.K.	0.2751	0.7602	−0.0065	−0.2340	0.6593	0.7040	0.6533

LITERATURE CITED

1. *Business Week* (March 13, 1978), pp. 62–68.
2. *IMF International Financial Statistics,* various issues.
3. Levhari, David, and Haim Levy. "The Capital Asset Pricing Model and the Investment Horizon." *The Review of Economics and Statistics,* 59 (February 1977), 92–104.
4. Levy, Haim. "Portfolio Performance and the Investment Horizon." *Management Science,* 18 (August 1972), B645–53.
5. Levy, Haim, and Marshall Sarnat. "Exchange Rate Risk and the Optimal Diversification of Foreign Currency Holdings." *Journal of Money, Credit, and Banking,* 10 (November 1978), 453–63.
6. Lintner, John. "Security Prices, Risk and Maximal Gains from Diversification." *Journal of Finance,* 20 (December 1965), 587–615.
7. Markowitz, Harry M. "Portfolio Selection." *Journal of Finance,* 7 (March 1952), 77–91.

Israel	Italy	Japan	Netherlands	Norway	S. Africa	Sweden	Switzerland	U.K.
0.0072	0.1944	0.2059	0.3758	0.3051	0.2757	0.2776	0.3338	0.2235
−0.0021	0.4945	0.3534	0.9641	0.8790	0.3220	0.8677	0.7987	0.6145
−0.0012	0.0209	−0.0069	0.0045	0.0257	−0.0269	−0.0004	−0.0022	−0.0303
−0.0394	−0.1267	−0.0054	0.1198	0.1204	−0.0241	0.0966	0.0250	0.0029
0.0329	0.4957	0.3830	0.9292	0.8940	0.3242	0.9050	0.7833	0.5871
0.0392	0.5904	0.2953	0.8170	0.7798	0.2748	0.7697	0.7184	0.5912
−0.0298	0.4628	0.3542	0.9466	0.8724	0.3553	0.8607	0.8114	0.5656
1.0000	−0.300	−0.0281	−0.0122	−0.0347	0.1077	0.0275	−0.1018	0.0567
−0.0300	1.0000	0.1831	0.5244	0.4383	0.1239	0.5018	0.4962	0.4761
−0.0281	0.1831	1.0000	0.3365	0.3480	0.1333	0.3115	0.3431	0.2476
−0.0122	0.5244	0.3365	1.0000	0.8545	0.3442	0.8496	0.7938	0.5942
−0.0347	0.4383	0.3480	0.8545	1.0000	0.3098	0.8803	0.7488	0.5351
0.1077	0.1239	0.1333	0.3442	0.3098	1.0000	0.2306	0.3119	0.2235
0.0275	0.5018	0.3115	0.8496	0.8803	0.2306	1.0000	0.7096	0.5394
−0.1018	0.4962	0.3431	0.7938	0.7488	0.3119	0.7096	1.0000	0.5361
0.0567	0.4761	0.2476	0.5942	0.5351	0.2235	0.5394	0.5361	1.0000
−0.1077	0.2823	0.4018	0.3339	0.3172	0.3839	0.2592	0.3641	0.2386
−0.2151	0.5219	0.6038	0.9691	0.9262	0.3092	0.9229	0.8441	0.6109
0.0091	0.0843	0.0872	0.0604	0.0599	0.0374	0.0267	0.0501	0.0213
−0.0802	−0.2333	0.0226	0.0357	0.1368	−0.1658	0.1674	0.0432	−0.2046
−0.1915	0.5160	0.6176	0.9533	0.9291	0.2839	0.9378	0.8582	0.5842
−0.1406	0.5963	0.6403	0.7923	0.7013	0.2405	0.7846	0.7246	0.6418
−0.1735	0.4638	0.5468	0.9375	0.9118	0.3272	0.8917	0.8700	0.5610
1.0000	−0.1681	−0.1350	−0.1904	−0.2318	0.0492	−0.1912	−0.3592	−0.2208
−0.1681	1.0000	0.5063	0.5733	0.4222	0.0343	0.5193	0.4395	0.5832
−0.1350	0.5063	1.0000	0.5538	0.5460	0.2250	0.5496	0.6229	0.6193
−0.1904	0.5733	0.5538	1.0000	0.9038	0.2426	0.9171	0.8117	0.5732
−0.2318	0.4222	0.5460	0.9038	1.0000	0.2996	0.9145	0.8565	0.5782
0.0492	0.0343	0.2250	0.2426	0.2996	1.0000	0.2024	0.2096	0.2472
−0.1912	0.5193	0.5496	0.9171	0.9145	0.2024	1.0000	0.7814	0.5016
−0.3592	0.4395	0.6229	0.8117	0.8565	0.2096	0.7814	1.0000	0.6415
−0.2208	0.5832	0.6193	0.5732	0.5782	0.2472	0.5016	0.6415	1.0000
0.2316	0.1351	0.2971	0.1387	0.0351	0.4116	−0.0060	0.1966	0.2751
−0.2438	0.5917	0.4991	0.9794	0.9122	0.4610	0.8822	0.8051	0.7602
−0.0122	−0.0298	0.0943	0.0894	0.1111	0.1061	0.0489	0.1432	−0.0065
0.0909	−0.4304	−0.0704	−0.1670	−0.0849	−0.3049	−0.0354	−0.1089	−0.2340
−0.1416	0.5409	0.5259	0.9499	0.9156	0.5441	0.9093	0.8509	0.6593
−0.1414	0.6572	0.6472	0.8499	0.7494	0.4260	0.8677	0.8114	0.7040
−0.1214	0.4129	0.4675	0.9348	0.9229	0.6201	0.8413	0.8538	0.6533
1.0000	−0.1706	−0.2809	−0.1976	−0.1457	0.2354	−0.0035	−0.4899	−0.4495
−0.1706	1.0000	0.5823	0.5172	0.3023	0.2940	0.4753	0.4655	0.6966
−0.2809	0.5823	1.0000	0.4571	0.3229	0.2523	0.4844	0.5295	0.4956
−0.1976	0.5172	0.4571	1.0000	0.9160	0.5189	0.8741	0.8026	0.7493
−0.1457	0.3023	0.3229	0.9160	1.0000	0.5399	0.8700	0.7643	0.5235
0.2354	0.2940	0.2523	0.5189	0.5399	1.0000	0.3771	0.4162	0.3334
−0.0035	0.4753	0.4844	0.8741	0.8700	0.3771	1.0000	0.6899	0.4856
−0.4899	0.4655	0.5295	0.8026	0.7643	0.4162	0.6899	1.0000	0.7267
−0.4495	0.6966	0.4956	0.7493	0.5235	0.3334	0.4856	0.7267	1.0000

8. Roll, Richard. "A Critique of the Asset Pricing Theory's Tests, Part I: On Past and Potential Testability of the Theory." *Journal of Financial Economics,* 4 (March 1977), 129–76.

9. Sharpe, William F. "Capital Asset Prices: A Theory of Market Equilibrium Under Conditions of Risk." *Journal of Finance,* 19 (September 1964), 425–42.

10. Tobin, James. "Liquidity Preference as Behavior Towards Risk." *Review of Economic Studies,* 25 (February 1958), 65–86.

JOHN T. CUDDINGTON*

Money, Income, and Causality in the United Kingdom

An Empirical Reexamination

1. INTRODUCTION

SINCE THE REDUCED-FORM ECONOMETRIC EXERCISES of Friedman and Meiselman [2], considerable research has been undertaken to determine the nature of the relationship running from money to income as well as the importance of "reverse causation" from income to money. Using an empirically testable defintion of causality proposed by Granger [4], Sims [7] developed an econometric technique to test for unidirectional causality in a two-variable system. In an application to U.S. nominal GNP and money data from 1949.III to 1968.IV, he reported that "the main empirical finding is that the hypothesis that causality is unidirectional from money to income agrees with the postwar U.S. data, whereas the hypothesis that causality is unidirectional from income to money is rejected" [7, p. 540].

To examine the generality of Sims's results, Williams, Goodhart, and Gowland [8] (W-G-G) undertook a similar study using U.K. data from 1958.I to 1971.III, a period when the Bretton Woods fixed exchange rate system prevailed. They found that neither the causal relationship from money to income nor reverse causality from

*This is a condensed version of Stanford University CREG Research Memorandum No. 234 with the same title. Helpful comments and suggestions from Paul Evans, Edgar Feige, Bert Hickman, and Michael Parkin are gratefully acknowledged. I would like to thank Beth Van Zummerman for computational assistance in the preliminary stages of this study.

JOHN T. CUDDINGTON *is assistant professor of economics, Stanford University.*

0022-2879/81/0881-0342$00.50/0
JOURNAL OF MONEY, CREDIT, AND BANKING, vol. 13, no. 3 (August 1981)

income to money was significant. Rejection of the first hypothesis was decisive but rejection of the second was marginal at the 5 percent significance level. W-G-G conclude that "this suggests at least the possibility of unidirectional causality from G.D.P. to M_n" [8, p. 421]. As they point out at the beginning of their paper,

> There were a number of reasons for doubting whether Sims' results would hold within a U.K. context. Unlike the United States, the United Kingdom is a relatively small, open economy which during the observation period maintained a regime of fixed exchange rates. Under such circumstances the private sector can more easily adjust their money holdings to their incomes by transfers of funds over the exchanges (subject to exchange control), than in a virtually closed economy such as the U.S. Furthermore the conduct of monetary policy during the 1960s was influenced by the precepts of the Radcliffe Committee Report that 'The authorities thus have to regard the structure of interest rates rather than the supply of money as the centre-piece of the monetary mechanism' (p. 135). In so far as the authorities primarily aim to regulate the structure of interest rates, movements in the money stock can be expected to respond to movements in nominal income. [8, p. 417]

In an attempt to draw together the findings of Sims for the U.S. and W-G-G for the U.K., Putnam and Wilford [6] (P-W) recently suggested the use of a monetary model of the balance of payments, noting the differing roles of the two countries under the Bretton Woods fixed exchange rate system. They claim, "the ability of the reserve currency country to create international reserve assets plays the primary role in explaining the asymmetrical nature of the system and the empirical results of Sims, and Williams, Goodhart, and Gowland" [6, p. 423]. The present paper puts their conjecture to the empirical test. It also examines the alternative explanation that the Bank of England attempts to control interest rates rather than the monetary base.

2. METHODOLOGY

Throughout this study the Granger causal detection method, rather than the asymptotically equivalent test proposed by Sims, is employed. The choice was based on two considerations. First, W-G-G used the Sims test and obtained inconclusive results regarding the causal linkages between U.K. money and income. It seemed worthwhile to apply the Granger test to the same data base for comparative purposes. Second, recent research has shown that the Sims test is extremely sensitive to changes in the prefiltering procedure (see [1, p. 532]). A recent paper by Geweke, Meese, and Dent [3, p. 38] comes out in favor of the Granger test over the Sims test on the basis of analytical results as well as simulation exercises.

Granger's procedure implies that if y is not caused by x, then lagged values of x should be of no assistance in predicting y once the past history of y has been taken into account. Consequently, in a regression of y on its own lagged values and lagged values of x, the latter variables should not be statistically significant. To ensure that the hypothesis tests are not biased by trends or seasonal fluctuations in the time series, a constant, a time trend, and seasonal dummies were included in all regressions reported in this paper.

It should be emphasized that all causality tests in this paper are *bivariate* in nature. Consequently, the possibility exists of spuriously detecting causality between two variables due to the omission of additional variables that are causally prior to either of the two variables under consideration. Nevertheless, the use of the bivariate causal detection framework should certainly not be discarded as a useless tool for the applied econometrician.

3. MONEY-INCOME CAUSALITY IN THE U.K.

Granger causal detection method is applied to British data from 1958.I to 1971. III. In order to test whether money (M_{uk}) "causes" nominal income (Y_{uk}), income is regressed on four of its lagged values and four lagged values of money.[1] A second regression reverses the role of M_{uk} and Y_{uk} in order to test the hypothesis that income does not cause money. The results are reported in Table 1. Taken together these tests indicate that there is statistically significant unidirectional causality running from U.K. income to U.K. money—just the opposite of what Sims found for the U.S. These results reinforce the tentative conclusions reached by W-G-G regarding reverse causality in the U.K.

TABLE 1

MONEY-INCOME CAUSALITY IN THE U.K. (1958.I–1971.III)

	$F(4,38)$	$\bar{R}^2$
1. M_{uk} does not cause Y_{uk}	1.61	0.995
2. Y_{uk} does not cause M_{uk}	5.32*	0.994

NOTE: The critical values for F (4.38) at the 1 percent and 5 percent levels are 3.86 and 2.62, respectively.
*Significant at the 1 percent level.

4. THE MONETARY MODEL

Having confirmed W-G-G's results, the monetary model suggested by P-W is now examined. The model has the following implications:

1. "The reserve currency country can control its money supply, while other countries cannot" [6, p. 425].
2. "The reserve currency country can influence its price level, while other countries must accept prices as determined on unified world markets" [6, p. 425].
3. Monetary expansion in the reserve currency country will cause prices and (nominal) incomes in all countries to increase.

[1]Premature truncation of the lag length of the dependent variable can bias the causality tests. To guard against such "spurious causality," preliminary tests on the lag lengths were carried out. For each variable in the paper, four and eight lag autoregressive representations were estimated. In all cases, the joint hypothesis that the lags five through eight are not significantly different from zero could not be rejected. Hence, four lags are used throughout.

4. The resultant increase in money demand in non-reserve-currency (NRC) countries leads to balance of payments surpluses.
5. For an NRC country, a balance of payments surplus causes an increase in the domestic money supply, implying no sterlization at least in the long run.
6. From a position of monetary equilibrium *if* an NRC country attempts to increase its money supply, there will be a deterioration in the balance of payments. (The resultant reserve outflow ultimately returns the money supply to its original level.)

These implications may be recast as a number of testable hypotheses. Implication 1 suggests that the U.S. money supply is exogenous, at least from the point of view of the U.K. and other NRC countries. In contrast, the U.K. money supply cannot be controlled by British monetary authorities. Ultimately, it depends on U.S. monetary policy via the inflow or outflow of foreign exchange reserves. This suggests two hypotheses.

Hypothesis 1. The U.S. money supply is exogenous with respect to changes in the U.K. money supply, implying that M_{uk} does not Granger-cause M_{us}.

Hypothesis 2. M_{us} Granger-causes M_{uk}.

Table 2 reports on tests of these and other hypotheses from the monetary model using the 1958.I to 1971.III data base employed by W-G-G. As predicted by the theory, the U.S. money supply is found to be exogenous with respect to the U.K. money supply. Also, the causal effect of M_{us} and M_{uk} is significant at the 5 percent (but not the 1 percent) level.

TABLE 2

GRANGER TESTS FOR THE MONETARY MODEL OF A SMALL OPEN ECONOMY (1958.I–1971.III)

	Monetary Model predicts	$F(4,38)$ Ratio	$\bar{R}^2$
1. M_{uk} does not cause M_{us}	accept	1.83	0.999
2. M_{us} does not cause M_{uk}	reject	2.66*	0.992
3. M_{us} does not cause P_{us}	reject	6.59**	0.999
4. M_{uk} does not cause P_{uk}	accept	1.33	0.996
5. M_{us} does not cause P_{uk}	reject	3.95**	0.997
6. M_{us} does not cause Y_{uk}	reject	0.70	0.994
7. M_{us} does not cause BP_{uk}	reject	2.98*	0.469
8. P_{uk} does not cause BP_{uk}	reject	2.66*	0.460
9. Y_{uk} does not cause BP_{uk}	reject	3.50*	0.490
10. BP_{uk} does not cause M_{uk}	reject	1.20	0.991
11. M_{uk} does not cause BP_{uk}		0.95	0.336

NOTE: All regressions include four lagged values of the dependent and independent variables, a constant, time trend, and seasonal dummies.
*Significant at the 5 percent level. $F_{0.05}(4,38) = 2.62$.
**Significant at the 1 percent level. $F_{0.01}(4,38) = 3.86$.

Implication 2 of P-W's model leads to two additional hypotheses concerning the ability of monetary authorities in reserve and non-reserve-currency countries to affect prices, which are determined on unified world markets. First, U.S. monetary policy should affect U.S. prices and hence prices in world markets.

Hypothesis 3. M_{us} Granger-causes P_{us}.

The appropriate F-statistic is 6.59, indicating a significant causal effect running from money to prices in the U.S. Second, monetary policy in the U.K., because it is a small NRC country, should have a negligible effect on world and British prices.

Hypothesis 4. M_{uk} does not Granger-cause P_{uk}.

As Table 2 indicates, this hypothesis is not rejected at the 5 percent significance level (F = 1.33). This is consistent with the monetary model. It should be noted, however, that this last hypothesis, unlike hypotheses 1 and 2, depends only on the assumption that the U.K. is a small open economy. It says nothing about the dominant role of the U.S. under the Bretton Woods system, which P-W emphasize. Their presumption leads to more specific hypotheses.

Hypothesis 5. M_{us} Granger-causes prices in the U.K. (P_{uk}), assuming unified world markets for tradable goods.

Hypothesis 6. M_{us} Granger-causes nominal GNP in the U.K. (Y_{uk}).

The causal relationship between U.S. money and U.K. prices is significant at the 1 percent level indicating strong support for the global monetarist model. No causal effect of M_{us} on British GNP was detected, however, in apparent contradiction of the model. This last result has also been obtained by Mixon, Pratt, and Wallace [5] using the period 1962.I–1970.IV.

Several other *U.S.* variables, namely nominal GNP, prices, and the interest rate, which are presumably caused by M_{us} and which might possibly have a causal effect on British GNP, were considered. All significant causal effects that were discovered are reported in Figure 1.

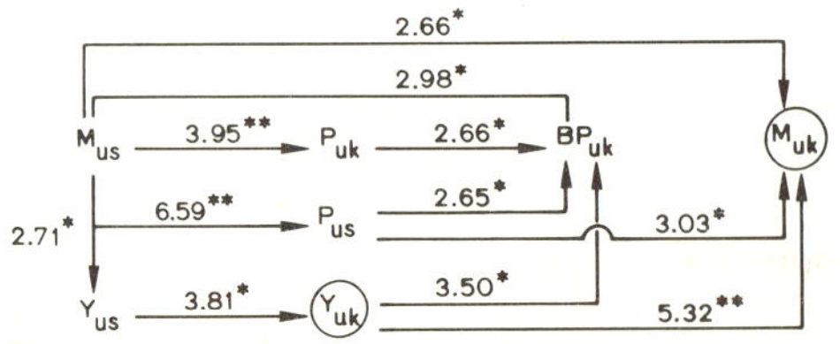

FIG. 1. Empirically Significant Causal Effects Among Variables of the Monetary Model of Putnam and Wilford. *Note*: The arrows indicate *all* of the significant causal relationships among the included variables. The corresponding numbers are the appropriate F-ratios for the test of the null hypothesis that there is no causality between the two variables. *Significant at the 5 percent level. ** Significant at the 1 percent level.

Returning to implications 3 and 4 above, U.S. monetary expansion causes a balance of payments surplus in the United Kingdom according to the monetary model. By raising U.K. prices and income, U.S. monetary expansion raises U.K. demand for nominal money balances. This demand is met by reducing expenditure on goods, services, and financial assets thereby inducing an inflow of foreign exchange reserves (which augments the domestic monetary base in the absence of sterilization). Thus,

Hypothesis 7. M_{us} Granger-causes BP_{uk}, the U.K. balance of payments.

Table 2 shows that the statistical hypothesis that M_{us} does not cause BP_{uk} is rejected at the 5 percent level, though it is not rejected at the 1 percent level.

Of course, even in the absence of a dominant reserve-currency country like the United States, the monetary theory of the balance of payments predicts that any changes in prices and income in the U.K. affect money demand, and, therefore, the balance of payments. This implies the following hypotheses:

Hypothesis 8. P_{uk} Granger-causes BP_{uk}.

Hypothesis 9. Y_{uk} Granger-causes BP_{uk}.

Once again the tests indicate that we can reject the hypothesis of no causality from P_{uk} or Y_{uk} to BP_{uk} at the 5 percent level, as predicted by the theory.

To continue our empirical investigation of P-W's model, implication 5 conjectures a relationship between the U.K. balance of payments and its money supply. In the absence of sterilization, the foreign reserve inflow (outflow) associated with a balance of payments surplus (deficit) implies an immediate (i.e., contemporaneous) effect on the monetary base. No *causal* effect from the balance of payments to the monetary *base* should exist. Unless multiple credit creation on the monetary base occurs instantaneously, however, the balance of payments will have a causal effect, not just a contemporaneous effect, on the domestic money supply. Thus, making the usual assumption of no sterilization yields,

Hypothesis 10. BP_{uk} Granger-causes M_{uk}.

The test of this hypothesis, reported in Table 2, revealed no statistically significant relationship running from BP_{uk} to M_{uk}. This result is particularly unexpected in light of our findings above that M_{us} caused M_{uk} (hypothesis 2) and also that M_{us} caused BP_{uk} (hypothesis 7). Reconciliation of these test results for hypotheses 2, 7, and 10 with the monetary model would require that reserve inflows affect the British money supply *instantly*, that is, without a time lag, so that no temporal effect involving BP_{uk} and M_{uk} occurs. This seems unlikely given that nature of the multiple credit creation process.

Of course, one might alternatively conclude from the evidence of no causal effect from BP_{uk} and M_{uk} that sterilization operations are carried out continuously so that reserve flows have no perceptible effect on the money supply.

Implication 6 states that *if* the British monetary authority was to attempt to increase the money supply autonomously rather than just responding passively to reserve inflows and outflows, a causal relationship running from M_{uk} to BP_{uk} would be found. Of course, if the authorities avoid such autonomous action, either because they realize it is futile or alternatively because they are controlling interest rates rather than monetary aggregates, then no causal relation from M_{uk} to BP_{uk} would be observed. Alternatively, if monetary disturbances lead to virtually instantaneous portfolio adjustment through the capital account of the balance of payments, it is quite possible that only a contemporaneous, but no causal, relationship would be detected from M_{uk} to BP_{uk} even if monetary authorities do, in fact, act autonomously rather than merely accommodating reserve inflows and outflows.

Given this uncertainty about the conduct of monetary policy and the rapidity of portfolio adjustment, it is clear that neither the presence nor absence of causality from M_{uk} to BP_{uk} is inconsistent with P-W's model. A test of this causal relationship is nonetheless interesting in light of the other tests reported above. It turns out that the null hypothesis that there is no causality from M_{uk} to BP_{uk} cannot be rejected regardless of the level of significance ($F = 0.948$).

The results of the tests of hypotheses obtained from the P-W model are summarized in Figure 1. That figure brings together all the causal links that have been detected at the 5 percent level. Except for the cases of M_{us} causing P_{uk} and Y_{uk} causing M_{uk}, none of these relationships was significant at the 1 percent level. The arrows in the figure indicate the direction of causality;[2] the accompanying numbers are the F-ratios, as reported in the text and tables.

The evidence presented in this section provides some empirical support for the monetary model. However, there remains room for skepticism. The absence of causal effects between M_{us} and Y_{uk}, BP_{uk} and M_{uk}, and M_{uk} and BP_{uk} would probably be unexpected a priori by most investigators attempting to verify the monetarist model. Nevertheless, the empirical evidence summarized in Figure 1 indicates that the existence of reverse causality from U.K. income to U.K. money observed by W-G-G can be explained by the fact that the U.K. is a small open economy in an international monetary system dominated by the United States, the primary reserve-currency country. Other explanations may, of course, also be consistent with the data.

5. THE INTEREST RATE MANAGEMENT HYPOTHESIS

Williams, Goodhart, and Gowland suggested a second reason why the causal effect of money on income might be weak in the United Kingdom, namely, the Bank of England may be attempting to control interest rates (or "credit conditions") rather than the monetary base, as recommended in the Radcliffe Report. Here we take the long-term government bond rate as the policy instrument and a proxy for credit conditions. (This appears justifiable in light of the results in Fig. 2.)

If the interest rate management (IRM) hypothesis is true, several causal relationships should be detectable. Interest rates should Granger-cause income through their effect on private-sector consumption, saving, and investment behavior. Income should not, however, cause interest rates. In fact, the appropriate British interest rate should not be Granger-caused by any economic variables in either the U.K. or

[2]The possibility of causality in both directions was considered for all pairs of U.K. variables. No cases of bidirectional causality emerged.

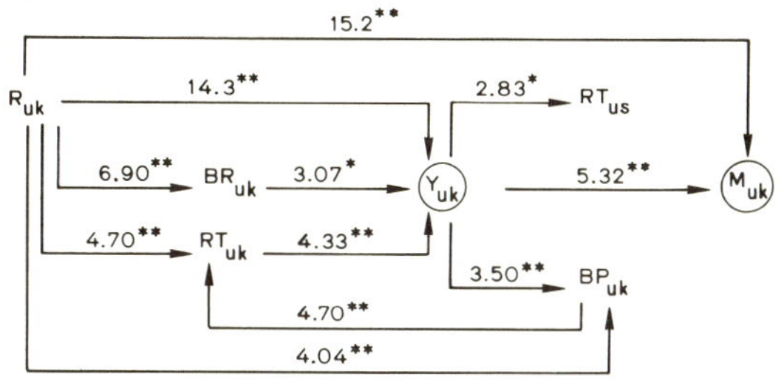

FIG. 2. Evidence on the Interest Rate Management Hypothesis. Interest rate variables: R_{uk} = U.K. long-term government bond yield; RT_{uk} = U.K. Treasury-bill rate; BR_{uk} = U.K. bank rate; RT_{us} = U.S. Treasury-bill rate. *Note*: The arrows indicate *all* significant causal relationships among the included variables as well as causal effects from U.S. interest rates (discount rate, T-bill rates, and long-term government bond rate) to each of the variables in the figure. None of the latter was significant. The corresponding numbers are the appropriate F-ratios for the test of the null hypothesis that there is no causality between the two variables. *Significant at the 5 percent level. **Significant at the 1 percent level.

the U.S. if it is truly an exogenously determined policy instrument.[3] In addition to affecting income, interest rates should also Granger-cause money in the U.K. due to the direct effect of interest rate changes on money demand as well as their indirect effect via income. The monetary authorities must passively adjust the money supply to meet money demand if they are to achieve their interest rate target (while at the same time maintaining the fixed exchange rate).

Figure 2 summarizes all causal relationships that were detected in the course of our examination of the interest rate management hypothesis. This hypothesis provides an alternative to the monetary model for explaining the reverse causality from U.K. income to money observed by W-G-G and confirmed in section 3 of this study. The level of significance of the causal relationships implied by the IRM hypothesis is very high, as the F-ratios testify.

6. CONCLUSIONS

This paper has summarized the results of an extensive search for bivariate causality relationships among money, income, prices, interest rates, and the balance of payments in the United Kingdom under the Bretton Woods system. The possibility of causal effects running from U.S. money, income, prices, and interest rates to any of the above-mentioned U.K. variables was also investigated. The objective of the exercise was to test alternative hypotheses that might account for the observed unidirectional relationship from income to money in the U.K. even though Sims [7] found the opposite relationship to prevail in the United States.

Two specific theories were entertained. The first, espoused by Putnam and Wil-

[3]Of course, if policymakers establish a feedback control rule for setting key interest variables, the interest rate will not be found to be exogenous.

ford, attributes the differing money-income relationships in the U.K. and the U.S. to the countries' differing roles under the Bretton Woods fixed exchange rate system. The second theory, suggested by Williams, Goodhart, and Gowland, is that "reverse causality" from income to money in the U.K. is due to the Bank of England's policy of controlling interest rates rather than the monetary base.

All significant causal relationships uncovered in the study of these two theories are summarized in Figures 1 and 2, respectively. If one was forced to choose between the interest rate management hypothesis and the monetary model as explanations of U.K. money-income causality, one would probably opt for the IRM hypothesis, given the evidence in sections 4 and 5. Fortunately, the models are not mutually exclusive alternatives, so a more eclectic explanation is possible. Tests of the monetary hypotheses have provided strong support for the view that the U.K. is an open economy whose price level and, to a lesser extent, its level of GNP are determined by external factors, particularly U.S. monetary policy. Yet U.K. monetary authorities remain able to significantly affect income, the balance of payments, and the domestic money supply through their ability to control domestic interest rates. Undoubtedly the existence of controls on U.K. capital outflows during the period under investigation gave authorities greater leeway in setting interest rates than might otherwise have been the case.

Taken together, the findings in Figures 1 and 2 provide a rather complete explanation of various influences contributing to the causal link from nominal GNP to money in the U.K. during the fixed exchange rate period. In addition to providing an explanation of the reserve causality, which has recently received attention in the literature, the figures suggest the nature of the interdependence among various macroeconomic variables in the United Kingdom. This information should be of use in building structural models of the British economy as it existed prior to 1971. Since that time important changes have occurred, including the widespread adoption of flexible exchange rates and the Bank of England's move to control the monetary base rather than credit conditions. Ultimately the judicious choice of macroeconomic policy must, of course, be based on structural information, not just the reduced-form exercises that characterize the money-income causality literature.

LITERATURE CITED

1. Feige, Edgar L., and Douglas K. Pearce. "The Causal Relationship between Money and Income: Some Caveats for Time Series Analysis." *Review of Economics and Statistics,* 61 (1979), 521-33.
2. Friedman, Milton, and David Meiselman. "The Relative Stability of Monetary Velocity and the Investment Multiplier in the U.S. 1897-1958." In *Stabilization Policies,* prepared for the Commission on Money and Credit, by Edgar Cory Brown et al., pp. 165-208. Englewood Cliffs, N.J.: Prentice-Hall, 1963.
3. Geweke, John, Richard Meese, and Warren T. Dent. "Comparing Alternative Tests of Causality in Temporal Systems: Analytical Results and Experimental Evidence." SSRI Workshop Series No. 7928, University of Wisconsin, 1979.

4. Granger, Clive W. J. "Investigating Causal Relations by Econometric Models and Cross-Spectral Methods." *Econometrica,* 37 (1969), 424-38.

5. Mixon, J. Wilson, Jr., Leila J. Pratt, and Myles S. Wallace. "Cross-National Money to Income Causality: U.S. Money to U.K. Income." *Journal of Money, Credit, and Banking,* 11 (November 1979), 419-26.

6. Putnam, Bluford H., and D. Sykes Wilford. "Money, Income and Causality in the United States and the United Kingdom: A Theoretical Explanation of Different Findings." *American Economic Review,* 68 (1978), 423-27.

7. Sims, Christopher A. "Money, Income, and Causality." *American Economic Review,* 62 (1972), 540-52.

8. Williams, David, Charles A. E. Goodhart, and David H. Gowland. "Money, Income, and Causality: The U.K. Experience." *American Economic Review,* 66 (1976), 417-23.

HERBERT M. KAUFMAN
DON E. SCHLAGENHAUF*

FNMA Auction Results as a Forecaster of Residential Mortgage Yields

1. INTRODUCTION

IN REPORTING THE RESULTS OF the April 28, 1980, Federal National Mortgage Association (FNMA) auction of four month commitments to buy mortgage loans, the *Wall Street Journal* in its issue of the next day said that "the trend of the yields is considered an indicator of future mortgage interest rates." Later in the same article they noted: "The [mortgage] lenders' bids reflect their expectations for future home-loan interest rates." These quotations summarize what might be called the general view, particularly in the financial press and in the financial community, that the FNMA auction results are good indicators of the future course of mortgage interest rates, especially during the period covered by the commitment (four months).

One reason that may underlie the belief, expressed in the quotation above, in the usefulness of the auction results as forecasters of mortgage interest rates, is that the mortgage market is assumed to be efficient. That is, FNMA auction results reflect all information at the time of the auction on the future course of mortgage rates and that the FNMA auction results themselves show up in other mortgage rates as well. However, a test of whether the efficient markets assumption is true in the case of the

*We wish to thank Raymond Lombra, V. Kerry Smith, and the anonymous referees for very useful comments, and Meg Schulman and Tracy Johnson for valuable research assistance.

HERBERT M. KAUFMAN *is professor, and* DON E. SCHLAGENHAUF *is assistant professor, Department of Economics, Arizona State University.*

0022-2879/81/0881-0352$00.50/0
JOURNAL OF MONEY, CREDIT, AND BANKING, vol. 13, no. 3 (August 1981)

mortgage market is beyond the scope of this paper. Rather, our object is to gauge whether or not the implied logic of viewing the auction results as good forecasting devices by the financial community makes sense. This issue can be considered quite independently of whether the mortgage market meets a statistical test of market efficiency.

The FNMA biweekly auctions are held to enable mortgage originators to secure commitments on their mortgages. Many of the customers of FNMA are mortgage bankers that are not depository institutions and really fulfill a brokerage function between borrowers and ultimate mortgage lenders. Thus these instutitions as well as traditional mortgage originators who wish to dispose of a portion of their mortgage holdings must seek outlets for these mortgages. They would prefer to sell their mortgages elsewhere as they have to pay a commitment fee to FNMA and meet other requirements if they actually deliver the mortgages to FNMA, but they need a guaranteed source of sale if they cannot find more attractive purchasers. Thus they enter the FNMA auction. Actually there are two auctions, one for conventional mortgage loans and the other for government-insured loans (FHA and VA). However, since these auctions are conducted in the same manner, we will for the present refer to them as "the auction." The bids made at the auction are ranked from low price to high price (or high yield to low yield) and FNMA, making reference to a number of factors, chooses the cut-off point on what they will accept. This sets the high auction yield, the low auction yield, and the average auction yield.[1] It is this latter variable that is generally regarded as a forecast of the future course of mortgage rates at least over the length of the commitment period.

The proposition that the average auction yield at FNMA auctions is a good forecaster of the average course of mortgage interest rates has never been tested to our knowledge. We will evaluate the forecasting performance of the FNMA auction results relative to two other forecasting devices. The first alternative is a very naïve forecast made by extrapolating the own rate of the particular mortgage category.[2] The second alternative employs the Box-Jenkins time series forecasting method. If FNMA auction results are a useful forecasting device, we would expect them to perform better than at least the first alternative. However to anticipate our conclusions, it turns out that FNMA auction results do substantially worse in forecasting the future course of mortgage interest rates than even the naïve forecast. The Box-Jenkins model does considerably better.

The paper is organized as follows. In section 2 the procedures utilized will be presented. Section 3 presents the results of the forecasting experiments. Finally the last section of the paper presents our conclusions and discusses the implications of our work for the forecasting of the mortgage interest rate.

[1]See [11] for a discussion of the FNMA auction. In addition, a number of studies of the mortgage market have been conducted which have included FNMA in various mortgage supply or housing starts equations (see, e.g., [3, 4, 7, 8, 13]). Perhaps the most widely known formal study of FNMA (along with the Federal Home Loan Bank System) is [14]. In addition, see recent papers by Jaffee and Rosen [9], Kaufman [10], Rosen [12], and Hendershott and Villani [6].

[2]Although we call this method "naïve" if one believed that the mortgage market was perfectly efficient it might be quite useful to use the rate to forecast. Nonetheless, it is not clear that the mortgage market is efficient and that simple extrapolation cannot be improved upon.

2. THE TECHNIQUE

It was mentioned above that there really are two FNMA auctions, one for conventional loans and one for those that are government insured. In the first model, we took the government underwritten auction results and used these to forecast one through four periods (months) ahead for the mortgage rate on FHA mortgage loans.[3] This series would be the most likely to be closely tracked by the results at the government underwritten auction, since that auction is concerned primarily with these loans.[4] However, for sake of comparison, we also used the government underwritten results of one-to-four period ahead forecasts of three conventional mortgage series. It would be expected that the government underwritten auction results would be a poorer predictor of conventional rates. However, this exercise led to some interesting anomalies, which will be noted in the next section when the results are presented. The first model also employed the results of the FNMA conventional auction to forecast the new and existing home conventional mortgage rates. Analogously to the government underwritten procedure, we also used the conventional results to forecast the FHA series.

The second model was a naïve model where the own rate at period t was used to forecast the mortgage rate in periods $t+1$ and $t+4$. This was done for the three conventional series and for the FHA series. It would be expected a priori that at a minimum, if the FNMA auction results are of any use to forecasting, they should do better than such a naïve extrapolative forecast. The fact that they did not leads to serious questions as to the usefulness of the auction results.

The third model was a Box-Jenkins ARIMA model for all series. The Box-Jenkins technique has now become widely known and utilized in economic forecasting so we need not devote a lot of time to reviewing the technique. Nonetheless, a brief review of the Box-Jenkins procedure is useful. This technique involves the use of the autoregressive integrated moving average (ARIMA) model for a time series. The general form of this model is expressed as

$$\emptyset_p(B)\phi_P(B^s)A^d A_s^D Y_t = \theta_q(B)\,\theta_Q(B^s)a_t,$$

where Y_t is the time series of interest; a_t is a white noise process, A^d and A_s^D are difference operators; $\emptyset_p(B)$, $\phi_P(B^s)$, $\theta_q(B)$, and $\theta_Q(B^s)$ are finite polynomials of degrees, p, P, q, and Q, respectively; and s represents the length of the seasonal effect. The Box-Jenkins approach is an interative model building approach. Identification and estimation comprise the first two stages in the procedure. Identification of the particular ARIMA form requires specification of the parameters p, P, d, D, q, and Q, while estimation is concerned with finding values of the resulting parameters in the polynomials. Since the procedures to identify and estimate an ARIMA $(p, d, q) \times (P, D, Q)_s$ can be found in Box and Jenkins [1], or Granger and

[3]All data sources and series definitions are presented in the Appendix.

[4]Although it also includes Veterans Administration-insured loans, these represent only a relatively small percentage of total offers at the auction.

Newbold [5], they will not be discussed here. Once the estimation stage is completed, diagnostic checks, the final stage, are applied to the residuals to determine whether the model provides an adequate representation of the time series. If the diagnostic checks indicate the model is inadequate, the iterative cycle is repeated until a suitable representation is found.

Box-Jenkins models were constructed for each of the four mortgage interest rate series utilized in this study. The estimated version of these models are presented in Table 1.[5] In the results section that follows it will be seen that the Box-Jenkins models did considerably better than the alternatives analyzed in this paper in forecasting the mortgage interest rate.

TABLE 1

BOX-JENKINS MODELS FOR THE VARIOUS INTEREST RATE SERIES (PERIOD JULY 1968–DECEMBER 1977)

Series	Estimated Model	Q-Statistic	Residual Mean Square	Residual Standard Error
FYFHA	$(1 + 0.2696B^6)(1 - 0.5127B)\ (1 - B)Y_t = a_t$	12.400	0.02553	0.16133
	(0.0963) (0.0868)	$d.f. = 22$		
EH	$(1 + 0.2434B^6)(1 - 0.7743B)\ (1 - B)Y_t = a_t$	26.867	0.00295	0.05483
	(0.0974) (0.0626)	$d.f. = 22$		
NH	$(1 - 0.6335B)\ (1 - B)Y_t = a_t$	23.8620	0.00405	0.06398
	(0.0753)	$d.f. = 23$		
HUD	$(1 + 0.3686B^6)(1 - 0.6085B)\ (1 - B)Y_t = a_t$	13.446	0.00779	0.08877
	(0.0952) (0.0804)	$d.f. = 22$		

The diagnostic checking stage of the model indicates that each model provides an adequate representation of the behavior of the relevant interest rate series. Since the residuals from the estimated Box-Jenkins model should be white noise, each of these residual autocorrelations should not be significantly different from zero. An examination of the autocorrelogram of the residuals for each model indicates a white noise process. In addition to examining residual autocorrelations, the Box and Pierce [2] test for randomness of the residuals can be applied.[6]

The relevant Q-statistics are also presented in Table 1 and are not significantly different from zero at 0.05 and 0.10 levels of significance. Thus the models appear to be adequate. The diagnostic check of overfitting was also applied to each estimated model. Again, there were no indications that the models were inadequate representations of the behavior of the various interest rate series.

[5]It should be noted that the autocorrelation and the partial autocorrelation functions suggest that an AR(1) Model is appropriate. The multiplicative models (Models 1, 2, and 4) evolved from an examination of the residual autocorrelations, which indicate a seasonal pattern was present.

[6]In order to apply the test, the Q-statistic must be formed. The formula for this is

$$Q = (N\text{-}D\text{-}d) \sum_{i=1}^{k} r_i^2 (\hat{a}_t)$$

where N is the number of observations, r_i is the autocorrelation of the residuals at the ith time lag, and D, d, P, p, Q, q are as defined previously. The statistic is approximately distributed as a χ^2 variate with $k-p-q-P-Q$ degrees of freedom. Thus, the null hypothesis of zero autocorrelation across all the residuals at k time lags can be tested. If the estimated ARIMA model cannot pass this test of adequacy, an alternative model must be entertained.

3. THE RESULTS

Table 2 presents the results for the FNMA auction average yield for forecasts one through four periods ahead. Two statistics are reported, the mean square error (MSE) and the mean square percentage error (MSPE). In addition, to these statistics a number of other measures of forecasting performances were calculated such as the root mean square error, the mean absolute error, and the Theil U statistic. These latter statistics are not reported since they yielded similar conclusions to the reported statistics.[7]

TABLE 2

COMPARISON OF FNMA AUCTION YIELDS WITH MORTGAGE YIELDS OVER THE FNMA COMMITMENT PERIOD (PERIOD JULY 1968–DECEMBER 1977)

Auction Type	Predicted Series		Mean Square Error	Mean Square Percentage Error
FNMAGU	EH	$t+1$	0.1512	0.0021
		$t+2$	0.1348	0.0018
		$t+3$	0.1427	0.0019
		$t+4$	0.1686	0.0024
FNMAC	EH	$t+1$	0.1579	0.0021
		$t+2$	0.1221	0.0016
		$t+3$	0.1086	0.0014
		$t+4$	0.1145	0.0014
FNMAGU	NH	$t+1$	0.1703	0.0023
		$t+2$	0.1561	0.0021
		$t+3$	0.1797	0.0025
		$t+4$	0.1599	0.0021
FNMAC	NH	$t+1$	0.2273	0.0030
		$t+2$	0.2012	0.0026
		$t+3$	0.1879	0.0024
		$t+4$	0.1888	0.0024
FNMAGU	FYFHA	$t+1$	0.0443	0.0006
		$t+2$	0.1183	0.0016
		$t+3$	0.2104	0.0028
		$t+4$	0.3064	0.0041
FNMAC	FYFHA	$t+1$	0.1197	0.0016
		$t+2$	0.1802	0.0023
		$t+3$	0.2546	0.0032
		$t+4$	0.3383	0.0042
FNMAGU	HUD	$t+1$	0.0982	0.0013
		$t+2$	0.1342	0.0017
		$t+3$	0.1809	0.0024
		$t+4$	0.2378	0.0032
FNMAC	HUD	$t+1$	0.0969	0.0012
		$t+2$	0.1283	0.0015
		$t+3$	0.1683	0.0020
		$t+4$	0.2192	0.0026

NOTE: See the Appendix for symbol definitions and data sources.

The first thing to note is that the errors do not always increase as the period being forecasted expands. This is somewhat surprising since it would be expected that when the bids are made to FNMA, they reflect all current information and this

[7]They are all available from the authors on request. In addition, only the MSE and MSPE will be reported for the other models discussed below. As in the first case, however, all statistics are available on request.

information is likely to be more appropriate to the next period than to a period four months ahead. The errors do reflect this increasing pattern for the government underwritten auction forecast of the FHA rate and for the conventional forecast of the HUD series. While the errors tend to be relatively small for the next period in the government underwritten sector, they tend to expand rather rapidly. This is particularly true if one looks at the mean square percentage error. In fact for the FHA series, the FNMA conventional result forecasts the FHA series almost as well as the government underwritten result in later periods. In general the conventional rate does better in forecasting the conventional series than the government underwritten in forecasting the government underwritten series, especially in later periods.[8] But here again there is an anomaly. The government underwritten series seems to do almost as well, especially in earlier periods, as the conventional auction results in forecasting the existing homes mortgage rate. The government underwritten series actually does better than the conventional auction result in forecasting new homes in the earlier periods and about as well later on. This is indeed a strange result but as there are no tests of significance to assess the differences, we just note these here.

TABLE 3

SIMPLE EXTRAPOLATION OF MORTGAGE SERIES OF TABLE 2 OVER THE FNMA COMMITMENT PERIOD. COMPARISON OF ACTUAL AND PREDICTED SERIES (PERIOD JULY 1968–DECEMBER 1977)

Predicted Series	Period	Mean Square Error	Mean Square Percentage Error
EH	$t+1$	0.0074	0.0001
	$t+2$	0.0262	0.0008
	$t+3$	0.0528	0.0008
	$t+4$	0.0838	0.0012
NH	$t+1$	0.0066	0.0001
	$t+2$	0.0219	0.0003
	$t+3$	0.0440	0.0007
	$t+4$	0.0707	0.0011
FYFHA	$t+1$	0.0366	0.0005
	$t+2$	0.1129	0.0014
	$t+3$	0.2035	0.0027
	$t+4$	0.2980	0.0040
HUD	$t+1$	0.0270	0.0003
	$t+2$	0.0556	0.0007
	$t+3$	0.0917	0.0012
	$t+4$	0.1311	0.0018

Furthermore, the size of these errors really tells us nothing as to the forecasting ability of the auction results until they are compared with other methods.

Table 3 presents the forecasts of the mortgage interest rates series for one to four periods ahead. These are own rate forecasts. For a forecasting device to be really useful, it would be expected to perform better than simple extrapolation. Unfortunately, as can be seen by perusing the table, the naïve forecast is almost always

[8]This is particularly interesting in that the conventional auction is much smaller than the government underwritten. FNMA started buying conventional loans only in 1972 and in May 1978 held about $8 billion of these loans compared to about $30 billion of government underwritten loans.

better than that of the comparable forecasts made by utilizing the FNMA auction results even a number of periods ahead. Notice particularly the mean square percentage errors on the conventional series. These are much improved over those generated by the FNMA conventional auction results. The government underwritten sector is somewhat less impressive, but even here it is better than that generated by the FNMA auction results. Clearly this is a blow to the generally accepted principle that the FNMA auction is a good indicator of the future mortgage interest rate. While trends may be indicated by the results, the auction results appear not to be useful as forecasters of rates. We will return to this later on.

Can the naïve forecast be improved upon? The answer is clearly yes when the results for the Box-Jenkins estimation are examined. These are contained in Table 4. Notice the substantially reduced errors using this method. Like some of the other

TABLE 4

Box-Jenkins Forecasts of Mortgage Series of Table 2 Over the FNMA Commitment Period. Comparison of Actual and Predicted Series (Period July 1968–December 1977)

Predicted Series	Period	Mean Square Error	Mean Square Percentage Error
EH	$t+1$	0.002949	0.000042
	$t+2$	0.013419	0.000193
	$t+3$	0.031653	0.000457
	$t+4$	0.058319	0.000838
NH	$t+1$	0.004057	0.000059
	$t+2$	0.013881	0.000206
	$t+3$	0.030918	0.000470
	$t+4$	0.055086	0.000847
FYFHA	$t+1$	0.025531	0.000332
	$t+2$	0.088818	0.001148
	$t+3$	0.170735	0.002239
	$t+4$	0.262990	0.003546
HUD	$t+1$	0.007797	0.000106
	$t+2$	0.028971	0.000391
	$t+3$	0.059454	0.000807
	$t+4$	0.095350	0.001308

results mentioned above, as would be expected these still show increases in errors as the period is extended but the order of the errors is of a much smaller magnitude. It is interesting to note that the results also show that the conventional rates are easier to forecast than the government underwritten rates. This may be due to the fact that since the government underwritten sector mortgages carry fixed note rates, information to the market is obscured and this interferes with the ability to forecast this sector.[9]

It may be useful to speculate on the reasons that the FNMA auction results appear to do so poorly in forecasting the mortgage rate. One possible explanation is that the average auction yield is computed after FNMA decides on the cut-off or stop-out

[9]In October 1975, trading began in Government National Mortgage Association (GNMA) futures contracts. Thus, approximately two years of futures trading overlaps the period investigated in this paper which ends in 1977. A referee suggested that a comparison between the performance of futures market yields relative to FNMA auction results, since the former is a true futures market, would be interesting

price (yield) at the auction. FNMA's decision on the number of bids it will accept is based on a number of factors that may not be totally or immediately relevant to the future course of mortgage interest rates (see [9]) and thus important information is lost. That is, FNMA's decision on the amount of bids to accept interferes with the generation of information about future mortgage rates. This may be particularly true if FNMA is attempting to influence the future course of rates by the amount of mortgages it accepts. It may be that if the average auction yield on all bids, rather than just successful bids, were generally available (it is not), this would prove more accurate as a forecasting tool. A second reason for the poor performance of the auction results as a forecasting device may be due to the fact that most of FNMA's customers are mortgage bankers who must finance their temporary holdings of mortgages at short-term interest rates until they sell them.[10] Thus their bids may simply indicate the status of the short-term market and the availability of alternative

and we agree. Thus data were gathered from the various issues of the *Wall Street Journal* for GNMA futures yields one month and four months before the contract expired. (Over the period 1976–1977 contracts traded on the Chicago Board of Trade for March, June, September, and December expirations.) To understand how we made our comparisons let us use the June 1976 contract as an example. We took the yield on the GNMA futures for the June 1976 contract as reported in March and May 1976. This gives us our four month (inclusive) and one month ahead results. (Although whether the March result is a true four month ahead forecast depends on how the series for March is centered, so there should be a caveat noted here. However, note that the GNMA contract expires near the end of the contract month.) Two different GNMA yields were utilized. The average of the results reported on the second and fourth Mondays of the month and alternatively the midpoint of the month were utilized. The former is used to somewhat approximate the biweekly FNMA auction process. These were then compared with the actual mortgage rates in the month of the contract using the four mortgage series that have been used throughout this paper. We had a total of seven GNMA contracts running from June 1976 to December 1977. The results for calculations of mean square errors and mean square percentage errors are presented below.

Mean Square and Mean Square Percentage Error Evaluation for GNMA Futures Contracts Yields 1976–77

	NH	EH	HUD	FYFHA
Average GNMA				
Futures Yield*				
One period ahead				
MSE	0.5538	0.5809	0.4660	0.2068
MSPE	0.0068	0.0071	0.0058	0.0027
Four periods ahead				
MSE	0.5298	0.5525	0.4527	0.2167
MSPE	0.0065	0.0068	0.0056	0.0028
Monthly Mid-point				
One period ahead				
MSE	0.5406	0.5683	0.4533	0.2029
MSPE	0.0066	0.0069	0.0056	0.0026
Four periods ahead				
MSE	0.5233	0.5474	0.4488	0.2153
MSPE	0.0064	0.0067	0.0056	0.0028

*Average of second and fourth Monday yields was utilized.

Notice that there are only two years of data and thus any conclusion to be drawn must be considered tentative. As would be expected since the GNMA contracts are for government-insured mortgages, they do best in forecasting the government-insured rate. However, the FYFHA series forecast, judged by a comparison of the mean square errors here with those for FNMA reported in Table 2, is superior to the FNMA results only for the four month ahead forecast.

[10]This is known as inventorying the mortgages. If short-term rates are high, mortgage bankers will be very eager to get rid of their mortgage holdings because high short rates imply that the yield between the mortgages they hold and short rates is negative or only slightly positive.

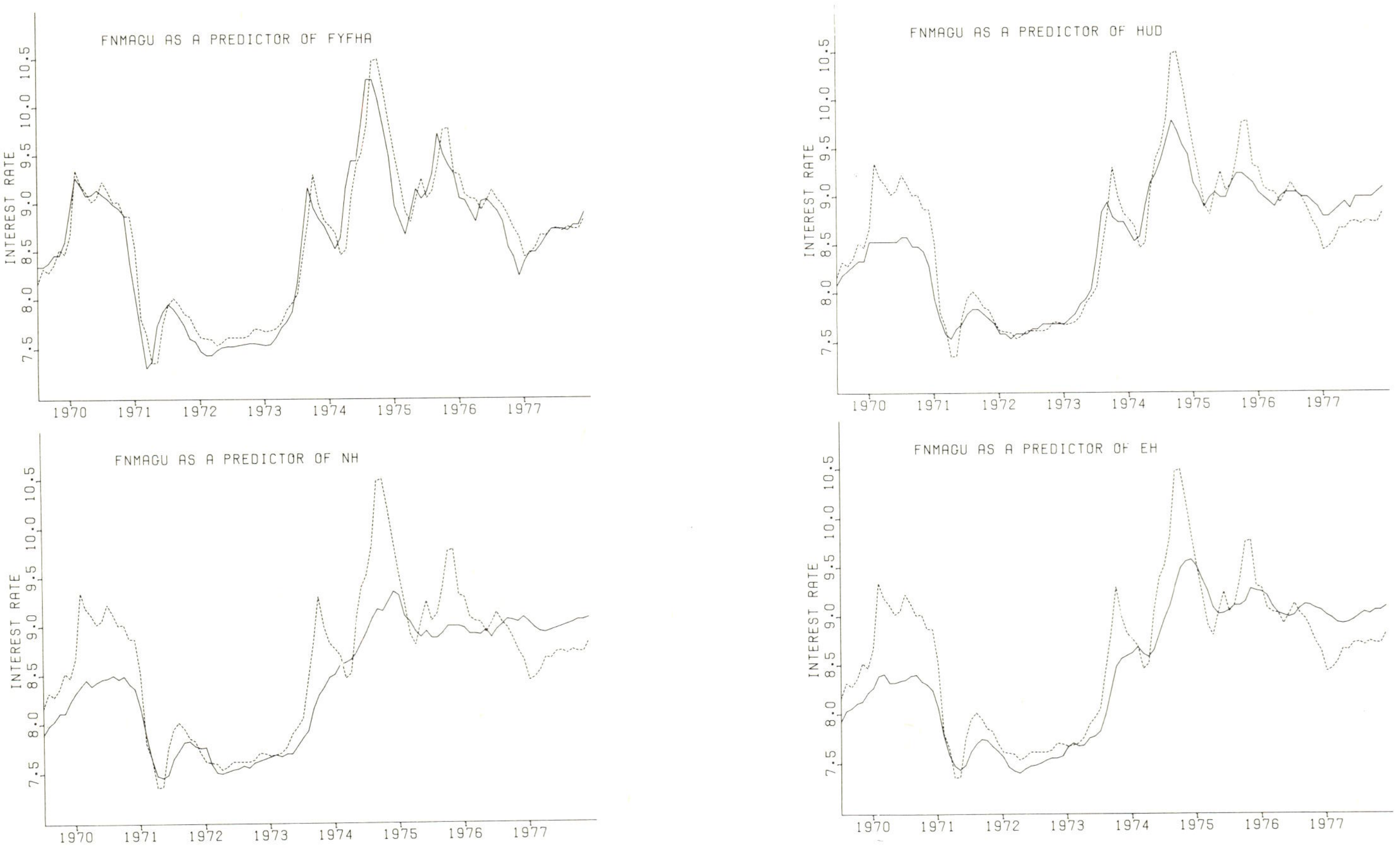

FIG. 1. Comparison of FNMA Auction Results with Mortgage Rate Series One Period Ahead. [*Key:* - - - - - Federal National Mortgage Association Government Underwritten (FNMAGU). ——Actual Mortgage Series: FHA insured mortgage rate (FYFHA); conventional mortgages, new homes (NH); conventional mortgages, new commitments (HUD); conventional mortgages, existing homes (EH).]

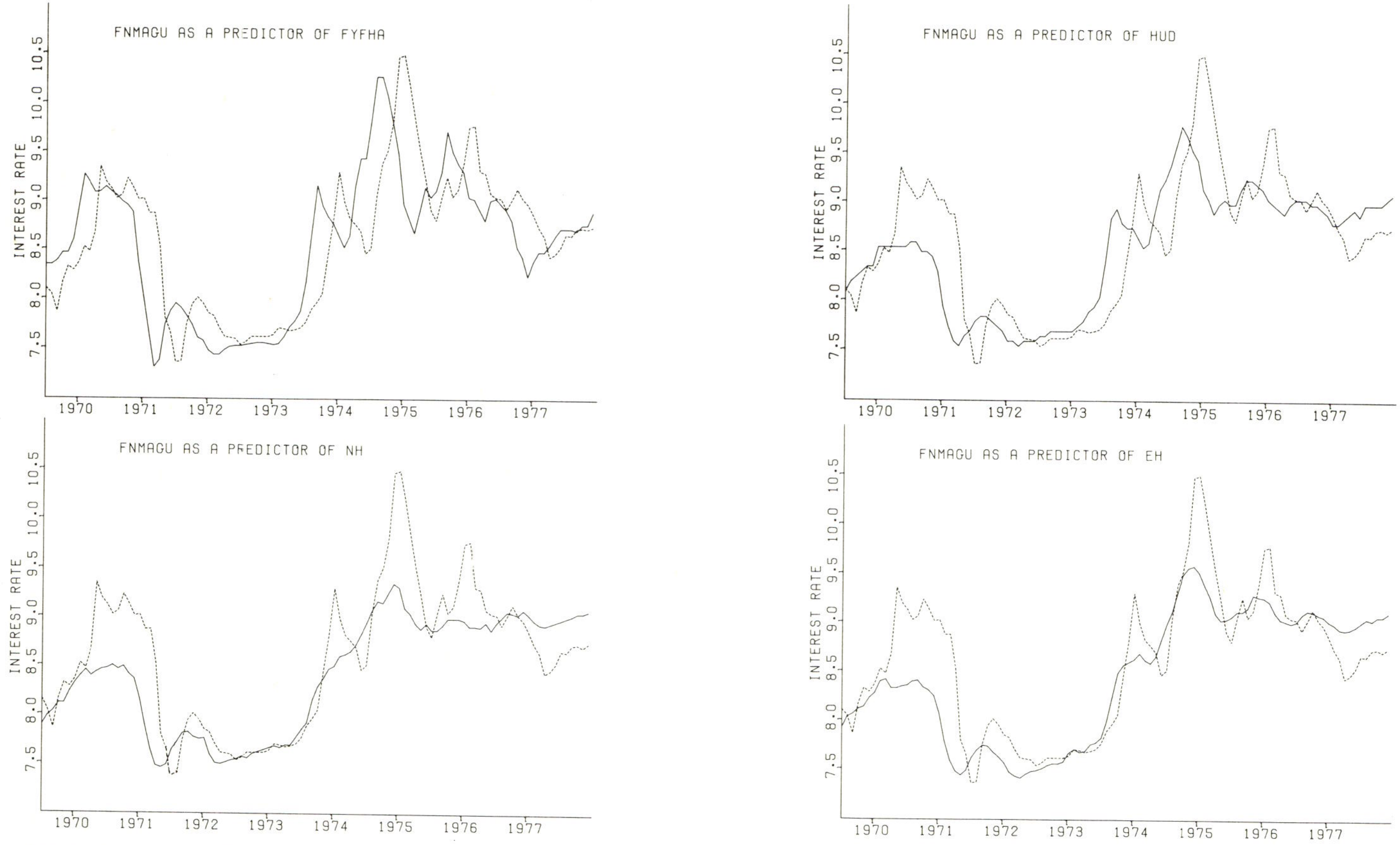

FIG. 2. Comparison of FNMA Auction Results with Mortgage Rate Series Four Periods Ahead. [*Key:* - - - - - Federal National Mortgage Association Government Underwritten (FNMAGU). ——Actual Mortgage Series: FHA insured mortgage rates (FYFHA); conventional mortgages, new homes (NH); conventional mortgages, new commitments (HUD); conventional mortgages, existing homes (EH).]

purchasers, factors that may not be related to the mortgage interest rate until some time has passed.

In light of the relatively poor performance of the FNMA auction results as mortgage rate forecasters reported in this paper, it is interesting to speculate, especially in view of the quotation from the *Wall Street Journal* given at the beginning of this paper, whether there is any systematic bias to the FNMA auction results that could be made use of by mortgage market participants to forecast mortgage market rates or trends.[11] To examine this question we have plotted in Figures 1 and 2 comparisons between the FNMA auction results and one and four period ahead actuals for the four mortgage series from July 1969 to December 1977. As the figures indicate there does appear to be some upward bias to the FNMA yields in general. Further the FNMA series seem to lag the mortgage series at turning points. Since these are forecast comparisons, the plots seem to imply that FNMA auction results are tracking current spot rates rather than forecasting rates. This evidence is consistent with the evidence above on the relatively poor performance of FNMA auction results as a forecaster.

TABLE 5

PERCENTAGE OVERPREDICTION OF FNMA AUCTION YIELDS COMPARED TO FUTURE SPOT MORTGAGE RATES

	FNMAGU (%)	FNMAC (%)
EH		
$t+1$	73	79
$t+2$	72	81
$t+3$	67	82
$t+4$	62	79
NH		
$t+1$	76	82
$t+2$	76	82
$t+3$	73	84
$t+4$	62	85
FYFHA		
$t+1$	64	85
$t+2$	58	81
$t+3$	50	79
$t+4$	54	75
HUD		
$t+1$	60	94
$t+2$	54	79
$t+3$	50	66
$t+4$	47	64

In addition to the plots, a more formal analysis for bias has been conducted. Table 5 presents for all observations, series, and forecast time frames the percentage of observations where the government underwritten auction and the conventional auction overpredicted the ensuing spot rate. The results confirm the findings of the plots. That is, FNMA auction results do on balance overpredict the actual yields, particularly the conventional auction results.[12] On balance therefore, while the

[11]We are grateful to the referees for suggesting this examination.

[12]Similar calculations were made for the Box-Jenkins and naïve forecast procedures. In the Box-Jenkins case there was approximate balance between overprediction and underprediction. For the naïve

auction results do tend to overpredict the future spot mortgage rates, the timing patterns indicated by the plots and the lack of overwhelming bias in the auction results appear to provide little systematic assistance to the mortgage market participant in forecasting rates or trends. This confirms our findings that the mortgage market participant would be better off using the naïve procedure and considerably better off using the Box-Jenkins approach.

4. CONCLUSIONS AND IMPLICATIONS

The results of this study are straightforward. The widely accepted notion that the FNMA auction results are a good forecaster of future mortgage rates appears not to be accurate. In addition, it appears that one could do better by simply extrapolating mortgage rates forward. However, there is an alternative. The Box-Jenkins procedure appears to be very useful as a forecasting methodology especially when the forecast period is not overly extended. In future work we will attempt to evaluate the Box-Jenkins technique as a forecasting device for mortgage interest rates by extending forecast periods and asking questions about its ability to pick up turning points—a usual criticism of Box-Jenkins techniques. Nonetheless, in the tests conducted, it appears to be much more effective than looking at the FNMA auction results. Whether it is better than a full-scale model of the mortgage market and mortgage rates remains for further study.

APPENDIX

Symbol Definitions and Data Sources

Series		Source
FNMAGU	FNMA Government Underwritten Auction Average Auction Yield	*Federal Reserve Bulletin*
FNMAC	FNMA Conventional Auction Average Auction Yield	*Federal Reserve Bulletin*
EH	Average Effective Interest Rate, Conventional Mortgages, Existing Homes	Federal Home Loan Bank Board *Journal*
NH	Average Effective Interest Rate, Conventional Mortgages, New Homes	Federal Home Loan Bank Board *Journal*
HUD	Average Contract Rates on New Commitments for Conventional First Mortgages	*Federal Reserve Bulletin*
FYFHA	FHA Insured Mortgage Rate	Federal Home Loan Bank Board *Journal*

forecast there was some evidence, but not strong, indicating underprediction. Further, the bias measure of the Theil decomposition procedure [15, pp. 33-36] was utilized and regressions of actual and predicted series run and the intercepts examined. Both methods confirmed the results above. Complete results are available from the authors on request.

LITERATURE CITED

1. Box, George E. P., and Gwilym M. Jenkins. *Time Series Analysis: Forecasting and Control*. San Francisco: Holden-Day, 1970.
2. Box, George E. P., and David A. Pierce. "Distribution of Residual Autocorrelations in Autoregressive-Integrated Moving Average Time Series Models." *Journal of the American Statistical Association,* 65 (December 1970), 1509-26.
3. Brady, Eugene. "An Econometric Analysis of the U.S. Residential Mortgage Market." Working Paper No. 11, Federal Home Loan Bank Board. Washington, D.C., November 1970.
4. Fair, Ray C. "Monthly Housing Starts." In *National Housing Models,* edited by R. Bruce Ricks. Lexington, Mass.: Lexington Books, 1973.
5. Granger, Clive W. J., and Paul Newbold. *Forecasting Economic Time Series*. New York: Academic Press, 1977.
6. Hendershott, Patric H., and Kevin E. Villani. "The Federally-Sponsored Credit Agencies: Their Behavior and Impact." In *Capital Markets and the Housing Sector,* edited by Robert M. Buckley, John A. Tuccillo, and Kevin E. Villani, pp. 291-309. Cambridge, Mass.: Ballinger Publishing Company, 1977.
7. Huang, David. "The Effect of Different Credit Policies on Housing Demand." In Volume III of *A Study of the Savings and Loan Industry,* edited by Irwin Friend, pp. 1211-39. Washington, D.C., 1969.
8. Jaffee, Dwight M. "An Econometric Model of the Mortgage Market." In *Savings Deposits, Mortgages and Housing,* edited by Edward M. Gramlich and Dwight M. Jaffee. Lexington, Mass.: Lexington Books, 1972.
9. Jaffee, Dwight M., and Kenneth Rosen. "Estimates of the Effectiveness of Stabilization Policies for the Mortgage Market." Financial Research Center Department of Economics, Research Memorandum No. 24, 1978.
10. Kaufman, Herbert M. "An Analysis of the Behavior of Federal Mortgage Market Agencies." *Journal of Money, Credit, and Banking,* 9 (May 1977), 349-55.
11. ______. "FNMA and Its Relationship to the Mortgage Market." *Journal of Bank Research,* in press.
12. Rosen, Kenneth. "Impact of FNMA on the Mortgage Market and Residential Construction." Paper presented at the ASSA Meetings, New York, 1979.
13. Rosen, Kenneth, and James Kearl. "A Model of Housing Starts, Mortgage Flows, and the Behavior of the Federal Home Loan Bank Board and the Federal National Mortgage Association." Joint Center for Urban Studies of the Massachusetts Institute of Technology and Harvard University, Paper No. 27, May 1974.
14. Silber, William L. "A Model of Federal Home Loan Bank System and Federal National Mortgage Association Behavior." *The Review of Economics and Statistics,* 55 (August 1973), 308-20.
15. Theil, Henri. *Applied Economic Forecasting*. Amsterdam: North-Holland, 1966.

NOTES, COMMENTS, REPLIES

The Growth of Organizational Forms of Foreign Banks in the U.S.

*A Note by Lawrence G. Goldberg and Anthony Saunders**

1. *Introduction*

In the 1970s foreign banks rapidly expanded their positions in the United States. In November 1972 the total assets of U.S. offices of foreign banks were $24.3 billion or 6.3 percent of the total assets of the weekly reporting banks. By March 1980 total assets had risen to $176.7 billion or 25.6 percent of the total assets of the weekly reporting banks. This dramatic increase in the importance of foreign banks led to the passage of the 1978 International Banking Act (IBA), which is designed to regulate the growth and entry of foreign banks in the U.S. In light of the recent foreign acquisition of the fifteenth largest and the proposed acquisition of the fourteenth largest domestic banks,[1] it is important to understand the factors affecting foreign bank growth, especially as foreign bank entry raises a number of important issues, in particular, competitive equity between domestic and foreign banks, interstate branching, and reciprocal treatment of U.S. banks abroad.

When entering the U.S. market, foreign banks may choose among various organizational forms. Because of changes in relative advantages and disadvantages, each organizational form has exhibited different patterns of growth over time. In this paper we examine the factors affecting the growth of the three most important organizational forms of foreign bank activity, agencies, branches, and subsidiaries. It is argued that differences in profitability, as measured by both current returns and costs, and expected future business should have affected the relative growth of the

*The authors would like to thank two anonymous referees for their comments and Theoharry Gramatikos and Helen Yu for their assistance in assembling the data. Partial funding for the project was provided by the program on International Banking at New York University and Salomon Brothers Center for Research into Financial Institutions.

[1]*Business Week,* July 28, 1980, p. 45.

LAWRENCE G. GOLDBERG *is associate professor of finance and economics, and* ANTHONY SAUNDERS *is assistant professor of finance, Graduate School of Business Administration, New York University.*

0022-2879/81/0881-0365$00.50/0

different organizational forms. In addition expectations of changes in the regulation of foreign banks in the U.S. should also have affected growth.[2]

Previous studies of foreign bank growth in the U.S. have been of two types. The first are largely descriptions of foreign bank activty [1, 6, 8]. The second have used time-series or cross-sectional data to test various hypotheses concerning the determinants of international banking [2, 3, 4]. The current paper extends this research by empirically examining the reasons for the growth of different organizational forms of foreign banks in the U.S.

In the following section we describe the main types of organizational forms of foreign banks, emphasizing permissible activities and regulatory restrictions. The main provisions of the IBA and the differential effects on the organizational forms are then discussed. Finally, a model of the growth of total assets for the three main organizational forms of foreign banks in the U.S. is developed and then tested.[3]

2. *Organizational Forms of Foreign Banks*

There are seven organizational forms that foreign banks may utilize.[4] In this paper we are concerned mainly with analyzing the growth of the three most important forms—agencies, branches, and subsidiaries—but here we will also briefly describe the other options open to foreign banks.

The most limited, but also the easiest to establish of the organizational forms, is the representative office. These offices cannot accept deposits nor make loans but can forward payments or loan papers to the home office. This form can serve as a precursor for a larger presence in the future.

Agencies are considered integral parts of foreign banks and until the passage of the International Banking Act were virtually immune from federal regulation. As can be seen from Table 1, in 1972 agencies were the most important organizational form of foreign bank activity. However, by 1980, while still largest in number, they were actually smaller than branches when measured by asset size. Agencies may make commercial and industrial loans but are prohibited from making consumer loans. They are not permitted to accept deposits although they do maintain "credit balances" that are very similar to deposits. The credit balance can represent an unused portion of a loan or a receipt from an international transaction. Most payments, however, cannot be made from these accounts. Agencies are financed primarily by funding from the parent bank or by borrowings in the Federal Funds or

[2]Entry of foreign banks into the U.S. by merger or de novo also raises antitrust issues. While in theory expectations regarding future changes in antitrust policy can be expected to affect choice of organizational form, measurement would be difficult, leading us to concentrate in our empirical work upon the effect of the IBA.

[3]Because of the unavailability of sufficiently disaggregated time-series data (for regression analysis) we do not distinguish in these tests between acquisitions and de novo entry nor between the region or market area of entry. In general, we might expect different behavior from the two types of entry. For example, acquisitions involve a ready-made deposit base and market share while de novo entry requires the bank to build up market share which may extend the interval until profits are realized. Nevertheless, Ogilvie has suggested that "roughly 80% of foreign bank asset growth is attributed to de novo expansion rather than to acquisitions" [6, p. 75].

[4]This discussion is based on [7, pp. 185–86; 5, pp. 786–87; 1, pp. 6–7].

TABLE 1

MAIN FORMS OF FOREIGN BANKS

	November 1972		March 1980	
	Total Assets	Number	Total Assets	Number
Agencies	13,635	50	62,227	165
Branches	5,302	26	85,889	127
Subsidiaries	4,064	25	25,788	37

SOURCE: Federal Reserve Board.
NOTE: Total assets are in millions of dollars.

interbank markets. Agencies usually emphasize financing of foreign trade, such as handling letters of credit and bills of exchange. Customers are mostly banks and businesses rather than individuals.

Investment companies engage in loan and investment activities and in many ways are very similar to agencies. They cannot accept deposits but like agencies maintain credit balances. They are of limited importance since they are only chartered in New York under the New York State Investment Company Act. Although they are the only organizational form permitted to deal in securities, they are often ignored in discussions of foreign bank activities since, as of March 1980, there were only six investment companies with total assets of less than $3 billion.

The International Banking Act also permitted foreign banks to establish Edge Act Corporations. These corporations are chartered by the Federal Reserve Board and specialize in international banking activities. The IBA expanded the powers of Edge Act Corporations, but their permitted scope of activities are similar to those of agencies. Agreement Corporations, a fifth alternative for foreign banks, are a state-chartered alternative to Edge Act Corporations but are of limited importance. There is only one foreign owned Agreement Corporation in existence today (in Texas). Furthermore, the passage of the IBA removed any remaining advantages of establishing Agreement Corporations rather than Edge Act Corporations.

The most important organizational form today (in terms of asset size) is the branch. Like the agency, the branch is considered to be an integral part of the parent bank, but unlike the agency it can offer a full range of banking services. Branches can accept deposits and make loans. Traditionally, their lending activity has emphasized U.S. subsidiaries of firms from the home country of the parent bank, but increasingly branches have become involved in the U.S. corporate market. Branches, like agencies, have been primarily wholesale operations.

The final form is the subsidiary. Subsidiaries have identical banking powers as domestic banks. Foreign banks can gain control of a subsidiary either through acquisition of an existing U.S. bank or by establishing a new bank. Many of the foreign subsidiaries are retail oriented. These banks are regulated in an identical fashion to domestic banks.

The data in Table 1 do not include some recent acquisitions of domestic banks, in particular the acquisition of Marine Midland Bank, the fifteenth largest in the country, by the Hong Kong and Shanghai Banking Corporation. In 1979 federal authorities approved this acquisition, but the New York State Banking Department denied the application. This induced Marine Midland to switch from a state to a national charter in order to circumvent state jurisdiction. More recently, in July 1980, Midland Bank, the third largest British bank, announced its intention to acquire Crocker National Bank, the fourteenth largest bank in the country. These acquisitions of large U.S. banks have alarmed many people and resulted in several proposals to impose more stringent limitations on foreign bank activity in the United States. Clearly, these trends only emphasize the importance of uncovering the factors affecting the expansion of foreign banks in the U.S., and, in particular, why the use of organizational form has varied over time.

3. *The International Banking Act*

The main purpose of the International Banking Act was to equalize the treatment of foreign and domestic banks. In changing the rules with respect to foreign banking activity, the act also altered the relative desirability of the organizational forms. The act has many provisions; some impact favorably and some unfavorably on the various forms.[5]

The IBA limits the multistate operations of foreign banks in order to equalize their position relative to domestic banks. Foreign banks with multistate operations in place can maintain them, but as of July 1978 new branches and agencies established by foreign banks outside their home states can only accept the same type of deposit accepted by Edge Act Corporations. This should reduce the relative attractiveness of branches and agencies.

Federal chartering for agencies and branches is established by the act. Branches and agencies electing this option can use Federal Reserve services such as check clearing. Unfavorable for branches and agencies, however, is the increased federal regulation and Federal Reserve authority to impose reserve requirements on all federal and state licensed branches and agencies (which took effect in September 1980). Prior to the act FDIC insurance was not available to foreign branches and agencies. However, the act makes FDIC insurance available to branches and agencies but actively requires FDIC insurance for all branches taking retail deposits (under $100,000). Since many branches will now pay FDIC premium assessments, they can no longer enjoy this relatively small cost advantage over domestic banks. However, their smaller depositors will now enjoy full deposit protection. This will probably allow branches to attract more retail deposits, increasing their attractiveness relative to subsidiaries. Foreign banks operating agencies and branches were also subjected to the nonbanking provisions of the Bank Holding Company Act of 1970 and thus could no longer engage in any new activities that were not permissible for domestic holding companies.

Finally, the powers of Edge Act Corporations were expanded and restrictions on foreign ownership were eased. Consequently, the act should encourage foreign

[5]See Segala [7] and Key and Brundy [5] for further discussion of the IBA.

establishment of Edge Act Corporations. In summary, with respect to branches and agencies, there are both favorable and unfavorable factors resulting from passage of the IBA, but, on balance, the unfavorable appear to be more important. Of the two, agencies should be most adversely affected since prior to the legislation they were virtually unregulated. Subsidiaries, since they were already regulated in the same fashion as domestic banks, should not have been significantly affected by the act.

4. *A Model of Foreign Bank Organizational Forms*

The model developed and tested below assumes that there are four basic motivating factors determining entry and expansion by foreign banks in a specific organizational form. The first factor is the current rate of profit (π). To the extent that foreign banks are profit maximizing firms a high level of profits for any of the three organizational forms would make entry and expansion attractive. However, the current profit rate is likely to offer only a partial explanation, especially if banks have longer-run profit objectives. Under such circumstances we might expect that anticipatory variables, which reflect future growth and profit opportunities, will be important to the foreign bank's management. It is hypothesized here that foreign bankers will form expectations as to the future growth of U.S. domestic business, the future growth of international business in the U.S., and the future course of U.S. regulatory policy. For example, anticipation that future regulatory policy will be restrictive, for a particular organizational form, is likely to inhibit entry and slow its rate of growth. Hence we specify that the size of each organizational form i at any moment t (a_{it}) will be dependent on current profitability (π_t), expected growth of domestic business (d_t^e), expected growth in international business (i_t^e), and expectations regarding U.S. regulation of foreign banks (r_t^e). Hence,

$$a_{it} = f(\pi_t, d_t^e, i_t^e, r_t^e). \tag{1}$$

We measure the dependent variable, the size of agencies, branches, and subsidiaries by the size of their total assets. Data on this variable for each organizational form has been published by the Board of Governors of the Federal Reserve System since 1972.IV and was available to us up until 1980.I. The first independent variable, π_t, presented a number of measurement problems. Specifically, it is extremely difficult to gain access to individual or even aggregate profit figures for foreign bank subsidiaries, branches, and agencies in the U.S. Consequently, we decided to measure current profitability by the estimated size of each organizational form's interest margin (or spread), s, in the prior quarter, where this spread is equal to the difference between the banks average interest revenue and its average interest expense. However, it should be recognized that the spread will tend to be a more volatile index of profits than profits calculated from end of year financial statements (such as the rate of return on equity). A full description of the estimation of the spread variable is provided in the Appendix. Using spread as an index of profitability, we expect, ceteris paribus, that as the spread widened for any of the organizational forms, asset size will have grown either through de novo entry or expansion by existing members of the organizational group.[6]

The three expectational variables also present measurement problems. The variable d_t^e, the expected growth of domestic business, was represented by the current rate of domestic investiment (I_t). This variable was selected on the grounds that expectations regarding the future growth of domestic U.S. loans, and in particular commercial and industrial loans, are likely to be highly correlated with I_t. Moreover, domestic investment tends to be a leading cyclical indicator of domestic business conditions and has been consistently employed to forecast future economic developments. Hence, growth of domestic investment is likely to generate expectations as to the future domestic demand for the services of foreign banks in the U.S. Quarterly data on gross domestic investment were derived from the *Survey of Current Business*.

For the foreign or international business expectations variable (i_t^e), we selected the ratio of U.S. imports (M_t) to U.S. GNP (Y_t). This ratio provides a measure of foreign firm penetration into U.S. markets. Since many foreign multinationals desire to retain links with their indigenous commercial banks, especially for the purposes of trade finance, it becomes desirable for foreign banks to set up a U.S. presence and to expand size as demand dictates. Clearly an increasing M_t/Y_t ratio implies an expanding rate of U.S. business activity by foreign firms and is indicative of the potential future demand for the international services of foreign banks in the U.S. The final expectations variable in the model is that relating to foreign bankers' expectations of future U.S. regulatory changes (r_t^e). Since we know that the IBA was passed in July 1978 we can measure expectations of that particular legislative change by employing a dummy variable. Specifically we might view the period leading up to the passage of the act as one in which foreign banks made appropriate adjustments to the impending regulatory change. For example, if the legislation was viewed as having a (net) negative impact on the organizational form, as is likely in the case of agencies, it should have reduced the rate of entry and expansion in anticipation of this effect. As the IBA was actively debated in Congress from the beginning of 1976 up until its passage in July 1978, we specified a dummy variable (D_t) that took the value of 0 between 1972.IV and 1975.IV and between 1978.IV and 1980.I, and a value of 1 between 1976.I and 1978.III. Use of this dummy will allow us to determine whether the IBA had a net restrictive effect on foreign banking and which of the organizational forms were most affected. The empirical form of equation (1) is specified as equation (2) below:

$$a_{it} = \beta_0 + \beta_1 S_{t-1} + \beta_2 I_t + \beta_3 (M/Y)_t + \beta_4 D_t + u_t. \tag{2}$$

[6]This appears to be a reasonable surrogate measure of profitability. Various bankers have argued that spread is a useful indicator of current bank profitability. See *New York Times*, July 29, 1980, p. D1.

TABLE 2

REGRESSION RESULTS

Agencies

$$a_{it} = -10004 + 8860.8 s^*_{t-1} + 69.896\, I_t^* + 22530\, (M/Y)_t^* - 7336.9\, D_t^*$$

$$(-1.768) \quad (4.453) \quad (5.864) \quad (2.751) \quad (-5.426) \qquad (3)$$

$$\bar{R}^2 = 0.901, \quad \text{D-W} = 1.265$$

Branches

$$a_{it} = -18422^* - 1748.2\, s_{t-1} + 285.8\, I_t^* + 45586\, (M/Y)_t - 8720.4\, D_t^*$$

$$(-2.465) \quad (0.486) \quad (7.356) \quad (0.207) \quad (-2.173) \qquad (4)$$

$$\bar{R}^2 = 0.788, \quad \text{D-W} = 1.346, \quad \hat{p} = 0.56$$

Subsidiaries

$$a_{it} = -47.383 - 145.42\, s_{t-1} + 70.202\, I_t^* - 20636\, (M/Y)_t - 1551.4\, D_t$$

$$(-0.026) \quad (-0.314) \quad (5.478) \quad (-0.311) \quad (-1.219) \qquad (5)$$

$$\bar{R}^2 = 0.611, \quad \text{D-W} = 1.501, \quad \hat{p} = 0.66$$

NOTE: t-statistics are in parentheses.
*Significant at the 5 percent level.

The model was estimated by generalized least squares. The results of the quarterly regressions for each organizational form are shown in Table 2.

Equation (3) presents the results for foreign agencies. As can be seen all four independent variables are statistically significant at the 5 percent level and have the expected signs. That is, an increase in the spread (profit) earned by agencies and in the domestic and foreign expectational variables had a significant positive effect on their size. Moreover, as was expected, the IBA dummy had a negative impact on agency expansion.

Equation (4) presents the results for branches. Two variables, the domestic business (I_t) and regulatory dummy (D_t) variables are statistically significant at the 5 percent level, while the foreign business and profit (or spread) variables are statistically insignificant. The relative importance of the domestic business variable compared to the international variable is explainable by the fact that branches were more oriented towards domestic U.S. business than were agencies. In particular, as explained in section 2, branches could undertake a number of domestic banking activities prohibited to agencies. The significant negative coefficient on the regulatory dummy is indicative of the fact that foreign bankers viewed the IBA as having a (net) negative impact on branches as well as on agencies. Finally the spread or profit variable is not statistically significant. There are a number of possible reasons for this. First, as discussed earlier, it is possible that because of its sensitivity to interest cycles, spread is not a very good measure of current profits. However, in the absence of detailed profit data for branches this possibility cannot really be evaluated. Second, foreign banks that set up branches may be concerned with longer-run profits and may place less emphasis on current (or short-run) profit maximization. In particular, since branches tend to be more permanent fixtures than agencies, usually requiring a greater infrastructure and longer-term commitment of resources by the foreign banks concerned, foreign owners may be willing to subordinate current or short-run profit objectives for longer-run profit considerations.

Equation (5) presents the results for foreign bank subsidiaries. As can be seen the results are similar, with one exception, to those for branches. Subsidiaries have tended to concentrate on domestic business rather than international finance, and this is reflected in the statistical significance of I_t and the insignificance of $(M/Y)_t$. Moreover, since subsidiaries are identical in regulatory structure to U.S. domestic banks, the establishment of subsidiaries tends to imply a longer-term commitment of resources with less stress on short-run profitability. Again this may explain the insignificance of the spread variable. Finally, the regulatory dummy variable is insignificantly different from zero. Hence, owners of foreign bank subsidiaries viewed the IBA as neither advantageous nor disadvantageous. This is not surprising since prior to the IBA subsidiaries were regulated on the same basis as domestic banks, the primary thrust of the IBA being aimed at agencies and branches.

5. *Conclusions*

This paper has sought to determine the variables impacting on the growth of different types of foreign banks in the U.S. All major organizational forms were identified, and the regulatory boundaries on their banking activities discussed. A model was developed that sought to explain the aggregate growth of the three main types of organizational forms. It was hypothesized that four factors could be expected to determine this growth: current profitability, expected future domestic business, expected future international business, and expected regulatory changes. The empirical results suggested that these factors tended to impact on agencies in a different manner from branches and subsidiaries, with agencies more affected by international business considerations and more concerned with current, or short-run, profitability. Also, the IBA appeared to have a negative affect on the underlying growth of agencies and branches leaving subsidiaries relatively unaffected.

APPENDIX

This appendix describes how the spread variable s (used as a surrogate for π_t in the paper) was derived from the balance-sheet data and available interest rates. As discussed in the paper the spread was defined as the difference between the weighted average return on assets and the weighted average cost of liabilities. These were measured using the definitions and assumptions described in equations (1) and (2) below.

Weighted Average Return of assets of organizational form i at time t

$$= \frac{\text{C \& I Loans}}{\text{Net Total Assets}} \times \text{Av. Prime Rate} + \frac{\text{Other Loans}}{\text{N.T.A.}} \times \text{Av. Prime Rate}$$

$$+ \frac{\text{Interbank Loans}}{\text{N.T.A.}} \times \begin{array}{l}\text{Average}\\ \text{Federal}\\ \text{Funds Rate}\end{array} + \frac{\text{Securities}}{\text{N.T.A.}} \times \begin{array}{l}\text{Average 6 Month}\\ \text{T. Bill Rate}\end{array}$$

$$+ \frac{\text{Clearing Balances}}{\text{N.T.A.}} \times \begin{array}{l}\text{Average 3 month}\\ \text{Commercial}\\ \text{Paper Rate}\end{array} + \frac{\begin{array}{l}\text{Due from Related}\\ \text{Institutions}\end{array}}{\text{N.T.A.}} \times \begin{array}{l}\text{Average}\\ \text{Euro Dollar}\\ \text{Rate}\end{array} \quad (1)$$

Weighted Average Interest Expense of organizational form i at time t

$$= \frac{\text{Non-Bank Deposits}}{\text{Net Total Liabilities}} \times \begin{array}{l}\text{Average Rate}\\ \text{on U.S. Time}\\ \text{Deposits}\end{array} + \frac{\begin{array}{l}\text{Borrowing from}\\ \text{Non-Banks}\end{array}}{\text{N.T.L.}} \times \begin{array}{l}\text{Average}\\ \text{Federal}\\ \text{Funds Rate}\end{array}$$

$$+ \frac{\begin{array}{l}\text{Interbank}\\ \text{Liabilities}\end{array}}{\text{N.T.L.}} \times \begin{array}{l}\text{Average}\\ \text{Federal}\\ \text{Funds Rate}\end{array} + \frac{\begin{array}{l}\text{Clearing}\\ \text{Liabilities}\end{array}}{\text{N.T.L.}} \times \begin{array}{l}\text{Average 3 month}\\ \text{Commercial}\\ \text{Paper Rate}\end{array}$$

$$+ \frac{\begin{array}{l}\text{Due to Related}\\ \text{Institutions}\end{array}}{\text{N.T.L.}} \times \begin{array}{l}\text{Average}\\ \text{Euro Dollar}\\ \text{Rate}\end{array} \quad (2)$$

Notes. Net total assets are defined as total assets—"other" assets (where other assets are not defined in the balance-sheet). Net total liabilities are defined as total liabilities—"other liabilities"—capital, and reserves. "Other assets" and "other liabilities" plus capital and reserves were fairly small in relation to total assets and liabilities (rarely more than 7 percent of the respective aggregates).

LITERATURE CITED

1. Comptroller General of the United States, General Accounting Office. *Considerable Increase in Foreign Banking in the United States since 1972*. Washington, D.C.: August 1979.

2. Fieleke, Norman. "The Growth of U.S. Banking Abroad: An Analytical Survey." In *Key Issues in International Banking*. Boston: Ballinger, 1977.

3. Goldberg, Lawrence G., and Anthony Saunders. "The Causes of U.S. Bank Expansion Overseas: The Case of Great Britain." *Journal of Money, Credit, and Banking*, 12 (November 1980, Part 1), 630–43.

4. ______. "The Determinants of Foreign Banking Activity in the United States." *Journal of Banking and Finance*, 5 (1981), 17–32.

5. Key, Sydney J., and James M. Brundy. "Implementation of the International Bank Act." *Federal Reserve Bulletin* (October 1979), 785–96.

6. Ogilvie, Nigel R. "Foreign Banks in the U.S. and Geographic Restrictions on Banking." *Journal of Bank Research* (Summer 1980), 72–79.

7. Segala, John P. "A Summary of the International Banking Act of 1978." *Economic Review* (January/February 1979), 185–90.

8. Terrell, Henry S., and Sydney J. Key. *The U.S. Activities of Foreign Banks: An Analytic Survey*. Washington, D.C.: Board of Governors of the Federal Reserve System, International Finance Division Paper No. 113, 1977.

Organizational Form and Risk in Bank-Affiliated Mortgage Companies

*A Note by John T. Rose and Roger D. Rutz**

1. INTRODUCTION

Although the Bank Holding Company (BHC) Act of 1956 restricted the nonbanking activities of registered multibank holding companies, federal regulation of BHC nonbanking activities expanded significantly when the act was amended in 1970. Most importantly, the 1970 Amendments brought one-bank holding companies, many of which had actively expanded into nonbanking activities during the late 1960s, under Federal Reserve regulation. In addition, the amendments broadened the Federal Reserve Board's authority to determine which nonbanking activities would be permissible for BHCs.

From 1971–79, the Federal Reserve Board permitted 19 nonbanking activities for BHCs and approved over 4,500 BHC applicants to engage in these activities. Interestingly, most of these so-called nonbanking activities are also permissible to national banks. Two principal considerations appear to explain the pattern of establishing traditional banking activities in BHC nonbank subsidiaries, rather than organizing the activities within the bank(s) of the BHC. First, BHC nonbank subsidiaries are generally exempt from geographic branching restrictions. Second, until perhaps recently, nonbank subsidiaries have generally been subject to less-intensive federal supervision than banks, as evidenced by the frequency of federal examinations. While insured banks have long been subject to annual or biannual examination by the bank's primary federal regulator, such frequent inspection of nonbank subsidiaries of BHCs was not instituted until 1978.[1,2]

*We wish to thank R. Michael Rice for providing the mortgage company data used in this study. We also extend thanks to Ronnie McWilliams for research assistance and Gloria Battle for clerical support. The views expressed are those of the authors and do not necessarily reflect the views of the Board of Governors or its staff.

[1]The Federal Reserve Board approved a program in 1976, establishing minimum guidelines for inspecting most BHCs at least once every three years. A formal program of annual inspections for large BHCs (above $300 million of consolidated assets) was instituted in 1978. (For further discussion of these programs, see the Federal Reserve Board's press release dated November 11, 1977, and Federal Reserve Board *Annual Reports* for the years 1976–79.)

[2]In addition to a less-intensive supervisory climate, the legal and regulatory apparatus may also favor the BHC nonbank subsidiary, at least for some bank-permissible nonbanking activities; see Childs [1].

JOHN T. ROSE *and* ROGER D. RUTZ *are economists, Board of Governors of the Federal Reserve System.*

0022-2879/81/0881-0375$00.50/0
JOURNAL OF MONEY, CREDIT, AND BANKING, vol. 13, no. 3 (August 1981)

This study explores the implications of these two considerations for the balance sheet risk exposure of one nonbanking activity—mortgage banking—which is permissible to both BHCs and national banks. Specifically, the study tests whether the balance sheet risk of bank-affiliated mortgage companies differs between mortgage companies operated as a subsidiary of a bank and those operated as a BHC nonbank subsidiary.[3] Mortgage banking is selected for two reasons. First, mortgage banking is one of the most important nonbanking activities in which BHCs are engaged. Second, sufficient data are available for mortgage companies that are subsidiaries of both BHCs and national banks so that statistical tests can be conducted.

Theoretically, spinning an activity out of a bank and into a BHC nonbank subsidiary should lead to an increase in the balance sheet risk of the activity since it is operated in a less-intensive supervisory climate. Greater geographic diversification, on the other hand, may be expected to have little effect on balance sheet risk,[4] except to the extent that it results in balance sheet adjustments by the parent holding company to maximize the BHC's overall risk-return preference function.

2. SAMPLE AND DATA

In order to compile a data base for testing purposes, each mortgage company on the *American Banker* list of the "100 Largest Mortgage Servicers in the U.S." for 1973 was asked to furnish copies of its annual "Financial Statement Survey" prepared for the Mortgage Bankers Association for each of the years 1973-77.[5] A total of twenty-four acceptable mortgage companies that either were bank-affiliated over the entire period 1973-77 or became affiliated after 1973 responded with usable financial statements covering at least two years of bank affiliation. Of these twenty-four companies, seventeen are nonbank subsidiaries of BHCs, and seven are subsidiaries of national banks which, in turn, are subsidiaries of BHCs.[6] By pooling all of the available data provided by these companies for the entire period 1973-77, the resultant sample includes sixty-two annual observations for mortgage banking subsidiaries of BHCs and twenty-four annual observations for mortgage banking subsidiaries of national banks.

3. REGRESSION MODEL

In order to test the impact of organizational structure on the balance sheet risk of bank-affiliated mortgage companies, the following multiple regression model is estimated in linear form:

[3]A preferred risk measure is the variance of a firm's earnings over time. However, variance-of-earnings data could not be computed for the sample mortgage companies.

[4]The effect of geographic diversification by a firm should be to reduce the time variance of the firm's earnings due to imperfect correlation of the time variability of earnings across geographic markets. However, this need have no effect on the firm's balance sheet structure.

[5]See *American Banker,* May 6, 1974.

[6]One respondent mortgage company was deleted because it is a subsidiary of a bank which is itself not a part of any BHC system. Some analysts have argued that BHCs may be more aggressive than their independent bank counterparts. Thus, we desired that all of the sample mortgage companies be affiliated with a bank that is itself a BHC subsidiary.

$$Y = f(X_1, X_2, X_3, X_4, X_5, X_6, X_{7j}),$$

where

Y = ratio of adjusted equity capital divided by risk assets of the mortgage company, where "risk assets" are defined as total assets minus cash, Federal National Mortgage Association stock, other marketable securities, and first mortgages, and "adjusted equity capital" is defined alternatively as equity capital plus 0.5 percent and 1.0 percent of the mortgage company's servicing portfolio

X_1 = dichotomous variable defined as one if the mortgage company is operated as a BHC nonbank subsidiary under Section 4(c)(8) of the amended BHC Act, and zero otherwise

X_2 = dichotomous variable defined as one if the mortgage company is operated as a BHC nonbank subsidiary under Section 4(a)(2) of the amended BHC Act, and zero otherwise

X_3 = asset size of the consolidated BHC with which the mortgage company is affiliated, in log form

X_4 = percentage change (in fractional form) in assets of the consolidated BHC with which the mortgage company is affiliated, over the two years prior to the observation date

X_5 = ratio of equity capital divided by risk assets of the consolidated BHC with which the mortgage company is affiliated, where "risk assets" are defined as total assets minus cash assets and U.S. Treasury and agency securities

X_6 = ratio of assets held by nonbank subsidiaries of the BHC with which the mortgage company is affiliated (less the assets of the mortgage company in the case where it is a nonbank subsidiary of the BHC), divided by total consolidated BHC assets

X_{7j} = four dichotomous variables, defined as one or zero, indicating year of observation, where j = 4, 5, 6, 7 for the years 1974–77.

Dependent Variable

The dependent variable, adjusted equity capital divided by risk assets, is a proxy for the overall balance sheet risk exposure of a mortgage company. The rationale behind this measure is that it relates the total net worth of the mortgage company to those assets with the greatest probability of default.

Traditional leverage ratios (for example, equity capital divided by total assets) are not appropriate measures of mortgage company risk for two reasons. First, such ratios ignore the value of the mortgage company's servicing portfolio which, although not represented on the mortgage company's balance sheet, usually represents the primary and most stable source of income and thus the most important "asset" a mortgage company possesses. A second deficiency of traditional leverage ratios relates to the transitory nature of a mortgage company's inventory of first mortgages. Because of variations over time in the rate of turnover of the first mortgage inventory, a mortgage company's total assets and any associated leverage ratio may fluctuate widely from time to time. Yet, because a mortgage company's inventory of first mortgages typically entails little or no default risk, the overall risk exposure of the mortgage company may remain unchanged.

The risk measure used in this study (Y) corrects for the difficulties outlined above, first, by adjusting equity capital upward to reflect the value of the mortgage company's servicing portfolio and, second, by adjusting total assets downward to exclude first mortgages and other relatively riskless assets.[7] The two adjusted measures of equity capital represent the likely range of net worth valuations based on historical sales prices for mortgage company servicing portfolios. Risk assets include primarily construction loans as well as other loans and assets, including land held for development.[8]

Independent Variables

Mortgage Company Organizational Form (X_1, X_2). Two dummy variables are included to capture the effects of the organizational form through which a BHC may operate a nonbank subsidiary. Most BHC mortgage banking subsidiaries are operated under Section 4(c)(8) of the amended BHC Act, which limits the nonbanking activities of a BHC to those permitted by the Federal Reserve Board. However, a number of mortgage banking subsidiaries of one-bank holding companies were acquired prior to the 1970 Amendments to the BHC Act and are, therefore, either permanently or temporarily (until December 31, 1980) "grandfathered" under Section 4(a)(2) of the act. Because these subsidiaries operate without federal restrictions on the activities in which they were engaged prior to the 1970 Amendments, they may be engaged in more activities than their Section 4(c)(8) counterparts, resulting in a somewhat different balance sheet structure. Still, both variables are expected to have negative coefficients, reflecting the less-intensive supervisory climate in which BHC nonbank subsidiaries operate, at least during the study period, relative to bank subsidiaries.[9]

Bank Holding Company Risk Preference (X_3, X_4, X_5). Differences among BHCs in risk preference should affect the BHC's equilibrium risk-return mix and, therefore, the risk exposure of the BHC's various activities, including mortgage banking. Three variables are defined to reflect differences among BHCs in their risk-return preference function. The first variable (X_3) represents consolidated BHC size and is expected to have a negative coefficient. Evidence by Mingo and Wolkowitz [4, especially n. 10] points to an inverse relationship between risk aversion and bank

[7]Mortgage loans held by a mortgage company are subject to interest rate risk, although this risk can be minimized by originating first mortgages with take-out commitments from permanent investors. A better measure of "risk assets" would perhaps exclude only those first mortgages made with take-out commitments; however, such data are not available for individual companies.

[8]For further discussion of the mortgage banking industry and this measure of mortgage company risk, see Rose and Rutz [6].

[9]As noted earlier, greater geographic diversification permitted to BHC nonbank subsidiaries is expected to have little, if any, direct effect on balance sheet risk. Diversification may result in some indirect effect if the parent holding company adjusts the balance sheet structure of its various subsidiaries in order to maximize the BHC's overall risk-return preference function; however, any such adjustments are expected to be minor.

size, and we expect a similar inverse relationship between risk aversion and BHC size. The logarithmic formulation of BHC size is used to allow for nonlinearity.

Short-term BHC growth (X_4) is also included to capture inter-holding company differences in risk preference. To the extent that rapid growth reflects aggressiveness and willingness to take risks, this should be manifested in greater risk exposure in the BHC's various activities.

A third measure of BHC risk preference is the leverage ratio of the consolidated holding company (X_5). Risk averse BHCs may be expected to have a relatively high consolidated ratio of equity capital to risk assets, in which case we may also expect a relatively high ratio of equity to risk assets in the various activities of the BHC.

Nonbank Subsidiary Organizational Form (X_6). In addition to mortgage banking, other bank-permissible activities, as well as some non-bank-permissible activities, may be established in BHC nonbank subsidiaries. The purpose of X_6, therefore, is to correct for inter-holding company differences in the amount of business of the mortgage company's parent holding company that is conducted through nonbank subsidiaries rather than through bank subsidiaries. To the extent that BHCs operate their subsidiaries as a single, integrated entity, as evidence [2, 3, 5] suggests, inter-holding company differences in organizational structure should impact on the risk exposure of individual subsidiaries as well as the overall risk exposure of the BHC system. A weakness of this variable, of course, is that it fails to allow for inter-holding company differences in the mix of activities conducted through nonbank subsidiaries. No particular sign is hypothesized for this variable.

Year 1974 to Year 1977 (X_{7j}). Because of the small number of cross-sectional observations for each year, the observations were pooled over the five years 1973–77. Four dichotomous (dummy) variables are included to capture any effects due to the year of observation.

4. REGRESSION RESULTS

Regression results were similar (in terms of statistical significance) for the two adjusted measures of mortgage company equity capital. Hence, results are presented only for the measure that includes 0.5 percent of the mortgage company's servicing portfolio (t-statistics in parentheses):

$$\begin{aligned}
Y = 3.196 \quad & \underset{(-4.379)^{**}}{-0.5973\,X_1} \quad \underset{(-3.997)^{**}}{-0.5785\,X_2} \quad \underset{(-2.308)^{*}}{-0.3398\,X_3} \quad \underset{(0.315)}{+0.1480\,X_4} \\
& \underset{(0.022)}{+0.0768\,X_5} \quad \underset{(-0.883)}{-1.609\,X_6} \quad \underset{(-1.115)}{-0.1919\,X_{74}} \quad \underset{(-0.414)}{-0.0896\,X_{75}} \quad \underset{(0.620)}{+0.1460\,X_{76}} \\
& \underset{(0.441)}{+0.0945\,X_{77}} \qquad \bar{R}^2 = 0.323.
\end{aligned}$$

(**Significant at 1 percent level; *Significant at 5 percent level.)

As shown, both variables X_1 and X_2 have expected negative, statistically significant coefficients, indicating greater balance sheet risk in mortgage companies operated as BHC nonbank subsidiaries.[10] "Grandfather" status appears to have no effect on Y; the coefficient of X_1 exceeds that of X_2 in absolute terms, but the difference is not statistically significant.

Among the other independent variables, only consolidated BHC size (X_3) has a statistically significant coefficient with the expected negative sign.[11] This is consistent with the hypothesis that larger BHCs are less risk averse than their smaller counterparts and, therefore, operate their various activities at a relatively higher risk level.

5. SUMMARY AND CONCLUSION

Statistical analysis indicates that mortgage companies operated as BHC nonbank subsidiaries tend to have greater balance sheet risk, as measured by the ratio of adjusted equity capital to risk assets, than mortgage companies operated as subsidiaries of banks. This is consistent with the argument that BHCs have been able to increase the risk level of their bank-permissible nonbanking activities by organizing them as nonbank subsidiaries which, in turn, have been allowed to operate in a less-intensive supervisory climate. Of course, to the extent that BHC nonbank subsidiaries have benefited from geographic diversification, their overall risk exposure, measured in terms of variance of earnings, may still have been reduced. Further empirical research is needed to confirm the importance of geographic diversification to the BHC form of organization.

LITERATURE CITED

1. Childs, Bradley D. "Bank Holding Company Acquisitions: The Role of Non-Banking Finance Affiliates." *The Magazine of Bank Administration,* 51 (August 1975), 30-33.
2. Mayne, Lucille S. "Bank Holding Company Characteristics and the Upstreaming of Bank Funds." *Journal of Money, Credit, and Banking,* 12 (May 1980), 209-14.
3. ______. "Funds Transfer Between Bank Holding Companies and Their Affiliates." *Journal of Bank Research,* 11 (Spring 1980), 20-27.
4. Mingo, John J., and Benjamin Wolkowitz. "The Relationship Between Bank Soundness and Bank Size." *Journal of Economics and Business,* 30 (Winter 1978), 119-23.
5. Rose, John T. "Bank Holding Companies As Operational Single Entities." In *The Bank Holding Company Movement to 1978: A Compendium,* pp. 69-93. Washington, D.C.: Board of Governors of the Federal Reserve System, September 1978.
6. Rose, John T., and Roger D. Rutz. "Analyzing the Risk of Mortgage Banking Firms." *The Journal of Commercial Bank Lending,* 62 (April 1980), 49-53.

[10]The model was also estimated using alternative leverage ratios as the dependent variable, including equity capital/total assets, equity capital/risk assets, and adjusted equity capital/total assets. Both variables X_1 and X_2 had negative, significant coefficients in every estimated equation; however, the $\bar{R}^2$ was reduced in these alternative model specifications.

[11]Multicollinearity among the independent variables does not appear to be a problem. The highest (absolute) simple correlation coefficient (r) between any two independent variables is -0.560 (X_1, X_2); between any two measures of BHC risk preference, -0.513 (X_3, X_5).

Inflation Expectations and the Specification of Demand for Money Equations

*A Note by Vittorio Corbo**

Introduction

The aim of this paper is to bring to light two problems found in much of the empirical work on the demand for money in countries with intermediate inflation and, in particular, in Chile. These are that the demand function itself has been wrongly specified and, second, that there has been a large overestimation of the lag involved in the process of determining the expected inflation rate. A consequence of the latter has been that, in periods of decreasing inflation, a "passive policy" of equalizing the money supply to the quantity of money demanded has, due to the underestimation of the latter, in practice been an "active policy" of reducing the level of economic activity.[1]

Section 2 develops the model to be estimated, and in section 3 the econometric results are reported and analyzed.

The Demand for Money Equation

A good summary of the large and growing literature on the demand for money can be found in [11] and [18]. In this paper, however, we use the conventional long-run demand for money function.

$$M^*(t) = L\,[Q^e(t),\, I^e(t)],$$

where $M^*(t)$ is the long-run demand for real money balances in period t; $Q^e(t)$ is the expected domestic product expressed in constant prices in period t; and $I^e(t)$ is the expected cost of holding money in period t.

*I am grateful to Jorge Cauas and Jean Marie Dufour for the useful discussions I have had with them on this material. I am indebted also to Jere Behrman, Phillip Cagan, Douglas Fisher, Jacob A. Frenkel, Morton Stelcner, and an anonymous referee of this journal for their helpful comments on a previous draft of the paper. My particular thanks go to Panagiotis Lazaridis, José M. Vrljicak, and Osvaldo Larrañaga for their devoted research assistance. Financial support was provided by a grant from The Servicio de Desarrollo Científico, Artístico y de Cooperación Internacional of the University of Chile.

[1]On monetary policy during 1965–70, see [9].

VITTORIO CORBO *is professor of economics, Concordia University and Catholic University of Chile.*

0022-2879/81/0881-0381$00.50/0

In this study two alternative specifications of the function L are considered

$$\ln M^*(t) = \phi_0 + \phi_1 \ln Q^e(t) + \phi_2 I^e(t) + u(t) \tag{1}$$

$$\ln M^*(t) = \mu_0 + \mu_1 \ln Q^e(t) + \mu_2 \ln I^e(t) + v(t), \tag{2}$$

where ϕ_0, ϕ_1, ϕ_2, μ_0, μ_1, μ_2 are parameters and $u(t)$ and $v(t)$ are random variables.

Equation (1) was suggested by Cagan [3] for countries with hyperinflation. This specification has also been used for developing countries with moderate to high inflation (see, e.g., [6, 7, 9, 15]). By contrast, equation (2) is frequently used for countries with relatively low rates of inflation (see, e.g., [11, 18]).

Due, however, to adjustment costs and/or the lack of a well-developed clearing mechanism in the money market, $M^*(t)$ is not directly observable. As in Chow [4], we introduce a lag adjustment process between actual and desired money stocks. This is represented by a logarithmic partial adjustment mechanism.

$$\ln M(t) - \ln M(t-1) = \gamma\,(\ln M^*(t) - \ln M(t-1)),$$

where $M(t)$ is the short-run demand for real money balances in period t.

Introducing equations (1) and (2) into the above equation, we obtain the following short-run demand for money functions:

$$\ln M(t) = \gamma\phi_0 + \gamma\,\phi_1 \ln Q^e(t) + \gamma\,\phi_2 I^e(t) + (1-\gamma)\ln M(t-1) + \gamma u(t) \tag{3}$$

$$\ln M(t) = \gamma\mu_0 + \gamma\mu_1 \ln Q^e(t) + \gamma\mu_2 \ln I^e(t) + (1-\gamma)\ln M(t-1) + \gamma\,v(t). \tag{4}$$

There remains, however, the problem of linking $I^e(t)$ and $Q^e(t)$ to observable variables. For $I^e(t)$, the cost of holding money can be divided into the real interest rate, r, and the rate of inflation, p. We make the further assumption, as in Deaver [6], Hynes [15], and Corbo [5], that the expected cost of holding money is formed by a Cagan-Nerlove adaptive expectation model. In other words,

$$I^e(t) - I^e(t-1) = \beta\,[I(t) - I^e(t-1)],$$

which implies that the expected cost of holding money can be expressed as a geometric distributed lag of the cost of holding money, such that

$$I^e(t) = \sum_{i=0}^{\infty} \beta\,(1-\beta)^i\, I(t-i), \qquad 0 < \beta < 2. \tag{5}$$

All previous studies have wrongly restricted β to be between zero and one. For the stability of equation (5) we require only the restrictions on β specified above.[2]

[2]I due this point to Jere Behrman.

Similarly, $Q^e(t)$ can be expressed in terms of actual output by assuming that

$$\ln Q^e(t) - \ln Q^e(t-1) = \delta\,[\ln Q(t) - \ln Q^e(t-1)].$$

Then, equation (3) is lagged by one period and multiplied by $(1-\delta)$. The result is subtracted from equation (3) yielding (3′). Similarly this is done for equation (4) yielding (4′).

$$\begin{aligned}\ln M(t) &= \gamma\,\delta\,\phi_0 + \gamma\delta\,\phi_1 \ln Q(t) + \gamma\,\phi_2\,[I^e(t) - (1-\delta)\,I^e\,(t-1)] \\ &\quad + [(1-\gamma) + (1-\delta)]\ln M(t-1) - (1-\gamma)(1-\delta)\ln M\,(t-2) \\ &\quad + \gamma[u(t) - (1-\delta)\,u(t-1)],\end{aligned} \tag{3'}$$

and

$$\begin{aligned}\ln M(t) &= \gamma\delta\mu_0 + \gamma\delta\mu_1 \ln Q(t) + \gamma\mu_2\,[\ln I^e(t) - (1-\delta)\ln I^e\,(t-1)] \\ &\quad + [(1-\gamma) + (1-\delta)]\ln M(t-1) - (1-\gamma)(1-\delta)\ln M(t-2) \\ &\quad + \gamma[v(t) - (1-\delta)\,v\,(t-1)].\end{aligned} \tag{4'}$$

The choice between models (3′) and (4′) is facilitated by the transformation procedure of Box and Cox [1] (see also [10]) since, in Box and Cox terminology, they are special cases of the following model:

$$\begin{aligned}\ln M(t) &= \gamma\delta\,\alpha_0 + \gamma\delta\,\alpha_1 \ln Q(t) \\ &\quad + \gamma\alpha_2\left[\frac{(I^e(t))^\lambda - 1}{\lambda} - (1-\delta)\,\frac{(I^e(t-1)^\lambda - 1}{\lambda}\right] + [(1-\gamma) \\ &\quad + (1-\delta)]\ln M(t-1) - (1-\gamma)(1-\delta)\ln M(t-2) + \epsilon\,(t),\end{aligned} \tag{6}$$

where α_0, α_1, α_2, δ, γ, and λ are parameters, and $\epsilon(t)$ is a random error. By setting $\lambda = 1$ in equation (6), we obtain model (3′). In the limit as λ approaches zero we obtain model (4′). The choice between these two models is, thus, a question of estimating equation (6) and testing separately the hypotheses of $\lambda = 1$ and $\lambda = 0$.

The Empirical Results

If the disturbances $\epsilon(t)$ in equation (6) are independent and identically normally distributed, the maximum likelihood estimates (*ML*) will be consistent and asymptotically efficient, but, if there exists autocorrelation between the disturbances, the presence of a lagged endogenous variable as a regressor means that they will not be consistent. The latter problem is dealt with here by using the *ML* method to estimate equation (6) on the assumption of first-order autocorrelation in the disturbances with the parameter of this autoregressive process being estimated jointly with the other parameters of the equation.

The definition of $I^e(t)$ constitutes a further difficulty since it leads to an infinite lag on $I(t)$ on the right-hand side of equation (6). The specific nonlinearity of $I^e(t)$ precludes reducing this lag to a finite series of terms, and here we adopt the solution suggested by Cagan [3] of truncating the series prior to searching for the value of β

in the interval (0,2) that maximizes the likelihood function (see also [12]). In this case, we take the series back to the first quarter of 1950. The estimations are made for the period 1960.III to 1970.IV and in all of them we set $r = 0.02$.[3]

The maximum likelihood estimates of equation (6) with different restrictions on the parameters are given in Table 1. In the most general case, the maximum of the likelihood function was found for $\beta = 1.41$. In equations (3′) and (4′), λ is restricted to take the value 1 (variable elasticity demand equation) and 0 (constant elasticity equation), respectively, and to test for these restrictions we use the likelihood ratio test. Since the properties of *ML* estimation are only asymptotic, the test is an approximation for our sample of forty-two observations. The results of the test under alternative null hypothesis are given in the last column of Table 1. The critical value of the ratio at a 5 percent level of significance with one degree of freedom is 3.84. For $\lambda = 1$, we calculated a value of 7.36 and for $\lambda = 0$, a value of 0.74. Thus, we can reject the first hypothesis but not the second. Our data are, thus, in agreement with the double-log model and incompatible with the semi-log version, a finding that throws doubt on the usual specification of the demand for money equation for countries with intermediate rates of inflation.

The estimates obtained for equation (4′) could, however, be questioned because of the assumption of a constant β. In particular, it is possible to argue that there may exist a relationship between β and changes in the rate of inflation. To investigate this, following Koot [17], we assumed β to be a linear function of the cost of holding money and of the absolute value of the first difference in this variable.

$$\beta_t = \beta_0 + \beta_1 I(t) + \beta_2 |I(t) - I(t-1)|. \tag{7}$$

In our specification of equation (4′) the test could not be performed directly because of the form in which β enters. Hence, we tested for nonconstant β in an equation slightly different from equation (4′). We used a log linear adaptive expectations model for $I^e(t)$ and substituted in the β of equation (7). The results of this slighty modified version were very similar to those reported in Table 1. A likelihood ratio test indicated that the null hypothesis that $\beta_1 = \beta_2 = 0$ could not be rejected.[4]

Finally, we tested for the stability of equation (4′). For this purpose we used a set of tests based on the standarized recursive residuals. All tests were performed using a 5 percent significance level. To deal with the problem of autocorrelation and the presence of a lagged endogenous variable as in Dufour [8], we applied these tests conditional on the values of β, γ, δ, and ρ from the last row of Table 1.

First, using the Brown, Durbin, and Evans [2] CUSUM and CUSUM square tests we found that the null hypothesis of a stable function could not be rejected. Second, using the Harvey and Phillip [14] test for heteroscedasticity in the variance of the error of (4′), the null hypothesis of homoscedasticity could not be rejected. Third,

[3]Data sources, measurements, and definitions of the variables are available from the author on request.

[4]The computed test statistic was 0.59. We also worked with an alternative formulation of equation (7) in which β_t was a quadratic function of $I(t)$. The results were similar and the null hypothesis of a constant β_t could also not be rejected.

TABLE 1

DEMAND FOR MONEY EQUATIONS: 1960.III–1970.IV

	α_0	α_1	α_2	γ	δ	λ	β	ρ	Log of Likelihood Function	R^2	D-W	Likelihood Ratio
Equation (6)	−18.426	2.113	−0.541	0.188	0.674	0.227	1.41	−0.223	83.3415	0.982	1.90	
	(2.848)	(0.298)	(0.469)	(0.072)	(0.288)	(0.249)		(0.281)				
Equation (3′)	−21.321	2.119	−4.308	0.155	0.814	1	1.45	−0.098	79.6628	0.978	1.92	7.36
(equation (6) with $\lambda = 1$)	(4.625)	(0.371)	(2.288)	(0.075)	(0.437)			(0.425)				
Equation (4′)	−18.045	2.111	−0.264	0.205	0.604	0	1.38	−0.324	82.9727	0.982	1.89	0.74
(equation (6) with $\lambda = 0$)	(2.587)	(0.287)	(0.107)	(0.075)	(0.246)			(0.228)				

NOTES: The values in brackets are the standard errors of the coefficients. The likelihood ratio is computed as $-2\,[\ln L\,(\Omega) - \ln L\,(\Omega)]$, where $\ln L\,(\Omega)$ is the log of the likelihood function with the restriction on the parameters incorporated, and $\ln L\,(\Omega)$ is the log of the likelihood function without restriction on the parameters.

using the Phillip and Harvey [19] test for autocorrelation we found that we could not reject the null hypothesis of no autocorrelation. Finally, there remains a special case of instability—possible misspecification of equation (4′). To test for this we used the Harvey and Collier [13] test for systematic over- or underprediction. Again, we found that the null hypothesis of lack of systematic over- or underprediction could not be rejected.[5] We are, therefore, able to conclude that there is no evidence of either instability or misspecification in the estimated demand for money equation.

One of our most important findings is the high estimated value of β. In equation (4′), the estimated value of β is 1.38, which implies that the process of forming price expectations (eq. (5)) is stable but with oscillations. The very high weight attached to the present rate of inflation (1.38) is also noteworthy since it means that, in Chile, economic agents rapidly become aware of the dynamics of the inflationary process and can even overshoot the existing rate of inflation when estimating the expected rate.[6]

The second interesting finding of this study is the high estimated value of γ, which is 0.205. This implies an average lag of 3.88 quarter in the adjustment of actual to desired money balances. These results contrast quite sharply with the extremely low βs and γs estimated or assumed by other authors. Using Chilean quarterly data for the period 1932–55, Deaver [6], using an equation similar to our equation (3′) above with $\gamma = 1$, estimated a value of β of 0.1 for the entire period. Hynes [15], using Chilean annual data for the period 1935–60, estimated an equation linear in all the variables. His estimate of β was 0.5 and of δ was 0.4. This implies average lags substantially longer than the ones obtained in this study.

Finally, in a recent study with quarterly data for the period 1962–76, Khan [16] estimated an equation of the type of our equation (3′) for eleven LDCs excluding Chile. He added a term for flow disequilibrium in the money market. He reported estimated β values from 0.4 to 0.9 and γ values ranging from 0.015 to 0.459. The average value of β was 0.67 and the average value of γ was 0.10 with nine values below it. This implies a very long average lag in the adjustment of money balances.

The difficulty with these studies is that they arbitrarily start with a Cagan-type demand for money function without testing for its appropriateness. Our results show that such a test may lead to quite different estimates of the speed of adjustment. Thus, our equation (3′) (the one rejected by the test) yields an estimated γ of 0.155 and an average lag of 5.5 quarters, significantly longer than the 3.8 quarters obtained using equation (4′).

LITERATURE CITED

1. Box, George E. P., and David R. Cox. "An Analysis of Transformations." *Journal of the Royal Statistical Society,* Series B, 26 (1964), 211–43.
2. Brown, R. L., James Durbin, and James M. Evans. "Techniques for Testing the Con-

[5]The results of all the stability tests are available from the author on request.

[6]In equation (4′) of Table 1, we also tested the null hypothesis that $\beta = 1.0$ (expected inflation equals the existing rate), but the likelihood ratio test gave 5.06 and the hypothesis was thus rejected.

stancy of Regression Relationships Over Time." *Journal of the Royal Statistical Society,* Series B, 37 (1975), 149-92.

3. Cagan, Phillip. "The Monetary Dynamics of Hyperinflation." In *Studies in the Quantity Theory of Money,* edited by Milton Friedman, pp. 25-117. Chicago, Ill.: University of Chicago Press, 1956.
4. Chow, Gregory C. "On the Long-Run and Short-Run Demand for Money." *Journal of Political Economy,* 74 (April 1966), 111-31.
5. Corbo, Vittorio L. *Inflation in Developing Countries: An Econometric Study of Chilean Inflation.* Amsterdam: North-Holland, 1974.
6. Deaver, John V. "The Chilean Inflation and the Demand for Money." In *Varieties of Monetary Experiences,* edited by David Mieselman, pp. 7-67. Chicago, Ill.: University of Chicago Press, 1970.
7. Diz, Adolfo C. "Money and Prices in Argentina 1935-62." In *Varieties of Monetary Experiences,* edited by David Mieselman, pp. 69-162. Chicago, Ill.: University of Chicago Press, 1970.
8. Dufour, Jean Marie. "Methods for Specification Analysis with Macroeconomic Applications." Ph.D. dissertation, University of Chicago, 1979.
9. Ffrench-Davis, Ricardo. "Economic Policies and Stabilization Programs, Chile 1959-1969." Ph.D. dissertation, University of Chicago, 1970.
10. Frenkel, Jacob A. "The Forward Exchange Rate, Expectations and the Demand for Money: The German Hyperinflation." *American Economic Review,* 67 (September 1977), 653-70.
11. Goldfeld, Stephen M. "The Demand for Money Revisited." *Brookings Papers on Economic Activity,* 3 (1973), 577-638.
12. Griliches, Zvi. "Distributed Lags: A Survey." *Econometrica,* 35 (January 1967), 16-49.
13. Harvey, Andrew C., and Patrick Collier. "Testing for Functional Misspecification in Regression Analysis." *Journal of Econometrics,* 6 (July 1977), 103-19.
14. Harvey, Andrew C., and Garry D. A. Phillip. "A Comparison of the Power of Some Tests for Heteroscedasticity in the General Linear Model." *Journal of Econometrics,* 2 (December 1974), 307-16.
15. Hynes, Alan. "The Demand for Money and Monetary Adjustments in Chile." *The Review of Economic Studies,* 34 (July 1967), 285-93.
16. Khan, Mohsin S. "Monetary Shocks and the Dynamics of Inflation." *IMF Staff Papers,* 27 (June 1980), 250-84.
17. Koot, Ronald S. "Nonconstant Coefficients of Expectation and the Recent Demand for Money." *Journal of Monetary Economics,* 1 (July 1975), 375-82.
18. Laidler, David E. W. *The Demand for Money: Theories and Evidence.* Second edition. New York: Dun-Donnelly, 1977.
19. Phillip, Garry D. A., and Andrew C. Harvey. "A Simple Test for Serial Correlation in Regression Analysis." *Journal of the American Statistical Association,* 69 (December 1974), 935-39.
20. Theil, Henri. *Principles of Econometrics.* New York: Wiley, 1971.

Indirect Evidence on the Efficacy of Selective Credit Controls: The Case of Consumer Credit

*A Note by Brian A. Maris**

This note reports the results of an empirical analysis designed to test whether or not expenditures on consumer durables (*DG*) are responsive to changes in consumer credit extensions (*CC*). The technique used is the Sims test for causality [8]. The lack of a causal relation from *CC* to *DG* would indicate controls on this type of credit are unlikely to be effective in influencing durable goods expenditures, while a result showing causality from *CC* to *DG* can be interpreted as support for the efficacy of such controls.

The Sims's test for causality involves regressing variable *X* on first, current, and lagged values of *Y*, and then current, lagged, and leading values of *Y*. The process is repeated, reversing *X* and *Y*. Significant coefficients on future values of *Y*, taken as a group, combined with insignificance for future values of *X*, allow a conclusion of unidirectional causality from *X* to *Y*.[1]

Two conditions are necessary for the results of this test to be valid. The residuals of the regressions containing leading values must be white noise, and X_t and Y_t must be covariance stationary. In order to test residuals for autocorrelation of greater than first degree, the Box and Pierce test is employed. The hypothesis is that the residuals are not autocorrelated, and it is rejected if $x^2 > x^2$ (0.95).

Data are quarterly and seasonally adjusted.[2] To achieve covariance stationary

*This note was written while the author was a visiting research scholar, Office of Policy and Economic Research, Federal Home Loan Bank Board. The author is grateful to Henry Cassidy, Barry Falk, and anonymous referees for helpful comments. However, I alone am responsible for the analysis and interpretation, including any remaining errors. This note does not represent policy or opinion of the Federal Home Bank Board or the Office of Policy and Economic Research.

[1]Pierce [6] has shown that tests for causal relations may be biased toward a finding of no relationship. However, Granger [3] has shown that there is no theoretical reason why this must be so, and Sims [9] points out that Pierce's results are due to the estimation technique that he used and are not generally valid.

[2]The two data series used in the analysis are "Personal Consumption Expenditures—Durable Goods" (seasonally adjusted at annual rates, in current dollars; U.S. Department of Commerce), and "Consumer Credit Extended—Total" (seasonally adjusted at monthly rates, in current dollars; Board of Governors). The monthly consumer credit data were summed by quarters for the analysis. It has been shown [1] that seasonal adjustment of a data series may eliminate nonseasonal cycles from the data. If so, it seems likely that this would bias the results of the analysis toward a finding of no causal relationship. Since the analysis reported in this note shows causality running both ways, neither this nor the potential bias addressed in note 1 appear to have materially affected the results.

Brian A. Maris *is assistant professor, Department of Economics and Finance, University of Wisconsin, La Crosse.*

0022-2879/81/0881-0388$00.50/0
Journal of Money, Credit, and Banking, vol. 13, no. 3 (August 1981)

processes and white noise residuals, the variables were converted into natural logs and filtered, following the approach outlined in [10].[3] Before accepting the transformations as adequate, one must test the residuals of regressions between transformed series for randomness, as noted above. Results of these tests are reported in Table 1. The transformations were successful in generating random residuals in each of the regressions reported.

TABLE 1

SUMMARY OF REGRESSIONS

Regression Equations	$\bar{R}^2$	F Due to Regression	SEE	$d.f.$	X^2	F-Test on Leading Values
1. $DG_t = f(CC_t, \ldots, CC_{t-8})$	0.52	13.84*	0.03279	100	5.14	
2. $DG_t = f(CC_{t+4}, \ldots, CC_{t-8})$	0.54	10.64*	0.03210	96	6.08	2.09*
3. $CC_t = f(DG_t, \ldots, DG_{t-8})$	0.48	12.08*	0.02802	100	10.17	
4. $CC_t = f(DG_{t+4}, \ldots, DG_{t-8})$	0.54	10.72*	0.02638	96	9.35	4.20*

NOTES: DG = expenditures on consumer durable goods; CC = consumer credit extensions. All series are quarterly, filtered as described in the text. Sample period: 1952.III–1977.III.
*Significant at 10 percent level.

The results of the analysis are summarized in Table 1. Lag lengths of eight past and four future values were used because they were believed to be sufficiently long to capture whatever relationships exist. Since there are no simple techniques to specify the lag lengths, they were set a priori and used for all equations.[4]

As shown on line 4 of Table 1, when CC is regressed on DG, coefficients on leading values of DG are significant at the 10 percent level, as are coefficients for future values of CC when included in regressions of DG on CC (eq. (2)). Also, the F-test indicates that in both cases the regressions of DG and CC on lagged values only of the other are significant (eqq. (1) and (3)). These results show evidence of causation running both ways between DG and CC. This rules out the possibility that the correlation between CC and DG is one-way from expenditures to credit and suggests that changes in consumer credit extensions do affect expenditures on durable goods. This, in turn, suggests that measures influencing the allocation of credit to consumers may affect the distribution of expenditures. The experience in the second quarter of 1980, in response to the Carter administration's restrictions on consumer credit, is quite consistent with this interpretation of the results. A caveat is in order, however. It is possible that the effects obtained running from CC to DG may be the result of total credit rather than consumer credit, with consumer credit acting as a proxy for total credit. In this case the results do not demonstrate the efficacy of credit allocation policies. Unfortunately, there is no easy way to disentangle total and consumer credit effects.

The results of this analysis support conclusions of some earlier investigators [2,7] that selective credit policies can alter expenditure patterns. However, Hamburger and Zwick, based on analysis of the 1948–52 period of selective controls in the U.S. concluded that "the installment credit controls . . . had no significant effect on the

[3]The filter $(1-0.75B)^2$, where B is a shift operator (i.e., $B^i X_t = X_{t-i}$), used by Sims in [8] was tried for CC; this transformation was not sufficient. For DG a simpler filter was adequate. The filters used were: for DG, $(1-B)$; for CC, $(1-B)(1-0.2B^2+0.3B^4)$.

[4]Regression coefficients are available from the author on request.

level of consumer durable expenditures'' [4, p. 1562]. They suggest in [5] that consumers and lenders respond to selective controls by substituting uncontrolled forms of credit. The results of the analysis reported in Table 1 do not support the conclusions of Hamburger and Zwick unless, as suggested above, *CC* is serving as a proxy for total credit. In that case the analysis would not detect the type of substitution referred to by Hamburger and Zwick.

LITERATURE CITED

1. Auerback, Robert D., and Jack L. Rutner. ''The Misspecification of a Nonseasonal Cycle as a Seasonal by the X-11 Seasonal Adjustment Program.'' *Review of Economics and Statistics* (November 1978), 601-3.
2. Cohen, Jacob. ''Integrating the Real and Financial via the Linkage of Financial Flow.'' *Journal of Finance* (March 1968), 151-83.
3. Granger, Clive W. J. ''Comment.'' *Journal of the American Statistical Association* (March 1977), 22-23.
4. Hamburger, Michael J., and Burton Zwick. ''Installment Credit Controls, Consumer Expenditures and the Allocation of Real Resources.'' *Journal of Finance* (December 1977), 1557-69.
5. ______. ''The Efficacy of Selective Credit Policies: An Alternative Test.'' *Journal of Money, Credit, and Banking,* 11 (February 1979), 106-10.
6. Pierce, David A. ''Relationships—and the Lack Thereof—Between Economic Time Series, with Special Reference to Money and Interest Rates.'' *Journal of the American Statistical Association* (March 1977), 11-22.
7. Silber, William L. ''Selective Credit Policies: A Survey.'' *Banca Nationale del Lavoro Quarterly Review* (December 1973), 328-51.
8. Sims, Christopher A. ''Money, Income, and Causality.'' *American Economic Review* (September 1972), 540-52.
9. ______. ''Comment.'' *Journal of the American Statistical Association* (March 1977), 23-24.
10. Williams, David, Charles A. E. Goodhart, and David H. Gowland. ''Money and Causality: the U.K. Experience.'' *American Economic Review* (June 1976), 417-23.

On the Revenue Maximizing Rate of Inflation

*A Comment by David Chappell**

In an influential paper Cathcart [1] derived an expression for the inflation rate which maximizes the present value of government revenue. It is the purpose of this brief comment to show that the Cathcart result is incorrect and to derive the correct result.

The Cathcart model may be described by the following equations.

$$g = (p + \lambda - a\dot{\pi})k \tag{1}$$

$$k = k_0 e^{-a\pi} \text{ (real balance demand function)} \tag{2}$$

$$\dot{\pi} = b(p - \pi) \text{ (adaptive expectations),} \tag{3}$$

where

g = government revenue from inflation as a proportion of income
p = actual rate of inflation
π = expected rate of inflation
$k\ (\pi)$ = desired and actual ratio of real balances to real income
k_0 = $k(0)$, a positive constant
λ = constant exogenous growth rate of real output
a and b = positive constants.

Substituting equations (2) and (3) into (1) we derive

$$g = (\pi + \dot{\pi}/\delta + \lambda)k_0 e^{-a\pi}, \tag{4}$$

where $\delta \equiv b/1(1 - ab)$. Cathcart then employs calculus of variations to solve the problem of maximizing:

*The author is grateful for the comments of two anonymous referees on an earlier version of this comment, but the usual caveat applies.

DAVID CHAPPELL *is Esmée Fairbairn Senior Research Fellow in Economics, University of Sheffield.*

0022-2879/81/0881-0391$00.50/0

$$J \equiv h \int_0^{\infty} g(\pi,\dot{\pi}) e^{-\phi t} dt, \tag{5}$$

where $\phi > 0$ is a discount rate assumed equal to the real rate of return on capital. The solution of the Euler equation is

$$\pi(t) = (1/a) + (\phi/\delta) - \lambda = \text{constant}, \tag{6}$$

which implies that, in equilibrium, both actual and expected rates are the constant given in equation (6). Substituting (6) into (5) and integrating, we derive.

$$J = \left(\frac{1}{a\phi} + \frac{1}{\delta} \right) k_0 e^{(a\lambda - 1 - a\phi/\delta)}. \tag{7}$$

That this result is suboptimal may be seen from the following arguments. First, note that since $p + \lambda + a\pi = m$ (the proportional rate of change of the money supply), it follows that

$$g = m g_0 e^{-a\pi} \tag{8}$$

and

$$\dot{\pi} = \delta\,(m - \pi - \lambda). \tag{9}$$

Second, in Cathcart's stylized model there is no restriction on the rate of change of the money supply. Consequently the revenue maximizing rate of inflation may be attained instantaneously by means of a large, once-and-for-all, change in the rate of growth of the money supply at $t = 0$. (Mathematically, this is attained by the use of a Dirac delta function impulse.) Since the optimal rate of inflation is a constant, it follows that $\dot{\pi} = 0$ and $m = \pi + \lambda$ (for all but the first instant of time). Consequently, the revenue maximizing rate of inflation is found by maximizing

$$V = (\pi + \lambda) k_0 e^{-a\pi}, \tag{10}$$

which gives the correct result,

$$\pi = (1/a) - \lambda \text{ and } m = (1/a). \tag{11}$$

Substituting equations (11) and (8) into (5) and integrating we finally derive

$$J^* = \frac{k_0 e^{(a\lambda - 1)}}{a\phi}, \tag{12}$$

which is the true maximum and is strictly greater than the expression for J in equation (7).

LITERATURE CITED

1. Cathcart, Charles D. "Monetary Dynamics, Growth, and the Efficiency of Inflationary Finance." *Journal of Money, Credit, and Banking*, 6 (May 1974), 169–90.

BOOK REVIEWS

Essays in Post-Keynesian Inflation

Edited by James H. Gapinski and Charles E. Rockwood. Cambridge, Mass.: Ballinger, 1979. xvii + 340 pp. $16.50

*A Review Essay by Preston J. Miller**

The essays in this volume address in an informal way the causes and cures for "stagflation," the concurrence of high unemployment and high inflation. The essays are based on presentations from a conference in honor of Abba P. Lerner held at Florida State University on March 28–30, 1979. Although the book suffers from many deficiencies, it does succeed in laying out two very different points of view on the stagflation issue. After presenting a general overview of the book, I describe and evaluate the two views, which I label post-Keynesian and neoclassical.

Overview

Because of the book's many deficiencies, readers must assume much of the burden of investigation and analysis. One deficiency is the book's lack of focus. Although the essays are supposed to be directed at the stagflation issue, they are, in fact, very wide ranging in subject matter. Thus, seven major sections in the book are needed to group sixteen essays, and topics range from Elizabeth Bailey's discussion of the experience of the Civil Aeronautics Board in deregulating airlines, to Martin Bronfenbrenner's derivation of the Marshall-Lerner condition, to Ray Canterbery's discourse on lexicographic preference orderings. Because of this lack of focus, the reader must determine what the major issues are and then sift and sort through the pages to find the main arguments on opposing sides of the issues.

Another deficiency is the lack of rigor in the authors' arguments. The essays are intended to be informal and are not meant to be potential journal articles. This informality, however, seems to give license to unsubstantiated arguments and inane comments. Different points of view are drawn neither from coherent models with tested implications nor from observations of systematic regularities in the data. Readers, then, are forced to draw on their own knowledge of theoretical and empiri-

*The views expressed herein are solely those of the author and do not necessarily represent the views of the Federal Reserve Bank of Minneapolis or the Federal Reserve System.

PRESTON J. MILLER *is economist, Federal Reserve Bank of Minneapolis.*

0022-2879/81/0881-0393$00.50/0
JOURNAL OF MONEY, CREDIT, AND BANKING, vol. 13, no. 3 (August 1981)

cal evidence to determine the merits of contrasting arguments. In addition, this informality allows some incredible statements to be printed. We read, for instance, from Leonard Rapping that "in periods of uncertainty asset holders have no basis upon which to formulate price expectations" (p. 51), from Canterbery that "the productive efficiency condition is no longer relevant" (p. 79), from David Colander that the rational expectations hypothesis "makes price stability maintenance impossible" (p. 203), and from Abba Lerner that "the neoclassical clarification . . . only makes it more clear that it is starvation that is the instrument depended upon to turn the deflation of employment into a deflation of money wage demands" (p. 228). And the list could go on and on.

Yet another deficiency is the failure to pursue or resolve differences of opinion. The editors, in their summary, suggest that the contributors were in fundamental agreement on the major issues, but nothing could be further from the truth: some contributors, such as Kenneth Boulding and Don Patinkin, argue that inflation is caused by expansionary monetary and fiscal policies, while others, such as Lerner and Sidney Weinbraub, argue that such policies are passive in the inflation process. Some, such as Boulding, Mancur Olson, and Patinkin, question the value of distinguishing between demand-pull and cost-push inflation, while others, such as William Baumol, Tibor Scitovsky, and Irvin Sobel, consider that distinction to be crucial. Some, such as Boulding, Patinkin, and Edmund Phelps, question the efficacy of incomes policies, while others, such as Baumol, Lerner, Charles Rockwood, and Weintraub, view such policies as essential in fighting stagflation. Some serious criticisms are leveled on opposing points of view, but these criticisms go unanswered. Again, the reader must rely on evidence from other sources to judge the validity of the criticisms.

Despite the deficiencies, the book does have merit. The main value is the sharp contrast that it provides between the post-Keynesian and neoclassical views on stagflation. Prominent economists are present from each school of thought, and their essays are sprinkled with interesting insights, observations, and logical points.

Description of the Two Views of Stagflation

The post-Keynesian view of stagflation begins with an explanation for ordinary inflation. According to post-Keynesians, inflation is a disequilibrium phenomenon. As Scitovsky states, "All forms and types of inflation are due to some kind of incompatibility: demand-pull inflation to the excess of aggregate demand over the maximum available supply, cost-push inflation to the excess of the sum of income claims over the total income generated" (p. 5). (The recognition of cost-push inflation in addition to demand-pull inflation is what distinguishes post-Keynesians from ordinary Keynesians.) Since demand-pull inflation occurs only with a high degree of resource utilization, stagflation—inflation with a low degree of resource utilization—must be explained by post-Keynesians as cost-push inflation.

The cost-push view of inflation assumes both wages and prices are administered in noncompetitive markets. Nominal wages are set by labor unions. In the traditional cost-push view, unions set wages to increase labor's share of income. According to Lerner, unions also set wages defensively to maintain labor's share of income in the face of exogenous expectations of future inflation. In both cases, the level of wages is assumed to be determined by factors outside the theory. Canterbery states that "the wage rate selection is a political decision" (p. 99), and Sobel attributes to Lerner the position that "the power of trade unions over wages . . . has become too great to allow the policy of determining wages by collective bargaining" (p. 267). In the case of defensive wage-setting, again according to Sobel, "Expectational inflation can be triggered by any number of causes" (p. 280) and "That type of inflation leads to what [Lerner] terms defensive behavior, that is, the attempt to raise wages and prices in order to defend one's own relative position in the face of an expected price increase" (p. 280).

While unions are assumed to set wages either offensively to increase labor's share of income or defensively to maintain labor's share in the face of expected inflation, firms are assumed to administer prices to keep profits a constant share of income. Scitovsky states that "if producers set product prices by adding a percentage profit mark-up to marginal costs, then their gross profit becomes an irreducible proportion of the Gross National Product" (p. 6), while Weintraub contends that "of the 'great ratios' of economics [the mark-up of prices over unit labor costs] is most nearly constant" (p. 233).

The demand-pull and cost-push explanations of inflation taken together suggest an L-shaped Phillips curve. At a low unemployment rate, for which all individuals in the labor force without jobs are frictionally unemployed, the Phillips curve is vertical. An increase in aggregate demand at this low unemployment rate results solely in higher inflation via demand-pull. For a whole range of higher unemployment rates, inflation is exogenously determined by cost-push factors. Thus, inflation rates on the Phillips curve to the right of the frictional unemployment rate are caused by cost-push and are consistent with stagflation. Lerner is quoted by Sobel on the shape of the Phillips curve:

> It is questionable whether we can obtain a general reduction in prices at the cost of lower levels of employment. We can get higher or lower levels of employment by providing higher or lower levels of spending, but between the politically and morally impermissible catastrophic depression that crushes [cost-push] inflation and the excessive demand of [demand-pull] inflation the effects on prices and inflation are questionable. (p. 271)

Although Lerner's views might be considered a bit extreme—even for post-Keynesians—they do reveal two generally held beliefs from this school of thought: (1) aggregate demand policies affect inflation only through the Phillips curve relationship by changing the unemployment rate, and (2) the Phillips curve is very flat over a wide range of unemployment rates above the frictional rate.

On the first point Weintraub asserts, "Only indirectly, and via a roundabout channel, can money have a price level incident: if tight money creates enough unemployment, the money policy can slow down the annual increments in money wages. This, to be sure, is good Phillips curve doctrine: unemployment is the route through which money policy can affect the price level" (p. 234). On the second point Rockwood reports, "Arthur Okun has concluded that each $200 billion reduction in real output, under a period of gradual restraint, would produce a reduction of only between .6 and 1.8 points in the basic inflation rate for the 1980s" (p. 163).

Optimal aggregate demand policy in this post-Keynesian view consists of choosing the point on the Phillips curve that maximizes social welfare. With an essentially L-shaped Phillips curve and with a social distaste for both inflation and unemployment, optimal policy is to aim always for full employment (the frictional unemployment rate).

Since post-Keynesian aggregate demand policy throws in the towel against inflation, direct government intervention is advocated to deal with this problem. Thus, we have Rockwood's controls, Weintraub's Tax-Based Incomes Policy (TIP), and Lerner-Colander's Market Anti-inflation Plan (MAP). Lerner is reported by Sobel to offer one justification for government interventions of this type, "In administered price industries, since the normal mark-up could be added to wage increases, an increase in wage costs meant an increase in money profits resulting in much lesser resistance if not acquiescence by management to inflationary wage demands. Given this inability or unwillingness by the two parties to countervail each other's power, Lerner viewed government, the other countervailing power, as needed to constrain people from ultimately hurting themselves" (p. 269). In other words, since pricing in noncompetitive markets is nonoptimal, government intervention in the pricing process can improve things. Baumol offers a second justification based on what he perceives to be an externality problem in pricing decisions: "There may be some reluctance on the part of the owner of any particular factor of production to permit a reduction in its remuneration, for while the reduction in remuneration will adversely affect him directly, any benefits resulting from a subsequent reduction in prices and the consequent increase in the scale of operations of industry will only partially accrue to him" (p. 64).

The contrasting view of stagflation, which I call neoclassical, can be described simply. First, it views inflation as an equilibrium process. Agents maximize utility or profits subject to prices which are taken as given, and markets clear. Inflation occurs when the stock of money or stock of federal debt grows too fast. Boulding states, "Inflation is a fairly deliberate policy on the part of government" (p. 24), and Patinkin claims "Inflation everywhere and anywhere is a monetary phenomenon" (p. 128).

Neoclassical economists do not believe the Phillips curve represents the policymaker's choice set. A perceived change to more expansionary aggregate demand policies is believed to increase prices while having little effect on real variables, such as output and employment. The stagflation of 1970s, then, can be explained by a deliberate and perceived move on the part of government to more expansionary policies. Boulding observes, "From 1970 on, however, we witness a most alarming escalation in the federal deficit, . . . and this factor is undoubtedly responsible for the acceleration in inflation that we see after 1970 . . . there is a very strong tendency for a public debt either to be monetized or to be regarded as liquid assets" (p. 25).

With the view that aggregate demand policies affect the inflation rate, but have little effect on real variables, neoclassical economists believe such policies should be made to ensure a noninflationary environment. Because such policies are expected to be successful in curtailing inflation and because the price system is viewed to be efficient, no direct government intervention in the pricing process is deemed necessary.

Evaluation of the Two Views of Stagflation

I find the cost-push view weak at every point along the line. While my sympathies lie with the neoclassical view, that view suggests the cure for inflation or stagflation is beyond the realm of economics.

The post-Keynesian view of inflation as a disequilibrium process makes that theory incomplete. It does not suffice, for instance, to posit that prices change proportionately to excess demand; the factor of proportionality must also be specified. More generally, an equilibrium is a specific solution to a game that describes how goods are produced and allocated. When the game is not solved—when demand is different from supply or when factor demands are greater than income—there is lacking an explanation for how production and allocation are decided.

The cost-push view of wage determination is incomplete and at variance with the data. As Olson writes, "the usual cost-push arguments are manifestly unsatisfactory. These accounts ascribe higher prices or wages to the monopoly power of big business or big unions, but they usually offer no explanation of why there should be continuing inflation, or why there should be more inflation in one period than another. The typical cost-push argument does not explain why an organization with market power would not choose whatever price or wage it found most advantageous as soon as it obtained the monopoly power, after which point it would have no more reason to increase prices than a pure competitor . . . [the cost-push arguments] must also be accompanied by some account of why monetary or fiscal authorities would provide increased demand after the alleged cost-push had increased wages and prices, so that the cost-push would culminate in inflation rather than in unemployed resources" (pp. 141–42). And Phelps observes, "The contention that unions and employers predesignate a path of real wages for existing employees over the rest of their working lives, revising it upwards on occasion, but never downwards by one iota, does not seem to me to be a very accurate description of money wage behavior in the United States over recent years. It does not stand up very well, at least in my eyes, to the almost experimental evidence offered by the supply shocks in oil and food of 1973–74, especially if one takes account of the end of the last stage of wage controls in the spring of 1974" (p. 188).

The view that prices are simply marked up from unit labor costs also does not hold up. If one attempts to run a regression of the price level on a distributed lag of unit labor costs, one finds that causation runs both ways—not just from costs to prices as this view suggests. A regression of prices on wages does reveal onc-way causation, but the evidence suggests that such a relationship is not invariant to government policy interventions.[1]

The view that estimated Phillips curves present policymakers with their relevant choice set is not tenable. First, the curves are not stable. As Rapping states, "I would not express the position in terms of the deterioration in the trade-off between inflation and unemployment (i.e., a shifting Phillips curve). This vehicle of expression implies a stability and predictability in the underlying process that simply does not exist" (p. 46). Estimates of the cost of anti-inflation policies that are based on historically unstable Phillips curves, such as Okun's, are meaningless. Moreover, the view that monetary and fiscal policies affect inflation only through changes in the unemployment rate also is not supported. Litterman and Sargent have shown that as much as 50 percent of the movement in prices is uncorrelated with movements in real variables.[2]

Furthermore, since the post-Keynesian view does not incorporate a theory of

[1]See [2].
[2]See [3].

valued money, it attributes no cost to inflation. The lack of a theory of money is a shortcoming, because as Patinkin states, "The price level is the inverse of the purchasing power or value of money" (p. 128). Without valued money, the costs to inflation are not evident. Sobel attributes to Lerner "The position taken is that inflation is dangerous and must be controlled not primarily because it engenders high welfare losses, but because it generates pressure upon policymakers which would induce them to allow or even pursue deflationary monetary and fiscal policies at less than full employment" (p. 269).

Finally, I find the case for incomes policies far from convincing. First, their main justification is that the alternative of deflationary monetary and fiscal policies is too costly. But those estimates of cost based on historical Phillips curves are hardly reliable. Second, the justification based on externalities in pricing decisions is wrong. It confuses the interdependence of budget sets, which Baumol describes, with interdependence of objective functions. The first is not an externalities problem while the second is. Third, such policies are costly in terms of administration and economic efficiency, which Lerner and Weintraub admit. Fourth, it is questionable that they would work. As Boulding states, "We certainly cannot assume that schemes devised merely to restrain the rise of money prices and money-wages would necessarily hold back inflation if Congress were in a deficit-spending mood for other reasons" (pp. 26–27). Finally, it is not evident that an incomes policy can be designed to correct the inefficiencies caused by pricing in noncompetitive markets. As Phelps ponders, "But there is a question, at least in my mind, whether we have the wit to use any of these methods with a high degree of success" (p. 179).

The neoclassical view of stagflation, in my mind, escapes most of these criticisms. It is based on a coherent theory, which completely describes the environment within which agents operate, agents' decision-making processes, the operation of markets, and the allocation of goods in equilibrium. Moreover, it does provide a theory of endogenously valued fiat money.[3] The theory seems capable of explaining regularities in the data,[4] and there have been cases in history where governments have credibly altered their monetary and fiscal policies and have caused inflation to subside without causing disastrous effects on output.[5]

The question remains, as Patinkin puts it, "Is the quantity of money an exogenous variable or is it an endogenous variable? . . . political leaders and ministers of finance have, from time immemorial, known how to print money. Why do they sometimes suddenly decide to print more?" (p. 28)

An answer is suggested from two considerations. The first is that in the neoclassical view, inflation acts like a tax. By issuing more money or bonds the government takes command over more resources, and the inflation that results lowers the value of existing nonindexed nominal assets. By affecting marginal conditions, the inflation tax distorts, as do other taxes. The second is Rapping's contention that "continuous inflation is often a reflection of a weak or disoriented government lacking sufficient power to impose solutions" (p. 35).

Greater use of the inflation tax would then come about as the government increased expenditures to appease special interest groups. Patinkin observes, for instance, that "inflations usually are connected with expanded government budgets" (p. 129). As the government spent more, it would have to tax more. It

[3]See, for example, [4, 7, 8].
[4]See, for example, [1, 5, 6].
[5]Rapping provides one example of France in the mid-1920s, but there are others.

would increase the use of the inflation tax either because both it and explicit taxes should optimally increase to finance the additional expenditures, or because it is easier for a weak government to passively raise the inflation tax than to deliberately raise explicit taxes.

If this answer is right, then the solution to inflation is largely political and not economic. It requires a stronger government. As Rapping states, "In a general sense, stabilization in the large means institutional change, not demand management" (p. 47).

Summary

Unfortunately, there is little reason for either post-Keynesians or neoclassicists to expect any near-term relief from stagflation. Post-Keynesians are likely to point to the unfavorable outlook for nominal wages based on the extraordinary inflation rates we have recently experienced. Neoclassicists are likely to point to an apparent lack of political resolve to adopt disciplined monetary and fiscal policies. Thus, the stagflation issue addressed in this book is likely to remain topical for some time to come. It is a shame that the contribution this book could have made on this issue is so diminished by its poor organization and exposition.

LITERATURE CITED

1. Barro, Robert J. "Unanticipated Money, Output, and the Price Level in the United States." *Journal of Political Economy,* 86 (August 1978), 549–80.
2. Geweke, John. "Wage and Price Dynamics in U.S. Manufacturing." In *New Methods in Business Cycle Research: Proceedings from a Conference,* pp. 111–56. Minneapolis: Federal Reserve Bank of Minneapolis, 1977.
3. Litterman, Robert B., and Thomas J. Sargent. "Detecting Neutral Price Level Changes and Effects of Aggregate Demand With Index Models." *Federal Reserve Bank of Minneapolis Working Paper 125,* revised November 1979.
4. Lucas, Robert E., Jr. "Expectations and the Neutrality of Money." *Journal of Economic Theory,* 4 (April 1972), 103–24.
5. Lucas, Robert E., Jr., and Thomas J. Sargent. "After Keynesian Macroeconomics." *Federal Reserve Bank of Minneapolis Quarterly Review,* (Spring 1979), 1–16.
6. Sargent, Thomas J. "A Classical Macroeconometric Model for the United States." *Journal of Political Economy,* 84 (April 1976), 207–37.
7. Townsend, Robert M. "Models of Money with Spatially Separated Agents." In *Models of Monetary Economics,* edited by John H. Kareken and Neil Wallace, pp. 265–303. Minneapolis: Federal Reserve Bank of Minneapolis, 1980.
8. Wallace, Neil. "The Overlapping Generations Model of Fiat Money." In *Models of Monetary Economics,* edited by John H. Kareken and Neil Wallace, pp. 49–82. Minneapolis: Federal Reserve Bank of Minneapolis, 1980.

The Development of Economic Policy: Financial Institution Reform, by Sidney J. Jones. Ann Arbor, Mich.: University of Michigan, 1979. xii + 360 pp. $12.50

The stated objective is to "review an example of the government's decision-making process as a framework within which to analyze the development of national economic policy." Dr. Jones uses the issue of financial institution reform in the post-1970 period as a special case study of the government's decision-making process. He concludes that comprehensive legislative reform focusing on broad, interrelated issues and problems is generally doomed to failure because of the divisive efforts of key special interest groups and legislative and executive procedural weaknesses.

The book is divided into three parts. The first part (chaps. 2–3) summarizes the competitive structure of major deposit-type financial institutions (commercial banks, savings and loans, mutual savings banks, and credit unions) and the problems faced by these institutions in an environment of fluctuating interest rates and deposit interest rate controls. The review of the financial intermediary system and government regulation provides a background for understanding the reform efforts and the desire for self-preservation by each type of private financial intermediary.

The second part of the book (chaps. 4–10) presents an informative, descriptive review of post-1970 studies and legislation related to financial reform. Chapter 4 focuses on the formation, operation, and recommendations of the President's Commission on Financial Structure and Regulation (Hunt Commission). The commission recommended a comprehensive framework of flexible financial institutions that would select operating policies according to the choices of managers and owners rather than statutory requirements. Although the recommendations were aimed at allowing private market forces to replace regulatory shackles, they were not politically feasible.

Chapters 5–7 present an excellent summary of the Financial Instituions Act of 1973 including the responses of financial institutions and such other market forces as consumer interest groups, organized labor, and the housing industry. The 1973 Act was introduced twenty-two months after the Hunt Commission Report and followed the philosophy and included many of the proposals from the Hunt Commission and the Commission on Money and Credit. The goal of the act was to "increase competition and stabilize financial conditions by expanding deposit flexibility and broadening the lending and investment powers of financial intermediaries without obstructing the attainment of important national housing objectives." Despite its focus on needed comprehensive financial reform, the act was opposed by major interest groups and was not voted on by either the House or the Senate.

Chapter 8 reviews the Financial Institutions Act of 1975, which included substantial portions of the 1973 Act and the Hunt Commission recommendations. The Senate passed an amended bill in December 1975, but the House instituted a broader financial reform study and did not vote on the act. Chapter 9 describes the abortive effort with the Financial Reform Act of 1976 and the FINE Study. Although the House considered a substitute bill to the 1975 Act, the process was abandoned during the summer of 1976 because of the Presidential election.

Chapter 10 summarizes the legislative results of financial reform. Dr. Jones contends that the financial institution reform case study demonstrates three facts about our modern political system: (1) the federal government has increasingly intervened in the private market process; (2) the structure of government often leads to delay of responsible and workable decisions; and (3) the present fragmented approach to government decision making dilutes the quality of analysis and confuses the assignment of authority and responsibility.

The third part of the book (chaps. 11–14) analyzes the potential contribution of presidential commissions, congressional hearings, and executive office task forces to the government's decision-making process. Dr. Jones concludes that while presidential commissions can provide necessary background for executive branch and congressional efforts, they have not been very effective as a catalyst for legislation. Congressional hearings tend to ignore fundamental issues, to place excessive emphasis on details, and to produce patchwork results.

The final chapter summarizes the advantages and disadvantages of the government's decision-making process but provides few specific recommendations for improvement. Dr. Jones concludes that piecemeal legislation is prevalent because "incremental gradualism avoids the political risks of comprehensive change." He cites the conflicts caused by major trade associations, attempts at consensus, the periodic need for reflection, and the differing motivations of government employees and government agencies as barriers to effective legislation.

The book offers an excellent, relatively objective bibliography of financial institution reform legislation from 1970 to 1976. Dr. Jones broad experience in government and his direct association with financial institution reform legislation give him a valuable perspective on the government's decision-making process. He uses the perspective very effectively. He utilizes a case study relating to one specific type of reform to provide evidence on the process of governmental decision making, and he draws important implications for all aspects of national economic policy. Unfortunately, he provides no feasible alternatives.

DAVID W. COLE

Ohio State University

The Economics of the Eurocurrency System, by George W. McKenzie. New York: Halsted Press, 1976. 141 pp. $15.95

George W. McKenzie has attempted to provide an introductory text on the economics of the Eurocurrency system that might appeal to both undergraduate and graduate students.

By way of overall assessment, I would be quite reluctant to adopt the book as the sole text for introducing students to the Eurocurrency system, although I believe chapters 2, 4, 5, and 6, which are fairly standard in their treatment of the subject at hand, should form part of a reading list on the Eurocurrency system in courses on domestic and international finance.

Perhaps the main limitation of the book is that it does not develop a complete conceptual framework for dealing with the Eurocurrency system in the context of the post-World War II trend toward increasing economic and financial interdependence. Although the introductory discussion (chap. 2) of the effects of the Eurocurrency system on the domestic banking sector and the balance of payments focuses on some of the linkages between foreign exchange markets, domestic money supplies, international reserves, balance of payments positions, etc., it fails to take the next logical step of developing a conceptual framework that encapsulates some of these linkages.

At the start of chapter 3, McKenzie poses two questions, namely: (1) What factors determine the currency of denomination of assets or liabilities held by individuals, business, and financial institutions? and (2) What factors determine the country where these assets or liabilities are created? His response is a simple time preference model of capital flows (chap. 3) and a discussion of financial intermediation in a world of uncertainty in terms of which the development of the Eurocurrency system is seen as the logical outcome of financial innovation in the context of such uncertainty (chap. 4).

What McKenzie seems to be groping for is a more complete conceptual framework—perhaps a general equilibrium (or disequilibrium) portfolio model. Such a framework would not only allow him to explain things like asset preferences and risk spreading but also would allow more explicit recognition of the precise nature of flows between domestic and offshore money and capital markets. Such a framework would also allow consideration of some of the other features of the Eurocurrency system with which McKenzie tries to deal but fails to integrate adequately, including interest rate linkages, balance of payments effects, divergent monetary policies and conditions, the effects of differences in banking regulations and capital controls, and so on. Specifically, McKenzie would have been able to present a more orderly discussion of the growth and development of the markets, and to more readily emphasize the significance of divergent monetary policies and divergent exchange, capital, and banking controls to that growth. By introducing transaction costs explicitly into such a general equilibrium framework it is also possible to explain the overall pattern of flows, as well as certain structural features of the markets. For example, why have cities such as London or Singapore emerged as financial centers.

The discussion in chapter 5 of some of the implications of the Euromarkets for conventional measures of money stock is a very useful one. McKenzie focuses on what he calls a "functional" definition of money whereby concern is with "the role of money, as a medium of exchange, in supporting overall economic activity." According to this view the appropriate concept of money is one that takes account of all deposits owned by residents of a particular country irrespective of the location or currency of denomination of these deposits. By implication, if international transactions are important and domestic (nonbank) residents hold significant foreign balances, then the domestic money stock measure will significantly understate balances held as media of exchange. Unfortunately, McKenzie's discussion seems to concentrate on bank deposits, both time and demand, rather than on the whole spectrum of deposits held domestically and internationally, which could be ranked according to liquidity.

Furthermore, there is an even more fundamental question of whether it is appropriate, from the point of view of aggregate economic activity, to concentrate only on gross measures of liquidity (like nonbank holdings of particular classes of deposits), independently of the other side of the (nonbank resident's) balance sheet. Presumably the total balance sheet position is also an important determinant of spending behavior. To take an extreme example, the spending behavior of an individual with (say) a $1,000 demand deposit would be different if he also has a liability of $1,000 due tomorrow, than if his $1,000 liability is due to be repaid in five years. This suggests that it may be important to look at the net as well as the gross liquidity position of the nonbank sector. This point may be of even more significance in the context of the Euromarkets if the Euromarket institutions who are supplying the Eurocurrency deposits operate in a fundamentally different way from their domestic counterparts [2].

In chapter 6, McKenzie summarizes five alternative approaches to the question of the Eurocurrency deposit multiplier but, unfortunately, stops short of a detailed comparison. His discussion begins with a textbook exposition of the closed economy fixed coefficient multiplier and ends with a description of a model developed by this author and Sakakibara [1] that attempts to make the portfolio choices of Eurocurrency borrowers and lenders explicit.

The essence of this approach is that the so-called "multiplier" may in fact have a maximum value of unity in the absence of the central bank redepositing in the market because of portfolio shifts induced by interest rate changes as funds flow between domestic and Eurocurrency markets. It is unfortunate that McKenzie's endorsement of the portfolio approach and the significance of interest rate adjustments did not carry over to his discussion of such topics as capital flows and market linkages. His discussion of the multiplier process itself could also have been improved if a more complete discussion of central bank redepositing had been included.

To some extent McKenzie's neglect of the determination of Eurocurrency interest rates simply reflects the state of the literature. The macro linkages between the Euromarkets and domestic banking and monetary sectors and foreign exchange markets are worthy of careful consideration, not only as to linkages at particular maturity levels across markets, but also as to term structure linkages. With the ready availability of interest rate and exchange rate data it is somewhat surprising that the area has received so little attention. Apart from these macro aspects, there are important micro questions concerning how individual Eurobanks set their deposit and lending rates, and in particular how they quote their margins above the London interbank offer rate (LIBOR) in their lending operations. Analysis of creditworthiness and default risks is still very much in its early days. However, the experience of recent years has demonstrated that it has an important dynamic as well as static aspect; credit appraisals (and therefore margins) determined in the light of market conditions at a point in time have appeared quite inappropriate at later times as market conditions have changed and therefore credit exposures have varied.

At the policy level, there are also a number of issues that do not receive adequate attention from McKenzie. The most important concern the implications of the development of the Eurocurrency markets for domestic policy autonomy and the now perennial question of controlling international banking. A conceptual framework that captures the macro and micro implications of the development of the Eurocurrency system is an essential prerequisite for adequate consideration of these policy questions.

LITERATURE CITED

1. Hewson, John, and Eisuke Sakakibara. "The Eurodollar Deposit Multiplier." *International Monetary Fund Staff Papers,* 2 (1974), 307–28.
2. Niehans, Jürg, and John Hewson. "The Eurodollar Market and Monetary Theory." *Journal of Money, Credit, and Banking,* 8 (February 1976), 1–27.

JOHN R. HEWSON

University of New South Wales

Rational Expectations and Monetary Policy, by Jac J. Sijben. Alphen aan den Rijn, The Netherlands: Sijthoff and Noordhoff, 1980. x + 144 pp. $37.50

This slim volume provides a critical summary of the recent developments in macroeconomic theory that are frequently, although sometimes inappropriately, described as rational expectations analyses. Sijben—associate professor of monetary economics at the University of Tilberg (The Netherlands)—focuses on the implications of these theoretical developments for monetary policy.

Overall, *Rational Expectations and Monetary Policy* is a readable, nontechnical discussion, apparently directed at policymakers and other application-oriented economists. The author organizes his discussion in five main parts: (i) the monetarist controversy, (ii) classical models of expectations, (iii) the expectations augmented Phillips curve, (iv) the theory of rational expectations, and (v) a critical review of rational expectations analyses. Sijben's basic view of monetary policy is characteristic of other recent discussions of the interaction of monetary policy and expectations. "Therefore it may be concluded that as far as in practice there is talk about a learning process, about the existence in an institutional respect of long-term contracts with some rigidity of wages and prices, about positive information costs and superior information by monetary authorities, it will still be possible to mitigate fluctuations in economic activity by using an active monetary policy" (p. 105). In this review we try to clarify the relationship between recent developments in macroeconomics and policy while arguing that Sijben's justifications for active monetary policy are not well-founded either theoretically or empirically.

Equilibrium Business Cycle Models and Policy Irrelevance—The "rational expectations" analyses of Lucas [6] and Barro [1] involve four central hypotheses: (1) the neutrality of "perceived" monetary inflation, either in the weak form of zero degree homogeneity of supply and demand functions, or in the strong form ("super neutrality") of the invariance of real magnitudes to sustained inflation; (2) market clearing or, more particularly, the assumption that agents execute all perceived mutually beneficial trades; (3) rational expectations based on imperfect information regarding current real and nominal aggregates that is common to the participants of a given market, and (4) monetary authorities with information that is a subset of that known by the private sector. Following Lucas, we use the term "equilibrium business cycle model" to describe models that incorporate market clearing and rational expectations. The above four hypotheses jointly are sufficient to imply a "policy irrelevance proposition" for the systematic component of monetary policy, similar to that advanced by Sargent and Wallace [8]. Departures from any of these hypotheses can overturn the policy irrelevance proposition; for example, Fischer's [3] analysis of preset nominal wages or the Sargent and Wallace analysis of superior information for the monetary authority. However, the discussions by McCallum [7] and others make clear that certain relaxations of the four hypotheses can be made which maintain the policy irrelevance proposition. Thus, ultimately, the importance of the policy irrelevance proposition must be judged within the context of a specific positive model of business fluctuations that is consistent with the central empirical regularities of the aggregate economy.

Aggregate Information, Neutrality, and Policy—The equilibrium business cycle models of Lucas and Barro are frequently criticized for assuming that agents have access to an unreasonably large amount of information about the structure of the economy, the decision rules of the monetary authority, and the relevant aggregate exogenous variables. For example, Sijben argues "a first point of criticism pertains to the crucial assumption of the rational-expectations theory implying that economic agents have at their disposal all the relevant information and make use of this efficiently in building up their inflation expectations" (p. 89). However, on such a priori grounds, it can be argued that the informational requirements of the Lucas and Barro models are overly restrictive. For example, in order to serve adequately as a positive model of business fluctuations in which unanticipated nominal shifts are an important source of impulses, this class of models must impose apparently artifical limitations on the information that agents have concerning nominal aggregates. In particular, agents are assumed to observe neither an aggregate price level nor the money supply contemporaneously. That is, it seems plausible that the informational restrictions of the theory are too strong rather than too weak.

Moreover, in order to analyze how different information structures affect the policy irrelevance proposition, it is not sufficient to claim that the informational requirements of a particular model are "unreasonable." As pointed out in the previous section, the effect of informational restrictions on the policy irrelevance proposition can be analyzed only within the context of a specific model in which the information structure is specified not only for the agents, but for the monetary authorities as well. Thus, the appropriate positive response to "unreasonable" a priori assumptions is to formulate an economic model that specifies an alternative information structure and, subsequently, to develop and execute tests derived from these assumptions.

Feasibility versus Desirability of Stabilization Policy—If the policy irrelevance proposition does not hold, it does not necessarily follow that it is desirable to engage in stabilization policy. This point has been stressed by Lucas [6, pp. 1139–40] and more recently by Kydland and Prescott [5]. In particular, a rationalization of active stabilization policy requires an identification of the sources of private sector failure similar to that typically required in other analyses of government intervention. In Keynesian models, for example, the source of private sector failure is sluggish adjustments to nominal disturbances ("wage rigidity"). In this case, the rationalization of activitist monetary policy is clear. However, if the policy irrelevance proposition fails because of departures from any of the four key hypotheses outlined above, then the form of a desirable stabilization policy is usually not obvious. In particular, construction of desirable policies requires detailed quantitative information (for example, on wage contracts and information structures) that economists do not possess at present.

Learning Behavior, Positive Economics, and Policy—The rational expectations hypothesis has frequently been criticized as applicable only to a stationary environment, neglecting the learning that characterizes the transition process. At a general level, however, it is possible to disagree with this criticism. For example, Taylor [9] and Friedman [4] have analyzed particular forms of learning behavior during the transition to rational expectations, modeling shifts in the monetary policy rule, and other components of the economic structure. Essentially, proponents of activitist monetary policy rely on the argument that the monetary authority has superior knowledge of the evolution of the economic system and can use its knowledge during the transition process to achieve desirable results, even if there is no gain in the new rational expectations equilibrium. Sijben appears to adopt this "eclectic view" of rational expectations and monetary policy which emphasizes learning behavior: "after a time-consuming learning process this procedure converges to a . . . rational expectations equilibrium. During this transition period some importance can still be attributed to a macroeconomic stabilization policy" (p. 105). To justify such an argument, it is necessary to first demonstrate the appropriateness of a specific model of learning behavior *and* the superior nature of the information available to the monetary authorities within a *positive* model of business fluctuations. Second, it is also necessary to demonstrate the desirability of active monetary policy, as discussed above. For example, an alternative to an active monetary policy during such a situation is merely to have the authorities announce whatever "superior" knowledge they happen to have and allow the private sector to act accordingly.

With respect to the first necessary condition, it bears emphasizing that there is no empirical evidence that learning behavior plays an important role in the positive analysis of business fluctuations. In early versions of Barro's [2] study of the relationship between unemployment and unanticipated money growth, for example, estimated specifications with time varying parameters and procedures for updating parameter estimates were used in an effort to incorporate evolutionary behavior in the money supply rule. The overall evaluation of these elaborate calculations were that they did not significantly alter the basic empirical findings. Thus, before learning behavior can be used as a foundation for policy, it must be incorporated into a positive model of business fluctuations.

Rationalizing Stabilization Policies—Sijben and other recent critics of equilibrium business cycle models and the implied policy irrelevance proposition apparently believe that the dismissal of certain models on a priori grounds can rationalize conventional stabilization policies. However, from our viewpoint, the only valid ground for dismissal is that the predictions of these models are inconsistent with the facts. In this light, it is particularly distressing that in a book which emphasizes the policy implications and practical relevance of recent developments in macroeconomics, there is virtually no discussion of empirical tests of the propositions of either equilibrium business cycle models or alternative theories of macroeconomic fluctuations.

Further, whatever the ultimate empirical judgment on current theories of fluctuations, the basis on which future stabilization policy must be evaluated and justified has changed. Taylor [10], for example, constructs and estimates a rational expectations model of fluctuations in which stabilization policies can be utilized. However, the types of models that lead to feasible stabilization policies do not necessarily imply that standard Keynesian policy prescriptions are desirable.

Thus, a necessary condition for rationalizing active policy is the development of a positive model of business fluctuations that is consistent with the facts. It is such a model that will ultimately determine the relevance of policy and the role it should play.

LITERATURE CITED

1. Barro, Robert J. "Rational Expectations and the Role of Monetary Policy." *Journal of Monetary Economics* (January 1976), 1-32.

2. ______. "Unanticipated Money Growth and Unemployment in the U.S." *American Economic Review* (March 1977), 101-15.

3. Fischer, Stanley. "Long-term Contracts, Rational Expectations and the Optimal Money Supply Rule." *Journal of Political Economy* (February 1977), 191-205.

4. Friedman, Benjamin. "Optimal Expectations and the Extreme Information Assumptions of 'Rational Expectations' Macromodels." *Journal of Monetary Economics* (January 1979), 23-41.

5. Kydland, Finn E., and Edward C. Prescott. "A Competitive Theory of Fluctuations and the Feasibility and Desirability of Stabilization Policy." In *Rational Expectations and Economic Policy,* edited by Stanley Fischer. Chicago: University of Chicago Press, 1980.

6. Lucas, Robert E., Jr. "An Equilibrium Model of the Business Cycle." *Journal of Political Economy* (December 1975), 1113-44.

7. McCallum, Bennett. "Price-Level Stickiness and the Feasibility of Monetary Stabilization Policy with Rational Expectations." *Journal of Political Economy* (June 1977), 627-34.

8. Sargent, Thomas, and Neil Wallace. "'Rational' Expectations, the Optimal Monetary Instrument, and the Optimal Money Supply Rule." *Journal of Political Economy* (April 1975), 241-55.

9. Taylor, John B. "Monetary Policy During a Transition to Rational Expectations." *Journal of Political Economy* (October 1975), 1009-21.

10. ______. "Estimation and Control of a Macroeconomic Model with Rational Expectations." *Econometrica* (September 1979), 1267-86.

ROBERT G. KING
CHARLES I. PLOSSER

University of Rochester

Social Security Versus Private Saving, edited by George von Furstenberg. Cambridge, Mass.: Ballinger, 1979. xx + 435 pp. $35.00

This volume is the first in a trilogy reporting results of studies on capital, investment, and saving sponsored by the American Council of Life Insurance. George von Furstenberg both directed the research program and edited these volumes with obvious effectiveness. The current volume focuses on a question popularized by Martin Feldstein: Does a pay-as-you-go social security system significantly reduce private saving?

It is widely supposed that if this question is answered affirmatively, then something should be done to reform the social security program. But even if it is granted that a reduced domestic capital stock—or reduced domestic ownership of an open economy's capital stock—is undesirable, then it need not follow that the social security system need be neutral in its effects. Both the editor's introduction and an excellent chapter on debt neutrality by Willem Buiter and James Tobin place the effects of social security on saving in the proper context of the overall effects of government consumption and investment spending, borrowing, and taxation. This context also suggests different approaches to Feldstein's original question, such as why would future benefits be more fully anticipated than future taxes?

A number of time-series studies of the United States have demonstrated that almost any effect of social security on aggregate private saving is consistent with the data and some form of the consumption function. The volume's contribution to this literature by Bulent Gultekin and Dennis Logue certainly does not change that opinion. The problem is simple: After World War II the various social security scale variables are essentially proportional to permanent income, and before the war they are essentially zero. Thus the coefficient on the variable will reflect any scale shift in saving between the prewar and postwar data, but only the very brave are able to draw firm conclusions from that evidence.

Foreign evidence is the best hope of obtaining additional degrees of freedom so the editor commissioned studies of Canada, Sweden, the United Kingdom, France, and Germany. The case study approach taken was not generally fruitful, however, with the exception of the chapters on Canada by Michael Denny and Samuel Rea, Jr., and on Sweden by Aleksander Markowski and Edward Palmer. In those two cases analysis and data were of high quality and there were significant variations in the social security programs. In Canada a strong retirement effect was noted and private saving if anything increased. A *funded* program in Sweden reduced private saving but not by as much as the fund increased aggregate saving. This is consistent with a story in which people value promised benefits by less than the fund accumulated to pay them and tells us little about a pay-as-you-go system. The other national studies were disappointing at best. One example will suffice. The authors of the German study marvel at the growth of personal saving due to tax incentives and then consider the decline in corporate saving (retained earnings) as a separate matter, completely missing that the tax laws imply a shift of the form of financing. Still to be written is a really definitive international cross-section/time-series analysis.

A concluding section of the book considers age structure effects on saving, and presents life-cycle and overlapping-generations models. None of these three chapters makes much of a contribution to the main theme of the book, though they have some interest in themselves. This reviewer supposes that they were part of the larger project that did not quite fit any of the other volumes either.

Some authors, as might be supposed given the sponsors, did devote some time to the influence of social security programs on the composition of private saving. They confirmed the existing conclusion in the literature: that social security programs can crowd out private provision of annuities by pension funds and insurance companies regardless of any effect on aggregate private saving.

The strengths of the book more than compensate for its weaknesses. The first two chapters are of general interest to macroeconomists and the next three at least to specialists in saving and consumption. Together these make up over half the book and that is a pretty fair batting average.

MICHAEL R. DARBY

University of California, Los Angeles

Ohio State
University Press

November
1981

JOURNAL OF MONEY, CREDIT AND BANKING

US ISSN 0022-2879

JOURNAL OF MONEY, CREDIT AND BANKING

ISSN 0022-2879.

JOURNAL OF MONEY, CREDIT AND BANKING

VOLUME XIII NUMBER 4 NOVEMBER 1981

ARTICLES

The "Rationality" of Money Supply Expectations and the Short-Run Response of Interest Rates to Monetary Surprises *Jacob Grossman* 409

Monetary Accommodation of Supply Shocks under Rational Expectations *Alan S. Blinder* 425

Long-Term Contracts and the Effectiveness of Demand and Supply Policies *Gary C. Fethke and Andrew J. Policano* 439

Bank Collapse and Depression *John Bryant* 454

Expense-Preference Behavior in the Savings and Loan Industry *James A. Verbrugge and John S. Jahera, Jr.* 465

A Reinterpretation of the Modern Theory of Forward Exchange Rates *E. Dwight Phaup* 477

NOTES, COMMENTS, REPLIES

The New Monetary Aggregates *A Comment by William A. Barnett* 485

Adjustment Lags Versus Information Lags: A Test of Alternative Explanations of the Phillips Curve Phenomenon *A Comment by Jacob A. Frenkel* 490

Adjustment Lags Versus Information Lags: A Test of Alternative Explanations of the Phillips Curve Phenomenon *A Reply by Charles R. Nelson* 494

Inflation and Real Growth: Some Empirical Results *A Note by Dennis E. Logue and Richard James Sweeney* 497

BOOK REVIEWS

Modelling the International Transmission Mechanism, edited by John A. Sawyer *A Review Essay by John T. Cuddington* 502

Expected Utility Hypotheses and the Allais Paradox, edited by Maurice Allais and Ole Hagen *Reviewed by Rubin Saposnik* 507

(*continued*)

International Lending, Risk and the Euro-Markets, by Anthony Angelini, Maximo Eng, and Francis A. Lees
The Financing of Long-Term Development, The Institute of Bankers
Reviewed by Ruth Wiener Arad 508

Demand for Financial Assets: An Econometric Study of the U.K. Personal Sector by D. K. Bhattacharyya *Reviewed by Varouj A. Aivazian* 513

The Regulation of Financial Institutions, Federal Reserve Bank of Boston
Reviewed by Robert A. Taggart, Jr. 515

Quest for World Monetary Order: The Gold-Dollar System and Its Aftermath, by Milton Gilbert *Reviewed by Liam P. Ebrill* 518

Models of Monetary Economies, edited by John H. Kareken and Neil Wallace
Reviewed by Stephen J. Turnovsky 520

Capitalism and Socialism: A Theological Inquiry, edited by Michael Novak
Reviewed by Tetsunori Koizumi 522

The Australian Monetary System in the 1970s, edited by Michael G. Porter
Reviewed by Thomas Havrilesky 525

Currency and Economic Reform, West Germany After World War II: A Symposium, edited by Rudolf Richter *Reviewed by William T. Gavin* 526

Selected Papers of Allan Sproul, edited by Lawrence S. Ritter
Reviewed by Lester V. Chandler 529

The Failure of the Franklin National Bank: Challenge to the International Banking System, by Joan Edelman Spero *Reviewed by Benjamin J. Klebaner* 530

The Impact of the Federal Reserve System's Monetary Policies on the Nation's Economy (Second Report), Staff Report of the Subcommittee on Domestic Monetary Policy of the Committee on Banking, Finance and Urban Affairs
Reviewed by Robert L. Hetzel 533

The European Monetary System: Its Promise and Prospects edited by Philip H. Trezise *Reviewed by Joly Dixon* 535

Housing and Investment in an Inflationary World: Theory and Evidence by John Tuccillo *Reviewed by Ronald L. Racster* 537

Zwei Generationen im deutschen Bankwesen 1833–1914 by Hermann and Paul Wallich *Reviewed by Benedikt Fehr* 538

Domestic and Multinational Banking, by Rae Weston
Reviewed by E. Victor Morgan 540

Annual Index 543

JOURNAL OF MONEY, CREDIT, AND BANKING (ISSN 0022-2879). Published quarterly in February, May, August, and November by the Ohio State University Press, 2070 Neil Avenue, Columbus, Ohio 43210. Richard C. Rose, Managing Editor; Kummi Ranjit, Production Editor; Lisa Satterfield Rookard, Assistant Editor; Lois Fausnaugh, Subscriptions Manager; Jeanette White, Secretary to the Editor, Department of Economics, Ohio State University. Second-class postage paid at Columbus, Ohio, and at additional mailing offices.

JACOB GROSSMAN*

The "Rationality" of Money Supply Expectations and the Short-Run Response of Interest Rates to Monetary Surprises

1. INTRODUCTION

THE PURPOSE OF THIS PAPER is to use weekly survey data to study the "rationality" of money supply expectations and the short-run response of interest rates to monetary announcements. Each Thursday at 4:00 P.M. the Federal Reserve System (Fed) announces changes in the monetary aggregates (M1 and M2) for the preceding statement week ending on Wednesday. Since September 1977, a private firm (Money Market Services Inc.) surveys twice a week about sixty government dealers for their expectations of the weekly M1 change. The first survey is done on Tuesday, two days before the announcement, and the second one is done on Thursday, the day of the announcement.

The first part of the paper studies the "rationality" of the Tuesday and Thursday expectations. It turns out that the Tuesday expectations, the revision of expectations from Tuesday to Thursday, and the Thursday expectations efficiently embed available information. Also, the results indicate that the survey expectations utilize all the information in a time series model and in addition contain autonomous (nonextrapolative) information. This evidence contrasts sharply with other survey data on

*I am grateful to Phillip Cagan, Paul Wachtel, Meir Schneller, Stan Jonas, and an anonymous referee for very helpful comments and suggestions, to Ernie Theurer for some econometric suggestions and to Barry Gonder for excellent research assistance. In addition, I am especially grateful to Bob Jones from Money Market Services Inc. for supplying the survey data on money supply expectations and giving his permission for me to use them in this analysis. The research reported here was carried out for the most part while I was at the Federal Reserve Bank of New York. The opinions expressed here are my own.

JACOB GROSSMAN *is director of financial futures, ACLI International Commodity Services, Inc., White Plains, New York.*

0022-2879/81/1181-0409$00.50/0
JOURNAL OF MONEY, CREDIT, AND BANKING, vol. 13, no. 4 (November 1981)

expectations (such as the Livingston survey on future inflation as reported in Pesando [25] and Pearce [24], and the Goldsmith-Nagan survey on future interest rates as reported in Friedman [10]) which shows that time series models contain more information than the survey expectations.

The weekly announcements on changes in M1 contain information on future monetary policy which in turn immediately affects market interest rates. Hence, in the second part of the paper, I study the short-run response of interest rates to the monetary announcements.

In efficient markets, anticipated changes are already embedded in rates and *only* the *un*anticipated, or surprise, changes are relevant. This hypothesis is easily accepted by the data. Further, under rational expectations, the effect of the surprise component on interest rates should reflect the System's techniques of operation (or policy rule) in implementing monetary policy. This has several empirical implications which also receive strong support from the data.

The paper extends earlier empirical contributions (Barro [2, 3] and Grossman [13]) to the recent theoretical literature on monetary models with rational expectations (Lucas [16, 17, 18, 19] Sargent and Wallace [26, 27] and Barro [1]) as well as to the related literature on market efficiency (as reviewed, e.g., in Fama [7]). A key assumption in the above models is that expectations of the monetary policy rule are "rational." Here I provide supportive evidence on this assumption by pointing out the efficiency of money supply expectations and the "rational" response of interest rates to the monetary announcements, in the sense of correctly incorporating the policy rule in operation. As a side product, the paper presents new evidence on the efficiency of the Treasury bill market.

The paper is organized as follows: section 2 tests the "rationality" of money supply expectations, section 3 studies and tests the response of interest rates to the monetary announcements, and section 4 briefly summarizes the findings and discusses their implications.

2. TESTS OF THE "RATIONALITY" OF MONEY SUPPLY EXPECTATIONS

An expectation is rational in Muth's sense [23] if the subjective expectation of a particular variable is equal to its corresponding mathematical expectation. More generally, if individuals do not have all the information used in the model, expectations are rational if they are optimal predictions based on the information available to the individual. Thus, there are two key properties of rational money supply expectations: (1) unbiasedness and (2) efficiency, in the sense of incorporating all available information. I shall test these two properties in turn.

A. Tests of Unbiasedness

A standard test of unbiasedness would be to regress the actual weekly change in M1, *DM*, on the anticipated change, *DMF*, as follows:

$$DM_t = a + bDMF_t + u_t, \quad (1)$$

where u_t is a zero-mean finite-variance disturbance term which is serially uncorrelated. If *DMF* is an unbiased forecast of *DM,* then (i) the constant term in equation (1) should not differ significantly from zero, (ii) the slope coefficient should not differ significantly from unity and, (iii) the residuals should be serially uncorrelated. Equation (1) was estimated for both the Tuesday and Thursday expectations (*DMF.Tu* and *DMF.Th,* respectively) for the sample period (September 21, 1977 to September 26, 1979) and two subperiods. The results are reported in Table 1. Also reported in Table 1 are the t-statistics of the hypothesis that $b = 1$ and the F-statistics of the joint hypothesis that $a=0$ *and* $b=1$.

TABLE 1

RESULTS OF OLS UNBIASEDNESS TESTS
$DM = a + bDMF. + u$

Independent Variable	a	b	SEE	D-W	SSE	R^2	$\bar{R}^2$	Test statistics: $b = 1$	Test statistics: F-statistic Ho: $(a,b)=(0,1)$
September 21, 1977 to September 26, 1979									
DMF.Tu	−0.52	1.18	1.61	1.86	270.9	0.41	0.41	1.31	(3.97)*
	(−2.82)**	(8.56)**							
DMF.Th	−0.469	1.14	1.55	1.84	250.6	0.46	0.45	1.16	(3.73)*
	(−2.73)**	(9.36)**							
September 21, 1977 to September 20, 1978									
DMF.Tu	−0.35	1.18	1.46	1.81	109.4	0.54	0.53	1.16	1.41
	(−1.59)	(7.74)							
DMF.Th	−0.34	1.14	1.46	1.90	109.6	0.54	0.53	0.96	1.22
	(−1.52)	(7.76)							
September 27, 1978 to September 26, 1979									
DMF.Tu	−0.71	1.22	1.76	1.91	158.7	0.29	0.28	0.81	2.80
	(−2.22)*	(4.56)**							
DMF.Th	−0.61	1.15	1.65	1.81	139.1	0.38	0.36	0.73	2.68
	(−2.23)*	(5.55)**							

NOTES: *DM* is the actual (first announced) weekly change in M1, *DMF.Tu* and *DMF.Th* are the Tuesday and the Thursday expectations, respectively. SEE is the standard error, D-W is the Durbin-Watson statistic and SSE is the sum of squared errors. The value of the t-statistic at the 5 percent level is 1.99, and of the F-statistic is 3.09 at the 5 percent and 4.82 at the 1 percent level.
*Significant at the 5 percent level.
**Significant at the 1 percent level.

For the entire sample period, the slope coefficient is insignificantly different from unity. However, the constant term is significantly less than zero. As a result, the joint hypothesis of $(a,b) = (0,1)$ can be rejected at the 5 percent level, though not at the 1 percent level. Note that the constant term is significantly different from zero only in the second subperiod (September 27, 1978 to September 26, 1979). As a result, removal of the bias would not have significantly affected the accuracy of the forecast. To see this, consider

$$DMF.Th^c = -0.469 + 1.14DMF.Th, \quad (2)$$

where $DMF.Th^c$ is the linearly corrected Thursday forecast for the whole sample period. The root mean square error (RMSE) of $DMF.Th^c$ is \$1.54 billion, about \$50 million (or 3 percent) less than the RMSE of *DMF.Th*. This difference is not statistically significant.[1]

Finally, note in Table 1 that in all cases the Durbin-Watson statistics are consistent with the hypothesis of the absence of first-order autocorrelated residuals and an examination of higher order correlations shows that no correlation of any order is significant.[2]

B. Tests of the Efficiency

1. Tests of Errors' Orthogonality to Available Information. A second key property of rational expectations is that they incorporate efficiently all available information. Thus, any information fully incorporated in this sense will be uncorrelated with the errors associated with rational expectations. A test of efficiency is therefore to examine the orthogonality of ex post prediction errors to any relevant information set I_i, $i=1,\ldots,n$. That is, run

$$DM_t = a + bDMF_t + u_t, \tag{3}$$

and test whether

$$E(\hat{u}_t / I_{it-1}) = 0, \qquad \text{for } i=1,\ldots,n \tag{4}$$

where I_{it-1} is the information set i which is available at $t-1$.[3,4]

[1]Further, since the coefficients in equation (2) embed the observations for the entire period, the actual difference is even smaller.

[2]An alternative test of unbiasedness is by a Theil decomposition of the mean square error as follows:

$$U^M = \frac{(\overline{DM} - \overline{DMF})^2}{MSE}, \quad U^R = \frac{(1-b)^2 \text{ VAR } (DMF)}{MSE}, \text{ and } U^D = \frac{(1-R^2) \text{ VAR } (DM)}{MSE},$$

where *DM* and *DMF* are the announced and anticipated weekly change in M1, *MSE* is the mean square error, $\overline{DM}$ and $\overline{DMF}$ are the sample mean of *DM* and *DMF*, *b* is the regression slope of *DM* on *DMF*, VAR(*DMF*) and VAR(*DM*) are the sample variances of *DMF* and *DM*, and *R* is correlation between *DM* and *DMF*. U^M is called the bias proportion, U^R the regression proportion, and U^D the disturbance proportion. Granger and Newbold [12] show that unbiased forecasts should have values of U^M and U^R close to zero, and therefore, U^D should be close to 1. The results (in percent) for the Tuesday forecast are $U^M = 5.5$, $U^R = 1.5$, and $U^D = 92.9$. For the Thursday forecast the results are $U^M = 5.5$, $U^R = 1.17$, and $U^D = 93.3$. The Granger and Newbold conditions of unbiasedness are therefore satisfied.

[3]Note that the test is biased toward rejecting the hypothesis of efficiency since the coefficients in (3) (which determine $\hat{u}$) embed the observations for the entire sample period. Thus, it is possible that (4) can be rejected for (say) I_k, but the effect of I_k on $\hat{u}$ is significant only toward the end of the sample period. In this case, the adjusted forecast (say, DMF^a) which incorporates the information in I_k will be only marginally superior to *DMF* itself. Put differently, if the effect of I_k on $\hat{u}$ is increasing in time or unstable, (4) can be rejected but the information value in I_k for forecasting purposes is of limited use.

[4]An alternative test would be to run

$$DM_t = a' + b'DMF_t + c'I_{it-1} + u' \tag{3'}$$

and test whether $c'=0$. The two tests are identical if *DMF* is orthogonal to I_{it-1}. Otherwise, the *b* in (3) may also reflect the information in I_{it-1} which would tend to bias the results of (2) toward accepting the hypothesis of efficiency. In this respect, (3′) is a more stringent test of efficiency. It turns out, however, that the results are almost identical, which implies that *DMF* is orthogonal to the information sets.

Although in principle one should test an infinite number of possible information sets, this will be meaningless given a stated number of degrees of freedom. Instead the tests presented here consider information sets which are frequently used in predicting weekly changes in M1. Consider then the information sets, first with respect to the Tuesday expectations (*DMF.Tu*) and then with respect to the Thursday expectations (*DMF.Th*).

The Tuesday expectations should embed (1) the information content in past values of weekly changes in M1; (2) the information which is released each Thursday following the close of each statement week and which directly relate to the M1 changes which will be announced a week later—they include the weekly average data on float, the monetary base, net private demand deposits for all New York City banks (released by the New York Clearing House), and adjusted demand deposits for ten large NYC banks (from the weekly condition report) showing Wednesday to Wednesday changes;[5,6] (3) other, more general information which (in some way) may help predict *DM*. Here I have included weekly average changes in the federal funds rate and in business loans.

Since the above information should be embedded in the Tuesday expectations, equation (3) was estimated for the *DMF.Tu* for the sample period September 21, 1977 to September 26, 1979 and the regression result (taken from Table 1) is

$$DM_t = -0.517 + 1.179 DMF.Tu_t + \hat{u}.Tu_t , \tag{5}$$

and $\hat{u}.Tu_t$ was regressed in turn on the above variables,

$$\hat{u}.Tu_t = a_0 + \sum_{j=0}^{s} a_{ij} I_{it-j} . \qquad i=1, \ldots n \tag{6}$$

The hypothesis of efficiency is that a_{ij}s $= 0$ for each i.

Equation (6) was estimated for each information set with contemporaneous and 4 lagged values ($s=4$). The F-statistics are presented in Table 2. As we can see, all the F-statistics are insignificantly different from zero.[7]. Thus, the evidence supports the hypothesis that the Tuesday expectations efficiently embed available information.

There is one important set of information which is released on Wednesday following the Tuesday forecast and a day before the M1 release on Thursday. This is the adjusted demand deposits for all weekly reporting banks (from the H.4.2 release).

[5]The information on the Wednesday figure of adjusted demand deposits for ten large NYC banks is examined together with the weekly average NYC clearinghouse data for traces of any large extraseasonal deposit flows. Changes in adjusted demand deposits at NYC banks provide a good clue to any current deposit flows which are not consistent with normal seasonal M1 patterns. (See Sivesind [28] for a good description as to how the market uses the different sets of information to produce the forecast.)

[6]The Thursday releases contain other relevant information, such as adjusted demand deposits at large Chicago banks, deposits data published by other regional clearing houses, and Treasury balances at Federal Reserve Banks. I have included, however, the key items. In the next section, I assess the entire set of (autonomous) information in a different way.

[7]I have also included all the information sets (I_is) in one equation. The F-statistic for all contemporaneous values was 0.86 and the F-statistic for contemporaneous and lagged values was 0.90. Both Fs are insignificant.

This information, therefore, should not be embedded in Tuesday expectations. That is, this variable when substituted for I_i in (6) should have a contemporaneous coefficient which is significantly different from zero, though coefficients of lagged values should be equal to zero. The regression result for current values is (t-values in parentheses)

$$\hat{u}.Tu_t = \underset{(0.011)}{0.0028} + \underset{(2.71)^{**}}{0.13}\, D.DDAWRB_t, \qquad \text{D-W} = 1.89 \tag{7}$$

where $D.DDAWRB$ is weekly changes in adjusted demand deposits for all weekly reporting banks. (An F-test on the lagged values is 0.96 which is insignificant.) Thus, as expected, the Tuesday forecast does not embed this information.

TABLE 2

F-STATISTICS OF THE HYPOTHESIS THAT PREDICTION ERRORS ARE ORTHOGONAL TO INFORMATION SETS

Weekly Average *Changes* in Available Information Sets (I_i)	$\sum_{j=0}^{4} I_{it-j}$ F-statistic
Lagged M1*	1.4
Float	0.50
Monetary base†	1.11
Net private demand deposits at all NYC banks	1.09
Adjusted demand deposits at ten large NYC banks‡	1.50
Federal fund rate	1.40
Business loans	0.74

NOTE: The critical value at the 5 percent level is 2.30.
*For lagged M1 changes, I have used $DM(-1)$, $DM(-2)$, $DM(-3)$, $DM(-52)$ and $DM(-53)$. This particular lag structure is explained in the next section (2.2).
†The monetary base is defined as total reserves plus the currency component of M1 plus nonmember banks vault cash.
‡Adjusted demand deposits are all demand deposits except U.S. government and commercial banks in the U.S. less cash items in process of collection. The figures are Wednesday to Wednesday changes.

Since $D.DDAWRB$ is released on Wednesday afternoon, the revision of expectations from Tuesday to Thursday (i.e., $DMF.Th$-$DMF.Tu$) should be significantly affected by it. The regression result is

$$DMF.Th_t - DMF.Tu_t = \underset{(-0.529)}{-0.018} + \underset{(4.24)^{**}}{0.048}\, D.DDAWRB_t. \qquad \text{D-W} = 1.83 \tag{8}$$

A one billion dollar increase in adjusted demand deposits at all weekly reporting banks will revise upward the Tuesday expectations by \$48 million. The coefficient is highly significant.

Finally, since this information should be fully incorporated in the Thursday forecast, the Thursday forecast error should be orthogonal to it. Thus, the regression result of equation (3) for the Thursday forecast (taken from Table 1) is

$$DM_t = -0.468 + 1.14\, DMF.Th + \hat{u}.Th_t, \qquad (9)$$
$$\quad (-2.72)^{**} \quad (9.37)^{*}$$

and then

$$\hat{u}.Th_t = 0.0018 + 0.089\, D.DDAWRB_t. \qquad \text{D-W} = 1.91 \qquad (10)$$
$$\quad (0.012) \quad (1.79)$$

The coefficient of $D.DDAWRB$ is insignificant at the 5 percent level. An F-test on the coefficient of $D.DDAWRB_t$ and 4 lagged values is 1.29, which is again insignificant.

In sum, the evidence supports the hypothesis that expectations of weekly M1 changes are efficient, where efficiency is defined in terms of prediction errors orthogonality to available information. The Tuesday expectations, the change in expectations from Tuesday to Thursday, and the Thursday expectations are in strong agreement with the hypothesis.

2. *Relative Efficiency Criteria.* Expectations, when unobserved, are usually generated in the literature by an autoregressive process. Thus, an alternative definition of efficiency is for the survey expectations to be *at least* as good a forecast as a prediction derived merely from extrapolation of past values of the series itself.[8]

I have fitted different time series (ARIMA- and autoregressive-type) models to the data (time period: January 2, 1972 to September 26, 1979) and the best fit is obtained from an unconstrained autoregressive process of the following form:

$$DM_t = a_0 + a_1 DM_{t-1} + a_2 DM_{t-2} + a_3 DM_{t-3} + a_4 DM_{t-52} + a_5 DM_{t-53}, \qquad (11)$$

where DM is the first announced weekly change in M1.[9] DM_{t-52} and DM_{t-53} apparently reflect imperfect seasonal adjustment. Equation (11) was estimated for the period January 2, 1972 to September 14, 1977 and the regression result is (t-values in parentheses)[10]

$$DM_t = \underset{(3.16)^{**}}{0.31} - \underset{(-6.44)^{**}}{0.41 DM_{t-1}} - \underset{(-2.9)^{**}}{0.19 DM_{t-2}} - \underset{(-2.12)^{*}}{0.13 DM_{t-3}}$$
$$+ \underset{(3.77)^{**}}{0.25 DM_{t-52}} + \underset{(3.22)^{**}}{0.22 DM_{t-53}} \qquad (12)$$

$$\text{SEE} = 1.37,\ \text{D-W} = 1.97,\ R^2 = 0.20,\ F(5{,}235) = 13.06$$

[8]This definition of efficiency is used in Mincer and Zarnowitz [20, pp. 21-32].

[9]It is interesting to note that the correlation between *DM* and the finally revised figures is zero. The benchmark revision essentially takes all the information content ("noise") out of *DM* and simply introduces some trend to it.

[10]A Chow test indicated that this lag structure was stable over different subperiods.

One way to proceed would be to extrapolate (statically) equation (12) for the sample period September 21, 1977 to September 26, 1979 and to compare the extrapolated values to the survey forecast. This method however will not be entirely appropriate since the coefficients in (12), which generate the extrapolated values, are estimated with data only until September 21, 1977 (the beginning of the sample period), and it fails to use the observations on DM which became available during the sample period. This deficiency can be easily corrected as follows: suppose that DM is available for $t = 1,2,\ldots,T$ (in our case t = January 3, 1973 and T = September 14, 1977). Equation (11) is estimated for the period 1 to T and the regression coefficients are used to generate $\widehat{DM}_{T+1}$ ($T + 1$ = September 21, 1977). At the end of $T+1$, equation (11) is rerun for the period 1 to $T+1$ and its (this time different) regression coefficients are used to obtain $\widehat{DM}_{T+2}$ ($T+2$ = September 28, 1977). This procedure is repeated up to the end of the sample period, each week equation (11) is reestimated with one additional observation, the predicted value is derived and so on. In this way, the regression coefficients contain all the currently available information on DM. This sequential-type method was used and the extrapolated values are denoted as DMX.[11,12]

First, I have computed the relative mean square error. That is, $E(DM - DMF)^2/E(DM - DMX)^2$. For DMF to be efficient, the ratio should be ≤ 1. The ratio is $2.534/3.475 = 0.729$.

Second, I have computed the partial correlation coefficients. $R_{DM,DMF.DMX}$ is the partial correlation of DM and DMF given DMX and it measures the predictive power in DMF which is not based on extrapolation. $R_{DM,DMX.DMF}$ is the partial correlation of DM and DMX given DMF and it measures the extent to which available extrapolative information is not utilized by DMF. If the survey expectations are efficient, $R_{DM,DMF.DMX} > 0$ and $R_{DM,DMX.DMF} = 0$. That is, DMF utilizes all available extrapolative information and in addition contains autonomous (nonextrapolative) information.[13] The results are $R_{DM,DMF.DMX} = 0.57$ and $R_{DM,DMX.DMF} = 0$. Alternatively, this result can be easily seen by running the regression

$$DM_t = a_0 + a_1 DMF + a_2 DMX. \tag{13}$$

If DMF is efficient, $a_1 > 0$ and $a_2 = 0$. The regression result is

$$\underset{}{DM_t} = \underset{(-2.69)^{**}}{-0.466} + \underset{(6.95)^{**}}{1.126}DMF + \underset{(0.13)}{0.027}DMX. \tag{14}$$

[11] I have also tried an alternative sequential method in which each week the latest observation is added and the earliest one is dropped, the regression is reestimated and extrapolated one week ahead, and so on. This would be a way of counting recent observations more heavily. The results, however, are unchanged. (For a more detailed description of the two types of sequential methods, see Grossman [13, pp. 1073–76].) Also, I have generated predicted values from the coefficients of equation (12) as well as from a set of coefficients estimated for the period January 2, 1973 to September 26, 1979. Again, the results are unchanged. The reason for the similarity of the results is because the coefficients of (12) remain stable when the new observations for the period September 21, 1977 to September 26, 1979 are added. As a result, all of the methods give essentially the same results.

[12] I have used the chi-square test to check that the residuals derived from the sequential method were white noise. The hypothesis that the result is white noise cannot be rejected.

[13] The type of autonomous information was discussed in the previous section and in Table 2.

Thus, the hypothesis of efficiency is accepted.

The above discussion clearly shows that *DMF* utilizes all available extrapolative information and in addition contains autonomous information. Thus, we might next ask what proportion of *DMF* is due to extrapolative information and what proportion is due to autonomous information. To answer this, estimate

$$DMF = a_0 + a_1 DM_{t-1} + a_2 DM_{t-2} + a_3 DM_{t-3} + a_4 DM_{t-52} + a_5 DM_{t-53} + u_t , \qquad (15)$$

and denote $\widehat{DMF}$, the predicted values of (15), as an estimate of the extrapolative component of *DMF*, and $\hat{u}_t$ as an estimate of the autonomous component of *DMF*.[14] Since (15) constitutes an orthogonal decomposition of the forecast into an extrapolative and autonomous component, $R^2_{DM,\widehat{DMF}} + R^2_{DM,\hat{u}} = R^2_{DM,DMF}$, the ratios $R^2_{DM,\widehat{DMF}}/R^2_{DM,DMF}$ and $R^2_{DM,\hat{u}}/R^2_{DM,DMF}$ can be used to measure the net contribution of the extrapolative and autonomous component, respectively, to the forecasting efficiency of *DMF*. The results show that 45 percent is contributed by the extrapolative component and 55 percent by the autonomous component.[15]

In this section, the survey expectations are said to be efficient if they predict *DM* *at least* as good as a forecast generated from extrapolating past values of *DM*. The results clearly show that the Thursday expectations utilize all available extrapolative information and in addition contain autonomous (nonextrapolative) information. More specifically, about 45 percent of the information in the Thursday expectations is extrapolative and 55 percent of the information is autonomous. This evidence contrasts sharply with other surveys' data on expectations, such as the Livingston survey on future inflation as reported in Pesando [25] and Pearce [24] and the Goldsmith-Nagan survey on future interest rates as reported in Friedman [10], which show that time series models contain more information than survey expectations.

The weekly announcements of changes in M1 contain information on future monetary policy which in turn immediately affects market interest rates. Hence, in

[14]It is clear that $\widehat{DMF}$ is different from *DMX* since the implicit weights allocated to the various past values of *DM* in formulating $\widehat{DMF}$ are different from the weights which determine *DMX*.

[15]Another test of efficiency which is frequently used in the literature (as in Pesando [25], Mullineaux [22], and Friedman [10] is to estimate

$$DM_t = a_0 + \sum_{i=1}^{3} a_i DM_{t-i} + \sum_{i=52}^{53} a_i DM_{t-i} + u_1 \qquad (11)$$

$$DMF_t = a_0' + \sum_{i=1}^{3} a_i' DM_{t-1} + \sum_{i=52}^{53} a_i' DM_{t-i} + u_2 \qquad (15)$$

and to define efficiency as the null hypothesis that $a_i = a_i'$, $i = 0,1,2,3,52,53$. As Friedman [10] argues this test is robust to the possibility that the market used information other than past *DM* in forming expectations because under the efficiency hypothesis omitted regressors lead to the same bias in both sets of estimated coefficients. However, the test does suffer from heteroscedasticity. The variance of *DMF* is about one-third the variance of *DM* (as is expected under rational expectations). The standard error of (11) is twice as big as the standard error of (15). Hence, I have multiplied all the variables in (15) (dependent and independent variables) by 2. This equalized the standard errors in the two equations. The resultant *F*-statistic is 0.76 which is insignificant. Thus, the hypothesis of efficiency defined as $a_i = a_i'$ cannot be rejected.

the next section, I study the short-run response of interest rates to the monetary announcements.

3. THE SHORT-RUN RESPONSE OF INTEREST RATES TO MONETARY ANNOUNCEMENTS

A. The Model

In efficient markets, interest rates should already embed (or "discount") the anticipated part of the announced change in M1 and *only* the *un*anticipated, or the surprise, part should have an effect. This hypothesis can be easily tested by regressing.

$$Di = a_0 + a_1 DMR + a_2 DMF.Th, \tag{16}$$

where Di is the change in interest rate from (ideally) just before to just after the announcement, $DMF.Th$ is the Thursday expectations, and DMR is the surprise component defined as the actual change minus the expected change, e.g., DM-$DMF.Th$. Thus, the first hypothesis is that $a_2 = 0$ and $a_1 \neq 0$.

The effect of DMR on Di (i.e., the sign of a_1) should reflect, under rational expectations, the anticipated policy response to the monetary surprise.[16] Since the Fed has essentially no informational advantage over the public with respect to the weekly changes in M1, it reacts to the incoming monetary data *after* they have been released to the public.[17] It is this possible reaction by the Fed to the unanticipated change in M1—unanticipated by both the Fed and the public—that triggers the rates response.[18] Thus, in order to understand the nature of the response of interest rates to the monetary surprise, it will be necessary at first to briefly describe the Fed operating procedures in implementing monetary policy which prevailed during the sample period.[19]

The directives given by the Federal Open Market Committee (FOMC) to the Federal Reserve Bank of New York retained the same basic format over the period.[20] After each monthly meeting, the FOMC instructed the manager to raise

[16]This dependency of the behavioral parameter a_1 on the System's techniques of operation in implementing monetary policy (as analyzed and tested below) is one specific example of Lucas's [19] insight about the dependency of the behavioral parameters on the policy parameters in structural macro models under rational expectations.

[17]The only informational advantage that the Fed has are preliminary data which it receives each Thursday for the statement week just ended. These preliminary estimates, based mainly on the Federal Reserve Balance sheet and on six days of data supplied by large, reserve-city member banks and five days of data from a sample of about three hundred country banks, are not released to the public. However these data are subject to large errors. The final figure is known to the Fed only a few hours before it is released. At times, the Fed may seek confirmation of trend by looking at the preliminary data, but this is at most a side source.

[18]The economic rational (as distinct from the legal one) of publishing weekly data on the monetary aggregates has never been spelled out by the Fed. I will comment on it briefly in note 25.

[19]The targeting and control procedures for 1977 and 1978 are outlined in more detail in [9]. Information for 1979 can be found in Federal Reserve Bulletins, which contain the proceedings of FOMC meetings during 1979.

[20]This format of operation has remained unchanged throughout most of the 1970s. On October 6, 1979 (which is outside our sample period), the Fed announced a basic change in its operating procedures. It

(lower) the federal funds rate within a band of tolerance (generally, 1/2 percentage point) whenever growth rates of M1 and M2 for the two-month period ending the month after the meeting appeared to approach or exceed the upper (lower) bands specified for these aggregates.[21,22] The FOMC also indicated how the manager was to vary his objective for the federal fund rate if incoming data caused revision in the projections of M1 and M2 relative to their ranges.[23] This was done by specifying either an ''aggregates'' directive, which called for responding to significant deviations of the aggregates from the midpoints of their two-month ranges, or a ''money market'' directive, calling for a response only if projected growth was closely approaching or moving beyond the upper, or lower, bounds specified for M1 and M2.[24] As a result, an ''aggregate'' directive increased the likelihood that the funds rate would rise quicker in response to indications of monetary growth which is higher than expected.[25]

Thus, it is the possible shifts in the System's weekly objective for the federal funds rate as incoming data on the monetary aggregates become available that trigger a positive (negative) interest rate response to an unanticipated increase (decrease) in the money supply. More specifically, the larger the surprise, the greater the likelihood of a revision in the projections of the growth in the monetary aggregates relative to their ranges and hence the greater the likelihood of a change (possibly a greater change) in the federal funds rate. Hence, interest rates will respond nonlinearly to monetary surprises (e.g., double the surprise will more than double the response of rates). Finally, while the above discussion might suggest that positive surprises are likely to raise rates as negative surprises are likely to reduce them, this has actually *not* been the case. There is clear evidence to suggest that over the period the System's manager was more responsive to relatively high than to relatively low monetary growth rates. Therefore, the Fed was more likely to raise

---

entails direct control of bank reserves rather than the federal fund rate. This change will most likely strengthen the argument and empirical estimates presented here.

[21]In addition, up until February 1979, once each quarter the FOMC publicly specified long-run objective for monetary growth, expressed in terms of four-quarter growth ranges based on the average level in the quarter just ended. The short-term (two-month) tolerance ranges often deviated from the long-term targets because the FOMC was trying to offset past unexpected deviations or to anticipate factors which may temporarily affect short-term growth. As a result, the two-month tolerance range had large fluctuations on a month to month basis (at times, several percentage points). From February 1979, the FOMC specifies the long-run (annual) objective for the monetary aggregates once a year.

[22]With few notable expectations (which will be discussed shortly), in comparing projected behavior against the ranges of tolerance, the Desk was expected to weigh M1 and M2 about equally.

[23]The Committee often established a two-month tolerance range for the aggregates that had midpoints below the growth actually expected for them at the time of its meeting.

[24]During 1978, the Committee used an ''aggregates'' directive half of the time. During 1979, the majority of the directives were ''money market'' directives.

[25]The minutes of the FOMC meetings are not made public until thirty days after each meeting. Thus, neither the directive nor the two-month tolerance range for the monetary aggregates nor the band of tolerance for the federal fund rate is publicly available at the time of the weekly announcement. The theoretical argument for not publishing the minutes immediately would probably be along the line of policy deception (which would however also call for not publishing weekly data on the monetary aggregates). If the monetary authority has better information about its monetary rule, there is the possibility of controlling money so as to fool the public. Taylor [29] presents a model in which there is an optimal, nonzero amount of this deception. Barro [1] however shows that this situation would seem most likely to arise when the policymakers lack a consistent objective function. Also, in Grossman [14] I have shown that a systematic ''trickery'' policy is not feasible.

rates in the face of positive surprises than to reduce them in the face of negative ones.[26] This apparent asymmetry was due to changes in the financial structure, payment mechanism and regulatory constraints which introduced a (largely unknown) downward bias to observed M1.[27]

In sum, I am interested in testing the following hypotheses: (1) *only* the *un*anticipated part of the weekly change in M1 affects interest rates. The effect of unanticipated money on rates is positive. (2) Interest rates respond nonlinearly to monetary surprises. (3) The response of rates to positive and negative monetary surprises is asymmetric, e.g., rates will rise more in response to a (given size) positive surprise than they will decline in response to a negative surprise.

B. Estimation

Table 3 reports estimates of equation (16), which is rewritten here for convenience

$$Di = a_0 + a_1 DMR + a_2 DMF.Th. \qquad (16)$$

The first hypothesis is that $a_1 > 0$ and $a_2 = 0$. *Di* is measured as the change in rates from 3:30 P.M. (the closing rates on the Federal Reserve Bank of New York quote sheet) to 5:00 P.M. (the closing rates on Telerate data base). It is important to isolate the announcement effect as much as possible because other factors come into play which may either wash the effect away or (in some way) bias the coefficients.[28] I have used three different rates, 3-, 6-, and 12-month Treasury bill rates, and two sample periods so that the effect can be studied across maturities and over time.[29]

The results from Table 3 can be summarized as follows. (1) In all cases, the effect of anticipated money (*DMF.Th*) on interest rates (*Di*) is *in*significantly different from zero.[30] Since, in efficient markets, rates should indeed embed anticipated money changes, the results provide new evidence on the efficiency of the Treasury bill market.[31] (2) The effect of unanticipated money (*DMR*) on rates is positive and

[26]At times, the Committee specified only an upper bound for the two-month growth of M1 or directing the manager to avoid having the fund rate decline when the aggregate weakened.

[27]Such financial "innovations" which reduced observed M1 include RP's, NOW and ATS accounts, money market mutual funds, offshore Eurodollars and others. For a good review of this issue, see Wenninger and Sivesind [31].

[28]For instance, the use of the opening rates on Friday at 9:30 A.M. would involve mixing the surprise effect on rates, not only with overnight developments, but also with the frequent release of important economic statistics (such as unemployment and price inflation) on Friday at 9:00 A.M. before the market opens. Further, the economic statistics which are released on Friday morning might also influence the Fed behavior so that the market is now anticipating the Fed reaction, not only to the monetary surprise, but to the new economic statistics as well.

[29]It would have been interesting to use the rates on Treasury bonds as well. However, the closing rates on Treasury bonds in Telerate data base are taken at about the same time as the Fed closing quotes, before the announcement. I am not aware of any other source of data.

[30]Conrad [6] estimated an equation of the same form as (16) (from 1972 to 1977) and found that the effect of anticipated money was significant. However, Conrad generated anticipated money from an essentially autoregressive model and he used changes in rates from Thursday afternoon to Friday morning. As a result, both his variables are deficient. (Other studies, such as Berkman [4], Sivesind [28] and Urich [30], suffer from the same shortcoming.)

[31]A different type of evidence on the efficiency of the Treasury bill market is provided in Hamburger and Platt [15] and Fama [8].

(with one exception) significantly different from zero at the 1 percent level.[32] The significant positive coefficient reflects the System's technique of operation; when money is growing faster (slower) than expected, money growth may approach or exceed the upper (lower) specified band and may thereby bring about tightening (loosening) by the Fed. Thus, the public correctly incorporates the policy rule which is used by the Fed.[33] (3) The effect of unanticipated money is increasing with the bill maturity (especially in the latter time period) which suggests that short- and longer-

TABLE 3

THE EFFECT OF ANTICIPATED (*DMF.Th*) AND UNANTICIPATED (*DMR*) WEEKLY CHANGES IN M1 ON CHANGES IN INTEREST RATES

Dependent Variable	Constant	*DMF.Th*	*DMR*	$\bar{R}^2$	SEE	D-W	*F*-test
Whole Sample Period: September 21, 1977 to September 26, 1979							
*Di*3	0.0048	−0.0018	0.0083	0.16	0.029	1.86	(10.02)**
	(1.37)	(−0.73)	(4.32)**				
*Di*6	0.0053	−0.0009	0.0082	0.22	0.023	2.26	(14.86)**
	(1.94)	(−0.49)	(5.45)**				
*Di*12	0.0060	−0.0028	0.0093	0.25	0.024	2.24	(17.2)**
	(2.06)*	(−1.38)	(5.81)**				
Subperiod 1: September 21, 1977 to September 20, 1978							
*Di*3	0.0011	0.0014	0.0084	0.10	0.031	1.91	(3.84)*
	(0.21)	(0.40)	(2.69)**				
*Di*6	0.0016	−0.0012	0.0055	0.10	0.020	2.15	(3.69)*
	(0.48)	(−0.54)	(2.7)**				
*Di*12	0.0021	−0.004	0.0069	0.16	0.023	2.36	(5.83)**
	(0.56)	(−1.80)	(3.06)**				
Subperiod 2: September 27, 1978 to September 26, 1979							
*Di*3	0.0087	−0.0026	0.0086	0.21	0.027	1.84	(7.05)**
	(1.79)	(0.70)	(3.60)**				
*Di*6	0.0097	−0.0004	0.011	0.32	0.025	2.38	(11.95)**
	(2.18)*	(−0.11)	(4.88)**				
*Di*12	0.010	−0.0002	0.012	0.36	0.025	2.15	(13.8)**
	(2.27)*	(−0.06)	(5.24)**				

NOTES: *Di*3, *Di*6, *Di*12 are changes in interest rates (in percent) on 3-, 6-, and 12-month Treasury bills, respectively, from 3:30 P.M. to 5:00 P.M. each Thursday for the period September 21, 1977 to September 26, 1979. *DMF.Th* and *DMR* are measured in billions of dollars. (See the text for the construction of these variables.) *t*-values are in parentheses below the coefficients.
*Significant at the 5 percent level.
**Significant at the 1 percent level.

term rates respond (at least) equally quickly to new information on future monetary policy.[34] This result put into question the term structure equations of structural macro models in which innovations in money affect only short rates at first, and long rates with considerable lag. If both short- and long-term rates respond to

[32]The surprise effect, though highly significant, is nevertheless small. For a $1 billion increase in unanticipated money, the average effect varies between 0.6 and 1.2. basis points. At times, however, the effect can be over 10 basis points. Note also that *DMR* can only explain (at most) 20 percent of the variance of *Di*.

[33]The positive effect of unanticipated money on rates is nontraditional in that the Keynesian liquidity function predicts that an increase in money will *reduce* rates. However, the traditional liquidity function makes no distinction between anticipated and unanticipated increases in the money supply. This distinction however is critical. It is still true that when the Fed buys securities and supplies reserves, rates decline. However, the upward adjustment of rates to an increase in the money supply is now much faster than in the past. The long lag in the adjustment of rates to money expansion as suggested in Friedman and Schwartz [11] and Cagan [5] has been considerably shortened.

[34]Even though I was unable to present direct evidence on Treasury bonds, it is clear to market observants that bonds respond as quickly as bills to monetary surprises.

innovations in money at the same time (as the evidence suggests), the effects of monetary policy on the economy occur much faster than is suggested in structural macro models (a point emphasized in Mishkin [21]).

Note also in Table 3 that the effect of *DMR* on *Di* is greater and more significant in the latter time period (especially for *Di*6 and *Di*12). Since the mean of *DMR* in period 2 is twice as big as its mean in period 1,[35] this result is consistent with the hypothesis that rates respond nonlinearly to monetary surprises.[36]

TABLE 4

THE EFFECT OF POSITIVE (*DMRP*) AND NEGATIVE (*DMRN*) MONEY SURPRISES ON CHANGES IN INTEREST RATES

Dependent Variable	Constant	*DMRP*	*DMRN*	$\bar{R}^2$	*F*-test
*Di*3	−0.014	0.021		0.12	(6.25)*
	(−1.10)	(2.50)*			
*Di*3	−0.003		0.002	0.009	(0.48)
	(−0.53)		(0.69)		
*Di*6	−0.002	0.011		0.19	(10.24)**
	(−0.40)	(3.19)**			
*Di*6	0.001		0.010	0.08	(6.5)*
	(1.75)		(2.55)**		
*Di*12	−0.006	0.015		0.18	(9.81)**
	(−0.82)	(3.13)**			
*Di*12	0.0007		0.007	0.05	(3.96)
	(0.110)		(1.99)		

NOTES: There are 39 positive surprises (DMRP) and 58 negative surprises (*DMRN*). The Durbin-Watson statistics (D-W) is omitted since it is inappropriate when there are gaps between observations. *t*-values are in parentheses below the coefficients.
*Significant at the 5 percent level.
**Significant at the 1 percent level.

Finally, I have tested for asymmetry by running separate regressions for positive and negative surprises and the results are presented in Table 4. The hypothesis is that positive surprises produce greater and more significant effect on interest rates than negative surprises. The effect of the positive surprise (DMRP) on the 3-month rate (*Di*3) is ten times bigger than the effect of the negative surprise (*DMRN*). In fact, the effect of *DMRN* is essentially zero. For the 6-month rate, the effect of *DMRP* is more significant, though of the same size as *DMRN*. For the 12-month rate, the effect of *DMRP* is twice as big and more significant.[37] Thus, the results support this hypothesis as well.

4. CONCLUSION

The key ingredients of "modern" monetary models are the distinction between anticipated and unanticipated money changes and the assumption of rational expectations. These two ingredients, when embedded in standard macro models, deliver results on the ineffectiveness of monetary policy which are drastically different from

[35]The mean of *DMR* in period 2 is $500 million and its mean in period 1 is $250 million.
[36]The respective slopes, however, are not significantly different from one another.
[37]It is interesting though that the effect of *DMRN* on *Di* is increasing with maturity.

Keynesian models. In particular they show that only unanticipated money has a "real" effect. This hypothesis has received empirical support in Barro [2, 3] and Grossman [13, 14].

This paper extends the above empirical studies by pointing out the efficiency of money supply expectations and the "rational" response of interest rates to monetary announcements. More specifically, rates respond *only* to monetary surprises, in a way which correctly incorporates the policy rule in operations. Thus, the paper lends additional, and independent, support to the rational expectations monetary models.

LITERATURE CITED

1. Barro, Robert J. "Rational Expectations and the Role of Monetary Policy." *Journal of Monetary Economics,* 2 (January 1976), 1-32.
2. ———. "Unanticipated Money Growth and Unemployment in the United States." *American Economic Review,* 67 (March 1977), 101-15.
3. ———. "Unanticipated Money, Output, and the Price Level in the United States." *Journal of Political Economy,* 86 (August 1978) 549-80.
4. Berkman, Neil. "On the Significance of Weekly Changes in M1." *New England Economic Review* (May-June 1978), 5-22.
5. Cagan, Phillip. *Channels of Monetary Effects on Interest Rates.* New York: Columbia University Press for National Bureau of Economic Research, 1972.
6. Conrad, William E., Jr. "Initial Treasury Bill Market Response to Money Stock Announcement." Processed. Board of Governors of the Federal Reserve System, 1978.
7. Fama, Eugene F. "Efficient Capital Markets: A Review of Theory and Empirical Work." *Journal of Finance,* 25 (May 1970), 383-417.
8. ———. "Forward Rates as Predictors of Future Spot Rates." *Journal of Financial Economics,* 3 (1976), 361-77.
9. Federal Reserve Bank of New York. "Monetary Policy and Open Market Operations in 1977," and ". . . in 1978." *Quarterly Review,* Federal Reserve Bank of New York (Spring 1978), 41-54, and (Spring 1979), 53-67.
10. Friedman, Benjamin M. "Survey Evidence on the 'Rationality' of Interest Rate Expectations." *National Bureau of Economic Research,* Working Paper No. 261 (July 1978).
11. Friedman, Milton, and Anna J. Schwartz. "Money and Business Cycles." *Review of Economic and Statistics,* supp. 45 (February 1963), 32-64.
12. Granger, Clive W. J., and Paul Newbold. *Forecasting Economic Times Series.* New York: Academic Press, 1977.
13. Grossman, Jacob. "Nominal Demand Policy and Short-Run Fluctuations in Unemployment and Prices in the United States." *Journal of Political Economy,* 87 (October 1979), 1063-85.
14. ———. "A Test of the Feasibility of a Systematic 'Trickery' Demand Policy." Federal Reserve Bank of New York, 1980, processed.
15. Hamburger, Michael J., and Elliott N. Platt. "The Expectations Hypothesis and the Efficiency of the Treasury Bill Market." *The Review of Economics and Statistics,* 57 (May 1975), 190-99.
16. Lucas, Robert E., Jr. "Expectations and the Neutrality of Money." *Journal of Economic Theory,* 4 (April 1972), 103-24.

17. ______. "Some International Evidence on Output-Inflation Tradeoff." *American Economic Review,* 63 (June 1973), 326–34.

18. ______. "An Equilibrium Model of the Business Cycle." *Journal of Political Economy,* 83 (December 1975), 1113–44.

19. ______. "Econometric Policy Evaluation: A Critique." In *The Phillips Curve and Labor Markets,* Carnegie-Rochester Conference Series on Public Policy, Vol. 1, edited by Karl Brunner and Allan H. Meltzer, pp. 19–46. Amsterdam: North-Holland, 1976.

20. Mincer, Jacob, and Victor Zarnowitz. "The Evaluation of Economic Forecasts." In *Economic Forecasts and Expectations: Analyses of Forecasting Behavior and Performance,* edited by Jacob Mincer. New York: Columbia University Press for National Bureau of Economic Research, 1969.

21. Mishkin, Frederic S. "Efficient-Markets Theory: Implications for Monetary Policy." In *Brooking Papers on Economic Activity,* Vol. 3, edited by Arthur M. Okun and George Perry, pp. 707–52. Washington, D.C.: Brookings Institution, 1978.

22. Mullineaux, Donald J. "On Testing for Rationality: Another Look at the Livingston Price Expectations Data." *Journal of Political Economy,* 86 (April 1978), 329–36.

23. Muth, John F. "Rational Expectations and the Theory of Price Movements." *Econometrica,* 29 (July 1961), 315–35.

24. Pearce, Douglas K. "Comparing Survey and Rational Measures of Expected Inflation: Forecast Performance and Interest Rate Effects." *Journal of Money, Credit, and Banking,* 11 (November 1979), 447–56.

25. Pesando, James E. "A Note on the Rationality of the Livingston Price Expectations." *Journal of Political Economy,* 83 (August 1975), 849–58.

26. Sargent, Thomas J., and Neil Wallace. " 'Rational' Expectations, the Optimal Monetary Instrument, and the Optimal Money Supply Rule." *Journal of Political Economy,* 83 (April 1975), 241–54.

27. ______. "Rational Expectations and the Theory of Economic Policy." *Journal of Monetary Economics,* 2 (April 1976), 169–83.

28. Sivesind, Charles M. "Efficient Markets and the Reaction of Securities Markets to the Weekly M1 Announcement." Federal Reserve Bank of New York, 1978, processed.

29. Taylor, John B. "Monetary Policy During a Transition to Rational Expectations." *Journal of Political Economy,* 83 (October 1975), 1009–21.

30. Urich, Thomas J. "The Information Content of Weekly Money Supply Announcements." New York University, June 1979, processed.

31. Wenninger, John A., and Charles M. Sivesind. "Defining Money for a Changing Financial System." *Quarterly Review,* Federal Reserve Bank of New York (Spring 1979), 1–9.

ALAN S. BLINDER*

Monetary Accommodation of Supply Shocks under Rational Expectations

1. THE ISSUE

WHEN THE ECONOMY IS BUFFETED by inflationary shocks from the supply side, should monetary policy turn "accommodative," that is, should the money supply be expanded in order to "finance" the higher prices? Or should it turn contractionary to combat the inflation? There are obviously both positive and normative aspects to this question. Most of this paper focuses on the following question in positive economics: If an accommodating policy is pursued, what will be the effects on output and prices? More specifically, is there an exploitable trade-off between inflation and unemployment? For the most part, we shall find that there is such a trade-off despite rational expectations. The next logical question is then the normative one: Should this trade-off be exploited and, if so, in which direction? This, naturally, is a far more difficult question, and I offer here no more than some suggestive remarks.

Theoretical analysis of the Keynesian variety generally leads to the conclusion that there is an exploitable trade-off in the short run,[1] and empirical estimates of the dimensions of this trade-off typically find large output effects and small price effects

*I am grateful for the helpful comments of Joseph G. Altonji, David Begg, Gregory C. Chow, Jonathan Eaton, Stephen M. Goldfeld, Bennett T. McCallum, John B. Taylor, a referee, and especially Julio Rotemberg; but I wish to stress that none of them is implicated in the conclusions. Research support from the National Science Foundation is gratefully acknowledged, as is research assistance from C. Robin Lindsey. This draft has benefited from comments received at the University of Chicago Money Workshop, at the Seminar on Inflation in Rio de Janeiro, December 1980, and at a meeting of the National Bureau of Economic Research's program in economic fluctuations.

[1]See, for example, [4, 8, 9, 15].

ALAN S. BLINDER *is professor of economics, Princeton University.*

0022-2879/81/1181-0425$00.50/0
JOURNAL OF MONEY, CREDIT, AND BANKING, vol. 13, no. 4 (November 1981)

from monetary accommodation in the short run.[2] This bit of positive analysis invites the normative conclusion that supply shocks should be accommodated.

But a number of economists have questioned these theoretical and empirical results on the ground that they fail to deal properly with inflationary expectations. Often appealing to some sort of ''rational expectations'' arguments, these economists deny that there is an exploitable trade-off and therefore oppose monetary accommodation. For example, Barro writes: ''Adverse shifts like the oil and agricultural crises will reduce output and cause painful relative adjustments no matter what the reaction of the monetary authority. Added monetary noise would only complicate and lengthen the process of adjustment'' [3, p. 26]. The implication seems to be that the authorities should stick to a constant money growth rule and ignore any supply shocks that may occur.

In dealing with the expectationists' arguments, I will divide them (somewhat artificially) into two groups. Arguments in the first group, which I call ''present disaster'' arguments, allege that econometric models err by understating the reaction of inflationary expectations. For example, it is claimed that a policy of monetary accommodation would increase inflationary expectations, shift the short-run Phillips curve upward, and defeat the purpose of the expansionary policy.

Arguments in the second group, which I call ''future disaster'' arguments, are more subtle, but also more elusive. The idea is that by informing private agents that it will accommodate supply shocks in the future, the monetary authority would exacerbate the downward rigidity of wages and prices, thus making it more difficult to deal with future supply shocks. Such arguments are cases of the Lucas [12] econometric policy critique, since they suggest that policy changes will cause parameter shifts.

Neither of these arguments is implausible on its face. The problem is that it is hard to know how to evaluate them until they are formalized in theoretical models and then tested empirically. This paper takes one small step in that direction by augmenting two popular macro models with rational expectations so that they are capable of dealing with supply shocks, and then examining both the present and future disaster arguments in the context of each.

2. BASIC IDEAS AND MODEL STRUCTURE

The two models presented here extend the analyses of well-known papers by Lucas [11] and Fischer [7]. Into each model I introduce an imported intermediate good, called oil, which is used as an input in the production of domestic output, but is neither produced domestically nor consumed directly. The real price of oil reduces both aggregate supply and aggregate demand. The origin of the effect on aggregate supply is obvious: an increase in the price of an imported factor of production reduces the ''optimal'' or ''natural'' rate of domestic output. Aggregate demand is affected because a rise in the real price of oil represents a transfer of

[2]See, for example, [1, 4, 5, 6, 13].

resources to foreign oil suppliers. In line with what actually appears to have happened in 1974 and again in 1979, it is assumed that the owners of the oil (henceforth, OPEC) have low marginal propensities to spend. So this redistribution lowers total demand.

The two models are used to address the following questions: Should the central bank deviate from its constant growth rate rule when there is a supply shock?[3] If so, in which direction? What would be the consequences of such deviations in both the short and long runs?

The oil market is modeled as a strict monopoly in which OPEC unilaterally sets the price of oil and the U.S. decides how much to buy at this price. I make no attempt to explain OPEC's pricing decision, but rather treat its target *real* price as exogenous. It is significant, however, that OPEC seeks to achieve this target by posting a fixed *nominal* price that is based on its expectation of what the price level in industrial countries will be. Specifically, if R_t is the (log of the) nominal price of oil and r_t is the (log of the) target real price, OPEC is assumed to set

$$R_t = r_t + {}_{t-1}\hat{P}_t, \tag{1}$$

where P_t is the (log of the) price level and ${}_{t-1}\hat{P}_t$ is OPEC's expectation of P_t.

The goods market is the standard one for domestic output, which is assumed to be competitive and to clear each period. Both Lucas [11] and Fischer [7] used the quantity theory with random velocity as their specification of aggregate demand, and I modify this only slightly to allow for the aforementioned distribution effects on demand. Thus[4]

$$y_t = m_t - P_t + v_t - c(R_t - P_t), \tag{2}$$

where y_t is (the log of) real output, m_t is the (log of the) money stock, and v_t is a white noise velocity shock.

The two models differ on their supply sides. In Lucas's [11] analysis agents do not know the current price level, and each must infer it from the information available to him—his own price and his knowledge of the probability distribution of the aggregate price level as of time $t-1$. Lucas solved a signal extraction problem to derive the supply function

$$y_t = k_t + \alpha(P_t - {}_{t-1}P_t) + e_t,$$

where ${}_{t-1}P_t$ is the *domestic* expectation of P_t, k_t is the (log of the) natural rate of output, and e_t is a white noise disturbance term. In this paper, I add one further

[3]I have argued elsewhere [4, chap. 8] that adherence to a fixed money growth rule is a fairly accurate characterization of what the Federal Reserve did after the 1973–74 oil price shock. It also seems to be the sort of policy response called for by Barro in the quotation in section 1. By contrast, many "Keynesian" economists advocated at that time and since a more accommodative policy.

[4]At the cost of slightly more notational complexity, some arbitrary positive coefficient, rather than 1.0, could appear in front of real balances in (2).

piece of data to agents' information set: the (log of the) current nominal price of oil, R_t. As shown in an appendix available on request, this leads to the following amendment to the Lucas supply function:

$$y_t = k_t + \alpha(P_t - {}_{t-1}P_t) - \delta(R_t - P_t) + e_t. \tag{3}$$

Fischer derived a rather similar supply function by a very different route. In his model, half the firms pay money wages that were set last period, and half pay money wages that were set two periods ago. When we extend that model to allow for energy as a second factor of production, the supply function for firms that set their wages in period $t-i$ becomes

$$y_{it} = k_{it} - \alpha({}_{t-i}W_t - P_t) - \delta(R_t - P_t) + e_{it}, \qquad i = 1,2 \tag{4}$$

where ${}_{t-i}W_t$ is the (log of the) nominal contract wage for period t set in period $t-i$. Since money wages are set one and two periods in advance, the labor market need not clear each period. It is not surprising that this model of the labor market gives monetary policy leverage that it lacks in the extended Lucas model. Specifically, Fischer assumed that money wages are proportional to expected prices, and normalized the factor of proportionality to unity: ${}_{t-i}W = {}_{t-i}P_t$. That is, the bargaining process was assumed to lead to a target real wage. In the presence of a second factor, it appears logical to allow the target real wage to be influenced by the expected real price of oil, so Fischer's specification of money wages is augmented to

$${}_{t-i}W_t = {}_{t-i}P_t - \gamma_{t-i}r_t, \qquad i = 1,2 \tag{5}$$

where γ is a positive constant reflecting the effect of higher energy prices on the demand for labor.[5]

Substituting (5) for wages into (4), and assuming that $i=1$ for half the economy and $i=2$ for the other half, the following aggregate supply function is derived:

$$y_t = k_t + \tfrac{\alpha}{2}(P_t - {}_{t-1}P_t) + \tfrac{\alpha}{2}(P_t - {}_{t-2}P_t) - \delta(R_t - P_t) + \tfrac{\alpha\gamma}{2}({}_{t-1}r_t + {}_{t-2}r_t) + e_t. \tag{6}$$

Notice the crucial role of the parameter γ, which indicates the responsiveness of the contract wage to the expected price of oil. If there is no such responsiveness ($\gamma=0$), the elasticity of output to a fully anticipated energy shock is $-\delta$. However, when $\gamma > 0$, the elasticity is only $-(\delta-\alpha\gamma)$, which is smaller. The reason is clear enough. Part of the problem of adjusting to an energy shock is getting real wages down to the level dictated by the reduced marginal productivity of labor. To the extent that labor

[5]Equation (5) is derived rigorously from microfoundations later. Note that if $\gamma = \delta/\alpha$, then a rise in the price of oil would leave output unchanged (see (4)). Thus it is clear that $\gamma < \delta/\alpha$.

and management do this voluntarily ($\gamma > 0$), employment and output will not have to fall as much as if they do not ($\gamma = 0$).

Monetary policy is assumed to follow a rule like

$$m_t = k_t + \beta(R_t - {}_{t-1}R_t) + b_{t-1}R_t. \tag{7}$$

If $b = \beta = 0$, this is the constant growth rate rule. Any rule with b and/or β positive will be considered "accommodating."

Finally, all agents are assumed to have rational expectations. However, OPEC has an information set that is slightly superior to the information set shared by domestic agents and the monetary authority. Specifically, at time $t-1$ OPEC knows the nominal price of oil that it will post at time t, but neither private agents nor the central bank have this piece of information. Since (7) is deterministic, this means that OPEC can forecast m_t one period ahead without error, while domestic agents cannot.

3. DIMENSIONS OF THE "PRESENT DISASTER" ARGUMENT

The Extended Lucas Model

In analyzing the short-run effects of monetary policy, I begin with the extended Lucas model because of its simpler structure. The model is solved by equating y_t in (2) and (3) and using the OPEC pricing rule (1) and the monetary rule (7). Some tedious algebra establishes that

$$_{t-1}P_t = \frac{b+\delta-c}{1-b} \; {}_{t-1}r_t \tag{8}$$

$$_{t-1}\hat{P}_t = {}_{t-1}P_t + \frac{\beta+\delta-c}{1+\alpha-\beta} \; (r_t - {}_{t-1}r_t) \tag{9}$$

$$P_t - {}_{t-1}P_t = \left(\frac{\beta+\delta-c}{1+\alpha-\beta}\right)(r_t - {}_{t-1}r_t) + \eta_t, \tag{10}$$

where $\eta_t = [(v_t - e_t)/(1+\alpha+\delta-c)]$. Therefore output is

$$y_t = (k_t - \delta_{t-1}r_t) + \left[\frac{\alpha(\beta+\delta-c)}{1+\alpha-\beta} - \delta\right] \; (r_t - {}_{t-1}r_t) + u_t, \tag{11}$$

where $u_t = (\alpha+\delta)\eta_t + e_t$.

These equations make several points quite obvious. First, observe that an increase in the relative price of oil decreases both aggregate supply and aggregate demand. It will be inflationary in a market clearing model only if δ exceeds c. Second, note that a policy of trying to offset anticipated OPEC price hikes completely through money creation ($b = 1$) is not viable. It leads to an indeterminate price level because OPEC anticipates the policy. Third, and more importantly, there is no reason in this model to accommodate such a shock at all. In fact, since positive values of b yield no output gains (see (11)), but cause anticipated inflation (see (8)), b should be *negative* if there is any cost at all of anticipated inflation. More specifically, setting $b = c-\delta$ (which is negative if the supply shock is inflationary) would appear optimal in this model, just as the expectationists have claimed.[6]

The issue of how to respond to *unanticipated* OPEC shocks is both more interesting and more complex. First consider (11) in the case that the money supply does not react to unanticipated oil price shocks ($\beta=0$). The coefficient of $r_t - {}_{t-1}r_t$ is then $-(\delta+\alpha c)/(1+\alpha)$, which is less negative than $-\delta$ as long as $\delta > c$. That is, with no monetary reaction real output would fall *less* in response to an unanticipated oil shock than to an anticipated one, but it would certainly fall.[7]

The positive economics of a β different from zero are clear; but the normative aspects are not. Equations (10) and (11) clearly show that making β positive will mute the output response to OPEC and exaggerate the price response. That is, there is a trade-off of the sort suggested by "Keynesian" models. Of course, this trade-off might be exploited in the opposite direction; by making β negative, the monetary authority can exaggerate the output drop and mitigate the price increase that results from an unanticipated OPEC shock.

Which type of response is advisable? It would seem to depend on whether unanticipated OPEC price hikes are temporary or permanent. Suppose first that all changes in the real price of oil are permanent, that is, OPEC follows a random walk pricing strategy. Then the first term in (11) is $k_t - \delta r_{t-1}$ while the natural rate of output for period t is $k_t - \delta r_t$, which is smaller if $r_t > r_{t-1}$. If it is optimal to keep output as close as possible to the natural rate, then the monetary authority should reduce output further by making β negative. Specifically, by setting $\beta = c-\delta < 0$, the monetary authority can keep y_t equal to $k_t - \delta r_t$ each period (except for unavoidable noise). Since this would also eliminate the unanticipated inflation emanating from the OPEC shock, it would appear to be the optimal policy response.[8]

The prescription is not so clear, however, if unanticipated OPEC shocks are transitory. For example, suppose that r_t deviates randomly from a deterministic trend, $\bar{r}_t$. Then the first term in (11) is $k_t - \delta \bar{r}_t$, which would appear to have some claim to the title "natural rate" because all unanticipated OPEC shocks are white noise. In this case, it can be argued that output should not be allowed to respond to unanticipated OPEC shocks, and should instead be stabilized around $k_t - \delta \bar{r}_t$.[9] To do this, it is necessary to make β positive, that is, to pursue an accommodative policy. However, complete stabilization of output is not optimal unless there is no social cost from unanticipated inflation. As just observed, there is a trade-off and the optimal choice of β must balance output stabilization against price stabilization.

In sum, if the unanticipated component of the OPEC shock is permanent (and

[6] See [3, p. 26, n. 51].

[7] Alternatively, if $c > \delta$, real output falls more in response to an unanticipated shock.

[8] If $c > \delta$, then $\beta = c-\delta$ calls for an accommodating policy response to fight *deflation* and stabilize output.

[9] The argument tacitly relies on the existence of some costs of changing output from period to period, which do not appear explicitly in the model.

$\delta > c$), it would appear optimal to contract the money supply in response, thereby eliminating unanticipated inflation and keeping output as close as possible to the natural rate. However, if the unanticipated component of the OPEC shock is transitory, an accommodative policy could be optimal; the optimal monetary policy response depends on the relative social costs of output and price fluctuations.

Readers familiar with the Lucas model may find it surprising that there is room for activist monetary policy in this model whereas there is none in the standard Lucas model. The reason is pretty clear. *By hypothesis,* OPEC introduces a disturbance that is recognized *contemporaneously* by the monetary authority.[10] Since R_t pushes P_t up, this additional information gives the authority some ability to react to the contemporaneous price-level disturbance. This is an ability the central bank would use even in the standard Lucas model without OPEC—if only it had it.

Before turning to the Fischer model, let me raise one further possibility—that it might be possible to "cheat" OPEC by inflation even though OPEC has rational expectations and knows the monetary rule. This, of course, is not possible if OPEC prices according to (1). Suppose instead that it prices according to

$$R_t = r_t + \omega_{t-1}\hat{P}_t + (1-\omega)_{t-1}Z_t, \tag{12}$$

where $0 < \omega < 1$ and where ${}_{t-1}Z_t$ is the price level of the rest of the industrial world (excluding the United States) converted into U.S. dollars by the exchange rate. What is the rationale for (12)?

Note that while OPEC fixes the price of oil in U.S. dollars, it presumably cares about the *purchasing power* of the nominal price it sets, not in terms of U.S. prices alone, but in terms of world prices. If OPEC directs a fraction ω of its purchases to U.S. goods and a fraction $(1-\omega)$ to other countries, then (12) is consistent with rational expectations, for then ${}_{t-1}\hat{P}_t + (1-\omega)_{t-1}Z_t$ is the price index OPEC expects to pay. The question then becomes: Under what conditions will ${}_{t-1}Z_t$ fail to rise proportionately with the anticipated U.S. price level? First, it matters whether we are talking about the policy response of the U.S. *acting alone* or of the whole non-OPEC world *acting in unison.* If all countries follow a cooperative policy and move their money supplies together, ${}_{t-1}Z_t$ will probably move proportionately with ${}_{t-1}\hat{P}_t$, and we are essentially back to the case $\omega = 1$. Personally, however, I find this scenario of coordinated monetary policy somewhat fanciful.

Consider instead the case where *only* the U.S. alters its money supply in response to a higher nominal price of oil. The price levels in other countries (measured in their own currencies) ought then to be approximately unaffected by the U.S. money supply; but the exchange value of the dollar should depreciate or appreciate, depending on whether the U.S. money stock rises or falls. In fact, if purchasing power parity held in the very short run, then the exchange rate would immediately move point for point with the price level differential between the U.S. and the rest of the world, so ${}_{t-1}Z_t$ would again become proportional to ${}_{t-1}\hat{P}_t$. However, I think we

[10]And also by everyone else. There is no issue of informational asymmetry here.

may safely assume that purchasing power parity does *not* hold in the very short run. In this case, the fraction ω in (12) can be expected to be less than unity.

Since in the short run it seems unlikely either that national economic policies will be perfectly synchronized or that purchasing power parity will hold, the implications of $\omega < 1$ seem worth exploring briefly even though ω will almost surely be unity in the long run. To keep things as simple as possible, consider the extreme case where $\omega = 0$, so that R_t becomes an exogenous nominal variable.[11] Under the same monetary rule as before, the model with $\omega = 0$ produces the following solutions:

$$ {}_{t-1}P_t = \frac{b+\delta-c}{1+\delta-c}\ {}_{t-1}R_t \tag{13} $$

$$ P_t - {}_{t-1}P_t = \left(\frac{\beta+\delta-c}{1+\alpha+\delta-c} \right) (R_t - {}_{t-1}R_t) + \eta_t \tag{14} $$

$$ y_t = k_t - \frac{\delta(1-b)}{1+\delta-c}\ {}_{t-1}R_t + \left[\frac{(\alpha+\delta)\ (\beta+\delta-c)}{1+\alpha+\delta-c} - \delta \right] (R_t - {}_{t-1}R_t) + u_t . \tag{15} $$

The dimensions of the policy problem with respect to unanticipated OPEC shocks are much the same as they were in the previous case (with $\omega = 1$), except that OPEC is now characterized by its nominal price rather than its real price. The situation with respect to *anticipated* OPEC shocks is, however, quite different. Clearly, (13) shows once again that any monetary accommodation of an OPEC hike will be inflationary. However, (15) now shows that such a policy will, in effect, raise the natural rate of output, $k_t - \delta\ [(1-b)/(1+\delta+c)]_{t-1}R_t$. There is, then, an output-inflation trade-off for accommodating an anticipated OPEC shock when $\omega < 1$.

This trade-off, of course, is only a short-run phenomenon. OPEC's price cannot be independent of the U.S. price level in the long-run because (13) implies that the real price OPEC expects to receive from its sales is a decreasing function of b. Furthermore, the factors that rationalize $\omega < 1$ cannot be expected to persist in the long run. Nonetheless, macroeconomists should not have to be reminded that the short run also matters.

The Extended Fischer Model

One new dimension of the accommodation issue arises when we turn to the richer structure available in the Fischer model: there may be shocks that while now anticipated were unanticipated when some old contracts were written. To concentrate on this issue, I solve the extended Fischer model—consisting of equations (1), (2), (6), and (7)—under the extra assumption that $r_t = {}_{t-1}r_t$. The term $r_t - {}_{t-1}r_t$

[11]This does *not* mean that R_t is fixed for long periods of time in nominal terms, but only that R_t does not react *contemporaneously* to either P_t or its expectation.

that appeared in equations (8)-(11) is assumed away because it has the same effects here as in the Lucas model. I concentrate instead on the revision of expectations that takes place between time $t-2$ and time $t-1$. Some laborious algebra leads to the following equations:

$$P_t - {}_{t-2}P_t = \frac{b+\delta-\gamma_1-c}{1+\alpha/2-b}\,({}_{t-1}r_t - {}_{t-2}r_t) + \eta_t \tag{16}$$

$$y_t = k_t - (\delta - \alpha\gamma)\,{}_{t-2}r_t + \left[\frac{(\alpha/2)(b+\delta-\gamma_1-c)}{1+(\alpha/2)-b} - (\delta-\gamma_1)\right]({}_{t-1}r_t - {}_{t-2}r_t) + u_t, \tag{17}$$

where $\gamma_1 \equiv (\alpha/2)\gamma$.

Equation (17) shows that a positive value of b will help offset the output-reducing effects of a shock that was anticipated in $t-1$ but was not anticipated in $t-2$. But equation (16) shows that a negative value of b will help offset its inflationary consequences. A trade-off exists.

The optimal choice of b would seem to depend on whether the new information contained in ${}_{t-1}r_t - {}_{t-2}r_t$ is viewed as permanent or transitory (and also on γ). If the revision in expectations is viewed as something that changes the natural rate (because it is permanent), output stabilization would lead us to set b at the value that makes the coefficient of ${}_{t-1}r_t - {}_{t-2}r_t$ in (17) equal to $-(\delta-\alpha\gamma)$. This might imply a positive (accommodating) or a negative (antiaccommodating) value of b, depending on the size of γ. If b turns out to be negative (which will be the case if γ is near zero), then both price stabilization and output stabilization call for setting b below zero, that is, for an antiaccommodative policy. If, however, b turns out to be positive (as will be the case if γ is large enough), then price stabilization calls for a negative b while output stabilization calls for a positive b. The standard sort of trade-off therefore arises in selecting an optimal b.

Suppose on the other hand that the new information contained in ${}_{t-1}r_t - {}_{t-2}r_t$ is not deemed as something that changes the natural rate of output (Sheik Yamani catches cold?). Then output can be insulated from this noise by setting b so as to make the coefficient of ${}_{t-1}r_t - {}_{t-2}r_t$ in (17) equal to zero. This implies a positive value of b. Since price stabilization always calls for negative b, the trade-off is with us again.

Notice the crucial interaction between the degree to which private agents voluntarily lower real wages in response to anticipated OPEC shocks ($\gamma_1 = (\alpha/2)\gamma$) and the optimal degree of accommodation. The larger is γ the less accommodation is optimal, and the reason is clear. If labor and management do not lower real wages enough, then with fixed nominal wage contracts the monetary authorities can help out by causing more inflation than was originally anticipated. This observation naturally raises the question of how private agents determine γ—a question I investigate in the next section.

4. DIMENSIONS OF THE "FUTURE DISASTER" ARGUMENT

In general, then, the dimensions of the present disaster problem are much the same in the extended Fischer model as they were in the extended Lucas model. It is when we come to consider the "future disaster" argument, that is, the Lucas [12] problem of policy-dependent parameters, that critical differences between the two models emerge.

The Extended Lucas Model

Two aspects of the future disaster argument seem to arise in the context of the extended Lucas model. Most obviously, the behavior of the central bank may influence the parameter ω in OPEC's pricing rule (12). Specifically, if it becomes known (or suspected) that the Fed will aggressively accommodate any nominal OPEC shock (i.e., b will be high), OPEC may decide to abandon its nominal pricing policy and try to establish a real price instead. In this case, a policy of accommodating an anticipated OPEC price increase might reap some gains at first (while $\omega < 1$) but leave us with a more vexing problem later (when $\omega = 1$). This would undercut, but not necessarily eliminate, the case for accommodation.[12]

Secondly, it was noted earlier than an activist monetary response to unanticipated OPEC price changes is advisable because of the informational content of R_t as a predictor of the price level. This informational content, however, depends critically on the correlation between R_t and P_t; and this correlation, in turn, depends in a fundamental way on the policy rule being followed. Lucas's econometric policy critique makes us suspect that the parameters of the aggregate supply function (3) might not be invariant to the policy rule.

This possibility is explored in an appendix available on request, where the following is established. Under the class of monetary rules considered here, neither α nor δ in equation (3) is structural in Lucas's sense. Both depend on the policy rule. More specifically, it is shown that as policy becomes more accommodating toward unanticipated shocks (i.e., as β rises), α falls and δ rises (the sum of $\alpha+\delta$ remains the same). Since the inherent difficulties caused by OPEC shocks depend directly on the size of the parameter δ, the future disaster argument clearly undercuts any possible case for accommodation.

How important is this problem quantitatively? The appendix establishes that

$$\frac{\partial \delta}{\partial \beta} = \frac{a[\sigma_z^2/(\sigma_z^2+\sigma_\eta^2)]}{1+d-c}, \tag{18}$$

where a and d are, respectively, the elasticities of output with respect to the perceived relative price of output and the relative price of oil in the *micro* supply function (see the appendix for details); σ_z^2 is the variance of relative prices; and σ_η^2 is

[12] The reasoning behind this sentence is precisely parallel to that in Hall [10] and Phelps [14] in a related context.

the portion of the variance of absolute prices that does not stem from energy shocks. The derivative in (18) may be ''large'' or ''small,'' depending on the values of several parameters. The issue thus seems open empirically and potentially quite important.

The Extended Fischer Model

Things are quite different in the extended Fischer model. Since the aggregate supply function (6) is not derived from optimal information processing, there is no reason to think that α or δ, which are technological constants, should change when policy changes. There is, however, a natural place to look for parameter shifts.

It is a plausible conjecture—and one that seems to be part of the ''oral tradition'' against accommodation—that the parameter γ might depend on the policy rule. Specifically, since γ indicates the degree to which real wages are responsive to OPEC's price, the future disaster argument suggests that γ might fall if the central bank pursues an accommodative policy. Since higher values of γ help insulate the economy from OPEC shocks, this conjecture, if true, would be important.

Is it true? To examine it, we need to provide explicit microfoundations for the wage-setting equation (5). The remainder of this section sketches how this can be done and the appendix provides the details. Contrary to the frequent assertion, γ turns out to be structural in Lucas's sense: it is independent of the policy rule.

The model is a simple one contrived to ''fit'' the requirements of the Fischer model; that is, to lead to log-linear decision rules that set money wages in advance and permit firms to vary the level of employment ex post. Specifically, I assume that workers and firms agree in period t on the *money* wages that will prevail in periods $t+1$ and $t+2$, and that workers cede to firms the right to determine the level of employment later on. (This appears, incidentally, to be a moderately realistic form of contract.) Agents make these decisions without knowledge of the future values of the two relative prices (real wage and real price of oil) but with the knowledge of the distributions of the relevant random variables. The essence of the ''future disaster'' problem is that, for any chosen money wage, monetary policy influences the joint density of the two relative prices, and the issue is whether policy therefore changes the nature of the contract agreement.

I assume that the money wage is chosen Pareto optimally, that is, to maximize a weighted sum of expected profits and expected utility of workers. When the future period arrives, assuming a Cobb-Douglas production function with weights s_1 on labor and s_2 on energy, the firm will demand labor according to

$$l = \text{const.} - \frac{s_2}{1-s_1-s_2} r - \frac{1-s_2}{1-s_1-s_2} (W\text{-}P), \tag{19}$$

which defines l, the log of employment, as a random variable from today's perspective.

When period $t+1$ or $t+2$ arrives, workers will supply the labor indicated in (19) and spend their earnings on domestic goods. If the direct utility function is $U = -a_1 l + (1+a_1)X$, where X is (the log of) consumption, then the indirect utility function is[13]

$$V = \text{const.} + \left(a_1 - \frac{s_1}{1-s_1-s_2} \right)(W\text{-}P) - \left(\frac{s_2}{1-s_1-s_2} \right) r .$$

A Pareto-optimal wage bargain maximizes the following weighted sum for some value of Θ:

$$E(\text{profits}) + \Theta E(V),$$

where $E(\cdot)$ is the expectation operator. Maximizing with respect to the money wage, and remembering that firms are always equating marginal products with factor prices ex post, leads after some algebra to

$$W = E(P) - (s_2/s_1)E(r) + \text{constant}, \tag{20}$$

where the constant depends on Θ. Equation (20) is precisely of the form (5) with $\gamma = s_2/s_1$. The model therefore implies that γ is independent of the policy rule despite the clear effect of policy on Var(P) and Cov(P,r).

What was wrong with the intuition that suggested that the covariance "mattered"? The answer is that while the covariance between P and r is relevant to the *variability* of the profits and to the *variability* of utility, it does not affect the *expected values* of either. Thus, if workers maximize expected utility and firms maximize expected profits, behavior will be independent of monetary policy.[14]

5. CONCLUSIONS

1. Where *unanticipated* OPEC shocks are concerned, there is always an exploitable inflation-employment trade-off in the short run. But this does not imply that accommodation is optimal. In fact, to the extent that unanticipated OPEC shocks are permanent, it appears optimal to *reduce* the money supply after a supply shock. Accommodation might be optimal, however, if unanticipated OPEC shocks are transitory.

2. Where *anticipated* OPEC shocks are concerned, conclusions depend more on the specifics of each model. In the extended Lucas model, the only potential case for accommodation rests on OPEC's nominal price not adjusting fully to the anticipated

[13] I assume $a_1 > [s_2/(1-s_1-s_2)]$ so that workers prefer higher wages, despite the lower employment that higher wages imply.

[14] This is not quite true. The constant in (20) *does* depend on the policy rule. Omitting a constant from (5) in the macro model is tantamount to embedding it in the "natural rate of output," k_t. Thus policy *does* affect the natural rate, as shown previously by Azariadis [2]. Azariadis's analysis suggests that stabilization policy may reduce the variance of output but also may reduce its mean. "Optimal" policy presumably must balance these two factors.

U.S. price level. I argued that such a situation is likely to prevail in the short run, but not in the long. In the extended Fischer model, there might be a case for accommodating OPEC shocks that are currently *anticipated,* but were *unanticipated* when some existing contracts were struck. Whether or not the optimal policy response is accommodating depends both on how permanent OPEC shocks are (permanent shocks call for less accommodation) and on how sensitive the contracted target real wage is to the anticipated real price of oil (smaller sensitivities call for more accommodation).

3. Great differences between the two models emerge when we come to consider the "future disaster" argument because the extended Lucas model turns on the informational structure while the extended Fischer model turns on fixed nominal contracts. In the Lucas model, a more accommodative policy increases the usefulness of the nominal price of oil as a predictor of the aggregate price level, and hence increases the sensitivity of output to OPEC shocks. By contrast, in the Fischer model, a plausible model of the labor contract leads to the conclusion that the parameters are invariant to the policy rule.

4. While a number of different cases have been considered (two different models, long run versus short run, anticipated versus unanticipated shocks) a general conclusion seems to be that doing nothing is unlikely to be the optimal monetary response to a supply shock. However, it is far from clear that increasing the money supply is the optimal response if the goods market clears instantly and expectations are rational. Indeed, if supply shocks are permanent, it seems likely that antiaccommodative policies are optimal under such circumstances.

LITERATURE CITED

1. Ando, Albert K., and Carl Palash. "Some Stabilization Problems of 1971–75, with an Application of Optimal Control Algorithms." In *Frontiers of Quantitative Economics,* Vol. 3, edited by Michael Intriligator. Amsterdam: North-Holland, 1976.
2. Azariadis, Costas C. "A Re-Examination of Natural Rate Theory." *American Economic Review,* in press.
3. Barro, Robert J. "Rational Expectations and the Role of Monetary Policy." *Journal of Monetary Economics,* 2 (January 1976), 1–32.
4. Blinder, Alan S. *Economic Policy and the Great Stagflation.* New York: Academic Press, 1979.
5. ______. "Supply Shock Inflation: Money, Expectations, and Accommodation." In *Development in an Inflationary World,* edited by M. June Flanders and Assaf Razin. New York: Academic Press, 1980.
6. Eckstein, Otto. *The Great Recession.* Amsterdam: North-Holland, 1978.
7. Fischer, Stanley. "Long-Term Contracts, Rational Expectations, and the Optimal Money Supply Rule." *Journal of Political Economy,* 85 (February 1977), 191–205.
8. Gordon, Robert J. "Alternative Responses of Policy to External Supply Shocks." *Brookings Papers on Economic Activity,* 1 (1975), 183–204.
9. Gramlich, Edward M. "Macro Policy Responses to Price Shocks." *Brookings Papers on Economic Activity,* 1 (1979), 125–66.

10. Hall, Robert E. "The Phillips Curve and Macroeconomic Policy." In *The Phillips Curve and Labor Markets,* edited by Karl Brunner and Allan H. Meltzer. The Carnegie-Rochester Conference Series, Vol. 1. Amsterdam: North-Holland, 1976.

11. Lucas, Robert E., Jr. "Some International Evidence on Output-Inflation Trade-Offs." *American Economic Review,* 63 (June 1973), 326–34.

12. ______. "Econometric Policy Evaluation: A Critique." In *The Phillips Curve and Labor Markets,* edited by Karl Brunner and Allan H. Meltzer. The Carnegie-Rochester Conference Series, Vol. 1. Amsterdam: North-Holland, 1976.

13. Perry, George L. "Policy Alternatives for 1974." *Brookings Papers on Economic Activity,* 1 (1975), 222-35.

14. Phelps, Edmund S. *Inflation Policy and Unemployment Theory.* New York: Norton, 1972.

15. ______. "Commodity-Supply Shock and Full-Employment Monetary Policy." *Journal of Money, Credit, and Banking,* 10 (May 1978), 206–21.

GARY C. FETHKE
ANDREW J. POLICANO*

Long-Term Contracts and the Effectiveness of Demand and Supply Policies

IN RECENT YEARS, the economy has been characterized by simultaneous labor-market slack, accelerating inflation, and a progression of real shocks. In response to these events, nontraditional aggregate control measures have been introduced that seek to affect the supply side of the economy. These policies include controls on wages and prices, general and targeted employment credits and wage subsidies, and tax-based incomes policies. This paper compares the effectiveness of monetary policy and one type of supply-management policy in controlling fluctuations in output and the price level. The supply-side program, which is a variant of the employment tax credit, acts directly on the firm's cost of labor and, thereby, on aggregate supply. Monetary policy, on the other hand, directly affects aggregate demand and only indirectly affects the firm's cost of labor through its impact on the price level. Since these programs have different transmission mechanisms, a principal question of the analysis concerns whether they exhibit differences in their ability to respond to demand versus supply shocks. An additional question addressed by the analysis concerns the interaction between the length of wage contracts and the policy parameters.

The framework consists of log-linear representations of aggregate demand and supply functions that are subject to random disturbances. Fluctuations in output occur as a consequence of both the random disturbances and the underlying wage rigidity caused by long-term contracts. The presence of long-term contracts is

*The authors are grateful for research support provided by the Upjohn Institute for Employment Research, and we have also benefited from constructive comments by an anonymous referee. Policano was at the University of Iowa when this paper was written.

GARY C. FETHKE *is associate professor of management science and economics, University of Iowa.* ANDREW J. POLICANO *is professor of economics, Fordham University.*

0022-2879/81/1181-0439$00.50/0

justified by the existence of costs associated with establishing perfectly contingent contracts. Private agents, in setting wage contracts, are assumed to develop rational forecasts of unobserved variables based on information concerning both the aggregate model and the policy feedback rules. The ability of the public authority to affect real variables derives from an assumed cost advantage on the part of the authority over private agents in reacting to recent shocks.

The results of the analysis relate to both the relative effectiveness of the demand and supply policies and the optimality and nature of the long-term wage contract structure. First, we show that the employment tax credit and monetary policy are equally effective in offsetting fluctuations in output. This result derives from the observation that both policy strategies affect the real wage and, thereby, can undo the effects of the preset contract. Monetary policy works on the real wage by changing aggregate demand and the price level, while the employment credit directly changes the real wage by providing a wage subsidy (or tax) to employers. Thus, while the transmission mechanisms of the policies differ, they have identical effects on the variances of employment and output. A further important result concerns the impact of the two policy alternatives on the variability of the price level. When shocks to the economy originate on the demand side, the monetary rule that stabilizes output implies smaller fluctuations in the price level than does the supply-side policy. This result occurs because both the increment to the money supply and the demand disturbance enter the demand equation, and the demand disturbance can be directly neutralized by changing the money supply. On the other hand, the employment credit, which acts directly on the real cost of labor, can effectively neutralize the impact of supply disturbances but will only work indirectly in counteracting demand shocks.

In addition to comparing the two policy regimes, we also examine the dependency of the optimal policy responses on the model's parameters and evaluate the economy's capacity to self-equilibrate in response to random disturbances in aggregate demand and supply. Interestingly, for certain parameter values, the system containing overlapping wage contracts will equilibrate in response to aggregate disturbances without policy intervention. Finally, with respect to the long-term contract structure, we show that the contract length depends on the parameters of the model, including the parameters of the policy feedback rules. This implies that it is not generally correct to assume that multiperiod contracts are invariant with respect to changes in government policy.

The paper contains five sections. Section 1 develops the aggregate framework, and section 2 examines the output stabilizing effects of employment-credit policy. Sections 3 and 4 compare the output and price fluctuations implied by the use of monetary and employment-credit policy. Finally, section 5 examines the interaction between the length of the contract and the policy feedback rules.

1. THE AGGREGATE FRAMEWORK

This section develops a stochastic aggregate model that includes employment-tax-credit and monetary-policy variables. We assume that economic agents form rational expectations of unobserved variables; consequently, systematic policy will have no impact on real variables unless there exists either an informational asymmetry between the authority and private agents or some form of price or wage rigidity. We adopt the rigid-wage assumption based on the considerable evidence for the United States and Canada that supports the existence of fixed-term nominal wage contracts [17, 18]. This literature suggests that a primary source of wage rigidity is the existence of transaction costs associated with either spot market or contingent contract determination of real wages.[1] The contract scheme utilized is similar to that developed by Fischer [8], which posits a long-term nominal wage setting process.[2]

The model contains the following equations:

$$Y_t^S = \epsilon_1(W_t - P_t - S_t) + \epsilon_2 Z_t, \qquad \epsilon_1 < 0, \epsilon_2 > 0, \epsilon_1 + \epsilon_2 = 1 \quad \text{(aggregate supply)} \tag{1}$$

$$Y_t^D = \phi_1(M_t - P_t) + \phi_2 V_t, \qquad \phi_1, \phi_2 > 0 \text{ (aggregate demand)} \tag{2}$$

$${}_{t-i}W_t = {}_{t-i}P_t + {}_{t-i}S_t + {}_{t-i}Z_t \text{ (wage contract equation)} \tag{3}$$

$$V_t = \rho_1 V_{t-1} + \mu_t, \qquad 0 < \rho_1 < 1 \text{ (stochastic demand process)} \tag{4a}$$

$$Z_t = \rho_2 Z_{t-1} + \eta_t, \qquad 0 < \rho_2 < 1 \text{ (stochastic supply process)} \tag{4b}$$

$$S_t = \sum_{i=1}^{\infty} (a_i V_{t-i} + a_i^* Z_{t-i}) \text{(employment-tax-credit rule)} \tag{5a}$$

$$M_t = \sum_{i=1}^{\infty} (b_i V_{t-i} + b_i^* Z_{t-i}) \text{ (monetary-policy rule).} \tag{5b}$$

Equations (1)–(5) describe an aggregate system that is consistent with a wide range of structural models. The variables are measured in logarithmic form; output, Y_t^S, and the money supply, M_t, are deviations from their respective full-employment levels (trends); W_t and P_t are logarithms of the wage rate and price level; S_t is the employment-tax-credit rate.[3]

[1]Unless transactions costs exist, it is difficult to explain the existence of labor contracts that fix nominal wages. Wachter and Williamson [21] argue that "obligational" contracts arise where labor skills are idiosyncratic and where bounds on rationality effectively eliminate the possible formulation of complete contingent contracts. They also argue that wage stickiness associated with obligational exchange implies that policy can alter real output even where agents form rational expectations. See Azariadis [2] for a discussion of the effects of costly information on aggregate variables, Taylor [20] for a development of the dynamic implications of staggered contracts, and McCallum [15] for a discussion of pricing decisions that lead to aggregate price rigidity.

[2]There are at least two alternative frameworks that can be used to analyze the macroeconomic effects of employment-credit policy. First, equilibrium models with multi-input production functions are used to examine the substitutability between inputs and the overall employment, investment, and output responses of the program [4, 13, 14]. Second, disaggregated Phillips curve models with low- and high-wage workers are used to assess the impact of the credit on the firm's substitution between less productive low-wage workers and high-wage workers [3, 11]. Our view is consistent with a homogeneous labor force and nominal wage rigidity [6, 7, 12].

[3]A stylized representation of the aggregate model follows:

Equation (1) represents an aggregate supply equation that results from inserting the profit-maximizing condition for determining the demand for labor into an aggregate production function which, in turn, depends on a random productivity disturbance and variable labor. Any event that increases the effective real cost of labor, $W_t - P_t - S_t$, will reduce output; thus firms operate on their notional supply curves. The random disturbance to output, Z_t, is characterized by equation (4b) as a first-order autoregressive process, where the innovation, η_t, is identically and independently distributed with zero mean and constant variance, σ_η^2.

Aggregate demand, Y_t^D, as described by equation (2), depends on real balances, $M_t - P_t$, and a stochastic process, V_t. The classical, quantity equation is the special case where $\phi_1 = \phi_2 = 1$. The ϕ's represent composites of underlying demand parameters, which we assume to be invariant to the employment-credit or monetary-policy rules. The random term, V_t, is a stationary, first-order autoregressive process, equation (4a). The innovation, μ_t, has a zero mean and constant variance, σ_μ^2, is serially independent, and is distributed independently of η_t.

The wage-setting process, equation (3), assumes that the nominal wage is set to equate the expected supply and demand for labor.[4] Thus, the contract specifies that the wage be set at period $t - i$ for period t to accord with the expected price, ${}_{t-i}P_t$, the expected employment credit, ${}_{t-i}S_t$, and the expected real disturbance, ${}_{t-i}Z_t$, where ${}_{t-i}X_t$ is the expectation of the variable X_t formulated at time $t - i$. When the random disturbances are realized, employment is determined ex post by labor demand; fluctuations in employment and output occur because the real wage in period t differs from that anticipated when the multiperiod contract is negotiated.

The policy rules are given by equations (5a) and (5b). The authority is described as being able to observe *past* values of V_t and Z_t and then reacts through changes in the money supply or the tax-credit rate to counter the effects of these disturbances

---

$$Y_t = \lambda L_t + Z_t, \quad 0 \leq \lambda \leq 1 \text{ (aggregate production function)} \tag{i}$$

$$L_t^D = \left(\frac{1}{\lambda - 1}\right)(W_t - P_t - S_t) + \left(\frac{1}{1 - \lambda}\right) Z_t \text{ (demand for labor)} \tag{ii}$$

$$L_t^s = \beta(W_t - P_t), \quad 0 \leq \beta \leq \infty \text{ (supply of labor)} \tag{iii}$$

$$Y_t = \frac{\pi_2}{1 - \pi_1} r_t + \frac{1}{1 - \pi_1} V_t, \quad 0 \leq \pi_1 \leq 1,\ \pi_2 < 0 \text{ (}IS\text{ function)} \tag{iv}$$

$$M_t - P_t = \pi_3 Y_t + \pi_4 r_t, \quad 0 < \pi_3,\ \pi_4 < 0 \text{ (}LM\text{ function)}. \tag{v}$$

In the above, r_t is the nominal rate of interest, λ is the elasticity of output with respect to labor, β is the elasticity of labor supply with respect to the real wage, π_1 is the income elasticity of consumption, π_2 is the interest elasticity of investment, and π_3 and π_4 are, respectively, the income and interest elasticities of the demand for money. Employment in each period is determined by labor demand, $L_t = L_t^D$, thus substituting (ii) into (i) yields equation (1), that is, $Y_t^s = \epsilon_1(W_t - P_t - S_t) + \epsilon_2 Z_t$, $\epsilon_1 = \lambda/\lambda - 1 < 0$, $\epsilon_2 = 1/1 - \lambda > 0$, and $\epsilon_1 + \epsilon_2 = 1$. Eliminating r_t from equations (iv) and (v) yields

$$Y_T^D = \frac{\pi_2}{\pi_2\pi_3 + \pi_4(1-\pi_1)}(M_t - P_t) + \frac{\pi_4}{\pi_2\pi_3 + \pi_4(1-\pi_1)} V_t,$$

which corresponds to equation (2).

[4]The elasticity of labor supply, β, is assumed to be zero; equating labor demand and supply implies that $W_t = P_t + S_t + Z_t$. If $\beta \neq 0$, then $W_t = P_t + [\epsilon_2/(\epsilon_2 + \beta)](S_t + Z_t)$. These contract structures differ from that introduced by Fischer [8], which assumes that agents seek a constant real wage even when the economy is subject to real disturbances.

on output. The policy determined parameters, a_i and b_i, depend, via an expected loss function, on the behavioral properties of the model. Contracting agents rely on the authority to intercede to clear the labor market, and there is no attempt by the authority to fool private agents. Specifically, agents expect the authority to offset any disturbances for which the contract has made no contingencies. Thus, in our view, private agents permit the authority to affect the real wage because it is less costly for the authority to achieve the socially desired outcome than it is for private agents to undertake more frequent contracting.

2. OUTPUT STABILIZATION IMPLICATIONS OF EMPLOYMENT-TAX-CREDIT POLICY

This section considers the effectiveness of employment-tax-credit policy in controlling fluctuations in output; the next section examines a pure monetary-policy alternative. To solve the aggregate framework, that is, to derive expressions for P_t and Y_t that do not contain conditional expectations, we implement the rational expectations hypothesis. We assume that agents know the structure of the aggregate system and past values of V_t and Z_t. They do not observe current values of output or the price level, nor do they observe current innovations to Y_t^D or Y_t^S. The price level adjusts each period to clear the commodity market and, thus, we equate Y_t^D and Y_t^S and solve for P_t. This expression for P_t is then utilized to derive the expectation of the price level in period t based on information available at earlier periods.

Before equating Y_t^D and Y_t^S, we first eliminate the nominal wage rate from the system. Specifically, the actual wage rate in period t, W_t, is a weighted sum of wage contracts negotiated at periods $t-1, t-2, \ldots, t-\tau^*$, where τ^* is the length of the contract. In general, τ^* is affected by the parameters of the policy feedback rules, and we analyze this relationship in section 5. To facilitate the analysis, however, all contracts are assumed to be two periods long. Firms are identical except for the timing of contract negotiation, with α_t being the fraction of total contracts negotiated at period t. From equation (3), we obtain the current nominal wage rate[5]

$$W_t = \alpha({}_{t-1}P_t + {}_{t-1}S_t + {}_{t-1}Z_t) + (1-\alpha)({}_{t-2}P_t + {}_{t-2}S_t + {}_{t-2}Z_t). \quad (6)$$

Equation (6) implies that the employment credit enters the wage-setting equation, and that credit adjustment by the fiscal authority can exert a direct impact on the real cost of labor and real output. In this respect, the employment credit program differs from traditional monetary policy, which has no *direct* impact on aggregate supply.

Substituting equation (6) into the aggregate output relationship, equation (1), yields

$$Y_t^S = {}_{t-1}Z_t + \epsilon_1 \{({}_{t-1}P_t - P_t) + (1-\alpha)[({}_{t-2}P_t - {}_{t-1}P_t) + ({}_{t-2}S_t - S_t) + ({}_{t-2}Z_t - {}_{t-1}Z_t)]\} + \epsilon_2(Z_t - {}_{t-1}Z_t). \quad (7)$$

[5]In the following, we assume, for simplicity, that α is constant through time. Ashenfelter and Pencavel

In deriving this expression, agents negotiating contracts at $t - 1$ and the authority are presumed to be equally knowledgeable, with the authority following the systematic credit rule, equation (5a); this implies that ${}_{t-1}S_t = S_t$.

We assume that the credit program is financed by changes in the money supply.[6] Specifically, $M_t = \pi_0 S_t$, where π_0 is a positive constant that approximates the ratio of the money supply increment to the credit rate. Substituting $M_t = \pi_0 S_t$ into equation (2) yields

$$Y_t^D = \phi_3 S_t - \phi_1 P_t + \phi_2 V_t, \tag{2'}$$

where $\phi_3 = \pi_0 \phi_1 > 0$. An equation for the aggregate price level results from setting equation (2′) equal to equation (7) and then solving for P_t:

$$P_t = (\epsilon_1 - \phi_1)^{-1}\{\epsilon_1[{}_{t-1}P_t + (1-\alpha)(({}_{t-2}P_t - {}_{t-1}P_t) + ({}_{t-2}S_t - S_t) + ({}_{t-2}Z_t - {}_{t-1}Z_t))] - \phi_3 S_t - \phi_2 V_t + {}_{t-1}Z_t + \epsilon_2(Z_t - {}_{t-1}Z_t)\}. \tag{8}$$

From equation (8), the expectation of P_t based on information available at time $t-2$ is

$$_{t-2}P_t = \phi_1^{-1}(\phi_{3\,t-2}S_t + \phi_{2\,t-2}V_t - {}_{t-2}Z_t). \tag{9}$$

Since agents forming expectations at $t-1$ know ${}_{t-2}P_t$, we substitute equation (9) into equation (8) and use the resultant expression to derive ${}_{t-1}P_t$:

$$_{t-1}P_t = [\phi_1 - (1-\alpha)\epsilon_1]^{-1}[(\phi_3 + (1-\alpha)\epsilon_1)S_t - (\phi_1^{-1}(1-\alpha)\epsilon_1(\phi_1 + \phi_3))_{t-2}S_t + \phi_{2\,t-1}V_t - (\phi_1^{-1}\phi_2(1-\alpha)\epsilon_1)_{t-2}V_t - (\epsilon_2 + \alpha\epsilon_1)_{t-1}Z_t + (\phi_1^{-1}(1-\alpha)\epsilon_1(1-\phi_1))_{t-2}Z_t]. \tag{10}$$

Finally, substituting for the terms ${}_{t-1}P_t - P_t$, ${}_{t-2}P_t - {}_{t-1}P_t$, ${}_{t-2}S_t - S_t$, ${}_{t-2}Z_t - {}_{t-1}Z_t$, and $Z_t - {}_{t-1}Z_t$ in equation (7), using equations (8), (9), (10), (4a), (4b), and (5a), yields the reduced-form expression for output that depends on current and past demand and supply shocks:

$$Y_t^S = (\epsilon_1 - \phi_1)^{-1}(\phi_2\epsilon_1\mu_t - \phi_1\epsilon_2\eta_t) + \sum_{i=2}^{\infty}\rho_2^i\eta_{t-i} - (\phi_1 - (1-\alpha)\epsilon_1)^{-1}\epsilon_1(1-\alpha)[(\phi_3 + \phi_1)a_1 + \phi_2\rho_1]\mu_{t-1} - (\phi_1 - (1-\alpha)\epsilon_1)^{-1}[\epsilon_1(1-\alpha)(\phi_1 + \phi_3)a_1^* - (\epsilon_2 + \alpha\epsilon_1)\phi_1\rho_2]\eta_{t-1}. \tag{11}$$

---

[1] find that this assumption is reasonably accurate based on British data; Smith and Wilton [19], however, find little support for this hypothesis using Canadian data.

[6]Other financing strategies, including changes in government expenditure, income taxes, and the deficit are considered in [6]; these alternatives do not affect the qualitative nature of the results.

The lagged innovation terms, μ_{t-1} and η_{t-1}, appear in equation (11) as a consequence of the two-period contracting process. Specifically, the authority can observe and respond to *realized* disturbances, thus it can completely offset the impact of these disturbances on current output by appropriate selection of a_1 and a_1^*. The values of the policy parameters for $i \geqslant 2$ do not enter equation (11) and are set equal to zero.

The expected loss function for credit and monetary policy will be represented by the mean-squared discrepancy of output from the level, $Y_t^* = Z_t$, associated with a frictionless system. Policy acts only to nullify unanticipated fluctuations in output that are associated with the multiperiod wage contracts and is not permitted to fool private agents by exploiting wage rigidity. Using equation (11), the expected loss in output is represented by the following expression:

$$E[(Y_t^S - Y_t^*)^2] = \left(\frac{\epsilon_1}{\epsilon_1 - \phi_1}\right)^2 (\phi_2^2\sigma_\mu^2 + (1 - \phi_1)^2\sigma_\eta^2)$$

$$+ \left(\frac{\epsilon_1(1-\alpha)}{\phi_1 - (1-\alpha)\epsilon_1}\right)^2 [((\phi_1 + \phi_3)a_1 + \phi_2\rho_1)^2\sigma_\mu^2$$

$$+ ((\phi_1 + \phi_3)a_1^* - (1 - \phi_1)\rho_2)^2\sigma_\eta^2]. \qquad (12)$$

Since a_1 and a_1^* only enter the second term in equation (12), the values of a_1 and a_1^* that set this term equal to zero will minimize expected loss. These values are given by

$$a_1 = \frac{-\phi_2\rho_1}{\phi_1 + \phi_3} \qquad (13)$$

and

$$a_1^* = \frac{(1 - \phi_1)\rho_2}{\phi_1 + \phi_3} \qquad (14)$$

Examination of equations (13) and (14) indicates that the optimal employment-credit rules depend on the autoregressive weights ρ_1 and ρ_2. If $\rho_1 = \rho_2 = 0$, then aggregate shocks affect the system only in the current period, and a_1 and a_1^* are equal to zero. In this case, because the authority has no information concerning current shocks, there is no role for discretionary policy. In addition to ρ_1, the optimal rule in response to demand-side shocks, equation (13), depends on the demand elasticities represented by ϕ_1, ϕ_2, and ϕ_3. Specifically, ϕ_1 is the absolute value of the price elasticity of demand. If ϕ_1 is relatively large, then the price change in response to any demand-side disturbance exerts a relatively large stabilizing impact on both aggregate demand and the level of output. Thus, the larger is ϕ_1 the smaller is the change in the credit required to offset the initial disturbance. Next, the larger is ϕ_2, the greater is the impact on Y_t^D of any demand-side disturbance and the larger is the change in the credit required to stabilize output. Finally, the larger is ϕ_3, the greater is the impact on Y_t^D of any change in the credit and the smaller is the change in the credit required to stabilize output.

The optimal rule in response to supply-side disturbances also depends on the parameters ϕ_1 and ϕ_3. In addition, the sign of the change in the credit required to offset supply-side shocks depends on the sign of $(1 - \phi_1)$. If ϕ_1 equals unity, the aggregate demand specification, equation (2), reduces to the quantity equation, and there is no role for discretionary response to supply-side disturbances. For example, consider a downturn in Y_t^S and the subsequent price increase. With a partially rigid nominal wage, the price increase reduces the real cost of labor, and employment and output tend to recover. In the special case where $\phi_1 = 1$, this price increase induces an increase in employment that clears the labor market and moves output to its new equilibrium level. Thus, discretionary reaction is unnecessary. If ϕ_1 is less than unity, the price response induces both employment and output to overshoot their new equilibrium levels, and a decrease in the credit is necessary. Realistic parameter values for the elasticities that determine ϕ_1 suggest that ϕ_1 is greater than unity.[7] In this case, the price response to an initial supply disturbance is not sufficient to obtain the new equilibrium values of output and employment, and an increase in the credit is the appropriate response to a random decline in aggregate supply.

Assuming that the optimal employment credit rules are adopted in each period, we obtain the minimum mean-squared error of output by substituting equations (13) and (14) into equation (12):

$$\min E[(Y_t^S - Y_t^*)^2] = \left(\frac{\epsilon_1}{\epsilon_1 - \phi_1}\right)^2 [\phi_2^2\sigma_\mu^2 + (1 - \phi_1)^2\sigma_\eta^2]. \tag{15}$$

This expression represents the movements in output around Y_t^* that cannot be offset by systematic employment-tax-credit policy.

3. OUTPUT STABILIZATION IMPLICATIONS OF A PURE MONETARY POLICY

This section contrasts the effectiveness of monetary policy with that of employment-tax-credit policy in controlling fluctuations in output. Under a pure monetary policy, $S_t = 0$ in equations (1)–(5) and equation (5b) replaces (5a); otherwise, the system remains the same. Following an analysis similar to that presented in the preceding section, the reduced-form representation for the level of real output is given by

[7]Consideration of demand-side parameters has generally been overlooked in the analysis of supply-side disturbances. For example, Fischer [8] and Gray [9] use simple quantity equations to represent aggregate demand. A notable exception is Phelps [16], who obtains a result similar to our condition concerning ϕ_1. In particular, from note 3, $\phi_1 > 1$ implies that $\pi_2(1-\pi_3) > \pi_4(1-\pi_1)$, where $\pi_1 > 0$ is the income elasticity of consumption, $\pi_2 < 0$ is the interest elasticity of investment, and $\pi_3 > 0$ and $\pi_4 < 0$ are the income and interest elasticities of money demand. A sufficient condition for $\phi_1 > 1$ is $\pi_3 \geq 1$, which is consistent with long-term estimates of this elasticity.

$$Y_t^S = (\epsilon_1 - \phi_1)^{-1}(\epsilon_1\phi_2\mu_t - \epsilon_2\phi_1\eta_t) + \sum_{i=2}^{\infty} \rho_2^i \eta_{t-i}$$

$$- \epsilon_1(1-\alpha)(\phi_1 - (1-\alpha)\epsilon_1)^{-1}[\phi_1 b_1 + \phi_2\rho_1]\mu_{t-1}$$

$$+ \phi_1(\phi_1 - (1-\alpha)\epsilon_1)^{-1}[(\epsilon_2 + \alpha\epsilon_1)\rho_2 - (1-\alpha)\epsilon_1 b_1^*]\eta_{t-1}, \quad (16)$$

where the ϕ_i's are defined as in section 1. As with employment-credit policy, the existence of wage contracts indicates that appropriate selection of b_1 and b_1^* by the monetary authority can offset the impact of previous disturbances on the level of output. Again, the policy parameters for $i \geqslant 2$ do not enter the aggregate supply equation and are set equal to zero.

The expected loss in output under the monetary-policy regime is given by

$$E[(Y_t^S - Y_t^*)^2] = \left(\frac{\epsilon_1}{\epsilon_1 - \phi_1}\right)^2 [\phi_2^2\sigma_\mu^2 + (1-\phi_1)^2\sigma_\eta^2]$$

$$+ \left(\frac{\epsilon_1}{\phi_1 - (1-\alpha)\epsilon_1}\right)^2 (\phi_1 b_1 + \phi_2\rho_1)^2\sigma_\mu^2$$

$$+ \left(\frac{\epsilon_1}{\phi_1 - (1-\alpha)\epsilon_1}\right)^2 (\phi_1 b_1^* - (1-\phi_1)\rho_2)^2\sigma_\eta^2, \quad (17)$$

where $Y_t^* = Z_t$ is the output rate associated with a frictionless economy. The values, b_1 and b_1^*, that minimize expected loss are given by

$$b_1 = \frac{-\phi_2\rho_1}{\phi_1} \quad (18)$$

and

$$b_1^* = \frac{(1-\phi_1)\rho_2}{\phi_1} \quad . \quad (19)$$

The optimal policy parameters again depend on the demand elasticities and on the autoregressive parameters, ρ_1 and ρ_2. Equation (18) implies that, in response to demand disturbances, the required change in M_t is relatively small if ϕ_2, the effect of the disturbance on Y_t^D, is small, or if ϕ_1, the effect on Y_t^D of changes in the price level, is relatively large. Equation (19) implies that the direction of the monetary change in response to supply-side shifts depends, as does the credit response, on the sign of $(1 - \phi_1)$. Again, for the case where ϕ_1 is greater than unity, a decrease in Y_t^S implies that an increase in the money supply is necessary to stabilize output.

Substituting the rules given by equations (18) and (19) into equation (17), we obtain the minimum expected loss implied by monetary policy, which is identical to the expected output loss under employment-credit policy, equation (15). This result is a consequence of the assumptions that the monetary and fiscal authorities possess identical information and that both agents follow the same general strategy in reacting to random disturbances. Thus, if the policy objective is to control fluctuations in output, policymakers should be indifferent between monetary policy and the employment-tax-credit program. The choice between the two strategies must depend on other criteria, including the practical problems associated with implementing the rules, the lag structure, and the variance in the price level implied by each regime. In section 4, we consider one of these criteria, namely, the implications for the variance of the price level.

4. PRICE IMPLICATIONS OF THE ALTERNATIVE STRATEGIES

To compare fluctuations in the price level between the two strategies, the optimal rules for minimizing the mean-squared discrepancy in output are inserted into the reduced-form equations for the price level. For the employment credit, we substitute the expressions for ${}_{t-2}P_t$, ${}_{t-1}P_t$, and ${}_{t-2}S_t$ into equation (8) to obtain an expression for P_t that depends on the employment-credit rules and present and past innovations to aggregate demand and supply. We then insert equations (13) and (14) into P_t and derive the asymptotic variance of the price level associated with the use of employment-credit policy,[8]

$$\mathrm{Var}(P|S) = \left(\frac{-\phi_2}{\epsilon_1-\phi_1}\right)^2 \sigma_\mu^2 + \left(\frac{\phi_2\rho_1}{\phi_1+\phi_3}\right)^2 \frac{\sigma_\mu^2}{1-\rho_1^2} + \left(\frac{\epsilon_2}{\epsilon_1-\phi_1}\right)^2 \sigma_\eta^2 + \left(\frac{1-\phi_1}{\phi_1+\phi_2}\right) \frac{\rho_2^2\sigma_\eta^2}{1-\rho_2^2} . \quad (20)$$

Following the same methodology, we substitute the optimal monetary policy rules, equations (18) and (19), into the reduced-form expression for P_t. Solving for the asymptotic variance of the price level associated with the use of monetary policy we obtain

$$\mathrm{Var}(P|M) = \left(\frac{-\phi_2}{\epsilon_1-\phi_1}\right)^2 \sigma_\mu^2 + \left(\frac{\epsilon_2}{\epsilon_1-\phi_1}\right) \sigma_\eta^2 + \left(\frac{\rho_2^2}{1-\rho_2^2}\right) \sigma_\eta^2 . \quad (21)$$

It is useful to consider the implications of equations (20) and (21) by separately analyzing demand and supply shocks. When the system is only subject to demand-side shocks, $\sigma_\eta^2 = 0$, equation (18), the optimal monetary-policy rule implies a smaller variability in the price level than does the corresponding optimal tax-credit

[8]The stochastic processes that drive the system, V_t and Z_t, are stationary; the parameters of the model conform to stability requirements; and the policy variables, M_t and S_t, are determined on the basis of stationary processes. These conditions and assumptions imply that all variables in the system can be represented as univariate, stationary stochastic processes. This property ensures the existence of finite means and variances for each endogenous variable, including P_t.

strategy. The essential idea is that with flexible prices, contractions in aggregate demand are deflationary. The monetary-policy rule acts to offset the decrease in the price level by directly stimulating aggregate demand. The increase in demand acts to nullify the deflationary impact of the demand disturbance. Thus, when shocks to the system originate on the demand side, optimal monetary policy directed at stabilizing fluctuations in output will also act to stabilize fluctuations in the price level.

In contrast, implementation of the optimal employment-tax-credit rule in response to a contraction in demand directly increases aggregate supply. This increase tends to reinforce the deflationary pressure caused by the initial shock. While the employment-tax-credit policy also increases aggregate demand through the increase in the money supply that finances the program, the credit-induced increase in aggregate supply implies that output stabilization is achieved with a larger price variance than that implied by optimal monetary policy. As a result, when shocks to the system originate on the demand side, the optimal employment-tax-credit rule implies greater variability in the price level than does the optimal monetary-policy rule.

Next, assume that $\sigma_{\mu}^2 = 0$, which implies that only supply-side disturbances affect the system. Examination of the terms containing σ_{η}^2 in equations (20) and (21) reveals that for the case in which ϕ_1 exceeds unity, the optimal employment-tax-credit rule, equation (14), implies smaller variation in the price level than does the corresponding money-supply rule, equation (19). The essential idea is that contractions in aggregate supply cause an increase in the price level. Optimal monetary policy, which acts to stabilize output by stimulating aggregate demand, precipitates a further increase in the price level. Alternatively, in response to a contraction in supply, the optimal employment-credit rule, while also affecting aggregate demand, acts to directly increase aggregate supply. As a result, the price variability implied by the use of the credit is smaller than that implied by the use of monetary policy.

The efficacy of either monetary or employment-tax-credit policy depends on the assumption that the policy authorities can correctly identify the source and magnitude of recent aggregate disturbances. In reality, the policy authorities may not directly observe the disturbances, μ_{t-1} and η_{t-1}. They may, in the present context, observe the joint impact of these disturbances on output and the price level, and this information can be used to obtain an estimate of the actual disturbance currently affecting the system. A downturn in aggregate supply, for example, will cause a simultaneous increase in the price level and decrease in output. Consequently, if a simultaneous increase in P_t and decrease in Y_t is observed, the appropriate policy response is to increase the credit. Alternatively, a downturn in aggregate demand will cause a simultaneous decrease in both P_t and Y_t. If this combination is observed, then the appropriate policy response is an expansion of the money supply.[9]

[9]Fethke and Policano [5] consider a case in which the monetary authority observes the price level but cannot distinguish the individual disturbances affecting the aggregate system. This analysis shows that a discretionary policy can be implemented that dominates a passive policy even when information is limited.

5. THE NATURE OF THE LONG-TERM CONTRACT STRUCTURE

Although the above analysis assumes that the contract specification is exogenous, the results yield insight concerning the nature of the contract and the rationale for nominal wage rigidity. This section examines the variation in output that is attributed to not having current information, and the interaction between the determination of the length of the contract and the policy feedback rules.

A. The Importance of Current Information

One implication of the above analysis is that the implementation of optimal feedback rules yields an expected loss, equation (15), which is not equal to zero. The essential idea is that it is too costly for either private agents or the authority to collect information concerning the current innovations μ_t and η_t. If agents form contracts that attach contingencies to the current innovations, or, if the authority reacts to these innovations immediately, then the expected deviations from Y_t^* will be zero. Consequently, equation (15) can be interpreted as the variation in output that results from not collecting this information.

The magnitude of the minimum mean-squared error in output, equation (15), depends on the elasticity of aggregate supply, ϵ_1, the elasticity of aggregate demand, ϕ_1, and the variances of the demand and supply innovations, σ_μ^2 and σ_η^2, respectively. An increase in the absolute value of ϵ_1 will increase the minimum loss for all nonzero, finite values of ϕ_1 and ϕ_2. In particular, as aggregate supply becomes more elastic, a given decrease in aggregate demand leads to a larger decline in output and a smaller decrease in price than will occur if supply is less elastic. The effect on minimum output loss of changes in ϕ_1 depends on whether $\phi_1 > 1$, which we argue is the most likely case, and the source of the aggregate disturbance. When the economy experiences only supply disturbances, $\sigma_\mu^2 = 0$, and $\phi_1 > 1$, then an increase in the absolute value of ϕ_1 will increase the minimum loss. Specifically, as demand becomes more elastic, a given decrease in aggregate supply leads to a greater decline in output and a smaller increase in the price level than when demand is less elastic. If, however, the economy is subject to only demand disturbances, $\sigma_\eta^2 = 0$ and $\phi_1 > 1$, then an increase in ϕ_1 will decrease minimum loss. In this case, the more elastic is demand, the less will be the decline in output following a demand shock, and the more this shock will be absorbed by changes in the aggregate price level. These cases indicate that minimum loss in output is smaller if aggregate supply elasticity is low, aggregate demand elasticity is high, and the economy is primarily subjected to demand-side disturbances. Minimum loss is larger when supply elasticity is high, demand elasticity is high, and when disturbances originate on the supply side of the economy.

B. The Wage Contract Structure and the Optimal Feedback Rules

While we assume to this point that wage contracts overlap and are two periods in length, the contract length more generally depends on the feedback rules, equations (5a) or (5b). In this section, we develop the nature of this dependency under the assumption that the employment tax credit is in effect. For expositional ease, we assume V_t and Z_t are continuous time equivalents of random walks ($\rho_1 = \rho_2 = 1$) and that contracts are nonoverlapping.

We adopt a framework similar to that developed by Gray [10] in which we determine the contract length, τ^*, that minimizes the per-period expected loss, $\psi(\tau)$, associated with both the deviations in W_t from ${}_{t-1}W_t$ and a cost of adjustment, C:

$$\psi(\tau) = \frac{1}{\tau}\left[\int_0^\tau E({}_{t-h}W_t - {}_{t-1}W_t)^2 dh + C\right] . \tag{22}$$

From equation (3), the expectation of W_t based on information available at period $t-h$ is given by ${}_{t-h}W_t = {}_{t-h}P_t + {}_{t-h}Z_t + {}_{t-h}S_t$. Substituting ${}_{t-h}W_t$ for W_t in the aggregate supply expression, equation (1), and setting this expression equal to Y_t^D from equation (2′), we obtain the market clearing price

$$P_t = \left(\frac{\phi_2}{\phi_1 - \epsilon_1}\right) V_t - \left(\frac{\epsilon_2}{\phi_1 - \epsilon_1}\right) Z_t + \left(\frac{\phi_3 + \epsilon_1}{\phi_1 - \epsilon_1}\right) S_t - \left(\frac{\epsilon_1}{\phi_1 - \epsilon_1}\right) ({}_{t-h}P_t + {}_{t-h}Z_t + {}_{t-h}S_t).$$

The above equation yields expressions for ${}_{t-h}P_t$ and ${}_{t-1}P_t$ that are then used to determine the difference, ${}_{t-h}W_t - {}_{t-1}W_t$. The minimization problem can finally be represented as follows:

$$\min_{(\tau)} \psi(\tau) = \frac{1}{\tau}\left\{\int_0^\tau \left[\left(\frac{(\phi_1+\phi_3)a_1 + \phi_2}{\phi_1 - \epsilon_1}\right) h\sigma_\mu^2 + \left(\frac{(\phi_1+\phi_3)a_1^* - (1-\phi_1)}{\phi_1 - \epsilon_1}\right) h\sigma_\eta^2\right] dh + C\right\} . \tag{23}$$

The value of τ that minimizes $\psi(\tau)$ is given by

$$\tau^* = \left[\frac{2C}{\left(\frac{-\phi_2 - (\phi_1+\phi_3)a_1}{\phi_1 - \epsilon_1}\right)^2 \sigma_\mu^2 + \left(\frac{(1-\phi_1) - (\phi_1+\phi_3)a_1^*}{\phi_1 - \epsilon_1}\right)^2 \sigma_n^2}\right]^{\frac{1}{2}} . \tag{24}$$

If $a_1 = a_1^* = 0$, the optimal contract length depends directly on the adjustment cost and indirectly on the variances, σ_μ^2 and σ_η^2. Alternatively, when a_1 and a_1^* are set according to equations (13) and (14), the denominator of equation (24) is zero and the optimal contract length is infinite. In effect, if agents expect the authority to react, period-by-period, to offset unanticipated shocks in aggregate demand and supply, then it is optimal to fix the nominal wage for all future periods.[10] This result

[10]The existence of overlapping contracts does not alter this result. For example, when wage contracts are three periods long and overlap, with $\alpha_1 + \alpha_2 + \alpha_3 = 1$, the difference, ${}_{t-3}W_t - {}_{t-1}W_t$, is

is consistent with the underlying presumption in our analysis that agents preset wages and permit the authority to react to offset the adverse effects of disturbances for which no contingencies have been made.

LITERATURE CITED

1. Ashenfelter, Orley C., and John H. Pencavel. "Wage Changes and Frequency of Wage Settlements." *Economica,* 42 (May 1975), 162-70.
2. Azariadis, Costas C. "Naïve Contracts and Information Lags in the Monetary Mechanism." Unpublished manuscript, University of Pennsylvania, October 1978.
3. Bailey, Martin N., and James Tobin. "Macroeconomic Effects of Selective Public Employment and Wage Subsidies." *Brookings Papers on Economic Activity,* 2 (1977), 511-44.
4. Bishop, John H. "The General Equilibrium Impact of Alternative Antipoverty Strategies." *Industrial and Labor Relations Review,* 32 (January 1979), 205-23.
5. Fethke, Gary C., and Andrew J. Policano. "Co-operative Policy Responses by Public and Private Agents to Aggregate Disturbances." *Economica,* 48 (May 1981).
6. Fethke, Gary C., Andrew J. Policano, and Samuel H. Williamson. *An Investigation of the Conceptual and Quantitative Impact of Employment Tax Credits.* Kalamazoo, Mich.: W. E. Upjohn Institute for Employment Research, 1978.
7. ______. "Macroeconomic Implications of Employment Tax Credit Policy." *Southern Economic Journal,* 46 (October 1979), 513-27.
8. Fischer, Stanley. "Long-term Contracts, Rational Expectations, and the Optimal Money Supply Rule." *Journal of Political Economy,* 85 (February 1977), 191-205.
9. Gray, Joanna A. "Wage Indexation: A Macroeconomic Approach." *Journal of Monetary Economics,* 2 (April 1976), 221-35.
10. ______. "On Indexation and Contract Length." *Journal of Political Economy,* 86 (February 1978), 1-18.
11. Johnson, George E. "The Potential Efficacy of Labor Market Policy." Discussion Paper 105. Ann Arbor, Mich.: Institute of Public Policy Studies, University of Michigan, January 1977.
12. Kaldor, Nicholas L. "Wage Subsidies as a Remedy for Unemployment." *Journal of Political Economy,* 44 (December 1936), 721-42.
13. Kesselman, Jonathan R., Samuel H. Williamson, and Ernst R. Berndt. "Tax Credits for Employment Rather than Investment." *American Economic Review,* 67 (June 1977), 339-49.
14. Kopits, George F. "Wage Subsidies and Employment: An Analysis of the French

---

$$
{}_{t-3}W_t - {}_{t-1}W_t = -\left(\frac{\alpha_2(1-\epsilon_1\alpha_3)}{\phi_1 - (1-\alpha)\epsilon_1}\right)[(\phi_1+\phi_3)a_1+\phi_2\rho_1]u_{t-1}+[(\phi_1+\phi_3)a_1^*-(1-\phi_1)\rho_2]\eta_{t-1}
$$

$$
-\left(\frac{\alpha_3}{\phi_1 - (1-\alpha)\epsilon_1}\right)\{[(\phi_1+\phi_3)a_1+\phi_2\rho_1](\rho_1\mu_{t-2}+\mu_{t-1})
$$

$$
+[(\phi_1+\phi_3)a_1^*-(1-\phi_1)\rho_2](\rho_2\eta_{t-2}+\eta_{t-1})\}.
$$

Clearly, use of the rules, equations (13) and (14), will completely offset the effects of demand and supply shocks. This result extends to overlapping wage contracts of any length, and the optimal contract length is infinite.

Experience.'' *Staff Papers, International Monetary Fund,* 25 (September 1978), 494-527.

15. McCallum, Bennett T. ''Price-Level Stickiness and the Feasibility of Monetary Stabilization Policy with Rational Expectations.'' *Journal of Political Economy,* 85 (June 1977), 627-34.
16. Phelps, Edmund S. ''Commodity-Supply Shock and Full Employment Monetary Policy.'' *Journal of Money, Credit, and Banking,* 10 (May 1978), 206-21.
17. Riddel, William C. ''The Empirical Foundations of the Phillips Curve: Evidence from Canadian Wage Contract Data.'' *Econometrica,* 47 (January 1979), 1-24.
18. Sachs, Jeffrey D. ''Wages, Profits, and Macroeconomic Adjustment: A Comparative Study.'' *Brookings Papers on Economic Activity,* 2 (1979), 269-319.
19. Smith, Philip M., and David A. Wilton. ''Wage Changes: The Frequency of Wage Settlements, the Variability of Contract Length and 'Locked-In' Wage Adjustments.'' *Economica,* 45 (August 1978), 305-10.
20. Taylor, John B. ''Aggregate Dynamics and Staggered Contracts.'' *Journal of Political Economy,* 88 (February 1980), 1-23.
21. Wachter, Michael L., and Oliver E. Williamson. ''Obligational Markets and the Mechanics of Inflation.'' *The Bell Journal of Economics,* 9 (Autumn 1978), 549-71.

JOHN BRYANT*

Bank Collapse and Depression

THE RECURRENT BANKING PANICS of the nineteenth century and the Great Depression of the 1930s are widely viewed as failures of our economic system. Moreover, such events are far from unique to U.S. monetary history (see, e.g., [11, pp. 402–11]). However, a fully satisfactory explanation for these events has not been provided (see e.g., [12]).

Although no fully satisfactory explanation for banking panics and depression has emerged, existing theory gives guidance in searching for one. One natural place to look for an explanation for failure of our economic system is known failures in the economic model of Walrasian equilibrium. Paul Samuelson introduced a failure to Walrasian equilibrium in his pure consumption-loans model [15]. He showed that with overlapping generations of finite-lived individuals in a model with no last period, the Walrasian equilibrium need not be Pareto optimal. Moreover, he introduced the concept of a negative net worth entity, the "social contrivance" of fiat (unbacked) money, the use of which makes everyone better off and yields Pareto optimality. We might, then, model recurrent banking panics and depression as recurrent and once-and-for-all collapse of a fiat money system, respectively. In section 4 it is demonstrated that such collapse of a fiat money system can generate reduced production and employment.

*This paper was presented to the Federal Reserve System Committee on Financial Analysis, Minneapolis, June 1980. I wish to thank discussant Neil Berkman, committee members, and anonymous referees of this journal for valuable comments. In addition, I wish to thank David Cass for introducing me to this class of models, Robert Lucas and Thomas Sargent for comments on an earlier version, and most especially my colleague Neil Wallace for a stimulating and productive association over the past three years. Errors are my responsibility alone. Views expressed do not necessarily represent those of the Federal Reserve System.

JOHN BRYANT *is senior economist, Research Department, Federal Reserve Bank of Minneapolis, and associate professor of economics, Rice University.*

0022-2879/81/1181-0454$00.50/0

There are, however, several problems with modeling banking panics and depression as collapses of a fiat money system. First, one must determine what events precipitate a collapse of a fiat money system and why. The collapse of a negative net worth entity causes a net loss, and therefore is something economic agents seek to avoid. Second, the fiat money model of section 4 has the property that with reinstitution of a fiat money system, the economy revives instantly and completely. The introduction of a negative net worth entity generates excess profits and is entered into at once. However, during the Great Depression deposit insurance and additional bank regulations were introduced, actions that might have reinstituted banks' role as providers of fiat money. Unfortunately, the economy remained depressed. Last, very generally, fiat money is a solution to the capital overaccumulation problem of the competitive economy (see [16] and sec. 4). In models more elaborate than Samuelson's, fiat money has value because its existence keeps the economy from accumulating too much capital. This suggests that the collapse of a fiat money system causes a period of overaccumulation of capital. It seems wrong to treat the banking panics and Great Depression as periods of high demand for investment.

The above remarks suggest that one look for a model with the "social contrivance" of a positive net worth entity that solves a capital underaccumulation problem. Cass and Yaari [10, p. 363], in an elaboration of Samuelson's model, briefly introduce just such a positive net worth entity.[1] The possibility of such an entity arises in a model of overlapping generations of finite-lived individuals with no *first* period. This entity has just the symmetric properties one would expect. Because it is a positive net worth entity, economic agents gain from its collapse, they lose from initiating it, and if constrained to reinstitute it following a collapse, they do so to the smallest extent possible. Lastly, collapse of the net worth entity causes a drop in the demand for investment.

All the above facts stem from a basic observation on the positive net worth entity. In Samuelson's model, given that otherwise there will be no fiat money in the future, it is Pareto improving to introduce fiat money and maintain it for all time. Symmetrically, in a model with the positive net worth entity, it is Pareto superior that there *will have always been* this entity than that it will have never existed.

Now we turn to a simple model on the positive net worth "social contrivance." Naturally, to get simplicity one must trade off realism. Therefore we then turn to elaborations of the model that, hopefully, clarify its implications for the real world.

1. THE MODEL

The simple model is one without production, employment, or investment of any kind. It is a pure exchange model. Time is discrete and without beginning or end. $N > 0$ individuals are born each period, and they live two periods. An individual born

[1]Phelps and Pollak [13] demonstrate the possibility of capital underaccumulation when individuals are "imperfectly altruistic." In Samuelson's model, individuals are totally unaltruistic, and it is more parsimonious to stay in the tradition of independent utility functions. For further discussion of Samuelson's model, see [2, 6, 9, 18].

in period t is of the tth generatioı.. There is a single transferable but nonstorable consumption good. Each individual is endowed with $L > O$ units of this consumption good in her second period of life, but is endowed with nothing in her first period of life. Let C_1 and C_2 be an individual's consumption of the consumption good in her two periods of life. Every individual has the same utility function $U(C_1, C_2) = \sqrt{C_1} + \sqrt{C_2}$.

As the model stands, there is no possibility of exchange. Everyone simply consumes L in her second period of life and gets $\sqrt{L}$ as utility. Notice, however, that if *every* old person hands over half her endowment to a young person, then everyone consumes $L/2$ in each period of life and gets $2\sqrt{L/2} = \sqrt{2}\,\sqrt{L} > \sqrt{L}$ as utility. Because there is no first old person, no one is hurt in this scheme. But suppose that individuals of generation t suddenly decide to hand over no goods. Previous generations still get $C_1 = L/2$, $C_2 = L/2$. However, generation t gets $C_1 = L/2$, $C_2 = L$. Generation $t+1$ gets $C_1 = 0$, $C_2 = L$. Clearly, generation $t+1$ will not start the string of gifts again, because all it can do thereby is lose second-period consumption.[2] So all future generations get $C_1 = 0$, $C_2 = L$. These observations explain the existence and properties of the positive net worth "social contrivance."

The "social contrivance" of a positive net worth entity allows the economy to converge to the $C_1 = L/2$, $C_2 = L/2$ allocation. Let us suggestively call this entity the "banking system." The banking system behaves as follows. Each period it takes delivery from the old on promises for goods issued when they were young. Then the banks sell these gooɑ. to the current young competitively for promises to deliver goods in the following period. The net worth of the banking system is the value of the promises of future delivery that it holds.

Let P_t be the units of goods that a young person of generation t gets for the promise of one unit of goods next period. Each individual is a price taker and takes P_t as given. Let b_t be the units of goods promised by a typical individual of generation t. Let us generalize our model just a bit, and assume that every individual of generation t is endowed with $L_t > 0$ when old. Then the problem of the young individual of generation t is

$$\max_{b_t} \sqrt{P_t b_t} + \sqrt{L_t - b_t}.$$

This is solved uniquely by b_t satisfying

$$P_t/b_t = 1/(L - b_t). \tag{1}$$

While the individual views herself as choosing b_t given P_t, the actual amount of goods purchased, $NP_t b_t$, is determined by the promises to deliver issued by genera-

[2]Notice, however, that $\partial U[0,L]/\partial C_2 = 1/2\sqrt{L} < \partial U[0,L]/\partial C_1 = \infty$. If generation $t+1$ cares at all about generation $t+2$ (except lexicographically), they have motive for a *social* decision to restart the string of gifts. In Phelps and Pollak [13] terms, if individuals are imperfectly altruistic in any degree, they desire restarting (see [7]).

tion $t-1$. Therefore, in equilibrium, the price P_t is determined by $NP_t b_t = Nb_{t-1}$. Plugging this equilibrium condition into (1) and rearranging yields

$$b_t / b_{t-1} = (L_t - b_t)/b_t. \tag{2}$$

Expression (2) is very suggestive. It has the following immediate implications for $b_{t-1} > 0$:

$$b_t > b_{t-1} \text{ iff } b_t < \tfrac{1}{2} L_t \tag{3}$$

$$b_t < b_{t-1} \text{ iff } b_t > \tfrac{1}{2} L_t \tag{4}$$

$$b_t = b_{t-1} \text{ iff } b_t = \tfrac{1}{2} L_t. \tag{5}$$

Suppose as assumed earlier that $L_t = L$ for all t. Then (2)–(5) imply that a nonzero sequence $\{b_t\}$ is either monotonically increasing with limit $L/2$, monotonically decreasing with limit $L/2$, or constant at $L/2$.

Expression (2) is a quadratic in b_t that has positive root

$$b_t = \tfrac{1}{2}[\sqrt{(b_{t-1})^2 + 4L_t b_{t-1}} - b_{t-1}]. \tag{6}$$

Notice from (6) that $b_{t-1} = 0$ implies $b_t = 0$; that if $b_{t-1} > 0$, b_t is increasing in L_t; and b_t is increasing in b_{t-1}. Moreover, if the sequence $\{L_t\}$ is increasing without bound, then a nonzero sequence $\{b_t\}$ is also increasing without bound.

We have assumed that each generation honors its promises to deliver goods. But suppose generation t fails to do so. It, of course, is better off. Generation $t+1$ is worse off, but it cannot be said that generation t broke a promise to generation $t+1$, because generation $t+1$ was not alive when any promises were issued. Perhaps it can be said that generation t has broken its promise to generation $t-1$. But generation $t-1$ does not care whether the promise is broken. No individual in her individual capacity has a claim against individuals of generation t. The banking system is, indeed, a social contrivance.

We have named our positive net worth entity "banking system." To maintain the net worth, the banking system must be regulated.[3] If the regulation is perfect, we get our solution. Instead, let us suppose that the regulation is imperfect. Specifically, let us assume that at the cost of K units of second-period consumption an individual can avoid meeting $\alpha \cdot 100$, $1 \geq \alpha > 0$, percent of her promised delivery. An individual of generation t exercises this option if the benefit of avoidance exceeds the cost as indicated in equation (7).

[3]If banks are privately owned, bankers have the same motivation to extract the net worth as do the other members of their generation. The bank owner may, for example, extract the net worth by making a "bad" loan to herself. In the model extraction of the net worth of the bank does not hurt the bank owner, but the individuals who would have subsequently used the bank's services. Note that the owner of any asset tries to extract its net worth, possibly by selling it. In the model it is in the social interest to keep the banker (or anyone else) from extracting the bank's net worth.

$$\alpha b_t - K > 0. \tag{7}$$

When the individual exercises her option to avoid delivery, she extracts a portion of the net worth of the banking system. We call this event a ''banking panic,'' as all individuals do so at the same time.

Now let us examine the behavior of our model with imperfect regulation. First, assume, once again, that $L_t = L$ for all t. Then $\{b_t\}$ approaches $L/2$ monotonically. Let us assume $\{b_t\}$ approaches $L/2$ from below. Then for any $K < L/2$ and any $\alpha > 2K/L$ there will come a time when this condition (7) is met.[4] If the fixed cost of avoidance is not high enough, and the percentage of indebtedness avoidable is too high, a banking panic inevitably results. Indeed, with $\alpha < 1$, this occurs repeatedly. With each banking panic b is reduced below $(1-\alpha)\ L/2$, but then climbs smoothly back towards $L/2$. If $\alpha = 1$, there is one terminating banking panic, and b remains at zero thereafter. Second, assume that $\{L_t\}$ is increasing without bound. Then $\{b_t\}$ also is increasing without bound. Therefore, for *any* $\alpha > 0$, $K > 0$, there will come a time when the individual exercises the partial delivery option.

2. INTERPRETATION OF THE MODEL

As long as one accepts the interpretation of the positive net worth entity as the banking system and the mass choice of the partial delivery option as panic, then we have a model of recurrent and a once-and-for-all banking panic. An explanation of decreased investment demand was also promised. Naturally, one would want an explanation for reduced production and employment as well. As the model has no production, no labor, and no capital, it clearly requires some elaboration to generate such explanations.

First, let us consider the banking panic. It is, of course, not at all a stretch of the imagination that banks play a role in facilitating borrowing and lending. Nor is it a stretch of the imagination that they are regulated positive net worth entities. However, the imperfection of regulation may seem unlikely in this simple model. Nor can it be claimed that a coherent model of the process of regulation is presented here or elsewhere. Indeed the imposition of ad hoc imperfection can only indicate possibilities. The ultimate goal is a coherent model of regulation in which the regulation is generated endogenously.[5] However, intuitively it does seem very possible that in reality actual regulation is not perfect. In the first place, the regulation of financial insitutions may not have been purposefully designed to protect net worth. Moreover, the world is much more complex than our model, making appropriate regulation less obvious. Also, according to the model, all market participants, both regulated banker (lender) and borrowers, have motive to circumvent the regulation, to

[4] $\alpha b_t - K = (2K/L)b_t - K + (\alpha - 2K/L)b_t \rightarrow (\alpha - 2K/L)L/2 > 0$ as $t \rightarrow \infty$.
[5] Bryant [5] takes a small step in this direction.

make the regulator's job difficult. They may, for example, overstate the value of a bank's portfolio of loans by understating the associated risk. The role of regulation is not well understood, and perfect regulation is not both feasible and costless.

In our banking panic a whole generation is made better off by circumventing regulation. This does not seem an accurate characterization of the Great Depression, for example. The essence of what the model is capturing is that for each transaction taken separately, all the participants have motive to circumvent the regulation. More generally, most or all individuals may be better off if regulation cannot be circumvented, but individuals in each of their transactions have motive to circumvent the regulation. All individuals want a viable banking system, but each banker must be competitive in offering deals, and each bank customer tries to get the best deals she can. In the Appendix we briefly sketch a model of spatial separation having such properties (see [17] for a discussion of models of spatial separation).

Usually one associates banking panics with runs on deposits rather than with the massive loan defaults of the model. Section 3 presents a version of the model in which an anticipation of massive loan defaults generates a run on deposits. Moreover, it is demonstrated that bank liabilities taking the form of deposits (rather than shares in the bank's portfolio) renders the model unstable. Section 4 also includes a model with banking panics that do not involve loan defaults.

Now we turn to production, employment, and investment. The model is easily modified to have endowments of labor and production technology. Moreover, input of labor today producing goods tomorrow can be interpreted as the result of a technology involving capital. Very generally, capital is a means of using today's labor to produce goods more efficiently tomorrow. That is what the $(0, L)$ endowment pattern is capturing, the trade-off of labor today for goods tomorrow available to those who enter the economy. In such a production model, the banking panic can produce reduced production, reduced employment, and reduced demand for capital, as is illustrated in section 4. Moreover, an increasing $\{L_t\}$ sequence can be interpreted as an advancing economy, an economy using higher and higher technology. Very generally, an advancing economy is one that produces a more and more favorable rate of exchange of labor today for goods tomorrow.

Now we turn to the elaborations of the simple model.

3. BORROWING, LENDING, AND DEPOSITS

In period t, $N_t > 0$ two-period-lived identical individuals (borrowers) are born, each endowed with L units of the consumption good in her second period of life, but endowed with nothing in her first period of life. At the same time $n > 0$ two-period-lived identical individuals (lenders) are born, each endowed with L units of the consumption good in her first period of life, but endowed with nothing in her second period of life. The positive net worth entity, the banking system, of section 1 exists. Every individual has the same utility function $U(C_1,C_2) = \sqrt{C_1} + \sqrt{C_2}$.

The N_t borrowers solve the same problem as the individuals in section 1. Let l_t be the units of goods promised to a typical lender of generation t. Then the problem of the young lender of generation t is

$$\max_{l_t} \sqrt{L-P_t l_t} + \sqrt{l_t}.$$

This is uniquely solved by $l_t = L/[P_t(1+P_t)]$. Let us define $Z_t = N_t b_t - nl_t$. Z_t is the aggregate net worth of the banking system. The equilibruim condition is $P_t Z_t = Z_{t-1}$. Plugging in the expressions for optimal b_t and l_t and rearranging yields

$$Z_t/Z_{t-1} = [N_t L - Z_t]/[Z_t + LnZ_t/Z_{t-1}], \tag{2'}$$

which should be compared with expression (2) of section 1. Using the same analysis as in section 1 we conclude that $Z_t \gtreqless Z_{t-1}$ implies $Z_t \lesseqgtr (N_t - n)L/2$. Moreover, if $N_t = N > n$ for all t, then $\{Z_t\} > 0$ is converging monotonically to $(N-n)L/2$. In the limit the lenders just ''net out,'' and we are reduced to our original problem. Lastly, (2′) is a quadratic in Z_t, which always has a positive root for $Z_{t-1} > 0$.

Suppose, however, that lenders are only allowed to make deposits, that they face a gross rate of return of one by external constraint.[6] Moreover, the banking system is constrained to issue all deposits demanded. Then $l_t = L/2$. Borrowers still face a gross rate of return of $1/P_t$. Let $Y_t = Z_t + nL/2 = N_t b_t$. The equilibrium condition now is $P_t Y_t = Y_{t-1}$. Substituting in the expression for optimal b_t and $l_t = L/2$ and rearranging yields

$$Y_t/Y_{t-1} = [N_t L - Y_t]/Y_t, \tag{2''}$$

which is equation (2) of section 1 with Y_t replacing b_t and $N_t L$ replacing L_t. For $N_t = N > n$ the system converges to $Y_t = NL/2$ or $Z_t = [N-n]L/2$ as above (the path is different, of course).

However, while (2″) is a quadratic in Y_t which always has a positive root for $Y_{t-1} > 0$, this root need not imply that $Z_t = Y_t - nL/2 \geqslant 0$!

Let $Y_{t-1} = \bar{N}L/2$. Then for $N_t < (1/2)\,[1+n/\bar{N}]n$, $Z_t < 0$. As Z_t is the net worth of the banking system, $Z_t \geqslant 0$ is required for solvency. If $Z_t < 0 < Z_{t-1}$ then $P_t > 1$, the rate of interest is negative, and the banking system cannot pay off on all its deposits, except by generating the negative net worth entity fiat money. If solvency is required, fiat money generation impossible, then nonprice allocation must replace price allocation, which seems a reasonable description of a run on deposits. The restriction that bank liabilities be deposits has rendered the system unstable; a low realization of N_t causes a bank run.

[6] Bryant [5] presents a model generating deposits endogenously.

4. PRODUCTION, EMPLOYMENT, AND INVESTMENT

$N > 0$ identical individuals are born each period, and they live two periods. In her first period an individual is endowed with L units of nontransferable leisure, while in the second she is endowed with nothing. There is a technology available to the individual to transform leisure hours into a capital good (K) 1 − 1 this period. This "one horse shay" capital good is exhausted in the subsequent period to produce, by itself, $(1+r)$, $r > 0$, units of transferable but nonstorable consumption good. The consumption good cannot be used to produce the capital good.[7] In the first period of life the consumption good and leisure are perfect substitutes in the utility function of the individual where one hour of leisure equals one unit of consumption good.[8] The banking system of section 1 exists. Let C_1 and C_2 be an individual's consumption of the consumption good and leisure in her two periods of life. Every individual has the same utility function $U(C_1,C_2) = \sqrt{C_1} + \sqrt{C_2}$.

The problem of the young individual of generation t is

$$\max_{K_t,b_t} \sqrt{L-K_t+P_tb_t} + \sqrt{(1+r)K_t-b_t}$$

subject to $K_t \leq$ L.

If the constraint is not binding, it is clear that in equilibrium $(P_tb_t=b_{t-1})$ $P_t = 1/[1+r]$, and b_t grows at the rate r. The unconstrained maximum is solved by $K_t = [1+r]\ L/[2+r] + b_{t-1}$ (after substitution for the equilibrium condition). This satisfies the constraint for $b_{t-1} \leq L/[2+r]$. In other words, for $b_{t-1} < L/[2+r]$ there is reduced production, reduced employment, and reduced demand for capital.

If the constraint is binding, $K_t = L$, the individual's problem becomes

$$\max_{b_t} \sqrt{P_tb_t} + \sqrt{(1+r)L-b_t},$$

which is identically the problem in section 1 with $(1+r)L$ replacing L_t.

Now let us briefly consider fiat money and a version of the capital overaccumulation problem.[9] In the simple model without production or investment of section 1, the possibility of valued fiat money arises when individuals are endowed with the consumption good in their first period of life rather than in their second. Similarly,

[7]The role of this assumption is to limit the size of the economy.

[8]Alternatively, the individual can produce the consumption good from leisure 1 − 1 "at home," out of the economy, and leisure does not enter the utility function. This is a simple form of the nonconvexity of labor choice found in the "new-new" labor economics (see [1, 3]). In this model there is "underemployment" rather than "unemployment." This I view as a technicality successfully addressed in the "new-new" labor economics.

[9]In the capital overaccumulation problem of growth theory, in all but the optimal nonmonetary equilibrium there is unexploited profit opportunity in the issuance of fiat money [16]. In this model the unique nonmonetary equilibrium has unexploited profit opportunity in the issuance of fiat money, and there is an optimal valued fiat money equilibrium.

in the model of production, employment, and investment of this section, the possibility of valued fiat money arises when the individual has better current period production possibilities than next period production possibilities. Specifically, let us assume that $-1 < r < 0$. This implies $\{b_t\}$ is a sequence approaching zero. At $b_{t-1} = 0$, $K_t = [1+r]L/[2+r]$. This we refer to as the nonmonetary equilibrium. Next, let us assume that individuals can transform leisure into the consumption good 1−1 in their first period of life. Lastly, we assume that the "social contrivance" of fiat money exists. Individuals can transform leisure into the consumption good, and then exchange the consumption good for fiat money with the previous generation, and so on.

The value of fiat money to the individual depends upon her assumption of the value of fiat money to the next generation. For simplicity we consider only stationary equilibria, ones in which the value of money is the same for all generations, the noninflationary equilibria. There are two such equilibria, one in which the value of fiat money is zero, the nonmonetary equilibrium, and one in which it is positive, the monetary equilibrium. In the monetary equilibrium as $r < 0$, $K = 0$, and valued fiat money has solved the problem of the accumulation of relatively unproductive capital (in this model, any capital is too much). Let m_t be the individual's real balances. Then the problem of the young individual of generation t is

$$\max_{m_t} \sqrt{L-m_t} + \sqrt{m_t},$$

which is solved by $m_t = L/2 > [1+r]L/[2+r]$. In the monetary equilibrium employment is higher than in the nonmonetary equilibrium. Notice also that the money equilibrium is devoid of dynamics, it does not depend upon initial conditions. We take a banking panic to be a surprise shift from the monetary to the nonmonetary equilibrium. A banking panic causes reduced production and employment, but increased demand for capital.[10]

The question remains of why a banking panic would occur in the fiat money model, why there is a "jump" between equilibria. In [4] it is argued that only the nonmonetary equilibrium obtains unless a positive minimum value of fiat money is guaranteed, presumably by an authority to tax future generations.[11] A banking panic then occurs when paper that was thought to be guaranteed is discovered not to be guaranteed. With this interpretation the Great Depression occurred when individuals discovered that the Federal Reserve System did not guarantee deposits. The question remains of why the U.S. economy did not immediately recover with the creation of the FDIC. It is possible that the relatively undeveloped ($r<0$) economies of the nineteenth century were subject to this kind of panic, while the advanced ($r>0$) economies of the twentieth century were subject to that of section 1.

[10]Perhaps gold is the relatively unproductive capital.

[11]Notice that such a guarantee "knocks out" not only the nonmonetary equilibrium, but nonstationary monetary equilibria as well.

APPENDIX

Spatial Separation

Each day N infinitely-lived individuals start on an unending "trail." All along the trail are sites. Each site has two sections, a and b. Each section has room for N individuals. They are allocated on a first come, first served basis. Each individual must spend two periods at a site and then move to the next site. On period t, $L_t > 0$ consumption goods are provided free to each individual at every section b. Nothing is provided to section a. The consumption goods cannot be transported between sites, but can be transported between sections of a site. There is a regulated "bank." Each individual at a section (a) bids for the handouts from section (b) with promises of handouts next period. The bank enforces promises. However, at the cost of destroying k goods, an individual can avoid her obligation.

Consider an individual of generation t. Let her consumption of the consumption good at section a and b, respectively, in site j be C_j^a, C_j^b. Then, for any i, j with $i > j$, and for any compact constraint see $T \subset R_+^4$, she chooses C_j^a, C_j^b, C_i^a, C_i^b in T to maximize the function

$$U_t\,(C_j^a, C_j^b, C_i^a, C_i^b; i, j) = \sqrt{C_j^a} + \sqrt{C_j^b} + \sqrt{C_i^a} + \sqrt{C_i^b}.$$

Banking panics make all individuals worse off.

LITERATURE CITED

1. Azariadis, Costas C. "Implicit Contracts and Underemployment Equilibria." *Journal of Political Economy,* 83 (December 1975), 1183–1202.
2. Balasko, Yves, and Karl Shell. "The Overlapping-Generations Model, I: The Case of Pure Exchange Without Money." Caress Working Paper No. 79-21, 1980.
3. Bryant, John. "An Annotation of Implicit Contracts and Underemployment Equilibria." *Journal of Political Economy,* 86 (December 1978), 1159–60.
4. ______. "Games and Economics: A General Solution and Particular Applications." Minneapolis, Minn.: Federal Reserve Bank of Minneapolis, Staff Report No. 57, 1980.
5. ______. "A Model of Reserves, Bank Runs, and Deposit Insurance." *Journal of Banking and Finance,* 4 (1980), 335–44.
6. ______. "Transaction Demand for Money and Moral Hazard." In *Models of Monetary Economies: Proceedings and Contributions from Participants of a December 1978 Conference Sponsored by the Federal Reserve Bank of Minneapolis,* edited by John H. Kareken and Neil Wallace, pp. 233–41. Minneapolis, Minn.: Federal Reserve Bank of Minneapolis, 1980.
7. ______. "The Competitive Provision of Fiat Money." *Journal of Banking and Finance,* in press.
8. Bryant, John, and Neil Wallace. "Open-Market Operations in a Model of Regulated, Insured Intermediaries." *Journal of Political Economy,* 88 (February 1980), 146–73.
9. Cass, David, and Karl Shell. "In Defense of a Basic Approach." In *Models of Monetary*

Economies: Proceedings and Contributions from Participants of a December 1978 Conference Sponsored by the Federal Reserve Bank of Minneapolis, edited by John H. Kareken and Neil Wallace, pp. 251-60. Minneapolis, Minn.: Federal Reserve Bank of Minneapolis, 1980.

10. Cass, David, and Menahem E. Yaari. "A Re-Examination of the Pure Consumption Loans Model." *Journal of Political Economy,* 74 (August 1966), 353-67.

11. Del Mar, Alexander. *A History of the Monetary Systems of France, and Other European States.* New York: Cambridge Encyclopedia, 1903.

12. Lucas, Robert E., Jr., and Leonard A. Rapping. "Unemployment in the Great Depression: Is There a Full Explanation?" *Journal of Political Economy,* 80 (January/February 1972), 186-91.

13. Phelps, Edmund S., and Robert A. Pollak. "On Second-Best National Saving and Game-Equilibrium Growth." *The Review of Economic Studies,* 35 (April 1968), 185-99.

14. Salop, Steven. "An Equilibrium Model of Private Credit Chainletters." Federal Reserve Board, Working Paper, 1979.

15. Samuelson, Paul A. "An Exact Consumption-Loan Model of Interest With or Without the Social Contrivance of Money." *Journal of Political Economy,* 66 (December 1958), 467-82.

16. Thompson, Earl A. "Debt Instruments in Both Macroeconomic Theory and Capital Theory." *American Economic Review,* 57 (December 1967), 1196-1210.

17. Townsend, Robert M. "Models of Money with Spatially Separated Agents." In *Models of Monetary Economies: Proceedings and Contributions from Participants of a December 1978 Conference Sponsored by the Federal Reserve Bank of Minneapolis,* edited by John H. Kareken and Neil Wallace, pp. 265-303. Minneapolis, Minn.: Federal Reserve Bank of Minneapolis, 1980.

18. Wallace, Neil. "The Overlapping Generations Model of Fiat Money." In *Models of Monetary Economies: Proceedings and Contributions from Participants of a December 1978 Conference Sponsored by the Federal Reserve Bank of Minneapolis,* edited by John H. Kareken and Neil Wallace, pp. 49-82. Minneapolis, Minn.: Federal Reserve Bank of Minneapolis, 1980.

JAMES A. VERBRUGGE
JOHN S. JAHERA, JR.*

Expense-Preference Behavior in the Savings and Loan Industry

1. INTRODUCTION

NEOCLASSICAL MICROECONOMIC THEORY traditionally has assumed that the decision process in the firm is guided by the objective of profit maximization. A number of economists have suggested, however, that managers may pursue goals which maximize personal utility rather than firm profitability [1, 10, 11, 23, 24]. Conditions under which managerial discretion may be substituted for profit maximization include weak competition in the product or service market, a high degree of regulation, and the separation of ownership and control. Under these conditions, managers have greater opportunity to indulge in discretionary expenditures and the pursuit of managerial emoluments. That is, managers may seek to achieve a higher level of personal utility via higher salaries, additional staff, and other perquisites for which they have positive preferences. In general, this results in an expansion of expenditures beyond the profit-maximizing level and a suboptimal (X-inefficient) use of resources within the firm.

The expense-preference theory of the firm recently received considerable support by the work of Edwards [3] in which he developed a test to distinguish between expense-preference and profit maximizing behavior. Upon application of this test to the banking industry, Edwards found that the number of employees and bank expenditures on wages and salaries are higher in noncompetitive banking markets;

*An earlier version of this paper was presented at the annual meeting of the Financial Management Association, October 1979, Boston.

JAMES A. VERBRUGGE *is professor of finance, University of Georgia.* JOHN S. JAHERA, JR., *is assistant professor of finance, Auburn University.*

0022-2879/81/1181-0465$00.50/0
JOURNAL OF MONEY, CREDIT, AND BANKING, vol. 13, no. 4 (November 1981)

that is, results consistent with expense-preference behavior. Extensions of this test by Hannan [5] and Hannan and Mavinga [6] provide additional support for the expense-preference theory.

This paper tests for expense-preference behavior in savings-and-loan associations (SLAs). The savings and loan industry is characterized by several conditions conducive to expense-preference behavior. First, SLAs are highly regulated, similar to commercial banks, with regulated interest rates, strictly controlled entry and exit, barriers to merging and branching, and imperfections in both the savings and the lending market. Second, the industry is characterized by the presence of both stock and mutual forms of organization. Because mutual institutions do not have "owners" in the traditional meaning of the term, managers of such organizations do not face ownership pressure similar to that experienced by managers of stock associations. The absence of such pressure may enable mutual managers to engage in various forms of expense-preference behavior. Furthermore, since mutual managers cannot benefit from the privileges of stock ownership, they may tend to indulge in operating expenditures for which they have positive preferences.[1] Taggart [21] provided evidence of such behavior in mutual savings banks in a study showing that the imposition of deposit-rate ceilings on mutual savings banks generated a windfall gain which was dissipated through increased operating expenses over the years immediately following the establishment of the ceilings. In general, these tendencies toward managerial discretionary behavior may result in higher overall operating expenses, higher personnel expenditures, lower reported profitability, and less risky portfolios for mutual than for stock organizations [2, 7, 8, 15, 22]. Since many stock and mutual associations operate in the same geographic market, it represents a unique opportunity to test for the expense-preference tendencies under identical external market situations.

In this paper, we concentrate on the hypothesis that mutual SLAs exhibit tendencies toward higher personnel expenditures than stock associations, and also that associations in more concentrated markets engage in expense-preference behavior as compared to associations in more competitive markets. We also address the issue regarding mutual versus stock behavior in concentrated markets and mutual versus stock behavior in more competitive markets. The model used is derived from Edwards [3].

2. METHODOLOGICAL FRAMEWORK

A. Models of Expense-Preference Behavior

Expense-preference theory has generally been approached in two ways. First, under the severable-decision model, it is assumed that managers make separate

[1]A number of empirical studies on the effects of separation of ownership and control have been conducted. Findings from these studies range from no significant differences in corporate performance to significantly higher levels of profit performance in owner controlled firms. Recent studies in this area include Kamerschen [9], McEachern [12, 13], McKean and Kania [14], Palmer [16], and Sorenson [20]. The issue has also been addressed recently for the banking industry by Glassman and Rhoades [4].

decisions regarding the maximization of firm profits and the maximization of managerial utility. That is, managers initially make all decisions in accordance with the profit-maximization principle, and then allocate the earnings into reported profits and the utility-maximizing expenses such as higher salaries, larger staffs, and other perquisites. Alternatively, in the joint-decision approach, managers are assumed to treat the profit and utility decisions as a single utility-maximizing decision. That is, managers are assumed to expand output beyond the profit-maximizing level, and to use a higher ratio of labor input than expected in a profit-maximizing situation. In contrast, under the severable model, output, prices, and nonlabor inputs are assumed to be at the profit-maximizing levels. In both approaches, however, labor expenditures are expected to be greater than they would be if expense-preference tendencies did not exist [3].

B. Test Equations

Since expense-preference behavior should be reflected in higher labor expenditures, a test for expense-preference can be based upon the firm's demand for labor. Following Edwards [3], the demand for labor model is[2]

$$\ln L = \beta_0 + \beta_1 \ln W + \beta_2 \ln k + \beta_3 \ln X + \beta_4 C, \tag{1}$$

where L is the number of employees, W is the wage rate, k is the cost of capital, X represents various nonprice factors influencing the demand for labor, and C is a market concentration measure. In the Edwards paper, the test of expense-preference is the coefficient of the market concentration variable. A positive coefficient implies expense preference behavior since it suggests that firms with monopoly power do have higher personnel expenditures than firms in more competitive markets.

Because expense-preference tendencies are hypothesized to originate from the absence of competitive pressure in the product or service market and from the lack of ownership influence in the mutual form of organization, it is important that the market structure and form of organization effects be isolated. To test for the influence of both market concentration and form of organization on personnel expenditures, equation (1) is modified as follows:

$$\ln TW = \beta_0 + \beta_1 \ln W + \beta_2 \ln Y + \beta_3 \ln LD + \beta_4 \ln D + \beta_5 \ln OFF + \beta_6 \ln SZ + \beta_7 C + \beta_8 MS, \tag{2}$$

where TW is the total wages and salaries paid by each association in the sample.[3]

In this test equation, the variables of particular interest are the market concentration measure (C) and the stock-mutual dummy variable (MS) which represents the form of organization and is assigned the value of one for a mutual association and zero for a stock association. A positive coefficient for the MS variable will imply

[2]The variables are expressed as natural logarithms (ln).

[3]Since data on the total number of labor units employed by each association are not available, the total expenditure on wages and salaries (total personnel expense) is used as the dependent variable.

expense-preference behavior since it suggests that mutual associations have higher personnel expenditures than stock associations. Similarly, a positive coefficient for the concentration variable suggests that in noncompetitive markets associations engage in expense-preference behavior via higher personnel expenditures. We also test for the possibility of an interaction effect between market concentration and form of organization. That is, mutual associations in noncompetitive markets may have greater leeway to indulge in expense-preference tendencies than mutuals in less concentrated markets. A positive coefficient on the interaction term ($C \cdot MS$) will indicate such expense-preference behavior on the part of mutuals in concentrated markets.[4]

The remaining variables in equation (2) are similar to those used in the studies by Edwards [3], Hannan [5], and Hannan and Mavinga [6]. The variable W is the hourly manufacturing wage rate in the association's SMSA. Wage rates paid by financial institutions are not used for several reasons. First, if SLAs do exhibit expense-preference behavior, SLA wage rates would be biased upward. Second, the only wage and salary data available are the total expenditures for all personnel. In general, we expect that all wage rates vary together because of labor mobility among professions and occupations within a market area.[5] Following conventional theory, the demand for labor should be negatively related to the wage rate.

We use total personal income in the SMSA market area as a measure of nonprice demand variable [3, 5, 6]. It is expected to be positively related to the demand for labor. Several individual firm factors influencing the demand for labor also are included in equation (2). To the extent that individual SLAs have different loan and deposit mixes, they are likely to employ different quantities of labor. Two variables are used to control for differences in asset and deposit composition. LD is defined as the mortgage-to-deposit ratio for the individual association and D is defined as the ratio of passbook savings to total deposits for each SLA in the sample. Since both higher lending ratios and higher ratios of more volatile short-term passbook savings accounts require greater amounts of labor, we expect both LD and D to be positively related to personnel expenditures. The number of offices (OFF) operated by each association is also expected to be positively related to TW. For example, a $300 million association with five branches should incur higher costs than a similar size SLA with only one branch. Finally, the influence of size on personnel costs is accounted for by the inclusion of the variable total deposits (SZ) and is expected to be positively related to labor costs.

Several alternative measures of market concentration (C) for each SMSA in the sample are utilized. These are (1) the five-firm concentration ratio (ALL) for SLAs and commercial banks (time deposits only and excluding large CDs), (2) the three-

[4]The recent study by Hannan and Mavinga [6] finds that manager-controlled banks operating in noncompetitive markets spend more on inputs likely to be preferred by managers than do owner-controlled banks in similar situations. Their findings are based on an interaction term in the test equation.

[5]The cost of capital, k, is not included in the equation. It has been commonly assumed in recent studies that this is constant across firms due to regulatory influences. However, the implicit cost of owner-pressure would suggest a higher cost of equity capital or net worth for stock associations. Moreover, such data are not readily available.

firm concentration ratio (*CSL*) for SLAs only, and (3) the Herfindahl Index (*HFL*) for SLAs in the SMSA. For these ratios, higher levels of concentration are expected to be associated with higher personnel expenditures. Finally, for a multistate sample of SLAs, we also experimented with a discrete concentration measure on the assumption that concentration levels in the market must achieve some critical or threshold level before monopolistic tendencies and expense preferences become significant. In this case, the concentration ratio for SLAs only was used and was assigned the value of one when concentration reached the critical level and zero otherwise. The critical level of concentration was estimated by means of Quandt's [17, 18] switching technique.

C. Sample Firms and Data

The data used to estimate equation (2) consist of observations for 116 SLAs in California (60 stock and 56 mutuals) with deposits of more than $10 million for the years 1974, 1975, and 1976. California represents an ideal situation in which to test for expense-preference tendencies in the industry because stock and mutual associations operate side-by-side under similar market conditions.[6] For tests reported in Table 2, the sample of associations is expanded to include 330 associations located in California, Ohio, and Texas.

All data for individual associations are obtained from reports of condition submitted to the Federal Home Loan Bank Board for the three years. Hourly wage rates are obtained from U.S. Bureau of the Census data, and information on market structure from the FHLBB and FDIC reports on deposits by SMSA.

3. EMPIRICAL FINDINGS

All equations are estimated using the ordinary least squares (OLS) estimation technique. Table 1 contains the results for the sample of California associations using alternative measures of market structure.

The equations reported in Table 1 perform quite well. The $\bar{R}^2$ values are consistently above 90 percent and the signs of the regression coefficients for the independent variables conform to a priori expectations in most cases. The coefficient for the wage rate variable (*W*) is negative and significant in nearly all cases. The coefficient for the income variable (*Y*) is positive but not significant. The coefficients for the output homeogeneity variables, the mortgage-deposit ratio (*LD*) and the passbook ratio (*D*), are positive and significant as expected. The relationship between the number of offices operated by the association (*OFF*) and personnel expenditures is also positive and significant as hypothesized. Similarly, the size variable, total deposits (*SZ*), is positively related to personnel costs.

As outlined above, expense-preference tendencies may originate from two

[6]More than 50 percent of the industry stock resources are concentrated in California SLAs. Within the state, approximately two-thirds of state industry resources are in the stock associations.

TABLE 1

EXPENSE-PREFERENCE REGRESSIONS, 1974–76: CALIFORNIA SAVINGS AND LOAN ASSOCIATIONS

Year	*Y*	*W*	*LD*	*D*	*OFF*	*SZ*	*ALL*	*CSL*	*HFL*	*MS*	Constant	$\bar{R}^2$
1974	0.011	−0.381	0.947	0.432	0.480	0.614	−0.382			0.272	1.872	0.967
	(0.35)	(−1.18)	(3.21)*	(2.47)*	(7.72)*	(13.29)*	(−0.97)			(6.33)*	(2.03)*	
1975	0.016	−0.403	0.684	0.376	0.534	0.584	−0.351			0.269	2.378	0.969
	(0.51)	(−1.34)	(1.72)**	(2.17)*	(7.84)*	(11.45)*	(−0.92)			(6.34)*	(2.35)*	
1976	0.022	−0.557	0.574	0.491	0.607	0.530	−0.144			0.252	3.600	0.962
	(0.67)	(−1.81)**	(1.41)	(2.57)*	(8.21)*	(10.10)*	(−0.35)			(5.24)*	(3.31)*	
1974	0.026	−0.537	0.959	0.463	0.477	0.617		−0.094		0.272	1.797	0.967
	(0.92)	(−1.96)*	(3.24)*	(2.69)*	(7.65)*	(13.32)*		(−0.39)		(6.28)*	(1.91)**	
1975	0.033	−0.537	0.708	0.402	0.530	0.586		−0.046		0.267	2.270	0.968
	(1.13)	(−2.03)*	(1.78)**	(2.34)*	(7.77)*	(11.46)*		(−0.20)		(6.27)*	(2.20)*	
1976	0.045	−0.586	0.608	0.530	0.602	0.532		0.190		0.250	3.280	0.963
	(1.51)	(−2.12)*	(1.49)	(2.80)*	(8.16)*	(10.17)*		(0.78)		(5.20)*	(2.96)*	
1974	0.024	−0.532	0.955	0.456	0.477	0.616			−0.211	0.272	1.800	0.967
	(0.81)	(−1.90)**	(3.22)*	(2.62)*	(7.66)*	(13.31)*			(−0.50)	(6.29)*	(1.94)**	
1975	0.027	−0.531	0.707	0.392	0.531	0.585			−0.213	0.268	2.318	0.968
	(0.88)	(−2.01)*	(1.78)**	(2.27)*	(7.79)*	(11.46)*			(−0.51)	(6.30)*	(2.27)*	
1976	0.045	−0.597	0.599	0.538	0.602	0.534			0.315	0.249	3.313	0.963
	(1.49)	(−2.16)*	(1.47)	(2.81)*	(8.15)*	(10.18)*			(0.77)	(5.18)*	(3.02)*	

NOTES: *t*-ratios are in parentheses. Variable definitions: *Y* = total personal income in the SMSA; *W* = hourly wage rate; *LD* = mortgage to deposit ratio for each SLA; *D* = passbook savings to total savings for each SLA; *OFF* = number of offices for each SLA; *SZ* = total deposits for each SLA; *ALL* = five-firm concentration ratio for commercial banks and SLAs; *CSL* = three-firm concentration ratio for SLAs; *HFL* = Herfindahl Index for SLAs; *MS* = mutual-stock dummy variable.

*Significant at the 5 percent level.

**Significant at the 10 percent level.

sources; greater personnel expenditures resulting from concentrated markets and from the behavior of mutual SLA managers as opposed to stock SLA managers. As shown in Table 1, the hypothesized positive relationship between personnel and market concentration does not appear for the sample of California associations. Given the characteristics of the California market, this is not surprising. The existence of statewide branching for both commercial banks and SLAs has virtually eliminated sheltered markets since financial institutions are allowed to operate wherever they choose. Thus, California markets tend to be quite competitive overall.

However, in all equations there is strong evidence of expense-preference behavior from the mutual form of organization. The coefficients for the form of organization variable (*MS*) are positive and highly significant with *t*-ratios exceeding 5.0 in all equations. Thus, there is support for the view that managers of mutual organizations indulge in higher expenditures on personnel. This finding is consistent with the reported profit figures (return on assets) for stock and mutual associations which reveal consistently lower ROA for mutual associations.[7]

Although the market concentration variable is not significant, there is the possibility that there may be interaction between the mutual-stock effect and market concentration. That is, in more concentrated markets, mutual managers may exhibit greater monopolistic tendencies (greater tendencies to engage in expense-preference behavior) than stock managers. In tests not shown in Table 1, an interaction term, defined as the market concentration variable times the mutual-stock dummy variable, was introduced into the equation. If such an interaction effect is present, the coefficient on the interaction term should be positive. The interaction effect was tested for each year for each of the three market concentration measures. In all cases, the coefficient for the interaction term was not statistically significant.[8] This

[7]The differences in expenditures across stock and mutual categories can also be observed in simple cost ratios for all stock and all mutual SLAs in California for the three year-period:

	Personnel expenditures ÷ Average assets		*Total operating expense ÷ Average assets*	
	Mutual SLAs	Stock SLAs	Mutual SLAs	Stock SLAs
1974	0.68%	0.42%	1.41%	1.00%
1975	0.70%	0.45%	1.45%	1.05%
1976	0.73%	0.47%	1.49%	1.12%

Profitability (return on average assets, net income divided by average assets) and capital positions (net worth to savings) of the stock and mutual groups are:

	Mutual SLAs		Stock SLAs	
	ROA	*NW/S*	*ROA*	*NW/S*
1974	0.38%	8.11%	0.70%	9.26%
1975	0.51%	7.14%	0.66%	8.30%
1976	0.74%	6.84%	0.94%	7.69%

Data are from *Combined Financial Statements for FSLIC-Insured Associations, 1974–1976*, FHLBB.

[8]The regression equations were also estimated without a size variable (*SZ*) as in Hannan [5] and Edwards [3]. The results were similar to those shown in Table 1. That is, the coefficient for *MS* was positive and significant, the concentration coefficient was not significant, and the interaction term was not significant. Also, the equations were estimated without the number of offices (*LOFF*) variable but with the size variable (*SZ*) included. Once again, the results were similar to those reported in Table 1.

is not surprising since few California markets are highly concentrated. The implication is that even in more competitive markets, managers of mutual associations exhibit expense-preference tendencies, although, as will be shown later, such tendencies are more pronounced in markets with higher levels of concentration.

Equation (2) was also estimated using a sample of more than 300 SLAs from three separate states. These results are shown in Table 2 and are similar to those reported in Table 1. The coefficients for the income variable (Y), mortgage-deposit ratio (LD), number of offices (OFF), and total deposits (SZ) carry the expected signs and are statistically significant. The coefficients for the wage rate variable (W) and deposit composition (D) have the expected signs but are not significant.

In the tests of expense-preference behavior, the coefficients for the market concentration ratio (ALL) and the mutual-stock variable (MS) are positive but each is significant in only one year. The most interesting finding is the result of the test for an interaction effect between concentration and form of organization. As outlined above, the presence of more concentrated (less competitive) markets may generate more leeway for mutual managers to engage in expense-preference tendencies than in more competitive markets. If so, the coefficient for the interaction term should be positive. As shown in Table 2, the coefficient for the interaction variable ($MS \times ALL$) is positive and significant in each of the three years. This suggests that mutual managers may react differently than stock managers to increases in market concentration. That is, in markets which are less competitive, mutual SLAs indulge in greater preferences for higher personnel expenditures than stock SLAs.

Additional confirmation of expense-preference effects of the mutual form of organization is provided by the results of two tests not reported in the tables. In the first test, equation (2) was initially estimated using Quandt's switching technique to find the critical level of concentration in the SLA deposit market, but without the mutual-stock variable MS. The sample of firms then was split into two subsamples: one consisting of firms in markets above the critical level and the other of firms below the critical level. Equation (2) was estimated on the two samples separately with the MS variable included. This test allowed us to examine for the presence of expense-preference effects of the mutual form of organization in markets above and below the critical level of concentration. In the markets above the critical level, the coefficients for the MS variable were consistently positive and significant. That is, in the highly concentrated markets, there was significant evidence of expense-preference behavior. For the equation estimated on firms in markets below the critical level, the coefficients for the MS variable were also positive but only one was significant at the 10 percent level. Thus, there was evidence, albeit weaker, of expense-preference behavior in the more competitive markets. These findings suggest that when market pressures from rival associations are more intense, there is less opportunity for mutual managers to indulge in expense-preference behavior. Further information is provided by the second test in which equation (2) was estimated only for non-California associations. The concentration ratio was assigned the value of 1 if concentration was above the critical level, and was assigned

TABLE 2

EXPENSE-PREFERENCE REGRESSIONS, 1974–76: MULTISTATE SAMPLE

Year	*Y*	*W*	*LD*	*D*	*OFF*	*SZ*	*ALL*	*MS*	*MS* × *ALL*	Constant	$\bar{R}^2$
1974	0.053	−0.169	0.690	0.035	0.396	0.672	0.051	0.054		−0.186	0.926
	(2.12)*	(−1.18)	(2.67)*	(0.47)	(7.68)*	(20.07)*	(0.25)	(1.37)		(−0.28)	
1975	0.064	−0.077	0.642	0.053	0.422	0.665	0.248	0.070		−0.374	0.925
	(2.52)*	(−0.51)	(2.31)*	(0.72)	(7.49)*	(18.40)*	(1.18)	(1.80)**		(−0.53)	
1976	0.074	−0.100	0.121	0.057	0.403	0.693	0.498	0.044		−0.985	0.947
	(3.61)*	(−0.84)	(0.53)	(0.95)	(8.26)*	(22.24)*	(2.76)*	(1.32)		(−1.62)	
1974	0.051	−0.179	0.678	0.042	0.390	0.676	−0.235	−0.256	0.642	−0.075	0.928
	(2.05)*	(−1.26)	(2.64)*	(0.57)	(7.59)*	(20.28)*	(−0.97)	(−1.74)**	(2.18)*	(−0.11)	
1975	0.061	−0.094	0.639	0.061	0.416	0.688	−0.079	−0.281	0.729	−0.214	0.926
	(2.42)*	(−0.62)	(2.32)*	(0.83)	(7.43)*	(18.62)*	(−0.32)	(−1.88)**	(2.43)*	(−0.30)	
1976	0.072	−0.111	0.108	0.062	0.399	0.695	0.273	−0.195	0.497	−0.862	0.948
	(3.52)*	(−0.94)	(0.47)	(1.03)	(8.22)*	(22.39)*	(1.28)	(−1.55)	(1.98)*	(−1.42)	

NOTES: *t*-ratios are in parentheses. Variable definitions: *Y* = total personal income in the SMSA; *W* = hourly wage rate; *LD* = mortgage to deposit ratio for each SLA; *D* = passbook savings to total savings for each SLA; *OFF* = number of offices for each SLA; *SZ* = total deposits for each SLA; *ALL* = five-firm concentration ratio for commercial banks and SLAs; *MS* = mutual-stock dummy variable; *MS* × *ALL* = interaction term, stock-mutual dummy times *ALL*.

*Significant at the 5 percent level.

**Significant at the 10 percent level.

the value of 0 for markets below the critical level. The stock-mutual variable (*MS*) was then multiplied times the dummy variable for concentration to form an interaction term. A positive coefficient on the interaction term would then reveal greater personnel expenditures by mutuals in markets above the critical level of concentration. In all cases, the coefficient was positive and significant.[9]

In summary, the findings from the various tests presented provide considerable support for the contention that expense-preference behavior exists in mutual SLAs. When the traditional ownership, profit-maximization influences are not present, mutual managers appear to engage in expense-preference tendencies. That is, there is evidence of considerable managerial discretion in the allocation of resources within the mutual SLA, both because of the mutual form of organization and (in some cases) a market concentration and form of organization interaction effect.[10] Further research is warranted to determine if these expense-preference tendencies extend to other expense categories in addition to personnel expenditures. The study by Hannan and Mavinga [6] suggests that this may be true for manager-controlled banks in more concentrated markets.

4. CONCLUSIONS AND IMPLICATIONS

The purpose of this paper has been to analyze the nature of discretionary managerial behavior in the savings-and-loan industry. By testing for expense-preference tendencies in a sample of California SLAs and a sample of SLAs in several states, it has been shown that mutual SLA managers do have significant preferences for higher personnel expenditures. These results are consistent with those found in recent studies of the financial-services industry [3, 5, 6, 21, 22].[11]

These findings are important for several reasons. First, they lend further support to the view that expense-preference behavior may be more appropriate than profit-maximization in describing managerial behavior in regulated industries. Second, they suggest that a significant social cost, in the form of *X*-inefficiency, exists in the mutual form of organization. Third, along with other current efforts to deregulate the industry, acceleration of the conversion movements from the mutual to the stock form of organization should result in improvement in resource-use efficiency. However, additional studies of the behavior of converting associations must be conducted to provide evidence on this issue.

[9]Several tests for possible interaction between branching and market concentration and between branching and form of organization were conducted. The tests did not reveal any significant interaction efects.

[10]These results are consistent with a study by Verbrugge and Goldstein [22] which finds that profitability is consistently lower in mutual SLAs than in comparable stock SLAs and that mutual managers also indulge in risk-reduction preferences by holding lower-risk loan portfolios.

[11]In a recent study Rhoades [19] concludes that the expense-preference hypothesis in banking is not supported by the evidence. However, his test equation is not consistent with that used by Edwards [3], Hannan [5], Hannan and Mavinga [6], and this study. Furthermore, careful examination of his results does reveal evidence of expense-preference behavior in several of his equations on salary expenditures and asset to employee ratios.

LITERATURE CITED

1. Alchian, Armen A., and Reuben A. Kessel. "Competition, Monopoly and the Pursuit of Pecuniary Gain." In *Aspects of Labor Economics*. A Conference of the Universities—National Bureau Committee for Economic Research Conference, 1960. Princeton, N.J.: National Bureau of Economic Research, 1962.

2. Brigham, Eugene F., and R. Richardson Petit. "Effects of Structure on Performance in the Savings and Loan Industry." In *Study of The Savings and Loan Industry*, Vol. 3, edited by Irwin Friend, pp. 971-1209. Washington, D.C.: U.S. Government Printing Office, 1969.

3. Edwards, Franklin R. "Managerial Objectives in Regulated Industries: Expense Preference Behavior in Banking." *Journal of Political Economy*, 85 (February 1977), 147-62.

4. Glassman, Cynthia A., and Stephen A. Rhoades. "Owner vs. Manager Control Effects on Bank Performance." *Review of Economics and Statistics*, 62 (May 1980), 263-70.

5. Hannan, Timothy H. "Expense-Preference Behavior in Banking: A Reexamination." *Journal of Political Economy*, 87 (August 1979), 891-95.

6. Hannan, Timothy H., and Ferdinand Mavinga. "Expense Preference and Managerial Control: The Case of the Banking Firm." *The Bell Journal of Economics*, 11 (Autumn 1980), 671-82.

7. Hester, Donald D. "An Empirical Analysis of Risk-Taking by Firms in the Savings and Loan Industry." In *Risk and Uncertainty*, edited by Karl Borch and Jan Mossin, pp. 33-61. New York: St. Martin's Press, 1968.

8. ______. *Stock and Mutual Associations in the Savings and Loan Industry*. Washington, D.C.: Federal Home Loan Bank Board, 1968.

9. Kamerschen, David R. "The Influence of Ownership and Control on Profit Rates." *American Economic Review*, 58 (June 1968), 432-47.

10. Leibenstein, Harvey. "Allocative Efficiency Vs. 'X-Efficiency.'" *American Economic Review*, 56 (June 1966), 392-415.

11. ______. "Aspects of the X-Efficiency Theory of the Firm." *The Bell Journal of Economics*, 6 (Autumn 1975), 580-606.

12. McEachern, William A. *Managerial Control and Performance*. Lexington, Mass.: Lexington Books, 1975.

13. ______. "Corporate Control and Risk." *Economic Inquiry*, 14 (June 1976), 270-78.

14. McKean, John R., and John J. Kania. "An Industry Approach to Owner-Manager Control and Profit Performance." *Journal of Business*, 51 (April 1978), 327-42.

15. Nicols, Alfred. *Management and Control in the Mutual Savings and Loan Association*. Lexington, Mass.: Lexington Books, 1972.

16. Palmer, John R. "The Profit-Performance Effects of the Separation of Ownership from Control in Large U.S. Industrial Corporations." *Bell Journal of Economics and Management Science*, 4 (Spring 1973), 293-303.

17. Quandt, Richard E. "The Estimation of the Parameters of a Linear Regression System Obeying Two Separate Regimes." *Journal of the American Statistical Association*, 53 (December 1958), 873-80.

18. ______. "Tests of the Hypothesis that a Linear Regression System Obeys Two Separate Regimes." *Journal of the American Statistical Association*, 55 (June 1960), 324-30.

19. Rhoades, Stephen A. "Monopoly and Expense Preference Behavior: An Empirical Investigation of a Behaviorialist Hypothesis." *Southern Economic Journal*, 47 (October 1980), 419-32.

20. Sorenson, Robert. ''The Separation of Ownership and Control and Firm Performance: An Empirical Analysis.'' *Southern Economic Journal,* 41 (July 1974), 145–48.

21. Taggart, Robert A., Jr. ''Effects of Deposit Rate Ceilings: The Evidence From Massachusetts Savings Banks.'' *Journal of Money, Credit, and Banking,* 10 (May 1978), 139–57.

22. Verbrugge, James A., and Steven J. Goldstein. ''Risk, Return, and Managerial Objective: Some Evidence From the Savings and Loan Industry.'' Invited Research Working Paper No. 28, Office of Policy and Economic Research, Federal Home Loan Bank Board, November, 1979; also, *Journal of Financial Research,* in press.

23. Williamson, Oliver E. ''Managerial Discretion and Business Behavior.'' *American Economic Review,* 53 (December 1963), 1032–57.

24. ______. *The Economics of Discretionary Behavior: Managerial Objectives in a Theory of the Firm.* Englewood Cliffs, N.J.: Prentice-Hall, 1967.

E. DWIGHT PHAUP*

A Reinterpretation of the Modern Theory of Forward Exchange Rates

1. INTRODUCTION

THE MODERN THEORY of forward exchange rate determination (MT) has been widely, although not unanimously, accepted as an improvement over the traditional interest rate parity theory (IRPT). The latter theory contends that in equilibruim the forward rate F will equal (except for transactions costs) the interest parity forward rate F^*.[1] Covered interest arbitrage (CIA) is a primary (but, as shall be seen, not the only) force insuring this equilibrium condition for the forward market. For example, if F exceeds F^*, then covering arbitrageurs borrow (or forego lending) in the domestic country, purchase the foreign currency on the spot market, lend abroad at the foreign interest rate, and simultaneously sell the foreign currency (including interest) on the forward market. These transactions cause F to decline and/or F^* to increase until equilibrium is restored.

Motivated in part by early empirical studies of the IRPT which found evidence of apparent deviations of F from F^* and by the intuitively appealing argument that expectations (or speculation) can also influence F, the MT suggests that the equilibrium forward rate is better explained as a weighted average of F^* and the expected

*The helpful comments of the referees are gratefully acknowledged.

[1]All exchange rates are expressed as the domestic currency price of foreign exchange. F^* is defined as SR, where S is the current spot exchange rate and $R = (1+rd)/(1+rf)$ where rd and rf are the interest rates on comparable domestic and foreign assets, respectively. Forward exchange rates and expected future exchange rates (introduced later) as well as interest rates are all of the same maturity. For treatments of the MT, see [9, 11, 17, 19].

E. DWIGHT PHAUP *is associate professor of economics, Union College, Schenectady, New York.*

0022-2879/81/1181-0477$00.50/0

future spot rate (Se). That is, the MT seeks to incorporate expectations into the determinants of F and to do so in such a way as to explain why F can diverge from F^*.

Whether the MT yields an equilibrium forward rate which is in fact different from F^* has been questioned previously. In particular, several studies have contended that separate forces will cause Se and F^* to take the same value, so that regardless of the weights (which sum to unity) attached to each variable, F still remains equal to F^* (see [8, 14, 20]). In light of the continued support that the MT has enjoyed, this critique (which relies on the purchasing power parity theory and a Fisherian approach to nominal interest rates) has evidently not been fully accepted.

In this paper, another reason (based only on the assumption of profit-maximizing behavior) for believing that F must equal F^* is presented. Specifically the primary conclusion of the MT (that F can diverge from F^*) is shown to rely on the assumption that alternative forms of speculation do not substitute freely for one another; further, the usual justifications for the assumption are found to be flawed. The next section briefly reviews the MT and the assumption it requires to be differentiated from the IRPT. Section 3 then considers the strength of the justifications for the assumption and section 4 provides some conclusions.

2. THE MT AND ITS ASSUMPTIONS

As noted above, most versions of the MT focus on covered interest arbitrage and forward speculation as determining forces of the forward rate. As was also mentioned, arbitrageurs' excess demand for forward foreign exchange (XD_a) depends on the relationship between F and F^*; specifically, their excess demand can be expressed as

$$XD_a = \alpha(F^* - F), \qquad \alpha > 0, \tag{1}$$

where α is regarded as less than infinitely large for a variety of possible reasons (see, inter alia, [2, 13, 16]).

Equilibrium among forward speculators occurs when F is equal to the expected spot rate, Se. If Se is greater than F, speculators will purchase foreign exchange forward at F with the intention of later selling it at Se. Consequently, the excess demand for forward foreign exchange by speculators is represented as

$$XD_s = \beta(Se - F), \qquad \beta > 0. \tag{2}$$

The coefficient β or the slope of the forward speculative schedule is also regarded as being less than infinitely large, to reflect the assumption of risk aversion.

Equilibrium in the forward market requires that $XD_a + XD_s = 0$; using equation (1) and equation (2) this condition can be solved for F as follows:

$$F = [\alpha/(\alpha+\beta)]\ F^* + [\beta/(\alpha+\beta)]\ Se. \tag{3}$$

According to equation (3), F can deviate from F^* whenever β is not dwarfed by α and F^* is not equal to Se; ostensibly, of course, such cases do occur since otherwise the MT would revert to the IRPT where F equals F^*. This paper is concerned with the assumption necessary to establish that β is not consistently dominated by α.

To develop the discussion, note that a potential speculator can take an open position in foreign exchange in two ways. First, a net long position can be attained by purchasing foreign currency on the forward market at F. Second, if the dollar value of that open position is, say, y-dollars, an equivalent long position can be assumed by borrowing $y/(1+rd)$ dollars, converting them to the foreign currency at $1/S$ and investing the foreign exchange at rf; the dollar price per unit of foreign exchange so acquired is F^*.[2] Thus, the forward market and the combined spot and money markets[3] offer two alternative methods for purchasing or selling claims to foreign exchange in the future at respective prices of F and F^*.[4]

Given that there exists a high degree of substitutability between the available options and that market participants are profit-maximizers, then F must equal F^*. Suppose, for example, that initially $Se > F > F^*$—a condition which according to the MT could characterize equilibrium in the forward market. In such a situation, speculators who have a choice of purchasing a future claim in the foreign currency at a price of F or of F^* would obviously select the more profitable route of spot speculation at the lower unit cost of F^*. With arbitrageurs dominating the forward market (selling forward) and speculators concentrating their activities on the spot market (buying), F and F^* would be equated; only then would speculators be indifferent about the options available to them.[5,6] Recast in terms of the MT, F cannot deviate from F^* since otherwise spot speculation would be more profitable than forward speculation and speculators would abandon the forward market; i.e., β would equal zero.[7] Hence, to prevent β from being equal to zero (and F from equaling F^*), the MT must assume that the alternative forms of speculation do not

[2]The positions are equivalent in the sense that at the time of maturity, the speculator's maximum potential loss is y-dollars in both instances.

[3]Following the usual practice, speculating through the combined spot and financial markets will be referred to as spot speculation.

[4]Similarly, traders seeking to close otherwise exposed positions have two options: to hedge through the forward market (at F) or through the spot and money markets; in the latter case, it can be shown that the unit price of hedging a future foreign exchange claim or obligation is F^* (see, e.g., [15]).

[5]Again, the argument is fully applicable to trader-hedgers. If F exceeded F^*, covering exporters would hedge (sell) future claims on foreign exchange at F while importers would hedge (purchase future claims) through the spot and money markets at F^*. Thus, arbitrageurs and covering exporters would both be selling forward, as speculators and covering importers would both be buying spot.

[6]Although, for expositional convenience, the above explanations have been couched in terms of a situation where $Se>F>F^*$, the conclusions are the same if the inequality signs are reversed. For example, if $Se<F<F^*$, then speculation would still only occur on the spot market; the direction of speculative and arbitrage flows would, however, be the reverse of that described in the text.

[7]Tsiang [18] has argued that F need not always fall between F^* and Se, so that a case where, for example, $Se > F^* > F$ is possible; in that situation forward speculation could be more profitable than spot speculation. Clearly, given equation (3), for that case to exist, F must be influenced by some variable other than F^* and Se alone. To supply the extra factor, Tsiang argues that if all traders hedge on the forward market and if exports are sufficiently greater than imports, then F can be less than both F^* and Se. As described in notes 4 and 5, however, to assume that all hedging occurs on the forward market when $F^* > F$ is to impose irrationality on exporters who could sell claims on future foreign exchange at F^*. Profit-maximizing behavior by exporters and importers would therefore cause F to rise and F^* to fall until $F = F^*$, at which point hedgers would also be indifferent between their options.

freely substitute for one another. The justifications for such an assumption are considered in the next section.

3. SUBSTITUTABILITY BETWEEN THE OPTIONS

In a seminal article in the MT literature, Tsiang [19] deals with spot speculation in two ways. First, he argues that it can be shown to be equivalent to a combined CIA-forward speculation operation and hence can be subsumed into those two activities which have already been treated. That is, spot speculation, which is essentially an uncovered interest arbitrage transaction, can be regarded as equivalent to the speculator covering his open position by an appropriate forward sale (a CIA action) and then reassuming his speculative position by purchasing from himself the forward exchange "sold as an arbitrageur." In terms of equation (1) and equation (2), the given volume of spot speculation is added to both XD_a and XD_s so that the solution for F given by equation (3) is unaffected.

This equivalence convention is a convenient device for handling spot speculation once the level of such speculation is known, but it does not address the implications for a high degree of substitutability between spot and forward speculation. That is, if all speculation occurs on the spot market while F is temporarily different from F^*, there is nothing "wrong" with treating it as a combined operation, but the convention itself does not change the fact that F must equal F^* in equilibrium. The reason for focusing on this perhaps obvious point is that the equivalence convention has conceivably obscured the importance of the substitutability question since it can misleadingly give the impression that spot speculation has been fully "accounted for"; clearly, such an impression is incorrect.[8]

The second comment Tsiang makes about spot speculation is more germane to the substitutability issue. After describing the equivalence idea, he writes "speculators . . . will speculate in spot exchange only if they find it cheaper to perform the implicit interest arbitrage themselves rather than leave it to the professional arbitragers, i.e., banks. In other words, unless they find that they can carry the speculative stock and spot exchange at a lower net interest and liquidity cost than the banks, they will prefer to concentrate on speculative operations in the forward market only" [19, p. 92].

This approach is unsatisfactory, however, because the decision-making process of the speculator only involves comparing the returns on the two speculative options available to him and not his returns from a given operation to the returns of another agent on that same transaction. If, for example, Se is \$0.60/DM, F is equal to \$0.58/DM and F^* for the speculator is \$0.55/DM, it would not matter to the speculator that a banker could arbitrage (because, e.g., of a narrower bid-ask spread

[8]For similar reasons, invoking the notion that hedging through the spot market can be treated as equivalent to a combined CIA-forward hedging operation and hence that spot market hedging is fully "accounted for" is also incorrect.

in the interbank market) at an F^* rate of \$0.54/DM; for the speculator, his most profitable option remains to speculate through the spot market.

On the other hand, if Tsiang is suggesting that the transactions costs of spot speculation are greater than those associated with forward speculation, then F and F^* could diverge by the amount of the cost differential. The effect of transactions costs for interest rate parity has, however, long been recognized and, besides, the ability to shift between the two modes of speculation still implies that outside a band around F^* (representing the extra transactions costs), β equals zero.[9]

Another possible explanation of why forward speculation may be preferred to spot speculation is attributed to Stoll (by Aliber [2]). The reasoning here is that speculators prefer the forward market because they can achieve a more highly leveraged position than is possible with spot speculation. Simply put, the speculator prefers the forward market because the use of his own funds is not required. Aside from the likelihood that due to margin requirements or compensating balances the forward speculator will in fact have to commit his own resources, Aliber's response is that if the speculator can borrow the funds he requires, he can become just as leveraged as through the forward market. Of course, it may be contended that banks would be more willing to supply foreign currency through the forward market but such an argument, as Aliber notes, tends to rely on a market imperfection in the supply of speculative funds. For example, assume that speculators arrange for speculative positions through their banks. If the banks are to avoid a speculative posture in, say, agreeing to sell speculators foreign currency on the forward market, they must simultaneously arrange to have the required foreign exchange available on the appropriate due date. The simplest and least expensive way to obtain the needed foreign exchange is through an arbitrage operation (where the foreign currency will be sold forward to the speculator); further, in a competitive market, the price that the banks should charge would be F^* (plus some transactions fee perhaps embedded in the bid-ask spread). Alternatively, if speculators chose to use the spot market, they could arrange with their bank to have the proceeds of a domestic loan deposited in a foreign branch of the bank. In both cases, the banks have no net open position in foreign exchange and both involve a shift of spot assets abroad; consequently, it is not clear why the banks would prefer to accommodate the forward rather than the spot position. Further, if the above description does reflect the bank's operations (see [3] for a supporting view and [4] for further discussion), then it explains why banks are believed to base their forward exchange quotes on the interest parity forward rate and provides another reason why F should equal F^* (except for transactions costs).

Aliber [2] offers a third explanation of why speculators may prefer the forward market. Spot speculation, he argues, involves not only exchange rate risk but also a political risk not found in forward speculation. The nature of this political risk is in

[9]Given recent estimates of these transactions costs, the associated band would appear to be narrow. See [6, 7].

the possibility that exchange controls may be imposed which would prevent the repatriation of assets held abroad or would constrain the return that could be earned on foreign assets (see [5]). Since, according to Aliber, speculators prefer to specialize in exchange risk and allow arbitrageurs to concentrate on political risk, speculators will prefer the forward market.

In assessing this explanation, note that calculation of the interest parity forward rate requires that interest rates on comparable financial assets be employed, where comparability refers, inter alia, to risk characteristics. To suggest that F may not equal F^* or that forward speculation may be preferred to spot speculation when assets with different risk characterisitics are used to determine F^* is also recognized in the interest parity literature. Aliber's contribution to this literature is to identify another factor—political risk—which prevents otherwise similar assets from in fact being precisely comparable (see [20, p. 29]). Put differently, Aliber's point does not change the fact that when interest rates on assets which are fully comparable (including in terms of risk) are chosen to calculate F^*, equilibrium still requires that F equal F^*; that Aliber and others have found that F is so close to F^* when the latter is measured using comparable Eurocurrency rates is testimony to this position.[10]

4. IMPLICATIONS AND CONCLUSIONS

In order for the forward rate to diverge from F^* in the manner described by the MT, it is necessary to demonstrate that the options for obtaining or selling claims to foreign currency in the future do not freely substitute for one another. As noted in the previous section, however, explanations for why one option may be preferred to another rely either on the existence of market imperfections or on using the returns on foreign and domestic assets which are not fully comparable to calculate F^*. It was also noted (n. 10) that when returns on comparable assets have been employed in empirical studies to determine F^*, the results have been consistent with the presence of a high degree of substitutability between the options. That is, both an analysis of the nonsubstitutability assumption and the available empirical evidence suggest that the assumption is not easily defended.

Still, one might argue that studies which tend to show that F is equal to F^* can be incorporated into the MT, since it does allow for the possibility that β is zero (or very small relative to α). The problem with defending the MT on these grounds is that in its popular interpretation, if β is equal to zero the implication is that speculation plays no role in determining F (e.g., [11, 17]). Clearly, however, speculation can still influence F even when β is equal to zero and $F = F^*$. If, for example, *Se*

[10]See, for example, [6, 7, 10, 12]. For a discussion of other issues surrounding Aliber's paper, see Dooley and Isard [5] who note that one source of differences between F and F^* when the latter is measured with domestic (instead of Eurocurrency) interest rates are existing capital controls (vis-à-vis possible new controls with which Aliber was concerned). Dooley and Isard's empirical results also indicated that political risk premia failed to be a factor shortly after the adoption of floating exchange rates and the dismantling of capital controls. For additional discussions of factors that can interfere with interest parity, see [1; 20, pp. 28–31].

increases, speculators will purchase the foreign currency on both the spot and forward markets in such a fashion as to drive up F and (through S and/or the relevant interest rates) F^* in the same amount, so as to keep the expected net marginal returns from each speculative approach equal. In short, although an alleged advantage of the MT over the IRPT is that the former better allows for capturing the influence of speculative sentiment on F, in fact it can obscure that effect. In this regard, the MT can be misleading and is thereby less instructive than the IRPT.

LITERATURE CITED

1. Agmon, Tamir, and Saul Bronfield. "The International Mobility of Short-Term Arbitrage Capital." *Journal of Business Finance and Accounting,* 2 (Spring 1975), 269-77.
2. Aliber, Robert Z. "The Interest Rate Parity Theorem: A Reinterpretation." *Journal of Political Economy,* 81 (November/December 1973), 1451-59.
3. Allen, William A. "A Note on Uncertainty, Tranactions Costs and Interest Parity." *Journal of Monetary Economics,* 3 (July 1977), 367-73.
4. Deardorff, Alan V. "One-Way Arbitrage and Its Implications for the Foreign Exchange Markets." *Journal of Political Economy,* 87 (April 1979), 351-64.
5. Dooley, Michael P., and Peter Isard. "Capital Controls, Political Risk and Deviations from Interest-Rate Parity." *Journal of Political Economy,* 88 (April 1980), 370-84.
6. Frenkel, Jacob A., and Richard M. Levich. "Covered Interest Arbitrage: Unexploited Profits?" *Journal of Political Economy,* 83 (April 1975), 325-38.
7. ______. "Transactions Costs and Interest Arbitrage: Tranquil versus Turbulent Periods." *Journal of Political Economy,* 85 (December 1977), 1209-26.
8. Giddy, Ian H. "An Integrated Theory of Exchange Rate Equilibrium." *Journal of Financial and Quantitative Analysis,* 11 (December 1976), 883-92.
9. Grubel, Herbert G. "A Multicountry Model of Forward Exchange: Theory, Policy and Empirical Evidence, 1955-1961." *Yale Economic Essays,* 3 (Spring 1963), 105-69.
10. Marston, Richard C. "Interest Arbitrage in the Euro-Currency Markets." *European Economic Review,* 7 (January 1976), 1-14.
11. McCallum, Bennett T. "The Role of Speculation in the Canadian Forward Exchange Market: Some Estimates Assuming Rational Expectations." *Review of Economics and Statistics,* 59 (May 1977), 145-51.
12. McCormick, Frank E. "Covered Interest Arbitrage: Unexploited Profits? Comment." *Journal of Political Economy,* 87 (April 1979), 411-17.
13. Officer, Lawrence H., and Thomas D. Willett. "The Covered-Arbitrage Schedule: A Critical Survey of Recent Developments." *Journal of Money, Credit, and Banking,* 2 (May 1970), 247-57.
14. Pippenger, John E. "Spot Rates, Forward Rates, and Interest-Rate Differentials." *Journal of Money, Credit, and Banking,* 4 (May 1972), 375-83.
15. Spraos, John. "The Theory of Forward Exchange and Recent Practice." *The Manchester School of Economics and Social Studies,* 21 (May 1953) 87-117.
16. Stoll, Hans R. "Causes of Deviations from Interest Parity." *Journal of Money, Credit, and Banking,* 4 (February 1972), 113-17.

17. ______. "An Empirical Study of the Forward Exchange Market under Fixed and Flexible Exchange Rate Systems." *Canadian Journal of Economics,* 1 (February 1965), 55–78.

18. Tsiang, Sho C. "Spot Speculation, Forward Speculation and Arbitrage: A Clarification and Reply." *American Economic Review,* 63 (December 1973), 999–1002.

19. ______. "The Theory of Forward Exchange and Effects of Government Intervention on the Forward Exchange Market." *IMF Staff Papers,* 7 (April 1959), 75–106.

20. Yeager, Leland B. *International Monetary Relations: Theory, History and Policy.* 2d ed. New York: Harper and Row, 1976.

NOTES, COMMENTS, REPLIES

The New Monetary Aggregates

*A Comment by William A. Barnett**

In a recent paper published in this journal, Berkman [10] disputed the usefulness of the new (chained Törnquist-Theil) Divisia quantity indexes of the economy's flow of monetary services, which just have begun to become available within the Federal Reserve System.[1] While a few of his comments have some merit, his criticisms are largely based upon a faulty understanding of aggregation theory, and he thereby fails to see the forest for the trees.

The Forest

The need for proper use of aggregation and index number theory in monetary aggregation has been known for years. For example, Friedman and Schwartz proposed

> regarding each asset as a joint product having different degrees of moneyness and defining the quantity of money as the weighted sum of the aggregate value of all assets, the weights for individual assets varying from zero to unity with a weight of unity assigned to that asset or assets regarded as having the largest quantity of moneyness per dollar of aggregate value. . . . We conjecture that that approach deserves and will get much more attention than it has so far received. [12, pp. 151–52]

We now have known how to construct that aggregate in a rigorous and unique manner derived directly from aggregation theory, since the Jorgensonian user cost of the services of monetary assets was derived by Barnett [1]. Regarding the simple sum (arithmetic average) index, Fisher concluded over half a century ago that "the simple arithmetic average produces one of the very worst of index numbers, and if this book has no other effect than to lead to the total abandonment of the simple

*I have benefited from comments on this note by Paul A. Spindt, Edward K. Offenbacher, Jared J. Enzler, and an anonymous referee. The views expressed herein are solely those of the author and do not necessarily represent the views of the Board of Governors of the Federal Reserve System.

[1]The monthly reports from Paul A. Spindt and me are available outside the system only upon request. The research supporting their design and construction is available in [2, 5, 6, 7, 8]. The first official source of the new data will be [9].

WILLIAM A. BARNETT *is economist, Division of Research and Statistics, Board of Governors of the Federal Reserve System.*

0022-2879/81/1181-0485$00.50/0 ©1981 Ohio State University Press
JOURNAL OF MONEY, CREDIT, AND BANKING, vol. 13, no. 4 (November 1981)

arithmetic type of index number, it will have served a useful purpose" [11, p. 29]. We agree with Fisher that "the simple arithmetic [index] should not be used under any circumstances" [11, p. 361].

Aggregating over currency and small time deposits by simple summation to acquire a monetary aggregate is no more reasonable than aggregating over subway trains and roller skates by simple summation (rather than through the Commerce Department's Laspeyres quantity index) to acquire an aggregate of transportation vehicles. As another example, suppose the money supply were measured by the Board's current highest level simple sum aggregate, *L*, which contains most of the national debt of short and intermediate maturity. All of that portion of the national debt could be monetized (bought up, burned, and paid for with freshly printed currency) without increasing either taxes or the "money supply," *L*.[2] However, the new Divisia index over the components of *L* would rise at about the same rate as the resulting explosive hyperinflation in prices.

On the other hand, the many problems associated with policies that target very low level aggregates result from the inability of such aggregates to internalize pure substitution effects occurring within the economy's transactions technology (or within any of its weakly separable blocks).

The Trees

Berkman's primary criticism is that the "technique Barnett used to estimate the elasticities required is not widely understood, nor are his estimates (and hence his aggregate definitions themselves) likely to remain unchanged by other researchers. Econometric difficulties aside, the elasticities are likely to change abruptly and unpredictably from time to time with changes in the regulatory environment" [10, p. 151]. In fact the Divisia index contains no parameters at all. *No* elasticities appear in the index. Hence the choice between the existing naïve simple sum index and a chained Divisia quantity index (or a Fisher ideal, or Laspeyres, or Paasche, or any other reputable index) cannot be based upon "econometric difficulties" or upon presumed variability over time of some parameters, which do not even exist in any of these indices.[3] Berkman's ciriticism is particularly surprising when compared

[2]Strictly speaking, this example would require a 100 percent reserves system.

[3]The estimation of parameters in Barnett's [2] research on the subject served two purposes. First, estimation of intensity parameters and elasticity of substitution parameters was required to test the necessary and sufficient conditions for simple sum aggregation. The conditions are perfect substitutability in identical ratios, that is, indistinguishable goods. We need not fear that someone will someday find that currency and nonnegotiable certificates of deposit are indistinguishable goods. While such observations hardly require empirical support, the empirical evidence that does exist (Barnett [2] and Offenbacher [13]) appears to remain applicable over long periods of time.

Second, as Berkman correctly observed, "the individual items to be included in the aggregate must be selected, a problem that either implicitly or explicitly involves the estimation of the elasticities of substitution among the various potential components" [10, p. 150]. This observation is true regardless of whether we use simple sum or Divisia indexes to compute the aggregate, once its components have been selected. In fact in the new aggregates that Spindt and I are now supplying, we are using precisely the same components as are used with the Board's simple sum aggregates. With those same components, we are computing and supplying both the simple sum and the Divisia quantity index, neither of which contains *any* parameters.

with his statement that the new Divisia indices "are relatively easy to construct, since the only information required to compute the weights is the commercial paper rate, a long term bond rate, and the relevant own rates of interest" [10, p. 151]. Those weights vary continuously over time and depend only upon measurable data. Surely there is no ambiguity in the difference in definitions of "measurable variables" and "estimable parameters."

Berkman's other criticism is that "estimation of own rates of interest required to compute the weights presents formidable conceptual and technical difficulties." Computation of own rates of return is a measurement problem and not an estimation problem. Indeed much careful work has gone into the acquisition of own rate data to permit us to begin supplying high quality Divisia quantity aggregates of the supply of monetary services. We were not deterred by "formidable conceptual and technical difficulties." In fact the major data problems, rather than being interest rate data acquisition problems, were problems resulting from unavailability at the Board of maturity breakdowns for some component quantities, which already are in the simple sum aggregates. Fortunately governmental agencies commonly do not fail to provide data on the grounds that initiation of any quality data series usually requires considerable work. Furthermore, we have found that the new Divisia indexes are very robust to changes in plausible data measurement procedures, when judged relative to the really large shift encountered when converting from the simple sum to the Divisia quantity index.

In addition to Berkman's two primary objections discussed above, he also has a few other objections. Berkman asserts that "there may be concern (however unfounded) over the potential for self-serving weight changes in a variable presumably under the control of the agency that constructs the data." Again, the chained Divisia index contains no parameters that can be determined at our discretion. The index depends solely upon data, as is true for any reputable index number or for the simple sum index. The growth rate of the Divisia index is a weighted average of the growth rates of its components. But the growth rate of a simple sum index also is a weighted average of its components. The growth rate weights of the Divisia index reduce to those of the simple sum index if the own rates of return on all components are equal—in which case all components are perfect substitutes (see [2]). The growth rate weights in either case depend upon the component quantities. If the Board were so inclined, it could tamper with those component quantities far more easily than it could tamper with interest rates, since the Board is the source of the component quantity data, but other agencies frequently are the sources of the rate data. Furthermore, the index number formula as well as the component quantity and own rate series would be publicly available. As a result, alteration of the procedure would be publicly detectable.

In constructing fixed-based price indexes, the Bureau of Labor Statistics (BLS) and Commerce Department use methods that could be altered much more easily than our chained Divisia quantity index construction. Yet would anyone seriously suggest that the CPI (a Laspeyres index) or the implicit price deflator (a Paasche index) be computed as the arithmetic average of its component prices? In that case the BLS and the Commerce Department would not have to gather quantity data, which could be falsified to understate the inflation rate.

In short, the Board's ability (or lack thereof) to tamper with an aggregate in a self-serving manner has nothing whatever to do with the selection between parameter-free index number formulas (such as the simple sum or Divisia). All such formulas depend only upon data, which cannot be rendered tamper-proof by the subsequent application of an index number formula. If, however, Board "accountability" were imposed through a legislated money growth rule, Congress might specify that the index be constructed and periodically updated by a governmental statistical bureau, such as the BLS, that has no direct interest other than the purely statistical one. That possibility, suggested to me by an anonymous referee, would be equally as applicable (or inapplicable) regardless of whether Congress defined its money growth rule in terms of a simple sum or chained Divisia index.

Berkman's discussion of the aggregation conditions for selection of components bears no evident relationship with the conditions for consistent aggregation (pp. 150–51). By quoting me out of context, Berkman has failed (undoubtedly inadvertently) to distinguish between the conditions for consistent aggregation (defined as the "Aggregation Conditions" [2, p. 35]) and the conditions for linearity of the aggregator function (defined as the "Linearity Conditions" [3, p. 38]).

Berkman asserts that I accept simple sum aggregation over transaction balances. In some of my original research on the use of aggregation theory in monetary aggregation, I did sum over transactions balances for reasons described in [3]. However, such simplifying assumptions were not appropriate in constructing the now available monthly Divisia aggregates, and hence (in accordance with [14]) we have imputed an implicit rate of return to demand deposits. Robustness to that imputation (even if set to zero) is high, since the failure of the simple sum aggregates becomes pronounced only when aggregation is carried to the level of M2 or higher.

The Conclusions

Simple sum aggregates do not and cannot accurately indicate the quantity of monetary services being provided to the economy. Properly constructed quantity index numbers can. Monetary aggregates should be no less competently constructed than aggregates long available for other economic variables, such as commodity quantities or prices.

LITERATURE CITED

1. Barnett, William A. "The User Cost of Money." *Economics Letters,* 1 (1978), 145–49.

2. ______. "Economic Monetary Aggregation: An Application of Aggregation and Index Number Theory." *Journal of Econometrics,* 14 (September 1980), 11–48.

3. ______. "Economic Monetary Aggregates: Reply." *Journal of Econometrics,* 14 (September 1980), 57–59.

4. ———. "Divisia Indices." In *Encyclopedia of Statistical Sciences,* edited by Norman Johnson and Samuel Kotz. New York: Wiley, forthcoming.

5. ———. *Consumer Demand and Labor Supply: Goods, Monetary Assets, and Time.* Amsterdam: North-Holland, 1981.

6. Barnett, William A., Edward Offenbacher, and Paul Spindt. "New Concepts of Aggregated Money." *Journal of Finance* (Proceedings of the AEA-AFA Denver Meetings), 36 (May 1981), 497-505.

7. Barnett, William A., and Paul A. Spindt. "The Velocity Behavior and Information Content of Divisia Monetary Aggregates." *Economics Letters,* 4 (1979), 51-57.

8. ———. "The Information Content of Divisia Monetary Quantity Indices." Special Studies Paper 146. Washington, D.C.: Federal Reserve Board, 1980.

9. ———. "Divisia Monetary Aggregates: Data and Historical Behavior." Processed. Washington, D.C.: Federal Reserve Board Staff Study, Publications Services, Federal Reserve Board, 1981.

10. Berkman, Neil G. "The New Monetary Aggregates: A Critical Appraisal." *Journal of Money, Credit, and Banking,* 12, pt. 1 (May 1980), 135-54.

11. Fisher, Irving. *The Making of Index Numbers: A Study of Their Varieties, Tests, and Reliability.* Boston: Houghton Mifflin, 1922.

12. Friedman, Milton, and Anna J. Schwartz. *Monetary Statistics of the United States: Estimates, Sources, Methods.* New York: National Bureau of Economic Research, 1970.

13. Offenbacher, Edward K. "The Substitutability of Monetary Assets." Ph.D. dissertation, University of Chicago, 1979.

14. Startz, Richard. "Implicit Interest on Demand Deposits." *Journal of Monetary Economics,* 5 (October 1979), 515-34.

Adjustment Lags Versus Information Lags: A Test of Alternative Explanations of the Phillips Curve Phenomenon

*A Comment by Jacob A. Frenkel**

In a recent paper in this journal, Charles R. Nelson [2] argued that

> Interestingly, Hume was clearly of the opinion that the *level* of activity would be raised *permanently* by a steady increase in the quantity of money, prices and wages. Hume was therefore a believer in a stable, long-run Phillips curve and perhaps the only serious economist to have so committed himself in print! [2, p. 2]

In this note I argue that Nelson's inference is invalid and that in fact there is evidence that Hume *did not* believe in a stable, long-run Phillips curve. In justifying his inference Nelson claims that in his 1752 essay "Of Money" Hume argued

> that though the high price of commodities be a necessary consequence of the encrease of gold and silver, yet it follows not immediately upon that encrease. It is easy to trace the money in its progress through the whole commonwealth; where we shall find, that it must first quicken the diligence of every individual, before it increase the price of labour. [Hume, as presented in Nelson 2, p. 2]

Unfortunately this quotation from Hume is imprecise. It combines two sentences, one from the beginning and one from the end of Hume's original paragraph, but it leaves out the entire material which Hume included in between these two sentences. The part which was left out is critical in that it clarifies what exactly was meant by Hume. The material which was left out makes it clear that the rise in the quantity of money will exert real output effects only in the short run during which individuals do not fully perceive the situation. Hume's complete original paragraph (starting and ending at the same place as Nelson's quotation) reads

> that though the high price of commodities be a necessary consequence of the encrease of gold and silver, yet it follows not immediately upon that encrease; but some time is required before the money circulates through the whole state, and makes its effect be felt on all ranks of people. *At first, no alteration is perceived;* by degrees of price rises,

*I wish to acknowledge useful comments from Robert E. Lucas, Jr. and financial support from a National Science Foundation grant SOC78-14480. The views expressed are those of the author and not necessarily those of the National Bureau of Economic Research.

Jacob A. Frenkel *is professor of economics, University of Chicago, and research associate, National Bureau of Economic Research.*

0022-2879/81/1181-0490$00.50/0
Journal of Money, Credit, and Banking, vol. 13, no. 4 (November 1981)

> first of one commodity, then of another; till the whole at last reaches a just proportion with the new quantity of specie which is in the kingdom. In my opinion *it is only in this interval or intermediate situation,* between the acquisition of money and rise in prices, that the encreasing quantity of gold and silver is favourable to industry. When any quantity of money is imported into a nation, it is not at first dispersed into many hands, but is confined to the coffers of a few persons, who immediately seek to employ it to advantage. Here are a set of manufacturers or merchants, we shall suppose, who have received returns of gold and silver for goods which they sent to Cadiz. They are thereby enabled to employ more workmen than formerly, who never dream of demanding higher wages, but are glad of employment from such good paymasters. If workmen become scarce, the manufacturer gives higher wages, but at first requires an encrease of labour; and this is willingly submitted to by the artisan, who can now eat and drink better, to compensate his additional toil and fatigue. He carries his money to market, where he finds every thing at the same price as formerly, but returns with greater quantity and of better kinds, for the use of his family. The farmer and gardener, finding, that all their commodities are taken off, apply themselves with alacrity to the raising more; and at the same time can afford to take better and more cloths from their tradesmen, whose price is the same as formerly, and their industry only whetted by so much new gain. It is easy to trace the money in its progress through the whole commonwealth; where we shall find, that it must first quicken the diligence of every individual before it encrease the price of labour. [1, pp. 37–38, italics mine]

From the above it seems clear that Hume's view is that "the encreasing quantity of gold and silver is favourable to industry" only because "at first no alteration is perceived" but that its real effects are confined only to "this interval or intermediate situation." It is difficult to see how these statements are consistent with the assertion that Hume was "a believer in a stable, long-run Phillips curve."

Hume considered explicitly the possibility of exploiting the facts of a sluggish adjustment of prices and wages and pursuing "a gradual and universal encrease of the denomination of money." He thus considered the following experiment

> Were all our money, for instance, recoined, and a penny's worth of silver taken from every shilling, the new shilling would probably purchase every thing that could have been bought by the old; the prices of everything would thereby be insensibly diminished; foreign trade enlived; and domestic industry, by the circulation of a great number of pounds and shillings, would receive some encrease and encouragement. [1, p. 39, n. 1]

Having outlined this experiment, he was aware that it could succeed in raising the level of economic activity only as long as it succeeded in misleading individuals and in disguising the actual course of policy. He thus continued the previous sentence by noting that:

> In executing such a project, it would be better to make the new shilling pass for 24 halfpence, in order to preserve the illusion, and make it be taken for the same.

The implication is that in the long run such a policy cannot be viable.

It is relevant to note, however, that there are several sentences in Hume's writing's which, when viewed in isolation, may leave the impression that monetary policy can have long-run employment effects (e.g., [1, p. 40]). In interpreting such sentences it is important to read things in their context. In the present case the relevant context seems to be other parts of the same article as well as Hume's other writings. The general methodological principle for the study of the history of economic thought was put forcefully by Don Patinkin [3, pp. 125–26]. Accordingly, the study of the history of doctrine should be looked at as an empirical study. The historians of thought are like econometricians fitting a multivariate regression to a man's writings. There are always points that are off the regression line and the question is whether these are random departures or the reflection of a systematic influence that the historian has not taken into account. Obviously, the difficult problem is to decide what is the regression line and what is the chance phrase or even a mistake, whose departure from the regression should not alter our views about the main tendency of the writer's thought.

In the present case I believe that the overwhelming general tendency of Hume's writings and one of the most important characteristics of his monetary theory has been the proposition concerning the neutrality of money. Indeed, in the very first paragraph of his 1752 essay "Of Money" he stated:

> If we consider any one kingdom by itself, it is evident, that the greater or less plenty of money is of no consequence; since the prices of commodities are always proportioned to the plenty of money, and a crown in HARRY VII's time served the same purpose as a pound does at present [1, p. 33]

As is clear, in this context monetary policy exerts no long-run real effects.

As a matter of fact Hume went even further. He recognized that in an open economy under a fixed exchange rate the monetary authorities cannot even determine the rate of growth of the *nominal* money stock. Establishing one of the fundamental tenets of the monetary approach to the balance of payments he demonstrated in his classic essay "Of the Balance of Trade" that the nominal money stock is endogenous. Consider, for example, his famous experiment:

> Suppose four-fifths of all the money in Great Britain to be annihilated in one night, and the nation reduced to the same condition, with regard to specie, as in the reigns of the HARRYS and EDWARDS, what would be the consequence? Must not the price of all labour and commodities sink in proportion, and everything be sold as cheap as they were in those ages? What nation could then dispute with us in any foreign market, or pretend to navigate or to sell manufactures at the same price, which to us would afford sufficient profit? In how little time, therefore, must this bring back the money which we had lost, and raise us to the level of all the neighbouring nations? Where, after we arrived, we immediately lose the advantage of the cheapness of labour and commodities; and the farther flowing of money is stopped by our fulness and repletion. [1, pp. 62–63]

Hume was aware, of course, that the monetary authority might try to alter the quantity of money but he believed that such efforts must be futile. This was the main analytical argument in his attempts to expose the logical fallacies of the mercantilism. There is a "natural distribution of specie" which is operative like a law of nature:

> All water, wherever it communicates, remains always at a level. Ask naturalists the reason; they tell you, that, were it to be raised in any one place, the superior gravity of that part not being balanced, must depress it, till it meet a counterpoise. [1, pp. 62–63]

To sum up, it is believed that, contrary to Nelson's assertion, there is no convincing evidence that David Hume believed in a stable long-run Phillips curve. Furthermore, recognizing that the economy is open to international trade, one of his main points was that under fixed exchange rates the monetary authority even loses its full control over the *nominal* money stock.

LITERATURE CITED

1. Hume, David. *Political Discourses*. Edinburgh, 1752. As reprinted in *David Hume Writings on Economics,* by Eugene Rotwein. London: Nelson, 1955.
2. Nelson, Charles R. "Adjustment Lags Versus Information Lags: A Test of Alternative Explanations of the Phillips Curve Phenomenon." *Journal of Money, Credit, and Banking,* 13 (February 1981), 1-11.
3. Patinkin, Don, and J. Clark Leith (eds.). *Keynes, Cambridge and the General Theory.* Toronto: University of Toronto Press, 1978.

Adjustment Lags Versus Information Lags: A Test of Alternative Explanations of the Phillips Curve Phenomenon

*A Reply by Charles R. Nelson**

Jacob A. Frenkel [1] has challenged my statement [3, p. 2] that David Hume was "a believer in stable, long-run Phillips curves." While I stand by my assertion and hope to convince the reader that it is accurate, I think thay any occasion to bring Hume's insightful essay, titled "Of Money" [2], to the attention of modern economists is well worthwhile. Indeed, we have remarkably little to add to Hume's explanation of how an "encrease of gold and silver" will "quicken the diligence of every individual, before it encrease the price of labour" in the long paragraph quoted by Frenkel.

Hume was careful to distinguish between the effect of alternative *levels* of the quantity of money and the effect of a *changing* quantity of money. He clearly regarded the level to be of little or no real consequence, as is evident from the additional quotes provided by Frenkel. Attributing the observation that money serves only as a unit of measure to the Scythian Anacharsis, Hume states that

> where coin is in greater plenty; as a greater quantity of it is required to represent the same quantity of goods; it can have no effect, either good or bad, taking a nation within itself. [2, p. 37]

Hume felt obliged, however, to explain what he regarded as an historical fact of the time, namely:

> But notwithstanding this conclusion, which must be allowed just, it is certain, that, since the discovery of the mines in America, industry has encreased in all the nations of Europe, except in the possessors of those mines; and this may justly be ascribed, amongst other reasons, to the encrease of gold and silver. Accordingly, we find, that, in every kingdom, into which money begins to flow in greater abundance than formerly, every thing takes a new face: labour and industry gain life; the merchant becomes more enterprising, the manufacturer more diligent and skilful, and even the farmer follows his plough with greater alacrity and attention. This is not easily to be accounted for, if we consider only the influence which a greater abundance of coin has

*I am grateful for support from the National Science Foundation under Grant SOC-7906948.

CHARLES R. NELSON *is professor and chairman, Department of Economics, University of Washington.*

0022-2879/81/1181-0494$00.50/0
JOURNAL OF MONEY, CREDIT, AND BANKING, vol. 13, no. 4 (November 1981)

> in the kingdom itself, by heightening the price of commodities, and obliging every one to pay a greater number of these little yellow or white pieces for every thing he purchases. And as to foreign trade, it appears, that great plenty of money is rather disadvantageous, by raising the price of every kind of labour. [2, p. 37]

Note that Hume is talking about a sustained increase in the quantity of money dating from "the discovery of mines in America." The next paragraph contains the lengthy passage quoted by Frenkel, but begins with

> To account, then, for this phenomenon, we must consider, that though the high price of commodities be a necessary consequence of the increase of gold and silver, yet it follows not immediately upon that encrease. . . . [2, pp. 37–38]

After a short paragraph in which he gives an example of prices lagging an increase in money in the France of Louis XIV, Hume concludes that

> From the whole of this reasoning we may conclude, that it is of no manner of consequence, with regard to the domestic happiness of a state, whether money be in a greater or less quantity. The good policy of the magistrate consists only in keeping it, if possible, still encreasing; because, by that means, he keeps alive a spirit of industry in the nation, and encreases the stock of labour, in which consists all real power and riches.[1] [2, pp. 39–40]

This advice to "our speculative politicians" leaves no doubt in my mind that Hume regarded only the rate of change of money as having real significance, but of such significance as to allow a long-run trade-off between output and inflation. There is nothing in Hume's analysis of monetary dynamics which implies that the trade-off cannot be sustained, since what he describes in the long paragraph quoted by Frenkel is a process of adjustment from one *level* to another, not from one *rate of change* to another. His conclusion follows consistently from his analysis. Viewed as a defense of the quantity theory against mercantilism, however, "Of Money" is not entirely satisfying. Eugene Rotwein concludes in his illuminating analysis of Hume's position that

> Hume has directed attention away from the "plenty of money" as such to the dynamics of monetary change, but in the process he has seriously undermined the basis of his attack on the mercantilist position. [4, p. lxv]

What David Hume has bequeathed to us then is not a quaint foretelling of the Phelps/Friedman natural-rate hypothesis but rather a marvelously clear example of the distinction between comparative statics and dynamics in the setting of monetary theory.

LITERATURE CITED

1. Frenkel, Jacob A. "Adjustment Lags Versus Information Lags: A Test of Alternative Explanations of the Phillips Curve Phenomenon. A Comment." *Journal of Money, Credit, and Banking,* 13 (November 1981), 490–93.

[1]The two sentences which I quoted from that paragraph were separated in the typescript by quotation marks. These were omitted by the typesetter, an error which I overlooked in proofing the galleys.

2. Hume, David. ''Of Money.'' As reprinted in *David Hume: Writings on Economics,* by Eugene Rotwein. Madison: University of Wisconsin, 1970.

3. Nelson, Charles R. ''Adjustment Lags Versus Information Lags: A Test of Alternative Explanations of the Phillips Curve Phenomenon.'' *Journal of Money, Credit, and Banking,* 13 (February 1981), 1-11.

4. Rotwein, Eugene. *David Hume: Writings on Economics*. Madison: University of Wisconsin, 1970.

Inflation and Real Growth: Some Empirical Results

*A Note by Dennis E. Logue and Richard James Sweeney**

1. Introduction

What is the relationship between the average rate of inflation and the variability of real economic growth? Recent studies by Gordon [3], Okun [7], Logue and Willett [6], Klein [5], and Jaffee and Kleiman [4] have attempted to fill some of the gaps in our knowledge of inflation's effect on the economy; these studies have generally demonstrated the positive empirical relationship between the rate of inflation and its variability or unpredictability. Such heightened uncertainty may produce greater variability of real growth which, in turn, undoubtedly increases welfare costs. Using annual data for twenty-four countries, we find a positive relationship between the mean inflation rate and the variability of real economic growth. This finding strengthens the commonly held belief that inflation is undesirable on welfare grounds.

2. The Influence of Inflation on the Stability of Real Output Growth

A number of considerations suggest a positive relationship between higher average rates of inflation and greater variability (or uncertainty) of inflation, which in turn leads to greater uncertainty in production, investment, and marketing decisions, and greater variability in real growth. One leading candidate (suggested by Okun [7]) is that at a high average rate of price change, a country is likely to be less consistent in its application of fiscal and financial policies as it tries various approaches to control inflation and bring it within a politically tolerable range while simultaneously attempting not to violate other political constraints—for example, low nominal interest rates on home mortgages. Judging by recent U.S. experience, high average rates of inflation are more likely to elicit stop-go policies than more moderate rates. Similarly, in Okun's analogy, much as a speeding car is more difficult to control than a slow moving one (for, among other reasons, the spacing

*We are grateful to Richard Bower, Michael Parkin, Bulent Gultekin, Richard Rogalski, Seha Tinic, Richard West, and Thomas D. Willett for comments on an earlier draft. We also found the comments by the referee, Milton Friedman, quite helpful. We, however, accept responsibility for any remaining errors.

DENNIS E. LOGUE *is professor, Amos Tuck School of Business Administration, Dartmouth College.* RICHARD JAMES SWEENEY *is professor of economics, Claremont Men's College.*

0022-2879/81/1181-0497$00.50/0

between random shocks is diminished, hence so is the time the driver has to react), higher rates of inflation are more difficult to keep under control.

In addition to this macro conjecture, recent empirical work by Parks [8] and others has shown that high inflation tends to produce large variations in relative prices. Such large variations may themselves lead to higher variability in real growth. One simple explanation of the connection between the two follows.

Producers operating in a highly inflationary economy receive distorted signals concerning demand for their goods and hence distorted signals concerning whether new plants ought to be opened and the expansion of production economically justified. With a surge in nominal income, a producer may experience a rise in product demand. Whether the increase in demand is a consequence of the producer's failure to raise prices relative to the new inflation bloated nominal income or a result of a real shift in consumer demand preferences may be indistinguishable to any given producer. Some producers may guess the former and raise prices; others may guess the latter and build additional capacity. To the extent that such guesses are wrong, abnormally large fluctuations in relative prices may follow. More importantly, to the extent relative price variation creates additional producer uncertainty, it is highly likely that the inability to distinguish real shifts in demand from "nominal" shifts, real growth in investment, and all other economic activity for that matter will be more variable than it would be in an environment where less guessing as to the source of an increase in nominal demand was necessary.

Apart from the relative price change phenomenon, there are other reasons to suspect a relationship between inflation and the variability of real growth. For example, models with a stable inflation-unemployment trade-off imply a positive relationship between the variability of inflation and the variability of real activity.[1] Additionally, any increase in uncertainty is likely to induce sufficient ebbs and flows in consumer/investor confidence to hamper smooth decision making.

The rate of inflation and its variability has an uncertain effect on the average rate of growth of real output in the long run.[2] On the one hand, one might argue that the only operative constraints on long run growth are really long run supplies of factors. If the economy's factor supplies grow at 3 percent per annum, then over the longer run the economy will grow at 3 percent, whatever the inflation rate. On the other hand, the level and variability of the inflation rate may have strong effects on the average level of factor use—the time path of the natural logarithm of real output will shift down with an increase in average inflation. High inflation could lead to a prolonged reduction in the rate of growth as a result of an induced reluctance to invest with highly uncertain real returns. Alternatively, the growth rate may not be noticeably affected, but the economy could always operate at a lower *level* of

[1]Suppose $(\Delta P/P)t = a - b\, Nu_t + e_t,\ a,\ b > 0$, where $\Delta P/P$ is the inflation rate, Nu the unemployment rate, and e an error term independent of Nu. Then, $\sigma^2 \Delta P/P = b^2\, \sigma Nu^2 + \sigma e^2$, $[(d\sigma^2 Nu)/(d\sigma^2 \Delta P/P)] > 0$.

[2]Since countries can be expected to have different underlying growth potentials even at equal inflation rates, the results shown are unlikely to shed much light on the effect of inflation on the *average* growth rate; *average* inflation, however, is unlikely to be the dominant influence on a country's trend growth rate.

activity than it might otherwise achieve. This question, unfortunately, remains open.[3]

One possible empirical experiment might involve examining the experience in each of several countries using a time series approach and relating inflation and its variability to production variability. Unfortunately, a neat measure of the next period's uncertainty that might be suitable for use in such a time series test is not available. Accordingly, we have chosen cross-sectional tests using data from countries that are members of the OECD.

Three simple empirical tests were carried out. Annual data on the rate of consumer price change (CPI) and the *rate* of real growth in industrial production (RGIP) for twenty-four countries[4] for the period 1950 through 1971 were obtained from the Data Resources Incorporated (DRI) data bank. The period was truncated so that confounding effects of floating exchange rates and the world energy situation would be eliminated. From these rates of change, means (—) and standard deviations (σ) were computed.

The following quite simple cross-sectional relationships are implied by our view of the inflation process.[5]

$$\sigma CPI_i = a_0 + a_1 \overline{CPI_i} + \epsilon_i \tag{1}$$

$$\overline{RGIP_i} = b_0 + b_1 \overline{CPI_i} + \epsilon_i \tag{2}$$

$$\overline{RGIP_i} = c_0 + c_1 \sigma CPI_i + \epsilon_i \tag{3}$$

$$^{\sigma}RGIP_i = d_0 + d_1 \overline{CPI_i} + \epsilon_i \tag{4}$$

$$^{\sigma}RGIP_i = e_0 + e_1 \sigma CPI_i + \epsilon_i . \tag{5}$$

We anticipate on the basis of theory and in view of prior empirical work by Gordon [3], Okun [7], and Logue and Willett [6] that $a_1 > 0$. The coefficients b_1 and c_1 should equal zero, in view of the fact that the average long-run growth rate should be unaffected by inflation. Further, we expect both d_1 and e_1 to be positive.

Results shown in Table 1 provide support for each of our contentions.

3. *Conclusions*

Although this study is merely suggestive, two new empirical regularities emerged. First, the mean rate of inflation (and the variability of inflation, to which

[3]Recent work by Fama [1] shows a negative relationship between inflation and real economic activity in the U.S. But further confirmation of the innovative work is necessary before a strong judgment can be made.

[4]Countries included were the United States, the United Kingdom, Austria, Belgium, Denmark, France, Germany, Italy, Luxembourg, the Netherlands, Norway, Sweden, Canada, Japan, Greece, Iceland, Portugal, Australia, Finland, Switzerland, Ireland, Spain, New Zealand, and Turkey.

[5]The specifications of these cross-section regressions can be derived from a number of models. For example, if Phillips curve slope coefficients are equal across countries, these regressions follow. While this assumption is unlikely to be exactly valid, note that random variations in these parameters across countries will bias our estimates downward and will understate the significance of the relationship.

TABLE 1

RELATIONS BETWEEN REAL GROWTH RATES AND INFLATION

	Independent Variables			
Dependent Variable	Constant	$\overline{CPI}$	$^{\sigma}CPI$	R^2_{adj}
$^{\sigma}CPI$	−0.143	0.844		0.74
	(−0.26)	(7.65)*		
$\overline{RGIP}$(a)	4.58	0.211		
	(3.58)*	(0.814)		−0.016
(b)	4.80		0.198	
	(4.31)*		(0.73)	−0.023
$^{\sigma}RGIP$(a)	−0.534	1.40		0.23
	(−0.21)	(2.67)*		
(b)	−1.18		1.89	
	(−0.60)		(3.97)*	0.41

NOTE: t-values are in parentheses below variables.
*Significantly different from zero at the 95 percent confidence level.

the mean is closely related) has little influence on the average growth rate of real output. However, the period investigated was one marked by comparatively high degrees of price stability. Hence, there may have been insufficient variation in the variables to yield definite conclusions about the influence of inflation on growth. Second, and quite significant, the variability in real growth seems to be strongly related to the rate of inflation. Finally, a subsidiary finding is further empirical confirmation that there tends to be a strong positive association between the average rate of inflation and its variability.

Inflation breeds uncertainty in many forms. At very high rates of inflation, the decisions facing producers, consumers, investors, and laborers are made considerably more difficult than they would otherwise be. Indeed, given the uncertainty induced by inflation, it does not seem unreasonable to suggest that the inflation-unemployment trade-off may actually slope upwards. And in this regard our work supports Friedman's [2] views.

While a great deal of progress has been made in recent years in analyzing the microeconomic foundations of inflation and unemployment, our results suggest the importance of devoting greater explicit attention to the effects of inflation on uncertainty and variability in output. There may also be important implications for the analysis of investment. For example, proxies for the uncertainty as to future inflation rates might be appropriately included in neoclassical models of investment behavior, thus perhaps sharpening the predictive ability of those models and giving added insight into the uncertainty effects of inflation.

LITERATURE CITED

1. Fama, Eugene F. "Inflation, Output, and Money." CRSP Working Paper No. 39. Chicago: Graduate School of Business, University of Chicago, May 1980.
2. Friedman, Milton. "Nobel Lecture: Inflation and Unemployment." *Journal of Political Economy,* 85 (June 1977), 451–72.

3. Gordon, Robert J. "Steady Anticipated Inflation: Mirage or Oasis?" *Brookings Papers on Economic Activity,* 2 (1971), 499-510.

4. Jaffee, Dwight E., and Edward Kleiman. "The Welfare Implications of Uneven Inflation." I.E.A. Conference on Inflation Theory and Anti-Inflation Policy, Saltsjobaden, Sweden, 1975.

5. Klein, Benjamin. "Our New Monetary Standard: The Measurement and Effects of Price Uncertainty, 1880-1973." *Economic Inquiry,* 13 (December 1975), 461-84.

6. Logue, Dennis E., and Thomas D. Willett. "A Note on the Relation Between the Rate and Variability of Inflation." *Economica,* 43 (May 1976), 151-58.

7. Okun, Arthur M. "The Mirage of Steady Inflation." *Brookings Papers on Economic Activity,* 2 (1971), 485-98.

8. Parks, Richard W. "Inflation and Relative Price Variability." *Journal of Political Economy,* 86 (February 1978), 79-95.

BOOK REVIEWS

Modelling the International Transmission Mechanism

Edited by John A. Sawyer. Amsterdam: North-Holland, 1979. x + 423 pp. $73.00

A Review Essay by John T. Cuddington

"This is the third in a series of volumes arising out of Project LINK, an international research project designed to integrate national econometric models in order to improve predictions of the effects of various policies and events upon world trade and to deepen understanding of how international fluctuations are transmitted" (p. vii). The book reports on LINK research undertaken since the publication of the earlier volumes by Ball [1] and Waelbroeck [2] up to the summer of 1977. It is full of model-building exercises, tests of the adequacy of those models, their forecasting abilities, and simulation exercises. Consequently, it makes for slow, difficult, and sometimes tedious reading for those who have not invested a considerable amount of time becoming familiar with the LINK system.

Although the introductory chapter by editor John Sawyer sketches the contributions in the first two volumes before summarizing the articles in the present one, this reader found it annoying not to have a more complete description of the LINK system at the outset so that the importance of the various articles could be better understood and assessed more critically. In fairness to the editor, he references summary statements of the LINK system which appeared in the first volume. Nevertheless, a brief recapitulation would greatly increase the readability of the book for the uninitiated reader. Given the high cost of the individual volumes (this one is $73) greater independence would also be worthwhile.

The reader who is unfamiliar with the primary features of the LINK system would benefit greatly from reading the introductory sections of chapter 10 (pp. 219–20), chapter 5 (pp. 97–107), chapter 4 (pp. 73–75), and the introductory chapter before embarking on the rest of parts 1–3.

As the aforementioned pages reveal, "The core of the Project LINK system is formed from the union of thirteen medium to large scale econometric models of the most important industrialized countries. . . . Many of the models predate the Link project itself. . . . Moreover, with but one exception each of the models was con-

JOHN T. CUDDINGTON *is assistant professor of economics, Stanford University.*

0022-2879/81/1181-0502$00.50/0
JOURNAL OF MONEY, CREDIT, AND BANKING, vol. 13, no. 4 (November 1981)

ceived, designed, estimated, and continues to be maintained in the country which is modeled'' (Johnson, p. 219). As Hickman and Lima point out, ''These country models are largely dynamic systems of Keynesian lineage. Output is proximately determined by real effective demand. In most of the models inverted production functions determine employment as a function of output. Wages are usually explained by a Phillips curve and prices by a mark-up hypothesis. In addition, import or export prices are also a direct determinant of domestic prices in most cases. Money matters for prices in most of the models because interest rates or liquid assets affect aggregate demand and hence the excess demand for labor and the rate of change of money wages and prices . . ., however, there is considerable variety in the monetary specifications of the models'' (p. 98). In addition to the thirteen major industrial country models, the LINK system includes ''a small system of models for developing regions . . ., a model for the USSR and a model for the other socialist countries together. The rest of the world, which is nontrivial in size, is treated in one block and is called the ROW model'' (Klein-Tishler, p. 74).

Although the individual models can be used separately for comparative single-country simulation exercises (the ''pre-LINK'' mode), one of the objectives of the LINK project has been to link these models together through their trade flows in a systematic way. To do this, equations explaining export volumes and import prices (if they are not assumed to be exogenous) in the individual country models are suppressed. The LINK system then endogenizes countries' export volumes and import prices by linking the national models through merchandise trade flows and solving the models simultaneously, recognizing that one country's (or region's) imports must be another's exports, and that one country's import price must be a weighted average of the export prices of her supplying countries (Gana et al., p. 9). This is not done by modeling the export supplies and import demands for each country separately to explain all bilateral trade flows. Such an approach would be intractable given the large number of countries and regions included in LINK even if commodity groups are highly aggregated. LINK disaggregates total trade into four commodity groups: (1) food, beverages, and tobacco—SITC 0+1; (2) raw materials—SITC 2+4; (3) fuels—SITC 3; and (4) manufactures and others—SITC 5-9.

Instead LINK employs a ''trade share matrix'' approach whereby a country's *i*'s exports of a particular commodity group are assumed to be a weighted average of all other countries' imports of those commodities. The weight given to each country *j*'s imports is equal to the share of the *i*th country's exports in the *j*th country's imports. The procedure ensures that the world total of calculated (as opposed to actual) exports for each commodity group equals the total amount of imports generated by all of the country/region models. Of course, if the original country model specifies both an import and an export function, there is no reason that the export level predicted by that export function will be the same as that predicted by the trade share matrix approach. To ensure that the LINK system is internally consistent, the export functions in the individual models were suppressed in the ''post-LINK'' mode. Using the same trade share matrices (for each commodity group), countries' import prices are generated as a trade-weighted average of the export prices of their various suppliers.

As Gana et al. explain, ''exports and the import prices predicted by the trade share matrix approach are fed back into the country models. This will cause a series of adjustments in the endogenous variables of the individual country models, including both imports and export prices. On the basis of this information, the exports and import prices are updated again using the trade share matrix. This process is continued until convergence is obtained'' (p. 11). Klein and Tishler point out that ''the use of such a system requires that imports and exports (quantities and prices) of all individual models are expressed in the same units of measurement. So, while each model solves for import volumes and export prices in its own currency units, conversion equations in U.S. dollars were introduced so as to make possible the use of the trade model. *This is the main point at which exchange rates enter the system.* Solutions for export volumes and import prices are subsequently converted back to the individual model's currency after they leave the LINK module and re-enter the individual country/region models'' (p. 75, emphasis mine).

Having briefly outlined the current nature of the LINK system, I turn to the individual papers. Part 1 is devoted to the use of the LINK system for forecasting world trade. The first article by Gana et al., entitled ''Alternative Approaches to the Linkage of National Econometric Models,'' discusses four different methods of generating the trade share matrices used in linking the country models. The conceptual ''approach'' to linkage remains the same in each case, however. Each of the four methods was used in making dynamic two-period forecasts of export and import volumes and prices for 1971 and 1972. The results are compared to actual values for those years. The authors conclude that the LINK model's predictions for import and export prices are not sensitive to the linkage method employed, whereas import and export volumes are.

The following paper by Johnson and Klein provides a detailed error analysis of the LINK system based on single period and dynamic forecasts. A paper by Klein and Tishler then presents a simplified version of the world trade model designed for long-term forecasting as opposed to the short-term horizon of the full system.

Part 2 presents a number of simulation exercises undertaken by participants in the LINK project since *The Models of Project LINK* [2]. The Hickman-Lima paper (''Price Determination and the Transmission of Inflation in the LINK System'') investigates the effects of exogenous wage shocks in each of the major industrial countries and the extent to which they are transmitted internationally. The introductory sections of their paper comparing the specification of the wage and price equations in each country model are extremely interesting. They provide a valuable summary of current practices for modeling the ''supply-side'' in various medium- to large-scale macroeconometric models.

The remaining two papers in part 2 consider various stabilization policies, some of which were proposed in 1975–76 to stimulate the world economy. Weinberg's paper simulates three policy options: (1) revaluation by groups of ''strong'' currency countries, (2) fiscal stimuli in the stronger countries (that presumably had idle capacity), and (3) a nominal transfer of purchasing power to the developing countries. The emphasis is on the effects of these policies on foreigners as well as on the domestic economy. The first two policies he finds have only small repercussion effects—in contrast to the conjectures of much 1975–76 policy discussion advocating a ''locomotive'' approach to world economic recovery. The transfer payment simulations indicated, however, that ''substantial real gains can be realized by the introduction of new nominal purchasing power into the world economy'' (p. 135). Unfortunately, this simulation makes the unrealistic assumption that the exogenous transfer of wealth to the LDCs comes from an unspecified source. Weinberg's assertion that "this transfer could represent the gift of profits from the sales of IMF gold reserves to the developing regions" (p. 130) is unacceptable because there is no attempt to model the effect that the requisite gold sales would have on the purchasing nations. A preferable approach would have been to consider a transfer from a developed country(ies) within the model rather than some autonomous agent such as the IMF, which is outside the model.

The Klein, Su, and Beaumont paper examines the effects of "Coordination of International Fiscal Policies and Exchange Rate Revaluations" by conducting a number of simulations where several countries embark on a fiscal expansion and/or revalue their exchange rates simultaneously. While these exercises are interesting in themselves, this reviewer objects to the implication that what is being discussed is policy "coordination." The latter presumably involves an ongoing commitment to harmonize policy, not merely a one-time policy action undertaken simultaneously in several nations.

Part 3 on "Country and Commodity Models in the LINK System" pursues two lines of research. The first involves efforts to improve the specification of the various aggregate regional models representing groups of LDCs, centrally planned economies, and the ROW, which comprises the smaller developed economies that are not modeled individually in LINK. The second line of research attempts to incorporate primary commodity models into the LINK system.

Since 1972 when a set of four fully specified regional models for the LDCs were incorporated into the LINK, it has become necessary to make substantial changes in the country aggregations to take account of the realities of the world oil situation. The Glowacki-Ruffing paper reports on recent model modifications. In contrast to the earlier versions, prices of primary commodities have now been endogenized through the addition of simple two-equation reduced-form commodity models.

Keith Johnson's paper describes a set of small individual models for each of the small developed countries that are presently represented by the ROW model. Costa and Menshikov describe evolving LINK procedures for modeling the six centrally planned Eastern European countries.

The remaining papers in part 3, like the Glowacki-Ruffing paper on LDCs, recognize the growing importance of world commodity market developments on the international economy. Sawyer and Obidegwu demonstrate how a commodity market model can be incorporated into a developed economy's macro model, using a copper-nickel model and the TRACE model of the Canadian economy. A paper by Adams takes on the task of integrating the process of price determination for primary commodities into LINK. This is accomplished combining a total of twenty-three existing models for thirty commodities to form the COMLINK model, which can then be used in tandem with the LINK system. At the present time, the most important commodity, petroleum, is not included in COMLINK. Exploratory simulations indicate that although real economic activity (as well as commodity prices, trade, and domestic prices) is influenced by the inclusion of COMLINK in the world trade model, "the impact on domestic economies is quite small, as is the impact of feedback on the commodity markets themselves" (p. 293). Although research on this topic is unfinished, this revelation suggests that the fruits of such labor may be rather limited.

Part 4 is directed towards the eventual resolution of what I see as the major deficiencies of the LINK model: its failure to allow for flexible exchange rates and international capital flows. As two of the authors point out, ''Work is progressing on the capital account, but meanwhile the simulations with the present system must be evaluated without endogenous feedbacks from payments imbalances to domestic money stocks and without international linkages of interest rates through capital markets. Exchange rates are also exogenous in the system, and the multipliers must be interpreted accordingly as applying to a regime of fixed or managed floating rates'' (p. 98). Even this is a sympathetic interpretation of the adequacy of exchange rates in the LINK system. Unlike a numeraire, an exchange rate cannot just be decreed to be fixed by the model builder. A country's commitment to an exchange rate target imposes constraints, sometimes extremely limiting ones, on domestic and foreign monetary authorities. It is unsatisfactory just to assume fixed rates and then allow monetary authorities all the latitude that they would have in a completely closed economy. It is essential that international financial markets be modeled explicitly before the domestic and international implications of fixed or dirty/clean floating rates can be fully understood.

Furthermore, any model that permits countries' trade balances to be nonzero (which the LINK system certainly does) automatically implies that there must be equal and offsetting (private and official) capital flows, according to well-known balance of payments accounting identities. Thus, there is an implicit specification of total international capital flows in the LINK system. The problem is that, being implicit, the specification is likely to be far from what any economic model builder would deem acceptable.

The papers in part 4 (''Future Development of the National Models: Monetary Sector and Capital Flows'') acknowledge the unsophisticated state of the financial sectors in many of the national models in the LINK system. None of the papers, however, deals with the LINK system directly. A paper by Ball and Burns focuses on the importance of ensuring that economic models have a long-run portfolio equilibrium consistent with their balance of payments and government deficit financing specifications. Their discussion mirrors the plea for stock-flow consistency that simple monetarist and portfolio models of the balance of payments have emphasized. Lybeck, Häggström, and Järnhäll follow up on this theme by empirically testing four possible specifications (two ''monetarist'' and two ''portfolio'' models) of international capital flows for Sweden, 1967–75. Krelle, Conrad, Grisse, and Martiensen provide an interim report on the development of a sophisticated monetary sector with endogenous exchange rates for the Bonn forecasting model of the German economy. Using the model, the effects of domestic monetary and fiscal policy changes and external disturbances are simulated.

Much difficult work remains if the LINK model is to embody recent theoretical developments in international monetary economics. ''The LINK system is now in the process of being extended to include capital flows and to make exchange rates endogenous. In many cases this requires further developments of the monetary sectors of the (individual country) models'' (p. 5). It is this reviewer's suspicion that an adequate characterization of national financial markets and international capital flows will reveal much about the international transmission of real as well as monetary disturbances. It is hard to imagine, for example, how the international effects of oil price hikes can be properly analyzed without acknowledging the concomitant financial transfers and recycling problem.

This book should prove to be an important reference work for those with an ongoing interest in large-scale macroeconometric model building.

LITERATURE CITED

1. Ball, Robert J. (ed.). *The International Linkage of National Economic Models*. Amsterdam: North-Holland, 1973.

2. Waelbroeck, Jean L. (ed.). *The Models of Project LINK*. Amsterdam: North-Holland, 1976.

Expected Utility Hypotheses and the Allais Paradox, edited by Maurice Allais and Ole Hagen. Hingham, Mass.: D. Reidel Publishing Co., 1979. vii + 714 pp. $86.85

This volume is concerned with the controversy, initiated by Maurice Allais in 1952, over the von Neumann-Morgenstern approach to decision making in the presence of risk. (The von Neumann-Morgenstern position is also identified as that of the ''American School'' and the ''Neo-Bernoullian Position'' throughout the volume).

The volume is presented in five parts. Part 1 consists of a foreword by Allais and an introductory survey by Ole Hagen.

''The Foundations of a Positive Theory of Choice Involving Risk and a Critique of the Postulates and Axioms of the American School,'' a paper running about 120 pages, which presents Allais's 1952 position, constitutes part 2 of the volume.

Part 3 consists of five papers presenting—and defending—the Neo-Bernoullian position. Yakov Amihud opens part 3 with a paper arguing that Allais and Hagen have misinterpreted the von Neumann-Morgenstern theory and that the Allais-Hagen theory itself is ''lacking in predictive power.'' De Finetti—in a one-page statement—reaffirms his faith in the von Neuman-Morgenstern theory. Marschak compares the Allais and ''American School'' theories and argues that neither theory is going to describe completely observed behavior. Marschak emphasizes the normative aspect of both theories and suggests that perhaps what is needed is education to train people to act in accordance with axioms that define rational behavior. Morgenstern, in an essay entitled ''Some Reflections on Utility'' criticizes Allais and the other detractors of the von Neumann-Morgenstern theory for focusing their criticisms on the axioms of the theory. Part 3 concludes by a rejoinder by Amihud to comments of Allais on Amihud's position.

Part 4 entitled ''Contemporary Views on the Neo-Bernoullian Theory and the Allais Paradox'' opens with a paper by Karl Borch on stochastic dominance, in which Borch points out that first-order stochastic dominance is the main axiom (''axiom of absolute preference'') in Allais's model. A. Camacho presents an axiom set on the preference ordering of infinite sequences of a finite number of prizes and derives utility indices for these prizes. In particular Camacho's results appear to be consistent with a claim made by Allais. Cyert and DeGroot in ''Adaptive Utility'' utilize this approach to cope with inconsistencies of the Allais paradox variety. Fishburn sets forth a weaker axiom system than von Neumann-Morgenstern used, but points out that the inconsistencies discovered by Allais and others still cannot be precluded. Gorovitz modifies the St. Petersburg paradox by putting a bound on payoffs, and notes that the "puzzle" persists that it is "reasonable" to refuse to play. Ole Hagen offers a model that predicts paradoxes of the Allais type and presents results of experiments with school teachers that exhibit deviation from behavior predicted by the von Neumann-Morgenstern model. Leinfellner and Booth discuss two approaches to decision making called "naturalistic" and "intuitionistic." MacCrimmon and Larsson compare the axiom systems of von Neumann-Morgenstern, Marschak, Savage, and Arrow in the first part of their paper "Utility Theory: Axioms versus 'Paradoxes.'" They go on to perform experiments which yield "paradoxical" results, but the rate of violation of the utility axioms decreases sharply as the probability and payoff parameters are varied away from critical levels. Menges concludes part 4 of the volume with a discussion of six decision models which are distinguished from each other on the basis of whether: (1) consequences are "original" or "transferred" (e.g., outcome = "original," utility of outcome = "transferred") and (2) probabilities are a priori or a posteriori or subjective.

Part 5 consists of a restatement by Allais of his position, a criticism of post-1952 theories of the "American School," and a rebuttal of critics of his theory.

Perhaps MacGrimmon and Larsson get to the essence of the controversy best when they say that, given violations of axioms, three options exist: (1) "maintain the choices . . . and conclude that the axioms are not relevant, (2) change their choices to bring them in line with the axioms, or (3) change the theory to make it consistent with their choices."

RUBIN SAPOSNIK
University of Kentucky

International Lending, Risk and the Euro-Markets, by Anthony Angelini, Maximo Eng, and Francis A. Lees. New York: Wiley, 1979. xi + 213 pp. $19.95

The Financing of Long-Term Development, The Institute of Bankers, London: The Institute of Bankers, 1979. xi + 206 pp. £7.50

International Lending, Risk and Euro-Markets deals with five principal issues: the history of lending since the beginning of the century, the changing role of commercial banks in international lending, lending to less-developed countries (LDCs), risk analysis, and the prospects for new forms of lending.

The historical review highlights the major changes that have taken place in "circumstances, participants, lending activities and results." Until World War I, England was the principal source of international financing; since then, the U.S.A. has risen to a position of dominance. After 1973, the accumulation of OPEC surpluses has brought about major changes in international lending and has greatly strengthened the role of the Euromarket.

Commitment on the part of developed countries (DCs) to the promotion of global welfare is a new phenomenon and has become apparent only after World War II: the

Marshall Plan, Truman's Point-Four foreign aid program and its successors, aid programs of DCs, and concessionary financing through international funding institutions are some of the principal manifestations of this commitment. During the 1945–60 period, concessionary financing has become a major factor in funding development; the United States alone spent close to $100 billion on foreign aid.

Prior to World War I, investments in LDCs were predominantly (80 percent) of a portfolio nature, whereas in recent transfers, loans to governments became predominant. The role of commercial banks in loans to LDCs was negligible until World War II: since the mid-1970s, it has kept at, or above, the 40 percent level. The sudden influx into commercial banks of huge short-term deposits from OPEC countries and the relending of a substantial portion of these deposits as medium-term loans to LDCs have created a potentially dangerous discrepancy between maturity profiles. Defaulting is still insignificant; but the fact that it has occurred in the past following every major political and economic upheaval is causing uneasiness in banking circles.

The various routines employed by financing institutions to analyze *country* risks are treated extensively by the authors. They stress that if commercial lending will in the future have to be extended to cover program funding also, commercial banks will have to supplement country risk analysis by program risk analysis. Also reviewed are innovative procedures that might become necessary to cope with the rapidly growing financial requirements of LDCs in the 1980s.

The Financing of Long-Term Development comprises eight papers presented by prestigious academic teachers and practitioners in August 1979, at the 32nd International Banking Summer School at Cambridge.

Sir Jeremy Mores's opening essay points out that lending risks associated with LDC development seem larger than they really are, since the big borrowers are mostly the newly industrializing countries (NICs), which have succeeded in rapidly expanding their exports. However, with the anticipated shift of emphasis to investments in the traditional sector and the poorer LDCs, risks are liable to increase.

Professor Peter Odell's paper on global energy needs presents the interesting thesis that our current estimate of the distribution of global oil and gas reserves is a product of historic accident and commerical bias. He sees no reason to doubt that substantial reserves exist in many of the underexplored countries, especially in some LDCs. The development of these additional reserves could sustain a primarily fossil-fuel-based energy economy until the end of the first quarter of the twenty-first century and arrest monopolistic rises of oil price.

Dr. Wilfred Guth stresses the existence in LDCs of institutional limitations to the efficient absorption of investment capital. He warns against yielding to LDC pressures to adopt less-selective loan procedures which would reduce efficiency in the allocation and utilization of funds. Dr. Guth sees the problem of financing in the 1980s less in the expansion of the volume of LDC borrowing than in the discrepancy in maturities between bank deposits and loans.

Quentin Morris's paper points out that investments in large energy-related projects, requiring capital outlays in the billion-dollar range, might be difficult to finance. In his opinion, the U.S. financial market is better adapted for this scale of financing. Professor David T. Llewellyn differentiates between financial and real resources transfer. He calls attention to the disturbing fact that, by 1985, debt servicing will absorb more than one half of total financial transfers to LDCs. His conclusion is that "no reasonable solution will emerge without a major political commitment by . . . the industrialized world to accept the transfer of real resources." Deryl Vander Weyer doubts that the preconditions for the requisite expansion of capital transfers to LDCs in the 1980s could, in fact, be met and that Eurocredits could continue to expand at the rate achieved during the last few years.

Although both books deal with the transfer of funds from DCs to cover the financial requirements of LDCs, the different background of the authors has led to different analytical perspectives. *The Financing of Long-Term Development,* written by practitioners for practitioners, deals with the actual changes that have recently occurred in the international financial system and attempts to anticipate problems that probably will have to be faced in the early 1980s. *International Lending, Risks and Euro-Markets,* written by academic analysts, reviews the same problems within a broader historic framework, with special emphasis on the changing role of the Euromarkets in international lending and on the increasing need of strengthening risk analysis.

In spite of differences in emphasis and perspective, the authors of both books arrive at similar conclusions. The steep rise in the balance of trade deficits resulting from rises in oil prices, the growing capital requirements of development, and the increase in the loan servicing burden have substantially augmented the need of LDCs for external financing. Because official development aid (ODA) rose only slightly during the late 1970s (17 percent in real terms between 1975 and 1980), LDCs had to have an increasing recourse to commercial sources to meet their financial requirements. At the same time, the need for recycling the large petrodollar surpluses created by OPEC since the mid-1970s has vastly increased the availability of short-term capital from commercial banks.

This has brought about a radical change in the sources of financing for LDC development. Private banks have become the principal instrument of financing LDCs. In 1978, out of a total flow of $56.8 billion from DAC (Development Assistance Committee) countries to LDCs, only $18.3 billion represented official development aid (ODA). The 1970 figures were $15.8 billion and $6.8 billion, respectively.

Increased capital flows to LDCs have undoubtedly contributed to their impressive average growth rates. In the 1970–80 decade, the GNP of LDCs increased at an annual rate of 5.2 percent (in real terms), as compared with 3.4 percent in DCs. However, it must be borne in mind that these average growth rates mask an unequal distribution within the LDC bloc: growth rates in the higher- and middle-income LDCs were considerably higher than those in the lower-income countries.

The rapid increase in short-term borrowing of LDCs in the second half of the 1970s will substantially increase their loan servicing burden in the coming years; some LDCs might find this burden unbearably difficult to sustain.

Problems of LDC financing in the 1980s are liable to be more exacting than those encountered in the 1970s. According to a 1979 World Bank forecast, the external financing requirements of LDCs may, by 1985, reach the figure of about $250 billion, out of which more than one-half might be needed for debt servicing. To meet such financial requirements and to keep debt servicing burdens at sustainable levels, ODA, and other forms of public-sources financing, will have to be expanded and new forms of commercial financing will have to be explored.

In spite of the satisfactory debt servicing performances of the principal borrowing countries in the 1970s, banks are preoccupied with the potentially damaging repercussions to the international financial market should one of the principal borrowing countries fail to meet its financial obligations. In the 1980s, risk and risk reduction are likely to become dominant issues. To achieve a reduction of risks to a point where the stability of the international financial system would be ensured, new policies will have to be devised, both at the borrowing and at the lending end. This is also the conclusion of the Independent Commission on International Development Issues under the chairmanship of Willy Brandt whose concrete suggestions on the matter deserve attention.

The great flexibility and adaptability demonstrated during the 1970s by the international financial community may justify the degree of optimism that the authors of both books profess regarding prospects for the 1980s. Nonetheless, and as far as one can venture to predict, the 1980s promise to be more demanding than the 1970s, and new problems will have to be dealt with both on the supply side (sources of funds) and on the demand side (capital needs and lending risks). The growth of the principal demand components (current account deficits), parallel with the expected growth of supply (primarily OPEC surpluses), suggest, however, that an equilibrium could somehow evolve in due course.

The bulk of financing will probably have to be handled by private banks, in which a considerable portion of OPEC surpluses will presumably continue to be invested. As in the 1970s, private banks will, with increasing apprehension, primarily cater to the needs of the more credit-worthy borrowers. This will leave the handling of loans for the fifty to eighty poorer LDCs to international institutions (IMF, World Bank, regional banks, bilateral aid). International institutions might, however, find it difficult to raise sufficient funds to finance these countries' current account deficits as well as their development projects, these coming on top of the current account deficits of middle- and high-income LDCs and of some DCs.

On the supply side, the 1980 OPEC current account surplus is estimated at around $100 billion. By the end of September 1979 the main international banks had foreign deposits of over $1,000 billion, representing a doubling within a four-year period. The future size of OPEC surpluses will depend principally on the prices and volumes of exports and imports of the OPEC countries. Forecasting OPEC pricing policies has proven an unrewarding task; however, a safe guess would be that—contingencies apart—OPEC will, from time to time, adjust prices and volumes to ensure a hefty current account surplus with the rest of the world. Moreover, imports of the main oil exporters with relatively small populations may be assumed not to grow as rapidly as they did in the mid-1970s.

As for the financial requirements of DCs, funds will, above all, be needed to finance their current account deficits with OPEC. Huge investments will also be required for their "depetroleumization." Trade with the Eastern bloc will likewise require considerable financing. Investment requirements for general economic growth may prove to be modest.

The financing demands of LDCs will be associated with a number of essential needs including: current account deficits, estimated to reach $50 billion in 1980; development projects, and especially projects to cater for the "basic needs" of the less-developed areas in the LDCs; projects in the fields of energy, mineral resources development, and infrastructure; and industrial development projects and associated infrastructure, especially in the newly industrializing countries (NICs).

Something more than incremental institutional adaptation of the international market will be needed. In the words of the Brandt Commission Report: "There is serious doubt as to whether adjustments to international balance of payments problems and the management of world liquidity and debt can be achieved adequately by the existing machinery" (*North-South: A Program for Survival* [London: Pan Books, 1980], p. 261). Institutional innovations might have to extend, as hinted at by the authors of both books, to a broader application of new types of cooperation and division of labor between international financing institutions and private banks, including joint financing ventures of public and private capital. Forms and conditions of this cooperation would have to ensure adequate capital transfers, while discouraging private banks from subscribing unwarranted risks and prospective borrowers from applying for loans that cannot be justified on economic grounds and such that these countries may be unable to service.

A number of additional approaches might have to be explored to reconcile the financial needs of LDCs with the stability requirements of the international market. OPEC depositors ought to be urged to accept longer maturities; after all, they should be interested in the stability of the financial market as much as the private banks in which most of their surpluses will be deposited. Access of the poorer LDCs to the financial market could be improved and their debt servicing burdens lightened if some concessionary funds were used to subsidize interest rates for "basic needs" projects. The Brandt Commission has arrived at similar conclusions, urging that concessionary funds be used to subsidize interest rates so that poorer countries can also take advantage of commercial bank loans (*North-South: A Program for Survival,* p. 275).

The IMF might have to moderate the deflationary conditions it specifies for the approval of loans. The *Economist* put it neatly (March 15, 1980) when it argued that in the 1980s the emphasis in IMF programs ought to be changed from adjustment (synonymous with deflation) to efficiency (which should mean faster growth), and that as long as OPEC can price-fix itself a large surplus, the health of the world financial system actually needs economies that grow fast enough to service their foreign debts, not ones that deflate far enough to throw off deficits.

In conclusion, what emerges from this discussion is that international financial institutions will have to rise to their responsibility of acting as guardians of the world economy; as such, they will have to promote and support economic growth in LDCs—and especially growth aimed at "basic needs"—whatever short-term ledger entries on the deficit side this might involve. This would be sound global economic policy; it might, even in the medium term, prove to be also sound accounting policy.

The adaptation of the international financial system to the not fully predictable needs of the 1980s is predicated upon many hypothetical "ifs." However, past performance should not refute cautious optimism, if two fundamental conditions can be fulfilled. On the lending side, the chief protagonists, that is, public and commercial lending institutions, would have to reach consensus on new ways of mutual cooperation that would ensure adequate capital flows to LDCs, without endangering the solvency and the stability of the system. On the borrowing side, lower- and medium-income LDCs would have to opt for using their share in these flows, above all for investments for short- and medium-term programs, aimed primarily at meeting the basic needs of their populations.

RUTH WIENER ARAD

Tel-Aviv University

Demand for Financial Assets: An Econometric Study of the U.K. Personal Sector, by D. K. Bhattacharyya. Farnborough, England: Saxon House, 1978. ix + 197 pp. $21.00

This monograph is based on the author's Ph.D. thesis that was submitted to the University of Essex in 1975. Its aim is to estimate the demand for financial assets in the U.K. personal sector. The assets studied include money, near-monies, stocks, and long-term debt. The primary purpose of the study is to measure the degree of substitutability between the different financial assets in the personal sector's portfolio. Bhattacharyya's methodology involves an optimization approach utilizing various portfolio equilibrium models. Estimates of substitutability relations among financial assets in the personal sector balance sheet provide information on the degree of money near-money substitutability and, hence, on the appropriate definition of money, in addition to information on the impact of monetary policy. The study also tests the appropriateness of alternative portfolio model specifications.

The monograph is divided into six chapters. Chapter 1 is a very cursory and unenlightening description of what is to follow. Chapter 2 repeats Chetty's well-known study on the substitutability of near-monies—what the author calls, in standard British nomenclature, capital-certain assets—using a ten-year quarterly data base (1955–66) provided by R. J. Barret, M. R. Gray, and J. M. Parkin ("The Demand for Financial Assets by the Personal Sector of the U.K. Economy," in *Modelling the Economy,* G. A. Renton [London: Heinemann Educational Books, 1975]). The capital-certain assets include demand deposits, deposits with Building Societies, Trustee Savings Bank and Ordinary Savings Bank deposits, National Savings Certificates, and Defense/Development bonds. Two classifications of less liquid assets, namely, government marketable bonds and company and overseas (equity) securities, are also included in the study. To avoid the criticisms leveled at the Chetty study, the author respecifies the wealth constraint properly and utilizes two-stage least squares and nonlinear estimation procedures to get around the problems of simultaneous equations bias and of constraints on the parameters. Although the author finds that his elasticity of substitution estimates between the different capital-certain assets are not very robust across the various estimation techniques, he is nevertheless able to conclude that Building Society and Trustee Savings Bank deposits are closer substitutes for money than demand deposits. One important conclusion from chapter 2 is that deposits with nonbank financial intermediaries have a significant impact on monetary policy. The analysis of this section also provides a basis of comparison with the portfolio model specifications developed in the subsequent chapters.

The remainder of the monograph extends the analysis by placing the asset demand problem into a portfolio framework. In chapter 3, which forms the bulk of the study, asset demand functions are developed within the single-period mean-variance portfolio framework. (A very sketchy and nonrigorous theoretical justification of the mean-variance framework is provided.) Asset-substitution relationships are derived and estimated using a variety of econometric specification techniques. The performance of models based on alternative specifications of the mean-variance utility function is also examined. Initially, empirical results are obtained on substitution relationships between capital-certain assets. The findings confirm the results of chapter 2 that Building Society and Trustee Savings Bank deposits are closer substitutes to money than demand deposits. Subsequently, the effect of aggregation on asset demand functions is examined by considering demand relationships for three aggregate classifications of financial assets, namely, all capital-certain assets, total government securities, and company and overseas securities. The empirical results here are quite sensitive to the actual specifications used. Nevertheless, they indicate that a portfolio decision model based on the exponential utility function is superior in terms of forecasting than one based on quadratic utility. The results also indicate that the most empirically plausible specification of the individual's objective function is one where terminal wealth is maximized in real terms.

Chapter 4 utilizes a multiperiod portfolio model involving dynamic programming. It is assumed that the individual decision maker's objective is to maximize the discounted utility of consumption flow over a finite time horizon. Furthermore, it is assumed that the investor has a target terminal wealth and exogenously given initial wealth, and that he evaluates and adjusts his portfolio at the end of each accounting period on the basis of state variable values at each stage. The empirical implementation is through an approximation to the optimum portfolio model developed and focuses on only the three broad classes of assets already treated in chapter 3. The main conclusion that emerges (which indirectly supports Friedman's view) is that the demand for assets is primarily determined by total financial wealth rather than rates of return.

A major shortcoming of the framework used in chapter 3 is that it relies totally on pecuniary returns (within the mean-variance framework) to analyze portfolio choice, ignoring the impact of nonpecuniary returns on portfolio choice. Yet an analysis of the demand for liquidity should ideally provide a more general specification allowing for liquidity and other nonpecuniary asset characteristics. The final model, presented in chapter 5, makes some attempt at remedying this deficiency by combining the less restrictive Chetty framework of chapter 2 and the mean-variance framework of chapter 3 within a general Lancaster characteristics framework. However, the integration is not altogether satisfactory because it is assumed that nonpecuniary returns on assets are proportional to the level of asset holdings—an approach that fails to incorporate liquidity considerations. The empirical specification is through a log-linear approximation with the focus on the set of capital-certain assets studied earlier. The results are highly tentative but seem to match those of chapters 2 and 3.

The results of the study are difficult to disentangle and interpret given the variety of different theoretical and empirical techniques that are utilized. Chapter 6, the concluding chapter, represents a very weak attempt at synthesizing the results. It is therefore difficult to derive strong public policy implications—both on the issue of money near-money substitutability and on the more general portfolio substitution properties so important to monetary policy—from the study. Nevertheless, the study is to be admired for its quantitative rigor and should prove very useful to researchers interested in the many facets relating to the empirical implementation of portfolio models.

VAROUJ A. AIVAZIAN
McMaster University

The Regulation of Financial Institutions, Federal Reserve Bank of Boston, Conference Series No. 21. Boston: Federal Reserve Bank of Boston, 1980. 266 pp. Free upon request

For more than a decade, the Federal Reserve Bank of Boston has been sponsoring a series of conferences on economic issues of current public policy interest. The theme of a recent conference was the regulation of financial institutions, and this proceedings volume contains eight papers, as well as discussants' comments, covering a variety of aspects of the subject.

As one should expect from a two-day conference, coverage of this broad topic is far from comprehensive. The conference organizers chose studies that treat relatively limited issues in some depth rather than a set of surveys, and hence the book will be of greater interest to specialists than to those seeking an overview of the subject.

Nevertheless, the papers represent two broad categories of regulation that appear in the economy generally as well as the financial institutions sphere. The first, or ''traditional'' type of regulation is typically aimed at maintaining some form of stability in a particular industry through the use of price and entry controls and sometimes financial soundness requirements. Among nonfinancial industries, examples would include regulation of railroads and trucking by the Interstate Commerce Commission and, until recently at least, of airlines by the Civil Aeronautics Board. Among financial institutions, much of the regulation of the banking, thrift, and insurance industries has been of the traditional type. In both spheres, traditional regulation has tended to resolve perceived conflicts between stability and competition on the side of stability. Traditional forms of regulation, however, have been the most frequent targets of deregulation efforts in recent years.

The other broad category, sometimes referred to as ''social'' regulation, is typically of more recent origin and has been rapidly proliferating. Frequently emphasizing the primacy of ''human'' over economic rights, this type of regulation cuts across industry lines to protect various consumer or worker groups from what are perceived to be socially undesirable practices by firms. In the nonfinancial sphere, examples include the work of the Consumer Product Safety Commission, the Occupational Safety and Health Administration, and the Equal Opportunity Commission, while among financial institutions, much of recent legislation aimed at consumer and mortgage lending practices is of this type.

Of the eight papers in this volume, three concern themselves with traditional forms of regulation, and the rest deal with social regulation. In the first group are a paper on the effects of Regulation Q on savings bank solvency by Richard Kopcke and Geoffrey Woglom, a paper on bank capital adequacy by Sherman Maisel, and a paper on capital requirements for entry in the property and liability insurance industry by J. D. Hammond and Arnold Shapiro. All three exhibit the "traditional" concern with the trade-off between competition and stability.

The Kopcke and Woglom paper attempts to compute "current value," or market value composite balance sheets for Connecticut mutual savings banks in order to determine the degree of solvency protection afforded them by deposit rate ceilings during the volatile interest rate periods of the late sixties and seventies. The basic idea behind the analysis is that while rising interest rates reduce the value of long-term savings bank assets, they also reduce the true value of rate-constrained savings deposits below their face value. In the absence of deposit rate ceilings, by contrast, short-term deposits will pay higher rates, and hence the market value of their net worth will be lower during such periods. Their conclusion from these calculations is that ceilings have provided "limited but critical, aid" to savings banks during high interest rate periods, but that this protection has tended to erode over time as more avenues for disintermediation have opened.

The calculations are, of course, fraught with perils, many of which are brought out either by the authors themselves or in the discussion by Donald Tucker. Despite such difficulties, however, the paper's basic conclusions accord with theory and intuition. Of particular interest are a set of calculations indicating that better matching of the term structure of savings bank assets and liabilities would have a greater salutary effect on net worth than deposit rate ceilings have ever had.

The papers by Maisel and by Hammond and Shapiro are complementary to each other since both discuss the usefulness of statistics and portfolio theory in helping regulators define and measure adequate capital for financial institutions. The ultimate aim of the Maisel paper is to use these analytical tools to determine fair deposit insurance premia for commercial banks, thereby reducing the moral hazard element inherent in the current system. This, in turn, would reduce the need for detailed portfolio regulation, and banks could be left free to take greater risks as long as they paid an appropriate premium for doing so. Among the conclusions emerging from an analysis of commercial bank loss experience are that the entire bank portfolio must be considered as a unit and that interest rate risk is a very significant and perhaps neglected element of overall bank risk. The paper by Hammond and Shapiro analyzes the loss experience of property and liability insurance companies, although in this case the aim is to improve the basis for setting entry capital requirements. Again, it is found that a company's total portfolio of risks rather than the risk of individual lines of insurance is the appropriate focus for regulatory attention. In addition, the authors' evidence suggests that smaller insurance companies are incapable of operating at the same premium-to-capital ratios that larger companies have while at the same time maintaining comparable safety.

Since the authors of both these papers direct their primary attention toward specific details of their studies, the discussion by Robert Merton is particularly useful in providing a broader view of the common issues, including the rationale for capital regulation.

In the remaining papers, the focus turns away from stability and toward the effects of a variety of measures, both state and federal, aimed at ensuring fair treatment of individual debtors by creditor financial institutions. Three of the papers—those by William Brandt and Robert Shay, by Richard Peterson, and by William Dunkelberg and Robin DeMagistris—are concerned with consumer credit regulation while the other two—those by James Barth, Joseph Cordes, and Anthony

Yezer and by George Benston—deal with "redlining" in the mortgage market. It seems a fair generalization that a more extensive and accepted body of research exists on topics in "traditional" regulation than on those in "social" regulation, even though social regulation has expanded more rapidly in recent years. In that light, these five papers on social regulatory issues are a welcome addition to the literature. At the same time, however, the papers help to illustrate why this is the less developed branch of the regulatory literature, for not only do the usual problems of modeling and measuring the relevant concepts seem especially acute in this area, but even the issues themselves are difficult to define.

Both Barth, Cordes, and Yezer and Benston, for example, go to some pains to give an economic definition of redlining: denial of mortgage credit to particular areas of cities for reasons unrelated to cost or risk. To discussant Robert Schaefer, on the other hand, redlining consists of "attributing the average behavior of some groups to the individual" even though such a practice might be justified on purely economic grounds. With this difference in definitions, however, debate over the existence of redlining is guaranteed to go unresolved. To find redlining under the economic definition entails disentangling all profit-maximizing elements from lenders' behavior and coming up with evidence of pure discrimination. In view of the difficulties inherent in performing this disentangling, it does not seem surprising that despite strenuous modeling efforts by Barth, Cordes, and Yezer and an exhaustive (as well as somewhat exhausting) survey of previous studies by Benston, no conclusive evidence of redlining is uncovered. Under Schaefer's alternative view of redlining, by contrast, the practice exists in some form almost by definition, since the very process of credit evaluation proceeds by using average experience across time or space to predict the credit-worthiness of a particular individual.

Such problems of definition appear better resolved in the papers on consumer credit, but the problems of modeling and measurement are no less severe. All three papers have in common a reliance on survey data. The paper by Brandt and Shay, for instance, uses a survey of consumer perceptions of credit discrimination and finds that those who felt they had been discriminated against were somewhat more likely to have been denied credit at least once, but eventually wound up obtaining about the same dollar amount of credit as others with similar socioeconomic characteristics. The ensuing discussion by Carol Greenwald is illustrative of the quasi-religious tone of debate over such social regulatory issues. Among other measurement difficulties, she cites the problem that many victims of credit discrimination may not have been aware of it.

Finally, the papers by Peterson and by Dunkelberg and DeMagistris are companion pieces, both stemming from a large study underway at Purdue's Credit Research Center and both examining the interactive effects of usury ceilings and creditor remedy restrictions on the price and quantity of consumer credit. In general, the results of both studies are consistent with theoretical predictions: low usury ceilings and tight creditor remedy restrictions, for example, are found to reduce the supply of credit. As in the redlining studies, however, adequately modeling the credit-granting process is sufficiently difficult that not all the conclusions are as sharp as one might hope.

In summary, this volume provides a representative, if somewhat selective view of the current state of research on financial institution regulatory issues. One overall feeling that the reader is left with, perhaps because so many of the papers are preliminary summaries of larger studies, is that there is room for a great deal more work, particularly on topics in social regulation. The reader who seeks much resolution of issues from this book will come away disappointed. A second overall impression is that the conference would have benefited from either an introductory or summary piece on the broad issues in financial institutions regulation to provide more of a context for the remaining papers. As it stands, the book has a somewhat disjointed quality. Studies of two broad categories of regulation are interspersed with one another, and the two categories deal with separate issues. One category has been growing in recent years while the other has come under increasing attack, and the reader cannot help puzzling over what, if any, is the relationship between them.

ROBERT A. TAGGART, JR.
Northwestern University

Quest for World Monetary Order: The Gold-Dollar System and Its Aftermath, by Milton Gilbert with posthumous editing by Peter Oppenheimer and Michael Dealtry. New York: Wiley, 1980. xvii + 255 pp. $19.95

As the title suggests, this book presents an assessment of the course of the International Monetary System in the post-World War II era. The author, the late Milton Gilbert, was economic advisor of the Bank for International Settlements, which, of course, makes him an unusually qualified commentator on this topic. The volume breaks down into four parts. In the first of these is presented a taxonomy of the causes and potential cures of balance of payments disequilibria together with a discussion of developments in the total supply and composition of international reserves. The second part of the book has individual chapters charting the course of the pound sterling, the French franc, and the deutsche mark. The third, and in many ways the most important, part devotes a number of chapters to the U.S. dollar, both on its own account and also with a view to assessing its changing role in the International Monetary System. In particular, the author concentrates on the relationship between gold and the dollar. There follows a final part in which the conclusions of the author concerning reform are presented. In this final section, one gets the impression that Mr. Gilbert feels that a major reason for the troubles experienced by the International Monetary System during the 1970s was the unwillingness of the United States to increase the dollar price of gold. This does not mean that Mr. Gilbert would be happy with a system of freely floating exchange rates. Given his emphasis on the need for an orderly creation of international reserve assets (as opposed to the need for improving adjustment mechanisms), he places great store in maintaining a stable dollar. Further, he feels that gold will continue to have a major role to play in the system.

The strengths of this volume lie in its description of the course of exchange rate behavior over the post-World War II era and in its reporting of the opinions (and mistakes) of the principal actors, such as the directors of the various Central Banks. These strengths would lead me to recommend it as a supplementary text to undergraduates taking a course in International Monetary Economics. My one reservation in this respect is that I find it puzzling that a volume such as this would have no explicit discussion of the role of the Japanese yen.

I find those sections of the book that present the author's theoretical perspective on the workings of the system to be weaker than other sections. There is a tendency merely to present a taxonomy of potential effects on the balance of payments of a given country. There appears to be no model in the background with which the author could organize his thoughts. This lack of a coherent general theoretical framework has the following, not unrelated, implications. First, the author *effectively* fails to recognize that the need to supply reserves and the nature of the international adjustment mechanism are inextricably intertwined. For example, the more flexible the adjustment mechanisms, the less the need for reserves. The author on occasion tends to treat the two separately and perhaps also pays excessive attention to the latter. This is most obviously the case when he discusses Triffin's analysis as laid out in the latter's *Gold and the Dollar Crisis* [New Haven: Yale University Press, 1960]. In this, Triffin pointed out the dilemma of having a system where increases in the supply of international reserves depended on the United States running an overall deficit in its balance of payments, notwithstanding the fact that this must inevitably call into question the dollar's convertibility into gold at $35 per ounce. Triffin ruled out floating exchange rates as a solution, preferring instead to adopt a modified version of the Keynes plan to reform the IMF. Mr. Gilbert extends Triffin's analysis by arguing, as mentioned above, that during the period the fundamental disequilibrium of the system lay in the undervaluation of gold. However, by concentrating on Triffin's analysis, he fails to emphasize the great importance that must be attached to improving adjustment mechanisms in individual countries to ease the transition to balance of payments equilibrium.

Second, a coherent framework would allow one to analyze the implications of structural change. While the U.S. dollar continues to be important, it is most likely the case that its role is now that of primus inter pares. Given the emergence of currency blocks due to this structural change, much greater exchange rate flexibility may be essential, that is, the growth of Europe and Japan as economic powers, with a concomitant ability for independent action, inevitably places a greater strain on available adjustment mechanisms. Indeed the need for an improvement in adjustment mechanisms has become all the more acute, in the short-term at least, due to the arrival of OPEC. Mr. Gilbert is, of course, correct in pointing out that this new situation in general, and the growth in importance of such currencies as the deutsche mark in particular, implies that the composition of international reserves will continue to be an issue in the 1980s.

Finally, the taxonomic approach is most likely responsible for the theory chapters and the historical chapters being somewhat unrelated.

By way of a summary, I find Mr. Gilbert's volume to be interesting, particularly as far as its historical perspective is concerned. It is envisaged as an updating and correction of Triffin's analysis and, as such, is a useful addition to that literature. It does, however, suffer from the deficiency of paying insufficient attention both to the role of adjustment mechanisms in ensuring the attainment of equilibrium and to the link that exists between the adjustment mechanisms used and the volume of reserves required by the International Monetary System.

LIAM P. EBRILL

Cornell University

Models of Monetary Economies, edited by John H. Kareken and Neil Wallace. Minneapolis: Federal Reserve Bank of Minneapolis, 1980. vii + 313 pp. $5.00

This collection of essays developed out of a conference having the title of the volume and held at the Federal Reserve Bank of Minneapolis in December 1978. Following an introduction by the editors, the volume consists of two parts. The first half consists of four papers presented at the conference, together with their formal discussion. The second half contains seven papers included as postconference contributions, which are related to the topics discussed at the conference.

The theme of the conference and of the essays in this volume is in trying to explain the existence of fiat money and in the development of models that generate endogenously a role for money. The basic question is the old one of explaining why fiat money has value. To some extent the volume is a debate between proponents of the overlapping generations model as a natural framework for generating a need for money, and those who find the traditional explanations to be adequate. The volume does not deal, at least in any length, with issues related to monetary policy.

The introductory essay by John Kareken and Neil Wallace begins by taking issue with conventional macroeconomic models, arguing that they are inconsistent or that they have too few implications. Inconsistencies of the traditional models are common in various contexts and Kareken and Wallace identify a particularly important one, where the distributions on yields generated by a model are not in general consistent with those of the underlying model. However, it is not clear, at least to this reviewer, that primitive specifications often adopted in macroeconomics—those specified without direct reference to some underlying optimization—necessarily yield too few implications. It would seem that the extent of the implications will depend upon the assumptions that one imposes; the less restrictive they are the weaker the implications and vice versa. Kareken and Wallace present an argument for the overlapping generations model, providing the theme for the rest of the volume. They find it to be attractive because it assigns a very natural role to money, that is, intergenerational transfers.

The first paper of the conference itself, by David Cass, Masahiro Okuno, and Itzhak Zilcha, deals with the first basic theorem of welfare economics in the overlapping generations framework developed in Samuelson's famous 1958 paper. In this paper Samuelson showed that in an overlapping generations model with all households identical, there may be *no* competitive equilibrium which is Pareto optimal, although Pareto optimality may be restored with the introduction of fiat money. The Cass-Okuno-Zilcha paper is essentially a generalization of Samuelson's model and is concerned with determining the robustness of certain propositions with respect to various assumptions. In particular, once heterogeneous households are introduced, counterexamples to the Samuelson propositions, or propositions derivable under Samuelson's assumptions, are obtained. For example, it is no longer clear that the existence of fiat money as a store of value is necessary to support the Pareto optimality of competitive equilibrium.

In a paper entitled "The Overlapping Generations Model of Fiat Money," Neil Wallace develops in great detail his framework for generating the need for money. He begins by defining two characteristics of fiat money: inconvertability and intrinsic uselessness. By the former it is meant that the issuer does not promise to convert the money into anything else; by the latter, fiat money is never wanted for its own sake, but only for the claim it yields over other goods and services. This of course runs counter to the procedure often adopted of inserting money into utility functions. With these assumptions, the usual factors that generate value for an ordinary commodity do not apply for fiat money. Thus, in order to generate a reason for the existence of money one requires a friction to be introduced into the Walrasian model. For this, Wallace develops the overlapping generations model. The essential argument is that providing for consumption in old age by personal accumulation may be inefficient. A more efficient way of achieving this is for workers to acquire a fiat store of value when they are young which they sell for consumption goods when they are old. Wallace argues that this provides a rich theory of fiat money and that the approach has important implications for practical issues in monetary policy. These relate to questions such as: the effects of varying the proportion of money to bonds in government debt and the determinacy (or indeterminacy) of the exchange rate.

The first two papers are discussed by James Tobin and José Scheinkman. In his comments, Tobin takes issue with the general argument put forward by Wallace for the overlapping generations model as an explanation of fiat money. He expresses several doubts, including the availability of alternative assets (e.g., land) for intergenerational transfers, the existence of social security schemes as a means for consumption in old age, etc. He agrees that the overlapping generations model does capture one essential feature of money, namely that "its value to me today depends upon its value to you tomorrow, which depends upon its value to someone else the next day, and so on into the endless future." But it does not capture the feature of money arising from its use in transactions and as a unit of account. Tobin's argument for money proceeds generally along more traditional lines. The brief comment by Scheinkman focuses on two specific points arising in the formal model developed by Wallace, the more important being the "tenuousness" of the equilibrium in the overlapping generations model. In fact he notes a kind of "super Inada condition," which if it holds suffices to rule out this problem.

The second pair of conference papers are by Martin Shubik and Robert Lucas. These present alternative approaches to determining endogenous theories of money. Shubik introduces money into a rather complicated multigenerational economy, specified as a noncooperative game. The Lucas paper generates a need for money by considering an economy in which there are two classes of people, producers and traders (shoppers). Since one cannot produce and trade at the same time, it turns out to be optimal for agents to pair off into household units consisting of one producer and one trader. Under the assumptions he introduces, the most efficient way to carry out exchanges is for each household to be endowed with a certain amount of some perfectly divisible object called money, with exchanges taking place in a particular, specified way.

While the Shubik and Lucas models are both rather specific, the discussion of these papers by Leonid Hurwicz and Frank Hahn deals with more general issues. Hurwicz contrasts the endogenous theory of money characterizing the conference with a more historical explanation. He is also somewhat skeptical of the overlapping generations model. In the latter part of his comments he raises an interesting question concerning the optimal design of economic institutions. The institutional framework is a question that economists typically take for granted, and Hurwicz asks, if we were to solve a particular model for the institutional optimum would we invent the Federal Reserve System? Hahn in somewhat related comments asks not how money gets into the system, but how are the existing institutions to survive? He also raises questions about the Walrasian equilibrium concept, upon which much of the existing literature is based.

The second half of the book contains the postconference contributions. Five of these papers (William Brock and José Scheinkman, John Bryant, David Cass, David Cass and Karl Shell, Robert Townsend) deal with various aspects of the overlapping generations model. Several of these are rather technical analyses of particular issues within that framework. Probably of greatest general interest is the paper by Cass and Shell which argues very strongly for the overlapping generations approach, on the grounds that it is the "only genuinely dynamic basically disaggregate framework available."

The technical sophistication of the papers in this volume is high. It is not easy reading and the general reader may find that in some cases the summaries and discussion suffice to give an indication of the main issues involved. Perhaps the main contribution of the volume is to give prominence to the overlapping generations model as a potential contribution to monetary theory. While the model has been in the literature for many years, I suspect that most economists, including monetary economists, regard it as a specialized model in capital and growth theory. Whether or not one is persuaded by all the arguments put forward by the proponents of the overlapping generations model, after reading this volume one cannot help but feel that it provides an important framework for understanding the role of money in a dynamic economy.

STEPHEN J. TURNOVKSY
Australian National University

Capitalism and Socialism: A Theological Inquiry, edited by Michael Novak. Washington, D.C.: American Enterprise Institute, 1979, 193 pp. $4.75

Are religious values at stake under capitalism and socialism today? How one responds to this question will no doubt depend on how one perceives capitalism and socialism as they exist in the world today. There is no question that the spiritual roots of both capitalism and socialism can be traced back to the Judeo-Christian theology. For an old-fashioned social scientist whose training included the required reading of Tawney [3] and Weber [4], a revelation that each economic system carries its own definite theological implications should come as no surprise. However, for a new breed of social scientists who take pride in practicing their disciplines as branches of social engineering, the relevation may come as somewhat of a puzzle. Indeed, some may even respond by asking, Why bother about theological implications? Why not get down to the mundane issues of the world today and try to solve them? And there is something to be said for this kind of pragmatic approach to the questions of comparative economic systems.

Brilliant as it was, Schumpeter's [2] classic treatise on the subject may have done a disservice to the social science profession with his almost complete neglect of the theological implications of capitalism and socialism. Once capitalism and socialism are defined, as Schumpeter did, as two alternative modes of organizing economic activities of production and distribution, the main focus is shifted away from the cultural issues to the economic ones regarding the relative performance of these two ''economic'' systems. In fact, such an economic interpretation can be extended, again as Schumpeter did, to the realm of politics by defining democracy as a competitive struggle for the people's vote, which, therefore, is compatible with both capitalism and socialism.

The book under review, published by the American Enterprise Institute, with its explicit concern about the theological implications of capitalism and socialism, is thus in sharp contrast to Schumpeter's treatment of the subject. Here capitalism and socialism are treated as two alternative modes of organizing and regulating human actions not only in the economic arena but also in the cultural arena. The fact that a theological inquiry is taken up in the year 1978 is a tribute to the persistence of the Tawney-Weber thesis that capitalism and socialism actually represent two ''cultural'' systems, two ways of life, with definite theological implications.

The book contains the texts of ten lectures delivered by seven speakers at the conference organized by the American Enterprise Institute and the Department of Religion at Syracuse University in July 1978. Irving Kristol, in his first lecture ''The Spiritual Roots of Capitalism and Socialism,'' offers an intriguing interpretation of these two cultural systems in terms of the orthodoxy-gnosticism duality that can be found in any religion. While attributing the appeal of socialism to its utopianism, which stems from its gnostic impulse, he finds in the same gnostic impulse a cause of the infertility of socialism with its calamitous failure in the realm of economics. In his second lecture ''The Disaffection from Capitalism,'' Kristol looks into the liberal impulse that has also played an important role in the development of both capitalistic and socialistic ideas during the Enlightenment. He identifies the crisis of capitalism today as that of belief. In particular, he points out how the very success of modern liberal democratic capitalism, with an ever-increasing role for the government in the economic arena, has led to the erosion of the Judeo-Christian morality.

Michael Novak, in his lecture ''Seven Theological Facets,'' offers a more comprehensive survey of the theological underpinnings of capitalism and socialism. He, as does Kristol, correctly points out how modern democratic capitalism has emerged from the Anglo-Scottish version of the Enlightenment, which inherited the Judeo-Christian tradition. However, its emphasis on individualism has undermined the sense of community on which prior Jewish-Christian cultures had thrived. Socialism, in a way, took off where capitalism had left off. As Peter Berger argues in his lecture ''Capitalism and Socialism: Ethical Assessment,'' the appeal of socialism lies mainly in the sense of restored community it promises to offer. However, the political leadership of socialist countries has yet to live up to this promise and to offer the degree of individual liberty enjoyed by the citizens of liberal democratic capitalist countries. Berger contends, in his second lecture ''Capitalism and Socialism: Empirical Facts,'' that the usual charges made against capitalism—inequality, exploitation, materialism, alienation—are not as well founded as they are presented by the critics of capitalism. His contention is based on his recognition of the important role now played by political distribution that complements the market mechanism. Penn Kemble carries Berger's thesis a step further in his lecture ''A Social Democratic View'' by arguing that what is valid in capitalism cannot be saved by capitalism alone. In particular, he recognizes a positive role for the public sector in setting the framework for promoting social democratic values while leaving to the private sector the role of promoting individualistic values.

The book contains three lectures on American capitalism: "American Exceptionalism" and "Religion in American Politics" by Seymour M. Lipset and "The Success of the American Economic System" by Ben J. Wattenberg. The title of the lecture "American Exceptionalism" is indicative of the author's intention to offer an explanation of why socialism has not taken root in the American soil, in this most industrialized capitalist economy, contrary to Marx's prediction. Lipset explains this exceptionalism in terms of the flexibility of the American two-party political system, which has been able to accommodate a wide spectrum of different values, including social welfare programs advocated by labor unions. From a theological perspective, American exceptionalism is due to the commitment to the Protestant moralism: We must do what is right. The upshot is that the Jews and the Catholics, who tend to be more sympathetic towards socialism in other countries, have to share with the Protestants in their support of individualism and antistatism. Ben Wattenberg develops in his lecture a defense of American capitalism, which includes, among other things, his perception of the positive role played by multinational corporations as supreme agents of human betterment.

The only "pagan" element of the book is found in the lecture by Muhammad Abdul-Rauf titled "The Islamic Doctrine of Economics and Contemporary Economic Thought." While other authors speak from the Judeo-Christian tradition of the West, the author of this lecture speaks from a different theological tradition that is currently searching for a meaningful way of building its economic foundation upon religious values. The piece is indeed a welcome addition to the book, for the author does an excellent job of explaining why the Islamic doctrine of economics cannot be meaningfully defined except within the framework of the Islamic value system, that the behavior of Islamic economic man cannot be meaningfully separated from his spiritual commitment. Read along with this lecture Schumacher's essay on Buddhist economics, and the reader should be convinced that economics can be very easily turned into an empty exercise if taken out of its metaeconomic framework. If this book serves to redirect the attention of social scientists to these broader cultural issues within which economic issues are embedded, then its publication can be judged as having been a worthwhile venture. Moreover, the economic reality of the world today cannot be understood unless we are prepared to take into account the diversity of cultures whose theological implications cannot be fully explained in terms of the Judeo-Christian tradition of the West.

Are religious values at stake under capitalism and socialism today? Not necessarily. Capitalism has evolved into what it is today by gradually shredding its religious heritage, while socialism has evolved into what it is today by denouncing religion as the opium of the masses. During the process, however, both capitalism and socialism have developed their own new implicit religious values. If a theological inquiry into capitalism and socialism is needed today, it is into the nature of these implicit religious values that have come to replace the old explicit religious values.

LITERATURE CITED

1. Schumacher, E. F. *Small Is Beautiful: A Study of Economics As If People Mattered.* London: Blond and Briggs, 1973.

2. Schumpeter, Josseph Alois. *Capitalism, Socialism and Democracy*. New York: Harper and Row, 1942.

3. Tawney, Richard Henry. *Religion and the Rise of Capitalism: A Historical Study*. Glouscester: Smith, 1929.

4. Weber, Max. *The Protestant Ethic and the Spirit of Capitalism*, translated by T. Parsons. London: Allen and Urwin, 1930.

TETSUNORI KOIZUMI

Ohio State University

The Australian Monetary System in the 1970s, edited by Michael G. Porter. Melbourne, Australia: Monash University, 1979. 244 pp.

In the western economies the 1970s were a turbulent decade. For many observers this turbulence so muddied the economic waters that they appeared deep. The perceptions of many policymakers and market participants during the decade were so often badly impaired by repeated disturbances that charges of a breakdown of economic theory were regularly heard. On such occasions a crash course on the state of economic knowledge is a good idea.

The present volume is the product of a conference held by Australian academics and policy advisers in order to clear the muddied water and demonstrate that economic reasoning still provides a useful support system for policymakers and market participants even in these turbulent times. Their efforts cover a breadth of issues ranging from the pure theory of how expectations affect outcomes under alternative monetary and exchange rate regimes to detailed descriptions of fundamental changes that have wracked Australian financial institutions.

Michael Porter's penetrating review of Australia's economic problems in the 1970s and Richard Snape's critical chronicling of Australian authorities' attempts to determine the exchange rate begin the volume. Stephen Turnovsky and Geoffrey Kingston presented a stimulating analysis of regressive exchange rate and adaptive inflationary expectations. While Snape and Porter focused on the impossibility of the authorities fixing simultaneously the money growth rate, the foreign exchange rate, the interest rate, and numerous other variables in equilibrium, and while Turnovsky and Kingston pointed out the adverse effects of abrupt changes in money supply growth, none of these three studies yields systematic insight into the reason behind shifts in any of the various policy targets and concomitant binges of excessive money supply growth.

Nevertheless, the masterful contribution by Michael Parkin and Robin Bade does shed light on the problem of money supply instability. The authors classified the central banks of twelve nations in terms of the type of linkage they had with their governments and reported correlations of the types of linkages with inflation, monetary instability, and the algebraic signs of the arguments of their respective reaction functions. According to these criteria, central bank autonomy, along Swiss and West German lines, seems to offer the most promise of monetary stability.

In stark contrast, the following study, in the institutionalist tradition, by Wolfgang Kasper, offers no hope for sound monetary management. Kasper enumerated changes in the structure of markets and the polity that he provokingly claimed to have vitiated stabilization policy. Similar to the cost push advocates, he overlooked obvious linkages between supply side shifts and subsequent monetary "validation."

A strong econometric focus emerged at the conference. One group of papers presented estimates of structural models. Neil Johnston rendered a skillful study of the impact of monetary policy on models of portfolio behavior for four sectors of the Australian financial system. Thomas Valentine provided some titillating estimates of money demand and money supply relations. Eric Kiernan, like Johnston, developed an interesting structural model of the financial system, only one that focused on money supply determination. Finally, Peter Jonson and John Taylor presented a complete model of the Australian economy.

In contrast to the preceding structural models, two papers dealt with "reduced form" estimation in the tradition of Friedman-Meiselman and Anderson-Jordan. Using cross-spectral analysis of time series since 1946, Kevin Davis and Mervyn Lewis found a closer relationship between money and output than between money and prices. Michael Burns, estimating the variability of the coefficients on policy variables in a reduced form model, discovered less variability in policy-response coefficients for Australia than for the United States.

There were also an interesting set of papers on the relationship between instruments and intermediate policy variables. Ian Sharpe and Paul Volker demonstrated the possibility of controlling M3 very closely and Paul Barry provided a study on the indicator problem à la Brunner and Meltzer.

Institutional-descriptive studies by Geoffrey Gloster and Roland Matrenza, Ken Mahar, and Gordon Bruns close the compendium. These papers deal, respectively, with the effects of financial controls on money supply variability, permanent building societies, and foreign exchange markets. The final study of the volume by Desmond Brook is a extraordinary proposal for a currency futures market.

The wide range of issues together with the fact that Australian economic experiences during the 1970s were so similar to that of other western economies indicates that there will be something exciting in this volume for everyone. Indeed, excitement generated by these papers is best gauged by the lively related commentary and discussions that are also published in the volume but, owing to space limitations, cannot be reviewed here.

THOMAS HAVRILESKY

Duke University

Currency and Economic Reform, West Germany After World War II: A Symposium, edited by Rudolf Richter, in cooperation with Terence W. Hutchinson, Ernst-Joachim Mestmäcker, Heinz Sauermann, and Wolfgang F. Stolper. Tübingen, Germany: J. C. B. Mohr (Paul Siebeck), 1979. viii + 236 pp. DM 54

This book is a collection of fifteen articles presented at a conference celebrating the thirtieth anniversary of the currency and economic reforms in West Germany. While no one denies the economic success of the West Germans following World

War II, economists still debate which policies were responsible for that success. Articles in this collection document economic events, political decisions, and intellectual discussions that surrounded the currency reform. Clearly, those who advocated an economic structure based on classical rather than Keynesian theories won the first round in the political arena. Beginning with the reforms in 1948, West Germans have spawned a unique set of institutions and ideas dealing with the role of socialist goals in a society that has an economic structure based on classical market principles.

The book is organized in six parts. The five articles in part 1 are primarily descriptive accounts of economic and political events leading up to the reform. The first three papers by Heinz Sauermann, Eckhard Wandel, and Jürgen Domes and Michael Wolffshon set the stage for the ideological debate that follows. This section also contains two papers dealing directly with other currency reforms. The first, by Otto Pfleiderer, compares the currency reform of 1948 to that of 1923. He notes the similar conditions present in both hyper- and suppressed inflations; that is, an excess supply of money, hoarding of goods, and a breakdown in the function of the market place. He emphasizes the importance of the government's credibility in both currency reforms, noting that this credibility was based on institutional constraints limiting the central bank's power to monetize government and private debt. The second paper, by Lloyd Metzler, is an historical document describing the currency reforms for five other European countries following World War II.

Part 2 consists of one article by Wolfgang F. Stolper and Karl W. Roskamp. This is a descriptive article covering the period from 1945 to 1960. While presenting a brief, well-written historical account of economic events, they introduce philosophical issues that are dicussed in parts 3 and 6. The authors suggest that Germany's economic experience has been labeled a "miracle" by those who would prefer to ignore its causes. They attribute West Germany's success to the government planning of economic forms rather than government planning of economic processes. They argue, following Walter Eucken, that it is not the quantity but the quality of government intervention that determines economic success.

Part 3 contains three papers dealing with economic philosophy and one historical document that includes the policy recommendations of the panel of West German economic advisors to the occupation forces. The policies enforced by the Allies were consistent with the recommendations of the majority of the panel.

The first paper by Christian Watrin surveys the historical origins and subsequent development of the principles which underlie the concept of the "Social Market Economy." The survey is excellent and well documented. In summing up, he describes the social market economy as a "permanent search for an economic and social framework, designed to encourage both an efficient production of the means of material well-being and personal freedom in a socially-balanced order" (p. 419). This description implies that the social market economy is an elusive ideal which may change over time. By calling it a search Watrin implies the need for ongoing economic legislation to correct flaws in the constitution defining the social-economic order. The purpose of a constitution is to protect the freedom of the individual from the democratic majority. One could readily argue that the currency reform was a success because it put in place an economic and legal framework which could not be easily changed.

In the second article of part 3, Terence W. Hutchinson attempts to evaluate the effect that economists and their ideas had on the programs adopted in 1948. He argues that the economic policies adopted in the currency reform ran counter to the ideas prevalent in Britain and in the U.S. While he acknowledges that the free-market principles embodied in the "neo-liberal" philosophy were closely related to the policies initiated by Ludwig Erhard, he claims that the acceptance of these policies was as much a function of circumstances as it was of economists' persuasion. He quotes at length well-known British and American economists who condemned the decisions made in 1948 because they ran counter to Keynesian ideas. He argues that it was mainly the force of outward circumstances that determined the structure of the economic reforms in West Germany. Government economic planning was associated with the Nazis, dictatorship, and the loss of World War II. The overriding desire for individual freedom did more to influence the structure of the reforms than did the ideas of the economists. In Britain and the U.S., winning the war gave credence to economic planning. Fear of another depression overrode fear of a powerful central government. Consequently, the ideas of Keynes and the structure needed to implement them were more readily accepted in these countries.

One of the issues debated in the post-reform era was whether social programs of the political left could be compatible with the free-market structure. Many, including Friedrich A. Hayek, argued that they could not be. The third paper in part 3 is a 1953 article by Franz Böhm which argues that because income distribution is partially a political problem even in a free market, a variety of alternative distribution schemes may be compatible with a free-market economy. He applauds the recognition by the political left that the free-market structure might be responsible for the high rate of growth Germany experienced following the currency reform.

Part 4 consists of a single article by Peter Schwerdtner describing the laws regulating labor unions. This brief account of institutions leaves one with the impression that the recent changes in the law have created the potential for stronger labor unions, which are likely to become obstacles to both domestic and foreign competitive forces.

Part 5 includes one historical document and two papers on international trade and relations. The first paper, by Henry C. Wallich and John F. Wilson, reviews the history of the balance of payments, lists various hypotheses attempting to explain thirty years of German surpluses, and concludes by offering insights of the authors. What is not mentioned is the institutional framework that almost necessarily mandated surpluses. Under Bundesbank Law the central bank was limited in the amount of credit that it could extend to the central government. Included in this limitation on credit was the central bank's portfolio of government securities. There was also a limit on lending to banks. The only source of the monetary base that could support monetary growth consistent with price stability and real growth was foreign reserves.

The second paper by Hans von der Groeben describes the interaction between West Germany and members of the European Economic Community. He argues that membership in the E.E.C. has caused West Germany as well as other members to pursue free-market principles out of necessity. Only market-oriented systems could be compatible unless some members were willing to give up political autonomy. He describes requirements placed by the E.E.C. on members in areas of antitrust policy, labor and capital mobility, and tax policy.

Throughout most of the articles in this symposium, one finds the notion that West

Germany's economic success was due not to the constancy but to the flexibility of the social market economy. At the same time one finds repeated warnings that current leaders may have forgotten the "lessons" of the past. In the concluding section, Peter Bernholz argues that it was the constitutional framework protecting individual freedom that was a prime reason for economic success. He goes on to claim that the flexibility and changes in the system over the last thirty years have usurped individual freedom and stifled economic activity. He presents episodal evidence to support the view that adjustments to the social order have weakened competition and increased the size of the government.

Overall, the papers are well written. Where translations are provided by other than the authors the style is fluent. This collection of articles is basically descriptive. As we in the U.S. formulate schemes to cure our economic ills, it is important to recall successful reforms. If the book is disappointing in any way, it is that there could have been more economic analysis to explain why specific reforms were successful and why some of the policies have been reversed. While Germany had fantastic growth in the 1950s and 1960s, it has also had a large deceleration in its annual growth rate over the last twenty years. Surely some of this deceleration can also be explained in terms of "economic reform."

WILLIAM T. GAVIN

Federal Reserve Bank of Cleveland

Selected Papers of Allan Sproul, edited by Lawrence S. Ritter. New York: Federal Reserve Bank of New York, 1980. xi + 233 pp. $3.50

Allan Sproul served the Federal Reserve System for thirty-six years, all but ten of them at the Federal Reserve Bank of New York. In 1920, soon after his graduation from the University of California, Berkeley, he joined the Federal Reserve Bank of San Francisco as head of its research department. While there he came to the attention of Governor Benjamin Strong and George L. Harrison of the New York Reserve Bank, who were so impressed that they offered him a job in 1928. He resisted for almost two years but finally yielded and joined the New York Bank at the beginning of March 1930. He became the third chief executive of the bank at the beginning of 1941, after George Harrison had resigned to enter private industry. Despite an offer of the presidency of the World Bank in 1946, which he declined, he remained in this office until mid-1956, when he resigned at the age of sixty, primarily for reasons of health. After more than twenty active years of retirement he died at age eighty-two. All the papers in this collection were written during his presidency of the New York Bank or during his retirement.

In selecting and presenting these papers, Professor Ritter has served us well. His brief biography of Sproul is excellent, his chapter introductions put the various papers in context, and his selection of papers is well designed to help us understand the man and his ideas.

Various developments during the 1930s and World War II, including the rapidly rising federal debt and problems of debt management, made it impossible for Sproul to play the dominant role that Benjamin Strong had played before his death in 1928. Some of these developments shifted power within the system from the reserve banks to the Federal Reserve Board; others shifted power from the Federal Reserve to the Treasury. Though not dominant, Sproul was one of the most influential officials in the Federal Reserve System during his fifteen years as president of the New York Bank. A big, rugged man with a vigorous tone of voice and a friendly smile, he made a favorable first impression, and that impression became even more favorable as further acquaintance revealed his high intellectual ability, his great fund of knowledge, his devotion to principle, his quick wit, his excellent speaking and writing style, and his willingness to fight for what he thought was right.

A few examples will suggest the nature of Sproul's approach to economic policy though they cannot do justice to the range of his ideas. He believed strongly that money not only matters but matters a lot; that money will not manage itself but must be managed; and that the dominant objective of monetary management should be to promote economic stability, including stability of the price level. But he was no "monetarist," as that term is interpreted today. For one thing, he would accord a stabilization role to fiscal policy as well as monetary policy. Also, he was adamantly opposed to inflexible rules that leave inadequate scope for discretionary human judgment. These papers provide the best available firsthand accounts of two historic controversies over monetary policy. One related to the policy followed during World War II and until March 1951, under which the Federal Reserve pegged prices and yields on government securities. Sproul strongly opposed this as an unconscionable constraint on the ability of the Federal Reserve to use its powers for stabilization purposes, and especially to combat inflation. The other related to an open-market policy called "bills only" or "bills usually," which was announced by the Federal Open Market Committee in March 1953 and abandoned only in February 1961. Under this policy the FOMC denied itself the use of purchases and sales of longer-term securities, except to correct disorderly markets, and confined its operations to the short end of the market. Sproul was bitterly opposed, not because he disapproved of current open-market policies but because he thought it very unwise for the Federal Reserve to limit its flexibility and capabilities by adopting an inflexible rule.

These papers also present Sproul's insightful comments on other subjects, such as gold standards, interest rate ceilings on deposits, the Vietnam War and its financing, and international financial aid.

These papers help explain why Sproul's contemporaries respected him so deeply. He was indeed an extraordinary man.

LESTER V. CHANDLER

Princeton University

The Failure of the Franklin National Bank: Challenge to the International Banking System, by Joan Edelman Spero. New York: Columbia University Press, 1980. xi + 235 pp. $14.95

The risks to the individual bank and the banking system attendant on the internationalization of the sixties and seventies are the focus of this monograph. Professor Joan Edelman Spero, a political scientist, investigates here in depth the foreign as well as domestic response to Franklin's collapse.

Franklin's failure in October 1974 occurred a decade after a number of major American banks started significant international operations. In this eventful decade, Franklin, which had been very successful as a retail bank in booming Nassau and Suffolk counties near New York City, sought further growth by expanding into Wall Street, broadening the scope of its activities, and aiming to compete effectively with the established giants.

Although the Fed had warned Franklin earlier about the adverse consequences of a possible denial, the holding company refused to withdraw the application to acquire Talcott National, a leading factoring concern. Andrew Brimmer, on the Board of Govenors at the time, viewed the 1974 denial to be "the single most important factor" making Franklin's survival prospect extremely uncertain [1, p. 122].

The Board of Governors had weighed the impact of a deposit drain, but the Fed also considered the undesirable effects of allowing leading banks to be controlled by a Sindona-type "configuration of arrangements," Brimmer noted [1, p. 126]. Sindona's Fasco International had acquired 21.6 percent of Franklin New York Corporation's shares from Loew's in July 1972. Within the Fed there had been mixed opinions as to the legal status of Sindona's control of Franklin [1, p. 123-24]. Professor Spero does not consider the Sindona connection to have been the major cause of Franklin's collapse, though she acknowledges that the tie accentuated other problems (p. 95).

In the wake of the severe 1974 recession, Franklin's loan portfolio had not deteriorated materially. Liquidity, not asset quality, was the basic problem, Comptroller of the Currency James Smith pointed out [5, p. 1968]. He testified that his agency underestimated the speed with which liquidity was transformed from a serious to an insoluble problem at a time of soaring money market rates, as lenders moved to quality [5, pp. 907, 921]. For that matter, Franklin's liquidity crisis was more severe than the Fed had expected, Dr. Spero notes (p. 126). A few days after the Talcott denial, Franklin announced huge losses from foreign exchange trading and government bond speculation. Alerted to Franklin's plight, the market responded by accelerating deposit withdrawal (largely by not renewing maturing CDs) and shrinking Franklin's other money market liabilities.

Between May and November 1974, Franklin "underwent a managed demise," in Dr. Spero's apt phrase. Comptroller Smith, convinced that a private sector solution had a reasonable prospect of success, did not immediately turn to the FDIC for an assisted merger. Viewing the comptroller's efforts along this line to have been unrealistic (p. 129), Dr. Spero does not take into account Smith's hope to salvage something for thousands of small shareholders and debenture holders [5, p. 912-14].

Former Secretary of the Treasury Kennedy was charged with putting together a merger on a commercial basis. By July 1, however, a quick unaided merger was out of the question, Kennedy informed the comptroller. The next day, Smith turned formally to the FDIC. A solution could have been arranged long before October 8, but this would have been "a financial disaster for the trust fund that the FDIC administers," according to FDIC chairman Frank Wille [5, pp. 1083-84].

Evidence that bank failures are "not unusual" is found in the closing of 635 banks between 1934 and the end of 1972. However, after 1942 an average of fewer than 5 a year failed; even small bank closings had become rare, very much below the rate of business failures.

The author endorses the view of Congressman Rosenthal that Franklin, the largest bank failure in American history, had been a case of regulatory neglect'' (pp. 185-86), with ''extremely weak'' supervision (p. 184). Comptroller Smith later conceded that his office had not acted aggressively enough to compel Franklin to institute needed changes uncovered by national bank examiners [5, p. 904].

The Office of the Comptroller of the Currency is also faulted for not limiting the size of Franklin's London branch operations (p. 185). This criticism does not take into account the fact that the branch was ''well-staffed,'' as Chairman Wille reported. Moreover, the $600 million loans on its books in the summer of 1974 were among the highest-yielding assets in Franklin's portfolio [5, p. 1070].

The Board of Governors and the Federal Reserve Bank of New York ''occasionally'' played divergent roles, we are told, Though the monograph is heavily footnoted, this tantalizing sentence is not, leaving us to guess.

After Franklin's collapse, the federal banking agencies instituted significant improvements in supervisory procedures. The new approach—mentioned only in passing (p. 187)—would ''never let a situation in a major money market bank develop to the point that it would be threatened with insolvency,'' Comptroller Smith told the Rosenthal subcommittee in June 1976 [6, p. 177].

Smith did qualify this claim with the proviso ''barring extreme circumstances in the financial market.'' Such conceivably might arise as a result of international financial complications. As Dr. Spero rightly emphasizes, for all the magnitude and effectiveness of international cooperation in the Franklin crisis, the international banking system remains ''susceptible to a crisis of confidence.'' Dr. Spero expresses concern about significant existing gaps with regard to such vital issues as responsibility for being lender of last resort and supervisor of foreign activities. There has yet to be a clear definition of central bank obligations on whom and when to assist. There exists unnecessary uncertainty under ''the present system of a vague but blanket assurance that central banks will support their big banks'' [2, p. 326]. Six years after Franklin, the economic summit Venice Conference endorsed the ''work in progress by our monetary authorities and the Bank for International Settlements designed to improve the supervision and security of the international banking system'' [3].

The very extensive bibliography includes regulatory agency and district court files, personal interviews with important officials and bankers here and abroad, in addition to numerous books and articles. However, neither Brimmer's essay, nor Joseph F. Sinkey, Jr.'s study, is mentioned [4].

Extensive litigation has generated vast additional materials after the research for this volume was completed. A former Franklin president, chairman, and largest shareholder were among the thirteen who were convicted or pleaded guilty to criminal charges. Sindona received a twenty-five-year sentence.

Further scholarly investigation into the tangled affairs of Franklin will have this study as an indispensable starting point. Meanwhile, Dr. Spero has done well to remind us that ''the management of international banking has a long way to go'' (p. 191).

LITERATURE CITED

1. Brimmer, Andrew F. "The Federal Reserve and the Failure of Franklin National Bank. A Case Study of Regulation." In *Business and the American Economy, 1776-2001,* edited by Jules Backman, pp. 108-39. New York: New York University Press, 1976.

2. Giddy, Ian H., and Deborah L. Allen. "International Competition in Bank Regulation." *Banca Nazionale del Lavoro Quarterly Review,* 130 (September 1979), 311-26.

3. *New York Times,* June 24, 1980.

4. Sinkey, Joseph F., Jr. "Identifying Large Problem/Failed Banks: The Case of Franklin National Bank of New York." *Journal of Financial and Quantitative Analysis,* 12 (December 1977), 779-800.

5. U.S. Congress, House Committee on Banking, Currency, and Housing, Subcommittee on Financial Institutions Supervision, Regulation, and Insurance, Hearings on H.R. 8024. *Bank Failures, Regulatory Reform, Financial Privacy,* Pts. 2, 3. Washington, D.C.: U.S. Government Printing Office, 1975.

6. U.S. Congress, House Committee on Government Operations, Commerce, Consumer, and Monetary Affairs Subcommittee, 94th Congress, 2d Session. Oversight Hearings Into the Effectiveness of Federal Bank Regulation (Franklin National Bank Failure). Washington, D.C.: U.S. Government Printing Office, 1976.

BENJAMIN J. KLEBANER*

City College of the City University of New York

*The reviewer is a regional economist with the Office of the Comptroller of the Currency, Second National Bank Region. The opinions expressed in this review are his, and in no way should be construed to represent those of the Office of the Comptroller of the Currency.

The Impact of the Federal Reserve System's Monetary Policies on the Nation's Economy (Second Report), Staff Report of the Subcommittee on Domestic Monetary Policy of the Committee on Banking, Finance and Urban Affairs, House of Representatives. 96th Congress, Second Session, December 1980. Washington, D.C.: U.S. Government Printing Office, 1980 xii + 51 pp.

This report, written by Robert Weintraub (former staff director of the Subcommittee on Domestic Monetary Policy), will make interesting reading for anyone who believes that Congress is solely a source of populist pressure on the Federal Reserve System. The gist of the report is contained in the following quotation from Chairman Parren Mitchell's letter of transmittal accompanying the report. "The impelling force underlying the persistent inflation which we have experienced . . . is an upward drift in the M1B money supply . . . inflation brings no gains either in output or employment. . . . I have strongly urged the Federal Reserve to set forth publicly a long run disinflationary track for M1B growth to which it adheres."

The first part of part 1 of the report reviews monetary policy and the performance of the economy from 1975 through 1980. In the second part, the author examines the behavior, in the post-Korean War period, of nominal and real GNP, the money supply (M1B), velocity, and the price level (GNP deflator). A number of relationships that are consistent with quantity-theory views are brought out through an examination of the data averaged over nonoverlapping, three-year intervals. The variability of growth in money and nominal GNP is high relative to the variability of growth in velocity. Money correlates well with nominal income on a contemporaneous basis and with the price level with a two-year lag.

There has been considerable conjecture that the public's demand function for narrowly defined monetary aggregates has become unstable in the 1970s due to the introduction of new liabilities by financial institutions. It is interesting to note in this respect that the evidence presented in part 1 lends no support to such conjecture.

A model of the economy is presented in part 2. Starting from a supply and demand equation for real GNP, reduced-form equations are derived for the rate of inflation and the rate of growth of real GNP. Although the author discusses why individual variables are included in the structural equations, he leaves for the reader the task of supplying a general, theoretical rationale for the model. For this reason, many readers will find the model ad hoc. The justification for the model must be that, when estimated using annual observations, it predicts well, not only for the within-sample period (1956 to 1975), but also for the out-of-sample period (1976 to 1980). The reduced forms do capture significant empirical relationships that existed among macroeconomic variables over the post-Korean War period.

From the estimation results of his model, the author draws a number of conclusions about post-Korean War empirical relationships. A given percentage change in the rate of growth of money produced, in the subsequent year, a similarly signed percentage change in real GNP growth of somewhat smaller magnitude. The impact of a change in money growth on inflation was delayed by two years. Four years were required before the rate of inflation fully reflected a change in the rate of growth of money. The rate of inflation enters into the reduced-form equation for real GNP growth in a way that indicates that the impact of a change in the growth of money on real GNP was ultimately offset by the indirect effects deriving from the change in money on the inflation rate. The results also indicate, for the period as a whole, little relationship between inflation and either unemployment or the budget deficit of the federal government. The author concludes that permanent high unemployment is not a prerequisite for low inflation and that deficits of the federal government do not cause inflation.

As a final exercise, the author simulates his model in order to determine the cost of restoring price stability. As one example, he assumes a sustained reduction, starting in 1981, in the rate of growth of M1B by 5 percentage points. Through the use of Okun's Law, he estimates that the unemployment rate would rise to a peak of 11.5 percent in 1984 versus 9 percent for a regime of constant money growth at the 1980 rate. The cumulative loss in output is $200 billion in 1980 dollars while inflation is reduced by 2.6 percentage points versus the constant money growth regime. After 1984, slower money growth generates further gains in reduced inflation and gains in reduced unemployment and faster real GNP growth as well. Compared to other estimates of the cost of reducing inflation, these estimates are moderate.

Proponents of the rational expectations–natural rate hypothesis may view these estimates as an upper bound to the cost of reducing inflation. If the empirical relationships estimated in this report incorporate the belief by the public that monetary policy is of a stop-go nature, and if the public were to become convinced that a new effort by the monetary authority to reduce inflation would be permanent, then the cost of restoring price stability would be less than what is indicated above. The author includes a qualitative discussion of the costs of allowing inflation to persist at its current level. He concludes that these costs are likely to be of a magnitude that outweighs the cost of restoring price stability.

ROBERT L. HETZEL

Federal Reserve Bank of Richmond

The European Monetary System: Its Promise and Prospects, edited by Philip H. Trezise. Washington, D.C.: The Brookings Institution, 1979. vii + 96 pp. $3.00

Jacques van Ypersele de Strihou, Michael Emerson, Henri Baquiast, Robert Triffin, and Christopher McMahon, authors of the five main essays in this volume can justly claim to be among the midwives if not the parents of the European Monetary System (EMS). Their papers were presented at a conference held at the Brookings Institution in April 1979, just after the belated start of the EMS. All strike an optimistic note in claiming that the system has good economic justifications, that it is well designed and flexible enough to cope with the main problems, and that it is complementary both to other developments in the Community and the international monetary system. McMahon concludes, in the most broad-ranging of the essays that "if the EMS did not exist, it—or something similar—would have to be invented." Such optimism is in sharp contrast to the caution and disbelief of the discussants: Ralph Bryant, Robert Solomon, Benjamin Cohen, and William Fellner. The most pessimistic, Benjamin Cohen, concludes that "the most probable outcome, therefore, is that the EMS, like its predecessor, will simply fail."

This small volume contains not only a concise description of the main features and aims of the EMS, but also a lively debate on whether it meets the necessary economic conditions for survival. The debate, as pointed out by Philip Trezise in his excellent introduction, is inconclusive, as its outcome ultimately hinges on the existence or lack of the indefinable and immeasurable quality of "political will." For the Europeans, the EMS itself is a demonstration of the existence of the quality; as Dr. Emminger, then president of the Bundesbank, said, "I see . . . in the EMS mainly a solemn declaration of intent that the Member States will be trying to harmonize, on a stable basis, their economic and monetary performance." The discussants on the other hand, perhaps with the history of past efforts towards monetary integration rather than the achievements of a new initiative in mind, take a more agnostic if not sceptical view.

The economic motivations for the EMS given by the authors concentrate on dissatisfaction with floating exchange rates. It is claimed that excessive exchange rate variability has led to higher inflation and lower growth than would have otherwise been expected. Emerson says: "By 1977 countries prone to both devaluation and revaluation had come to appreciate that erratic exchange rate movements were part of the reason the European economy was being constrained to subpotential economic performance." On the whole the discussants do not disagree, although Solomon says with some justification "that the sluggish performance of the so-called strong-currency countries in Europe in 1976–77 was the result of their domestic policies rather than of the appreciation of their exchange rates." The real disagreement is centered on whether the EMS offers a viable way of tackling the problems. The exchange rate arrangements are one of the major parts of the EMS but the crucial question of the degree of fixity is not fully answered. As well as recognizing that deep structural differences rule out irrevocably fixed exchange rates within Europe, all seemed to agree with Bryant, who comments on Van Ypersele's and Triffin's papers that, because changes are sometimes desirable and sometimes not depending upon the sort of disturbance to the system, an agnostic approach to exchange rate variability should be adopted. The authors, especially Baquiast, stress the differences between the EMS and the Bretton Woods System, and put considerable weight on the ability of one of its innovations, the divergence indicator, to ensure that the system will get the balance between too many and too few central rate realignments right. They also express the belief that this new mechanism will help ensure a satisfactory degree of symmetry of adjustment.

The authors stress that the EMS should not be seen only as an exchange rate system but should be considered in the light of developments both within the Community and in the international monetary system. Emerson says that the EMS is "deeply embedded in a whole range of Community institutions and their political, economic and financial mechanisms," and that this was not true for the "snake." He argues that the system is part of the whole process of convergence, which is the touchstone of the Community's present activity.

Triffin and McMahon see the EMS as "working with the grain of underlying economic and financial integration rather than against it." They argue that—regrettable though it may be, because the times of stability in the international monetary system have been times when there has been one dominant currency—the days of the dollar standard are over. The world is now on its way to becoming multipolar and may well end up with a system of regional currency blocks. The EMS would therefore simplify this world and facilitate a closer relationship between the monetary authorities on both sides of the Atlantic which would be preferable to the existing isolated crisis reactions. Some discussants, on the other hand, question the need to develop a new asset in the form of the ECU, and regard the lack of a dollar policy as potentially fatal.

Trezise in his introduction states that "only the course of events will determine whether the EMS will be another failed experiment or a long step toward ultimate European union." It is now possible to say, with the benefit of at least some hindsight, that it has been so far more success than failure. General economic performance especially as regards employment and inflation has not been satisfactory; but this is a worldwide problem. The exchange rate system has worked remarkably well achieving a high degree of stability as well as being flexible enough to accommodate three changes in parities; there has been increased coordination of monetary policies helped to some extent by the divergence indicator; and the ECU has played a significant role in Community settlements. The papers and discussion frequently return to the importance of economic convergence; and although emphasis differs, all would seem to agree that the transitional system which came into existence in March 1979 cannot by itself create convergence. The crucial question is the extent to which it will, as it develops, contribute towards that process. The main shortcoming of the volume is that the conference title of "promise and prospects" was interpreted too much in terms of failure or success of the exchange rate system, and apart from some mention of the increasing use of the ECU and of pooling of reserves, there is very little discussion of the possible developments of the EMS, and of how these can contribute to convergence.

The next stage of the EMS, again delayed though certainly not indefinitely, will involve the creation of a European Monetary Fund which could eventually become a European central bank. The exchange rate mechanism and its development must be considered together with the credit mechanisms, which were expanded at the start of the EMS but which remain practically unused. The way in which these mechanisms are consolidated and the amount of discretionary power given to the fund will be important in determining its nature. At the moment all the Community central banks hold ECUs, created through a system of three-month revolving swaps. With the rise in the price of gold, this system has resulted in a very rapid increase in the amount of ECU from around 25 billion to over 45 billion, which compares unfavorably even with the dollar reserve explosion to which Triffin refers in his paper. If the ECU is to be the reserve asset of a system which successfully aims at monetary stability, its creation both through the deposit of other reserve assets and through credit operations will have to be brought under control. The role that the fund will play in this process of control remains to be determined as do a number of factors affecting the attractiveness of the ECU reserve asset. The promise and prospects of the EMS depend upon the answers found to these questions and on the extent to which they contribute toward economic convergence in the Community.

JOLY DIXON

Commission of the European Communities

Housing and Investment in an Inflationary World: Theory and Evidence, by John Tuccillo. Washington, D.C.: The Urban Institute, 1980. 56 pp. $5.50

This brief monograph reviews much of the analyses of the effects of inflation on investment in housing. Housing is viewed by the author as primarily an investment good. In that context, investment in housing versus capital assets is examined; the affordability issue is discussed; and the manner in which government regulation of returns on financial assets affects the decision to invest in housing is debated.

The author begins by documenting increases in house prices relative to general price levels through 1978. Then, the effects of inflation and taxes on interest rates and the attractiveness of housing as an investment relative to other capital assets are examined. Inflation and the tax system tend to make corporate investment inferior to residential investment in terms of a real after-tax rate of return. Inflation increases the real after-tax rate of return on housing and reduces the rate for other assets. When the home is considered as an investment, affordability becomes a question of the rate of return to homeownership. Thus, inflation, by raising the real return on housing, increases the affordability of homeownership.

The effects of anticipated inflation on the household's decision to save is addressed, but no conclusion can be reached. Some increased savings are automatic in an inflationary period, when contribution to social security and pension plans increase. However, discretionary savings may fall if consumption increases in response to an inflationary psychology. If the increase in consumption is biased toward consumer durables, some savings occurs. On the other hand, if the inflation generates uncertainty, households may increase savings. If the after-tax real rate of interest is increased, savings should rise, but conflicting views exist on the connection between inflation and the real rate of interest. The author goes on to mention the "tilt" effect in the real payments on a mortgage, which increases households savings when nominal mortgage rates increase. Further, the author points out that savings decrease if households borrow against the equity in their homes and consume; if they buy durables and other assets, savings increase. Evidence indicates that borrowing against equity has occurred, but the disposition of the borrowed money is unknown. Finally, unanticipated inflation can unpredictably alter the household's consumption and savings.

Government regulation of returns on financial assets also are viewed as a factor in the shift to investment in housing. Interest rate ceilings on savings deposits have resulted in disintermediation and have weakened the government's ability to control the economy through monetary policy. The present phase-out of these regulations is seen as enabling the government to attain a greater measure of control and to heighten the competitiveness of corporate investment relative to housing. The author also speculates that the government's ability to control inflation may be weakened by the creation over time of a "proinflation constituency" of homeowners, because of housing's favored position as an investment.

Finally, a research agenda is suggested, which begins with three broad questions:

1. How has household wealth been affected by inflation, particularly as it is contained in owner-occupied housing? How have households adjusted to these changes?
2. How has the housing finance system accommodated a world in which the underlying rate of inflation has increased? What implications do these changes have for the conduct of public policy?
3. Has increased investment in housing affected the level of corporate investment? What are the implications of this for future growth and productivity?

RONALD L. RACSTER

Ohio State University

Zwei Generationen im deutschen Bankwesen 1833-1914, by Hermann and Paul Wallich. Frankfurt, West Germany: Fritz Knapp-Verlag, 1978. 432 pp. DM 78

The Institut für Bankhistorische Forschung Frankfurt/M. has taken upon itself the task of documenting the main developments in banking history. Among its publications are, on the one hand, outstanding scholarly works and, on the other, biographies and memoirs of distinguished bankers. The memoirs of two eminent bankers, who between them were observers of almost a hundred years of German and international banking, are published in the second volume of the series.

Hermann Wallich and his son Paul Wallich give the reader, through their personal recollections, an insight into their own opinions and attitudes and describe their social sphere and the economic circumstances of their time. The underlying theme of this book is the problem of reconciling individual ambition with the pressure of external events; by reason of their particular development the careers arising from the ambitions of these two men are of more than passing interest. The book is introduced with additional explanation and commentary by Henry C. Wallich, a grandson of Hermann Wallich, and presently a member of the Board of Governors of the Federal Reserve System.

Hermann Wallich's memoirs span the greater part of his life, from his birth in Bonn in 1833 to his retirement from the directorship of the Deutsche Bank in 1894. A descendant of an old Orthodox Jewish family, the memoirs show him as a man capable of clearheaded judgments both of himself and of the world around him. The later success of this self-made man rested on the dual foundations of this clear insight and a driving ambition. With typical candidness Hermann Wallich admits his own mistakes and makes clear what sacrifices he had to make for the sake of his career; in particular he regrets his renunciation of a carefree, happy youth—a time that was for him, in his own words, "embittered and poisoned" by his own ambition and sense of duty. Nevertheless, his good natured sense of humor never left him and shows itself in the anecdotes which enliven his memoirs. Following Wallich's career through his apprenticeship in the banking world of Cologne and Paris, to the island of Réunion in the Antilles, and to Shanghai, the reader is given an inside view of the business and banking practices of the day.

Wallich gives a vivid narration of his activities on the Antilles island Réunion, where he succeeded in reorganizing a suffered portfolio of agricultural mortgages for his Company Comptoir d'Escompte de Paris, coupled with a restoring of the shattered economy of this "Sugar Island." With regard to Wallich's life in Shanghai, the reader is faced with the complicated and unscrupulous business in the Far East around 1866. When he finally enjoyed a lucky transaction consisting of a very risky and difficult arrangement of arbitrage in bills, he made a remarkable contribution for better conditions in clearing the Far East business. His own comment nearly shows understatement: "Profit amounted to millions of Franks and ever since I have passed for the greatest banker in China."

In 1870, when the new type of incorporated banks was on the ascendant in its domination over private banks, Wallich agreed to be appointed a director of the newly founded incorporated Deutsche Bank AG at Berlin, the original task of which was to free Germany's overseas trade from the intermediation of Britain. The implementation of his plan, for which he showed himself to be eminently suited, became his life's mission. He wrote in his memoirs, with justifiable pride, "though my original project was modified by time and circumstances, I can nevertheless look back on my achievement with pride and satisfaction. Today, the Deutsche Bank, which I helped to build up, stands at the summit of its prosperity and in a leading position in German and especially in overseas trade." In 1894 Wallich gave up the position of director of the Deutsche Bank, and moved to the supervisory board, of which he continued to be a member until his death in 1928 at the age of ninety-five. After 1894 he had devoted himself particularly to the education of his two children, to whom he tried to offer everything that he himself had lacked in his youth.

Paul Wallich's memoirs cover only a relatively short period, from the beginning of his studies in 1901 to his departure to the war in 1914. Paul, who like his father was endowed with a clear intellect, set himself the aim of achieving in the social sphere the same success that his father had attained in the world of business. However, although he had been baptized into the Christian faith as a child, he was never fully accepted in a society gripped by anti-Semitism. The critical and occasionally bitter tone of his memoirs can be traced to the many unjustifiable slights and humiliations that he suffered. Paul Wallich describes himself and his acquaintances with unsparing frankness. The candidness that contributed to the father's success was transformed in the son, under the pressure of outside circumstances, into a talent for an occasionally destructive self-criticism.

Wallich describes his studies—among his teachers of national economics were Schmoller and Wagner—his training as an officer in the reserve, his various trainee positions at home and abroad, and his entry into business life in the Berliner Handelsgesellschaft. In the course of this narrative the reader makes the acquaintance of up to a hundred different people who crossed Wallich's path or influenced him in some way. In these variegated portraits in words can be found a reflection of the sensitive streak in Paul Wallich's character, a trait that is otherwise only allowed to show itself in an ironical guise, for example, in his more or less disparaging remarks about his own verse. So the reader gradually comes to know a man who in the words of his son Henry "initially with the help of his father's connections, but finally through his own efforts, built an exceptional career in the Berliner Handelsgesellschaft." The wide-ranging descriptions of the circumstances of his life, his friends, and his acquaintances will be of especial interest to those people who have had some personal connection or contact with those who figure in the book. In addition an interesting light is thrown on the banking business and practices of the time.

The different experiences in European banking and in the "New World" that the younger Wallich shows to his readers are probably typical of this era. Remembering practical experiences at European banking centers he gives a view of making money with small but safe interest margins and market profits, while the demonstration of his activities at the well-known New York bank Goldman Sachs & Co. reflects the more speculatory orientation of American banking. Detailed and inside information is given about complications in financing the construction of the London subway and about the most peculiar story of founding and financing Sears Roebuck & Co., the world's largest mail order house. Wallich's negotiations of "Vereinigung Berliner Banken und Bankiers"—better known as the "Stempelvereinigung"—along with his memories of other activities in "Berliner Handelsgesellschaft" are of special interest in banking history.

In later years, not treated in this book, but referred to in his son's introduction, Paul Wallich entered the Frankfurt firm of J. Dreyfus & Co. In 1937, the Nazi regime intensified its pressure on "non-Aryans" to such an extent that the bank had to be sold. In the face of the escalation of Nazi terror in 1938, Wallich evaded imminent arrest and took his own life, leaving as a testament moving farewell letters, which are appended to his son Henry's introduction.

These recollections by Hermann and Paul Wallich and the introduction by Henry Wallich allow the reader to come to know and understand two men who have had a decisive influence on commercial life. Through their personal approach, the reader is reminded that history, including economic history, is made by men, and that history itself consists of the history of individuals.

BENEDIKT FEHR

Freiburg i.Br.

Domestic and Multinational Banking, by Rae Weston. New York: Columbia University Press, 1980, 411 pp. $32.50

The author has set herself the nearly impossible task of providing, within a single book, a theory of bank behavior, domestic and international, with and without government regulation, and also a description of domestic bank regulation in many countries and of the movement towards multinational banking. It is not surprising that such an ambitious effort has not been wholly successful.

Part 1 sets out a theory of domestic bank behavior without any government regulation. It rejects what the author calls "the traditional portfolio paradigm" because of its "assumptions that a firm has an unlimited and riskless ability to borrow and that there are perfect financial markets." Instead, she argues that, "a more consistent interpretation of the variety of banking services may be provided if we regard the banker as a retailer of services." Though there are frequent references to "the retail paradigm," there is no clear statement of a theory of retailing (as distinct from the theory of the firm in any other activity) so it is not clear how the analogy contributes to the understanding of bank behavior. Despite the reference to "the variety of banking services," the formal diagrammatic model deals only with deposits, loans, profits, and earnings on free reserves and in terms of only one variable, the rate of interest. I did not find this analysis helpful.

Part 2, comprising nearly half the book, describes official regulation of banks in the major industrial companies of the noncommunist world and in a few developing countries including Egypt, Indonesia, and Papua New Guinea. In the few pages devoted to each country, Ms. Weston describes prudential regulations and regulations intended as tools of monetary policy, and gives a summary of recent developments in policy. For the countries with which I am personally familiar, the descriptions were broadly accurate, though with a few errors in detail.

In a comparatively short third part, Ms. Weston considers the effects of various kinds of regulation in relation to her theoretical model. Much of the comment reads like sound common sense, but the model does little to provide rigorous underpinning.

Part 4, entitled "The Move to Multinational Banking," consists of a description of moves into foreign operations by banks in Norway, the Netherlands, Japan, and the U.K. together with a discussion of the various types of risk involved in such operations. The description is so brief as to be little more than a record, with dates and places of the initiation or acquisition, of foreign operations by the banks concerned. There is no attempt to relate these moves either to banking theories or to the policies of governments, and there is no discussion of the moves of U.S. banks into foreign operations. The chapters on risk make good practical sense but, again, are not related to the theoretical model. Finally, part 5 contains a brief general discussion of the regulation of multinational banking, and of the regulations enforced by the United States and Canada.

The theoretical part of this book does not, in my opinion, provide an alternative, or even a useful complement, to "traditional" theories of the banking firm. The factual material is the product of a great deal of research. As already indicated, the coverage is so wide that detail is inevitably lacking but it provides a useful base from which students could launch inquiries into the comparative effects of banking regulations in different countries.

E. VICTOR MORGAN

University of Reading

ANNUAL INDEX

Volume XIII, 1981
February 1–134
May 135–272
August 273–408
November 409–547

Adjustment Lags Versus Information Lags: A Test of Alternative Explanations of the Phillips Curve Phenomenon, Charles R. Nelson, 1–11

Adjustment Lags Versus Information Lags: A Test of Alternative Explanations of the Phillips Curve Phenomenon, comment, Jacob A. Frenkel, 490–93

Adjustment Lags Versus Information Lags: A Test of Alternative Explanations of the Phillips Curve Phenomenon, reply, Charles R. Nelson, 494–96

Aivazian, Varouj A., book review, 513–15

Allais, Maurice, and Ole Hagen (eds.), *Expected Utility Hypotheses and the Allais Paradox,* reviewed, 507–8

Amihud, Yakov, A Possible Error in the Expectations Theory, rejoinder, 107–8

Ang, James, book review, 257–59

Angelini, Anthony, Maximo Eng, and Francis A. Lees, *International Lending, Risk and the Euro-Markets,* reviewed, 508–13

Arad, Ruth Wiener, book reviews, 508–13

Arzac, Enrique, Robert A. Schwartz, and David K. Whitcomb, The Leverage Structure of Interest Rates, 72–88

Australian Monetary System in the 1970s, The, Michael G. Porter (ed.), reviewed, 525–26

Ballendux, Frans J., and Marius J. L. Jonkhart, A Possible Error in the Expectations Theory, comment, 105–6

Bank Collapse and Depression, John Bryant, 454–64

Bank Credit Cards for EFTS: A Cost Benefit Analysis, Robert W. McLeod, reviewed, 264–65

Bank Failures of 1930–31, The, comment, Robert A. Stauffer, 109–13

Bankruptcy Risk in Financial Depository Intermediaries, Michael F. Koehn, reviewed, 117–18

Barnett, William A., The New Monetary Aggregates, comment, 485–89

Barrett, Richard N., Purchasing Power Parity and the Equilibrium Exchange Rate, 227–33

Bates, Timothy, and William Bradford, *Financing Black Economic Development,* reviewed, 114–15

Beedles, William L., and Nancy K. Buschmann, Describing Bank Equity Returns: The Year-by-Year Record, 241–47

Beenstock, Michael, and J. Andrew Longbottom, The Term Structure of Interest Rates in a Small Open Economy, 44–59

Bhattacharyya, D. K., *Demand for Financial Assets: An Econometric Study of the U.K. Personal Sector,* reviewed, 513–15

Bickelhaupt, David L., book review, 129–32

Black, Harold, book review, 114–15

Blinder, Alan S., Monetary Accommodation of Supply Shocks under Rational Expectations, 425–38

Borch, Karl H., book review, 117–18

Boughton, James M., book review, 259–62

Brittain, Bruce, International Currency Substitution and the Apparent Instability of Velocity in Some Western European Economies and in the United States, 135–55

Brownlee, Oswald H., book review, 269–71

Bryant, John, Bank Collapse and Depression, 454–64

Buschmann, Nancy K. *See* Beedles, William L.

Can the Reserves Approach to Monetary Control Really Work? James M. Johannes and Robert H. Rasche, 298–313

Capitalism and Socialism: A Theological Inquiry, Michael Novak (ed.), reviewed, 522–25

Cargill, Thomas F., A Tribute to Clark Warburton, 1896–1979, note, 89–93

Chandler, Lester V., book review, 529–30

Chappell, David, On the Revenue Maximizing Rate of Inflation, comment, 391–92

City Lights, E. Victor Morgan, Richard A. Brealey, Basil S. Yarney, and Paul Bareau, reviewed, 265–66

Clark, Peter B., book review, 254–57

Cole, David W., book review, 399–401

Composite Reserve Assets in the International

Composite Reserve—*continued*
Monetary System, Jacob S. Dreyer, reviewed, 254-57

Corbo, Vittorio, Inflation Expectations and the Specification of Demand for Money Equations, note, 381-87

Corporate Growth and Common Stock Risk, David R. Fewings, reviewed, 257-59

Cox, Charles C., book review, 132-34

Cuddington, John T., Money, Income, and Causality in the United Kingdom: An Empirical Reexamination, 342-51; review essay, 502-7

Currency and Economic Reform, West Germany After World War II: A Symposium, Rudolf Richter, reviewed, 526-29

Darby, Michael R., book review, 407-8

Demand for Financial Assets: An Econometric Study of the U.K. Personal Sector, D. K. Bhattacharyya, reviewed, 513-15

Describing Bank Equity Returns: The Year-by-Year Record, William L. Beedles and Nancy K. Buschmann, 241-47

Development of Economic Policy, The: Financing Institution Reform, Sidney J. Jones, reviewed, 399-401

Die deutsche Währung in der Weltwirtschaftskrise 1929-1933 (*The German Currency in the World Depression 1929-1933*), Jurgen Schiemann, reviewed, 267-69

Dixon, Joly, book review, 535-37

Domestic and Multinational Banking, Rae Weston, reviewed, 540-41

Dreyer, Jacob S., *Composite Reserve Assets in the International Monetary System,* reviewed, 254-57

Dudley, Leonard M., book review, 262-64

Dwyer, Gerald P., Jr., The Effects of the Banking Acts of 1933 and 1935 on Capital Investment in Commercial Banking, 192-204

Dynamic Analysis of the Impact of Fiscal Policy on the Money Supply, A, W. Douglas McMillin, 221-26

Ebrill, Liam P., book review, 518-19

Economics of the Eurocurrency System, The, George W. McKenzie, reviewed, 401-3

Effects of the Banking Acts of 1933 and 1935 on Capital Investment in Commercial Banking, The, Gerald P. Dwyer, Jr., 192-204

Equity Funding Papers, The, Lee J. Seidler, Frederick Andrews, and Marc J. Epstein, reviewed, 129-32

Essays in Post-Keynesian Inflation, James H. Gapinski and Charles E. Rockwood, reviewed, 393-99

Exchange Market Pressure During the 1970s in Argentina: An Application of the Girton-Roper Monetary Model, Nelson C. Modeste, 234-40

Expected Utility Hypotheses and the Allais Paradox, Maurice Allais and Ole Hagen (eds.), reviewed, 507-8

Expense-Preference Behavior in the Savings and Loan Industry, James A. Verbrugge and John S. Jahera, Jr., 465-76

European Monetary System: Its Promise and Prospects, The, Philip H. Trezise (ed.), reviewed, 535-37

Failure of the Franklin National Bank, The: Challenge to the International Banking System, Joan Edelman Spero, reviewed, 530-33

Federal Reserve Bank of Boston, *The Regulation of Financial Institutions,* reviewed, 515-18

Federal Reserve System and Control of the Money Supply in the 1970s, The, Robert L. Hetzel, 31-43

Fehr, Benedikt, book review, 538-40

Fethke, Gary C., and Andrew J. Policano, Long-Term Contracts and the Effectiveness of Demand and Supply Policies, 439-53

Fewings, David R., *Corporate Growth and Common Stock Risk,* reviewed, 257-59

Financing Black Economic Development, Timothy Bates and William Bradford, reviewed, 114-15

Financing of Long-Term Development, The, The Institute of Bankers, reviewed, 508-13

Fischer, Stanley (ed.), *Rational Expectations and Economic Policy,* reviewed, 248-53

Fletcher, Gordon A., book review, 265-66

FNMA Auction Results as a Forecaster of Residential Mortgage Yields, Herbert M. Kaufman and Don E. Schlagenhauf, 352-64

Frenkel, Jacob A., Adjustment Lags Versus Information Lags: A Test of Alternative Explanations of the Phillips Curve Phenomenon, comment, 490-93

Frydman, Roman, Sluggish Price Adjustments and the Effectiveness of Monetary Policy Under Rational Expectations, note, 94-102

Gale, William A., Temporal Variability of United States Consumer Price Index, 273-97

Gapinski, James H., and Charles E. Rockwood, *Essays in Post-Keynesian Inflation,* reviewed, 393-99

Gavin, William T., book review, 526-29

Gilbert, Milton, *Quest for World Monetary Order: The Gold-Dollar System and Its Aftermath,* reviewed, 518-19

Girton, Lance, and Don Roper, Theory and Implications of Currency Substitution, 12-30

Goldberg, Lawrence G., and Anthony Saunders, The Growth of Organizational Forms of Foreign Banks in the U.S., note, 365-74

Grossman, Jacob, The "Rationality" of Money Supply Expectations and the Short-Run Response of Interest Rates to Monetary Surprises, 409–24

Growth of Organizational Forms of Foreign Banks in the U.S., The, note, Lawrence G. Goldberg and Anthony Saunders, 365–74

Guindey, Guillaume, *The International Monetary Tangle: Myths and Realities,* reviewed, 115–17

Havrilesky, Thomas, book review, 525–26

Hetzel, Robert L., The Federal Reserve System and Control of the Money Supply in the 1970s, 31–43; book review, 533–35

Hewson, John R., book review, 401–3

Hodrick, Robert J., book review, 121–24

Housing and Investment in an Inflationary World: Theory and Evidence, John Tuccillo, reviewed, 537–38

Impact of tbe Federal Reserve System's Monetary Policies on the Nation's Economy (Second Report), The, Staff Report of the Subcommittee on Domestic Monetary Policy of the Committee on Banking, Finance and Urban Affairs, reviewed, 533–35

Indirect Evidence on the Efficacy of Selective Credit Controls: The Case of Consumer Credit, note, Brian A. Maris, 388–90

Inflation and Real Growth: Some Empirical Results, note, Dennis E. Logue and Richard James Sweeney, 497–501

Inflation and the Personal Income Tax: An International Perspective, Vito Tanzi, reviewed, 269–71

Inflation Expectations and the Specification of Demand for Money Equations, note, Vittorio Corbo, 381–87

Inflation: Global, International and National Aspects, Assar Lindbeck, reviewed, 259–62

Institute of Bankers, The, *The Financing of Long-Term Development,* reviewed, 508–13

International Currency Substitution and the Apparent Instability of Velocity in Some Western European Economies and in the United States, Bruce Brittain, 135–55

International Lending, Risk and the Euro-Markets, Anthony Angelini, Maximo Eng, and Francis A. Lees, reviewed, 508–13

International Monetary Tangle, The: Myths and Realities, Guillaume Guindey, reviewed, 115–17

Jahera, John S., Jr. *See* Verbrugge, James A.

Johannes, James M., and Robert H. Rasche, Can the Reserves Approach to Monetary Control Really Work?, 298–313

Jones, Sidney J., *The Development of Economic Policy: Financial Institution Reform,* reviewed, 399–401

Jonkhart, Marius J. L. *See* Ballendux, Frans J.

Kareken, John H., and Neil Wallace (eds.), *Models of Monetary Economies,* reviewed, 520–22

Kaufman, Herbert M., and Don E. Schlagenhauf, FNMA Auction Results as a Forecaster of Residential Mortgage Yields, 352–64

King, Robert G., and Charles I. Plosser, book review, 404–7

Klebaner, Benjamin J., book review, 530–33

Koehn, Michael F., *Bankruptcy Risk in Financial Depository Intermediaries,* reviewed, 117–18

Koizumi, Tetsunori, book review, 522–25

Kregel, Jan A., book review, 124–26

Landskroner, Yoram, and Nissan Liviatan, Risk Premia and the Sources of Inflation, 205–14

Laurent, Robert D., Reserve Requirements, Deposit Insurance, and Monetary Control, 314–24

Leverage Structure of Interest Rates, The, Enrique Arzac, Robert A. Schwartz, and David K. Whitcomb, 72–88

Levy, Haim, Optimal Portfolio of Foreign Currencies with Borrowing and Lending, 325–41

Lindbeck, Assar, *Inflation: Global, International and National Aspects,* reviewed, 259–62

Liviatan, Nissan. *See* Landskroner, Yoram

Logue, Dennis E., and Richard James Sweeney, Inflation and Real Growth: Some Empirical Results, note, 497–501

Longbottom, J. Andrew. *See* Beenstock, Michael

Long-Term Contracts and the Effectiveness of Demand and Supply Policies, Gary C. Fethke and Andrew J. Policano, 439–53

Mandell, Lewis, book review, 264–65

Maris, Brian A., Indirect Evidence on the Efficacy of Selective Credit Controls: The Case of Consumer Credit, note, 388–90

Markowski, Aleksander, *An Unformalized Forecasting Model,* reviewed, 118–21

Marshall, William J. *See* Yawitz, Jess B.

Martin, John P., and Alasdair Smith (eds.), *Trade and Payments Adjustment Under Flexible Exchange Rates,* reviewed, 262–64

McCafferty, Stephen A., review essay, 248–53

McCallum, Bennett T., Sluggish Price Adjustments and the Effectiveness of Monetary Policy Under Rational Expectations, reply, 103–4

McKenzie, George W., *The Economics of the Eurocurrency System,* reviewed, 401–3

McLeod, Robert W., *Bank Credit Cards for EFTS: A Cost Benefit Analysis,* reviewed, 264–65

McMillin, W. Douglas, A Dynamic Analysis of the Impact of Fiscal Policy on the Money Supply, 221–26

Measurement of the Real Rate of Interest and Re-

Measurement—*continued*
lated Problems in a World of Uncertainty, Stuart M. Turnbull, 177-91

Measuring the Effect of Callability on Bond Yields, Jess B. Yawitz and William J. Marshall, 60-71

Michael, Walther P., book review, 267-69

Miller, Preston J., review essay, 393-99

Minford, Patrick, *Substitution Effects, Speculation and Exchange Rate Stability,* reviewed, 121-24

Modelling the International Transmission Mechanism, John A. Sawyer (ed.), reviewed, 502-7

Models of Monetary Economies, John H. Kareken and Neil Wallace (eds.), reviewed, 520-22

Modeste, Nelson C., Exchange Market Pressure During the 1970s in Argentina: An Application of the Girton-Roper Monetary Model, 234-40

Monetary Accommodation of Supply Shocks under Rational Expectations, Alan S. Blinder, 425-38

Monetary Policy and Foreign Price Disturbances Under Flexible Exchange Rates: A Stochastic Approach, Stephen J. Turnovsky, 156-76

Money, Income, and Causality in the United Kingdom: An Empirical Reexamination, John T. Cuddington, 342-51

Morgan, E. Victor, book review, 540-41

Morgan, E. Victor, Richard A. Brealey, Basil S. Yamey, and Paul Bareau, *City Lights,* reviewed, 265-66

Müller-Groeling, Hubertus, book review, 127-29

Nelson, Charles R., Adjustment Lags Versus Information Lags: A Test of Alternative Explanations of the Phillips Curve Phenomenon, 1-11; Adjustment Lags Versus Information Lags: A Test of Alternative Explanations of the Phillips Curve Phenomenon, reply, 494-96

New Monetary Aggregates, The, comment, William A. Barnett, 485-89

Novak, Michael (ed.), *Capitalism and Socialism: A Theological Inquiry,* reviewed, 522-25

On the Generality of Keynesian Economics, Jukka Pekkarinen, reviewed, 124-26

On the Revenue Maximizing Rate of Inflation, comment, David Chappell, 391-92

Optimal Portfolio of Foreign Currencies with Borrowing and Lending, Haim Levy, 325-41

Organizational Form and Risk in Bank Affiliated Mortgage Companies, note, John T. Rose and Roger D. Rutz, 375-80

Pay Board's Progress, The: Wage Controls in Phase II, Arnold R. Weber and Daniel J. B. Mitchell, reviewed, 132-34

Pekkarinen, Jukka, *On the Generality of Keynesian Economics,* reviewed, 124-26

Phaup, E. Dwight, A Reinterpretation of the Modern Theory of Forward Exchange Rates, 477-84

Plosser, Charles I. *See* King, Robert G.

Policano, Andrew J. *See* Fethke, Gary C.

Porter, Michael G. (ed.), *The Australian Monetary System in the 1970s,* reviewed, 525-26

Possible Error in the Expectations Theory, A, comment, Frans J. Ballendux and Marius J. L. Jonkhart, 105

Possible Error in the Expectations Theory, A, rejoinder, Yakov Amihud, 107-8

Purchasing Power Parity and the Equilibrium Exchange Rate, Richard N. Barrett, 227-33

Quest for World Monetary Order: The Gold-Dollar System and Its Aftermath, Milton Gilbert, reviewed, 518-19

Racster, Ronald L., book review, 537-38

Rasche, Robert H. *See* Johannes, James M.

Rational Expectations and Economic Policy, Stanley Fischer (ed.), reviewed, 248-53

Rational Expectations and Monetary Policy, Jac J. Sijben, reviewed, 404-7

"Rationality" of Money Supply Expectations and the Short-Run Response of Interest Rates to Monetary Surprises, The, Jacob Grossman, 409-24

Reexamination of the Role of Stocks in the Consumption Function and the Transmission Mechanism, A, Geoffrey Woglom, 215-20

Regulation of Financial Institutions, The, Federal Reserve Bank of Boston, reviewed, 515-18

Reinterpretation of the Modern Theory of Forward Exchange Rates, A, E. Dwight Phaup, 477-84

Reserve Requirements, Deposit Insurance, and Monetary Control, Robert D. Laurent, 314-24

Richter, Rudolf, *Currency and Economic Reform, West Germany After World War II: A Symposium,* reviewed, 526-29

Risk Premia and the Sources of Inflation, Yoram Landskroner and Nissan Liviatan, 205-14

Ritter, Lawrence S. (ed.), *Selected Papers of Allan Sproul,* reviewed, 529-30

Roper, Don. *See* Girton, Lance

Rose, John T., and Roger D. Rutz, Organizational Form and Risk in Bank-Affiliated Mortgage Companies, note, 375-80

Rutz, Roger D. *See* Rose, John T.

Saposnik, Rubin, book review, 507-8

Saunders, Anthony. *See* Goldberg, Lawrence G.

Sawyer, John A. (ed.), *Modelling the Interna-*

tional Transmission Mechanism, reviewed, 502-7

Schiemann, Jürgen, *Die deutsche Währung in der Weltwirtschaftskrise 1929-1933 (The German Currency in the World Depression 1929-1933),* reviewed, 267-69

Schlagenhauf, Don E. *See* Kaufman, Herbert M.

Schmidt, Wilson E., *The U.S. Balance of Payments and the Sinking Dollar,* reviewed, 127-29

Schwartz, Robert A. *See* Arzac, Enrique

Seidler, Lee J., Frederick Andrews, and Marc J. Epstein, *The Equity Funding Papers,* reviewed, 129-32

Selected Papers of Allan Sproul, Lawrence S. Ritter (ed.), reviewed, 529-30

Sijben, Jac J., *Rational Expectations and Monetary Policy,* reviewed, 404-7

Sluggish Price Adjustments and the Effectiveness of Monetary Policy Under Rational Expectations, note, Roman Frydman, 94-102

Sluggish Price Adjustments and the Effectiveness of Monetary Policy Under Rational Expectations, reply, Bennett T. McCallum, 103-4

Smith, Gary, book review, 118-21

Smith, Harlan M., book review, 115-17

Social Security Versus Private Saving, George von Furstenberg, reviewed, 407-8

Spero, Joan Edelman, *The Failure of the Franklin National Bank: Challenge to the International Banking System,* reviewed, 530-33

Staff Report of the Subcommittee on Domestic Monetary Policy of the Committee on Banking, Finance and Urban Affairs, *The Impact of the Federal Reserve System's Monetary Policies on the Nation's Economy (Second Report),* reviewed, 533-35

Stauffer, Robert A., The Bank Failures of 1930-31, comment, 109-13.

Substitution Effects, Speculation and Exchange Rate Stability, Patrick Minford, reviewed, 121-24

Sweeney, Richard James. *See* Logue, Dennie E.

Taggart, Robert A., Jr., book review, 515-18

Tanzi, Vito, *Inflation and the Personal Income Tax: An International Perspective,* reviewed, 269-71

Temporal Variability of United States Consumer Price Index, William A. Gale, 273-97

Term Structure of Interest Rates in a Small Open Economy, The, Michael Beenstock and J. Andrew Longbottom, 44-59

Theory and Implications of Currency Substitution, Lance Girton and Don Roper, 12-30

Trade and Payments Adjustment Under Flexible Exchange Rates, John P. Martin and Alasdair Smith (eds.), reviewed, 262-64

Trezise, Philip H. (ed.), *The European Monetary System,* reviewed, 535-37

Tribute to Clark Warburton, 1896-1979, A, note, Thomas F. Cargill, 89-93

Tuccillo, John, *Housing and Investment in an Inflationary World: Theory and Evidence,* reviewed, 537-38

Turnbull, Stuart M., Measurement of the Real Rate of Interest and Related Problems in a World of Uncertainty, 177-91

Turnovsky, Stephen J., Monetary Policy and Foreign Price Disturbances Under Flexible Exchange Rates: A Stochastic Approach, 156-76; book review, 520-22

Unformalized Forecasting Model, An, Aleksander Markowski, reviewed, 118-21

U.S. Balance of Payments and the Sinking Dollar, The, Wilson E. Schmidt, reviewed, 127-29

Verbrugge, James A., and John S. Jahera, Jr., Expense-Preference Behavior in the Savings and Loan Industry, 465-76

von Furstenberg, George, *Social Security Versus Private Saving,* reviewed, 407-8

Wallich, Hermann and Paul, *Zwei Generationen im deutschen Bankwesen 1833-1914,* reviewed, 538-40

Weber, Arnold R., and Daniel J. B. Mitchell, *The Pay Board's Progress: Wage Controls in Phase II,* reviewed, 132-34

Weston, Rae, *Domestic and Multinational Banking,* reviewed, 540-41

Whitcomb, David K. *See* Arzac, Enrique

Woglom, Geoffrey, A Reexamination of the Role of Stocks in the Consumption Function and the Transmission Mechanism, 215-20

Yawitz, Jess B., and William J. Marshall, Measuring the Effect of Callability on Bond Yields, 60-71

Zwei Generationen im deutschen Bankwesen 1833-1914, Hermann and Paul Wallich, reviewed, 538-40